ACT OF TREASON

ACT OF TREASON

The Role of J. Edgar Hoover in the Assassination of President Kennedy

MARK NORTH

Carroll & Graf Publishers, Inc.
New York

First Carroll & Graf hardcover edition 1991
First Carroll & Graf paperback edition 1992

Carroll & Graf Publishers, Inc.
260 Fifth Avenue
New York, NY 10001

Library of Congress Cataloging-in-Publication Data

North, Mark.
    Act of treason : the role of J. Edgar Hoover in the assassination of
President Kennedy / by Mark North. — 1st Carroll & Graf ed.
        p.   cm.
    Includes bibliographical references and index.
    ISBN 0-88184-877-8 : $13.95
    1. Kennedy, John F. (John Fitzgerald), 1917–1963—Assassination.   2.
Hoover, J. Edgar (John Edgar), 1895–1972.   I. Title.
E842.9.N66   1991
364.1′524′0973—dc20   91-27049
                                                                           CIP

Manufactured in the United States of America

Excerpts from *Six Seconds in Dallas*, by Josiah Thompson, copyright ©
    1967.
Reprinted by permission of Bernard Geis Associates.

This book is dedicated to
my parents, Richard and
Marjory North; and my wife,
without whose love and
understanding this work
would not have been
possible.

For the balance of history

Author's Note

This work, the result of five years' effort, is a comprehensive analysis of all books, speeches, letters, government documents, articles, newspapers, interviews, and photographs in the available record pertaining to FBI director J. Edgar Hoover and the assassination of President John F. Kennedy. Much of the data herein is presented for the first time.

The book is structured primarily in chronicle form. My analysis within that portion is couched in present tense. This approach has been used because much of the source data consists of media material contemporaneous to that time. News items are identified as "press reports." It is also my feeling that the reader should view this crime in its context, its "time." Accordingly, some terminology may appear dated. The term "Cosa Nostra," for example, is the equivalent of "Mafia." Other such terminology is defined where used.

Each section is prefaced with an "Overview." Where necessary, additional analysis accompanies quoted material within a section in order to correlate or explain significant events.

The scope of this book is primarily limited to Hoover's actions and their impact upon President Kennedy and Vice President Johnson. The Director's machinations regarding Martin Luther King, Jr., and the Communist Party USA (CPUSA), although mentioned where relevant to this work, are largely the subject of other books.

Acknowledgments

First and foremost I would like to thank Wendy Brown. Her impeccable understanding of the English language, editorial skills, patience, and on many occasions simple willingness to listen were instrumental to the development of this book.

I would also like to thank my dear friend Constanze Frank of the Bookroom, in Santa Fe, New Mexico, for the unfailing encouragement she gave during this undertaking; but most importantly for the impetus provided during a fireside conversation one snowy afternoon that now seems like a million years ago.

Of great help was Bob Silverstein of Quicksilver Books, whose professionalism and expeditious manner led to the sale of this work.

Numerous librarians helped in various ways with the basic research. Though I cannot remember all the individual names, I am very appreciative of the efforts of the reference and interlibrary loan personnel at the following institutions: New Mexico State Library at Santa Fe, New Mexico, New Mexico State Supreme Court Law Library, Santa Fe Public Library (downtown facility), University of New Mexico, University of Arizona, University of Texas at Austin (PCL), and Lyndon B. Johnson Presidential Library, Austin, Texas.

The Library of Congress also proved to be a key source of information. When I could find data nowhere else, it was there. Specifically, I would like to thank Judith Brisker for her help in locating and obtaining photographic materials. I also thank Maura Porter of the John Fitzgerald Kennedy Library and Nat Andriani of Wide World Photos (i.e., Associated Press). Special Thanks to Ken Todd for assistance with photographs (University of Texas at Austin—PCL).

My appreciation goes to Dr. Robert Wiggins and his wife Allison for the use of their home during the initial drafting of the manuscript.

I thank Marina Oswald for permission to publish tax data related to her and Lee's 1962 income, and Dallas researcher Mary Ferrell for her invaluable assistance in this regard.

Finally, a great deal of credit belongs to my publisher, Carroll and Graf (including editorial assistant Laura Langlie), for reasons other than the obvious. Their willingness to confront the political issues raised by the ongoing crisis that is the Kennedy assassination, through such books as *Best Evidence* and *Crossfire*, is deserving of great praise—for the day the American publishing industry refuses to deal with these kinds of issues, this nation will be doomed.

COMMIT A CRIME
AND IT SEEMS AS IF A COAT OF SNOW FELL ON THE
   GROUND
SUCH AS REVEALS IN THE WOODS
WITH THE TRACK OF EVERY PARTRIDGE AND FOX
   AND SQUIRREL AND MOLE

YOU CANNOT RECALL THE SPOKEN WORD
YOU CANNOT WIPE OUT THE FOOT TRACK
YOU CANNOT DRAW UP THE LADDER
SO AS TO LEAVE NO INLET OR CLUE
—Emerson

Contents

Introduction

The purpose of this book is to reveal the true nature of the conspiracy that killed President John F. Kennedy and thereby explain the ongoing refusal of the U.S. Department of Justice to formally investigate and make public its findings.

In September 1962, as a result of data obtained through covert surveillance programs against the Mafia, then FBI director J. Edgar Hoover learned that a subcomponent of that organization, the Marcello family in New Orleans, Louisiana, had, in order to prevent its own destruction (through prosecutorial pressure resulting from the administration's war on organized crime) put out a contract on the life of John Kennedy. Despite specific statutory requirement, and his duty as an American citizen, Hoover did not inform his superiors within the Justice Department, or warn the Secret Service (a minuscule organization by comparison, which relied heavily upon the FBI for raw data concerning threats against the President). He withheld the data in part because he felt Kennedy was an indecisive, immoral liberal who, if left in place, would destroy the nation. But most important, he did this because JFK had made it known that he intended, by the end of his first term in office, to retire the Director and replace him with a man of his own, more liberal political philosophy. An integral part of Hoover's decision to aid the assassination of the President stemmed from the fact that by the fall of 1962 he held sufficient information to control then Vice President Lyndon Johnson, a longtime friend, were he to become President. Through data gleaned (and withheld from the Justice Department) from investigations of the Billie Sol Estes and soon-to-break Bobby Baker/Mafia scandals, Hoover had hopelessly compromised the Vice President. Johnson, a man then tremendously dissatisfied with his position in government, knew this.

As a result of Hoover's traitorous act, President Kennedy was assassinated, Johnson became President, and the Director obtained an Executive Order, on May 8, 1964, waiving his compulsory retirement.

The Warren Commission, consisting of longtime political insiders handpicked by Johnson to "satisfy themselves that the truth is known as far as it can be discovered," was made up of intelligent, knowledgeable men. Instructed by Johnson to look to Hoover as chief investigator, however, they were quickly stymied. From the outset, the Director refused to send representatives to Commission meetings, would not provide the raw data the event compelled them to examine, and repeatedly leaked to the press investigative "conclusions" supporting only the lone-nut thesis. On December 5, 1963, he formally, publicly, concluded that Oswald and Ruby had acted alone, independently of each other, and then demanded that the Commission issue a public statement agreeing with him. The members in turn, became deeply suspicious of his motivations. Like many Beltway officials, they had known of Hoover and JFK's hatred for each other long before the assassination, as well as of Kennedy's plan to retire the aging Director.

Forcing Johnson's hand with a public demand for raw FBI investigative reports on December 16, 1963, their suspicions concerning Hoover were confirmed by March 1964. To complicate matters, evidence pointing to Mafia complicity raised ominous questions with regard to Johnson himself. Through involvement with Senate aide Bobby Baker in the late 1950s and early 1960s, LBJ had effectively associated himself with some of the same people then deeply involved with mafiosi like Meyer Lansky, Santos Traficante, and Carlos Marcello. Mafiosi such as Edward Levinson and Benjamin Sigelbaum, and lobbyist Fred Black, along with Bobby Baker, were, by early 1964, themselves under Senate investigation. One Warren Commission member, Senator John Sherman Cooper, actually served concurrently on the Baker panel. The political reality of Hoover's act and Johnson's vulnerability came home.

Struck by the gravity of this truth, and pressured by Hoover and Johnson, the controlling faction within the Commission made the tragic decision to accept Hoover's lone-nut thesis and conceal the conspiracy from the public. Its chief counsel, J. Lee Rankin, a compromise choice of the Commission not known for any hard-line position on the Mafia, was prevented from exposing the Director. In all likelihood, preservation of institutional credibility was the paramount concern. Consider what the short-term public reaction would have been had it been revealed that the Director of the FBI, an ultraright figure of messianic bent and hero to many, had allowed the President, a highly popular man of the middle and left, to be assassinated primarily for personal gain.

The constitutional crisis in which the country found itself after the assassination was in part a consequence of the times. Prior to 1964, Hoover was a popular man. The public and news media were much more trusting of political leaders and knew almost nothing of Hoover's covert surveillance programs. They perceived only the public image of the Director, understanding little of his true ultraconservative nature and capabilities.

In fact, Hoover's act of treason required little personal effort and few participants. Word of the Marcello contract had reached him by way of encoded sealed AIRTEL from the Miami, Florida, field office, which had learned of the plan through a confidential informant within the Cuban exile community. In all likelihood, only the informant, field office contacts George Davis and/or Paul Scranton, their immediate supervisor, Miami Special-Agent-in-Charge Wesley Grapp, Hoover, and two top assistants knew of the report. In supplying the information to Hoover, Miami personnel simply followed FBI procedure and undoubtedly presumed Secret Service had been informed. And only when considered by Hoover in conjunction with other data from such field offices as New Orleans and Las Vegas did the true reality of the threat that was posed become apparent.

As the focal point for sensitive data on the Mafia from the field offices, Hoover, Associate Director Clyde Tolson, and Organized Crime Division chief Courtney Evans held a unique perspective. Their exclusive knowledge in this area developed as the natural consequence of a pyramid-shaped information-flow system designed to concentrate critical data in the hands of a conservative, tightly knit oligarchy. By Hoover's own directive, all sensitive reports on John Kennedy had long been kept out of the Bureau's Central Records System, secreted instead in his own personal (official and confidential) office files. Simply put, information of this nature was unknown to all outside the FBI and only a few within.

The Mafia, then as now, was a vicious, ruthless organization. Far from the glamorized entity the public thinks of today, its basic

philosophy dictated murder as a solution for most problems. Anyone perceived as a threat, whether a part of the organization or not,
was routinely killed. By fall 1962, Hoover was more aware of this
fact than most. A Bureau report describing the August 11, 1961,
torture slaying of informant William "Action" Jackson reveals this
brutal reality:

William "Action" Jackson—Coroner's Report:

Impaled on meat hook, doused with water. Cattle prod (elec-
trical) used in rectum and pubic area.
Shot.
Limbs cut (apparently with an ice pick).
Beaten about most of the body (apparently with baseball bats).
Severe body burns, inflicted with a blowtorch.
Incineration of the penis.

This was the nature of Mafia killings in the early 1960s. The press
typically "spared" the public the more gruesome details.

And where do we stand today on the murder of John F. Kennedy? The majority of Americans stopped believing the Warren Report decades ago. They continue to wait for the truth. And yet the
Justice Department remains silent. Has not this silence brought
about the very loss in credibility the Commission so feared in 1964?
In the years since the assassination, a virtual army of journalists,
writers, and congressional investigators have succeeded in making it
painfully clear that the President was killed by the Marcello organization. In 1979, the report of the House Select Committee on Assassinations (HSCA), the most intensive Congressional investigation in
U.S. history, implied in its conclusions this was likely the case.
These findings pointing to the Mafia were quickly attacked by the
Justice Department and FBI. Why?

An overwhelming body of evidence at the time of the assassination strongly suggested complicity on the part of the New Orleans
Mafia. Anyone who read newspapers during the Kennedy administration knew that the Mafia, especially the Marcello family, would
have liked nothing better than to see President Kennedy's efforts to
destroy them brought to an end. Why then, was, and is, the Justice
Department unwilling to consider the obvious? Logic should have
dictated the opposite. Shouldn't the assassination of the President,

under such obviously conspiratorial circumstances, have automatically triggered investigation and prosecution? Consider this: If the truth behind the Kennedy assassination had involved only a Mafia contract, would the Justice Department have kept it from us for twenty-eight years? Undoubtedly not. And yet they have done just that. In their minds, they have to. To do otherwise will implicate Hoover, but more importantly, the FBI as an institution.

This book then, is not about ill-conceived, macroassassination theories of national and/or international proportion. It is about historical reality. The military-industrial complex, the CIA, and the Soviet and Cuban governments play no direct role because they had none. In these pages, Lee Harvey Oswald will not be exposed as an international contract killer, CIA agent, or "kill-crazy-communist" because he was not. He was, in fact, one of history's most maligned figures—an uneducated, naïve young Marxist enlarged far beyond life by Hoover and the Warren Commission for the express purpose of misleading the American public and thereby concealing the truth.

In essence, this book is about what your government has yet to tell you about the assassination of John F. Kennedy, an event that continues to haunt us all. Do we not, after twenty-eight years, have the right, *the fundamental right,* to be told the truth? It is time for the lie to stop.

—Mark North
May 27, 1991

Over the long run,
the Public cannot
be fooled.

—J. Edgar Hoover

I

The Man:
Biographical profile of Hoover on
11/8/60

In order to understand the capabilities and motivations of J. Edgar Hoover, it is first necessary to define him. By this I mean definition within the relevant time frame—who he was on November 8, 1960.

At the time of JFK's narrow victory, Hoover was nearing age sixty-six, yet remained a vigorous man.[1] The youngest of four, he was five-foot-eleven, 190 pounds, with piercing, dark brown eyes.[2] His hair was thinning and gray. The staccato voice was gruff, with a slight Virginia accent.[3] His complexion was ruddy, jaw jutting, face pugnacious, walk brisk.[4] Typical work attire consisted of a navy-blue suit with handkerchief, white shirt, conservatively patterned tie, dark shoes, and a hat.[5] Special agents were required to dress in similar fashion.[6] Everyday jewelry (gold) consisted of a watch, cuff-links, tie pin, and blue sapphire ring worn on his wedding finger.[7] Overall, the image conveyed was one of calmness, authenticity, and strength.

Appearances aside, Hoover was, by any definition, also a borderline fanatic. Fiercely dedicated, exceedingly egotistical, opinionated and thin-skinned, he demanded dedication and excellence from all around him.[8] A lawyer and relentless perfectionist, he required minutely detailed reporting from his employees.[9] The Bureau was run with an iron hand, Hoover openly asserting to others that he *could not* be removed from his position.[10] By 1960 he had evolved into an ends-justify-the-means personality. Field offices were rarely visited, the Director taking a condescending view of SACs (special-agents-in-charge).[11] He would sign his notations and memos simply with the letter H in a blue ink he alone used.[12] He disliked the French, British, Dutch, and Australians, and felt that many people from all walks of life were "communist dupes."[13] Weak handshakes or sweaty palms were considered a bad sign.[14] He enjoyed teasing people, always getting the last laugh.[15] Instantaneous dislike arose for anyone who upstaged him or canceled an appointment.[16] Ironically, as a lifelong resident of D.C., he never voted in a presidential election.[17]

Hoover lived at 4936 30th Place NW, in an upper-middle-class neighborhood of Washington, D.C., known as Chevy Chase, which bordered on a large, well-kept greenbelt called Rock Creek Park.[18] The house was a red brick two-story and contained a basement. A walled yard included a rose garden and goldfish pond and was kept in immaculate condition.[19] The house was filled with memorabilia, honors and awards gathered over the decades.[20] Hoover had a passion for Oriental art, his personal collection containing over fifteen hundred jade, quartz, and ivory objects. The upstairs bedroom contained an Oriental dressing partition.[21] The dining-room window contained a stained-glass FBI emblem that caught the evening light.[22] A fire was kept burning almost year round.[23] The basement held a club room used to entertain his bachelor friends and was papered with nude photos and foldouts of various women.[24] There was a stereo that featured a light bar capable of flashing various colors.[25] Servants included a caretaker and cook/maid.[26] All repair and maintenance on his home was performed by FBI agents, in part for security reasons.[27] His neighbors thought him a wonderful man of impeccable standards, Hoover taking a serious, apparently grandfatherly interest in the young son of one.[28]

The position of Director afforded and required many things of him. Annual salary was approximately thirty thousand dollars.[29] Transportation anywhere by car was accomplished in an incredibly heavy, black, bulletproof Cadillac limousine. It was replaced annually.[30] Whenever riding in this car, he would place his hat on the left rear ledge of the back seat so as to "confuse" potential assassins.[31] Reportedly he received threats from around the country on a regular basis.[32] In my research, however, I could find no instance of physical attack upon him, in his car or anyplace else. Civic efforts included administrative work with the Boy Scouts and other youth organizations. Although apparently not overly involved, he was also a thirty-third-degree Mason.[33] Great formality was observed with regard to thank-you notes, Hoover harboring an intense dislike of form letters.[34] He saw to it that birthdays, weddings, and anniversaries of all his friends were always remembered. Reciprocation was expected.[35] At Christmas, cards were sent to close friends and to many others.[36] Friends considered him a congenial and witty personality.[37]

Examination of his private life reveals a more gentle, less formal side. Like many people, he enjoyed soothing music.[38] In the evening before dinner, he drank one or two Jack Daniel's, with soda.[39] When forced to travel, Hoover preferred trains to airplanes, never once leaving the continental U.S.[40] Injections of vitamins, possibly laced with amphetamines, were taken regularly.[41] Hobbies were gardening (he loved roses), collecting and selling antiques (C. G. Sloan's quarterly auctions) and watching horse races.[42] Occasionally he presented the winner's cup after the feature event (particularly at nearby Bowie).[43] He was a two-dollar bettor, stopping once he had lost ten.[44] Pets included two cairn terriers.[45] Tastes in art ran to Remington, literature allowed Kipling and Robert Service.[46] He also enjoyed light fiction and the Lawrence Welk show.[47] Neither he nor his constant companion Clyde Tolson (associate director) mixed with highly educated or intellectual types, though the latter held several patents. Light talk and privacy were apparently the rule.[48] They reportedly teased and insulted each other during conversation.[49] The 1930s and men like Dillinger were apparently favorite topics of discussion.[50] Hoover enjoyed sending, as well as receiving, flowers, requiring whenever he traveled a fresh bouquet in his hotel room.[51] Fastidious in nature, he demanded strict cleanliness, at home and in the office.[52] Lacking proficiency with firearms, he was physically involved in only one arrest.[53] Reading, listening to, or viewing pornographic material, whether mass produced or taken in evidence, was a favorite pastime.[54] Paradoxically, he was adamantly opposed to the use of lie detectors as a means of obtaining evidence.[55]

There is the distinct probability he was also a homosexual. Hoover never dated, living with his mother until he was forty-three, when she died.[56] His daily companion of nearly forty years was Clyde Tolson who, like Hoover, never married.[57] Hoover nicknamed him "Junior," while Tolson referred to him as "Eddie," "Speed," or "Boss."[58] They lived only blocks from each other, rode to and from work together, ate lunch and dinner together, went to the horse races nearly every Saturday, and dined at Hoover's on Sunday.[59] On Monday nights, Hoover ate dinner at Clyde's apartment.[60] They took semiannual vacations together—Miami in January (peak racing season) and La Jolla, California, in August, where they also attended the races, and Hoover received his annual physical. While on vacation, they shared the same bungalow.[61] Hoover kept secreted in his home, not discovered until his sudden death, a photo album containing pictures, apparently taken on vacations, of Clyde asleep in bed, either in pajamas or partial undress. An extraordinarily reticent individual, Tolson took great pains to avoid publicity. To this day, there is a general dislike of Hoover within the homosexual (male and female) population of this country, the common perception being that he and Tolson were "hypocritical" in this regard.[62] Those who suggested he and Clyde were homosexuals were "public rats, gutter-snipes, and degenerate pseudo-intellectuals (pronounced sway-do)."[63] From 1953 to his death in 1972 he personally directed an illegal nationwide surveillance program of homosexual rights groups.[64] There was a peculiar fixation with "impostors." Apparently the idea of people, particularly men, representing themselves publicly as something they were not, infuriated him.[65] A number of Hoover's friends were also homosexual, most notably the late Roy Cohn.[66] It seems apparent that Hoover's homosexuality contributed in some basic way to his hatred of President Kennedy. The latter's satyric life-style was a subject of intense concern to the Director.[67] In definitional terms then, Hoover and Tolson were basically an elderly, discreet homosexual couple, of tremendous political power, living and working inside the Beltway.

But this is only part of the picture. Hoover was also extremely moralistic. He did not use sexually oriented profanity, preferring at worst phrases like "13 karat son-of-a-bitch."[68] He once said of Martin Luther King, "I don't like the man. I've said so publicly and I had him up here for 45 minutes and I told him so privately. I don't think he is a good man."[69] Training sessions for special agents included numerous stories of recruits who had lost their jobs because of marital infidelity or alcohol abuse.[70] He opposed undercover operations for fear his agents would be corrupted.[71] In the case of one, a New Orleans case officer, his fears were justified.[72]

An unerring Presbyterian, in his youth he taught Sunday school and sang in the choir, hoping some day to become a minister.[73] Counted as a friend was Dr. Edward L. R. Elson, Senate and National Presbyterian chaplain.[74] This man was to later eulogize him at his death in 1972.[75] His favorite Bible verse was Micah 6:8, "He hath shown thee, O Man, what is good; and what doth the Lord require of thee, but to do justly, and to lose mercy, and to walk humbly with thy God?"[76] This is telling. If you read Micah in total you will, I believe, gain an insight into Hoover's personality. Micah deals with the dual concepts of an avenging God striking down a sinful man, and predictions of the Christ child; vengeful self-righteousness, messianic presence, and an absolute adherence to the concept of predestination. Despite this (or perhaps because of it), he rarely attended church in later years, and was not afraid of publicly attacking any religious sect that opposed his views on law and order.[77]

Politically Hoover was thoroughly conservative. Elements of the public and press with moderate to extreme left viewpoints were "pinkos, gadflies, pseudo-intellectuals and liberal eggheads."[78] He considered left-wing radicals mentally disturbed.[79] In contrast, Marine Corps discipline was to be admired.[80] Two guiding commandments for special agents were, "Never embarrass the Bureau" and "Look like an agent."[81] He believed that a person convicted of premeditated murder should always get the death penalty.[82] Rhetoric for those opposing his ideas on order in society included, "bleeding heart judges, sobsister parole boards, sentimental yammerheads, pseudo-intellectuals, so-called liberals and enemy [sic] of law and order."[83] General adversaries were "scavengers, garbage collectors, bums, rats, craven beasts, misfits, pinkos, vermin from the jails, slobs, kooks, rabble rousers and commies."[84] Any who suggested psychologically oriented treatment programs for juvenile delinquents were "muddleheaded sentimentalists."[85] A very close friend to Joe McCarthy, he distanced himself publicly only after the politician fell into disgrace.[86] His view of minorities was basically nineteenth century, as evidenced by his use of blacks as servants, chauffeur, and office bodyguard.[87] Not coincidentally, he felt all blacks were easily manipulated.[88]

Hoover's need for control of others was absolute. He intentionally structured the FBI bureaucracy in pyramid shape so as to ensure complete obedience from all employees. He kept a plaque in his office demanding absolute loyalty from all who worked for him.[89] Most considered him unpredictable, adding to their fear and willingness to cooperate.[90] "Defections" were rare. This bureaucratic system also guaranteed that all information of any political value eventually crossed his desk.[91] Ultimate decision-making authority lay exclusively with him, to the extent of overruling the collective judgment of his eleven assistants.[92] Through his efforts, the Bureau was exempted from the rules of the Civil Service Commission.[93] This was very significant. It meant that he could fire with prejudice, transfer without notice, demote, censure, or suspend without pay anyone in his organization, leaving employees with no effective redress of grievance. The courts almost always backed his personnel decisions. He used this power with considerable regularity. Favorite places to transfer agents (and thereby frustrate careers) who had in some way displeased him were Omaha, Oklahoma City, and *New Orleans*.[94] Most employees referred to him as "the Director," calling him "sir" when in his presence.[95] Memos were sometimes circulated to all agents to make a collective point.[96] A typical opening attack on an employee who had incurred his wrath was as follows: "I am amazed and astounded and completely at a loss to understand how a supposedly rational human being could commit an act of such colossal stupidity."[97] A former lieutenant colonel in the army reserve, Hoover labeled FBI headquarters "SOG," for Seat of Government.[98] Only scheduled visitors were allowed to see him. Before these people were brought in, he had any file on them pulled and placed before him. He would then skim their dossier, picking up minute facts to use in conversation. If he had someone in his office whom he was unsure of, he would launch into a rapid-fire, staccato monologue, dominating the conversation until the individual's time was up.[99] He tended to rant when discussing things he felt strongly about.[100] Any criticism of the FBI was taken personally.[101] Agents and others regularly sent him flattering memos, letters, and cards, which he reportedly enjoyed reading.[102] In arguments, even with superiors, he would stand his ground, displaying a short, volatile temper.[103] He perceived congressmen and senators as potential adversaries, keeping dossiers on those he did not trust.[104] Nearly all insiders in Washington considered him more powerful than the President, and many politicians lived in fear of him.[105] To control those he was unsure of, he used various forms of political blackmail. For example, if an investigation of any sort unearthed political dirt or information damaging to an individual or his family, Hoover would, through an intermediary (he always used intermediaries to accomplish tasks he felt were too risky to handle personally), confidentially brief the official, while simultaneously assuring him his secret was "safe" with the Bureau.[106] Some nicknamed him "the Librarian" because of the many dossiers he kept.[107] He regularly bypassed technical superiors and dealt directly with the President.[108] JFK was the first to prevent this practice.[109]

Hoover was also a consummate opportunist, providing derogatory information to public officials whenever they needed such to win reelection, ensure support on legislation, or obtain advantage in personal matters.[110] He was often apolitical if cooperation meant an opportunity for safely improving the Bureau's position.[111] He was considered very good at light talk, knowing at least a little about many subjects.[112] Any help or information provided by local and state police on investigations was usually readily accepted.[113] And yet, he would not provide information in return, apparently feeling that local agencies were either too corrupt or inept to trust.[114] Selection for specialized course work at the FBI Training Academy, highly valued by police organizations, was used by Hoover to ensure the allegiance of the IACP (International Association of Chiefs of Police).[115] Intelligence data was routinely withheld from other federal, state, and local agencies if it served to benefit him or the Bureau.[116] He developed a tradition of acquiring as much damaging information as possible on a President, his family, and friends. The fact that a Chief Executive had the technical power to simply replace him, without Congressional cooperation, did not prevent him from attempting blackmail.[117] The disciplining of an employee was often used to make a point to others working for the Bureau.[118] Favorable news stories, fed to him from the field and AP/UPI tickers at SOG, were automatically followed up with a personal letter thanking the editor.[119] Unfavorable stories earned a hostile reply or placement on the "no-contact" list.[120] Visitors to his office were always photographed with him and given an autographed print.[121] The presence of well-known or influential people in a tour group of FBI headquarters would be communicated to the Director, who would then invite them up for a personal meeting.[122] When public "threats" or "crises" arose, Hoover would not hesitate to "develop" them, ride forth to protect the masses, and thereby meet its need for heroes. He clearly understood the power and potential value of film as a form of evidence, and more than once manipulated it to create a totally false impression in the public mind. During the 1960 House Committee on Un-American Activities summer protest in

San Francisco, considerable footage was taken. After the demonstration was broken up by police, Hoover, in conjunction with HUAC, used media coverage to create a "documentary" entitled *Operation Abolition*. This film asserted that communists had manipulated American youth, inciting them to assault the authority of the federal government.[123] A jury of twelve did not agree.[124] Oddly, both Hoover and Tolson regularly allowed others to pay their dining tabs. For many years the two ate almost daily, sometimes twice daily, at a local restaurant called Harvey's, apparently never once paying for a meal.[125] When on vacation, it was the same.[126] Expenses incurred during inspection tours of field offices were paid for by local agents.[127]

The final primary component of the "definition" is public imagery or perception—who he was to his constituency. Understanding this is critical, for Hoover was a master at controlling and cultivating his public. He had realized early on that by creating a highly favorable public image, he could gain and retain a broad-based following. This, in turn, could be used to enhance job security and force cooperation on Capitol Hill. While his personal views were right to ultraright, he astutely projected an image that endeared him to "Middle America." Every field office employed people whose primary job was to read newspapers and other publications, reporting their contents to SOG if of interest or value to the Bureau.[128] Relationships with newspaper editors and other members of the press were carefully nurtured.[129] Hoover maintained a staff of correspondence personnel who carefully replied to all letters received.[130] Daily tours of SOG were conducted, highlighting the Bureau's performance and role in society.[131] Hoover wrote profusely in furtherance of this public "image," monthly penning an editorial for the *FBI Law Enforcement Bulletin* entitled "Message from the Director."[132] In addition, there was a monthly report on communism.[133] He wrote letters to children, civic organizations, and newspaper editors. Articles for Christian publications, business periodicals, and law reviews were common.[134] There were several books, although it remains unclear whether he wrote these unaided.[135] To news, magazine, and radio personalities he was sure of, he granted interviews. He gave speeches on radio.[136] In sensational cases, he sometimes staged "breaks" in the presence of certain newsmen, allowing them the "scoop."[137] There were regular appearances before patriotic organizations to give speeches and receive awards. The primary themes in all public addresses, writings, and interviews were communism, morality, and crime. He clearly understood that a single federal investigative force such as the Bureau had limited enforcement capabilities. He felt strongly that by projecting his views on these subjects, particularly to youth, he encouraged a more orderly, obedient society. Given the spiraling crime rate in the sixties and seventies, there is little reason to suppose it worked.

He did not believe that his public rhetoric applied personally, however, any more than many other officials of his day. Although very discreet, as previously noted he was probably a homosexual. After Hoover's death, at least one of his close friends admitted that Hoover had told him the "threat" of communism, in actuality, was much smaller than what he had stated publicly.[138] By his weekly activities at the race track, he supported organized gambling. He vacationed at the expense of others, including his own personnel. He often presented himself as ageless to his public, using dated, mass-circulated photos for articles and book releases. In contrast to his public "interest" in youth, he privately maintained an intense dislike of small children.[139] In essence he understood that by "appearing" to be the embodiment of Middle American values, he would in fact become indispensable to his public. This indispensability became of paramount concern with the election of John F. Kennedy to the presidency.

Hoover's workday began promptly at 6 A.M. with a brief workout on an exercise bicycle.[140] Breakfast usually consisted of bacon and eggs, fruit juice, and black coffee.[141] His chauffeur arrived at seven thirty sharp. From there they proceeded to Clyde's apartment, a few blocks away.[142] On balmy days Hoover had the limousine stop at 14th and Constitution, from which point he and Tolson would briskly walk the remaining blocks to the Justice Department.[143] They entered the building by nine.[144] Hoover's personal SAC laid out his morning mail and briefed him on the day's agenda.[145] This usually included meeting scheduled visitors, rendering special services to some.[146] At midday, Hoover and Tolson took the limousine to Harvey's for lunch at the nearby Mayflower Hotel. There, they were always served by the same waiter (a Cuban) and seated at the same table. Hoover usually greeted him with "Hello, Castro, ha, ha." Lunch often consisted of grapefruit, cottage cheese, and black coffee.[147] Upon returning to SOG, Hoover napped briefly on a couch in his office.[148] One assistant director in particular, named Cartha D.

DeLoach (an extremely loyal and aggressive individual in charge of the Crime Records Division), came to his office regularly. Apparently he acted as Hoover's personal liaison in delicate matters (e.g., the Johnson, Estes, and Baker scandals).[149] A portion of the day was spent working on articles, speeches, and letters. He also read copies of commendations and awards, almost all of which found their way into the *Congressional Record.*[150] Many times, such awards were presented to him in his outer, "official" office.[151] This same office was regularly used by Hoover to bestow honors on others (e.g., the John Edgar Hoover Award for Excellence in the Study of Law Enforcement).[152] Office photo sessions with visitors and those receiving awards were commonplace. Dramatic or important news items from the AP/UPI tickers would be brought to his office.[153] Depending on the time of year, he would review summary reports from the assistants concerning activities in their respective divisions.[154] Important or sensitive FBI intelligence reports could arrive from a field office at any hour of the day or day of the week, via encoded AIRTEL or Telex.[155] He often stayed past 5 P.M., taking work home on weekends.[156] Dinner, again usually at Harvey's, allowed a cocktail or two.[157] Hoover did not like being seen drinking in public, requiring Clyde to keep his drink concealed from view. How this was done is not clear. Either Clyde kept the drink in his lap, handing it to Hoover under the table, or Clyde appeared to be the only one drinking.[158] If dining out, they returned home by 9 P.M. When eating at Hoover's, they usually arrived by 6:30 P.M.[159] Every Tuesday, all the assistants, Tolson, and occasionally Hoover met in his outer office at a conference table to discuss ongoing projects or current situations. A vote was often taken on a given issue but was only effective if Hoover agreed with the majority. If he was not in attendance, one of the two assistants to the Director would write an executive memo to him detailing what was discussed, what decisions were made, and their recommendations.[160] On Saturdays, Tolson and two other men, Harry Duncan and George Allen, met at Hoover's for breakfast. After the Director's SAC delivered Bureau mail, the foursome set out for the track, two agents close behind in a support car. Once there, Hoover and Tolson retreated to their own skybox to watch the races.[161] Presumably lunch was taken in the executive lounge atop the enclosed stands. After the races, they went to one of the four's house for dinner.[162] On Sundays, Hoover occasionally went to church, but usually worked alone at home.[163]

Again, his SAC would deliver any important AIRTELs or Telexes.[164] When not dealing with paperwork, he spent time in his garden or simply took some sun.[165]

Hoover's fifth-floor office (room 5633) was designed to serve both as command center and stage. Impressive in size, it consisted of a long corridor and eight offices.[166] Upon entering the suite, one immediately encountered his personal bodyguard, Sam Noisette.[167] The anteroom was filled with memorabilia from bygone eras.[168] Turning to the left and walking down the corridor lined with plaques and commemorations of various honors, past three more support offices containing secretaries and locked "Official and Confidential" (i.e., political) files, one came to Hoover's stately "official" office. "Appropriately," it was larger than the attorney general's, Hoover's superior. The focal point of the room was a dark wood, government-issue desk with various phones and intercom systems atop it.[169] Brass pistol lamps sat on each end.[170] A small brass plaque inscribed with the phrase "Two feet on the ground are worth one in the mouth" perched front and center.[171] This desk was situated on a raised platform, which allowed him a subtle height advantage over seated visitors or personnel.[172] Two large American flags, one at either end of the desk, helped enhance the focus.[173] On the wall behind and above his desk was a massive FBI seal.[174] The room also contained memorabilia and locked filing cabinets.[175] There was a large fireplace built into the wall opposite his desk.[176] A doorway to the left of this led directly to the office of his executive secretary of forty years, Helen Gandy.[177] The walls were paneled and contained bookshelves.[178] A large, rectangular conference table occupied the center of the room.[179] Situated to the left of Hoover's desk were a bronze sculpture of an Indian on horseback and a potted plant. Large windows lining one wall were covered with venetian blinds and heavy dark curtains.[180] This then, was the public image his office conveyed. But there was more to it. Directly behind his desk and between the two flags was a set of heavy wooden doors, almost always closed when photographs were being taken. These led to a second, inner office. Apparently it was a private retreat (including bath), different in many respects from his outer office.[181] Schematics of his office suite depict this "inner" sanctum as being as large as his outer "public" office, yet photos appear to reveal a much smaller room.[182] It contained another desk and possibly a couch, perhaps the one Hoover used for afternoon naps.[183] The room had no windows and was an odd shape, a right-angled triangle. The desk was situated at the base, Hoover's back to the wall opposite the entrance.[184] There was also a television that had been specially wired so that its tubes were always on. With the set in a constant state of readiness, the screen would instantly leap to life with the flip of a switch. In the days before solid-state circuitry, this meant something to an impatient individual.[185] Like the outer office, there was a seal on the wall opposite the double-doored entrance.[186] While this inner sanctum clearly existed, photos were not generally allowed, and people did not discuss it directly. The public was kept ignorant of its existence, perhaps for security or merely for privacy. Overall though, one can see that Hoover's office environment was highly structured and controlled. No one was given access to him without his specific approval. His executive secretary screened all callers.[187] A hidden electronic buzzer system within arm's reach allowed Hoover instantaneous communication with all his assistants.[188] Assistants who, in turn, managed SOG, a Prussian-style bureaucracy that effectively monitored all field offices, domestic and foreign.

An examination of Hoover's later life reveals the existence of two distinctly different "personalities," one genuine, the other a façade designed almost exclusively to enhance his position as director. Within this façade an increasing paranoia is also apparent. Undoubtedly, as this progressed, those closest to him, people who worked and socialized with him, realized his objectivity and mental state were beginning to deteriorate. And yet, none of these individuals questioned his actions, much less tried to stop him.

II

The Bureaucracy:
Structure of FBI during Kennedy
administration

An examination of the bureaucratic structure of the FBI, as it then existed, is essential to understanding how Hoover was able to override the safeguards of his own system without being challenged. Designed personally by the Director, it concentrated power at the apex.

The base of the pyramid consisted of fifty-five field offices, resident support agencies in an additional five hundred cities and towns under direct field-office control, and foreign offices called LEGATs.[1] Almost one-half of the foreign-office personnel was stationed in Mexico, although there were eleven embassy offices worldwide.[2] Within these offices was a hierarchy that consisted of special agents, their immediate supervisors, and the ASAC (assistant special-agent-in-charge), all of whom were controlled by the special-agent-in-charge, or SAC.[3] The typical field agent (there were approximately fifty-nine hundred in all) was white, male, middle class, definitely anticommunist, conservative, ill-at-ease regarding minorities, and somewhat antiintellectual. There were many Irishmen, Mormons, and Southerners.[4] Physical appearance was important enough to require that file photos regularly be sent to SOG.[5] All followed a procedure book entitled *The FBI Manual of Instruction,* as well as *The Federal Rules of Criminal Procedure.*[6] These provided procedural interpretation of the federal statutes within FBI jurisdiction. The average agent had served ten years and was career oriented.[7] Despite this, he would likely meet personally with Hoover only two or three times before he retired.[8] A personal visit, allowed only in Hoover's "official" office environment, customarily required a small gift, usually pastry (green cakes) or ice cream.[9] SACs and ASACs, however, reported regularly to Hoover for in-depth performance reviews.[10] A SAC could send information directly to Hoover and vice versa, although he could not talk or meet with him without first gaining approval from one of the eleven assistants.[11] Field offices were required to submit reports to SOG, both in June and December.[12] These were designed to supply division chiefs and assistant directors with detailed information about active cases. In turn, Bureau mail was sent by air daily to each SAC. Included in the package were instructions for the office, detailed accounts of disciplinary action taken against errant agents, and case-related paperwork.[13] Additional controls were exerted by "inspectors" from SOG who could appear in a field office without warning.[14] Hoover also used covert informants, consisting of SOG personnel, who would visit field offices and then report directly to him, bypassing the assistants.[15] The existence of these informants was, however, known to the field.[16] SOG employed intricate cross-check methodology to verify accuracy of field-office statistics and reports.[17] "Locator sheets," issued daily, verified the whereabouts of key agency personnel.[18] SACs were not allowed to gather anywhere in large groups, with the exception of Quantico, Virginia, for in-service training.[19] It was considered inappropriate for field-office personnel to criticize assistant directors.[20] Ingrained in Bureau philosophy was the idea that each agent was personally accountable to Hoover for the quality of his work. This was highly significant because by 1960 Hoover's reputation had become international.[21] And yet, in terms of conviction rates, his department ranked third behind the Bureau of Narcotics and the IRS.[22] A letter to an agent or SAC addressing him by last name only (e.g., Mr. Jones), meant Hoover was angry.[23] His correspondence department apparently kept tabs on key events in agents' lives, sending them form letters with Hoover's "signature" on a regular basis.[24] In reality, special agents had very little discretionary power. All cases were viewed as having equal value and all agents carried comparable caseloads.[25] Each agent's "Time in Office" was carefully scrutinized to determine whether enough time was being spent on the streets, working cases.[26] Due to the ever-present possibility of transfer, agents were required to keep three "Offices of Preference" on file at SOG at all times.[27] Obviously these rigorous controls over the field added to the level of stress inherent in the work. In terms of overall job performance, however, the field was staffed with dedicated, quality personnel.[28] Disloyalty was rare.

The next tier in the pyramid was SOG itself, which occupied several large buildings scattered around Washington, D.C.[29] It was standard procedure for any special agent seeking promotion to serve for a time at this level, there being approximately four hundred field positions in D.C.[30] In addition to implementing Hoover's control methodology, SOG served, in effect, as a focal point for all information gathered by the field. Nine bureaucratic "divisions" sifted and utilized the incoming data. These divisions were broken into two basic categories, Investigative and Administrative.[31] The former included Domestic Intelligence, General Investigative, and Laboratory; the latter encompassing Identification, Crime Records (which handled public relations, letters, etc.), Training and Inspection (which split into two divisions between January 1962 and March 1963), Files, and Communications and Administrative.[32] Each was controlled by an assistant director, who was in turn controlled by the two assistants to the director.[33] It is the Investigative group of divisions that is of primary concern here, for the information that became the basis of Hoover's continuing power did not reach the Administrative, or filing divisions. Above the two assistants to the director sat Tolson, known simply as associate director.[34] Atop it all, of course, was Hoover. In total, there were nearly fourteen thousand FBI employees, almost one-half the total of the entire Justice Department.[35]

Men who occupied the position of assistant formed an elite group. Without exception, they had worked their way up the ranks through the years, personally observed and cultivated by Hoover. Seventy to eighty percent were already eligible for retirement, and all strongly supported his views.[36] The nine assistants communicated directly with the two assistants to the director, Tolson, or Hoover, and, of course, the field. While they all respected Hoover, none, with the exception of Tolson, liked him.[37] There was a significant amount of infighting among several, most notably Cartha DeLoach, William Sullivan, and Courtney Evans, all of whom may have been vying for the position of director in anticipation of Hoover's compulsory-retirement date.[38] Sullivan, an Irish Catholic, may have been promoted to the position of assistant in early 1961 in an attempt by Hoover to gain favor with President Kennedy.[39] As stated, DeLoach operated as "political" representative for Hoover in many situations, including a longstanding role as liaison to Vice President Johnson. Evans, in charge of the Organized Crime "division," (in reality a subdivision of General Investigative) served as liaison to the Attorney General, Robert Kennedy, and frequently traveled to regional conferences with him.[40] Alan Belmont, an assistant to the director (Investigative) was apparently considered by the others to be a man of genuine integrity.[41] Research suggests that he knew little of Hoover's machinations regarding President Kennedy.[42] Tolson operated as a hands-on, detail-oriented, day-to-day manager for Hoover, seeing practically everything that crossed his desk.[43] Hoover personally consulted with Tolson before making significant decisions.[44]

Undoubtedly, while esprit de corps was important, the primary force that motivated practically all beneath Hoover and Tolson was fear. This was true at least for those with any significant career time accumulated. Fear that they could be fired "with prejudice" and be unable to find another job. Fear of sudden transfer, forced home sales, and the uprooting of children. And, perhaps, even a certain amount of physical fear, of a man now larger than life.

III

The System:
FBI record keeping

The filing system designed by Hoover to help perpetuate his position and implement the investigatory function of the FBI encompassed three separate subsystems. Nonsensitive information, such as that dealing with kidnapping, bank robbery, car theft, and other local crime statistics, flowed from the field into the leviathan Central Records system.[1] Data that were the result of illegal or questionable activities (e.g., electronic surveillance programs such as ELSUR—electronic surveillance or COINTELPRO—counterintelligence programs) were funneled into the Special File Room, where only top SOG personnel were allowed access. Files kept in this room were not in any way a part of Central Records.[2] Lastly, there was Hoover's private system. This contained a combination of political dossiers, illegal surveillance product, information regarding ongoing covert operations, and his personal files (estate, tax, business, correspondence, etc.)[3] Information otherwise headed for Central Records or the Special File Room could be retained in Hoover's office files indefinitely.

Central Records personnel received, routed, classified, indexed, and serialized incoming data.[4] In all, there were over five million files accessed by an index system consisting of both numerically and alphabetically arranged cards, some fifty million in all.[5] The information contained therein fell into more than one hundred and fifty categories.[6] Basic subjects included were investigative, administrative, applicant, personnel, and general.[7] This system, though manually operated, allowed for quick retrieval of information.[8] The Central Records format was unique to federal government.[9] All information entering this system was processed through the Files

and Communications Division. From there, after sorting and classi-
fying, it would be duplicated and a copy sent to the responsible
division for use in everyday operations.[10] If necessary, a specific
piece of data could be expeditiously processed to a particular division.[11]

Information originated not only with the field, but from other
police agencies as well in the form of monthly crime-statistics reports.[12] Field offices stored this and other information in much the
same manner as Central Records. Data received would be classified,
copied, and filed, with the original forwarded to the agent assigned
the relevant case file.[13] In turn, this information, and the related
casework product, would be sent semiannually to SOG. Information that proved worthless, or that did not require any action
tended to remain in field-office files until such time as it could be
destroyed.[14]

A typical FBI document was numbered as follows: 92-2713-103:
"103" represented the number assigned to the item in the file;
"2713" meant it was part of the 2,713th file, in the "92nd" category
of files maintained by Central Records.[15] So, this document can be
identified as one relating to Carlos Marcello (2713), categorized
under the Mafia (92), representing item number 103 in his file.[16] By
implication, this last number reveals that the file contained at least
103 documents. The type of items that would be found in a formal,
indexed file such as this, one within reach of general FBI personnel,
would be information concerning his criminal record, background,
and family. Derogatory or threatening statements attributable to
him or his associates, or information concerning his political connections would not.[17] Such valuable data instead went to either the
Special File Room or Hoover's private files.

The Special File Room was located in the Files and Communications Division, which was controlled by W. S. Tavel throughout the
two years and ten months of the Kennedy administration.[18] Items
filed in this room were processed through Central Records in sealed
envelopes in order to prevent them from being read by clerical personnel.[19] This meant there had to be some special designation on the
outside of the package, perhaps only the name of the addressee.
Once in this subsystem it became a "June" file. Why the name June
was chosen is unknown. There were, however, two important events
that occurred every June, fiscal year end and biannual reporting
from the field.[20] There were about five-hundred such files, all con-

taining extremely sensitive information.[21] Basic subjects were technical surveillance (i.e., wiretap, "bug," film), sources and informants, and covert programs (ELSUR and COINTELPRO).[22] This is where the more volatile portion of Carlos Marcello's file would have been stored, along with all other such information on Mafia figures, corrupt officials, etc. It is not clear whether all of this information was maintained via the same "00-0000-000" numerical indexing system or by another, as were Hoover's "Official and Confidential" files. It is clear though that Hoover could cause information to be stored in the Special File Room, and thus kept out of Central Records, at will. Further, it could be so filed without the appropriate assistant knowing of its existence (e.g., sealed, encoded AIRTEL from SAC to Director, Central Records forwarding directly to Director's office, Director routing to either O & C files within his office or to Special File Room via sealed envelope). It was this room that contained the numerous transcripts derived from illegal electronic surveillance of key Mafia people prior to and during the Kennedy administration.

Data suitable for Hoover's private files were stored solely within his suite of offices under lock and key and the watchful eye of his executive assistant, Helen Gandy.[23] Only his division assistants were allowed to view items from these files and then only while in the Director's office. They would not attempt to examine such without his express approval.[24] Hoover's control of this information was absolute. An item entering this subsystem from the field usually arrived in the form of a sealed AIRTEL addressed "To the Director."[25] After analysis, it was dealt with in one of three ways. If he marked "PF" at the top, it became part of his personal files, and most likely placed in a "correspondence" section. If marked "O & C" it would be sent to the Official and Confidential files under the appropriate name or subject. Thirdly, it could simply be sent to the Special File Room.[26] In any event, the data would be effectively denied to Central Records, and thus kept from public disclosure. The parallel concepts of "PF" and "O & C" at first appeared meaningless. Undoubtedly, however, there originally was a purpose. Hoover's personal files did indeed contain information relevant only to him and Tolson, such as estate and tax matters, but they also contained O & C material.[27] Most likely it became a case of commingling over the years. It could also be that the designation PF simply alerted Miss Gandy to the fact that the document was to stay in the office, some final categorization being left to her. Given Hoover's control of these files and his tendency to work after 5 P.M., there can be little doubt that he filed some of these documents himself, eliminating the need for designation entirely. Possibly, placement of O & C material in the PF category served as some ultimate form of filing, placing the most sensitive items in the most sacrosanct files of all, Hoover's own.

This curious style of categorizing may represent little more than his ever-present need to ultimately define and control all valuable information that came to him. For in reality, what difference would it make to a Government Operations investigator whether damaging information regarding the assassination of John Kennedy were found in a PF, or an O & C file when both were contained in the same filing cabinet? It would seem too fine a distinction. Hoover could also circulate sensitive information among his assistants by sealed interoffice memorandum. By stamping or writing "Do Not File," "Route by Messenger," or "Route by Envelope" at the top right-hand corner of a document, he ensured that it would not be viewed by general personnel and would be returned to him after consideration by the addressee. Upon its return, he could do with it what he chose.[28] The field also used the "Do Not File" designation, with agents often illegally retaining a copy so stamped. Retention was based upon the idea that any document with such a stamp was probably valuable from a political or bureaucratic standpoint, perhaps even something that could be used to advantage upon return to the private sector.[29] As many agents continued using their FBI training by working in private investigative agencies after retirement, the idea is not without merit. Information of this sort would not be given a file number, nor most likely serialized. Rather, upon placement in the relevant O & C folder, a pink three-by-five index card would be prepared if one did not already exist. Such a card would be titled by name or subject and added to Miss Gandy's card file. The O & C files contained derogatory and nonderogatory categories. It was the same for PF files, only white three-by-five cards were used. Both colors were kept separately in alphabetical order and were cross-referenced.[30]

The contents of these files, kept in locked, vertical, four-drawer cabinets, as well as smaller wall cabinets, are both illuminating and disturbing. Hoover began compiling them during the 1920s and never stopped. There were at least 164 separate files in the O & C category at his death in 1972, including forty-eight on public officials, these in the "derogatory" category. There were also one and a half drawers of numbered documents from the Special File Room. Categories of information were policy and administrative matters, reference material, internal personal matters, sensitive sources, prominent persons, and miscellaneous. Lastly there were forty-five to forty-eight PF files, containing both personal and O & C material.[31]

The uses to which these documents were put by Hoover give one an idea of their specific content. By the FBI's own admission, they were used to aid politicians in reelection bids, circumvent federal constitutional processes, provide derogatory information on critics to various administration officials, force congressional opponents to cooperate on proposed legislation, discredit FBI critics, and conduct improper investigations.[32]

There were, of course, statutory requirements governing the handling and compilation of files by the FBI, the essence of which are summed up in the *Federal Records Act of 1950:*

> *Information from these files is disseminated to appropriate Federal,* state and local *agencies when the right and need to have access to this information exists—For example, to assist in the general crime prevention and detection efforts of the recipient agency. . . . In the event that a system of records* maintained by this [FBI] agency to carry out its functions *indicated* a violation or *potential violation of law,* civil, criminal . . . , and whether arising by general statute or particular program statute, . . . *the relevant records may be referred, as a routine use, to the appropriate agency,* whether federal, state or local, . . . charged with the responsibility of investigating or prosecuting such violation or charged with enforcing or implementing the statute. . . . (emphasis added).[33]

There was also the *FBI Handbook,* governing all special agents and their superiors, which stated:

> *Any information indicating the possibility of an attempt against the person or safety of the President,* members of the immediate family of the President, President-elect or Vice President *must be referred immediately by the most expeditious means of com-*

munication to the nearest office of the United States Secret Service. (emphasis added).[34]

And yet, in the case of Mafia death threats against President Kennedy, the above procedures were simply ignored by Hoover. Instead, the information went into his private files. That such a threat could be discovered in the field and then communicated only to him and one or two other top assistants, in violation of the above requirements, is appalling. There had to be, almost from the outset of the Kennedy administration, an overriding directive from Hoover to his SACs regarding any information obtained concerning President Kennedy. It is the only possible explanation, given the nature of the various threats and the above-described procedural controls. The issue of unquestioning loyalty is inescapable—loyalty best described by a former SAC: "We were FBI agents and J. Edgar Hoover was our leader—anybody else was down the line someplace."[35]

Alan Belmont, Assistant to the Director during the Kennedy administration, made the following telling remarks to the Warren Commission in 1964:

If, anywhere in the field, there is a matter which has some urgency, or there is a question of policy, it would and does come to my attention, and to the attention of Mr. Hoover. I am kept daily advised, as is Mr. Hoover, of all matters of policy or urgency or where there is a question of procedure. This is inherent in our system of close supervision.[36]

The above-described information-filing systems and related procedural regulations were in place and fully operational before and during the administration of President Kennedy.

IV

Means to an End: FBI intelligence-gathering techniques and programs

In order to understand the mechanics by which Hoover gained prior knowledge of Marcello's plan to assassinate the President, we must also examine FBI intelligence and data-gathering techniques.

To Hoover, the ideal source of information was a live informant. Accordingly all agents were encouraged to cultivate potential criminal informants or PCIs.[1] There were, in fact, many such men and women.[2] Typically they reported information to their official contact, usually the special agent assigned to work the related subject.[3] In exchange for data, they received a monthly stipend from the government. They were, in effect, special employees, some reliable, others simply bilking the system as a means of making a living.[4]

In addition, there were private investigative agencies, often owned by or employing ex-FBI agents. Typically an agency of this sort was located near an FBI office, which was in turn located in the local federal building.[5] The value of such an agency lay in the fact that it could provide information through otherwise illegal means. Many times, when an agent retired from the Bureau, he joined the Society of Former Special Agents of the Federal Bureau of Investigation. As with any other federal agency, inside contacts based upon prior association allowed former agents to continue using their skills after return to civilian life. Special agents did perform illegal break-ins, but the private investigative agency provided opportunity for more comprehensive use of this practice.[6] It was a lot safer. All former agents had, upon retirement, signed nondisclosure affidavits regarding case and procedural knowledge obtained while with the Bureau.[7] In spirit, this confidentiality conditioning further

enhanced their value as professional informants. Additionally, use
of these people allowed the avoidance of certain constitutional controls. All police-type entities were required to follow strict guide-
lines in the area of search and seizure, whereas private citizens were
not. The private agency employee would, at worst, commit trespass.
For example then, if the Bureau wanted information on an individual or group, but could not legally obtain it, it would contract with
the private agency and allow it to perform the necessary act of
placing the "bug." This relationship became truly symbiotic during
the administration of John F. Kennedy.[8] In fact, "the Society" so
appreciated Hoover that, on May 10, 1964, it presented him with a
lifesize bronze bust commending his fortieth year as director.[9] Apparently Hoover could control membership in this organization,
causing New Orleans District Attorney Jim Garrison to be struck
from its roles after the assassination.[10]

Another advantage of the private investigative contract was informant cover. In some cases, an individual being paid as an informant risked losing his value if it became known that he was in any
way connected with intelligence agencies such as the FBI. This
danger was minimized by having him report information gathered
to a contract agency instead. Lee Harvey Oswald is a good example.
As a publicly avowed, although somewhat naïve, young Marxist he
had value to the Bureau. While living in New Orleans in the summer of 1963, efforts were made to recruit him as an informant for
use in the Cuban exile community (second largest in the U.S.).[11] His
activism as a Marxist was legitimate, and it was hoped he would act
as a magnet, drawing toward him, or otherwise revealing the identities of, covert pro-Castroites operating in the New Orleans area.[12] In
an effort to accomplish this without directly involving the Bureau, a
private investigative agency being run by an ex-FBI SAC named
Guy Banister was contacted and made aware of Oswald's presence.[13] Oswald was philosophically opposed to those at the agency
but cooperated for the money and two other reasons, which will
become apparent in the course of reading this chronicle. He was
given the use of a small room in the building utilized by Banister,
near the offices of the New Orleans FBI.[14] Here he conducted his
pro-Cuban activities into September 1963.[15]

Electronic surveillance, code-named "ELSUR," became widespread after 1959 as a means of acquiring information on the Mafia
quickly and accurately.[16] There were two varieties, legal (if ap-

proved by the attorney general) telephonic wiretaps, and illegal "bugging" approved by Hoover.[17] The latter was by far the most effective and desirable, both because it provided quick results and because it allowed entire conversations to be taped, virtually any sound within range of a remote sensing device.[18] People not even connected with a person under surveillance could be recorded. These were commonly known as "walk-ins."[19] Bugs were illegally planted in the homes, apartments, hotel rooms, business offices, restaurants, and cars of the various leaders of the Mafia throughout the U.S. If a Mafia leader could not be bugged, then his associates were.[20]

The devices used were innocuous. Terms like "parasite transmitter, pit, Little Sentry, Tiny Tim, Tiny Tattler" and "high output crystal microphone" are illustrative. They were usually battery operated and weighed approximately one ounce. Adhesive strips allowed them to be hidden practically anywhere.[21] Once activated, the information they picked up would be relayed via FM signal (on a frequency banned by the FCC) to a nearby monitoring station, manned by special or contract agents, and recorded on tape. Some bugs were monitored twenty-four hours a day.[22] An obvious advantage of this type of surveillance was that by being covert (i.e., not known to Congress, the Executive, or Judiciary) the results could be kept from the American people. This allowed SOG to use the product for any purpose. Contrast this with a court, or Attorney-General-approved telephonic wiretap, which was subject to tight controls and public review.[23]

Only a handful of companies around the U.S. produced and marketed surveillance items. They often classified them by capability, such as Class A or Class B, the former restricted for use only in cases involving "national security" or "high crimes," whereas the latter were available to "authorized individuals from public agencies."[24] Special agents who did the monitoring were first trained by way of an internal FBI program called "sound school," where they learned how to interpret and process the information obtained.[25] Each bug they planted was given a code number. An example is "MM877-C," which pertained to a Miami, Florida, attorney then under surveillance, named A. I. Malnik.[26] Agents were undoubtedly briefed on the illegalities as well.

After recording the conversation on tape, the agent began processing it by preparing a written log of all conversations. If "politically" significant, involving for instance a death threat against some public official, a transcript would be prepared by the monitoring agent(s). Once the log and/or transcript was ready, the tape was usually erased, although Hoover kept in his possession, and used, actual tapes of sexual encounters involving various public officials.[27] The agent then turned the information over to his supervisor, who gave it to the SAC, who then completed the job by forwarding it to Hoover.[28] This was done in one of three ways: by Telex (i.e., two-way teletypewriter over phone lines), AIRTEL, or courier.[29] Every field office contained a radio room equipped with transmitting devices capable of sending voice or typed messages. High-speed teletype circuits allowed heavy volume. All such transmittals were encoded and ultimately delivered to Hoover in sealed envelopes.[30]

Once in the Director's hands, a death threat received from any of the above described "sources" required two further steps. Hoover was to 1) immediately contact the chief of the U.S. Secret Service, and 2) see to the physical conveyance of the supporting data to its Washington, D.C., headquarters. From there, the following course of action by the Secret Service would be taken. If the danger were imminent, the President's guard would be notified and a defensive posture initiated. If for example, instead, the threat dealt with an individual or group of individuals in another city, or a city that the President was scheduled to visit, the information would be put into a data bank called the PRS, which was located in an office in the Executive Building.[31] This system basically consisted of a large, nationwide index of municipalities. Prior to the President's visit, an "advance agent" would review all threats originating from the city in question, allowing the Service to take the necessary precautions to adequately protect the President.[32]

As the director of the investigative arm of the U.S. Department of Justice, the department spearheading the President's war on the Mafia, Hoover occupied a key position. Undoubtedly Kennedy understood this. By 1962, their intense dislike for each other was common knowledge in Washington political circles.[33] That Hoover worked in opposition to him behind the scenes was apparent.[34] Tragically JFK accepted this as the price of waiting for federal statute to "retire" the Director. Effectively denied access to Hoover's personal files and unaware of ELSUR, he could not know that the Director's "opposition" would assume treasonous proportions.

V

The Elements of Treason

Before turning to the chronicle itself, it is essential to examine the nature of Hoover's primary crime, that of treason.

Considered by the framers of the Constitution to be the gravest offense a citizen can commit, its elements are clearly defined. As stated in *Corpus Juris Secundum,* a standard legal text (See 87 C.J.S. 1, pp. 910–914. 1956 ed.) the act of treason is

1. *overt;*
2. committed with the *intent to betray the government;*
3. *performed in concert with others* "for the purpose of executing a treasonable design by force" (involves an *actual assemblage of men*);
4. in effect a *"forceable opposition . . . to the execution of public law* of the United States";
5. *"adhering to* [this nation's] *enemies, giving them aid and comfort."*

Hoover's "act," as will be revealed, can be summarized here briefly. By September 1962 he and at least one other top aide had learned that a cabal of criminals, the Marcello organization in New Orleans, themselves part of a national criminal syndicate known as the Mafia, were planning to assassinate President Kennedy. Hoover was under both statutory duty, as director, and constitutional duty, as a U.S. citizen, to prevent this. Instead, he concealed the existence of the plan from the Secret Service (*overt act*). He did this with the full knowledge that the assassination would topple the presidency (*intent to betray the government*). The "contract" had been put out by the Marcello organization (*assemblage of men*) in an attempt to prevent further prosecution by the U.S. Department of Justice and other federal agencies (*forceable opposition . . . to the execution of public law*). Under the guidance of the President and the Attorney General, these agencies had been waging war, on a national scale, against this entity. In failing to warn the President and Secret Service, Hoover and his aides, Clyde Tolson and Courtney Evans, enabled the "contract" to succeed (*performed in concert with others, adhering to . . . enemies*). Immediately after the assassination, Hoover and at least one of these same two officials undertook a systematic effort to prevent investigating bodies from learning of the "contract" (*giving them aid and comfort*), and thus their own role in the crime.

Note "the term 'enemies' applies to the subjects of a foreign power in a state of open hostility with the U.S." A formal state of "war" is not a requirement of this crime. Clearly the American variation of the Mafia, a criminal organization inherently foreign in concept, controlled by Sicilians and those of Sicilian descent, and at the time the subject of an intense national effort, constituted such an "enemy." Within the American Mafia itself, members of the Marcello organization were considered "purists," strict adherents to Sicilian methodology. Paradoxically, as a resident alien, Marcello was subject to U.S. law, and therefore, like the Director, committed treason in implementing the "contract."

FBI director Hoover, as an attorney who had worked with federal statute for decades, understood the elements of treason and was well aware of the gravity of such an act. With the information supplied above we turn now to election day, November 8, 1960.

VI

Chronicle—11/8/60 to 5/8/64

Cooperation

11/8/60 to 1/29/61

Overview

During the period 11/8/60 to 1/29/61, Hoover displays outward signs of cooperation with President Kennedy, publicly endorsing his choice of RFK for the attorney generalship and preventing use of the Bureau by the outgoing administration to investigate charges of vote fraud in the election.

Privately Hoover and Tolson have serious misgivings about the new President, perceiving him (firsthand) as decadent, overly liberal, and indecisive. In contrast, the Director's relationship with Lyndon Johnson continues to blossom.

Longtime detractors of Hoover begin to speak out, sensing that his tenure may well come to an end during the current administration. His compulsory retirement date is common knowledge.

The Director misjudges Attorney General Kennedy, operating under the assumption that JFK is the only relevant power. RFK's youth and inexperience surely enhance this perception.

With ELSUR already in operation, Hoover monitors the activities of Carlos Marcello, Santos Traficante, and associates like bookmaker Gilbert Beckley and Teamster Jimmy Hoffa.

In anticipation of Johnson's shift from Senate majority leader to Vice President, various individuals of dubious intent, such as Billie Sol Estes, Bobby Baker, and Edward Levinson begin positioning themselves around him to gain advantage. These men are well known to Hoover.

The use of Oswald's identity by an ex-Bureau official again surfaces.

The focus of Hoover's public rhetoric continues to be the threat of domestic communism.

In relevant part, Hoover's state of knowledge on election day about the key individuals and entities in this chronicle is as follows:

John F. Kennedy: His father, Joseph P. Kennedy, had obtained part of his fortune by supplying scotch whiskey to the Eastern seaboard during Prohibition with the help of organized crime, which in turn controlled distribution of illegal alcohol.[1] Hoover and JPK know each other well and are on good terms.[2] During World War II, JFK had had an affair with a woman named Inga Arvad, who was suspected by the FBI of being a Nazi sympathizer. His encounters with this woman had been recorded by the Bureau through elec-

tronic surveillance.[3] As a U.S. Senator in the 1950s, Kennedy had
been promiscuous even after his marriage, his affairs including married women. Surveillance compiled by the Bureau during spring and
summer 1960 had indicated that Kennedy's extramarital affairs were
ongoing.[4] Hoover assumes that such activities will make him extremely susceptible to political blackmail as President. He is a friend
of Frank Sinatra, who also serves as an intermediary between various Mafia leaders, such as Carlos Marcello (New Orleans), Santos
Traficante (Miami), and Sam Giancana (Chicago).[5] In August 1960,
JFK had remarked he would retain Hoover as FBI director if he
were elected President.[6] He is undoubtedly aware that Hoover
knows many things about his personal life, such as his severe back
problems and the fact he suffers from Addison's disease, as well as
his philanderings.[7] All of which causes Kennedy, in a certain sense,
to fear Hoover. Most important, Hoover understands that Kennedy,
even if he does not win reelection in November 1964, will remain
President until January 21, 1965, well past Hoover's compulsory
retirement date (1/1/65). This gives JFK the absolute power to either
allow his retirement simply by operation of law, or waive it via
Executive Order.

Lyndon Johnson: As a neighbor of Johnson's for nearly nineteen
years (they walk their dogs together), Hoover is close to him, understanding his personality and motivations as a politician.[8] While Senate majority leader during the 1950s, LBJ had used his position, in
part, to enrich himself. This had been accomplished by manipulating
legislation and circumventing constitutional safeguards with the
help of senatorial aide Bobby Baker, all in exchange for money and
financial opportunity. Through Baker and other aides, he has indirectly associated himself with various organized-crime figures.[9]
Since the 1950s Baker has been associated with Mafia functionary
Benjamin Sigelbaum, who in turn is tied to Mafia gambler Edward
Levinson. This individual is a major figure in off-track betting (horse
racing) in Newport, Kentucky, and casino gambling in Las Vegas,
Nevada (Fremont Hotel, others).[10] In 1959, Johnson and his wife
attended the opening of the Stardust Hotel and Casino in Las Vegas,
which is controlled by Mafia interests.[11] LBJ holds the power to
impede any investigation into his dealings in Texas and is linked to
white-collar criminals operating in the state. Billie Sol Estes is a
prime example. LBJ has used Hoover to obtain FBI name checks on
potential employees for his television and radio stations in Texas.[12]

These same stations are operating as a monopoly in South Central Texas, via Johnson's machinations with the FCC.[13] He, like Hoover, has little interest in prosecuting the Mafia.[14] Johnson has always used intermediaries to effectuate questionable goals.[15] While not publicly supporting any candidate for the presidency in 1960, Hoover had privately assisted LBJ's effort to obtain the nomination. Both Hoover and Tolson actually met with him at his Texas ranch on 11/9/59.[16] The Director knows that Johnson, a compromise vice-presidential candidate, does not care for John or Robert Kennedy and knows they, in turn hold LBJ in low regard.[17] Two letters from Johnson to Hoover in the months prior to election make apparent the close relationship between the two men. Excerpts are as follows:

July 25, 1960

Dear Edgar:

I very deeply appreciated your wonderful letter. Just to know that a distinguished public servant and very dear friend like you feels as you do, is richly rewarding to me personally. I only hope that I can live up to the trust of the people who have nominated me for this office—and to the confidence of J. Edgar Hoover.
Warmest regards.

Sincerely,
L

September 6, 1960

Dear Edgar:

Many thanks for your thought on my birthday. It's good to be remembered by your friends—and your neighbors!!
With warm regards.

Sincerely,
L[18]

While LBJ's correspondence is generally effusive, selected letters to Hoover have been utilized in this book where to do so makes clear the long-term, intimate nature of their relationship, as well as John-son's desire to see Hoover remain indefinitely as FBI director. See Appendix A and the photographic inset for an overall selection of their correspondence during the early 1960s.

The Mafia: Hoover has known of its general existence since the 1930s, using it as a source for political and criminal information.[19] Frank Costello, a major New York Mafia figure, had been used as a personal contact for many years, their meetings held in Central Park.[20] Hoover had pursued Mafia figures during the 1930s and early 1940s only because ordered to do so by FDR, and then only halfheartedly.[21] He clearly understands that many officials at all levels have been paid off by the organization. These same officials also have the ability to undercut his power base and thus job secu-rity. He is astute enough to prevent himself from being photo-graphed at race tracks with known Mafia figures. This is accom-plished with the aid of local special agents who can recognize those in the crowd the Director needs to avoid. This practice is adhered to at all tracks Hoover frequents.[22] He knows that the Mafia is con-trolled by a national "commission," which meets periodically to dictate policy to individual members.[23] Some members are difficult to control, men such as Joe Bonnano and Carlos Marcello. The latter holds the position of reigning over the oldest Mafia family in America, which affords him the right to operate outside the will of the commission in some instances.[24] In addition, a disproportionate number of Jewish immigrants work in association with the Mafia. Men such as New York's Meyer Lansky and Miami's Jesse Weiss operate as middlemen, aiding in critical monetary and political in-formation exchanges. Hoover probably knows that the CIA has been using the Chicago and Miami Mafia to engineer the assassina-tion of Fidel Castro, and that this is to take place sometime near the end of 1960. He also knows that JFK knows nothing of this.[25] Since September 1960 an ex-FBI agent named Ray Abbaticchio, as chair-man of the Nevada Gaming Control Board, has been circulating (presumably to Hoover as well) data on Las Vegas gamblers and their connections to the Mafia (i.e., men like Carlos Marcello, San-tos Traficante, and Sam Giancana).[26]

Carlos Marcello: Hoover knows Marcello has been involved in narcotics and gambling for many years and had once supplied Miami mobster Santos Traficante with the murder weapon for a "contract" in Tampa, Florida.[27] On 10/14/59 Hoover sent a memo to the New Orleans field office urging them to use electronic surveillance on Marcello in an effort to obtain more information, noting the success of other offices regarding other Mafia figures. He implied there had been little success getting data on him.[28] The Director had compiled a large file on Marcello from sources other than FBI field work, including the following: *1951—Kefauver Committee, 1957—McClellan Committee* report on organized crime, *New Orleans Crime Commission Reports, New York Crime Report* on the November 14, 1957, Apalachin meeting of the Cosa Nostra commission, *1959—McClellan Committee* testimony by Marcello, *1961 —Permanent Investigations Subcommittee,* and *Immigration and Naturalization Service* reports regarding Marcello's lack of citizenship and "undesirable" status.[29] Frank Costello (Hoover's Mafia liaison) had been one of Marcello's earliest supporters.[30]

"During the 1940s, Marcello became associated with New York Mafia leader Frank Costello. . . . Marcello's association with Costello in various Louisiana gambling activities had come about following a reported agreement between Costello and Senator Huey Long that allowed for the introduction of slot machines into New Orleans. . . . Marcello . . . also gained control of the . . . best known gambling casino in the New Orleans area, the Beverly Club. . . . [This] club brought [him] into partnership with . . . Meyer Lansky. By the late 1950s, the Nola Printing Co., of New Orleans, a gambling wire service controlled by Marcello . . . was serving bookmakers and relay centers throughout the state of Louisiana, as well as areas as diverse as Chicago . . . Miami, Hot Springs . . . Detroit . . . [Newport, Kentucky, and New York]."[31]

Meyer Lansky, an extremely powerful Mafia financier, maintains a close relationship with Edward Levinson. "Installed in key positions in the casinos were such Lansky friends as Clifford A. Jones, a former lieutenant governor of Nevada; Eddie Levinson, the Newport, Kentucky, graduate who had fronted for Lansky in several Las Vegas casinos, including the Sands and the Fremont. . . ."[32]

Hoover knows that Marcello, like most Mafia leaders, operates as follows: removed from actual operations, uses intermediaries to accomplish crimes, confers on finances and policy only with a small and trusted staff, which then carries out his directives; insulates himself from outside criminal exposure; uses associations, connections, and political contributions rather than outright bribes; maintains halo of respectability and culture, living comfortably in a neighborhood far from criminal operations; dresses conservatively, involves himself in charitable, cultural, and church service; and observes three caveats regarding police entities: 1) Public notoriety and high living attract unwelcome notice of ambitious prosecutors and investigators. 2) Crimes of violence against innocent victims or police tend to arouse even the most complacent. Obtain legal advice before acting in this area. 3) Violations of federal statutes expose one to attack from federal enforcement agencies whose resources and manpower far outweigh those of the Mafia. Again, get legal advice before acting in this area.[33]

Marcello and Traficante share the same attorney, G. Wray Gill, as well as the same doctor.[34] As liaison between them they use a mobster from Chicago named Dave Yaras (one of the participants in the "Action" Jackson torture slaying described in the Introduction).[35] The brother-in-law of Nofio Pecora (a close Marcello lieutenant) is D'Alton Smith, Marcello's closest adviser and front man. Smith is also associated with two Dallas friends of Jack Ruby. Pecora's wife is Marcello's secretary.[36] Marcello is funding a Cuban exile group in New Orleans called the CRC, which is controlled by Arcacha Smith. In all likelihood the bag man for these payments is a man named David Ferrie, himself a rabid supporter of the exiles.[37]

Hoover shares two friends with Marcello, although this may not be known to him at this time. These are Washington, D.C., lobbyist, Irving Davidson and Texas oil millionaire, Clint Murchison.[38]

In March 1960 Hoover received informant information from the New Orleans SAC suggesting that "Joe Fischetti" and other mobsters, all associated in some fashion with local mobster Marcello, were planning to support JFK for the presidency through the efforts of Frank Sinatra. Hoover then directed New Orleans to verify the accuracy of the story, but the office responded that it had no way of doing so.[39]

Given the Justice Department's ongoing investigation of Jimmy Hoffa, it is very possible that Hoover is also aware that on 9/26/60 Marcello contributed five hundred thousand dollars to Nixon's campaign through Hoffa and the Teamsters. ". . . Hoffa quietly made a trip to New Orleans to meet Carlos Marcello . . . Marcello had a suitcase filled . . . with cash. . . ."[40] Present was "Edward . . . Partin, . . . Secretary Treasurer of Teamsters Local 5 in Baton Rouge, Louisiana."[41]

Lee Harvey Oswald: Hoover knows that he had defected to the Soviet Union in September 1959, that he is an ex-Marine of low rank.[42] He also undoubtedly has Oswald's military file and knows his family background. On 6/3/60 Hoover sent a memo to the State Department entitled, "Lee Harvey Oswald, Internal Security," in which he stated, "Since there is a possibility that an impostor is using Oswald's birth certificate, any current information the Department of State may have concerning subject will be appreciated." The certificate had disappeared in New Orleans around the time of Oswald's defection to the Soviet Union.[43]

11/8/60—TUESDAY: Hoover works this day, as Election Day is not a holiday in D.C. (also one cannot vote in presidential elections if resident of D.C.). In the evening he follows the election returns closely. JFK wins narrowly. Hoover sets in motion a plan whereby he can obtain as much information as possible on JFK, all with an eye toward leverage. He feels Kennedy will be a president he can control. The President has been engaged in an affair with a woman named Judith Campbell for some months.[44] According to Assistant Director Sullivan, "Hoover was always gathering damaging material on Jack Kennedy, which the President, with his active social life, seemed more than willing to provide."[45]

Tolson states his dislike for both John and Robert Kennedy. "We'll be stuck with the Kennedy clan . . . till the year 2000."[46]

Harper's magazine (November) contains article entitled, "Why The Crime Syndicate Can't Be Touched." "The FBI was the coolest agency of all. J. Edgar Hoover at a national meeting of U.S. Attorneys decried the need for 'special groups' to fight organized crime. . . . The public was never told that the FBI gave us the cold shoulder." Regarding the Apalachian, New York, Mafia trial, the result of a police bust of a 1957 commission meeting of top mobsters, ". . . the reports were not produced until the federal court, at trial, directed the FBI to do so. . . . When we asked for copies of the reports, the G-men acted as if they had never heard of Apalachian." . . . In any event, Hoover seemed determined to stay clear of us, which was a certain way to avoid the stigma of failure. . . . Our report on the inadequacy of federal law enforcement was not made public when J. Edgar Hoover resented our implied criticism of the FBI's activities (or more precisely, 'inactivities') in the field of organized crime. . . . Mr. Hoover has indicated that he does not want the FBI to become a national police force, and shows no inclinations to expand the bureau's functions. . . . Basically this is espionage work which requires an espionage type approach. . . . To assign it a task that its revered Director opposes would seem unwise. . . . Yet something must be done on the national level, for the states will never be able to 'contain' syndicate crime."

11/9/60—WEDNESDAY: Hoover pens congratulatory letter to Johnson.

Dear Lyndon:

I would like to take this opportunity to extend my heartiest congratulations to you on your election as Vice President. . . . All of your friends in the FBI join me in wishing you every success, . . . and *we want you to know that we stand ready to be of aid whenever possible* [emphasis added].

With assurances of my highest esteem,

Sincerely,
Edgar[47]

11/10/60—THURSDAY: JFK announces "I have asked Mr. J. Edgar Hoover to stay on as director of the Federal Bureau of Investigation and he accepted. His tenure in the Federal service . . . stretch[es] all the way back to the Administration, I believe, of President Hoover, and the non-partisan nature of this post is well established."[48] Hoover has known since August. Kennedy personally feels he has done a good job, but, according to aide O'Donnell, ". . . [his] time had come and gone."[49] Earlier in the year Hoover supporters, fearing that Kennedy would not retain him, had attempted to provide for him. ". . . Congress passed a special act . . . which permits anyone who has served as head of the FBI for 30 years to retire at any time, on full pay of $22,000 a year for life."[50]

11/12/60—SATURDAY: Press reports: "The Republican National Committee yesterday sparked an investigation of purported presidential election frauds in 11 states. . . ."[51]

11/13/60—SUNDAY: Press reports: "GOP leaders in Illinois, where Mr. Kennedy held a lead of less than 8,000, were demanding recounts in Cook County (Chicago)."[52]

11/16/60—WEDNESDAY: Press reports: "Riding a wave of absentee ballots, Vice President Richard M. Nixon grabbed California's 32 electoral votes . . . and pared President-elect . . . Kennedy's popular vote . . . The switchover . . . boosted . . . Nixon's . . . total to 223. It dropped . . . Kennedy's from 332 to 300. . . . Kennedy flew [to Johnson City] late this afternoon . . ." to meet with LBJ.[53] Presumably they discuss the California setback as well as GOP vote fraud allegations in key states of Illinois and Texas.

11/19/60—SATURDAY: Press reports: "The Justice Dept. said . . . it has asked the FBI to investigate several alleged voting frauds in the presidential election. . . ."[54] Hoover is now in a difficult position. He must walk a fine line between placating Nixon (and the right) and not offending Kennedy, who in all likelihood has effectively become President.

Johnson sends note to Hoover:

> *You know how delighted I am by the news that you will continue in your present position. . . . This is a recognition* not only of your dedicated service during the past, but *of the continuing need for your service during the years which lie ahead* (emphasis added).[55]

11/20/60—SUNDAY: Press reports regarding FBI's investigation of the alleged vote fraud. "It would be several weeks before the FBI completes all the investigations and determines whether further federal action is warranted."[56] Note that 12/19/60 is the day the Electoral College officially counts the electoral vote and elects the President, four weeks away. This suggests Hoover will sidestep his dilemma by not reaching an investigative conclusion until after this vote, virtually assuring JFK the presidency.

11/23/60—WEDNESDAY: Press reports on FBI involvement in a D.C. investigation of the sex slaying of a little boy on November 14. Hoover orders "100 FBI agents" to investigate. For some reason he has committed 25 percent of his local force of special agents to work on a simple murder case.[57] Why this one, given the high crime rate in D.C. during this time, is unknown. However, Hoover's fascination with sex-related evidence cannot here be ignored. Bureau agents are often ordered into such cases, ostensibly on the pretext that the child has been kidnapped.

Press also reports on the GOP vote-fraud case in Chicago, stating "A shift of Illinois away from Sen. Kennedy would still leave him with 273 electoral votes—four more than the 269. But it could result in throwing the election into the House if enough Southern electors denied Sen. Kennedy their votes. Even so, the odds still favor Sen. Kennedy. In any such House showdown, each state's congressional delegation would cast one vote, to be decided by a majority of the delegation. The Democrats control twenty-nine state delegations compared to seventeen for the GOP. Four are evenly divided."[58]

12/1/60—THURSDAY: *Fortune* magazine (December) mentions LBJ in connection with a controversy surrounding a Navy contract which had been awarded, without competitive bidding, to Transport of Texas for work to be done in the Kwajalein islands. ". . . His role seems to have been that of an innocent bystander." The company apparently had little experience in this kind of overseas work. The contract ultimately went three times over budget. Gossip in Washington had suggested there was a political relationship between its president, Edgar M. Linkenhoger, and LBJ.[59] Johnson's protégé John Connally will shortly become Secretary of the Navy. Up to this point, Johnson, as a longtime member of the U.S. Senate, has served as a ". . . member of the House Naval Affairs Committee, . . . Senate Armed Services Committee, . . . Senate Preparedness Committee, . . . Space Committee, [and]Appropriations Subcommittee for the Armed Services." In this regard he is closely associated with future Warren Commission member Senator Richard Russell.[60]

12/4/60—SUNDAY: Press reports Texas GOP charge of vote fraud, and its claims that the state's twenty-four electoral votes belong to Nixon. Republicans prepare to ask for a federal injunction. ". . . Being investigated by the FBI for possible criminal prosecution . . . are reports of such things as voters being 'coerced and intimidated' by pistol-packing election officials; many cases of alleged 'fixed' voting machines; widespread disregard of the secret ballot; numerous instances of clearly illegal voting; disqualified ballots."[61] Delay here by Hoover has an ingratiating effect with LBJ.

12/12/60—MONDAY: The International Association of Chiefs of Police (IACP) disbands its Committee on Organized Crime as a result of pressure from Hoover. He had objected to its resolution to establish a national nerve center on syndicate crime. Its sponsor, Edward J. Allen, chairman of the IACP's Committee on Organized Crime, is discredited.[62]

12/13/60—TUESDAY: JFK offers RFK the position of Attorney General. "I want somebody who is going to be strong . . . I need you in this government."[63]

12/15/60—THURSDAY: Robert Kennedy pays a visit to outgoing Attorney General William P. Rogers at the Justice Building to discuss the possibility of accepting JFK's offer. Press reports, "After his meeting with Rogers, Robert lunched with Justice William O. Douglas and then returned for further conferences at the Justice Department."[64] Prior to taking the position, he also meets with Hoover, who, when asked, suggests RFK accept. The Director later confides to those around him that he thinks it is a bad idea, but feels his hands are tied because of JFK.[65]

Press reports on the coming inaugural (1/20/61).[66] Apparently Hoover is not invited, his name failing to appear on the roster of dignitaries who will be seated in the presidential stands. It is unclear why, perhaps protocol or simply security.

12/16/60—FRIDAY: JFK announces his selection of RFK as Attorney General then leaves for the Palm Beach, Florida, family home to relax.[67]

12/19/60—MONDAY: The electoral college meets in D.C. to cast the official vote in the election. The final count stands JFK 300, Nixon 219.[68]

12/22/60—THURSDAY: Hoover announces to the press that ". . . the Communists are completing final arrangements for a conference to be held in Chicago beginning 12/31 to formulate plans for a new national youth organization (New Horizons For Youth). In addition the Communists hope to repeat the success which they achieved on the west coast last May, in spearheading mob demonstrations by college students and other young people against a committee of Congress (HUAC)."[69] Note that by this time sixty-two of the demonstrators arrested have been freed, and the charges against them dropped. It was this event that spawned the film *Operation Abolition*.

12/28/60—WEDNESDAY: The *New Orleans States-Item* reports that "Attorney General designate Kennedy was planning specific actions against Marcello," and details RFK's plans to expedite deportation of the New Orleans Mafia leader, a foreigner previously ruled undesirable. As Marcello is the dominant economic and political power in Louisiana and influential in surrounding states, as well as Las Vegas, Hoover has the case monitored closely.

1/61—THIS MONTH: Covert (ELSUR) FBI surveillance of Detroit Teamsters reveals deep involvement between Jimmy Hoffa and the Mafia. The product of ELSUR, Hoover does not brief RFK on this intelligence after he becomes Attorney General.[70]

FBI and IRS, in New Orleans, Miami, and Newport, Kentucky, begin surveillance of Mafia gamblers (off-track betting) Sam di Piazza, Eugene Nolan, Louis Bagneris, Charles Perez, Harold Brouphy, and Anthony Glorioso of Louisiana; Gilbert Beckley and Alfred Mones of the Miami Beach area; Benjamin and Robert Lassoff and Myron Deckelbaum of Newport, Kentucky; Alfred Reyn of New York; and Peter J. Martino of Biloxi, Mississippi. All are Marcello functionaries operating a nationwide betting network through the illegal use of interstate phone services.[71] Nolan and di Piazza are particularly close to Marcello.[72] This operation is a primary source of income to the New Orleans mobster. Beckley is the key contact on the East Coast, working out of Newport, Miami Beach, and New York.[73]

1/10/61—TUESDAY: Hoover sends memo to RFK. "Dear Bob: [Communism poses] . . . a greater menace to the internal security of our Nation today than it ever has since it was first founded in this city in 1919."[74] Note Hoover's familiar, friendly approach to Kennedy. It is not known whether RFK believes communism poses any threat at this date, but his future actions imply he thinks little of Hoover's fears in this area. Absence of activity in the available record suggests that between now and January 26,

Hoover and Tolson are in Miami for peak racing events, this in keeping with longstanding annual tradition.

1/12/61—THURSDAY: FBI (New Orleans) SAC sends AIRTEL to Hoover regarding Marcello. He states a source has reported that Marcello is "extremely apprehensive and upset and has [been] since the *New Orleans States-Item* newspaper on 12/28/60 published a news story reporting that . . . Robert F. Kennedy stated he would expedite the deportation proceedings pending against Marcello after Kennedy takes office in January 1961."[75]

1/18/61—WEDNESDAY: FBI (Miami) special agent George E. Davis sends report to Hoover regarding a Cuban exile group called MIRR. (No. 97-4474). This agent, and another named Paul Scranton, deal regularly with informants in the local Cuban population.[76] Hoover had perceived early on the potential for pro-Castroite infiltration within large Cuban immigrant communities like those in Miami and New Orleans, and places a high priority on intelligence of this sort. This is in part because he believes Castro is a driving force in black unrest in the South.

White-collar Texas swindler Billie Sol Estes, between now and January 25, is in Washington, D.C., ostensibly for the inauguration. While there, he visits with LBJ. The Agriculture Department, which has been preparing to raise Estes's bond requirements quite substantially, reverses its policy, freezing the amount at 1960 levels. Estes is in fact involved in the fraudulent transfer of federal cotton allotments in order to obtain huge subsidies from the U.S. Agriculture Department, as well as mask equally fraudulent sale and lease-back transactions regarding nonexistent fertilizer storage tanks.[77]

1/18—1/20/61: LBJ aide Bobby Baker and North American Aviation lobbyist Fred Black meet Mafia functionary Ed Levinson at a preinauguration party in D.C., probably through Baker's friend, Benny Sigelbaum.[78] Black is a next-door neighbor to Johnson.

1/20/61—FRIDAY: At a New Orleans Ford dealership (Bolton Ford, Inc.) a group of men attempt to buy a number of trucks. ". . . The American first identified himself as 'Joseph Moore' but asked that the name 'Oswald' should go on the purchase documents. 'Oswald,' he said, was handling the money for his anti-Castro organization and would pay for the trucks if the deal went through. . . . The anti-Castro group [was the] 'Friends of Democratic Cuba.' In 1961 a leading light of that organization was Guy Banister—former FBI agent (Chicago SAC)."[79] Hoover's prior suspicions (6/3/60 memo) are confirmed when he learns of this second use of Oswald's identity. He orders the New Orleans field office to trace "Joseph Moore" and the Cuban exile group listed on the application. Recall that Oswald's birth certificate had been stolen from him around the time he defected to the Soviet Union. It has never been found. Obviously, with such a document one can assemble an entire identity. Various exile organizations, in conjunction with the CIA, are currently engaged in a military buildup in anticipation of the Bay of Pigs invasion. Two of Banister's friends, David Ferrie and Robert Maheu (an ex-FBI man), as CIA contract agents, are actively participating in the preparations. Why Banister's group associate Oswald's name (that of a known defector to Russia) with an organization purchasing trucks in anticipation of invading a Soviet satellite, remains unknown.

JFK is sworn in as President of the United States, and RFK as Attorney General. Very shortly the latter will provide Hoover with an initial list of Mafia figures targeted for prosecution, including Carlos Marcello.

1/22/61—SUNDAY: ". . . There were some seventy phone contacts between Judith [Campbell] and the White House between January 22, 1961, and March 22, 1962. . . . Miss Campbell . . . was also seeing [Chicago mafioso] Sam Giancana" on a regular basis.[80]

LATE THIS MONTH: Marcello may learn, through Chicago connections, of JFK's affair with Judith Campbell.[81]

Courtney Evans, FBI liaison to the Kennedys, supplies presidential aide Kenneth O'Donnell with FBI name-check reports on prospective administration appointees. The aide feels that many are nothing more than investigative smears designed to discredit administration selections. O'Donnell also feels that Hoover harbors a greater personal dislike for JFK than RFK.[82] One FBI assistant, Sullivan (Domestic Intelligence Division), will later maintain that Hoover feels JFK dislikes him from the beginning.[83]

As indicated by FBI Mafia file, 1961, Bureau No. 92-6054, between now and January 31 Marcello flies to D.C. to meet with whomever he can to try to prevent his deportation, as well as complain about the fact that his donations (through Catholic organizations) to Kennedy's campaign have not produced the desired results. While there, he calls at least one congressman, and sees Louisiana Senator Russell Long. The FBI (ELSUR) monitors all of this, probably via phone taps and bugs hidden in the mobster's Washington hotel room. This data is soon relayed to Hoover. Marcello also turns to Traficante, asking him to use his contacts with Frank Sinatra. Apparently the singer attempts to discuss the matter with the President, but fails as he will not listen.[84]

1/25/61—WEDNESDAY: U.S. Department of Agriculture employee, Henry Marshall, rules at a meeting of Southwest farm aid officials that Billie Sol Estes's existing transfers of federal cotton allotments are permissible. "Despite [his] suspicions . . . Marshall decided to pass along the approved transfer forms. . . ."[85]

1/26/61—THURSDAY: Deputy Chief of the Secret Service, Russell Daniel, retires from the number-two position after a thirty-two-year career. "Maybe it's time for me to retire. Maybe I'm getting old and soft."[86]

1/21—1/31/61: Hoover and Tolson go to RFK's office to pay initial courtesy call. Kennedy is already angry with Hoover, for a number of reasons: Hoover's absence in the days immediately after the inauguration has been taken as an insult; his successful opposition to Kennedy's idea of a national crime commission as a method of fighting the Mafia; and/or the fact RFK has been kept out of the FBI's fitness gym (he apparently worked out daily).[87] "Well, the Director said that when he and Mr. Tolson went in, Bobby was sitting in his shirtsleeves behind the desk throwing darts and kept doing it all the time they talked. In other words, he did not give the Director his undivided attention. The Director said he had served under a score of Attorneys General during his time in government and it was the most damnably undignified conduct he ever witnessed. He was especially disturbed because Bobby frequently missed the target and the dart stuck in the wall paneling." Hoover also refers to RFK as an "adolescent horse's ass." "He was like a child playing in a Dresden china shop. . . . It was pure desecration of . . . government property."[88] The two terminate their visit quickly, each undoubtedly outraged.

1/27/61—FRIDAY: After work, Hoover and Tolson attend a D.C. dinner and awards ceremony at the Army and Navy Club. The Director receives the " 'Vigilant Patriot Award' from the All-American Conference to Combat Communism" for an article he has written entitled, "One Nation's Response to Communism."[89] The essay had been translated and circulated abroad.

1/28/61—SATURDAY: Hoover and Tolson attend Bowie race track for the Burch Handicap. "In the absence of owner Mrs. William Coxe Wright, Samuel Dixon . . . accepted the Burch trophy from FBI bossman J. Edgar Hoover."[90]

1/29/61—SUNDAY: Hoover attends a White House reception for subcabinet-level officials, where he is greeted by JFK, as well as LBJ. "[The] . . . President . . . came downstairs and through the Green Room, unannounced. . . . *For the first time, there was a bar in the State Dining Room, with waiters to stir up martinis or pour vodka, Scotch, bourbon or champagne.* There were ash trays around the tables, and *for the first time, guests were allowed to smoke. . . .* The Chief Executive and First Lady slipped out . . . just as unobtrusively as they had walked into the East Room an hour and fifteen minutes earlier" (emphasis added).[91] In the course of my research, I found no other Kennedy administration social gathering attended by Hoover. Protocol alone does not explain his absence, for other officials of similar rank do appear on guest lists at various times.

Press reports theft of Kennedy in-law Peter Lawford's jewelry from a D.C. hotel during the inauguration, and the FBI's involvement in attempting to solve the case. "The story—hard enough to come by after the FBI's terse 'no comment' on the case. . . . . . . All records of the case . . . had been impounded by the FBI."[92]

Animosity

1/30 to 2/22/61

Overview

Standoff develops between Hoover and Attorney General Kennedy during the initial month of the new administration. The Director has him placed under around-the-clock surveillance. Perceiving the source of RFK's power, he begins verbally assaulting President Kennedy. The latter's immorality is the obvious focus of attack.

The Bureau suffers its first embarrassment, the apparent result of JFK's decision regarding a patronage position.

The Attorney General begins the implementation of the President's war on the Mafia by organizing and focusing the investigative power of the federal government. Hoover refuses to cooperate in this effort.

Oswald decides to return to the U.S. The Bureau continues its effort to discover who is using his identity in the Louisiana/Texas area.

Johnson's white-collar criminal activities and extreme egotism soon become apparent.

1/30/61—MONDAY: FBI (Rome LEGAT) ". . . forwarded to Hoover a copy of an interview with Alicia Purdon published in the Italian weekly 'Le Ore' concerning her alleged relationship with John Kennedy in 1951. . . . At Hoover's direction, a memo on the 'Le Ore' story was sent to Attorney General . . . Kennedy. . . . At the same time [he] directed that other charges—that [John]Kennedy was a sex pervert and that his wife had had an affair with a New York multimillionaire—be forwarded to the attorney general."[1]

LATE 1/61—EARLY 2/61:   Apparently as a result of his inability to penetrate Hoover's personal security (i.e., screened calls, restricted access), RFK directs the phone company to install a direct hotline from his to Hoover's office, including a buzzer device for summoning the Director. This is unprecedented. Installation occurs without warning while Hoover is in his office.[2]

RFK makes an unannounced entrance into Hoover's office, forcing an outgoing official, Luther Huston, to briefly delay his appointment with the Director. "I had arranged to see him at a particular time but I had to wait because the new Attorney General was there.

He hadn't called or made an appointment. He had just barged in. You don't do that with Mr. Hoover. Then my turn came and I'll tell you the maddest man I ever talked to was J. Edgar Hoover. He was steaming. If I could have printed what he said, I'd have had a scoop. Apparently Kennedy wanted to set up some kind of supplementary or overlapping group to take over some of the investigative work that the FBI had been doing. My surmise is that Mr. Hoover told Bobby, 'If you're going to do that, I can retire tomorrow. My pension is waiting.' Robert Kennedy wouldn't want to be responsible for being the man who caused Hoover to leave the Justice Department."[3] Hoover feels that RFK demeans the Justice Department with his casual manner, which includes rolled-up shirt sleeves, loosened tie, uncombed hair, unpressed clothes, and giving his dog, a black Labrador named Brumus, the run of the fifth floor.[4] Kennedy also occasionally brings his preschool-aged children to work. Hoover soon begins arguing with the A.G., defending the absence of minority personnel by claiming that RFK wants him to lower FBI standards. He vehemently denies the Mafia even exists. There are constant attempts to catch RFK doing anything that Hoover feels can be used to advantage. Apparently these efforts produce nothing. RFK begins a practice of requiring Hoover to prepare a formal memo every time he leaks a smear-type JFK story to the press. The Director's memos to RFK are now simply addressed "The Attorney General."

1/31/61—TUESDAY: ". . . Vice President Johnson wrote to Secretary of Agriculture Orville Freeman . . ." in behalf of Billie Sol Estes.[5]

2/61—THIS MONTH: Hoover attempts to move the buzzer phone to Miss Gandy's desk, but "when [RFK] first picked up the hotline . . . it was not Hoover but . . . Helen Gandy, who answered. 'When I pick up this phone, . . . there's only one man I want to talk to—get the phone on the Director's desk.' "[6]

RFK puts Walter Sheridan (ex-FBI) in charge of the labor/racketeering group, a part of the Organized Crime section at Justice. He also quadruples the size of the section and begins a policy of requiring Section Chief Hundley to circulate all information obtained regarding the Mafia among the twenty-seven federal agencies involved in crime detection and enforcement. In effect, he creates the very thing Hoover opposed, a national crime commission. Hoover refuses to provide data to this information-exchange program, although he quite willingly accepts it from the other agencies. RFK issues his initial hit list of Mafia figures, some forty individuals, to all twenty-seven agencies. Marcello is on the list.[7]

"Ward Jackson, a high official with Commercial Solvents, attended a business conference . . . in Washington . . . and enjoyed the special services of Clifford Carter and a visit with Vice President Johnson. . . ." This New York company is closely tied to Billie Sol Estes's Texas operation.[8] Carter and a man named Walter Jenkins are LBJ's personal aides.

2/1/61—WEDNESDAY: RFK is using, with some regularity, the hotline buzzer to summon Hoover, heightening tension between the two. Apparently RFK's aides begin complaining to him regarding Hoover's noncooperation policy. The A.G.'s response is to attempt to calm them by suggesting that by 1/1/65 Hoover will be retired.[9]

Oswald, in Minsk, makes an entry in his diary. "I mail my first request to American Embassy, Moscow, for reconsidering my position. I stated, I would like to go back to U.S."[10]

2/3/61—FRIDAY: "A spokesman [for the Retail Merchant's Credit Association of Fort Worth] revealed that within two weeks of the [Bolton Ford] truck purchasing incident the FBI twice inquired whether the association knew of business dealings by Oswald. . . . The inquiries immediately preceded Passport Office concern that 'there is an imposter using Oswald's identification data.' "[11]

2/4/61—SATURDAY: "Of all the Kennedy sacrileges against hallowed Hoover procedures . . . none angered the Director more than Bobby's habit of appearing at headquarters on weekends and requesting the duty agent to supply specific case files for his review. The Attorney General had never had direct access to FBI files; any request for files [was] to be made to Hoover, who would unilaterally determine what was and was not appropriate for A.G. review. . . . Kennedy's unpredictable weekend appearances required the Director . . . to spend Saturdays at the office, an unprecedented interference with his ironclad routine. . . . Once, Bobby had his children with him . . . when he was unexpectedly called to the White

House, and as he rushed out he had casually asked the Director to keep an eye on the kids. Hoover had sputtered about 'those brats' for weeks afterward. . . ."[12]

Press reports that JFK appointee, Charlie Merriweather, is of highly questionable character, stating "Hurried President Kennedy relied on the FBI in checking Merriweather's qualifications and the FBI must have been even more hurried when it made its report." Merriweather had allegedly been involved in land-transaction fraud at the expense of the taxpayer. "This is the man the FBI cleared to dole out millions from the Export-Import Bank."[13] The FBI name-check report to JFK on this man could well have contained these allegations. This adverse publicity would have angered Hoover.

2/13/61—MONDAY: FBI (New Orleans)—Longtime Marcello case agent Regis Kennedy prepares and sends yet another report on the mobster to Hoover. "Continued investigation of Carlos Marcello since Dec. 1957 has failed to develop vulnerable area wherein Marcello may be in violation of statutes within the FBI's jurisdiction."[14] This is Special Agent Kennedy's standard reply regarding Marcello, a reply Hoover has been reading biannually for years. Given Hoover's close friendship with Marcello mentor Frank Costello, acquiescence in this recurring response may be deliberate.

EARLY 2/61: RFK informs White House aides they are "to 'go through the Attorney General first' before arranging 'any' meetings with . . . officials . . . in the FBI."[15]

2/14/61—TUESDAY: Press reports that JFK has just instructed the Navy to retain Admiral Rickover past his mandatory retirement age, to take effect on 1/28/62. ". . . Rickover is being kept . . . beyond his normal retirement date at the direct request of President Kennedy. . . ."[16]

2/17/61—FRIDAY: "Friday night . . . was extremely foggy and wholly unfit for flying in the Austin, Texas, area. Vice President Johnson was at his Pedernales River Ranch, sixty-odd miles west in the Blanco County Hills. 'His plane,' . . . was . . . on the ramp at the Austin Airport; its pilot . . . Harold Teague and his copilot, Charles Williams . . . were . . . standing by. . . . Johnson ordered the plane flown to the ranch—where the paved strip was

lighted, but where no ground-control instruments had been installed, with only a two-way radio at the ranch for communication
with the plane. . . . the strip lights could not be seen and flying
was blind. . . . Teague consulted 'the tower' at Austin and was
advised against the flight. He then talked . . . by radio, with Lyndon at the ranch, telling him they should not try to make it. Johnson . . . exploded, venting his profanity upon the pilot, demanding to know 'what do you think I'm paying you for?' and again
ordering him to 'get that plane' to the ranch. . . . Vice President
Johnson's Convair roared into the murky night, above the hilly
terrain. . . . The charred ruins were found where the pilots, hopelessly groping down for lights they could not see, had at last flown
into a cedar-covered hill."

Oddly, word of the crash does not reach the news media until the
following Sunday. A controversy ensues regarding actual ownership
of the plane, title to which changes hands three days after the crash,
ultimately coming to rest in the hands of a corporation controlled
by a lawyer working for the LBJ Co.[17]

2/20/61—MONDAY: Secretary of Agriculture Freeman responds unfavorably to LBJ's letter in behalf of Estes's fraudulent
operation. "Freeman . . . pointed out that 'there have been some
abuses of the law in this regard.' "[18]

Political Confrontation

2/23/61 to 9/62

Overview

Hoover's political assault on President Kennedy develops on two fronts during this time. Through writings and public statements, he attempts to counter JFK's policies and programs, all the while covertly accumulating compromising data on his personal life. This he continuously feeds to the Attorney General, under the assumption it is passed along to the President.

Over the next eighteen months the Director and the Chief Executive clash repeatedly over basic issues of governmental philosophy. There are disagreements over the use of the Bureau in investigations involving the U.S. Post Office, Department of Defense, and private industry (i.e., the steel crisis). Kennedy implements a policy of pardon and early parole for certain criminals, many of whom Hoover originally helped convict. These include political foes of the Director. JFK also eliminates travel restrictions on Soviet visitors to the U.S., complicating the Director's domestic counterintelligence operations. Through the efforts of Secretary of Defense Robert McNamara, apparently with the acquiescence of President Kennedy, Hoover's propaganda film, *Operation Abolition,* is denounced and removed from circulation. In opposition to the Bureau's prosecrecy stance, the President openly campaigns for abolishment of government regulations allowing such. Herein lie seeds of the Freedom of Information Act (FOIA).

The President and the Director make heavy use of the media to denounce each other. Hoover belittles Kennedy's leadership skills after the latter fumbles the Bay of Pigs invasion. Through various speeches, the President exposes the Director's true, archconservative nature to the public. Ultrarightist General Edwin Walker resigns his post and becomes a focal point for political controversy. Hoover aligns himself with Walker, encouraging verbal attacks upon the President. Kennedy's actions, however, effectively reduce the credibility of the aging official. Hoover's aides and supporters (Clyde Tolson, Cartha DeLoach, George Sokolsky, various senators and congressmen, etc.) unleash a barrage of rhetoric against the administration. In turn, longtime Hoover critics and former agents speak out, describing the autocratic, and in many ways increasingly inefficient, nature of the Director's stewardship of the Bureau. As a result, press reports begin to surface, suggesting Kennedy will simply remove the bureaucrat. By early 1962, Hoover learns of JFK's plan to discard him on New Year's Day, 1965.

One bright spot for Hoover is the appointment of his longtime ally, Congressman John W. McCormack, to the position of Speaker of the House in January 1962. A Massachusetts political foe of JFK, he is now the third most powerful man in the U.S. behind Johnson.

Hoover monitors the President's personal life, hoping to obtain sufficient data to force him into waiving the Director's compulsory retirement. He learns of Kennedy's affairs with Marilyn Monroe and Judith Campbell, attempting via the latter to directly intimidate the President. Monroe, perhaps as a result of depression stemming from her short-term relationship with JFK, dies of a drug overdose in early August 1962. Toward the end of 1961, Hoover discovers that the Chief Executive's father had taken campaign donations from a Mafia member the Attorney General is then attempting to prosecute. Shortly after being confronted by the Kennedy brothers with the data, the family patriarch suffers a massive stroke.

Almost from the beginning, President Kennedy and Hoover disagree over the proper role of the Attorney General, the Director refusing to recognize his status as a superior. In an attempt to redirect the federal bureaucracy toward administration philosophy and goals, JFK begins a systematic program of replacing agency and department directors. These include, to name a few, top officials of the Secret Service, CIA, Immigration and Naturalization Service, National Security Agency, Joint Chiefs of Staff, and Bureau of Narcotics. Many of these officials are former FBI agents and long-time bureaucrats, some of whom have been in power for decades. In contrast, he issues Executive Orders waiving the retirement rules for those he feels are performing valuable services (i.e., Rickover and Waterman).

Martin Luther King, Jr., becomes a political issue, the Director hoping to undermine the President's position (Kennedy had publicly promoted the minister's civil-rights programs) by "proving" King is nothing more than a communist dupe. In doing so, Hoover hopes also to shore up his crumbling anticommunist propaganda platform.

Early on, JFK increases his personal security, dramatically building up the ranks of both the Secret Service and White House police. He develops an air of unpredictability as to his public appearances, at times adhering to published schedules and at others not. He maintains a very fast pace, often appearing where he is not expected. JFK forces Secret Service protection on a very unwilling Vice President Johnson. As a result of reports supplied by the Attorney General, Kennedy breaks with singer and Mafia functionary Frank Sinatra in the summer of 1962. Throughout this period, however, the President's personal life-style remains unchanged in many respects. Late hours are kept and private parties attended.

In spring 1962, Kennedy announces plans to seek a second term, and he privately informs Johnson of his intention to campaign in Texas at some point in furtherance of that goal.

Hoover continues to expand his electronic-surveillance coverage of the Mafia. Increasingly hostile rhetoric against the President and Attorney General is recorded and forwarded to the Director, who withholds it from the Department of Justice and Secret Service. The aging icon implements a large-scale surveillance program of Las Vegas casinos, in the process discovering a close relationship between the Mafia and Johnson's longtime protégé, Bobby Baker.

The personal pursuit of impostors (of varying degrees of importance) is evidenced by the arrest and prosecution of men posing as lawyers and foreign diplomats, as well as of one individual attempting to create the illusion of his own death. Hoover maintains his focus on King and Oswald, perhaps in part for the same reason (i.e., King's discreet philanderings, the use of Oswald's identity by anti-Castro forces in New Orleans).

In anticipation of his retirement, many groups and entities commend and otherwise heap praise upon the Director. In response to the retirement of Narcotics director Harry J. Anslinger, and the introduction of Senate Bill 3526 in July 1962 governing his own retirement, Hoover's public rhetoric changes. The dominant themes become immorality and organized crime. Publicly attacked in August 1962, the ferocity and accuracy of the verbal assault temporarily stuns both him and his supporters. His credibility suffers another blow.

During this time of confrontation, Marcello is subjected to the full force of John Kennedy's war on the Mafia. Despite intense behind-the-scenes efforts, in April 1961 he is deported. Upon illegal reentry, he is prosecuted for various offenses. The IRS begins investigation for tax fraud and liens are placed on his assets. The gambling arm (Beckley, et al.) of his empire is broken up via the arrest and prosecution of various functionaries around the country. For an in-depth analysis of this onslaught, see September 1962 in the chronicle.

His response to this is, in part, to align himself with members of the intelligence community, people involved with the FBI and CIA. Ultrarightists such as David Ferrie and Guy Banister are cultivated. When called to testify regarding his criminal activities, for a time he openly defies the federal government. The mobster unsuccessfully attempts to obtain employment for a key lieutenant (Sam Saia) with the Immigration and Naturalization Service in hopes of preventing future deportation. By mid-1962, associates such as Teamster Jimmy Hoffa and New York gambler Eddie McGrath are calling for the assassination of Robert Kennedy with explosives, under the assumption it will end the President's drive against them. By August, pretrial efforts of the Beckley group to obtain dismissal have failed. A trial date is set. Via ELSUR and other forms of surveillance, Hoover monitors most of the Marcello organization's reaction to all of this. As with other Mafia product, it is withheld from the proper authorities. The Director also makes no attempt to force New Orleans Marcello case officer Regis Kennedy to develop evidence against the mafioso. By September 1962, Marcello makes the decision to assassinate President Kennedy, hoping thereby to precipitate the removal of the Attorney General and alleviate pressure on his organization.

Johnson's machinations continue to become ever more complex as his relationship with Hoover grows. As Vice President he proves very illusive, almost secretive. He avoids the press entirely. Individuals with inside knowledge of Estes's activities and relationship with Johnson are murdered by persons unknown. When the overall scandal breaks, LBJ turns to the Director for help. He is not refused. As with Marcello, Hoover has monitored much of Estes's affairs. As the chief investigator in that case, the opportunity to gain control of Johnson is not missed. Through liaisons and private meetings the two become closer than ever. By withholding evidence from Texas officials and otherwise refusing to cooperate, Hoover prevents Johnson's political destruction. Despite this, rumors begin to develop to the effect that Johnson will be dumped from the 1964 presidential ticket. To counter this, Kennedy publicly endorses LBJ as his running mate.

Johnson protégé Bobby Baker becomes more deeply involved with Mafia gamblers Levinson and Sigelbaum. He enters contractual agreements (Serv-U Corp., Carousel Motor Inn) with the pair and in all likelihood conveys word of Johnson's dissatisfaction with the vice presidency to them. They, in turn, are in close contact with gambling associates of Marcello. Johnson himself publicly supports Baker's involvement with the Mafia by attending the gala opening of his East Coast resort, the Carousel. By authorizing ELSUR on Levinson, Hoover gains detailed knowledge of the man's relationship with the mob.

Attorney General Kennedy's efforts against the Mafia in the broader sense begin to produce results. New antiracketeering legislation is passed, causing considerable fear within the organization. He attempts to have his best-selling book on the Mafia, *The Enemy Within,* adapted to the screen but fails, much to the relief of Hoover, Marcello, and the Mafia in general. In 1962 there is another push for even tougher legislation. Kennedy orchestrates an all-out assault on Hoffa in an attempt to break him. There are numerous deportations of Mafia personnel. One functionary, Joseph Valachi, agrees to inform on the mob in exchange for protection.

The A.G. also focuses on Texas, partly because of Johnson's association with white collar crime. Besides the Estes scandal there are rice-allotment and oil scams that warrant investigation. All of this enrages Johnson, who quickly develops a strong dislike for RFK.

In the area of civil rights, Kennedy brings increasing pressure to bear on the state of Louisiana, causing intense concern in Marcello's home city of New Orleans. Local FBI offices take pains to make it clear that it is Kennedy's doing, not theirs.

RFK's power struggle with Hoover continues, the younger man repeatedly attempting to circumvent the Director by befriending Bureau officials in D.C. and around the country. Kennedy successfully deflates the specter of domestic communism created so artfully by Hoover over the decades. The large percentage of dues-paying Bureau informants within CPUSA is made apparent.

Oswald marries, corresponds with his mother, and, after obtaining permission from the Soviets and U.S. State Department, returns to the U.S. in June 1962 with wife and child. He is monitored by the Dallas FBI, undoubtedly at Hoover's request, but appears insignificant. Despite this, an attempt to recruit him as an informant is made. Like many defectors, he had become disillusioned with the realities of communist life.

In France, a cabal of political extremists attempts the assassination of President de Gaulle. In part for political reasons no doubt, de Gaulle instructs the government to move quickly against the conspirators, apprehending and prosecuting all concerned. The French people are fully informed of details surrounding the attack. Politics aside, the thoroughly public and expeditious manner in which the perpetrators are prosecuted demonstrates, in the literal sense, the optimal reaction of government to a conspiracy designed to topple it.

2/23/61—THURSDAY: Between 10 and 11:30 A.M., Hoover, in keeping with tradition, attends annual White House presentation of Young American Medal for Bravery award ceremony. Without warning, he confronts the President, bitterly complaining about the controls the latter has allowed the Attorney General to impose upon him. Hoover obviously has chosen this moment to bypass RFK and attempt to regain the upper hand. A threat to resign may be made at this point. He holds the President responsible for RFK's actions. The photograph capturing the moment is simply captioned, "FBI Director J. Edgar Hoover had two listeners . . . in President Kennedy and Attorney General Robert F. Kennedy. . . ."[1] The expression on JFK's face is one of embarrassment, intimidation, and fear. He fingers his wedding band nervously.

2/25/61—SATURDAY: *Memphis Commercial Appeal* reports "A flat FBI denial that J. Edgar Hoover intends to resign should put the quietus on all the rumors and gossip to that effect which have been going the rounds since President Kennedy was elected. . . . One so-called newsletter circulated recently throughout the country, in commenting on a prediction that the FBI's Director would 'be out by summer,' made the unequivocal statement that 'He and his boss, Attorney General Robert Kennedy, disagree too much, particularly on the FBI's proper role. . . . Only the Nation's enemies and its criminal underworld will regret that Mr.

Hoover is still going to be around officially to give them a hard way to go." Via FBI news-clipping department in the nearest field office, this article is on Hoover's desk within hours. Undoubtedly the article has been precipitated by his February 23 clash with JFK.

Press reports a story regarding JFK's World War II naval service, during which he sustained debilitating back injuries. "After seventeen years, President Kennedy has identified the man who saved him from death on a South Pacific island."[2]

Press reports on fact that Frank Costello, a New York Mafia crime figure "has just been stripped of his American citizenship by the Supreme Court and now faces deportation to Italy. . . ."[3]

3/61—THIS MONTH: Hoover article appears, "Protecting the Innocent—Law Enforcement's Sacred Task," which states in part, "The FBI is a fact-gathering agency. It does not . . . make recommendations or evaluations. In making its investigations the FBI is interested in obtaining the facts—accurately, completely and without interpretation."[4]

During this general time period, FBI (Philadelphia) ELSUR begins obtaining verbatim conversations of Philadelphia Mafia leader Angelo Bruno. "Bureau records . . . indicate that Marcello initiated various efforts to forestall or prevent the anticipated prompt deportation action. . . . According to the Philadelphia underworld leader, Marcello had enlisted his close Mafia associate, Santos Traficante of Florida, in the reported plan. Traficante in turn contacted Frank Sinatra to have the singer use his friendship with the Kennedy family on Marcello's behalf. This effort met with failure and may even have resulted in intensified Federal efforts against [him]."[5] Marcello's disappointment is made clear. Hoover must realize that Marcello now perceives the President as a formidable foe.

Robert Kennedy will later write of Hoover, "Every month or so he'd send somebody up or a memo . . . to give information on somebody I knew or a member of my family. . . ."[6]

U.S. Agriculture Department employee, William E. Morris, in Texas interviewing candidates for State Agriculture Advisory Committee, meets Billie Sol Estes for the first time. The Texan buys him a hundred-dollar hat. Estes foe Dr. John Dunn prepares an anonymous report for the FBI on his dealings. He soon makes it available to ex-FBI agent and commentator, Dan Smoot.[7]

3/3/61—FRIDAY: General Joseph M. Swing, director of the Immigration and Naturalization Service (INS), secretly informs Hoover and the New Orleans FBI that ". . . the Attorney General has been emphasizing . . . the importance of taking prompt action to deport notorious hoodlums. In this connection, the Marcello case is of particular interest. A final order of deportation has been entered against Marcello but this fact is being held in strictest confidence." In response, the New Orleans field office prepares a report on Marcello and his impending deportation.[8]

3/8/61—WEDNESDAY: Press reports that JFK will be depicted in a ". . . biographical story of his accomplishments as a skipper under fire in the Pacific. 'P.T. Boat 109' will deal with the 1943 episode in which a Japanese destroyer cut Lieutenant Kennedy's craft in two."[9] Hoover himself was partially responsible for JFK's transfer to the Pacific theater in World War II. This was because of JFK's affair with suspected Nazi sympathizer Inga Arvad, while stationed on the East Coast—an affair the Director had had monitored with electronic surveillance.[10]

3/9/61—THURSDAY: Press reports: "The FBI has begun a thorough probe of alleged illegal fund raising inside the Post Office during the last election. The money went to Republican campaign coffers."[11] Given Hoover's use of the same agency to screen subversive literature, as well as open certain individuals' mail, it is unlikely he has instigated this probe, or will willingly participate in it.

3/14/61—TUESDAY: United Services Organization, Inc., gives its annual award to Hoover for his ". . . unselfish contributions to the American heritage."[12]

3/17/61—FRIDAY: Press reports: "President Kennedy . . . ordered the Post Office . . . to stop holding up Communist propaganda received in the mail from abroad. 'A review . . . has disclosed that the program serves no useful intelligence function. . . .' "[13] This is a direct assault upon one of Hoover's fundamental beliefs.

3/18—3/23/61:   Hoover writes a memo concerning Hollywood producer Jerry Wald, who is planning to make a movie based on RFK's exposé of the Mafia through his best-selling book, *The Enemy Within.*[14] A movie of this nature is unsettling to Hoover. Revealing its long, successful history, and by implication Hoover's ambivalence, would prove very damaging.

3/24/61—FRIDAY: Hoover again comments in an internal memo regarding producer Jerry Wald.[15]

Press reports: "Vice President Lyndon B. Johnson doesn't want Secret Service agents following him around when he is in Washington. . . . Johnson told [Secret Service Chief Baughman] he didn't think it was necessary. . . ."[16] It would seem odd that the Vice President would not want such protection, but then again he also does not give press conferences.

3/25/61—SATURDAY: Baltimore FBI SAC, Edward Powers, announces that the Bureau will "interview the nine jurors who reinacted on a Baltimore TV show the deliberations which led to Ree's [a murderer's] conviction. . . ."[17] The concern is that such a reconstruction could jeopardize the case, currently on appeal. The FBI had been involved in the original investigation, and Hoover is angered by the chance that an evidentiary reinactment might distort the truth to the Bureau's disadvantage.

D.C. press reports: "Members of the Fairfax County School Board are . . . angry over a statement sent recently to the County school teachers saying the Board is 'anxious' that they see the film, 'Operation Abolition.' . . . There is a difference of opinion over the accuracy of the picture. . . . 'All true' says . . . J. Edgar Hoover."[18] Recall that the defendants in the protest, depicted as communist dupes in the film, are currently on trial in San Francisco. JFK is known to oppose the film's use.

3/27/61—MONDAY: ". . . Dan Smoot . . . forwarded to the bureau an anonymous fourteen-page memorandum on . . . Estes' chattel mortgages, storage tanks, and other documents on file at the Reeves County Courthouse."[19]

3/30/61—THURSDAY: FBI (New Orleans) or SOG (Hoover) generates another report on Marcello regarding his impending deportation, all in the context of General Swing's 3/3/61 memorandum.[20]

4/61—THIS MONTH: "Even in his anti-Castro activities, [Marcello functionary David] Ferrie may have served as a financial conduit for [the Mafia leader], as suggested by an FBI report of April 1961."[21]

4/3/61—MONDAY: *N.Y. Mirror* publishes an article regarding an interview with Harry Singer and Gerold Duncan, both formally with the late 1950s anti-Mafia federal task force known as the Wessel Group. "Hoover was very cool to the whole idea of the Attorney General's special group. He ordered that the FBI files, containing the very information we needed on organized crime, were to be closed to us. . . . Criticizing Hoover is a dangerous thing for anyone to do. . . . But honesty compels me to say that some of Hoover's ideas are sadly behind the times. . . ."

Newly censured FBI special agent William Turner writes to Senator Jacob Javits. He ". . . described the Bureau as an 'autocratic empire isolated by myth from outside inspection.' " In the coming months Hoover will fire the agent, who, in turn, moves to D.C. to contest the action. "[I] . . . called the office of Edward Bennett Williams and in his absence was connected with . . . Vincent J. Fuller. We arranged a conference. After I recounted the lengthy story . . . he exclaimed, 'It sounds like a Gestapo.' A few days later Fuller called to say that Williams would take the case. The famous attorney had received a quarter of a million dollars in defending . . . Jimmy Hoffa. . . ." The lawyer takes Turner's case for ". . . five hundred, a pittance compared to Williams' usual fees."[22] The case has been taken for a nominal fee because of the inside perspective of the Bureau Turner can provide.

4/4/61—TUESDAY: In New Orleans, "On the afternoon of April 4, . . . 8 years after he was ordered deported, Carlos Marcello was finally ejected from the United States. As he walked into the INS office in New Orleans for his regular appointment to report as an alien, he was arrested and handcuffed by INS officials. He was then rushed to the New Orleans airport and flown to Guatemala. Marcello's attorneys denounced the deportation later that day, terming it 'cruel and uncivilized,' and noted that their client had not been allowed to telephone his attorney or see his wife." FBI (New Orleans) prepares a report on the deportation and forwards it to Hoover.[23]

4/5/61—WEDNESDAY: Marcello, without luggage, and with little cash, is now temporarily stranded in Central America. "He quickly regained his composure, however, and soon was installed in a plush suite at the Biltmore Hotel, as his brothers flew in cash and clothes."[24]

Press reports RFK's statement that Marcello's "deportation was in strict accordance with the law."[25]

4/6/61—THURSDAY: Press reports that Marcello's attorneys "promptly asked the District Court here (New Orleans) to hold the Attorney General Robert F. Kennedy and Commissioner of Immigration J. M. Swing in contempt. They said that the Government decided long ago that Marcello was born in Tunis and that it was relying on a phony birth record when it got the warrant to deport him to Guatemala. In Guatemala . . . the Immigration Service was apparently as confused as everything else. Its men were at the wrong airport when the U.S. plane landed. As a result, Marcello slipped into the quiet obscurity he has sought for years but which he could never find because people kept talking about him when they talked about the Mafia, narcotics, gambling, police payoffs, and so on. An Immigration spokesman there, the Associated Press said, announced a Guatemala-wide search for Marcello. 'If he is a Guatemalan, we are going to arrest him, and if he isn't, we are going to deport him,' Ramon Alvardo vowed. The search didn't turn up Marcello but he dropped in at the Interior Ministry at mid-day yesterday. He was neither arrested nor deported and he went back to his hotel. His papers were in order, a government spokesman said. Marcello didn't say anything but it must have seemed like home. Back in Washington, Attorney General Kennedy learned about Marcello's ride after newsmen did. He wasn't happy about that but there didn't seem to be much he was going to do about it. When the Immigration Service asked Guatemala, Guatemala said yes. The Immigration Service then asked: Will you take him back? Guatemala said yes and Marcello went for a ride."[26]

4/7/61—FRIDAY: Press reports "Kohei Hanami, the man who sank President Kennedy's torpedo boat in WWII, has received a bronze medal commemorating the Presidential Inauguration. When Mr. Kennedy was elected, Mr. Hanami and surviving members of his crew sent congratulations."[27]

Press reports Marcello as saying "he wanted to go back to the United States. . . . Local newspapers published reports from the tiny village of San Jose Pinula labeling as 'false' the birth registration produced with Marcello's name there. Guatemalan newsmen in the interior said the birth registration had been 'planted' in the records a few weeks ago 'by a young North American who arrived at San Jose Pinula in a sports car.' "[28]

4/10/61—MONDAY: IRS files an ". . . $835,396 tax lien against [Marcello] and his wife," beginning a criminal investigation for tax fraud.[29]

Press reports story regarding an incident that occurred in Hoover's office earlier in the year. "Attorney General Kennedy was taking his children on a tour of the Justice Department when they ended up in the director's office. Mr. Hoover was away from his desk, below which the youngsters discovered a fascinating row of buttons. They did what came naturally and before the grown-ups knew what happened, two-thirds of the FBI top command hurried through the door."[30] Although reported in a humorous light, it is extremely unlikely that Hoover was anything but furious.

Press reports journalist's conversation, by phone, with Marcello in Guatemala City a day or so after his arrival. Marcello stated, " 'They had the plane already started when we arrived. . . . I [said I] would like to get some clothes, it's on the way to the airport. They wouldn't even talk to me. They had orders that they couldn't even talk. One guy offered me a cup of coffee.'. . . Marcello didn't know why the Guatemalan immigration authorities were bypassed and left cooling their heels at another airport. [A] Col. Batres whisked him off to an apartment house where they stayed overnight. Next day he reported to the immigration people, who had calmed down. 'They told me I am a Guatemalan citizen and can do what I want. . . .' He interrupted the phone interview to answer a knock at his door. It was his brother Sam, who had been searching all day for him. Marcello blamed Immigration Commissioner Joe Swing for his sudden deportation. 'He did the same thing a few years ago. I don't blame Kennedy; Swing is just trying to show him what he can do.' "[31] This last comment by Marcello is illuminating. Recall his strenuous political efforts earlier in the year when he traveled to D.C. in response to press reports that RFK intended to expedite his deportation after the inauguration, and the behind-the-scenes effort to use Sinatra to get to JFK to prevent the same. Given Marcello's understanding of power and bureaucracy, which has been based upon a lifetime of manipulations, a comment such as this is patently absurd. Bear in mind this phone conversation takes place just three weeks prior to a six-day jungle nightmare for Marcello and his attorney.

4/16/61—SUNDAY: Press reports on Justice Department response to Marcello attorney's contempt motion: "Special Assistant United States Attorney Gil Zimmerman filed affidavits to show Marcello was born in a tiny town in Guatemala, then taken to Tunis where he says he was born—in time for baptism about two months later. And in any case, the Justice Department claimed, law permits Marcello to be taken to any country that will accept him—as Guatemala has done. The department said no advance notice was given Marcello because of his 'general reputation' and the 'likelihood Marcello would abscond' if warned ahead of time."[32]

4/18/61—TUESDAY: The U.S. naval Bay of Pigs invasion force, launched only days before, is overwhelmed. This occurs because of faulty intelligence from the CIA regarding willingness of the population to rebel, failure of the Mafia/CIA assassination plot against Castro, a woefully inaccurate estimate of Castro's military strength, and indecisiveness on the part of JFK. Kennedy may also have had the perception that he was being consciously misled by both the CIA and the Joint Chiefs of Staff—in effect, attempting to maneuver him into large-scale use of American military might, rather than simply providing naval support to the exile brigade.

4/19/61—WEDNESDAY: Press reports: "New Orleans rackets figure Carlos Marcello was granted the right yesterday to have his fight to return to the United States considered by a three-judge Federal court."[33]

4/20/61—THURSDAY: Marcello associate ". . . [David] Ferrie admitted [to the FBI] that following the Bay of Pigs invasion, he had 'severely criticized' [President] Kennedy both in public and private. . . . 'He ought to be shot.' Ferrie also admitted that he had said anyone could hide in the bushes and shoot the President."[34]

Press reports on ongoing San Francisco HUAC protest trial: "A key witness in the City Hall riot trial yesterday contradicted House Un-American Activities Committee accounts of violence at the Committee's hearings here last May. The House Committee's accounts were contained in a printed report by FBI Director J. Edgar Hoover and in the narration of the Committee-sponsored film report called 'Operation Abolition.' "[35] Hoover is surely following this case closely, for his credibility is now squarely on the line.

4/24/61—MONDAY: Press reports on relationship between Hoover and RFK. "Attorney General Robert Kennedy is a Justice Department boss whom J. Edgar Hoover will never forget. Hoover is a careful man—a meticulous administrator whose personal appointments are scheduled with the precision of fine clockwork. Before a caller is received, Hoover knows all about him and has FBI files at hand, if necessary, to help. . . . Attorney General's informality is quite a shock. For Bobby Kennedy has taken to dropping in—unheralded and unannounced—and in his shirt sleeves, at that —when he has an FBI matter to discuss. If Hoover isn't there, he simply says 'I'll wait.' "[36]

Press reports that JFK "yesterday asked Congress to authorize full-time Secret Service protection for the Vice President . . . at all times whether or not he requested such protection. Protection is now provided the Vice President only at his request."[37] As noted, LBJ has already publicly stated he does not want protection, yet JFK is forcing it upon him. Publicly, at least, this action implies the President is security minded.

Press reports JFK has appointed CIA chief Allen Dulles and General Maxwell Taylor to a review panel exploring the causes of the U.S. failure at the Bay of Pigs. The article suggests Kennedy may reorganize the CIA. "It is also noted that the FBI—concerned now with only internal intelligence—is under Kennedy, and that the President has great confidence in his brother and may want him in on such an important reorganization study as the Taylor Review."[38] JFK is taking the first step toward review of many top officials and agencies.

4/25/61—TUESDAY: Press again reports on San Francisco HUAC protest trial. "The defense yesterday sought to support its contention that there was no student assault on any policeman at the City Hall riots last May. Five witnesses testified they saw none. . . . Murray Elwood, . . . Alleghany High School teacher supported Meisenbach's [the primary defendant] story. Murray said he watched police 'hosing and pulling people away and dragging them by the neck. They had clubs in their hands and were hitting with their fists,. . . . Then I saw an officer drop his club. I saw him crouched on the floor. Another officer slipped and fell. The floors were five inches deep in water.' The defense contends Schaumieffel [police officer Hoover contends was assaulted by communist dupes] was injured in a fall. Jane O'Grady, a University of California researcher, testified she saw no violence before hoses were turned on the crowd. Joseph F. Lewis, Sunnyvale attorney who was counsel for two witnesses called before the House Committee, also said he saw no student violence. Similar testimony was given by Sandra Levinson, . . . Stanford teaching assistant, and Fred Haines, a radio announcer in Berkeley."[39]

4/27/61—THURSDAY: Mafia leader (Chicago) Sam Giancana and mistress Judith Campbell are seen together at a wedding in Chicago.[40] Given the fact that the Chicago FBI is closely monitoring Giancana, the identity and background of this woman will be determined before long.

4/28/61—FRIDAY: San Francisco Assemblyman John A. O'Connell writes a letter to Hoover, accusing him of lying in regard to the student protest. "The pamphlet, published and distributed by the HUAC, clearly implies that there was no legitimate reason for any non-communists to oppose the Committee hearing. Many San Franciscans considered that a political judgement which was unfounded in fact and also outside the rightful scope of the supposedly non-political functions of your office."[41] This enrages Hoover, possibly prompting him to open a file on the assemblyman.

". . . The day after [Campbell] and Giancana went to the wedding . . . [she] was visited by the President, who was [there] for a fund-raising dinner, at her suite . . . in the Ambassador East Hotel. Though he stayed for only twenty minutes they were intimate."[42] Chicago FBI may well have monitored this encounter in some fashion.

5/61—THIS MONTH: ". . . During May 1961, a [CIA] field survey was completed wherein available public source data of adverse nature regarding officers and leaders of FPCC [Fair Play for Cuba Committee] was compiled and furnished (FBI executive) Mr. DeLoach for use in contacting his sources."[43]

President Kennedy's affair with Judith Campbell continues until at least February 1962. ". . . She allegedly visits [him] in [the] White House at least twenty times [while] she continues seeing Giancana. . . ."[44]

Press reports RFK ". . . will set up permanent racket squads to combat organized crime in New York, Chicago, Los Angeles and *Miami.* He has ordered U.S. Attorneys to give priority to probing organized crime in Cleveland, Detroit, Newark, *New Orleans,* Philadelphia, Pittsburgh, St. Louis, San Francisco and Tucson. Finally, Kennedy will form a 25-man mobile squad to move into any city where help is needed to prosecute the mobsters" (emphasis added).[45]

5/2/61—TUESDAY: ". . . Allegations [regarding the Estes case] were discussed by the Bureau with Lawrence Fuller, Assistant United States Attorney in El Paso. . . . Fuller thought at the time that there might be possible violations of the Federal Reserve Act, involving false financial statements or false notes to banks." Between now and July 3, agents also talk with ex-agent Dan Smoot regarding the case.[46]

5/3/61—WEDNESDAY: R. J. Meisenbach, defendant in the San Francisco HUAC protest trial, is acquitted of all charges. Hoover's credibility has suffered a major setback.[47] *The San Francisco Chronicle* publishes the text of Assemblyman O'Connell's letter to the aging official, in which he had effectively called him a liar. Given the jury's verdict, O'Connell is apparently correct.

JFK is presented with an honorary doctorate of laws in a ceremony at George Washington University, Hoover's alma mater.[48]

Press reports: ". . . growing pressure in Congress for a special joint committee on intelligence operations. A resolution proposing 'continuing studies' of the CIA and all other intelligence outfits [except the FBI] was formally introduced. . . ."[49]

5/4/61—THURSDAY: Marcello's jungle nightmare begins. Press reports: "Eight secret police picked up . . . Marcello at his hotel here (Guatemala City) late [Thursday] night, drove him to El Salvador's border in a station wagon and expelled him. . . . There was no confirmation available from El Salvador that Marcello had arrived there, . . . The accused racketeer was taken to the airport by police yesterday after President Miguel Ydigoras Fuentes ordered him sent back to the United States not later than 12:30 P.M. But none of the three airlines serving Guatemala would accept him as a passenger. Marcello's wife, their daughter, his brother Vicente and Vicente's wife were put aboard a U.S. plane yesterday. But Marcello was denied passage because he lacks a U.S. visa as well as a passport."[50] "Marcello and a lawyer who had come to help him, Michael Maroun, of Shreveport, Louisiana, were unceremoniously flown to an out-of-the-way village in the jungle of El Salvador, where they were left stranded. Salvadorian soldiers jailed and interrogated the two men for five days, then put them on a bus and took them twenty miles into the mountains, where they were again left to fend for themselves. Eight hours and seventeen miles later they reached a village. They were hardly prepared for the mountain hike, as they were dressed in silk shantung suits and alligator shoes. (A portly five-foot-two, Marcello fainted three times.) In the village they hired muchachos to lead them to an airport, but fearful that their guides had robbery and murder in mind, they took the first opportunity to flee back into the jungle. During a downhill scramble, Marcello fell and broke two ribs."[51]

Press reports: "President Kennedy yesterday formally ordered a full-scale review of this country's foreign intelligence effort."[52]

5/9/61—TUESDAY: Marcello and his attorney end their ordeal by reaching a small coastal town. There they arrange illegal reentry to the U.S. It was ". . . learned from a wiretap that Marcello was flown to Miami in a Dominican Republic Air Force jet. . . . The President of the Dominican Republic, General Raphael Trujillo, was known to be close to . . . Santos Traficante."[53] How Marcello gets from Miami to New Orleans remains unclear. Some will later claim David Ferrie, a pilot for Eastern Airlines, flew him back by light plane.

5/10/61—WEDNESDAY: *Washington Daily News* carries two articles regarding Hoover. "Now it operates in such a manner that no incoming President or Attorney General whatever his politics has any doubt about what he is going to do about it—he's going to keep Mr. Hoover in charge." Further, "Harry S. Truman probably was under the greatest pressure to fire Mr. Hoover and to cripple the FBI. HST wouldn't have dared even if he had wanted to do that."

5/14/61—SUNDAY: Press reports on strain between JFK and Joint Chiefs of Staff over Bay of Pigs fiasco. "It is evident that new faces will be seen in their posts in due course."[54]

5/17/61—WEDNESDAY: Press reports on RFK's testimony before the House Judiciary subcommittee regarding legislation against the Mafia. " '. . . They have outgrown local authorities. . . . . . . Only the Federal Government can curtail the flow of funds which permit the kingpins to live far from the scene'. . . . He submitted a statement by FBI Director J. Edgar Hoover, seconding his proposals, but Chairman Emmanuel Celler (D.-N.Y), said he would like to hear from Hoover personally. Celler said Hoover had declined an invitation to testify and asked Kennedy to try to 'change Mr. Hoover's attitude' so the committee can question him." The chairman notes the hearings will continue more than a week. Clearly Hoover does not want to be questioned under oath, for fear his self-imposed ignorance in this area will be revealed. Over the course of the next week, Hoover defies the committee, refusing to appear.[55]

5/19/61—FRIDAY: Press reports: "United States District Judge Alexander Holtzoff ruled . . . that the deportation of Carlos Marcello to Guatemala . . . was valid and legal. The judge . . . denied a motion by attorneys for Marcello that the deportation be declared illegal. The effect was to prevent Marcello's return to this country unless the ruling is overturned. Jack Wasserman, attorney for Marcello, told reporters that 'we will appeal, of course.' "[56] Marcello's whereabouts are unknown.

Press reports from Chicago: "The Federal Department of Justice has declared war on organized crime in Chicago. United States Attorney James P. O'Brien yesterday announced the formation of a

special prosecution unit in his office to war 'against organized criminal activity' in the Chicago area. O'Brien said the unit will 'rely
heavily on the resources' of the Federal Bureau of Investigation."[57]
Given the fact that the Justice Department is basically relying upon
Hoover to supply the information necessary to prosecute the Mafia,
one can only assume he is now clearly in position to dictate the
results.

5/21/61—SUNDAY: *Christian Beacon* publishes an article
claiming that the Kennedy administration has put pressure on Hoover, requiring him to instruct assistant director William Sullivan to
make speeches minimizing CPUSA (Communist Party-USA) influence over U.S. churches. In reality, it is more probable that RFK is
directing Sullivan's statements, simply bypassing Hoover. It appears that early on at least, Sullivan believes CPUSA poses little
threat.

5/22/61—MONDAY: Tolson's birthday.[58] The two probably
celebrate in some manner, just as they do on Hoover's birthday.
Interestingly, May 23, 1961, 1962, and 1963 show no activity on the
part of either man, suggesting some form of formal recognition of
the event. For many years, on Hoover's birthday the two traveled to
New York.

6/61—THIS MONTH: ". . . Ferrie often provided Arcacha
Smith with funds. . . .'He (Ferrie) had $100 bills around all the
time.' An FBI report of April indicated Marcello offered . . .
Smith a deal whereby Marcello would make a substantial donation
to the movement in return for concessions in Cuba after Castro's
overthrow. One explanation of Ferrie's ability to provide funds to
Arcacha Smith may be that he acted as Marcello's financial conduit."[59]

American National Bookstore News (June—July issue), published
by the National States Rights Party, denounces Hoover for, via
Sullivan, minimizing CPUSA influence in American churches.
"It just goes to prove that even J. Edgar Hoover, Director of
the Federal Bureau of Investigation—can be bought and was
bought!" More likely, as noted above RFK has instructed Sullivan

directly in the matter. Hoover is again embarrassed by the administration.

National Geographic article on the FBI is released. "The FBI: Public Friend Number One." Hoover is interviewed during the course of a tour of FBI headquarters, which probably occurred in early May. Bear in mind the fresh U.S. naval disaster at the Bay of Pigs, recent media stories of JFK's World War II naval service, plans for a movie about his wartime experiences (*PT 109*) and his current position as commander-in-chief of U.S. military forces. Hoover: ". . . Let's continue the navy analogy, and say that the FBI has a first-class crew, from my longtime friend, Associate Director Clyde Tolson, down to the newest clerical employee. I doubt that it could be equaled anywhere in the government." A more direct form of comment on JFK's leadership qualities would be hard to imagine. Not only is he attempting to make a joke of JFK as President, but he is also comparing himself as a leader. In effect Hoover is rhetorically placing himself and Clyde above the presidency. Hoover continues on other subjects, "As to the future, we have a number of factors to guide us. First and foremost, there is the law, which tells us where our jurisdiction lies. There is the Congress, which passes the laws and grants us the funds to operate. And there is the press, which stands to warn us if we get off base or fail to measure up to the standards expected of us. With these guideposts, I don't believe we can ever go too far wrong." Note he makes no reference to the branch of government that he is part of, and directly subordinate to—the Executive.

6/1/61—THURSDAY: Press reports sighting of Marcello in the Shreveport, Louisiana, area. ". . . Immigration authorities confirmed that Marcello, 51, had been in the Shreveport area recently, but it was not known how he got out of El Salvador. Patrick F. Duvall, special detail officer of the Immigration Service, said 'We'll stay here until we arrest him.' Duvall said Marcello was now sought on a felony charge—reentering the country without permission of the Justice Department."[60]

6/2/61—FRIDAY: ". . . Marcello's attorneys announced he had returned and was in hiding."[61] At this point RFK apparently makes the decision to order twenty federal officers to New Orleans to find and arrest the mobster. Both Kennedys must be concerned at this sudden and rather unfortunate turn of events.

Press reports: "The exact whereabouts of New Orleans rackets figure Carlos Marcello remained a mystery today, but immigration officials concentrated their search in the Shreveport area, apparently hoping to arrest and deport him again. Attorneys for the reputed underworld king of New Orleans confirmed in Washington today that Marcello returned to the country from Latin America two days ago. 'Marcello will be surrendered to the proper United States officials,' said David Carliner, Washington attorney. 'Then we will immediately apply to the District Court [in Shreveport] for his release on bond pending settlement of his case.' "[62]

Press reports: "A spokesman for the Central Intelligence Agency said Friday night he was 'laughing off' a report that Allen W. Dulles was planning to step down as agency director after President Kennedy returns from Europe. 'I would not take it seriously at all,' the official said."[63]

Press reports on Hoover's June message in the *FBI Law Enforcement Bulletin:* He ". . . said . . . that Bible-quoting 'misguided do-gooders' were advancing religious arguments for the abolition of the death penalty. '. . . [These people] frequently quote the Sixth Commandment, "Thou shalt not kill," to prove that capital punishment is wrong.' But, he said . . . Exodus . . . declares that 'he that smiteth a man, so that he die, shall be surely put to death.' "

6/3/61—SATURDAY: In Texas, U.S. Agriculture Department employee Henry Marshall is found murdered, shot numerous times with his own bolt-action rifle. "Five bullet holes were found in the body."[64] "Hoover . . . carefully followed the FBI's investigation into the mysterious death. . . . The information [he] obtained about Estes's activities and relations with Johnson is still unknown— the extensive documentation in Hoover's file [has been] withheld in its entirety."[65]

6/4/61—SUNDAY: RFK is seen standing at a newsstand near St. Matthew's Cathedral in D.C., just after mass. According to a press report, "The young man needed a haircut, and one sock was up over the cuff of his trousers as if he had dressed in a hurry. He kept thumbing through the New York Times as if he wanted to glean all the news. . . ."[66] Given the intense search for Marcello now under way in Louisiana, he may well be searching for any news reports on the subject.

6/5/61—MONDAY: Marcello ". . . voluntarily surrendered in New Orleans and was ordered held in an alien detention center at McAllen, Texas."[67]

Press reports U.S. Supreme Court ". . . said that the Communist Party must meet requirements of the Internal Security Act of 1950 by registering with the Attorney General."[68] This ruling has two very different effects. First, it appears to confirm what Hoover has been saying for years regarding the nature of the organization. But second, it now gives RFK the power to obtain and disclose the names of individual Party members. The FBI's heavy infiltration and use of paid informants within CPUSA makes such disclosures very dangerous for Hoover. Were the public to be told that a significant percentage of the membership actually consists of federal agents, a cherished program would be destroyed. Hoover's credibility would be further undermined in the eyes of his constituency. Predictably he shows little public reaction to this ruling.

6/7/61—WEDNESDAY: Press reports: "The Immigration Service reported . . . it has found a new country willing to accept Carlos Marcello. . . . The Government's attorney . . . declined to name the country in disclosing the development at a bail hearing for Marcello before the Board of Immigration Appeals."[69]

6/8/61—THURSDAY: Press: ". . . a Federal Grand Jury indicted Marcello for illegal reentry. . . ."[70]

6/16/61—FRIDAY: "On June 16 . . . the FBI received a report that . . . U.S. Senator [Russell Long] from Louisiana might have sought to intervene on Marcello's behalf [in his fight to avoid deportation]. This Senator had reportedly received 'financial aid from Marcello' in the past and was sponsoring a Louisiana official for a key INS . . . position from which assistance might be rendered." The official in question is Marcello bookmaker Sam Saia. "Given Saia's . . . ties to Frank Caracci, Joseph Campisi [both are Marcello lieutenants, the latter operating out of Dallas] and Marcello himself, his sponsorship for a federal post by Senator Long was disturbing."[71] As the New Orleans Mafia's top bookmaker, Saia is also closely associated with Marcello gamblers Sam di Piazza, Eugene Nolan, and Gilbert Beckley. Recall that these same individuals have been under surveillance since January in connection with illegal off-track betting. This surveillance may well be the source of this report. The event puts Hoover on notice that Marcello has the power to influence members of the U.S. Senate. He must now realize that Marcello is potentially a dangerous individual. Apparently the Director does not relay this information to RFK.

6/19/61—MONDAY: D.C. press reports: "Marine Capt. Earnest Brace . . . was acquitted . . . today of charges that he deliberately crashed his . . . training plane [in a bid to create the illusion of his death]. . . . Brace's plane crashed . . . last Jan. 3. After 10 days . . . [he] surrendered to the FBI in Baltimore."[72] This is the second case this year in which Hoover has been proved wrong by a jury, early indications of his declining credibility. Interestingly, both cases dealt with defendants supposedly rebelling against authority, followed by Hoover's attempt to mislabel them. Note also that Hoover had alleged that the pilot had planned to fool the public by assuming a false identity. The Director's fascination with impostors continues.

6/23/61—FRIDAY: Press reports: "John N. LaCorte, director of the Italian Historical Society of America, and Attorney General Kennedy stand beside a memorial to Charles J. Bonaparte, founder of the Federal Bureau of Investigation, at the unveiling rites yesterday in the Justice Department Building. Bonaparte, a grandson of Napoleon Bonaparte, was Attorney General in the administration of Theodore Roosevelt and founded the FBI in 1908." Hoover is not in the photograph, nor is he mentioned in the article.[73] Considering his preeminent position in the Bureau, his absence is surprising.

   D.C. press reports: "FBI charged that a man known for the past two years as L. A. Harris . . . fraudulently represented himself as an attorney duly admitted to practice here in 1955. FBI agents said they have been unable to locate him."[74] Despite its insignificance, Hoover follows this case personally. The fact that the man is impersonating an attorney, and is black, undoubtedly influences his decision to do so. Another impostor is exposed.

6/26/61—MONDAY: *Chicago American* reports, in article entitled "Ax Out For G-Man Hoover," ". . . There are so-called liberal personalities high among the New Frontiersmen . . . who have been cracking at Hoover and the FBI for many years. They are harassing him from the inside and intend to make him feel that, after 37 years on the job, life is too short to put up with their manipulations. Their aim is to frustrate him out of business. . . . Now, with the elevation of many of his chief detractors to the highest places in Government, including the *White House,* the harassment technique is organized and in motion" (emphasis added).

6/27/61—TUESDAY: Press reports "The Justice Department . . . announced the indictment at *New Orleans* of 13 gamblers on charges of using an illegal long-distance telephone hookup to conceal a nationwide horse-betting syndicate. Attorney General Robert F. Kennedy said a 20-count indictment returned by a Federal grand jury accused the men of conspiring to defraud the Government of taxes and cheat the American Telephone & Telegraph Co. of toll charges. Bookmaking and layoff betting were involved in the conspiracy, Kennedy said. It operated between 1952 and 1959 out of the following 10 cities: *New York, New Orleans and Baton Rouge,* La.; *Newport,* Ky.; *Biloxi, Miss.; Miami, Fla.;* Atlantic City, N.J.; *Las Vegas,* Nev.; Los Angeles and Chicago" (emphasis added). "The indictments named the following: Benjamin Lassoff, . . . Robert Lassoff, . . . and Myron Deckelbaum . . . of Cincinnati. *Gilbert L. Beckley,* . . . of Surfside, and *Alfred Mones,* . . . of Miami Beach, Fla. *Sam di Piazza,* 35, and *Louis E. Bagneris,* 60, of Arabi, La., a suburb of New Orleans; *Eugene A. Nolan,* 31, of Baton Rouge, and *Charles A. Perez,* 44; *Harold Brouphy,* 52, and *Anthony Glorioso,* 46, of New Orleans. *Alfred Reyn* . . . of New York. *Peter J. Martino,* 37, of Biloxi, Miss. District Judge Herbert W. Christenberry of New Orleans issued bench warrants for the thirteen and set bond at $25,000 each. Reyn was arrested in New York. . . . A Federal attorney . . . said *Reyn* had told him he *was arrested seven years ago in New Orleans on gambling charges,* but the case was dismissed. *The Lassoff brothers and Deckelbaum* surrendered in *Newport, Ky.* They were sent to jail in default of bonds pending a hearing July 6. The jury did not name the A.T.& T. employees who allegedly had been paid off by gamblers to fix the hook-ups. But the indictment described as co-conspirators, not defendants, . . . Al-

bert E. Bagneris and Vincent J. Caminita of New Orleans. . . .
The maximum penalty could be $11,000 in fines and ten years in jail
for each indictment" (emphasis added).[75]

Clearly, this is a major disruption of, and financial setback to, the
gambling arm of Marcello's organization (a half-billion-dollar-a-
year inflow). Sam di Piazza and Eugene Nolan are two of Marcello's top three bookmakers, handling lay-off bets in New Orleans and
Houston. Peter J. Martino is possibly related to John Martino, a
former Havana gambling casino employee with ties to both the Mafia (Traficante) and Cuban exiles.[76] Note that during the 1940s both
Meyer Lansky and Frank Costello worked with a man named "Big
Porky" Lassoff, possibly a relative of Benjamin and Robert.[77] In the
early 1960s Beckley operates the Newport, Kentucky, end of
Marcello's off-track betting operation from a Teamster-owned
house north of Miami Beach called Blair House. Hoffa himself
keeps an apartment in the building.[78] Nine of the thirteen indicted
live within areas directly controlled by either Marcello or Traficante. FBI is involved in this indictment. It is not known whether
ELSUR is in place at this point, although it appears that through
Saia the Bureau has some form of ongoing surveillance.

6/31/61—SATURDAY: The White House acknowledges to
the press "that an FBI investigation of a security leak could lead to
the persecution [sic] of a high Pentagon official . . . if FBI agents
discover who leaked secret plans about Berlin to the press. . . .
[Pierre] Salinger would not say that President Kennedy himself had
ordered the FBI investigation. Salinger said the FBI was asked to
find out who gave out the secret information and 'the entire circumstances relating to the passage of this information.' "[79] Use of the
Bureau in this manner places Hoover squarely at odds with the U.S.
military.

D.C. press reports: "Henry Winston, who was convicted in the
1949 Communist conspiracy trial and now is blind and in ill health,
was released from prison. . . . President Kennedy commuted the
sentence to the time Winston has served because Winston is blind
and faces possible surgery for a brain tumor. . . . [He] was organi-
zational secretary of the Communist Party in the United States.
. . . [and] was one of 11 top Communists convicted 12 years ago of
conspiracy to teach and advocate forcible overthrow of the Govern-

ment."[80] This action by JFK only antagonizes Hoover further, in his mind freeing enemies of the state.

7/61—THIS MONTH: Marcello aide David Ferrie presents a speech before the New Orleans Military Order of World Wars, entitled "Cuba—April 1961 Present, Future." ". . . As he was addressing the [group] he was asked to step down when the vehemence of his criticism of President Kennedy became excessive."[81]

7/2/61—SUNDAY: Press reports: "the President's decision on whether and how to streamline CIA is coming to a head. . . . The President has ordered the FBI to investigate news leaks about Berlin contingency planning. . . . Two broad changes in the intelligence establishment are currently under consideration by the White House. First is a proposal to merge the intelligence and research division of the State Department with CIA intelligence-gathering functions into a new agency. The second proposal would be to take away from CIA all operational functions, such as its organization of the invasion of Cuba by the anti-Castro exiles."[82]

7/3/61—MONDAY: Estes investigator, Dr. John Dunn, is interviewed by FBI agents. ". . . The bureau reported that [the] investigation had failed to turn up any violations of the Banking Act, [and] Mr. Fuller decided to drop the matter."[83]

7/6/61—THURSDAY: Hoover notifies the press of the arrest of Daniel J. Morgan, the impostor, in San Francisco. "FBI Director J. Edgar Hoover said that Morgan, charged with illegally representing himself as a Washington attorney, was seized by agents at a YMCA Hotel. . . ."[84]
Press reports White House announcement that ". . . the FBI still is investigating the 'leak' of information on American preparations to meet the Berlin crisis . . . insisting that it was aimed at finding the source of the leak and denying that it had anything to do with a Newsweek magazine story. . . . calling the FBI investigation a move to dramatize the Berlin crisis. . . . There was another . . . report in the New York Times that the FBI inquiry had aroused resentment among high Pentagon officials."[85] If true, antagonizing the Pentagon through such use of the FBI would raise fundamental issues in Hoover's mind. Consider his background as a

retired lieutenant colonel and strong supporter of Marine Corps discipline.

7/7/61—FRIDAY: D.C. press reports that JFK and his wife had recently previewed a newly released Italian film, *La Dolce Vita.* "They saw it two months ago at the White House. Upon special request of the President. . . . The three-hour-long film, which has won critical acclaim, and blame, too, for its picture of modern decadence. . . ."[86]

Senators Frank J. Lausche and Thomas H. Kuchel take to the Senate floor to defend Hoover regarding rumors of his impending replacement by JFK. Citing a recent news story, Lausche describes it as "inferring that in high places within our Federal Government there is a move to discredit and oust Mr. Hoover. . . . I cannot believe it, I hope it is not true." Senator Kuchel: "I look upon J. Edgar Hoover as one of the greatest Americans of this or any other generation." Gallery spectators applaud.[87]

7/11/61—TUESDAY: INS again rules Marcello an undesirable and orders him deported.[88]

7/12/61—WEDNESDAY: Chicago FBI interviews Giancana at O'Hare International Airport. He becomes angry, exclaiming, "I know all about the Kennedys . . . and one of these days . . . (I am) going to tell all."[89] A statement such as this only increases the intensity of FBI surveillance.

7/13/61—THURSDAY: FBI (New Orleans and SOG Crime Lab) fails to break an encoded message, which the A.G. had provided and ordered deciphered, from Marcello to one of his attorneys. The lab concludes, "because of the brevity of the text, no determination as to the meaning of the possible code . . . could be made. It is possible, however, that the names in the text . . . represent double meaning, wherein certain words are given arbitrary meaning by the correspondents." Apparently as a result of this, RFK begins criticizing the quality of FBI intelligence.[90]

Secretary of Defense Robert McNamara (a Kennedy appointee), presumably with JFK's acquiescence, has by now instructed that Hoover's discredited film, *Operation Abolition,* no longer be shown to U.S. military personnel.[91]

7/21/61—FRIDAY: The Senate Foreign Relations Committee releases a memorandum detailing the threat posed by internal military rightism, and "warned that right wing propaganda activities . . . may create 'important obstacles' to President Kennedy's programs. . . .'Running through all of them is a central theme that the primary, if not exclusive, danger to this country is internal Communist infiltration. . . . The Communist threat often is developed by equating social legislation with socialism, and the latter with communism. Much of the Administration's domestic legislative program . . . under this philosophy would be characterized as steps towards Communism' . . . It said this examination should try to determine whether 'these relationships do not amount to official support for a viewpoint in variance with that of the Administration.' "[92]

7/23/61—SUNDAY: D.C. press reports on "prized prestige symbols—the expensive official limousine. The undisputed top spot is held currently by the Federal Bureau of Investigation. . . . A $14,549.06 fully-armored, 1961 seven-passenger Cadillac limousine —not surprisingly placed at the disposal of Bureau Director J. Edgar Hoover. Only President Kennedy . . . rides around in a personal car that cost the taxpayers more. For more than 10 years the FBI has had permission to buy an armored car, initially for up to $10,000 but now 'without regard to the general purchase price limitation.' No other agency can show such a statement."[93]

7/24/61—MONDAY: Hoover's *Annual FBI Uniform Crime Report* is released. He states: "Crime reporting is an essential element of effective police work. It also carries with it, however, heavy responsibilities. . . . This is a personal responsibility. . . . It is imperative that we, the Federal Bureau of Investigation . . . do the utmost to produce the most useful information possible."

D.C. press reports: "U. E. Baughman, 55, chief of the United States Secret Service, is resigning, it was learned [Monday] night. After 34 years in the Secret Service, 13 as chief. . . . He has no plans for private employment at the moment."[94] Clearly JFK's program for systematically retiring longtime agency heads not in agreement with administration policy and goals is now in full swing.

7/25/61—TUESDAY: Hoover sends a memo to JFK aide, McGeorge Bundy, describing the FBI's "investigative programs." The report, requested by the President, makes no mention of illegal electronic surveillance programs such as ELSUR or COINTEL-PRO.[95]

D.C. press carries interview with Baughman. "I will say emphatically that there is no Mafia in this country and no national crime syndicate. Why don't those who talk about the Mafia name its leader or leaders? There has been no Mafia in this country for at least 40 years. Now about a national crime syndicate: I say there is no such thing, and I say it not simply as a personal judgment but on the basis of talks with other enforcement officials."[96] Given the realities of the threat posed by the Mafia at this time, Baughman's assertions are profoundly disturbing. It is small wonder he has been retired by the administration. Note his stated reliance on "other enforcement officials" as the basis for his belief. This rhetoric is nothing more than the standard Hoover line regarding the Mafia's supposed nonexistence.

7/26/61—WEDNESDAY: D.C. press reports: "The 1961 American Legion Boys' Nation yesterday unanimously endorsed President Kennedy's stand on Berlin. Later the youngsters were taken on a special tour of the White House. The delegates also toured FBI headquarters."[97]

7/31/61—MONDAY: White House announces to press "that Allen W. Dulles intends to retire as director of the Central Intelligence Agency by the end of this year. Press Secretary Pierre Salinger declined comment. . . ."[98]

8/1/61—TUESDAY: D.C. press runs a story on new Secret Service chief James J. Rowley, revealing he "joined the FBI in 1937, transferred to the Secret Service here in 1938 and was assigned to the White House."[99] Shortly after JFK's assassination, rumors will circulate to the effect that a feud between the Secret Service and the FBI had contributed to the disaster. It is not known why Rowley stayed with the FBI for such a brief period of time. It is known that Hoover does not like Bureau defectors. This choice can only exacerbate Hoover's dislike of Kennedy.

8/2/61—WEDNESDAY: D.C. press reports on Gerald Behn, newly appointed head of White House Secret Service Detail. "Behn said he considers his job of guarding the Presidents of the United States a 'pretty routine assignment' and added that providing for the safety of President Kennedy and his family presents no special problems."[100]

This night, Hoover and Tolson are in La Jolla, California, having just arrived for their annual respite. Press reports "A gunman robbed the swank Del Charrol [*sic*] Hotel of $150 [during the] night while guest J. Edgar Hoover slept in his bungalow about 200 yards away, police reported. The Director of the Federal Bureau of Investigation, taking his vacation here, has been a yearly visitor since 1938."[101] Hoover probably reacts angrily to this publicity, the implication being he is, so to speak, sleeping on the job.

8/3/61—THURSDAY: Press reports: "The administration is perfecting plans to strip from the Central Intelligence Agency its function of over-all intelligence evaluation. . . . The Department of Defense announced Wednesday that its intelligence operations were also being reorganized. . . . Its net result is largely to duplicate . . . *the scheme of organization now being proposed for the civilian intelligence agencies*" (emphasis added).[102]

8/4/61—FRIDAY: Hoover receives a U.S. Senate resolution commending his thirty-seven years of service, the "highest possible commendation."[103] It is difficult to believe that the Senate does not anticipate Hoover's impending retirement by JFK.

8/8/61—TUESDAY: Judith Campbell ". . . lunched with the President at the White House. They argued and were not intimate as Kennedy had hoped, according to her account. That evening, Giancana and Anthony Tisc, his son-in-law and the administrative assistant to Congressman . . . Roland Libonati, visited Campbell in room 353 of the Mayflower Hotel in Washington."[104] Given the fact that the FBI has Giancana under full-time surveillance, the connection between Campbell and JFK may now be known.

8/11/61—FRIDAY: Ferrie is ". . . arrested . . . for a crime against nature with a fifteen-year-old and indecent behavior with three other boys." He retains Marcello's personal attorney, G. Wray Gill, for his defense.[105]

8/13/61—SUNDAY: *Washington Post* reports: "The FBI today entered the search for the torture killers who stuffed the nude body of gangland "Juiceman" William (Action) Jackson into the trunk of his car and left it beneath Chicago's Loop. . . . He had been cut, kicked and beaten and there was a bullet hole in his left ear." In another article of the previous day, ". . . there were rope marks around his head and abdomen." This is the same individual described in the introduction to this book. Note the edited description of his wounds. The press does not know that Jackson was an FBI informant.

8/22/61—TUESDAY: New Orleans FBI probably interviews David Ferrie on this date, confirms his connections with CRC, the local Cuban exile group controlled by Arcacha Smith, and prepares a report.[106]
Newport, Kentucky, press reports: "Federal agents last night smashed their way into a bar they described as the headquarters for greater Cincinnati's numbers racket. . . . The Sportsman Bar. They arrested six persons and confiscated several thousand dollars, a number of guns . . . and gambling equipment."[107] Recall that Cincinnati area Mafia gamblers, Edward Levinson, et al., have already begun an association with LBJ protégé Bobby Baker and aviation lobbyist Fred Black. Not only a front man for Lansky interests in Las Vegas casinos (e.g., Sands), Levinson is also associated with Jimmy Hoffa through a Teamster loan used to construct Levinson's Fremont Hotel in that city. A number of airport hotels across the U.S., constructed by Airway Hotel, Inc., in which Levinson has an interest, were also funded, in part, by Teamster loans. He is also a close friend of Giancana.[108] Levinson and his brothers have spent many years helping to develop the Newport area gambling apparatus.

8/26/61—SATURDAY: In connection with the child-molestation charges against him ". . . Eastern Airlines suspended Ferrie indefinitely."[109] Up to this point he has been a pilot for the company.

8/27/61—SUNDAY: Hoover essay appears, written for the AP wire service, entitled "A Summons from the Boss." Hoover describes the moment on May 10, 1924, when he was offered the position of director of the Bureau of Investigation. "The attorney general did not want my resignation. To the contrary, he was naming me the bureau's director. . . . That so often is the case in our lives. We become nervous and apprehensive in the face of events which ultimately prove to be memorable, pleasant occasions." Considering the tenuous nature of the relationship Hoover now has with both the Attorney General and the President, this type of essay is truly bizarre. In effect, Hoover is saying his fears over job security are baseless. Perhaps the information he is now acquiring on the President has made him feel more secure.

8/30/61—WEDNESDAY: Ex-FBI agent Aaron Kohn, a member of the New Orleans Crime Commission, testifies in D.C. before the Permanent Investigations Subcommittee regarding Marcello. FBI shortly obtains a copy of his testimony, adding to their knowledge of the mafioso.[110]

8/31/61—THURSDAY: Press reports on Kohn's testimony before the Senate gambling hearing. "He said another $25,000 was contributed by associates of Carlos Marcello, . . . allegedly for permission to operate a racing wire. Marcello failed to respond to a subpoena to appear before the subcommittee yesterday. Earlier, C. Ray Edmonds, manager of Jefferson Downs race track at New Orleans, said he appealed to Marcello to help him quash wide-open bookmaking near his track. He said Marcello told him he 'would not go to his friends and ask them to close their businesses.' Senate Committee Chairman John L. McClellan . . . said Marcello would face a contempt citation if he did not appear before the investigating group next Thursday. Marcello's brother, Joseph, and Joseph Poretto, a Marcello associate, appeared but gave only their names and addresses before invoking the Fifth Amendment 52 times."[111] Carlos Marcello's open defiance of the U.S. Senate, for the second time (the first occurred during the 1950s) reveals the mind set of this individual regarding central authority. Hoover and his top advisers, as the only people aware of all the facts, realize the danger this man represents.

9/1/61—FRIDAY: *FBI Law Enforcement Bulletin* is released. Hoover's message deals with "the criminal marauders who have too long believed they can plunder our country unchallenged. . . . Every day which passes imbues the law enforcement officer with the knowledge . . . which will topple the empires of criminals as fast as they try to build them. This knowledge . . . is born of a growing brotherhood among law enforcement agencies. . . . Crime cannot long withstand such a rising tide of cooperative effort, and we in the law enforcement profession must nurture this idea, this philosophy, so that it may reach even greater heights. Mutual accomplishments can bring mutual satisfaction in a job well done."

Johnson sends a letter to Hoover, reiterating his belief that the Director should not be retired. ". . . I am grateful that I have good friends as you, upon whom I and our Nation may rely, to represent our best interests in the years ahead."[112]

9/7/61—THURSDAY: Marcello appears before McClellan's subcommittee on Senate Investigations upon advice of his attorneys, in order to avoid contempt of Congress. Photographed during testimony, the look of hatred in his eyes is blatant. Press: "Carlos Marcello, reputed former New Orleans underworld boss, muttered his name and New Orleans street address, then invoked the Fifth Amendment in reply to every other question. *He declined to answer questions about connections with the Nola printing company in New Orleans, a racing wire service,* or with a juke box and pinball machine company in Louisiana. Marcello is under $10,000 Federal bond on charges of illegal entry into the United States" (emphasis added).[113] The activities of the Nola printing company, indirectly controlled by Marcello, are also the subject of the Gilbert Beckley case, now pending. Interestingly, New York Mafia leader Vito Genovese, during World War II, ran a series of fraudulent operations in Nola, Italy.[114]

9/13/61—WEDNESDAY: D.C. press reports: "President Kennedy . . . signed into law three bills that give Federal, state, and local police powerful new weapons to crack down on underworld rackets ranging from the numbers game to narcotics traffic. . . . The most sweeping legislation of its kind in 30 years. The President signed the measures at a special White House ceremony attended by the Attorney General, FBI Director J. Edgar Hoover,

Chairman John L. McClellan . . . and members of Congress of both parties."[115] In the accompanying photograph Hoover stands at the back of the group looking on as JFK signs. All are smiling.

9/16/61—SATURDAY: Columnist and Hoover fan, George E. Sokolsky, writes, ". . . If anyone wants to know if a person was administrative assistant to J. Edgar Hoover or whether he was a chief of bureau in the FBI, let a letter of inquiry be written to the proper person and place. It will be found that I am not in error in the general view that if a person worked for the FBI he has no permanent license to advertise himself as very close to the equivalent of J. Edgar Hoover. If a man's work is worth-while, he does not need such an accolade."[116]

9/21/61—THURSDAY: Press reports: ". . . 33 of the 37 Federal agencies permit some kind of telephone monitoring. . . . . . . 17 do not always require that the other party be warned that what he is saying is being taken down. [There are] . . . indications of 'a dangerous drift toward a huge bureaucracy peering over the shoulder of the citizen.' "[117]

Hoover document "The Communist Party Line," prepared for the Senate Internal Security subcommittee, is released by Senator James O. Eastland. " 'The danger of indiscriminately alleging that someone is a Communist merely because his views on a particular issue . . . parallel the official [Communist] party line is obvious. . . . the . . . Party line . . . is . . . designed to . . . confuse the public by blending proposals ostensibly sponsored by the Communists with those of legitimate organizations.' . . . The uninformed citizen . . . 'may make the . . . assumption that anyone who advocates proposals similar to . . . the party line is automatically a Communist.' "[118] In effect, Hoover is making moderately liberal to liberal philosophy analogous with communism, while simultaneously cautioning his public not to assault those who espouse that view.

9/22/61—FRIDAY: FBI (New Orleans) prepares a five-page report on Marcello associate David Ferrie, detailing his involvement with the Civil Air Patrol, citing opinions of those who know him (Mrs. Dunn, Mrs. Nichols, Joseph Lisman), and recounting his be-

liefs regarding presidents who "sellout to the communists." By this
time they have also searched his home.[119]

9/23/61—SATURDAY: Press reports, "The House Government Information Subcommittee said . . . it has 'a powerful new
weapon'—presidential support—for the first time since it started
warring on secrecy in Government six years ago. '[The] . . . President . . . [has made an] unequivocal stand on freedom of information. . . . [The] . . . weight of the White House was added to
help re-establish the people's right to know. . . . A thin veneer of
new leadership, [however,] superimposed on the massive bureaucracy, is not enough to prevent secrecy-minded career officials from
equating secrecy with good government.' "[120]

9/27/61—WEDNESDAY: Press covers JFK's appointment
of John McCone as director of CIA. "The Chief Executive praised
McCone in a brief talk, but he praised the outgoing Dulles even
more warmly. He emphasized, too, that Dulles had promised him
after last November's election to stay on as CIA Director for a year,
and noted that the year will be up next month. 'I know of no man
who is a more courageous, selfless public servant . . . [I] want to
express my profound regret that at the age of 68, after 10 years in
this responsibility, that Mr. Dulles should be retiring. He has
agreed to continue to serve as a consultant to me on intelligence
matters, and therefore his long experience will be available to the
people of this country."[121] Note JFK's acute sensitivity to the idea
of Dulles's removal. Clearly he is very concerned with conservative
reaction to this move. It is small wonder he plans to let federal
statute retire Hoover.

9/28—10/5/61:   Hoover responds privately to an attack by
New York Herald Tribune columnist John Crosby, who has just
written a piece entitled "The FBI's Commercial." In the article
Crosby has accused Hoover of allowing the Mafia to flourish while
indulging in self-aggrandizement. As will later be noted by the *Saturday Evening Post,* "Instead of replying to Crosby, the FBI chief
wrote a bitter letter to Crosby's editor, assailing the column as 'de-
grading to the code of the journalistic profession,' and hinting that
Crosby had 'an ulterior purpose in mind.' "[122]

10/12/61—THURSDAY: JFK attacks ultrarightists in a speech at the University of North Carolina. "He said that if Americans remain undeterred by these [fanatics], if they can face up to risks and are purposeful, then '*we shall be neither Red nor dead, but alive and free.* . . . Those of you who regard my profession of political life with some disdain, should remember that it made it possible for me to move from being an obscure lieutenant in the United States Navy to Commander in Chief in 14 years, with very little technical competence' " (emphasis added).[123]

10/13/61—FRIDAY: Press details fact that soon-to-be-appointed Speaker of the House John McCormack and JFK view each other with personal disdain. "It is well known that McCormack . . . opposed President Kennedy's school-aid bill and foreign-aid program. What isn't known, however, is that McCormack made a deal with Louisiana Congressman Otto Passman, the foreign-aid critic, to help slash foreign aid. In return, Passman agreed to help round up Southern votes for McCormack to be speaker."[124] Hoover and McCormack are longtime friends.

10/16/61—MONDAY: Hoover loyalist George Sokolsky joins in the attack on critic Crosby. "It takes no courage to attack J. Edgar Hoover . . . John Crosby, a writer for the New York Herald Tribune, does precisely that in an article entitled 'The FBI's Commercial.' By what law is the FBI charged with police supervision of gambling, narcotics and industrial rackets? Gambling is, by law, none of the FBI's business except as a statistical item in uniform crime reporting. Narcotics are under the jurisdiction of the bureau of Narcotics . . . J. Edgar Hoover is opposed to a national police force, which easily becomes a militia. CROSBY ASKS: 'How many big shots of organized crime has the FBI arrested in the last five or ten years? Are they looking for any? Has the FBI any program for trapping any of those well-organized and enormously rich racketeers Mr. Kennedy talks about?' Under what laws does Crosby expect the FBI to make these arrests? I DO NOT know what John Crosby knows about what he calls the crime syndicate. Actually, most gangs of criminals engage in felonies and misdemeanors which are not covered by Federal law at all."[125]This defense of Hoover may well be the result of FBI coaching. When considered in light of ELSUR, COINTELPRO, and Hoover's growing body of personal knowledge about operations such as Marcello's, its naïveté becomes obvious.

10/17/61—TUESDAY: JFK tells speechwriter Arthur Schlesinger, "The three masters of public relations in the last half century have been Baruch, Hoover, and Allen Dulles."[126]

FBI (New York) ELSUR records mafioso Ray DeCarlo and another discussing Carlos Marcello: "Well, they're all greasers down there. They're all greenhorns. What have they got there? . . . I don't know if Carlos is Americanized. Is he? I know the kid is— Joey is. Most of them guys are all dyed-in-the-wool, you know, greenies. The old mustache mob."[127] This assessment of Marcello and his organization corresponds with Hoover's knowledge of their reputation as dangerously unpredictable, even among commission members.

Hoover makes public appearance in D.C. suburb of Silver Spring. Press: ". . . At the unveiling of a portrait of Silver Spring Boys' Club leader Harry F. Duncan. Hoover, a personal friend of Duncan, said it is preferable to build good citizens through boys' clubs than to rehabilitate broken lives. The ceremonies took place in the Harry F. Duncan building."[128] Recall that Duncan is a member of Hoover's weekly track racing group.

10/18/61—WEDNESDAY: ". . . Estes and his attorney visited [Mr. Tucker at] the [Agriculture] department to protest the investigation. . . . [He] declared that if [it] were not canceled, 'before night he would have a group consisting of about thirty-eight people including lawyers and accountants who would fly into Washington' and 'buy space in newspapers and magazines and go to New York and appear on television and embarrass the Administration. . . .' He mentioned the death of Henry Marshall. . . ."[129]

10/21/61—SATURDAY: Press reports on another black impostor. "Edward Lee Woods . . . who is accused of posing as an African diplomat . . . has been arrested in Wilmington, North Carolina, by the FBI. A spokesman said he would be returned to Providence to face a charge of making false statements."[130]

Assistant Director Cartha DeLoach, Hoover's trusted liaison man, addresses editorial writers in Virginia Beach, Virginia. "[He] . . . called on editorial writers tonight to 'lift their green eyeshades' and become more vigilant against Communist infiltration of their profession. '. . . A contrary record is still being written by a small segment of so-called journalistic enterprise . . . Some press representatives are spewing forth a stream of vilification which has the effect of helping to weaken our foundations of security . . . They are the true enemies of freedom of the press and have historically been in the vanguard of Communist conquerors who would destroy a free press. It is time for editorial writers to . . . ascend to a height where they can look beyond the border of their own area to see what other newspapers are doing. They should sound off loud and clear against the propagandists who are undermining all that patriotic men hold dear . . .' "[131] That there has recently been considerable press devoted to criticism of Hoover is undeniable. It is as if DeLoach is calling on the nation's editors to decide whether they are true Americans, or communists who will destroy the country by allowing criticism of the Bureau.

10/27/61—FRIDAY: U.S. Agriculture Department generates a 140-page internal report concerning Billie Sol Estes. "The . . . memorandum reported on a departmental investigation of . . . Estes' cotton operations. [It] also dealt with . . . accounts of . . . Estes' threats to go to top Administration officials if lower-echelon officials sought to interfere." [132] Obviously the department's administrators sense a political battle that can destroy careers and are preparing their interpretation of the facts accordingly.

10/29/61—SUNDAY: D.C. press reports: ". . . President Kennedy has been commuting the sentences of prison inmates at a rate four times greater than that of the Eisenhower Administration. One group is composed of those . . . suffering from terminal illnesses . . . The other group . . . is made up of those who are serving long terms but who have made successful efforts to improve themselves . . . . . . One of these cases . . . involved a man . . . convicted of robbing a bank in 1952. . . . He turned himself in to the FBI . . . was convicted and sentenced to 40 years in prison."[133]

Parade magazine runs an interview with RFK entitled "What's Wrong With the Two Dollar Bet?" Speaking of the A.G.'s recent successes, it states, "Tax agents, for instance, discovered an illegal telephone operation set up by big-time gamblers in *New Orleans*.

Although the tax evasion amounted only to small change, *Kennedy persuaded T-Men to cooperate with the FBI in building a case* against the gamblers. Result: 13 people have been indicted" (emphasis added). This revelation by RFK provides direct proof of FBI surveillance in the Beckley/di Piazza case and indictment on 6/27/ 61.

10/30/61—MONDAY: ". . . Attorney General Kennedy announced the indictment of Marcello by a Federal grand jury in New Orleans on charges of conspiracy in falsifying a Guatemalan birth certificate and committing perjury. Marcello's brother, Joseph was also charged in the alleged falsification of the birth certificate."[134]

FBI (New Orleans) prepares yet another report on Ferrie. "[He] has a group of young boys whom he supports and controls completely."[135]

11/61—THIS MONTH: FBI (Chicago) ELSUR succeeds in placing either wiretaps or bugs on Chicago Mafia leader and Marcello confidant, Sam Giancana.[136]

11/3/61—FRIDAY: Press reports "Maj. Gen. Edwin A. Walker announced last night he is quitting the Army because he feels its action in rebuking him and taking away his divisional command destroyed his usefulness in uniform. 'I must be free from the power of little men who, in the name of my country, punish loyal service to it.' Among other things, *Walker* was *accused* of having described *as 'definitely pink'* such well-known Americans as *President Harry S. Truman. . . . Walker said some people in this country* apparently *do not realize the Nation is at war with international communism*" (emphasis added).[137] Hoover, during the late 1940s and early 50s, had made a near identical, public denouncement of Truman.[138]

11/6/61—MONDAY: Hoover notes on UPI ticker quoting excerpts from an RFK speech that it sounds like "some of Bennetts's philosophy." Bennett is the director of the Bureau of Prisons, a man Hoover intensely dislikes because he feels he is soft on criminals.[139] Note this in the context of recent stories detailing JFK's early parole approach to some types of criminals.

11/7/61—TUESDAY: ". . . A check of [Campbell's] phone records turned up two calls to the White House—on November 7 and 15, 1961."[140]

11/11/61—SATURDAY: D.C. Hoover follower Sokolsky comments on General Walker's recent resignation. ". . . He has been unfairly treated . . . Who is responsible for the peculiar action that was taken concerning General Walker? . . . We need to know what is the motivation for this sort of thing."[141]

11/15/61—WEDNESDAY: Judith Campbell calls JFK at the White House.[142]

11/18/61—SATURDAY: JFK gives a speech before a Democratic Party fund raiser in Los Angeles. Press reports ". . . He said the extremists he had in mind were those who preach that the big danger for this Nation is not Communist imperialism abroad but Reds at home—Reds in the government itself. 'They equate the Democratic Party with the welfare state,' Mr. Kennedy continued, 'the welfare state with socialism, and socialism with this communism. But *you and I and most Americans take a different view of our peril. We know that it comes from without, not within. It must be met by quiet preparedness, no provocative speeches*' " (emphasis added).[143]

"The day after the Hilton reception the President visited the Lawfords at Santa Monica [California]. . . . Marilyn [Monroe's] makeup man drove her to meet [Kennedy] at the . . . beach house."[144]

11/20/61—MONDAY: Senator Henry Jackson (D), concluding a subcommittee study on national security, issues a personal statement. Per press: "He called for a clearer 'sense of direction' and a stronger effort to put the best people in key policy jobs. President Kennedy has . . . adopted several recommendations. . . . They include abolition of scores of inter-agency committees, centralization of authority in Cabinet officers. . . ."[145]

11/22/61—WEDNESDAY: S. Wesley Reynolds, security director of the National Security Agency (NSA), is fired. Press reports "[He is] . . . the second high official of the trouble-beset defense communications agency to be fired within two days. The 'requested' resignation of Maurice H. Klein, former NSA personnel director, was announced Monday." Reynolds is also an ex-FBI agent.[146]

D.C. press reports: "Gen. Joseph M. Swing, Commissioner of Immigration and Naturalization since 1954, has submitted his resignation to President Kennedy. The retention of Swing by the Kennedy Administration had brought sharp criticism from many liberals. . . . Swing ran into difficulties once with Attorney General Robert F. Kennedy when he summarily whisked New Orleans gambler Carlos Marcello out of the country. Kennedy said two days later that he would have handled the situation differently. The General . . . completed 50 years of government service last June. He is a former FBI agent. . . ."[147]

11/12—11/22/61: ". . . The FBI received a letter [dated 11/12/61] offering proof that the President was an adulterer, 'including photographs.' . . . Kennedy had allowed himself to be seen, with Marilyn (Monroe) at his side, at a reception in the Beverly Hilton Hotel."[148]

11/27/61—MONDAY: "Campbell was first interviewed . . . [by the FBI] in Palm Springs, California. Little of significance was developed from the interview. . . ."[149]

Press notes: "The big State Department shakeup puts the firm stamp of John F. Kennedy on that critical branch of government."[150]

12/61—THIS MONTH: "By the end of 1961, 121 [mafiosi] had been indicted. . . . The Justice Department went on to convict 96 in 1961 and 101 in 1962."[151]

12/1/61—FRIDAY: D.C. grand jury returns a twelve-count indictment against CPUSA for failure to register per Supreme Court order. This sets the stage for the release of names of individual Party members, a large percentage being FBI informants. RFK comments: " 'The Party apparently has cut down the number of its officers, eliminated dues payments in some areas, and greatly reduced the frequency of local meetings.' He said his information about the Party's activities had been gathered by the Federal Bureau of Investigation. The 12th count . . . charges that the Party failed to file a list of its members' names. . . ."[152]

ACLU releases a chronologically accurate version of *Operation Abolition*, further undermining Hoover's public version of the event. Press reports " 'Operation *Correction*' employs printed subtitles identifying the days on which the film sequences were taken. . . . Dramatic and noisy events occurring on Thursday and Saturday were woven into 'Operation Abolition' as if they were events immediately preceding the rioting climax on Friday" (emphasis added).[153]

12/3/61—SUNDAY: RFK, in an interview with Henry Brandon of the *London Sunday Times,* states regarding CPUSA, "It couldn't be more feeble and less of a threat, and besides its membership consists largely of FBI agents." A public acknowledgment of this sort by the Attorney General fundamentally undercuts Hoover's policy of anonymity regarding informants.

12/5/61—TUESDAY: D.C. press reports: "President Kennedy's Charlie yesterday claimed the District's No. 1 dog license. Meanwhile, the No. 2 tag had been given to Jefferson, a beagle owned by Vice President Lyndon B. Johnson. FBI Director J. Edgar Hoover had long held the No. 3 and 4 spots with his Cairn terriers, G-Boy and Tucker. So, when a 'tall, hatless man,' otherwise unidentified, came into the District Building from the White House yesterday, the Nos. 1 and 9 licenses were the only one-digit tags available."[154] Kennedy's personal interest in the dog tagging is, although trivial, intriguing. As will be shown, it continues to irritate him and will present the opportunity for symbolic gesture regarding Hoover and Johnson both.

Press: "President Kennedy today accepted the resignation of A. Gilmore Fluse as Assistant Secretary of the Treasury." He had served in that position since 1957.[155]

12/7/61—WEDNESDAY: Press reports: "President Kennedy gave New York police the slip last night when he stopped at a friend's apartment for a late party although he had promised to go straight home to the Carlyle Hotel."[156]

Hoover, in an evening ceremony, receives Mutual of Omaha's Criss Award "for outstanding contribution to personal security and safety of the American people." He also presents a prepared speech entitled "Faith to Be Free" in which he directly rebuts JFK's position, taken on November 18, concerning communism. *"The communist threat from without must not blind us to the communist threat from within.* The latter is reaching into the very heart of America through its espionage agents and a cunning, defiant, and lawless Communist Party, which is fanatically dedicated to the Marxist cause of world enslavement and destruction of the foundations of our Republic . . . America's emblem is the soaring eagle —not the blind and timid mole. *Fear, apologies, defeatism, and cowardice are alien to the thinking of true Americans! As for me, I would rather be DEAD than RED!"* (emphasis added). JFK, in his own speech, as previously quoted, had stated, "But you and I and most Americans take a different view of our peril. *We know that it comes from without, not within.* It must be met by quiet preparedness, no provocative speeches" (emphasis added).[157] See also 10/12/61.

12/8/61—FRIDAY: Press quotes other excerpts from Hoover's fiery speech: *"Unfortunately, we are plagued with some Soviet apologists who, time after time, would have us betray the cause of international freedom and justice by yielding to the Red fascists . . . on vital moral issues. . . . We are at war with the communists, and the sooner every red-blooded American realizes this the safer we will be"* (emphasis added).[158] This last sentence is a line taken from General Walker's 11/12/61 speech.

12/9/61—SATURDAY: FBI (Chicago) ELSUR records conversation between Mafia figures Giancana and Johnny Roselli. "On December 9, 11, and 21, 1961, FBI listening devices picked up conversations . . . that . . ." reveal the fact that Giancana had secretly made campaign contributions to JFK's presidential bid through Joseph Kennedy without the official's knowledge.[159] Presumably this has been done in an attempt to obtain protection from prosecution. This information is almost immediately sent by AIRTEL to Hoover.

12/12/61—TUESDAY: FBI (Chicago) ELSUR continues taping Giancana and Roselli. "He's got big ideas, Frank does, about being ambassador or something. You fuck them, you pay them, and then they're through. You got the right idea, Moe, so . . . fuck everybody . . . we'll use them every fucking way we can. They

only know one way. Now let them see the other side of you."
Roselli: "I had a chance to quiz (Sinatra in Vegas). . . . I said,
'Frankie, can I ask you one question?' He says, 'Johnny, I took
Sam's name, and wrote it down, and I told Bobby Kennedy, this is
my buddy. This is my buddy, this is what I want you to know, Bob.'
And he says, 'Johnny, he————.' " Giancana: "You could have
answered it yourself." This information is also sent by AIRTEL to
Hoover, who goes to RFK and informs him that Giancana has
contacted his father three times. The Director also states that Giancana has tried to use Sinatra to get to JFK to prevent prosecution.[160]

12/14/61—THURSDAY: Hoover sends memo to RFK telling of Giancana's secret campaign donation to JFK via JPK.[161]

12/15/61—FRIDAY: Hoover sends yet another memo to the
A.G. concerning Giancana.[162]
    The Agriculture Department's ". . . general counsel . . . ruled
that . . . Estes' 1961 [cotton] allotments were illegal" ". . . [and]
recommended to Mr. Murphy that [they] be canceled."[163]

12/15—12/17/61:   Johnson arranges a private dinner with
Hoover.[164]

12/17/61—SUNDAY: D.C. press reports: "Senate Democratic leader Mike Mansfield, Mont., said . . . that 'extreme right
wingers' pose a great threat to the security and welfare of the
United States. He also said their charge that the Communist threat
is greater from within than without indicates a lack of confidence in
J. Edgar Hoover and the FBI."[165]

12/18/61—MONDAY: This date is SOG's deadline for receipt of biannual reports from all field offices. All significant data
obtained within the last six months will now be forwarded to Hoover's assistants (e.g., Courtney Evans, Organized Crime Division.)
From this they will generate updated reports for personal review by
Hoover and Tolson.

12/19/61—TUESDAY: Quite possibly as a result of the confrontation by both JFK and RFK about campaign donations from
Giancana in previous days, Joseph Kennedy suffers a massive

stroke. Per press report: "Palm Beach, Fla. . . . President Kennedy flew here . . . to the bedside of his 73-year-old father . . . who is partially paralyzed following a stroke in the early afternoon. . . . Attorney General . . . Kennedy accompanied the President on his flight. . . ."[166] It is difficult to believe this is not a political disaster for Hoover. Having provided the allegation that may have precipitated the stroke, he will probably be held responsible in JFK's mind. This alone could well preclude any consideration of a retirement waiver from the President.

12/20/61—WEDNESDAY: Press reports "The Justice Department may take some direct action next month against Communist Party leaders for their failure to register as agents of a foreign power—the Soviet Union. . . . The government must prove in court that a given individual is a leader. *This could call for testimony from valuable informers within the party whose usefulness would then be lost to the FBI"* (emphasis added).[167]

". . . With Marcello free on a $10,000 bond, the five-member Board of Immigration Appeals upheld the deportation order against [him], denying another appeal by [his] attorneys that it be declared invalid."[168]

12/21/61—THURSDAY: Press report "COVINGTON, Ky . . . A Federal grand jury probing vice . . . indicted nine men today on charges of evading nearly $400,000 in gambling taxes on a 2-million dollar-a-year numbers racket. . . . Attorney General . . . Kennedy . . . said *the numbers racket (includes off-track betting) was operated out of the Sportsmen's Club in the gambling center of Newport, Ky.* . . . The defendants were . . . David . . . and Frank Andrews . . . ; Walter Owens . . . Louis Tye . . . Russell Malone . . . Willard Whitley . . . Gus Postel . . . Frank Andrioli . . . [and] Peter Andrews. . . . Kennedy said the nine were charged with conspiring to evade $387,555 in gambling excise taxes. . . . . . . *Teams of FBI and revenue agents began surveillance and undercover operations in Newport in May, he said. The Sportsmen's Club was raided Aug. 22"* (emphasis added).[169] Collateral indictments of members of the Beckley/di Piazza/Levinson group, controlled by Marcello and Lansky, continue.

12/61: ". . . The FBI . . . leased twenty-five telephone lines directly from the telephone company in Las Vegas, Nevada, to monitor telephone lines at the Desert Inn and other Las Vegas hotels. The lines were leased to the Henderson Novelty Company, a front with the same address as the Las Vegas FBI office." A massive ELSUR operation, it will continue into May 1963 without the A.G.'s knowledge.[170]

12/22/61—FRIDAY: ". . . Murphy decided to cancel [Estes's] allotments. Later the same day he overrode an adverse recommendation by the review and adjudication division . . . and directed the appointment of . . . [Estes] to the newly formalized cotton advisory committee." By now, two other Agriculture Department employees, Messrs. William E. Morris and James T. Ralph, have received money orders from Estes. The latter, while in D.C. during January 1962, meets with LBJ aide, Cliff Carter.[171]

12/24/61—SUNDAY: D.C. press reports: "The Communist Party in the United States has lost something like 90 percent in membership since it reached its peak numerical strength 17 years ago. This is an official estimate, prepared for the Washington Post by the Federal Bureau of Investigation of the Department of Justice. . . . The FBI estimates that the numerical strength of the Communist Party in the United States has now nose-dived to between 8,000 and 10,000. It is a paradox that, as the Communist Party in this country has grown weaker, the uproar against it by right-wing extremists has grown louder. President Kennedy, in recent speeches on the West Coast, tore into the extremists. . . . . . . Attorney General Robert F. Kennedy says that the right-wing extremists are '. . . a tremendous disturbance to our system of government.' . . . He has no sympathy for 'those, who in the name of fighting communism, sow seeds of suspicion and distrust by making false or irresponsible charges . . . against public officials . . . Congress, the Supreme Court and even the Presidency. . . . Kennedy says he is backed in this stand by a man who is a glamorous hero in the eyes of the John Birch Society and other extremist outfits, J. Edgar Hoover. . . . Kennedy said: 'As a vigilant, experienced American, who has real credentials as a Communist fighter—J. Edgar Hoover—has said, such actions play into communist hands and hinder, rather than aid, the fight against communism.' Why has the Communist

Party in the United States lost such an immense part of its membership? Although the FBI doesn't list it, the chief reason . . . is that the climate is not congenial for Reds. The FBI says that the Communist Party . . . is dangerous in spite of the great shrinkage in its membership, and adds: '. . . The Party, through the fanaticism of its members and strategic placement in key industries and groups, is able time after time to wield an influence far out of proportion to its actual numbers.' Attorney General Kennedy has been saying . . . 'If we think that the great problem in the United States now is the fact that there are 10,000 Communists here, if we think that that's what's going to destroy this country, we are in very bad shape . . .' " This article, when considered in light of Hoover's December 7 speech (which encouraged ultra-right extremism, inflated the communist threat, and attacked JFK's position on communism) reveals the depth of philosophical difference between the two men. Note that the Director is not actually quoted in this article. Undoubtedly he had little to do with its preparation as an official estimate for the *Washington Post,* a newspaper he loathes. By exposing the nonsubstantive nature of Hoover's claims regarding the size of the communist threat, the Kennedys hope to show that he is out of step with reality and the times.

12/25/61—MONDAY: Press carries excerpts from ex-Secret Service chief Baughman's new book about his exploits with the agency. "You know that three of our Presidents have been assassinated—and that the assassins were insane. Did you know that five others have come within a hair's-breadth of being murdered by mad individuals? Who makes these attempts, the successful ones, the nearly successful ones and the complete failures? They are all made by mentally disturbed people." He also details the 12/14/60 capture of an individual threatening President-elect Kennedy: "A letter was found on him which read in part: 'I believe that the Kennedys bought the Presidency and the White House. . . .' "[172] Interestingly, ex-CIA director Allen Dulles, at the initial meeting of the Warren Commission in December 1963, will provide members of that group with copies of a book, the thesis of which being that only lone nuts assassinate American presidents. History, of course, has shown that this was not the case in Lincoln's assassination, as well as the attempt on Truman. Circumstances surrounding Harding's sudden death remain unclear. The record in practically all other countries by this time is replete with reports of assassinations and attempts, committed by groups of individuals for completely sane, pragmatic reasons. A 1962 attempt on Charles de Gaulle by a group of ex-military officers will provide good example. That men such as Baughman or Dulles, both recently retired by Kennedy and both in the intelligence community, would feel it necessary to promote such a myth is disturbing.

12/29/61—FRIDAY: Press reports: "President Kennedy today accepted the resignation of Gen. C. P. Cabell as deputy director of the Central Intelligence Agency. Cabell has been deputy director since 1953."[173]

12/31/61—SUNDAY: Hoover by now is maintaining "in his office copies of numerous published pamphlets, news stories, and letters from right-wing activists accusing Kennedy of disloyalty."[174] JFK, meanwhile, has also made it clear to his aides that he does not intend to waive the statute requiring Hoover's retirement on 1/1/65.[175] Also, according to one of Hoover's assistants (William Sullivan), ". . . It was rumored that when JFK was reelected, Hoover would be out and Courtney Evans would become the new director. . . . Hoover heard that rumor too . . ." [176] This revelation concerning Evans is significant. It does not, however, change the fact that he remains in charge of the Bureau's Specialized Investigative (i.e., organized crime) Division until after the assassination.

By now, Johnson associates Bobby Baker and Fred Black have, along with Mafia functionaries Ed Levinson and Benny Sigelbaum, formed "Serve-U Corporation, [which] provided vending machines for the automatic dispensing of food and drink in companies working on [federal] government contracts. In the next two years, Serve-U was awarded the lion's share of the vending business at three major aerospace firms—*North American Aviation,* Northrop Corp., and . . . Space Technologies. At North American Aviation alone, [its] machines raked in $2.5 million annually in the company's California plants."[177] During the 1950s, "Representative Hebert of Louisiana called for hearings, got them, and found that there were . . . swarms of retired officers working for defense contractors— . . . 92 for *North American Aviation.* . . . A bill to regulate the activities of retired officers passed the House. In the Senate, Johnson, giving the military establishment the last year [1960] of his allegiance as Majority leader, saw that the bill was properly laid to rest without . . . action."[178] Note that LBJ, as Vice President, is heavily involved in aerospace work (NASA, etc.). Baker's and Black's opportunity to obtain the vending contracts described above stems from Johnson's prior senatorial work in awarding defense contracts to such companies.

1/62—THIS MONTH: Hoover qualifies his position on the Mafia by stating, "No single individual or coalition of racketeers dominates organized crime across the nation." With over a thousand special agents focusing now on the entity, the use of ELSUR is becoming pervasive.[179]

FBI (Chicago) ELSUR again records Giancana. He and an individual named John D'Arco discuss the pending Cook County (Chicago) sheriff's election and potential candidate, Roswell Spencer, a former FBI agent. Giancana: "Spencer is like Kennedy. He'll get what he wants out of you, but you won't get anything out of him." D'Arco: "That fucker Kennedy! Is Sinatra gonna work on . . . ?" Giancana: "No." D'Arco: "I heard that the President, when he is in California, is with Sinatra all the time." Giancana: "He can't get change of a quarter." D'Arco: "Sinatra can't?" Giancana: "That's right. Well they got the whip and they're in office and that's it . . . so they're gonna knock us guys out of the box and make us defenseless." [180] Like previous recordings, this is sent by AIRTEL to Hoover.

Congressman McCormack of Massachusetts, JFK opponent and Hoover friend of thirty-four years, is elected Speaker of the House.[181] Hoover considers this a very fortunate turn of events, as he is now closely aligned with the most powerful man in the country after Johnson.

Allegedly, Commercial Solvents, a New York–based company and Estes's main creditor, is under the influence of the Mafia. ". . . An FBI agent on the case revealed to a friend that Commercial Solvents [was] suspected of gangster connections. . . ." This is known to Hoover prior to 5/21/62.[182] If the allegation is true, Marcello may already be privy to details surrounding Estes's relationship with political powers in D.C., through New York connections such as Joe Bonnano, Frank Costello, Meyer Lansky, and members of the Beckley group.

1/1/62—MONDAY: Today is Hoover's sixty-seventh birth-day. In the January edition of the *FBI Law Enforcment Bulletin,* he writes, "By the exchange of valuable criminal intelligence informa-tion, the FBI and other Federal, State and local agencies are suc-cessfully penetrating the innermost sanctions of the criminal deity. . . . *Dissemination of criminal intelligence must be expeditious. Presently it is exchanged promptly by agencies involved and there is no delay in its reaching the proper authorities"* (emphasis added).

1/8/62—MONDAY: "A . . . [memo]from . . . Hoover [to RFK] stated the Bureau had learned that Stanley D. Levison, 'a member of the Communist Party, USA . . . is allegedly a close advisor to . . . Martin Luther King, Jr.' . . . This was the first time that the FBI had realized King and Levison were close friends. . . . The two . . . had known each other . . . well for over four years. . . . Levison's activities remained under extremely close surveillance throughout the remainder of 1954 and into the summer of 1955. Then, . . . [his] central role in secret CP financial deal-ings declined greatly. . . . Direct contact with Levison came to an end. The Bureau's interest in his activities noticeably slackened. . . . On November 27, 1959, the New York office recommended . . . that Levison be considered for recruitment as an informant. [He declined.]. . . . FBI's lack of interest . . . ended suddenly when it was learned in very early 1962 that [he] and King were close friends. . . ."[183] Given the public support provided King by JFK, part of Hoover's motivation to discredit the former could well be stemming from a perceived opportunity to damage the adminis-tration. In addition, by linking black unrest with CPUSA, Hoover can undercut the Kennedys' efforts to minimize the threat posed by that organization. This, in turn, might revitalize support for Hoo-ver's now flagging rhetoric concerning domestic communism. An-other reason could simply be Hoover's desire to bring to justice one more impostor. King's politics and reported philanderings, taken in combination with his status as both a member of the clergy and married man, enrage the Director.

1/9/62—TUESDAY: D.C. columnist George E. Sokolsky again heaps praise upon Hoover. "It is impossible to mix security and politics. J. Edgar Hoover succeeded in his management of the FBI because he stayed out of politics." Further, in almost surrealist fashion, he attempts to analyze the extreme left and right. "Many of the pro-Communists have found their way back to Washington. Surprisingly, some are found in right-wing anti-Communist movements where they are doing very well. There has been a very strong infiltration . . . with the object of breaking them into segments by internal quarrels as well as giving them a ridiculously extremist facade."[184]

1/12/62—FRIDAY: "Asst. Sec. of Labor Jerry R. Holleman . . . admitted . . . that he had asked Mr. Estes to pay for a dinner given . . . on Jan. 12 by Secretary of Labor . . . Goldberg in honor of Vice President Johnson."[185] At some point in the evening Estes meets with LBJ, obtaining a personal invitation to come to his private residence.

1/14/62—SUNDAY: Estes and other Texans attend afternoon reception at Johnson's house. "It was at this reception, . . . that [Johnson] met [with] Estes. . . . The Vice President is known to have had a brief conversation with [him]."[186]

1/15/62—MONDAY: Per LBJ's instructions, aide Walter Jenkins meets with Estes, informing him of the Vice President's willingness to again intervene on his behalf with Undersecretary of Agriculture Murphy. Shortly after this, Jenkins contacts Murphy by phone.[187]

1/16/62—TUESDAY: "Also there are records of three cashier's checks totaling $145,015, drawn Jan. 16 . . . against . . . Estes' account. . . . These are believed to be checks he took with him on a trip to Washington Jan. 16 to 20."[188]

1/18/62—THURSDAY: The Department of Agriculture ". . . wired Estes an order . . . raising his bond to $1,000,000 . . ." up from $700,000.[189]

1/20/62—SATURDAY: FBI, in a massive raid, shuts down a Reading, Pennsylvania, gambling casino controlled by the Bruno (Mafia) organization, headquartered in Philadelphia. Press reports: "More than 100 armed FBI agents ripped bars from windows and broke down the front door to surprise more than 100 patrons at three dice tables. They seized $55,000, arrested 100 . . . In Washington, J. Edgar Hoover, FBI director, said an investigation determined that the gambling games had been operated continuously since mid-November, 1961."[190] This bust may well be the result, in part, of ELSUR coverage on Angelo Bruno.

1/23/62—TUESDAY: Ex-FBI agent Jack Levine sends a forty-four page "Memo on the FBI" to Assistant Attorney General Herbert Miller (in charge of Criminal Division) in an attempt to expose and denounce Hoover.[191]

1/24/62—WEDNESDAY: Hoover testifies before the House Appropriations subcommittee regarding his annual Bureau budgetary request. During the course of this testimony, he discusses a variety of subjects. On communism he states it would be a serious mistake for the nation to "minimize the internal threat of communist activity." He is also upset about the fact that chronologically accurate and unedited versions of *Operation Abolition* have been made available to the public, while his own version has been withdrawn by JFK. On the Mafia: "The chart which I hand to the Committee shows the upward trend in the accomplishments in criminal cases directly attributable to FBI *confidential informants"* (emphasis added). Representative Rooney, perhaps realizing that Hoover is also talking about electronic surveillance, responds, "Do you want this in the record?" Hoover: "I have no objection, Mr. Chairman." Further, "For example, to date we have transmitted to the Department 4,896 reports covering the activities of approximately 1,800 criminal figures who are operating in this country. In addition, 417 specially prepared summaries reflecting detailed data as to the background and activities of racketeers operating throughout the country were made available to the Department for its assistance. Further, an intensive all-out investigation was launched early in 1961 on 40 [includes Marcello] of the most prominent and notorious racketeers in the country and we have initiated an intensive investigating operation against additional ones. . . . *During the course of our investigations, we develop many items of information which are of significance to other Federal . . . law enforcement agencies. This data is promptly disseminated to the appropriate agency [e.g. Secret Service] which can effectively take action on it. . . ."* (emphasis added). On Cuban refugees, Mr. Sikes: "With so many refugees, do you not have an almost impossible situation to detect the people who are sent here as agents for Castro?" Hoover: "It is a very difficult problem. (Discussion off the record)."[192]

1/25/62—THURSDAY: "Estes flew to Washington and . . . showed up at the Agriculture Department where, quite possibly through Johnson's influence with Undersecretary . . . Murphy, the higher bond was waived."[193]

1/26/62—FRIDAY: *Congressional Record* insertion of a Hoover article in *Retired Officer* magazine entitled "Communism and the Knowledge to Combat It," in which he remarks, "And communists are not liberals."

1/28/62—SUNDAY: Press: "Attorney General Robert F. Kennedy has named his chief aide . . . to lead the prosecution of top Communist Party officials. . . ."[194]
    Estes is informed by the Agriculture Department that he must produce "seller's certificates" in order to prove the legitimacy of cotton allotment transfers but is given no deadline for compliance. He provides none.[195]
    Johnson, at the White House, pontificates for the press. "I was proud when I stood beside the President on the steps of the Capitol one year ago and heard him plead with this Nation to 'begin now.' After a year at his side, I am prouder now than I was then."[196] Once he obtains the presidency, he will state instead that he "detested every minute" of his time as Vice President.[197]

2/62—THIS MONTH: "Ferrie . . . entered into [an] arrangement . . . with Guy Banister, a former FBI agent who ran a private investigative firm. By the terms of the agreement, Ferrie's work . . . included analyzing autopsy reports in payment for Banister's investigative services. Banister . . . handled [his] case 'personally.' " Banister also agrees to help in Ferrie's battle with Eastern Airlines.[198] This raises a very interesting question. To what extent is the New Orleans FBI aware of this connection? Ferrie has been under surveillance by them for some time. In addition, they regularly interact with Banister's agency, supplying him with contract work. In exchange, the ex-agent helps them monitor the local Cuban exile population.

The Cuban Revolutionary Council, a large, local exile organization controlled by Arcacha Smith, moves its offices to 544 Camp Street, New Orleans, as had Banister, whose agency develops background reports for Smith regarding CRC volunteers.[199] Considering the keen interest Hoover and the Bureau have in these groups, it is probable that Banister is supplying copies of these reports to the New Orleans field office.

A U.S. Border Patrol report ". . . alleges that Ferrie was the pilot who flew Carlos Marcello back into the United States from Guatemala. . . ."[200] This report, in keeping with the goals of the Attorney General's twenty-seven-agency task force, is probably made available to the FBI.

2/1/62—THURSDAY: FBI assistants Evans and Belmont discuss, via memo, the fact that RFK has installed a man named Paul Corbin on the Democratic National Committee. "It offended . . . Hoover, who [had] assured the press and the House Un-American Activities Committee that Corbin had been a Communist . . . The Attorney General, Courtney Evans told [Belmont], 'seems to have gone completely overboard in trying to defend Corbin.' "[201]

"Marilyn [Monroe] was one of several guests invited to be at the Lawford home . . . when the Attorney General and his wife [passed] through Los Angeles at the start of a world tour. . . . 'Sometime in the evening, she and Kennedy . . . had a very long . . . political talk. She . . . had asked [him] whether they were going to fire . . . Hoover—she was very outspoken against him—and Kennedy replied that he and the President didn't feel strong enough to do so, though they wanted to.' "[202]

2/2/62—FRIDAY: Press reports: "A bill that would legalize wiretapping by state and Federal law enforcement officers was sent to Congress by the Kennedy Administration yesterday. [Under the proposed law] . . . a Federal judge could issue a wiretap order upon the request of the Attorney General. . . . *[The] crimes are* murder . . . *transmission of gambling information,* interstate travel for racketeering purposes *and narcotics*" (emphasis added).[203]

D.C. press reports: "The manicured mobsters who rule Chicago's rackets have . . . departed for Miami, en masse. . . . . Crime czars from other cities are also converging upon Miami. The

best guess is that they are heading south . . . to discuss what to do
about Attorney General Robert Kennedy. . . . Using his influence
with the White House, he has united the feuding Federal enforcement agencies into the most formidable army of lawmen ever to
wage war upon organized crime. They now keep all the Nation's
top racketeers under constant scrutiny. . . ."[204]

2/7/62—WEDNESDAY: FBI SAC (Los Angeles) AIRTEL
to Hoover updating him on "the current status of the Bureau's
investigation of a group of prostitutes recently arrested by the Los
Angeles Police Department. . . . One of the madams had sent
'prostitutes to . . . John Kennedy and Frank Sinatra, after which
she received telephone calls from these two individuals to send
other girls to their associates' and that this had occurred 'just prior
to the opening day of the Democratic Convention in 1960.' When
Courtney Evans . . . later informed the attorney general of these
'allegations,' he reported back that Kennedy was 'most appreciative' of the briefing."[205]

2/9/62—FRIDAY: FBI (Philadelphia) ELSUR records local
Mafia boss Angelo Bruno and associate Weisberg discussing Hoover's recent gambling raid in Reading, Pennsylvania. Weisberg:
*"See what Kennedy done. With Kennedy a guy should take a knife, like
one of them other guys, and stab and kill the fucker, . . . somebody
should kill the fucker, I mean it. This is true, honest to God. . . . I
hope I get a week's notice. I'll kill. Right in the . . . White House.
Somebody's got to get rid of this fucker."* Bruno: "They are trying to
pass a federal law that you can't take the Fifth [Amendment.]
When they grant you immunity you can't take the Fifth." Weisberg:
"They are not going to pass that now." Bruno: "But they might"
(emphasis added).[206] This death threat against the President is very
shortly sent by AIRTEL to Hoover, who decides not to inform the
Secret Service or the Attorney General. He instead hides the information in the Bureau's confidential files. Electronic surveillance of
the Bruno organization continues. It is interesting to note that
elements within the Mafia clearly recognize that Hoover, and even
RFK, merely implement presidential policy. In Hoover's mind,
three points must by now have crystallized regarding JFK: 1) His
father, JPK, has taken campaign money from the Chicago Mafia;
2) Kennedy is a womanizer who has committed adultery with

Mafia-supplied prostitutes; and 3) He associates with a man, Frank Sinatra, used by the Mafia as a liaison. To a man of Hoover's mindset, the line between the Mafia and the President may have now become blurred. Given this, and his obsession with internal security, his perception of JFK as a leader must also, by this point, have been called into question.

Press reports: "Federal agents are now digging into the compost pile of California crime in search of federal violations. Many top racketeers, rather than risk a Federal rap, are taking to flight like so many startled quail. If the mobsters who flourish like bloated spiders on the profits of organized crime were to ape the FBI and publish their own list of Ten Most Wanted Men, there is no doubt whose picture would head it: That of Attorney General Kennedy."[207]

2/12/62—MONDAY: Pecos, Texas, newspaper, *The Pecos Independent and Enterprise* begins ". . . The devastating exposure that blew the Billie Sol Estes business sky high."

"The Estes matter began to plague Johnson in 1962, when a story in a Pecos, Texas, newspaper raised questions about the vice president's relations with Texas gubernatorial candidate John Connally and alleged that Johnson had lent Estes $5 million. . . . Because CBS had picked up the local news story, Johnson immediately contacted Hoover to ask 'if the Bureau could talk to the editor of the weekly newspaper in Pecos. . . .' Johnson identified the editor by name and said that 'people with that paper have played this [incriminating] tape to the [investigative reporter] for CBS.' . . . Hoover promised to 'get started on it right away.' Johnson and Hoover then discussed how best this could be done, the vice president inquiring 'what to do on these things except to call DeLoach.' 'That was the thing to do,' Hoover replied, and DeLoach apparently defanged the editor. Johnson also agreed that in the future 'he would have his assistant, Walter Jenkins, get in touch with Mr. DeLoach in such instances.' "[208]The FBI picks up the Estes case once again.

2/16/62—FRIDAY: *The New York Times,* a paper hated by Hoover, quotes excerpts from his recent *ABA* [American Bar Association] *Journal* article, "Shall It Be Law or Tyranny?" "We must remember that many non-communists may legitimately, on their own, oppose the same laws or take positions on issues of the day which are also held by the communists. Their opinions, though temporarily coinciding with the party line, do not make them communists."

2/17/62—SATURDAY: Hoover and Tolson attend Bowie for the $11,275 Southern Maryland Handicap. "The presentation of the trophy to Clyde Troutt, the trainer of Rare Rice, was made by J. Edgar Hoover. . . ."[209]

FBI SAC (Philadelphia) AIRTEL to Hoover containing more ELSUR product on Bruno. Maggio: ". . . the only reason [Robert F. Kennedy] won't leave, which I heard before, you see he wants Edgar Hoover out of that." Bruno: "Edgar Hoover." Maggio: *"He wants Edgar Hoover out of the FBI because he is a fairy, you know he is a fairy, I heard this before. . . ."* Bruno: *"Who?"* Maggio: *"Edgar Hoover is a fairy. . . . Listen to this. Hoover is not married and neither is his assistant, read back in his history."* Bruno: "His assistant?" (emphasis added).[210] Information about Hoover and Tolson's homosexuality is handled very carefully by SOG. It is not clear when or in what form Hoover or Tolson review this data. What *is* clearly significant here is that key Mafia figures have picked up on the fact that Kennedy wants Hoover removed. Given Bruno's close friendship with Traficante, and the latter's even closer association with Marcello, it is safe to assume that Marcello is also aware of JFK's plan to retire Hoover. One can only wonder at Hoover's reaction to this latest information.

D.C. press reports: "The big story social Washington has been buzzing about has . . . been . . . the big White House twist party when even the Secretary of Defense, to the amazement of his generals, twisted and when the President himself danced until 4:30 A.M."[211]

2/21/62—WEDNESDAY: The Freedoms Foundation announces that Hoover is the winner of the "George Washington Medal," his second award from the group in six years. The award is for "contributions to a better understanding of the American way of life."[212]

2/22/62—THURSDAY: George Washington's birthday, a federal holiday, permits Hoover to travel to Valley Forge to receive his medal and present an acceptance speech entitled "The Courage of Freemen." "Today as never before, America has need for men and women who possess the moral strength and courage of our forefathers. . . . . . . What we desperately need today is patriotism founded on a real understanding of the American ideal. . . . *In our Nation today,* the proper balance between the rights of the individual and those of *society is being undermined by* two major elements—*communism and organized crime*—two powerful and dangerous foes. *And we are hastening national disaster when we tolerate weaknesses in the administration of justice.* . . . Crime has a partner in forming the common denominator of a breakdown in moral behavior; it is the influence of godless communism. The basic answer to communism is moral. America has no place for those timid souls who urge 'appeasement at any price' nor those who chant the 'Better Red Than Dead' slogan. *We need men with a capacity for moral indignation, men of faith, men of conviction, men with the God-given strength and determination to uphold the cause of democracy. Nor does our strength stem from the pseudo liberals of* the extreme left . . ." (emphasis added).[213]

2/26/62—MONDAY: FBI (Dallas) Crime Condition Report is forwarded to SOG. With regard to the Mafia, it states, "There is no evidence of illegal activity by Joseph Francis Civello. . . . Texas is not a place where the mafia has the kind of control it has elsewhere." Civello is a Marcello lieutenant representing the latter in Dallas. Campisi and Jack Ruby are functionaries of the Civello organization.[214] Like Regis Kennedy in the New Orleans field office, the Dallas case officer(s) also do not see any threat from the mob. As the Beckley/di Piazza/Saia/Campisi investigation is beginning to show, such a statement is, at best, naïve.

2/27/62—TUESDAY: In another direct attempt to manipulate JFK, ". . . Hoover sent a memorandum to Robert Kennedy and Special Assistant to the President Kenneth O'Donnell stating . . . that during the FBI investigation of Roselli's role in [an illegal wiretap in Las Vegas] . . . the Bureau had found that he maintained a relationship with Judith Campbell, who had also been having affairs with Sam Giancana and President Kennedy—simultaneously."[215] Hoover also states ". . . The relationship between

Campbell and Mrs. Lincoln [Kennedy's secretary] or the purpose of these calls is not known."[216]

2/28/62—WEDNESDAY: Press reports: "The Secret Service is planning to put on an extra shift of agents to keep up with the fast moving man whose life they guard—President Kennedy. '. . . We could use another shift. We were contemplating establishing what we call a fourth shift because of the activities of the President. As you know, he is moving back and forth almost every weekend.' Rowley explained that when the President is on the move agents are withdrawn from the field to handle the extra workload of the White House detail. '. . . It is my hope that the Vice President would have a detail.' Rowley said that only two men are now assigned to protect Vice President Johnson, 'at his [Johnson's] request and not as a matter of law.' Rowley said that the number of threatening letters to the President increased by 52 percent in 1961."[217] Genuine lone-nut-type cases involving threats against the President usually take such form. Some also attempt to approach him personally in public, or enter the White House.

3/62—THIS MONTH: "With his problems mounting, Ferrie sought legal aid from New Orleans attorney G. Wray Gill, Sr. [He] . . . testified that he and Gill . . . entered into an agreement in March 1962 that Gill would represent Ferrie in his legal difficulties in return for Ferrie's research and investigative work on other cases for Gill."[218]
     FBI (Las Vegas) ELSUR discovers that "In March . . . $200,000 was skimmed from the Desert Inn alone. . . ."[219]
     Baker and Black cosign a $175,000 bank loan, along with Lansky's Las Vegas representatives Edward Levinson and Benny Sigelbaum.[220]

3/2/62—FRIDAY: D.C. press reports: "President Kennedy greeted a group of *Louisiana* beauty queens at the White House today, welcoming them to Washington, and spent several minutes chatting with them about the Mardi Gras Ball they are here to attend . . . tomorrow night" (emphasis added).[221] It would be interesting to know whether Marcello in any way influenced the selection of young women for this group, or if there was interaction between Kennedy and any of the women. There are a number of stories concerning supposed Mafia efforts to use the President's involvement with various women to blackmail him during his administration (e.g., Marilyn Monroe "wiretap" by West Coast mob, use of Judith Campbell by Chicago Mafia). Hoover, obviously, is not averse to the attempt.

3/5/62—MONDAY: Hoover receives from an "outraged patriot" a copy of the *London Sunday Times* interview with RFK in which the latter had disclosed the presence of numerous FBI agents within CPUSA.[222]

3/6/62—TUESDAY: FBI LEGAT (Mexico City) AIRTEL to Hoover regarding Marilyn Monroe. Unknowingly placed under electronic surveillance while visiting a friend south of the border, she had discussed her dinner February 1 with the Robert Kennedys at Lawford's house in Los Angeles. "The . . . document reports that Marilyn 'spent time with Robert Kennedy at Lawford's home,' and that they discussed political issues. . . . Marilyn confid[ed] that . . . [they] . . . discussed the Kennedys' desire to fire J. Edgar Hoover."[223] Receiving information in this manner from the field about his own impending retirement no doubt infuriates him. With regard to a purported RFK/Monroe affair, Hoover assistant William Sullivan later said, "The stories about RFK and Marilyn Monroe were just stories. The original . . . was invented by a so-called journalist, a right-wing zealot who had a history of spinning wild yarns. It spread like wildfire, of course, and J. Edgar Hoover was right there, gleefully fanning the flames."[224]

3/8/62—THURSDAY: Hoover dictates a letter thanking the sender of the *London Sunday Times* article. ". . . It was good of you to make this item available to me. . . ." With it he includes five quotes of his own on communism.[225]

3/9/62—FRIDAY: Press reports: "President Kennedy selected Maj. Gen. Marshall S. Carter today to be Deputy Director of the Central Intelligence Agency. The nomination must be confirmed by the Senate. The Carter appointment was the second major shift in the top ranks of the CIA since John A. McCone succeeded Allen W. Dulles as director last November. Two weeks ago Richard M. Helms, an assistant director, was named to succeed Richard M.

Bissell, Jr., who resigned as deputy director for plans."[226] JFK continues to systematically replace the CIA's top command with people more closely aligned to his own political philosophy.

3/13/62—TUESDAY: Hoover has a private lunch with President Kennedy in the residential section of the White House. This is one of five to seven such off-the-record luncheon meetings between the two. Usually arranged by RFK, it is not known what they discuss.[227] Given the animosity between the two, it is difficult to believe they are not extremely awkward.

FBI SOG internal memo from Evans to Belmont regarding his concern over the possibility of Hoffa informants within the Criminal Division of the Justice Department. Not surprisingly, this memo will later be found in Hoover's O & C (Official and Confidential) files. This day the press reports *"Defense attorneys for James R. Hoffa, seeking dismissal of a mail-fraud indictment, entered as evidence today a statement allegedly made by President Kennedy in a campaign debate with Richard M. Nixon. . . . The quotation, 'I'm not satisfied when I see men like Jimmy Hoffa, in charge of the largest union in the country, still free"* (emphasis added).[228]

D.C. press reports: "About a dozen youths held a sit-in demonstration for several hours today in Attorney General Robert F. Kennedy's outer office. They protested the Administration's civil rights policies. The group of Negroes and whites identified themselves to surprised Justice Department officials as members of the Student Non-Violent Coordinating Committee. They said they favored faster action in efforts to protect rights of Negroes. . . . They were seeking the release of three students held on criminal-anarchy charges by Louisiana authorities."[229] Hoover, his office located on the same floor, is probably very disturbed by this type of youthful protest.

3/17/62—SATURDAY: Maynard Wheeler, the president of Commercial Solvents, meets with Estes at his ". . . home in Pecos, Texas. . . ."[230]

3/18/62—SUNDAY: Press reports: "William T. Heffelfinger, the Treasury's highest-ranking career official with nearly forty-five years of service, will retire March 31. Mr. Heffelfinger, 58, gave no reason for his retirement. . . . He merely said, 'I am electing to voluntarily retire.' "[231]

3/19/62—MONDAY: Press reports: "Integrationists held a 2½-hour sit-in at the reception office of Attorney General Robert F. Kennedy today. . . . The sit-in . . . was the third in six days."[232]

3/20/62—TUESDAY: Press reports: "President Kennedy named Robert M. Ball of Baltimore today to be Commissioner of Social Security. . . . [He] . . . will succeed William L. Mitchell, who is retiring."[233]

3/22/62—THURSDAY: Hoover attends a White House ceremony for presentation of the Young American Medal For Bravery award. During a private luncheon with JFK he confronts him with a " '. . . restatement of information relating to telephone calls made to the President's Secretary from Judith Campbell's Los Angeles residence' on 7, 10, 13, and 14 November 1961 and 14 February 1962. The restatement conceded ignorance as to the nature of Campbell's relationship with Mrs. Lincoln but reported that an FBI informer 'of questionable reputation' had claimed that 'Campbell [was] the girl who was shacking up with John Kennedy in the East.' "[234] "Later that afternoon the President made his last call to the woman."[235] "O'Donnell, . . . present when the FBI Director met the President, later quoted Kennedy as saying, 'Get rid of that bastard. He's the biggest bore.' "[236] Hoover's confrontation of the President in this manner, given all that has transpired between the two in the last year, reveals his growing desperation. That JFK is apparently outwardly oblivious to Hoover's attempts at blackmail can only be a source of frustration.

3/23/62—FRIDAY: JFK and RFK fly to the West Coast. There, the President presents a speech at Berkeley wherein he states that the "great currents of history are carrying the world 'away from communism and toward national independence and freedom.' "[237] After the presentation ". . . Kennedy had planned to stay with Frank Sinatra in Palm Springs, but switched at the last minute to Bing Crosby's home in the same area. . . . Sinatra, mightily offended, expressed his wrath partly by breaking off relations with Peter Lawford."²³⁸ RFK has to be the motivating force behind this change in plans.

3/24/62—SATURDAY: JFK attends a dinner party at Sinatra's. ". . . Marilyn was there and . . . they were obviously together. . . . having a good time. . . ."²³⁹

Hoover and Tolson appear at Bowie for one of biggest events of the season, the $115,900 John B. Campbell Handicap. Also in attendance, as noted by the press, were "Vice President and Mrs. Johnson [who] headed a group of twelve that arrived at the track shortly before the third race. They were escorted to the Director's lounge, from which point they watched the races. The Vice President gave the elevator operator, Mrs. Edna Kreitzer, a pen bearing the inscription, 'Presented by the Vice President of the United States— Lyndon B. Johnson.' "²⁴⁰ Hoover and LBJ very probably meet, however briefly. The latter has apparently learned of the latest development in the Estes case and may well know of Estes's imminent arrest by the FBI. For the entirety of LBJ's tenure as Vice President, this is his only recorded visit to local tracks. Clearly his fear of exposure is becoming very real. Forever the opportunist, Hoover does not miss his chance to come to Johnson's aid.

Los Angeles press reports: "Attorney General Robert F. Kennedy said today that the greatest internal danger the United States faced from communism was 'espionage of Communist-bloc countries,' rather than the party itself. . . . *Mr. Kennedy said the Communist party of the United States as a political organization posed 'no danger.' He said it had 'been disregarded by the American people' and was under close scrutiny by the Federal Bureau of Investigation"* (emphasis added).²⁴¹

3/26/62—MONDAY: D.C. press reports: "The Republican National Committee criticized today a Secret Service request for fifty-eight more agents to protect President Kennedy. . . . . . . The committee asked if this request had anything to do with Mr. Kennedy's 'penchant for commuting from Hyannis Port, Palm Beach, Newport, and Middleburg.' "²⁴²

3/28/62—WEDNESDAY: As the press will soon reveal, "Frank Cain, of Pacific Finance, under oath swore that when he told Estes that the FBI was investigating him, Estes retorted: 'I can stop all that. I will get Lyndon Johnson on the phone,' and that night Estes added, 'I've got that investigation stopped." Estes calls LBJ aide Cliff Carter in an attempt to reach the Vice President. ". . . Three calls had been made to . . . Carter. . . . One call had gone to an unlisted number in Washington."[243]

By this point Estes has also met with associates of Jimmy Hoffa in an attempt to negotiate a twelve-million-dollar loan for his cotton allotment scheme (see 5/16/62).[244] News of the attempt would have gotten back to Traficante, and thus Marcello, both close supporters of Hoffa. Once Again, the New Orleans mobster is in a position to obtain inside information regarding Johnson's shady activities.

Press reports: "The Federal Government was urged today to dry up the 'huge profits' of organized gambling by striking at the bookmakers' intelligence network. . . . Senate Permanent Subcommittee on Investigations concluded that local law enforcement cannot cope with the 'grave internal threat of organized crime, much of it financed by gambling earnings.' They identified the key lay-off men, or bookmakers' bookmakers, as *Gilbert Beckley of Miami Beach, Florida, and Newport, Kentucky* . . . The report asked Congress to consider legislation to permit Federal, state, and local agencies to make legal wiretaps and to introduce the evidence in criminal prosecutions" (emphasis added).[245] Note the clear interconnection between Beckley and Levinson via Newport. In effect, the two gamblers are part of the same "intelligence network" and, like Lansky and Marcello, undoubtedly know each other well.

3/29/62—THURSDAY: Press reports: "Mr. Estes and three associates were indicted in Federal court at El Paso . . . for fraud."[246]

Press: "President Kennedy apparently disposed today of any doubts that he planned to seek a second term in 1964."[247]

Press: "Robert F. Kennedy . . . told Senators today he had strong evidence that *major public officials in communities in the South,* East, and West *'are on the payroll of big-time gamblers.'* Mr. Kennedy urged approval of an Administration bill that would permit Federal and state law-enforcement officials to tap wires, under court orders, when investigating a limited list of major crimes and to use the evidence in court. The Federal Bureau of Investigation now taps wires in national security cases, but it cannot use the evidence in court. Under the measure urged by Mr. Kennedy today, wiretapping by state law-enforcement officials would be limited to cases involving murder . . . bribery . . . or trafficking in narcotics. . . . Federal law enforcement would be permitted to wiretap in investigations of the same types of crime. . . . *Mr. Kennedy testified he believed enactment of the legislation would reduce the number of wiretaps and 'make individual rights of privacy far more secure than they are now. He said this was so because . . . an unauthorized wiretap would be a crime in itself,* regardless of any disclosure of the information. . . .' " (emphasis added).[248] Considered against the backdrop of Hoover's covert, ongoing electronic surveillance (EL-SUR) program, discussions such as the above appear ludicrous. Still, passage of the legislation would increase the risks involved in his use of such methods.

". . . there were strong suspicions that the Kennedys were . . . set to shunt Johnson aside in 1964 because of his connections with the Estes affair. It is known that FBI agents were working on this angle immediately after Billie Sol's arrest. Dr. Dunn had numerous calls from agents inquiring specifically for leads as to Johnson's connections, the agent in charge admitting that they 'had the green light' from Washington. . . ."[249] As the investigator in charge, Hoover is now in a position to allow public exposure of LBJ's role in the matter, or prevent the Justice Department from learning anything of it.

3/30/62—FRIDAY: Press reports "Robert Amory, Jr., has resigned as deputy director for intelligence in the Central Intelligence Agency, a post he has held since 1953."[250]

4/62—THIS MONTH: "Governor . . . Connally of Texas indicated that the idea of a Presidential visit to Texas arose first in the spring of 1962. . . . Johnson approached Connally with the information that the President wished to come to Texas for the purpose of fundraising."[251]

"Baker recalled the disasterous spring of 1962 when he was plunging money into the storm-damaged Carousel Motel (an East Coast casino club he had begun construction of during this time). . . . 'I went to the best friend I ever had around the Capitol . . . Vice President [Johnson].' "[252] The Senate aide may well have approached, or been approached by, gamblers Levinson et al. by this point.

Texas Argus magazine runs an article regarding LBJ's original election to the Senate and the nature of the "controlled vote" in southwest Texas.[253] "Controlled vote" here means, in part, purchased or falsified ballots.

4/2/62—MONDAY: Estes's CPA, George "Krutilek . . . [underwent] secret grilling by FBI agents. . . ."[254]

Press reports: "Texas Republican Chairman Tad Smith asked the United States House Government Operations Committee to determine if . . . Federal political influence was involved in the Estes case."[255]

Press reports in an unrelated, but nearly parallel, case to that of Marcello, "The Supreme Court denied a hearing today to Paul de Lucia of Chicago, who has been fighting deportation to Italy. Today's brief order lets stand as final the decision against de Lucia . . . last December. De Lucia, a naturalized citizen, who has had his citizenship revoked, has a criminal record."[256] As a resident alien with a criminal record, Marcello surely notes this case with considerable concern.

4/3/62—TUESDAY: An internal report ordered by RFK regarding Sinatra's ties to the Mafia reaches his desk. Marcello associate Joseph Fischetti (New Orleans and Chicago) is listed as a close friend. Hoover, through ELSUR, has known this since March 1960. "The nature of Sinatra's work may, on occasion, bring him into contact with underworld figures but this cannot account for his friendship and/or financial involvement with such people as Joe Fischetti and Rocco Fischetti. . . . No other entertainer appears to be mentioned nearly so frequently in connection with racketeers." The Attorney General will use this report as a basis for distancing both himself and the President from Sinatra within a few months.[257]

Press reports: "The House Judiciary Committee approved a bill today aimed at protecting informants in Federal criminal investigations. It would make it a crime to injure or threaten a person who furnishes information to the Federal Bureau of Investigation . . . in the course of an official investigation. Attorney General . . . Kennedy had asked that corrupt interference with an informant . . . be included as well as threats and violence but the committee refused to go that far."[258]

4/4/62—WEDNESDAY: "On the night of April 4 . . . at the western end of Texas, a ranchman came upon the body of George Krutilek in the sandhills near the town of Clint, slumped in his car with a hose from his exhaust stuck in the window. . . . The El Paso County pathologist . . . held that he . . . did not die from carbon monoxide poisoning."[259]

4/5/62—THURSDAY: D.C. press reports: "The Federal Bureau of Investigation disclosed today that it was *using more confidential informants* with increasingly successful results in criminal cases. Such informants were credited by J. Edgar Hoover, the FBI director, with a 'tremendous' contribution in the fight against crime. At the same time, *Mr. Hoover noted, his bureau's informants had supplied information that helped other Federal,* state and local *law-enforcement agencies to apprehend 2,640 persons. . . .*" (emphasis added). Hoover typically used the term "confidential informants" in internal memos to refer to ELSUR or COINTELPRO.[260]

Press: "A Federal grand jury indicted Billie Sol Estes, Texas financier, and three associates today on charges of committing fifty-seven acts of fraud." [261] LBJ is undoubtedly frightened by this latest turn of events.

4/10/62—TUESDAY: The "steel crisis" begins. Despite agreement with JFK not to raise prices, producers in fact do so. The President is furious, calling in RFK to consider the legal options.[262]

4/11/62—WEDNESDAY: Press reports: "At about 6 o'clock . . . Attorney General Kennedy ordered the Federal Bureau of Investigation to find out exactly what Mr. Edmund F. Martin had said." Martin is a steel company official. RFK orders that reporters who interviewed the official be questioned by agents in order to determine the accuracy of his statements. He also instructs Hoover to have agents interview the heads of the various steel companies.[263]

4/12/62—THURSDAY: An internal FBI memorandum from Evans to Belmont is generated regarding Hoover's authorization of ELSUR on Edward Levinson in Las Vegas, Nevada.[264] Obviously this has been done because of his deep involvement with both Mafia gambling and Johnson's protégé Bobby Baker. The Las Vegas ELSUR program has by this time generated considerable data on this individual, undoubtedly adding to Hoover's concerns regarding the Vice President.

In an obvious attempt to drive a wedge between President Kennedy and the press, Hoover orders agents to interview reporters in the predawn hours regarding Martin's statements. They do so, attempting to wake various individuals in the dead of night. The action creates a firestorm in the media, with accusations of "gestapo tactics" hurled at the administration. Hoover forwards a report concerning the night's work to RFK, who in turn relays the data to the President.[265] Conservative members of Congress seize upon the issue. Per press, "Republicans held the floor of the House of Representatives for more than six hours last night and into this morning in an extraordinary speech-making assault on the Kennedy Administration. Criticizing virtually every aspect of Administration policy, speaker after speaker contributed to the tide of oratory that began at 5:33 P.M. yesterday when the House ended its legislative routine and continued until 12:07 this morning."[266]Hoover is undoubtedly ecstatic. Marcello undoubtedly follows this carefully.

4/13/62—FRIDAY: U.S. Steel backs down, others follow suit, and the crisis ends. " 'Jack was very anxious to make peace with industry,' " RFK wrote a few days later.[267]

4/15/62—SUNDAY: Press reports: "The Customs Bureau has compiled figures that support the Kennedy Administration's contention that Communist propaganda in this country is a 'negligible' threat to national security. Republicans have charged that the Kennedy Administration has 'naïvely made concessions to the Communists' that have 'increased delivery of propaganda in this country ten-fold.' "[268]

4/15—5/31/62:   Apparently JFK's actions during the steel crisis have greatly antagonized high officials of the corporations involved. An American citizen in Moscow in June 1962 will meet and speak with a Mr. Williams Hill (National Steel) and one other man. "Mr. Hill was irate about Kennedy's use of the FBI for this purpose, and said that when he was in Washington, he'd complained to Mr. Hoover. According to Hill, Mr. Hoover responded: 'I have to do what Bobby Kennedy tells me to do.' "[269] Hoover evidently takes every opportunity to distance himself as much as possible from the effects of his and the administration's actions.

4/16/62—MONDAY: Press reports: "The Department of Agriculture today dismissed [an] . . . employee who was reported to have admitted receiving a gift hat from Billie Sol Estes. . . . William E. Morris . . . was discharged because he failed to make himself available to investigators who wanted to question him about his relations with Mr. Estes. Investigators could not find Mr. Morris over the weekend and he failed to report for work this morning. . . . . . . The Federal Bureau of Investigation had been asked to investigate their dealings. . . . The Republican National Committee said Mr. Estes was appointed by President Kennedy to the National Cotton Advisory Committee. 'Loaded with political TNT an FBI probe now under way may yet come to rest on the doorstep of the White House,' said the committee's publication, Battle Line."[270]

4/62—5/62:   Vice-presidential aide "Jenkins, on learning that Congressman Bill Cramer (R.-Fla.) was preparing impeachment proceedings based on the Vice President's and Mrs. Johnson's alleged association with Estes in two grain storage operations in Texas, asked DeLoach to have the FBI 'interview Cramer immediately.' Emphasizing that Hoover 'would, of course, want to be of every possible assistance to the Vice President,' DeLoach recommended that 'in [sic] this particular occasion it might be better if we received the information from a third party rather than from the Vice President's office.' The next morning *Thomas Corcoran, the lobbyist,* contacted DeLoach to report having learned that Cramer planned to initiate impeachment proceedings against the Vice President. DeLoach thereupon briefed Hoover, recommending that Cramer be 'immediately' interviewed as a 'legitimate responsibility in the current Estes investigation.' Hoover had concluded . . . 'We have already checked into the story told by Cramer and found it false; Cramer himself is a loud mouth; Corcoran is the devious "Tommy." ' . . . Jenkins recontacted DeLoach later that month to convey the Vice President's request for a meeting to discuss an editorial in *Farm and Ranch Magazine.* At the ensuing meeting approved by Hoover, Johnson denounced 'the false allegations [about his financial relations with Billie Sol Estes] made in the editorial,' offered evidence to challenge the allegations, and requested that Hoover have 'FBI Agents interview the editor of this magazine. . . .' DeLoach assured Johnson that 'the Director would want this done immediately,' and the Vice President expressed his 'appreciation.' Hoover thereupon referred the matter to the FBI's General Investigative Division 'for appropriate action,' demanding that it report back to 'the Vice President's office the results of the interview.' . . . Hoover's quiet helpfulness only encouraged Johnson to resort to the Bureau to silence his detractors, who, given his sleazy associates and wheeler-dealer style of operating, were legion. Accordingly, the Vice President was soon back at Hoover's doorstep, and the services went on" (emphasis added).[271]

4/28/62—SATURDAY: Press reports: "An aide to Vice President Johnson rejected today an inference that he attempted to use his influence to obtain a Federal job for a friend of Mr. Estes."[272]

Press reports: "The resignation of Dr. Haydn Williams as Deputy Assistant Secretary of Defense for International Security Affairs was announced today."[273]

5/1/62—TUESDAY: *FBI Law Enforcement Bulletin* is released. Hoover's topic is the coming Police Week, including Peace Officers' Memorial Day. "We . . . also take this occasion to renew our pledge to protect from peril the sacred principle of government by law."[274]

A Hoover essay appears in *Nation's Business:* "Why Reds Make Friends With Businessmen." "We can defeat the communists by working together as a team. That is our challenge."

Press reports: "ABILENE, KANSAS . . . Former President . . . Eisenhower said today that American concepts of . . . morality and decency were declining. . . . He singled out modern art and the twist dance craze for special scorn. More sternly, he denounced the use of 'vulgarity, sensuality, indeed, downright filth. . . . . . . Only Americans, only Americans can ever hurt us. His . . . listeners included . . . Vice President Johnson. . . ."[275]

5/2/62—WEDNESDAY: FBI (NY) ELSUR tapes Mafia leader (Genovese family) Michael Clemente. "Bob Kennedy won't stop today until he puts us all in jail all over the country. Until the commission meets and puts its foot down, things will be at a standstill."[276] This data is quickly sent by AIRTEL to Hoover, who again decides to withhold the information from the Attorney General and Secret Service. The transcript is consigned to his private files. Clearly JFK's war on the Mafia is having the desired effect.

Press reports: "Secretary of the Army Elvis J. Stahr, Jr., has resigned, . . . to become president of Indiana University."[277]

5/3/62—THURSDAY: Press reports: "A Roman Catholic educational film group has produced a documentary feature giving its interpretation of the controversial San Francisco riots during the 1960 Communist investigations by the House Committee on Un-American Activities. . . . 'Autopsy on Operation Abolition,' is the third film to be produced in 'answer' to 'Operation Abolition,' . . ."[278] Given that JFK, a Roman Catholic, has personally opposed *Operation Abolition* as untrue, Hoover would have viewed this development suspiciously.

Press: *"President Kennedy will go south* tomorrow to speak twice in New Orleans. . . ." (emphasis added).[279]

FBI (New York) ELSUR records conversation between Gilbert Beckley functionary Eddie McGrath "and a woman identified only as Jeane. What is this, Russia, you know what they did, *they went over to Gil's and said do you know that Gil is living with a girl in New York City,* why don't they come in and say this to me? . . . I'll say . . . *[since] when is fucking a federal offense,* and *if it is* a federal offense *I want the President of the United States indicted because I know he was whacking all those broads Sinatra brought him out. . . . If I could* just *hit Bob Kennedy . . . [with] . . . some kind of bomb that will explode I would gladly go to the penitentiary for the rest of my life,* believe me. . . .' "[280] This death threat is sent by AIRTEL to Hoover. As with other such ELSUR product, it is withheld from the Attorney General.

This particular threat is revealing for three reasons. First, it demonstrates the intimate level of communication between the Gilbert Beckley gambling network and the Marcello organization. Recall that Sinatra's relatives, the Fischettis, had worked with Marcello early on in an attempt to influence the President. In this context, Sinatra had introduced Kennedy to Judith Campbell. News of the subsequent affair has obviously been circulated among the bookmakers. Newport gambler Ed Levinson, as a major figure in the overall network, has surely been made aware of JFK's philanderings in this regard.

Second, it makes obvious the reach of this gambling organization. Beckley is deeply involved with bookmaking in New Orleans, yet he also operates in Newport, Miami, and New York City. Levinson, aside from his involvement with the Newport apparatus, is, as a Lansky functionary, actively pursuing interests in Las Vegas casinos, as well as developing business ties with the Vice President's closest associate.

And what of Johnson? Through Baker he is now indirectly associated with the Mafia. It begs the question. To what degree is LBJ aware of Baker's dealings with these people? Does he have any financial interest in the latter's affairs? And why is a man such as Levinson, with the money and connections he possesses, involved in a close business relationship with a senatorial aide? Undoubtedly it is the very organization from which Levinson is drawing his power that is driving the association. Baker has enough inside information concerning Johnson to compromise the vice presidency. By drawing the aide into direct association with the Mafia, his knowledge can be obtained and used to help the people Levinson represents gain immunity from prosecution.

Third, and most ominously, it betrays the growing desperation of the group. Individuals directly associated with Marcello, Lansky, and Hoffa functionaries are now coming to the conclusion that the Attorney General must somehow be stopped.

5/7/62—MONDAY: The Beckley court rules, "It is . . . ORDERED . . . that the trial of this case be . . . continued to Monday, August 13, 1962. . . ."[281] The gambler's battery of defense attorneys succeed in yet another delay, but time is beginning to run out.

Press reports: "Secretary Orville L. Freeman said today there was 'no evidence' that Billie Sol Estes had received special favors from the Department of Agriculture. The Federal Bureau of Investigation is . . . conducting an investigation at Mr. Freeman's request."[282]

5/9/62—WEDNESDAY: Press reports: "Penalties totaling $554,162.71 were levied by the Department of Agriculture today against Billie Sol Estes for violating Federal cotton planting allotments in 1961. Secretary of Labor Arthur J. Goldberg said he would investigate to determine if 'any impropriety' was involved in a suggestion made by an Assistant Secretary of Labor that Mr. Estes help to pay the bill for a dinner Mr. Goldberg gave Vice President Johnson last Jan. 12."[283]

Press: "President Kennedy said today that Vice President Johnson would be on the Democratic ticket again in 1964 'if he chooses to run.' This unusual presidential endorsement for a Vice President . . . was given. . . . However, few persons here who understand the strange logic of politics seemed likely to accept the President's statement as a binding commitment. . . . . . . *Rumors [are circulating] in Texas that Mr. Johnson might be dropped from the ticket in 1964.* Despite the President's reference to Mr. Johnson's great value to the Administration, *it is extremely difficult to find out what the Vice President's value is. This is largely because Mr. Johnson prefers it this way. He never holds a news conference; he keeps tight restraints over all information about his nonpublic activities; he rarely talks to reporters and, when he does, talks only off the record.* Even his confidential utterances are likely to be paeans to Mr. Kennedy" (emphasis added).[284]

5/10/62—THURSDAY: Today is Hoover's thirty-eighth anniversary as director. President Kennedy sends a congratulatory note. " 'I did not want May 10 to pass without expressing my congratulations on your 38th anniversary as director of the Federal Bureau of Investigation. . . . Yours is one of the most unusual and distinguished records in the history of government service.' . . . To forestall a cake-cutting ceremony in his honor, planned and announced by Bobby Kennedy, Hoover made it known that he was spending the day at his desk following his usual daily routine."[285]

Press reports: "A Philadelphia family left for the United States tonight after deciding against emigrating to the Soviet Union. David Paul Johnson and his wife and two children changed their minds because of the poor living conditions. . . . . . . Johnsons appealed to the embassy. Officials there said they would guarantee a loan. . . . Mr. Johnson told officials that he had been active in Communist causes in Philadelphia for the last eight years, although he never joined the Communist Party."[286] Interestingly, there are many such ill-fated immigrations during this period. Considered in this context, the Oswald family's imminent return to the U.S. will be seen for what it was, an insignificant event.

5/11/62—FRIDAY: Press reports: "Assistant Secretary of Labor Jerry R. Holleman resigned tonight, disclosing that he had
accepted a $1,000 gift from Billie Sol Estes. He said that the gift had
been 'personal' to help him cover 'living expenses.' Mr. Holleman, a
Texan himself, is the highest Kennedy Administration official yet to
be linked to Mr. Estes. . . . . . . The official admitted earlier this
week that he had asked Mr. Estes to pay for a dinner given here on
Jan. 12 . . . in honor of Vice President Johnson."[287]

5/16/62—WEDNESDAY: Press reports again regarding Estes: "Also there are records of three cashier's checks totaling
$145,015, drawn Jan. 16, 1962, against Mr. Estes' account at the First
National Bank of Pecos. These are believed to be checks he took
with him on a trip to Washington Jan. 16 to 20."[288] Another article
states: "It was reported today that the Senate investigators were
looking into published reports that Mr. Estes sought a $12,000,000
loan this year from welfare and pension funds of the International
Brotherhood of Teamsters. According to these reports, Mr. Estes
negotiated with James R. Hoffa, the union president, and other
teamster officials."[289]

5/17/62—THURSDAY: "President Kennedy disclosed today
that seventy-five agents of the Federal Bureau of Investigation were
investigating the Billie Sol Estes case.' " Kennedy makes the statement during a press conference. Further declaring, "I can assure you
that if any members of the Executive Branch are involved, any
improprieties shown, they will be immediately disciplined appropriately."[290]

5/18/62—FRIDAY: Press reports: "District Attorney Bryan
Russ today ordered a grand jury inquiry into the mystery death of
Henry Marshall. . . . In commenting on the case today Will Wilson, the state's attorney general, criticized Mr. Freeman's department for having been 'defensive.' 'We have been unable to find out
from the Department of Agriculture . . . what they have found out
about Marshall's death. We can't even get a report on the report that
the department was supposed to be making on the case.' "[291] Both
JFK and Secretary Freeman, whenever questioned about specifics in
the Estes case, continuously defer to the FBI, whose policy is not to
comment on a case in progress.

5/19/62—SATURDAY: The gala celebration of JFK's forty-fifth birthday is held in Madison Square Garden to raise funds for the Democratic Party. Marilyn Monroe attends. "John Kennedy sat in the Presidential box, feet up on the rail, chomping contentedly on a cigar. . . . Marilyn led the throng in a birthday chorus, and stepped away from the microphone. Then the President said, 'Thank you. I can now retire from politics after having had, ah, 'Happy Birthday' sung to me in such a sweet, wholesome way.' "[292]

5/21/62—MONDAY: The Beckley court rules again, this time consolidating all defense motions for final consideration. All ". . . Motions now pending . . . be, and the same are hereby, fixed for argument on Wednesday, June 20, 1962. . . ."[293]

5/22/62—TUESDAY: Press reports: "A medical examiner strongly indicated today that . . . an Agriculture Department figure in the Billie Sol Estes case had been murdered. . . . Autopsy indicated that Mr. Marshall . . . had been shot in the back." [294] In a related article of the same date "Justice of the Peace Leo Farmer, who [originally] pronounced [a] suicide verdict without ordering an autopsy, said tonight, 'I just don't have nothing to say now.' "[295]

5/24/62—THURSDAY: JFK, in response to a question from reporters regarding the Marshall murder, states, "Well, I think we should wait till the FBI has completed its investigation of the matter—I couldn't, Mr. Freeman is not—I don't think that the Texas local officials made a judgment in regard to the case which has been accepted until recently. Now the FBI and the local authorities are re-examining the case and we'll get a much better idea when that examination is complete."[296]

After analyzing the Agriculture Department's internal report on the Estes matter, Hoover had turned it (or parts) over to the Justice Department. Press reports in this regard, "The Justice Department said today it would turn over to the Robertson County jury pertinent parts of an Agriculture Department investigative report on Mr. Estes's cotton allotments. Herbert J. Miller, Jr., assistant Attorney General in charge of the criminal division, authorized full cooperation with the jury, a spokesman said. . . . *The Federal attorney at Dallas had conferred with State attorney general . . . about giving the jury 'excerpts of summaries' of parts of the report relating to*

Mr. Marshall" (emphasis added).[297] Just "what" parts the Justice Department is allowing the Texas officials to see is not clear. Nor is it clear what additional information Hoover provided the Justice Department when he forwarded the Agriculture Department report to RFK. Hoover has had the report for some time. With "75 agents" on the case, surely he has learned more of the matter by this point. The question that naturally arises is whether he has in some way exercised editorial control over the evidence before forwarding it to Attorney General Kennedy.

5/25/62—FRIDAY: LBJ flies to Austin, Texas, ostensibly to accept an honorary degree from his alma mater, Southwest Texas State College. The edited version of the Agriculture Department's report on Estes is due to arrive in Austin (at the Attorney General's office) the following day.[298] The *Chicago Tribune* reports on the Agriculture Department report, raising the issue of Estes's threats to "go to the top."

5/26/62—SATURDAY: Press reports: "Attorney General Robert F. Kennedy said excerpts from the confidential report were flown to Texas today."[299]

5/27/62—SUNDAY: Press reports: "The public-hearing phase of the confused and confusing Billie Sol Estes case opens tomorrow with Republicans hoping to place a major scandal on the Kennedy Administration's doorstep. Up to now, the Federal investigative efforts have been privately conducted."[300]

Press: "Vice President Johnson received an honorary Doctorate of Law degree and a standing ovation today at his alma mater, Southwest Texas State College. The Vice President heard the combined college choir and band perform a song written for the occasion, 'Let Us Now Praise Famous Men.' *He did not speak.* The Johnsons arrived in Texas Friday." (emphasis added).[301]Johnson's appearance in Texas at this particular time is significant. Note that the Agriculture Department report on Estes arrived in Austin the day before. Doubtless he feels the need to be present. That the Vice President would travel to Texas to receive an honorary degree from his alma mater and have nothing to say, is revealing. The focus of his visit is undoubtedly the report.

5/28/62—MONDAY: Press: "The grand jury trying to decide
whether the death of a Department of Agriculture official was murder or suicide accepted today a curtailed government report on
Billie Sol Estes' cotton allotment deals. The Government, fighting
to keep the jury from inspecting the full 175-page report, filed a
motion to quash a subpoena requiring officials to provide all the
documents. Will Wilson, Texas Attorney General, countered with a
demand that the Justice Department make reports by the Federal
Bureau of Investigation available on the puzzling death of Henry H.
Marshall, shot five times last June 3 while he was investigating
cotton allotments to Mr. Estes. . . . Mr. Wilson said the Government had submitted twenty-two pages of the larger report for the
grand jury to study. Harold B. Sanders, United States Attorney in
Dallas, said . . . 'The public interest would not be served by production of a document concerned with matters not pertinent to the
purpose of the jury.' Mr. Wilson said . . . 'we are in a situation
where we have to drag from them the report of his activities as if we
were pulling teeth. . . .' " The jury is being allowed to see only
13.5 percent of the report.[302]

   FBI (New Orleans) agent Regis Kennedy, the Marcello case officer, sends a report to Hoover on Sam Saia. Hoover had requested
the information sometime after the 6/27/61 indictment of the Beckley organization by the IRS. ". . . Special Agent Regis Kennedy
noted that the Internal Revenue Service had identified Saia as a
powerful gambling figure." He has also been described by the New
Orleans Crime Commission as "the biggest and most powerful operator of illegal handbooks and other forms of illegal gambling in the
city."[303]As previously stated, he is the link between men like Gilbert
Beckley, Sam di Piazza, Eugene Nolan, and Marcello. It is not
known what other data Hoover's surveillance system produced on
the interaction among these men between 6/27/61 and this date;
that he is keenly interested in information on this gambling network
is now undeniable.

   In an effort to counter growing suspicion concerning his links to
Estes, LBJ provides the press with a copy of a patronage letter he
sent the former on 12/28/60. "Vice President Johnson has told
friends privately that he had never had any dealings or communications with Mr. Estes. Mr. Johnson also has said privately that he
met Mr. Estes only once. . . . The Vice President said he wouldn't
know Mr. Estes if he saw him again. It was learned at the Depart-

ment of Agriculture that when Mr. Estes's empire collapsed, Mr. Johnson telephoned the Department of Agriculture, presumably to Secretary Freeman. He is said to have told Mr. Freeman that he had never heard of Mr. Estes except on the one occasion at his home."[304]

5/30/62—WEDNESDAY: Oswald writes a letter to his mother:

> Well, here we are in Moscow getting ready to leave for the U.S.A., I'll be sending a telegram or otherwise informing you as to where we shall embark and so forth, everything is O.K. so don't worry about us. We shall be leaving from Holland by ship for the U.S. on June 4th however I expect to stay over in New York for a day or so and also Washington D.C. for sightseeing.
>
> See you Soon
> Love XXX
> Lee[305]

5/31/62—THURSDAY: "Attorney General Robert F. Kennedy requested a Government agency today to label ten persons Communists and order them to register under the Internal Security Act of 1950. Today's action was the beginning of the third of three enforcement steps taken against the party by the Justice Department since last Oct. 9. 'I would like again to make it clear,' Mr. Kennedy said, 'that the registration requirements of the law do not outlaw the party. They do not forbid the party to do anything. *They simply require the party to register—to make public the identity of its officers and members and the sources of its finances'* " (emphasis added).[306] Kennedy's apparent goal is to reveal the names and number of FBI agents and informants within the Party, a large percentage of the total. Exposure of Party finances would also make public the strong level of financial support coming directly from the Bureau.

6/62—THIS MONTH: Judith Campbell ". . . and the President continued to be in touch with each other into June."[307]

Justice Department informant Edward Partin attends a meeting with Jimmy Hoffa in D.C., ". . . in which *Hoffa had talked about assassinating Robert Kennedy."*[308] *"The* first *plan,* the one Hoffa was then leaning toward, *involved fire bombing* Hickory Hill, *Robert Kennedy's Virginia estate, with extraordinarily lethal plastic explosives . . . 'The place will burn after it blows up.'* . . . The second plan was . . . a backup scheme . . . [Robert] Kennedy would be shot to death from a distance away; a single gunman would be enlisted to carry it out—someone without any traceable connection to Hoffa . . . ; a high-powered rifle with a telescopic sight would be the assassination weapon. *'Somebody needs to bump that son of a bitch off . . . Bobby Kennedy has got to go.'* "[309]

6/1/62—FRIDAY: Press reports: "Farmers in Oklahoma were told by an Estes employee that 'Estes was very influential, had strong political connections, had hunted quail with Vice President Johnson, and had been to the inauguration.' "[310]

6/5/62—TUESDAY: Press: "President Kennedy signed today an order permitting Dr. Alan T. Waterman to continue as director of the National Science Foundation beyond the retirement age of 70. Dr. Waterman was 70 yesterday. Without Mr. Kennedy's order he would have been required under the Civil Service Retirement Act to retire at the end of this month. Mr. Kennedy told Dr. Waterman that, as the first director of the foundation, he had 'guided it through the formative years to a position of importance as the primary Federal agency engaged in the support of general-purpose basic research and education in the sciences.' "[311]Note that this individual's situation is analogous to Hoover's. He has just obtained the very thing Hoover must have prior to 1/1/65, something President Kennedy has stated Hoover will under no circumstances receive.

6/6/62—WEDNESDAY: Press: "Senator John L. McClellan announced today that on June 27 his Permanent Investigations Subcommittee would start several weeks of public hearings in the Billie Sol Estes case."[312]

"A man identified as a Communist Party member by a congressional witness who joined the Party at the request of the Federal Bureau of Investigation disclosed last night he, too, was working for the FBI. Melvin F. Hardin . . . said he had been an informant for eight years. He said his wife, Virginia, had been a member since 1958 and both reported regularly to the FBI. Mrs. Julia Brown

. . . said the Hardins were members of the Communist Party in Cleveland. Edward E. Hargett, special-agent-in-charge of the FBI's Cleveland office, confirmed Mr. Hardin's story." [313] Revelations such as this are at once humorous and foreboding, making apparent the degree of FBI support within the organization.

6/7/62—THURSDAY: Press: Marcello's mentor, and Hoover's New York Mafia contact of many years, "Frank Costello petitioned the United States Court of Appeals yesterday to throw out an order for his deportation. The deportation ruling was based on Costello's conviction on two crimes involving moral turpitude. The gambler was convicted of evading income taxes for 1948 and 1949." [314] But for the fact that this man is a naturalized citizen, his situation is analogous to Marcello's.

6/9/62—SATURDAY: Press reports: "President Kennedy signed a bill today that permits hiring of eighty more White House police. The measure raises the ceiling on the uniformed police force to 250 from the level of 170 established in 1952." [315] Nearly a 50 percent increase, President Kennedy is clearly concerned with his and his family's security.

Fort Worth Star Telegram reports: "A former Ft. Worth resident who defected to the Soviet Union is on his way home by slow boat. *Lee Harvey Oswald,* 22, has his Russian wife and infant child with him. A U.S. embassy spokesman in Moscow said Friday Oswald applied to the embassy for a passport last autumn, the Associated Press reported [*sic*], At the same time he asked the Soviets for exit permits for himself, his wife and child. The formalities were completed last week and the three left Moscow by train, the spokesman said. They were to continue their trip to the United States by ship, but the spokesman said he did not know which ship or where it was sailing from. Oswald turned in his passport at the American embassy in Moscow Oct. 31, 1959, saying he would 'never return to the United States for any reason.' He apparently had gone to work at a factory in Minsk. Oswald, a former Marine, is a brother of R. L. Oswald of 7313 Davenport. His mother, Mrs. Marguerite Oswald, resides in Boyd" (emphasis added).

6/11/62—MONDAY: Press: "Junius Irving Scales, a former Communist party leader who is in prison for violation of the Smith

Act, asked President Kennedy today for a pardon or commutation of sentence."[316]

6/13/62—WEDNESDAY: Press: "Billie Sol Estes spent nearly two hours today with a Robertson County grand jury investigating the death of an Agriculture Department official. Mr. Estes answered a few questions. But he refused to answer most on the grounds he might incriminate himself. He was accompanied by . . . two lawyers, *John Cofer* of Austin and William Moore of Bryan. The party immediately went to the third-floor chambers of Judge Barron, where they remained for nearly an hour. Then followed an extraordinary hour-long session in the adjacent courtroom, during which Mr. Cofer sought to determine whether Mr. Estes' constitutional rights against self-incrimination were being jeopardized by the grand jury's subpoena" (emphasis added).[317] Cofer is also a friend of, and sometimes attorney for, LBJ.

Press: "A Teamster Union official said today that the wiretapping bill backed by Attorney General . . . Kennedy could be used as a 'club' to keep an administration in power. . . . Mr. Zagri told the House Judiciary Committee that both his office and home telephones and public pay phones within several blocks of the teamster's Washington headquarters, were now being tapped."[318]

Marilyn Monroe sends a telegram to RFK and his wife at home in Virginia declining an invitation to a dinner party in Los Angeles.[319]

6/14/62—THURSDAY: Oswald and his family arrive in Fort Worth, where they are met by his brother Robert. "The first few days after Lee's return to Ft. Worth, staying with his brother Robert, his wife Vada and the children, were full of those pleasant moments that come to hours of reunion."[320] Oswald is reportedly disappointed by the lack of press coverage at his arrival. He does not realize the insignificance of the event. The following week they will move in with his mother, where they stay until they can afford an apartment.[321] At the time Marina is described, perhaps unfairly, as a late sleeper, somewhat lethargic, and a bit egocentric.[322] With regard to this latter point it is difficult to know. The Russians are a proud people. And anyone coming from a cool climate to the Texas summer is immediately struck by the oppressive heat and humidity. It is indeed enough to make one "lethargic."

Press: "A group of heavily armed members of the Secret Army Organization was arrested in east-central France last night and to-day by security police officials who charged that the terrorists were plotting to assassinate President de Gaulle. General de Gaulle arrived in this region today on a speech-making tour. . . ."[323] Events unfolding in France this summer will demonstrate how public disclosure and prosecution of conspiracy can serve the long-term interests of any society.

6/15/62—FRIDAY: Hoover notes on an internal memo regarding JFK aide Schlesinger, a man he loathes (Hoover considers him an extreme leftist), "I understand better now the views of the A.G. since the latter is a great admirer of Schlesinger."[324]

Press: "A House subcommittee sought today to tie the Commercial Solvents Corporation, a financial backer of Billie Sol Estes, to anti-Administration lobbying efforts on Capitol Hill."[325] The press also reports regarding Estes's bankruptcy proceedings. "Mr. Estes' lawyer, John Cofer of Austin, then said a new plan was being worked on. He declined to give details, but it was understood to involve a new source of funds that could be used to satisfy the creditors."[326]

6/16/62—SATURDAY: Press: "It was understood that *the Justice Department,* which arrested Mr. Estes, *hoped to obtain a new indictment* against him *on the basis of additional data gained by seventy-five agents of the Federal Bureau of Investigation."*[327] RFK's relentless pursuit of Estes can only serve to further alienate LBJ from the Kennedys. Presumably unknown to RFK, however, is the fact that Johnson, in an attempt to protect himself, is maintaining a close liaison with Hoover concerning the case. It is also unlikely Kennedy knows of LBJ's friendship with Estes's attorney, John Cofer. Once again the situation raises the question of complicity on the part of Hoover. Simply put, how much data is he making available to the Justice Department? And how would Kennedy possibly know if information tying LBJ to Estes is being withheld?

6/18/62—MONDAY: Oswald attempts to transform notes concerning his stay in Russia into a book. " 'I saw your name in the telephone book,' he said. 'Can you do some typing for me?' [Pauline V.] Bates said she worked at brief intervals for the next few days typing the notes that he had made on various kinds and shapes of paper. Mostly, she said, they described the harshness of life in Russia. He told her he intended to solicit the help of a Ft. Worth engineer in publishing a book from his notes. Oswald, she said, insisted that it be kept secret and had her destroy the carbon copy she used." The notes amount to an across-the-board assault on daily communist life in Russia. The "engineer" Oswald refers to may possibly be George de Mohrenschildt (petroleum engineer) or Declan Ford (geologist). These are but two of several individuals the Oswalds will briefly associate with in the fall of 1962. Both men are members of the local "white Russian" exile community. [328] For more on de Mohrenschildt, see Marrs's *Crossfire,* p. 200.

6/19/62—TUESDAY: Press: "There has been friction between the F.B.I. and the Texas Rangers in their investigations of Mr. Marshall's death." The Rangers had previously stated, publicly, that Marshall's death was murder rather than suicide.[329]

6/20/62—WEDNESDAY: Oswald pays the typist ten dollars, abruptly ending his effort to write a book. After the assassination, Miss Bates will state that he appeared "nervous, fidgety."[330]

Press: "Complaining bitterly that the President and the Attorney General had pronounced him guilty before he was tried, Billie Sol Estes asked a Federal District Judge today to stop a grand jury from investigating him further. John Cofer . . . charged that . . . the President and Attorney General . . . had made it impossible for the grand jury to be unbiased."[331] The schism between LBJ and President Kennedy can only be growing with rhetoric such as this.

6/22/62—FRIDAY: Press: "The Communist party yesterday denounced a new law *signed by President Kennedy* this week making recruiting for the party a felony" (emphasis added).[332]

". . . Joseph Valachi, a prisoner in the U.S. penitentiary in Atlanta, seized a two-foot length of iron pipe, rushed a fellow inmate, John Saupp, and beat him to death. . . . The incident precipitated Valachi's break with . . . Cosa Nostra and his public testimony on the structure of organized crime."[333]

Eisenhower presents a speech at a Republican fund raiser. "Clearly such Administration policies and deeds invite our extensive criticism; we shall not neglect this critical function in our *free* society. My friends, the principles we follow are profoundly significant to *free Americans.* They are founded in an *unshakeable faith* in the people of our country. It is this faith that makes us cleave to constitutional government. It is likewise *our faith in the individual* that incites us to be vigilant sentinels of liberty" (emphasis added).[334] Hoover does not hesitate to heed this call, incorporating the "Faith In Freedom" concept into upcoming speeches. His ability to build upon popular themes introduced by other public figures of his day is nothing short of political genius.

Press: "A United States *defector from the highly secret National Security Agency in Washington* has become disillusioned with some aspects of Soviet life since his arrival two years ago. . . . [William H.] Martin said, however, that he was living comfortably and was willing to make the best of his new situation. He said he had married a Russian girl and was continuing studies toward a higher degree in mathematics. The 31-year-old statistician spoke willingly . . ." (emphasis added). [335] Cases such as this make obvious Oswald's situation. Unlike the young ex-Marine however, this individual very likely had information of value to the Soviets. This fact and his obvious educational background have undoubtedly afforded him better treatment. Oswald, uneducated and with little to offer, had discovered the harsh realities of Soviet factory life. During his stay in Russia he had worked long hours for low pay and an inadequate diet; hence his markedly aged appearance upon return to the U.S.

6/23/62—SATURDAY: Press: "An assistant state attorney general, reading from telephone company records, testified today on calls from Billie Sol Estes' telephones. These included calls to a member of Vice President Johnson's staff. . . . . . . Three calls had been made to Cliff Carter. . . . He indicated one call had gone to an unlisted number in Washington. . . . One call had been placed from an Estes' telephone March 28 to a 'Mr. Carter' at Arlington, Va. . . . Mr. Estes had talked six minutes to 'Mr. Carter.' . . . Two . . . calls had been made from Mr. Estes' telephones in Pecos to Henry Marshall."[336] The aide's response is found in another article of the same date. "Clifton C. Carter, a staff assistant to Vice President Johnson, said today he had received two or three telephone calls from Billie Sol Estes earlier this year, including one the day before Mr. Estes was arrested. 'I told him I knew nothing about it.' Mr. Carter said. He said Mr. Estes had asked him to call back if he found out anything. 'But I did not call back,' Mr. Carter said. 'I have no unlisted phone and I have never had one. My phone has always been listed in the Washington directory since I've been here.' "[337]

6/24/62—SUNDAY: Press: "Republicans have made plain that they intend to stay right on the Administration's tail about the activities of the West Texas financier. But this week the major inquiry will get under way when the Senate Permanent Subcommittee on Investigations, under the chairmanship of John McClellan, Democrat of Arkansas, begins hearings."[338]

6/25/62—MONDAY: Press: "Billie Sol Estes appeared in Texas District Court today and in a surprise move demanded an immediate trial on charges of stealing $827,577 in fertilizer tank deals. Mr. Estes appeared almost jovial in court. Mr. Estes' demand for quick trial, made through his lawyer, John Cofer, surprised Atty. General Will Wilson of Texas. *Mr. Estes . . . cannot be summoned to Washington to testify before a Congressional committee if he is being tried in Pecos, his hometown"* (emphasis added). [339] As LBJ's friend, Cofer's plan is clearly to prevent Estes from testifying in Washington. In conjunction with that goal, he will also prevent Estes from testifying during his trials in Texas. By use of this tactic, connections to federal officials such as Johnson can be concealed.

Marilyn Monroe, in Los Angeles, places a call to the Justice Department in an apparent attempt to reach Attorney General Kennedy.[340]

6/26/62—TUESDAY: "When Oswald returned to Texas, FBI agents seemed somewhat ignorant about his case and slow to react. Oswald's name had not been placed on the list of those . . . potentially disloyal. But the FBI had opened a 'security case' on [him] after his defection. . . ." Pursuant to a May 31 SOG directive, FBI in Dallas contacts Oswald, requesting his presence for a 1 P.M. interview at its field office. Oswald complies.[341] At this point he is destitute and in debt. Uneducated, he has been unable to capitalize on his experiences in Russia, either by writing a book or teaching Russian. His undesirable Marine Corps discharge will also prove to be an obstacle to quality employment. In addition, he has a wife and young daughter to support. Marina, unable to speak English, is also unemployed. At this time the U.S. economy is stagnant. At the interview, agents attempt to determine if Oswald is an international communist spy, under the assumption that his apparent socioeconomic status may be only an elaborate ruse. He is questioned about his activities in the Soviet Union, as well as his wife's background. If it is determined that his wife is in fact a communist spy, she can be deported. This point may well be subtly conveyed during the interview, simply to establish fear in Oswald. To be sure, much of this is standard procedure. Oswald becomes antagonistic, uncooperative. He is asked to inform the Bureau if he is contacted by any spies in Dallas. He refuses to submit to a lie detector test, and the interview ends. In all probability he feels considerable animosity toward the FBI at this point. Undoubtedly his activities are monitored, however briefly, to confirm his identity and intentions. Hoover himself has previously written of an impostor using Oswald's name in New Orleans, although by now he may well know of ex-FBI SAC Guy Banister's role in the matter (see chapter 4 and 1/20/61 of Chronicle). Oswald's first job after returning to America will be as a manual laborer in a local metal factory, working long hours for near subsistence wages.

6/27/62—WEDNESDAY: Attorney General Kennedy flies to Los Angeles. "An FBI report, partially censored for release to the public, reveals that the Attorney General conferred . . . with Jerry Wald, the would-be producer of Kennedy's 'The Enemy Within.' . . . 'There seems to be some question in the Attorney General's mind . . . as to whether this picture should be produced until after prosecutions in which James Hoffa is involved are completed.' " "On June 27, . . . Robert Kennedy [also] visited Marilyn at home in Los Angeles. . . ."[342] At this point she may well be threatening to go public regarding her brief affair with President Kennedy. As crisis manager during Kennedy's administration, he is now attempting to contain a situation created by JFK's shortsightedness.

Press: "In Pecos, Tex., a change of venue was ordered for Mr. Estes' trial on charges of felony theft. The action by a state district judge delayed the trial for at least a month. . . . The chief defense lawyer, John Cofer, immediately said he would file an objection to the change. He told the court: 'I am vigorously opposed to the moving of the trial from this county.' The court ordered the change on its own motion. There was no indication when the trial would resume. Mr. Cofer would have stood extremely good chances of winning either an acquittal or an instructed verdict in a trial here."[343]Clearly there are different forces at work here, but the effect is the same: Estes is being kept off the witness stand and away from Washington, D.C.

6/28/62—THURSDAY: FBI (Los Angeles) sends a report to Hoover detailing RFK's activities while in that city. This data will be in Assistant Director Evans's hands by July 3.[344]

Press: "The United States Court of Appeals . . . granted Henry Winston, the communist party leader, the right to sue the Government for alleged negligence in medical attention while he was in prison. Subsequently he lost his sight. His sentence was commuted by President Kennedy for compassionate reasons last June."[345]

Press reports on Estes and his attorneys. "He does nothing without the consent of his lawyers. . . . . . . His chief lawyer, John Cofer of Austin, said yesterday he was really not worried about Washington. 'They can't do anything to him there.' In Mr. Cofer he has a man whom many consider one of the top trial lawyers in Texas. [He] . . . has been active in Democratic politics. . . . How does Mr. Estes . . . afford obviously expensive legal counsel?"[346]

Hoover ". . . sent to the Department of Justice a summary report entitled, 'The Criminal Commission,' which documented the structure of the national syndicate of organized crime. From there on, the report was updated every six months."[347]

7/62—THIS MONTH: Attorney General Kennedy reportedly leaks the fact to press that Hoover will be subject to compulsory retirement statute (5 United States Code 2255, Sec. 5(a)) on 1/1/65.[348] This is not news to the press. What is significant is the fact that Kennedy has chosen to point this out at this time (see 7/10/62). In effect, the President, through the Attorney General, is telling the press that Hoover will not be given a waiver.

Bobby Baker's East Coast (Ocean City, Maryland) Carousel Motor Inn finally opens, with the probable assistance of Mafia money. Press: "Bob Baker went into the hotel business with a 50-state splash that opened his [motel/casino], six miles north of Ocean

City. . . . Guests watched the limousine arrival of Vice President Johnson. . . ." [349] Given the obvious closeness of Baker to Johnson, it is safe to assume at this point that the aide well knows of the Vice President's intense dislike for the Kennedys. It is not known whether Levinson and/or Sigelbaum are present at this gala event, but their absence would be surprising. The obvious question here is whether Baker, in turn, conveys word of Johnson's hatred to the two Mafia functionaries. Does Johnson, intentionally or inadvertently, do this directly? It is entirely possible that by this point the Vice President may already have been compromised through his ongoing association with Baker. An event such as this provides perfect opportunity to observe, and gain influence over, LBJ. As part of the gambling network, Levinson is squarely in position to convey anything learned to those most in need of such information, individuals like Meyer Lansky, Santos Traficante, Carlos Marcello, and Jimmy Hoffa.

7/1/62—SUNDAY: *FBI Law Enforcement Bulletin* is released. Hoover's Message is patriotism. "Unfortunately, in some circles today the apologetic approach to patriotism is becoming fashionable. Today, perhaps as never before, America has need for doers of extraordinary deeds. . . . We of law enforcement share in this noble cause. . . . Let us not fail the test of greatness."

D.C. press reports: "Harry J. Anslinger, 70 years old, one of the most controversial men in government, will retire soon, after thirty-two years as the first and only United States Commissioner of Narcotics. He would like to remain in office. He is backed generally by those who see drug addiction as chiefly a problem of law enforcement. He is opposed by those who view it as a problem to be solved by social reform and psychotherapy."[350] A more exact parallel to Hoover's own situation is not possible. He is, in fact, the harbinger of Hoover's approaching retirement. A clearer signal by President Kennedy cannot be sent.

7/2/62—MONDAY: Marilyn Monroe places two calls to the Attorney General.[351]

7/4/62—WEDNESDAY: Press: "A Federal investigation is under way into the alleged sale of Federal rice planting allotments in Texas. Secretary of Agriculture Orville Freeman has turned the case over to the Federal Bureau of Investigation. The rice case is somewhat similar to the one involving cotton allotments obtained by Mr. Estes. . . ."[352] It is not known whether LBJ is also involved in this scheme, but the continued targeting of his home state for such massive investigations can only serve to intensify his dislike for President Kennedy. Interestingly, rice-production areas in Texas are found primarily in the southeastern portion of the state and into Louisiana, Texas ranking second to the Bayou State in total production.

7/5/62—THURSDAY: Press: "Secretary of Agriculture Orville L. Freeman clashed with Republican Senators today during a hearing into the Billie Sol Estes case. *Senator Mundt, in particular, was skeptical about Mr. Freeman's assurances that neither the Federal Bureau of Investigation nor Congressional committees had uncovered 'any wrongdoing by anyone connected with the department* against whom prompt and effective action has not been taken' " (emphasis added).[353]

7/6/62—FRIDAY: Press: ". . . the United States is eliminating travel restrictions on all temporary Soviet visitors to this country."[354]

Press: "Two Federal farm officials from Oklahoma admitted to a Senate subcommittee today that they had each accepted $820 in cash from Billie Sol Estes. The admissions . . . came after the subcommittee heard preparatory testimony from *Alphonse F. Calabrese, its chief staff investigator in Texas. Mr. Calabrese, [is] a former agent for the Federal Bureau of Investigation. . . .*" (emphasis added).[355] Another investigation involving LBJ, and one that will also be controlled by Hoover, that of Bobby Baker, will also use ex-FBI agents as investigators. In both instances then, Hoover maintains direct, and quite possibly indirect, control over the investigative process.

7/8/62—SUNDAY: Press: "Security restrictions on President and Mrs. John F. Kennedy's estate, Glen Ora, will continue during July and August while the estate is subleased. . . ."[356]

7/10/62—TUESDAY: Senator Everett Dirksen takes the floor of the Senate to introduce Senate Bill 3526, which is designed to govern Hoover's replacement and provide the body with the power of "advice and consent" regarding future appointees. The bill also calls for limitation of term, with no reappointment. ". . . Strangely enough, the Director of the FBI is not legally required to be appointed by the President, *nor is confirmation by the Senate required*" (emphasis added).[357] A nearly identical bill will shortly be introduced in the House. In effect, Congress has just accepted the fact that Hoover will be retired by President Kennedy. Up to this point, their fear has been that he will replace the aging icon, as he has just replaced Anslinger, with a man unpalatable to the right. The Senate wants the control of "advice and consent" for so powerful a position as FBI director. As Hoover has demonstrated, the power of such an office can become almost the equal of congressional or presidential authority. Many in Congress, in fact, fear him. The Senate bill is formally received by LBJ, who refers it to committee. With Anslinger's "retirement" and this pivotal decision on the part of the Senate, Hoover has sustained a potentially fatal political blow. Johnson, who is becoming increasingly dependent upon him for his own survival, must be deeply worried by this development. Hoover, no doubt, recognizes his position and blames President Kennedy. The governing statute, 5 USC 2255-Sec.5(a), is worth quoting in relevant part:

> . . . an employee who shall have attained the age of seventy years and completed fifteen years of service shall be automatically separated from the service. The President may, by Executive Order, exempt from automatic separation under this section any employee, when, in his judgment, the public interest so requires.

Short of revising the statute to specifically exempt Hoover, there is little Congress can do. Any such legislation would surely be vetoed by President Kennedy. Perhaps as fearful of Hoover as is JFK, they are letting Kennedy shoulder the responsibility of the Director's retirement. With "advice and consent" the result, this legislation will give them the necessary input with regard to future directors. It is unlikely Hoover knew of both Anslinger's retirement and this legislation in advance, but within a few days he will respond. A direct appeal to his constituency will come in the form of a radio speech that can only be described as brilliant.

FBI (Dallas) SAC sends memo to Hoover regarding Oswald's refusal to submit to a lie detector test.[358]

Press: "The United States Department of Justice filed suit yesterday against Orleans [New Orleans] Parrish Registrar of Voters A. P. Gallinghouse in an effort to force him to make his records available to the Federal Bureau of Investigation."[359]

7/12/62—THURSDAY: Press first mentions the coming film, *The Manchurian Candidate,* which is set for fall release.[360] For those convinced that CIA/military intelligence was the key player in President Kennedy's assassination, this movie will become a cult classic. It is relevant here only in the context of one of the actors involved, Frank Sinatra. Given Sinatra's concurrently close ties to the Mafia, one can only speculate concerning his knowledge and feelings on the subject of Kennedy's assassination. Reportedly he will be instrumental in the suppression of this film from 1963 to 1987, at which time it will be re-released. Interestingly, Sinatra discussed the making of the film with President Kennedy prior to the end of their friendship in September 1962.[361]

7/13/62—FRIDAY: Press: "James R. *Hoffa said today that members of his union resent what he called President Kennedy's 'meddling' in labor relations.* Mr. Hoffa said that Teamsters generally regarded the President's appeal for wage restraint as the opening wedge to Government control of collective bargaining. *The Attorney General, he said, has been given more power than any man ever to hold that office. . . ."* (emphasis added).[362] Like Hoover and Marcello, Hoffa holds President Kennedy responsible for the actions of the Attorney General.

FBI LEGAT (Mexico City) sends security memo to Hoover regarding ongoing electronic surveillance of Monroe. The report quotes her ". . . as saying she had 'attended a luncheon at Peter Lawford's residence' with one of the Kennedy brothers."[363]

Press: "Jerry Wald, the motion picture producer, died tonight at his home in Beverly Hills. He was 49 years old."[364] RFK's vision of a high-budget film exposing the Mafia comes to an end. This is undoubtedly a great relief to Hoover, as well as to Marcello and Hoffa.

7/15/62—SUNDAY: Hoover responds to the retirement of
Anslinger (7/1), and the decision of Congress to effectively allow
his own retirement, by appealing directly to his perceived constituency, the American people. He appears on NBC's "Monitor" program. The topic is ostensibly communism and how to stop it:

> We in America are today facing a grave danger—that of
> international Communism—and you, as citizens . . . play an
> increasingly important part in protecting our Nation. Not long
> ago a student came to my office. He was an intelligent young
> man, well versed in the affairs of the world. I still remember
> one of his remarks. "I feel that most Americans, . . . young
> and old alike, simply are not aware of the terrible danger
> which Communism poses for us. We need to know more about
> this enemy." Do Americans today realize the dangers they
> face? Are we willing to do our share to keep our Nation from
> going the way of the Roman Empire? At this moment the
> Communists, spearheaded by Moscow, are attempting to de-
> stroy America. . . . Today a vast ideological battle is under
> way for the minds of men, women and young people. Nothing
> less is at stake than the very existence of our Judaic-Christian
> civilization—the values which have given meaning to our dem-
> ocratic way of life. . . . *We must know the dangers. We must
> know the enemy. Most of all, we must know the values of Amer-
> ican life we are defending. Just what do the Communists desire?
> Communism, despite its high-sounding double talk phrases, is a
> system designed to enslave mankind. . . . Today the Commu-
> nists are directing tremendous pressure to influence your think-
> ing.* The Communist Party of the United States is an integral
> arm of the international Communist movement. It is . . . a
> . . . conspiracy. . . . *Why are the Communists today appeal-
> ing so strongly to young people? The Communists realize that
> the young people will be the leaders of tomorrow. . . . They
> want to touch [their] thinking, to expose [them] to the deceitful
> double talk of their program. The very intensity of this Commu-
> nist effort to reach young people, however, shows how the enemy
> can be defeated. One of our best defenses . . . is the strong
> moral character of our young people.* In this fight against Com-
> munism, what are some of the qualities America expects from
> its young people? Let me mention a few: 1. *High ideals.* . . .

2. *Courage.* . . . 3. *Self-discipline.* . . . 4. *Enthusiasm.* . . .
5. *Integrity.* . . . Stay loyal to your high ideals. Never sully
them by dishonor, compromise, or expediency. In this worldwide ideological struggle, *how can you now best aid your country?* . . . Take every opportunity to *visit the historic shrines of
America.* . . . *Bunker Hill, Independence Hall, Valley Forge.*
The visits of Americans, especially young people, to Washington, D.C., are an excellent way to know your country better.
*We appreciate very much your coming to see our FBI headquar-
ters.* . . . Keep abreast of the news of the day, through your
newspapers and on radio and television. *What is occurring in
your country?* Stand firm for your convictions. Today the Communists are trying to convince you that freedom is old-fashioned and that their way of life is superior. *Know the strength
of our institutions of Government. Be ready to defend them.*
That is the challenge. Nothing will take the place of responsible knowledge in our fight against Communism—a knowledge
anchored in faith in God. *We can defeat Communism because
we have the superior values,* the superior way of life. The task
will not be easy. But we can win if each of us is willing to do
his share. We must meet Communism with facts, not hysteria.
Truth is our best weapon of attack. Not long ago I talked with
a special agent of the FBI who was facing a very difficult
problem. I can still remember the intensity of his eyes and the
determination in his face. *"I can meet this problem,"* he said,
*"because I am not going to give up." Yes, we in America are not
going to give up. We are going to win this battle—and in winning it, we are protecting liberty for all the generations yet to
come."* [emphasis added].

By expanding the war against communism to include the issue of
personal morality, Hoover accomplishes two things. First and foremost, he sends a thinly veiled threat to President Kennedy, a man
he considers to be immoral. Over the last eighteen months Hoover
has *covertly* attempted to blackmail Kennedy over the question of
morality, to no avail. Now, he is *publicly* suggesting that immorality
of any sort is the hallmark of communism. By this technique he can
attempt to use a public forum to blackmail JFK. Second, he succeeds in bringing home the "threat" of communism to the average
American in ways he can clearly understand. He suggests that com-

munism can be exposed simply by analyzing a person's personal morality. If he does not follow the highest ideals, he could well be suspect, an enemy of the people. Hoover is well aware that the perennially popular Eisenhower, only months before, had called for a reexamination of public morality in America, decrying the new permissiveness. Hoover has previously suggested publicly that while liberals in fact talk and act like communists, one must try to remember that they are not. By intimidating JFK in the areas in which he is perceived to be vulnerable, morality and communism, the Director can perhaps regain the upper hand.

Hoover then ties the morality issue to *patriotism,* while simultaneously attempting to equate himself, and the Bureau, with that of a national institution. His use of "we" and "our" is pervasive. He becomes the indispensable man on the white horse who will effectively lead the country to victory and safety, through morality and conservative philosophy.

He repeatedly suggests that CPUSA is targeting American youth. Consider this in light of President Kennedy's focus on youth, national fitness (e.g., fifty-mile hikes), vigor, and programs such as the Peace Corps and New Frontier. In a recent Rose Garden reception for foreign youth, Kennedy had been very nearly mobbed by the large, overly enthusiastic group.

The speech takes on added significance when considered in light of Kennedy's public campaign to deflate the dangers of the domestic communist threat.

Overall, however, this event reveals the desperation in Hoover's political position. Though masterfully delivered, his warnings regarding the dangers of domestic communism are not new. Public concern over the subject is waning. Whether JFK will be intimidated by this new tactic cannot be known. Hoover may well feel he has nothing to lose. To be sure, the Kennedys either listen to this speech or are soon informed of its contents by their advisers. But there is no public reaction by President Kennedy.

Marcello, a man now as desperate as Hoover, would not have missed the message sent by this speech. As one who has spent a lifetime subverting and manipulating public officials and systems, he has been intently studying the D.C. power structure ever since his sudden deportation in April 1961.

7/16/62—MONDAY: *St. Louis Globe Democrat* runs an article in reaction to the events surrounding Hoover, entitled "Who Will Fill Hoover's Shoes?" The story details S.3526, pointing out the fact that "J. Edgar Hoover . . . is 67 years old. He is only [29 months] away from the age of compulsory retirement—unless the President gives him a waiver. . . . This agency has been an effective guardian of the national security . . . for two reasons. One, it has kept above politics. Two, its able Director is also a vigilant anti-communist. . . . The head of the FBI is merely another civil servant whom the Attorney General can choose at will. . . . Presidential appointment and Senate approval is required for other major executive appointments. The Director of the FBI, who is vested with vast power as head of the Nation's chief investigative agency, certainly falls in that class."

Marilyn Monroe again attempts to reach RFK by phone this date.[365]

"Oswald . . . found a job, as a manual worker with a local metal factory, and began working long hours." He will hold the position into October, at which point he quits.[366]

7/17/62—TUESDAY: FBI (Philadelphia) ELSUR records mafioso Angelo Bruno. The topic of conversation is Carlos Marcello. Bruno reveals that Marcello had again approached Sinatra through Traficante, calling upon him to use what influence he had with President Kennedy's father. Reportedly the attempt had only made matters worse.[367] This recording reconfirms the close relationship shared by Marcello and Traficante. The transcript is sent by AIRTEL to Hoover.

After dozens of motions, resulting in more than one year of delay by an entire team of lawyers, the federal court in New Orleans rules against Marcello's people, Beckley et al. "IT IS ORDERED by the Court that all other Motions of all defendants be, and the same are, hearby DENIED."[368] The pretrial phase has now ended, and along with it the defendants' best hope of stopping their prosecution and imprisonment.

Monroe calls the Justice Department twice.[369]

7/18/62—WEDNESDAY: Senator Dirksen places the *St. Louis Globe Democrat* article defending Hoover into the *Congressional Record.*

7/20/62—FRIDAY: Hoover's speech on morality is read into the *Congressional Record* in its entirety.

Press reports: "Four new indictments were returned here today against Billie Sol Estes."[370]

Press: "President Kennedy announced today a major reshuffling of the military high command, with a new chairman of the Joint Chiefs of Staff and a new United States commander in Europe. Gen. Lauris Norstad, for the last six years the commander of United States and North Atlantic Treaty forces in Europe, will retire Nov. 1."[371] Though hardly predicated upon Hoover's speech, this action by President Kennedy is an effective response.

7/23/62—MONDAY: Washington Bureau *Gannett News Service* carries an article regarding Hoover's impending retirement. "John Edgar Hoover, the first and only Director of the Federal Bureau of Investigation, will be 68 years old on New Years Day. The mandatory retirement age under the law, unless a special exemption is granted by President Kennedy . . . is 70. . . . Associates claim that Hoover is in the best of health and that he has no intention of retiring in the forseeable future. There have been recurrent reports, however, that . . . Kennedy . . . might like to replace him with an appointee of [his] own choosing. Two names mentioned in this connection are those of Walter Sheridan . . . and Carmine Bellino. . . . Both are former FBI agents who worked under Attorney General . . . Kennedy when [he] was Chief Counsel of the Senate Rackets Investigating Committee 1957–60. . . . One of the first announcements that President Kennedy made [after winning the election] . . . was that he intended to retain the two top men in the vital Government Investigatory Agencies—Hoover at the FBI, . . . Dulles at the Central Intelligence Agency. Within less than a year, Dulles . . . was dismissed . . . blamed by White House aides for the Cuban invasion fiasco. . . . Hoover . . . has refused to allow [the FBI's] files to be used for political purposes." Note the individuals named as potential Hoover replacements; both are men who have worked closely with RFK in prior efforts to destroy the Mafia. These are undoubtedly people Marcello and Hoffa are all too familiar with.

Press reports: "Mr. Estes, has yet to appear here. But the McClellan panel expects to call him within three weeks."[372]

Press reports on the 7/10/62 Senate legislation: "To his surprise,

Senator Everett McKinley Dirksen of Illinois, the Republican minority leader, discovered that the director of the 13,776-employee
Federal Bureau of Investigation was not legally required to be appointed by the President. Nor is approval of his appointment by the
Senate required. The Illinois Senator promptly introduced a bill to
remedy the situation. *It would take effect, nowever, [sic] only after
the incumbent, J. Edgar Hoover, on duty since 1924, retires"* (emphasis added).[373]
Monroe calls the Justice Department.[374]

7/24/62—TUESDAY: Press: "Two Republican Representatives attacked testimony on the Billie Sol Estes case today given by
Donald A. Russell, director of Auditing for the Agriculture Department. Mr. Russell said a full account had been turned over to the
Justice Department for whatever action it chose to take."[375]

7/26/62—THURSDAY: Attorney General Kennedy arrives
in Los Angeles to present a speech before the National Insurance
Association. The FBI (Los Angeles) simultaneously receives an
anonymous death threat against him.[376]Pursuant to standard FBI
procedure, the threat is sent by AIRTEL to SOG. Because it is
effectively *public* in nature, Hoover has little choice but to dictate a
memo to the chief of Secret Service. This he does, and proper security precautions are taken. By this time, Hoover has accumulated
284 internal memos on the Attorney General as a result of Bureau
surveillance.
The Beckley court sets 8/7/62 for its pretrial conference.[377]
Press: "The Senate Rackets Subcommittee yesterday harshly condemned . . . Hoffa as a man who doesn't care whether . . . racketeers rob or steal members' money."[378]

7/27/62—FRIDAY: Press: "Coleman McSpadden . . . told a
court of inquiry that Mr. Estes had said that he was going to build a
10,000-bushel grain storage elevator at Hereford, Tex., and give an
eighth interest to Vice President Johnson. Mr. Johnson never has
been accused of any personal connection with . . . Mr. Estes. Mc
Spadden said Mr. Estes had told him he spent $100,000 a year on a
'situation' in Washington but never had explained what the situation was."[379]

Press: "The White House announced today the forthcoming retirement of three Army Generals."[380]

7/30/62—MONDAY: Press: "The Justice Department said
today that it was seeking contempt citations against thirteen Louisiana school officials for ignoring Federal court orders to desegregate
a trade school run by the state." A school official responds. "He
asserted that Federal Bureau of Investigation agents had questioned
him because of his segregationist activities. *An FBI [Baton Rouge]
spokesman said a routine investigation had been conducted at the
specific request of the Justice Department.*"[381] This statement by the
local FBI, which recurs regularly from this point forward, is an
attempt to explain their presence, and sends a signal to men like
Marcello. In essence, would the FBI even be pursuing the matter
but for the Kennedys?

Monroe calls the Justice Department, speaking for eight minutes
to either Kennedy or his secretary.[382]

7/31/62—TUESDAY: Press: "Senate Republicans gave their
unanimous endorsement today to legislation providing that future
directors of the Federal Bureau of Investigation be appointed by the
President and confirmed by the Senate. J. Edgar Hoover, the present director, took his job without Senate confirmation. He is still
three years away from 'possible mandatory retirement,' the Republicans noted."[383] Hoover is in fact two years, five months away from
certain retirement. Clearly the Republican senators are walking a
fine line. They do not want to antagonize Hoover or his constituency, but they are equally afraid he will be replaced by a liberal if
they fail to obtain "advice and consent" prior to 1/1/65. That Hoover will be out of power in less than twenty-seven months is accepted as a foregone conclusion, something he, too, now realizes.

8/62—THIS MONTH: FBI ELSUR records, ". . . in Au-
gust 1962 a series of telephone calls from Roselli to Chicago underworld leader Sam Giancana." Roselli also works in close association
with Marcello associate Santos Traficante.[384]

FBI (New York) obtains direct access to Mafia hit man Joseph
Valachi, who begins a dialogue with agents. He reveals the historical
background of the New York crime families, as well as details concerning typical family structure.[385]

8/1/62—WEDNESDAY: A Hoover essay appears in *Follow Up Reporter.* The article, "Communist Youth Campaign," equates communists with liberals. "The communist discusses his party's concern for civil rights and civil liberties and speaks of its work to promote world peace and international disarmament. He portrays his organization as the defender of the underdog and the weak."

FBI Law Enforcement Bulletin is released. Hoover's message is, ostensibly, the dangers of a rising crime rate. *"Indulgence and materialistic selfishness are eroding the tried and true American traditions of honesty, integrity and fair play.* . . . Action in the war against crime has never been so sorely needed" (emphasis added).

FBI (New York) ELSUR records Mafia financier Meyer Lansky discussing the Attorney General with his wife. He ". . . claim[ed] that Robert Kennedy was 'carrying on an affair with an El Paso, Texas, girl.' . . . Hoover dispatched Courtney Evans to apprise the attorney general of Lansky's allegation. Unimpressed . . . Robert Kennedy categorically denied ever having been in El Paso and declared that there 'was no basis in fact for the allegation.' "[386]

President Kennedy holds a press conference. There is no mention of Hoover's recent rhetoric or his impending retirement.[387]

8/3/62—FRIDAY: "At the Attorney General's request, a nineteen-page report on Sinatra was prepared and delivered. . . . While indicating no illegal activity by the entertainer, it documented his longstanding association with major mob figures. The report was forwarded to the President." The impetus for it was complaints from within RFK's staff. They had expressed frustration in their overall efforts because of the JFK/Sinatra social relationship. Apparently the final straw, JFK completes the break with the singer.[388] He has little choice. Should RFK's, or for that matter Hoover's, investigations inadvertently lead to the indictment of Sinatra, any connection with the President, even social, could prove very damaging. Reportedly Sinatra is so angered by the break that he personally destroys the helicopter landing pad he had installed near his Palm Springs home for JFK's occasional visits.[389] Shortly after this, Sinatra meets with both Giancana and Roselli, probably to apprise them of the relationship's termination. Marcello would have been quickly informed regarding the failure of Sinatra's effort on his, as well as others', behalf. Through Fischetti and Traficante, Marcello has spent considerable time, effort, and money attempting to gain immunity from prosecution, all to no avail. This latest set-back must be bitterly disappointing. Hoover follows the break very closely, sensing that the Mafia is fast becoming frustrated with the President's refusal to cooperate.

Press: "Attorney General . . . Kennedy, accompanied by his wife Ethel and four of their seven children, arrived in San Francisco . . . for a weekend prelude to a West Coast vacation. Kennedy will address a session of the American Bar Assn. convention in San Francisco Monday at 3 P.M. . . . He said he will hold a news conference at 9:30 A.M. Monday. After his San Francisco speech he and his family will go to Seattle."[390] This weekend he and his family will stay with friends, the Bates, on their ranch outside San Francisco.[391]

Marilyn Monroe calls the Justice Department, apparently attempting to reach RFK. Shortly after this she receives an injection from one of two physicians she is seeing, a Dr. Engelberg.[392] She may also have called the San Francisco hotel where RFK is registered, unaware that he is not there. The actress has another prescription filled this same day.[393] In addition to medication she receives from her two physicians, she also apparently has other sources, for a number of unmarked prescription bottles will be found in her bedroom at the time of her death.[394] Clearly she is depressed over her short-term relationship with JFK, but the fact that she has also been receiving a considerable variety of prescription drugs, from different sources, cannot be ignored. Nor is it clear that these sources are necessarily aware of each other. Add to this even a moderate amount of alcohol, an unstable personality, a succession of failed marriages and affairs, and the stage is set for depression and accidental drug overdose.

The president of Commercial Solvents, Maynard C. Wheeler, is indicted by a grand jury in Texas. Press: "Wheeler and Estes both were charged on two counts of conspiracy to fix the price of chemical fertilizer and two counts charging restraint of trade."[395]

8/4/62—SATURDAY: RFK and his family vacation at the Bates Ranch. [396] How, with the itinerary described above, the presence of his family, and commensurate publicity, Kennedy is supposed to have flown to Los Angeles this weekend for a secret encounter with the even more famous Monroe, undetected, is beyond comprehension. Bear in mind that Hoover has the A.G. under continuous surveillance, and maintains an open security file on

Monroe.[397] Had there been such a meeting, only hours before her death, the Director would have been squarely in position to obtain extremely compromising evidence against the A.G. And yet, to this day, no substantive proof of this supposed rendezvous has surfaced.

Monroe calls the St. Francis Hotel in San Francisco in an attempt to reach RFK, apparently speaking with a hotel operator.[398]

8/5/62—SUNDAY: Press reports Marilyn Monroe ". . . was found dead early today in the bedroom of her home. . . . Beside the bed was an empty bottle that had contained sleeping pills. Fourteen other bottles of medicines and tablets were on the night stand. Miss Monroe's physician had prescribed sleeping pills for her for three days. The actress had also been under the care of a psychoanalyst for a year, and had called him to her home last night. Miss Monroe left no notes, according to the police."[399]

This morning RFK and family attend church, spending the afternoon with friends at the ranch. The A.G. apparently has little to say, publicly, about Monroe's death.[400] It is entirely possible that upon arrival in San Francisco he had instructed Peter Lawford to keep the actress away from him and his family for the duration of the weekend. The Kennedy in-law is known to have been in contact with her the evening of her death. Upon learning of it, the actor may well have contacted RFK by phone. He, in turn, could easily have instructed him to remove anything connecting her with JFK from her residence. Lawford's role in the affair remains unclear to this day. If one examines the evidence and personal morality of JFK, the probability of an extramarital relationship with Monroe becomes apparent. Do the same with RFK and you will find nothing. He was the antithesis of his older brother in this regard. The record shows that Robert Kennedy spent a considerable amount of time during JFK's administration trying to contain news of the President's indiscretions and associations. There is no reason to believe this matter was any different.

8/1—8/5/62: FBI (New York) ELSUR again records Lansky conversing with his wife. "Bobby Kennedy, who has seven kids and is carrying on an affair with a girl in ? (possibly El Paso). Teddy [Lansky's wife] says it's all Frank Sinatra's fault and he is nothing but a procurer of women for those guys. Sinatra is the guy that gets them all together. Meyer says its not Sinatra's fault and it starts with the President and goes right down the line."[401]

8/6/62—MONDAY: W. H. Ferry, vice president of the Fund for the Republic, during a speech before the Western States Democratic Conference, launches a bitter attack on Hoover. Press: He ". . . accused . . . Hoover . . . of 'sententious poppycock' in building a false legend of communism's strength. . . . Ferry . . . said he was speaking of a 'mischief-making tapestry of legend and illusion if there ever was one.' He recalled President Kennedy's speech at Yale University urging that legends and myths about Government . . . be avoided. . . . The legend 'shrinks in the washing,' Mr. Ferry asserted. . . . He described . . . Hoover as 'the indubitable mandarin of anticommunism in the United States' and 'our official spy-swatter.' Mr. Hoover's warnings against Soviet espionage are 'an old line of the FBI chief,'. . . . 'Its success year after year is a tribute to the trance into which his sermons throw Americans, not excepting Congressmen,' '. . . In these persistent reports about espionage and sabotage, is he delicatedly [sic]telling us that he isn't up to the job, that Red spies are running loose despite his best efforts?' . . . 'Our institutions are nowhere nearly as fragile as Mr. Hoover thinks they are. . . .' "[402] Hoover supporters are stunned.

FBI (Los Angeles) SAC sends memo to Hoover regarding RFK's stay in California. Undoubtedly the L.A. SAC also filed a report on Monroe's death.[403]

8/7/62—TUESDAY: RFK, only hours after Ferry, addresses the same group as he travels through Seattle with his family. In a press conference afterward, he says of Hoover, "I hope he will continue to serve the country for many, many more years to come. I admired him and the FBI before I became Attorney General, but my admiration has increased tremendously after seeing his work close at hand."[404] Note that RFK chooses his words very carefully, not saying in what capacity he hopes Hoover will serve. Of course, he, like Hoover, knows that it is JFK who controls the Director's fate.

Press: "The Republican National Chairman, William E. Miller, branded today as 'virtually traitorous' the remarks made by W. H. Ferry about J. Edgar Hoover. John M. Bailey, Democratic National

Chairman, replied that his party 'believes in freedom of speech and is not afraid to be exposed to ideas with which it disagrees.' "[405]

The Beckley court sets 10/19/62 as the trial date for the defendants in Marcello's gambling network.[406]

8/10/62—FRIDAY: Lee and Marina move into their first apartment.[407]"One of Oswald's Dallas acquaintances, Teofil Meller, . . . had taken precautions before plunging into a relationship with a former defector. He said he had 'checked with the FBI, and they told him that Oswald was all right.' " Exactly how Meller is able to do this remains unclear, as Bureau files are confidential. He may have inside contacts with the Dallas field office. Oswald soon arranges to begin receiving FPCC (Fair Play for Cuba Committee) literature.[408]

Press: "Billie Sol Estes was indicted . . . for the sixth time since April. . . ."[409]

8/12/62—SUNDAY: Oswald writes to the Socialist Workers Party in NY concerning possible membership.[410]

8/14/62—TUESDAY: Congressman Thomas M. Pelly introduces H.R. 12898, which is nearly analogous to Senator Dirksen's July 10 bill governing Hoover's impending retirement.[411] Passage in the House will not come easy, for here Hoover has many friends.

8/15/62—WEDNESDAY: D.C. press reports: "The name . . . of Vice President Johnson . . . figured . . . in testimony before two congressional subcommittees investigating the Billie Sol Estes case. Spokesmen for Johnson immediately denied that he ever sought favors for Estes. *The Senate Investigations subcommittee made public an Agriculture Department memorandum that said* Johnson discussed the disputed Estes cotton allotments with Undersecretary of Agriculture Charles S. Murphy. But . . . John E. Bagwell . . . author of the memo, said that he was referring only to a discussion between Murphy and Walter Jenkins, one of Johnson's assistants. Jenkins later said that he had made a routine telephone call to Murphy last January after Estes and six other Texans asked Johnson's office for assistance on their cotton allotment problems. Bagwell . . . noted in the memo that Estes' efforts to obtain cotton allotments had 'created wide interest and comment from a number of persons,' including . . . Johnson. . . ."[412] This evening, LBJ telephones Agriculture Department employee Bagwell, ostensibly to obtain a copy of his 4/10/62 memo to Secretary of Agriculture Freeman regarding Estes and LBJ.[413] Such a call makes little sense considering the Vice President's inside contacts with Hoover, particularly in view of the fact that Secretary Freeman has stated publicly that all information on the case had previously been turned over to the FBI. More likely, Johnson is either seeking to learn just what Estes has told Bagwell or simply intimidate the official, or both. Note also that the subcommittee had made public copies of the report prior to Johnson's call.

8/16/62—THURSDAY: Hoover, vacationing in La Jolla, California, grants a rare interview. "Changing adult attitudes toward morality and religion were blamed here Wednesday by FBI director J. Edgar Hoover for a national increase in the juvenile crime rate. Hoover is vacationing here with Clyde Telson, [sic] assistant director. He said: 'The current incidence of juvenile crime, in my opinion, is simply a reflection of *the current moral climate in America. Relativism, expediency and materialism appear to be placing growing pressures on ethical behavior rooted in the moral absolutes derived from religious belief and past experience. We have ceased to emphasize moral behavior and in many instances have substituted for it something called "socially acceptable behavior." The line between right and wrong is no longer clear to growing numbers of young people.* . . . The child who is exposed to sound spiritual training seldom gets into trouble. . . . *If he eventually is to become a complete man, he needs the spiritual training which will provide him with moral armament to meet the temptations of a complex, mechanical, and increasingly materialistic age'* " (emphasis added).[414] Hoover expands on his morality theme, coining the phrase "moral armament." Consider this attack on adult immorality in light of his July 15 "Monitor" speech, in which he equated liberalism with immorality, and immorality with communism.

FBI (Dallas) again interviews Oswald, this time approaching him as he gets off work. The case officer, Agent John Fain, concludes that he poses no threat and closes his file.[415] To this point, Oswald has done nothing more than show an interest in socialist organizations and literature.

Press: "Reports that Vice President Johnson telephoned Mr.

Bagwell last night concerning his testimony were at first denied and then confirmed today by a spokesman for the Vice President. . . . The second time, the spokesman said that Mr. Johnson had merely asked Mr. Bagwell to send him a copy of his memorandum."[416]

8/18/62—SATURDAY: Press: "Henry L. Giordano, . . . was sworn in Friday as U.S. Commissioner of Narcotics and promptly declared war on narcotics peddlers and other criminals. Giordano's appointment brought to an end the 32-year tenure of Harry J. Anslinger, the first, and until Friday only, narcotics commissioner."[417] Note that Marcello has long been involved in the distribution of illegal narcotics.

For the second year in a row, Hoover's La Jolla hotel is robbed while he and Clyde sleep. Press: "Burglars broke into the fashionable Hotel Del Charro . . . where FBI chief J. Edgar Hoover is a guest, and took $30,000 worth of jewelry from rooms where occupants were sleeping, police reported. Many of the guests, like Hoover, are here for the racing season at Del Mar Race Track."[418]

8/19/62—SUNDAY: Press reports on RFK's push for additional anti-Mafia legislation. "The attorney general said three other pending measures also would be of great assistance in fighting crime. He listed them as: 1—Granting immunity to a union representative who has received bribes to compel his testimony against the person responsible for the payoff. 2—Protecting a person being questioned by the FBI or other agencies of government. . . . 3—A comprehensive new wiretapping bill, flatly forbidding tapping except when authorized for investigation of specific crimes. *He said the Justice Department has been able to prosecute cases not previously possible because information on hundreds of leading underworld figures has been consolidated in special files in the organized crime section. Passage of five anti-crime and racketeering bills, he said, has helped in the attack on illegal gambling, 'the keystone of organized crime' "* (emphasis added).[419] Marcello, Hoffa, Beckley et al., and Levinson, the unlucky subjects of recently passed anti-Mafia legislation, consider these new proposals particularly ominous.

Press: "President Kennedy capped his 33-hour visit here Sunday by delighting hundreds of bathers with an impromptu swim in the Pacific. Sunbathers were overwhelmed when Mr. Kennedy strode out of the canvas-draped fence of Peter Lawford's Santa Monica home in an unannounced public showing in blue boxer swim trunks shortly after 5 P.M. . . . The crowd cheered, applauded, touched and followed the deeply tanned and broadly smiling President in a pushing, shoving mass as he made his way to the surf. Several women went into the water with him fully dressed. . . . The crowd . . . soon swelled . . . to about 600 persons. Secret Service agents and police tried to surround him when he got to the beach, but children scuttled between their legs, women clung to him and everybody wanted to touch, talk and see him up close. He seemed to enjoy the friendly . . . attention, shaking hands with all he could, patting children's heads and flashing his wide grin as he strode back to the Lawford home. A short time later Mr. Kennedy left Lawford's home and retired to the Beverly Hilton presidential suite. During the evening, Kennedy ordered dinner. . . . The meal, [was] for nine persons. . . . [Names of] guests at the late dinner party, aside from Lawford, were not disclosed."[420]

8/22/62—WEDNESDAY: Press: "The Federal Bureau of Investigation, with vacationing director J. Edgar Hoover nearby, Tuesday entered the case involving the theft of some $50,000 in cash and jewels during the weekend in nearby La Jolla. . . . Hoover was asleep in his room at the Del Charro early Saturday during the burglaries."[421]

French press reports assassination attempt on French President de Gaulle. "According to M. Frey, the attack occurred at 8:10 P.M. about 300 yards from the village of Petit-Clamart on the route between Paris and Villacoublay. As the car carrying the President, Mme. de Gaulle and Col. Alain de Boissieu . . . passed the spot, at least three bursts were fired from automatic weapons. The escorting motorcyclists took cover momentarily and the two ambush cars sped away. . . . The President's car was hit about ten times, including *a slug* that *broke the* rear *window* near Mme. de Gaulle, another *less than two inches from the President's head.* . . . M. Frey said separate bursts of fire—about 120 to 150 bullets—came from groups around two cars sixty yards apart. . . . President Kennedy sent a message to President de Gaulle today expressing gratitude that the French President escaped unhurt" (emphasis added).[422]

Press: "Vice President Johnson left on his tour today with the best wishes of President Kennedy. But there was a bit of a slip in the wishes. The President said: 'We wish him well and extend to him our best wishes and hopes for a speedy recovery—er, return.'"[423]

8/23/62—THURSDAY: French press reports further regarding de Gaulle: "Investigators found that the technique of the ambush, with the President's car being submitted to a cross-fire from both sides of the road, indicated that it had been planned by soldiers. In the face of the well-planned attempts upon his life and numerous threats of assassination, President de Gaulle has maintained an air of icy disdain. He once said that the Secret Army Organization did not have the courage to kill him. In the face of enormous personal danger, he mixed freely with crowds. . . ."[424]

8/24/62—FRIDAY: Press: "A Justice Department official said today that no Communists had registered under the Internal Security Act of 1950. In addition Attorney General Robert F. Kennedy has petitioned the subversive Activites Control Board to order ten persons to register as members of the party. If the board grants Mr. Kennedy's request and the defendants fail to register, the department could move to have them indicted under the act."[425]

8/27/62—MONDAY: Press: "J. Edgar Hoover . . . will keynote the American Legion convention in *Las Vegas, Nev.,* National Commander Charles Bacon announced today. The convention begins Oct. 5 and is expected to draw 3,000 veterans . . ." (emphasis added).[426]

8/28/62—TUESDAY: Oswald places an order with the Socialist Workers Party in New York for literature regarding Trotsky.[427]

8/31/62—FRIDAY: Louisiana press reports: "Reporting threats of violence, Roman Catholic Church officials today closed Our Lady of Good Harbour School, desegregated two days ago. *Less than three hours later, the Federal Bureau of Investigation began an inquiry. The F.B.I. entered the case, it said, 'at the specific request of the Attorney General of the United States.'* The Federal move was viewed as a direct challenge to *Leander H. Perez,* [this man is at most only distantly related to the Charles A. Perez currently under indictment with the Beckley group] political leader of

Plaquemine Parish. The 71-year-old arch-segregationist was excommunicated last April for opposition to Catholic School desegregation."[428] This parish, representing southeast New Orleans and coastal areas, is directly adjacent to Jefferson Parish, where Marcello lives. Like Perez, Marcello is a strong segregationist.[429] Note that local FBI officials again make clear, publicly, the fact that the Attorney General is responsible for their presence.

8/62—9/11/62: Marcello, unable to withstand the combined effect of the numerous pressures mounting against him, makes the decision to put out a contract calling for the assassination of President Kennedy.[430] The essential factors that have triggered this desperate measure are: 1) he is personally under federal indictment; 2) the threat of deportation has become a reality. Efforts to place gambling lieutenant Saia on the appeals board of the INS, so as to prevent another deportation, have failed. Other Mafia members, foreigners such as himself, have, in fact, been deported; 3) he has not forgotten the public humiliation (and near fatal experiences) heaped upon him in April 1961, by the Attorney General. He has a personal score to settle; 4) the criminal division (CID) of the IRS is now examining his taxes for fraud; 5) the key officers of his gambling operation (Beckley et al.), the cornerstone of his financial empire, are under indictment, awaiting trial. Functionaries of that group (McGrath) have expressed a willingness and desire to assassinate the Attorney General (with explosives) in a desperate attempt to save themselves; 6) the U.S. Circuit Court of Appeals is ruling against Marcello in his attempt to overturn prior criminal convictions (convictions which form the basis of his undesirable status); 7) attempts to directly influence the President through Frank Sinatra have now failed, dashing hopes for a political solution; 8) many of his associates, men such as Hoffa and Traficante, are coming under surveillance and/or indictment. Hoffa himself has by now communicated to those around him (e.g., Louisiana aide Edward Partin; possibly Marcello bookmaker Gil Beckley through Miami) his desire to stop the A.G.'s prosecutorial onslaught by assassinating RFK (with explosives); 9) the Attorney General, at the direction of the President, is now calling for additional legislation which will eliminate protection allowed by the Fifth Amendment, in effect *compelling* Mafia members to testify against each other by way of immunity. Marcello has always taken the Fifth whenever called to testify; 10) The director of the Bureau of Narcotics has just been replaced with a man handpicked by JFK. Upon appointment the new director promptly declared war on the Mafia. Since the 1950s the mobster has obtained a significant portion of his income from trafficking in narcotics. "New Orleans don Carlos Marcello was able, with Lansky's help, to monopolize at least a third of the Cuban dope business;"[431] 11) the Attorney General is forcing desegregation on local schools, something Marcello, an avowed racist, strongly opposes; 12) and lastly, and perhaps most important, should the directorship of the FBI (like the Bureau of Narcotics) be placed in the hands of a man loyal to the President and Attorney General (an event sure to occur by 1/1/65), the full force of the agency will no doubt be turned against his organization. No longer disinterested (by agreement between Hoover and Costello?), the FBI would become his nemesis. In recent press stories two men strongly anti-Mafia, and closely aligned with the A.G., have been named as possible replacements. In short, Marcello is now facing deportation and/or imprisonment, loss of assets, and the destruction of his organization, as well as his way of life. Desperate straits call for desperate measures.

An integral part of this decision is also, undoubtedly, the opportunity it presents. As a man who has made a science of manipulating power structures, he has been studying the federal bureaucracy since 1961 in an attempt to save himself. He has realized that by placing the presidency in the hands of Lyndon Johnson he may well remedy the situation. It is common knowledge that LBJ has no interest in pursuing the Mafia. Through the gambling network (Levinson, Beckley, et al.) Marcello is now well aware of the Vice President's machinations with men such as Bobby Baker. Surely, as a longtime political insider, LBJ has some understanding of the significance of Baker's association with Mafia gamblers. Through these same people, Johnson may even have directly communicated his desire to become President (at the grand opening of the Carousel, or perhaps via neighbor Fred Black).

In his dealings with Estes, Johnson is now also associated with men who have murdered one man, federal official Henry Marshall, and perhaps another, Estes CPA Krutilek. Like many people, Marcello knows of the close relationship between the Vice President and J. Edgar Hoover. Simply by reading the papers, he would have perceived that Hoover is protecting the Vice President regarding the Estes scandal. As the man in control of evidence being gathered for the federal committee investigating the case, he can obviously withhold any information implicating Johnson. Marcello, given his criminal and political associations, may have detailed knowledge of Johnson's role in the affair. Recall Estes's effort to obtain money from Hoffa and allegations of Commercial Solvents' ties to the Mafia. The New Orleans mobster must be impressed by LBJ's ability to continuously sidestep the issues of bribery and graft. An examination of the Estes case leaves one with the clear impression that Lyndon Johnson has taken considerable sums of money from Estes in exchange for political protection.

Despite his power, however, rumors are beginning to circulate in Washington and Texas to the effect that Johnson will be dumped from the 1964 presidential ticket by President Kennedy. The Attorney General is pressing investigations of fraud in Johnson's home state, compiling evidence of his criminal activities. Very likely, this information will be used at the 1964 convention to replace him with a man more acceptable to the Kennedys. They may have little choice. Republicans, sensing the vulnerability created by Johnson's activities, plan to make full use of what information they can obtain prior to November 1964. In Marcello's mind then, Johnson, like Hoover, is very probably doomed politically.

Because of his near parallel situation, the Director is of considerable interest to Marcello. As stated, were Hoover's retirement to come about under Kennedy's watch, the consequences for the Mafia would be grave. Like many people, Marcello knows of the mutual hatred between Hoover and the Kennedys. He also knows that the aging icon does not intend to be retired, especially by a liberal such as JFK. Because of Costello's relationship with the Director, there may also be other, more sinister reasons to prevent the official's replacement.

From all this, a number of questions occur to Marcello. Were Lyndon Johnson and J. Edgar Hoover to become more permanent fixtures in Washington, D.C., through the assassination of President Kennedy, would not his own situation improve dramatically? This thought cannot have escaped him. Will two officials who so hate the Attorney General allow his continuance in power? Would this not allieviate the pressure on Hoffa and the gambling network? Obviously the assassination of the A.G., as called for by these associates, is no solution, and would only make matters worse (i.e., the full power of the presidency brought to bear against the Mafia). The

President himself has to be removed. Marcello has by now realized that if he does nothing, these questions may soon become academic, for his own position is rapidly becoming untenable.

The final question he addresses is, quite simply, how to get away with it. Here, classic gangland methodology comes into play. As detailed in David Scheim's *Contract on America,* Mafia assassinations of Chicago Mayor Anton Cermak and Robert F. Kennedy illustrate the "lone nut" approach. In basic terms, an individual not connected with the organization, providing an irrelevant but believable motive, is put in position to "assassinate" the official. All the while, a professional contract killer is also in position, waiting for the nut to open fire. Taking advantage of the momentary confusion and terror, he, in turn, guarantees the actual killing. Fading into the crowd, the assassin leaves the nut to take the blame. For a visual, and rather adroit, demonstration of this technique, one need only view the closing minutes of an obscure Italian film entitled *The Seduction of Mimi.* This picture details the "seduction" of one man into the ranks of the Sicilian Mafia, by way of assassination of a local official. A domestic film involving a concealed shooter is *The Man Who Shot Liberty Valance.* Undoubtedly Marcello's own situation calls for the use of the lone-nut approach if it is to have any chance at success. To do otherwise will only ensure direct exposure and the very destruction he is seeking to avoid.

With this decision, Marcello and his coconspirators are now in violation of a number of federal statutes that provide jurisdiction for the FBI. Paradoxically, Marcello's status as a resident alien provides legal basis for prosecution for the most serious offense, that of treason. In all, several statutes, as written in 1962, are applicable. They are as follows:

> *18 USC 2381. Treason.* Whoever, owing allegiance to the United States, . . . adheres to their enemies, giving them aid and comfort within the United States . . . is guilty of treason and shall suffer death. . . .

> *18 USC 2384. Seditious conspiracy.* If two or more persons . . . in any place subject to the jurisdiction of the United States, conspire to overthrow . . . the Government of the United States, . . . they shall each be fined not more than $20,000 or imprisoned not more than twenty years, or both.

18 USC 2385. Advocating overthrow of Government. Whoever knowingly or willfully advocates, abets, advises . . . over-throwing . . . the government of the United States . . . by the assassination of any officer of . . . such government . . . shall be fined not more than $20,000 or imprisoned not more than twenty years, or both. . . .

18 USC 372. Conspiracy to impede or injure officer. If two or more persons . . . conspire to prevent, by force, . . . any person . . . from holding any office . . . under the United States, or from discharging any duties thereof, . . . or to injure him in his person . . . on account of his lawful discharge of the duties of his office . . . such persons shall be fined not more than $5,000 or imprisoned not more than six years, or both.

There are additional offenses, both criminal and civil, of lesser weight involving civil rights, which have also been violated.[432]

9/62—THIS MONTH: Sometime prior to September 11, Marcello communicates with close friend Santos Traficante and discloses the fact that the contract has been put out.[433] Both men are under surveillance by the FBI, which quite possibly learns of the interaction, although not its purpose. As the two share many business interests and the same attorney, communication would not be unusual in and of itself.

Dallas FBI is informed of Oswald's subscription to the leftist newsletter *The Worker.*[434]

9/2/62—SUNDAY: Attorney General Kennedy appears on NBC's "Monitor" radio program. The topic is domestic communism and Hoover. RFK: "I think that the ineffectiveness of the Communist Party in the United States at the present time is due more to Mr. Hoover and the FBI than any other individual or group. . . . The Communist Party, I don't believe, has any political following in the United States. . . . It's . . . a disservice to say that there is a Communist under every bush or behind every tree. Or when the State Department or the Government does something with which you disagree to indicate it must be run by a bunch of Communists." The A.G.'s position, once again, is 180 degrees from that of Hoover's. This rebuttal, on the very same program the Director appeared on only weeks before, incenses him. The timing of this attack on Hoover, as will be seen, is unfortunate for President Kennedy.

9/3—9/5/62:   Estes ". . . conceived the idea that he could absolve himself by going on the stand and telling the whole truth about everything and everybody. It is known that Cofer disagreed. Estes then decided to fire Cofer and hire another, . . . Warren Burnett, of Odessa, for a fee of $30,000. But Cofer refused to be fired. He was already paid and by report he was adamant against spreading the . . . truth through confession. There was none."[435]

9/6/62—THURSDAY: French press reports: "Several persons were reported tonight to have been arrested in Paris and in the provinces in connection with the attempt to assassinate President de Gaulle August 22. . . . Security precautions for the President have been considerably increased. Jacques Foccart, Secretary General for African Affairs for the President, and Alexandre Sanguinetti, a senior official at the Interior Ministry, denied defense assertions, made yesterday, that they knew of the plot in advance. . . . A retired security officer, Col. Pierre Fourcaud, told the court that he had heard of a plot a few weeks before the attempt took place but had dismissed it as too fantastic."[436]

Press reports comments of one of Estes's attorneys: "Mr. Dennison said during questioning that he discussed Mr. Estes' affairs with . . . Walter Jenkins, administrative assistant to Vice President Lyndon B. Johnson."[437]

9/8/62—SATURDAY: French police arrest sixth suspect in the assassination attempt, revealing that ". . . seventeen more persons suspected of complicity in the attempt were being interrogated."[438]

Press: "A strong possibility arose today that Billie Sol Estes's appearance before Senate investigators will be postponed indefinitely at the request of Texas officials. The Pecos promoter has been scheduled to testify Wednesday before the Senate Investigations Subcommittee. . . . But Mr. Estes is slated to go to trial in Texas on Sept. 24. . . ."[439]

9/9/62—SUNDAY: Press again reports regarding the Senate's bill governing the replacement of Hoover. "Not one to rock a boat that has been stable for thirty-odd years—the incumbency of J. Edgar Hoover—Mr. Dirksen has proposed that after Mr. Hoover leaves, the job be made a Presidential appointment with a fifteen-year term, subject to the advice and consent of the Senate."[440] Here Dirksen's fear of antagonizing Hoover is made apparent.

9/10/62—MONDAY: Press: "Senators . . . agreed today to postpone questioning the Texas financier until after his trial on fraud charges."[441]

Johnson responds to a letter from Hoover. "Such kind expressions of friendship will be a great source of strength and happiness to me in the days ahead, and I am very grateful to you."[442]

Treason

9/62 to 11/22/63

Overview

At the outset of this time period Hoover learns of Marcello's plan to assassinate President Kennedy. Through an informant in Miami, Florida, and analysis of related files, he, Tolson, and probably Courtney Evans discover that Hoffa's earlier desires to kill the Attorney General have evolved into a contract on the life of JFK. Sensing the opportunity, Hoover shifts his efforts from attempting to gain political leverage over the President to ensuring the success of the contract. Word of the plot is withheld from the Secret Service. Emboldened by the new opportunity, Hoover shifts the primary focus of his rhetoric against the administration, openly tying the concepts of immorality and the Mafia with irresponsible leadership in government. JFK is directly compared to President Truman, a man Hoover had previously denounced as a communist. While in Las Vegas in October 1962 to present an address, he quite possibly meets with a Lansky/Levinson Mafia functionary (long time friend Del Webb), expressing his dissatisfaction with RFK and JFK. A West Coast informant (Becker) also learns of the contract, but is denounced and ignored by the Los Angeles field office (possibly for other reasons). Despite this, Hoover shows intense interest in the individual well into 1963. The aging official actively involves himself in long-range plans for a new FBI building in the Washington area. Even after directives from RFK to develop a case against Marcello, Hoover continues to ignore the mobster. Stubbornly apathetic Marcello case officer Regis Kennedy is left in place. During February 1963 Appropriations testimony Hoover perjures himself, twice, to avoid divulging the existence of ELSUR (and its commensurate illegalities) and the Marcello contract. Beginning in mid-March, he publicly states, not once but twice, his intention to avoid *compulsory* retirement. The Director continues to develop his relationship with the Vice President, as well as number-three man, Speaker McCormack. ELSUR coverage of Levinson, Baker, Black, and Sigelbaum increases in intensity. In June, the U.S. Senate passes legislation allowing for Hoover's retirement. Passage in the House stalls. Also by midyear, Tolson, possibly as a result of the stress related to foreknowledge of the assassination plan, begins suffering severe angina, which by summer's end necessitates open heart surgery. He is never the same. In July, Hoover informs a Lansky/

Sigelbaum functionary (Jesse Weiss) that he is intensely dissatisfied with RFK as A.G. Around the same time, close Hoover confidant Willis (from *Louisiana*), becomes head of the HUAC. He, too, in all likelihood is made aware of Hoover's desire for a change in the status quo. In the fall, Evans begins distancing himself from the Attorney General. During September, Hoover receives, from the Philadelphia field office, further confirmation of the coming hit, and again withholds the data from Secret Service. On October 31, Hoover and JFK have an off-the-record luncheon, after which Kennedy publicly endorses Johnson as his 1964 running mate. In early November the Secret Service is instructed to make preparations for the Dallas trip. Examination of the PRS file for that city reveals nothing, and the go-ahead is given to the President.

JFK continues to implement his political agenda, which from time to time brings him into conflict with Hoover. Efforts in behalf of freedom of information persist. Kennedy actually addresses the FBI National Academy, appearing as keynote speaker at its October graduation ceremony. There is no mention of a waiver for Hoover. At year's end the President pardons a longtime Hoover foe (communist Junius Scales), infuriating the Director. In April, Kennedy waives the retirement statute for friend Admiral Rickover, a decision under consideration for over a year. In May, JFK personally has Hoover's dogs retagged so that his own can be given the top three numbers in the District. Also this month, the government drops outstanding charges against 1950s opponents of Hoover, CPUSA officials. In late June, JFK personally advises Martin Luther King, Jr., that he is under electronic surveillance (COINTEL-PRO) by Hoover, in an attempt to deflate the Director's campaign against him. After Kennedy's public endorsement of King, Hoover renews efforts to tie the minister to CPUSA, via aide Stanley D. Levison. In mid-November the fundamentally different personal and political philosophies of the Director and the President surface for the last time when both address, only hours apart, the same group (Catholic Youth Organization) in New York City.

During spring, summer, and fall 1963 President Kennedy tours the country, speaking at political fund raisers. Open motorcades are common, the public responding warmly overall. In June, he arranges for a TV mini-series based upon his best-selling book *Profiles In Courage,* donating the proceeds ($351,000) to charity. This summer Oswald obtains the same book from a local library and reads it. In September, the President initiates reconciliation talks with Cuba via diplomatic aide, William Attwood. The press begins widespread coverage of the coming Texas trip. When asked about the Mafia in an October news conference, he avoids discussing the issue. The same month, Louisiana politicians openly begin to oppose his renomination for the presidency. At another news conference in November, he sidesteps questions concerning Johnson protégé Bobby Baker and Secretary of the Navy Fred Korth, both under increasing pressure due to scandal. In mid-month the Chief Executive, while in New York, attends another late-night, private party without the knowledge of his security people.

Battles with ex-agents Levine and Turner continue for Hoover into late 1962 and early 1963. Articles concerning his possible retirement abound. In April, an FBI agent is violently assaulted in New York by Mafia thugs (Foley incident), but, in extreme departure from standard policy, Hoover does not publicly react. Sometime during May, the Bureau's massive ELSUR coverage of Las Vegas casinos stops, having been discovered by the Mafia. By then however, Hoover has learned a great deal about Levinson and his associations. ELSUR, in August, inadvertently picks up conversations between the Mafia and Hoover friend Jesse Weiss, in which the latter describes Hoover's dissatisfaction with RFK to Sigelbaum associate Malnik. Special September and October reports make Hoover well aware of Oswald's activities. Just prior to a presidential motorcade into Philadelphia, Hoover apparently attempts to provoke assassination of JFK by local mafioso (Weisberg) through the arrest and public humiliation of certain members of that family. Two weeks before the assassination, the third most powerful official in the U.S., Speaker McCormack, also addresses the FBI National Academy, endorsing and heaping praise upon Hoover.

Marcello is nearly undone in September 1962 when Hoffa aide Partin reveals to Justice Department officials the Teamster's earlier threat to assassinate the A.G. with explosives. Because of Hoover, however, RFK learns nothing of the McGrath or Aleman reports, and does not make the connection to JFK. Certain members of the Beckley group avoid further participation in their trial, including close Marcello lieutenant di Piazza. Bureau surveillance of Ferrie continues, making his ties to Marcello more obvious. At the same time the relationship between the two and ex-SAC Banister flourishes. During early mid-1963, Jack Ruby is leveraged over club-related debts and outstanding taxes, becoming an active participant in the plan to kill the President. At the beginning of the year, New Orleans District Attorney Jim Garrison is actually prosecuted, and convicted of criminal defamation, by the very judges he works for after suggesting some are involved with the Mafia (i.e., Marcello). By May, Ruby is in regular communication with Marcello lieutenants concerning logistical details of the contract. In this context, he begins a liaison with Lansky/Levinson functionary Lewis McWillie, who operates out of the *Thunderbird Hotel* in Las Vegas. This is the same hotel Baker associate Clifford Jones is involved with. Jones works closely with Levinson. Also in May, possibly as a result of jury tampering, the Beckley group is found not guilty. Pursuit of Beckley himself however, continues well into the mid-1960s. On May 27 the U.S. Supreme Court denies cert. (i.e., refuses to consider) Marcello's case, dashing any hopes for salvation through legal avenues. At midsummer, Ruby's indebtedness to the IRS exceeds forty-one thousand dollars. During summer and fall, Marcello associate Traficante is recorded by ELSUR on four occasions, the mafioso expressing tremendous bitterness toward the Kennedys over the disruption of his gambling operations. The A.G. is not informed. During this same time period Ruby contacts Hoffa's East Coast Mafia representatives. Ferrie works closely with Marcello, ostensibly in regard to the latter's trial in New Orleans. One week prior to the assassination Ruby begins behaving as if his financial difficulties will shortly be resolved. Three occurrences in the days just before the killing, the Abilene, Cheramie, and Redbird Airport incidents, make apparent the imminent nature of the contract. Last-minute interactions between Ruby and various Mafia functionaries (Braden, Meyers, "Jeane," Gruber, and Campisi) cement his role in the conspiracy.

Throughout the fall of 1962 and into 1963, Johnson's relationship with Baker et al. continues to strengthen. In all likelihood the Vice President is compromised by the Mafia via Baker-supplied prostitutes, as well as prior business dealings. Hoover monitors this closely. In contrast, LBJ's ability to interact with both the President and Attorney General from a policy standpoint deteriorates dramatically. Scandals within the state of Texas, some involving Johnson, continue to surface (e.g., Estes, slant hole drilling, TV/FCC monopolies, suits against LBJ Co.). From early 1963 on, public rumors circulate suggesting Johnson will not be on the 1964 ticket. In March Johnson himself refuses to say whether he will seek renomination. In April he informs Texas media officials of Kennedy's plan to tour Texas in November. June brings an address before the FBI National Academy. He has nothing but glowing praise for Hoover. His reliance on the aging right-wing icon grows. A secret meeting in El Paso involving JFK, Johnson, and Governor Connally resolves details of the coming tour. On June 18, open hostility between the Vice President and A.G. breaks out. The two are bitter enemies after this. Sensing the possibility of public disclosure regarding data connecting Johnson to a Baker prostitute, Hoover, in August, quietly arranges her deportation. Privately Johnson attacks President Kennedy over his decision to sell wheat to the Russians. LBJ appointee Fred Korth resigns under pressure. The Vice President confides fears of removal from the 1964 ticket to the Director. At the end of October former LBJ Co. employees sue the corporation, alleging they have been swindled out of their retirement funds. New charges of impropriety (TFX contract) involving Johnson and Korth surface just three days before the murder of Kennedy.

The prosecution of Billie Sol Estes continues during late 1962 to fall 1963. Friends of Johnson arrange the purchase of the criminal's assets. Testimony before congressional committee finally comes, just ten days before the assassination. Estes repeatedly takes the Fifth, and the inquiry is hastily concluded. On November 18, Texas A.G. Waggoner Carr drops further attempts to prosecute New York Estes backer, Commercial Solvents.

In early 1963 Levinson et al., via Serve-U Corp., take control of Baker's East Coast resort, the Carousel. The Senate aide arranges a congressional junket to the Lansky-controlled Flamingo Hotel in Las Vegas during April. As summer progresses, his relationship with the mobsters continues to deepen. There are Carribean ventures and deals with Johnson and Hoover cronies, the oil-rich Murchisons. September 1963 sees the explosion of the Baker/Levinson scandal. Close connections between Johnson and the Mafia are effectively revealed. The relationship Levinson shares with Newport, Kentucky, gambling (i.e., Beckley) is made clear, as well as Baker's ties to Las Vegas casinos like the *Thunderbird*. Hoffa construction loans to the Mafia, used to build casinos controlled by

Lansky and Levinson are exposed. As the investigation unfolds, ex-
FBI agents are appointed to supervise the collection of evidence.

The impetus for much of what happens during the time of treason is
the ever-expanding war on the Mafia, spearheaded by Robert Kennedy. This puts even greater pressure on Hoover, Johnson, and
Marcello. Yet Marcello remains free. In early 1963 the A.G. appears as keynote speaker before the Fund for the Republic, the same
organization that had so viciously attacked Hoover in summer
1962. The Director is deeply offended. Hoffa, perhaps in an attempt
to blunt the A.G.'s drive against him, donates several hundred
thousand dollars to Hoover's favorite charity, the Boy Scouts. The
gift is made directly to the D.C. area council. On May 9 RFK
succeeds in obtaining an indictment against the Teamster, charging
him with jury tampering. The case will ultimately destroy the labor
leader and Mafia associate. Hoover and the A.G. clash directly over
the use of mob informant Valachi, the Director opposing public
exposure of the individual. Over the summer months, Louisiana
FBI offices effectively and publicly convey disinterest in the A.G.'s
civil-rights program. In August, Hoover sends a memo to Robert
Kennedy detailing the sex life of Martin Luther King. Although
shocked, he forwards the document to the President. Fall brings
renewed legislative requests from RFK to Congress in the area of
the Mafia.

General Walker works diligently to obtain more and more publicity.
The high point of this effort is seen in a staged attempt on his life in
April 1963. In France, prosecution of the de Gaulle conspirators
continues on course.

Lastly, there is Oswald. Most of his activities during the time leading up to the assassination deal simply with survival. He changes
jobs several times, arguing frequently with his wife. They move
repeatedly. He decides to become a revolutionary in the Cuban
cause, spending a considerable amount of time in furtherance of this
goal. There are public demonstrations and letter campaigns, association and attempted association with various left-wing organizations, all of which culminate in an unsuccessful effort to reach Cuba
via Mexico City in the fall of 1963. Newspapers reveal that many

other individuals attempt the same trip during 1963, some suc-
ceeding.

A move to New Orleans in April 1963 brings the young Marxist
into association with an FBI contract agency run by ex-SAC Guy
Banister. Through involvement with this group the young ex-
Marine gains publicity for his cause (FPCC). Unfortunately he unknowingly becomes a tool of the Marcello organization as well.
Through David Ferrie and others he is maneuvered into position to
take the blame for Kennedy's murder. The Bureau consistently
monitors him throughout most of 1963, perhaps using him as an
informant. Hoover is periodically updated on this individual as he
has shown a personal interest in the case. Both Oswald and his wife
attempt to obtain reentry visas to Russia, to no avail.

Oswald's passive nature becomes apparent during this period. At
times he appears somewhat inept, consistently displaying a low level
of manual dexterity (e.g., cannot drive a car). He purchases cheap
weapons for purposes of building an image as a revolutionary, although he never actually practices with them. During the summer
of 1963 he reads a great deal in an attempt to educate himself. His
literacy level, however, remains fairly low. After failing to reach
Cuba in September, he starts to settle down. Obtaining a job and a
room in Dallas (he and Marina now live apart), he begins treating
his wife better. She and their daughter reside with friends in Fort
Worth (the Paines). Oswald joins the ACLU. Marina has a second
child on October 20, 1963, which seems to have a maturing effect on
him (he also gains an exemption for tax purposes). After receiving
his first paycheck from the Texas School Book Depository in early
November, he contacts the IRS in an apparent attempt to begin the
process of obtaining an early tax refund and/or downward adjustment in his withholding rate. He continues to attempt to obtain a
visa to Cuba, actually gaining conditional approval, contingent
upon receipt of a Russian visa, shortly before the assassination.

In the context of the Marcello contract, an animated, overly aggressive Oswald look-alike surfaces in the Dallas area in October
and November. This is done in an attempt to make the real Oswald
appear to be a violent individual. His rifle is stolen in October,
possibly by Ruby associates, for the purpose of linking him with the
assassination after the fact. By coincidence, Oswald's job site is on
Kennedy's Dallas motorcade route. (Note, the use of Oswald's rifle
in the killing is enough to "implicate" him. Even if the motorcade

were to follow a route other than through Dealy Plaza, simply by keeping Oswald away from work and without an alibi, he can be framed for the assassination.) Marcello's contract killers position themselves in strategic locations in the immediate area of Dealy Plaza during the predawn hours of November 22, 1963, using Oswald's rifle in the ensuing fusillade.

On November 18, 1963, Oswald apparently calls the Russian embassy in Washington, D.C., trying to find out the status of his and his wife's visa applications. The Bureau monitors this. Spending the night with his wife in Fort Worth, on the morning of the assassination he oversleeps, narrowly avoiding missing his ride to work. He carries a bag of some sort into the Depository with him; its contents are unknown. The bag is light, thin, and short enough to tuck under one arm and cup in the hand, precluding the possibility that it contains a rifle (even disassembled). At the prodding of Marcello people (Ferrie et al.), it may contain some form of pro-Cuba protest material. At 12:30 P.M. (CST) President Kennedy is assassinated by at least two gunmen while Oswald eats lunch on the second floor of the Texas School Book Depository.

9/62—THIS MONTH: "Sometime in September of 1962, an old revolutionary colleague . . . told [wealthy Cuban exile Jose] Aleman [living in Miami, Florida] that [Santos] Traficante wanted to see him. [He] explained that Traficante felt indebted to Aleman's cousin . . . and wanted to express his gratitude by helping Aleman out of his financial difficulties. He was prepared to arrange a sizable loan from the Teamsters Union. Aleman's friend assured him that the loan . . . had already been cleared by Jimmy Hoffa himself. . . . [Traficante visited] . . . Aleman at the Scott Bryan and offered him the loan—$1.5 million to replace the ramshackle motel. . . . Aleman says Traficante spent most of the evening philosophizing. 'He spoke almost poetically about democracy and civil liberties.' But then he turned to the Kennedys: they were not honest, they took graft and they did not keep a bargain. He complained about their attacks on his friends, saying, *'Have you seen how his brother is hitting Hoffa,* a man who is a worker, who is not a millionaire, a friend of the blue collars? He doesn't know that this kind of encounter is very delicate. Mark my words, *this man Kennedy is in trouble, and he will get what is coming to him.'* Aleman . . . *argued that Kennedy would get reelected, and Traficante replied,*

'No, Jose, he is going to be hit.' " . . . "Aleman indicate[d] that
. . . Traficante made clear to him . . . that he was not guessing
about the killing; rather he was giving the impression that he knew
Kennedy was going to be killed. *Aleman did not believe [Traficante]
was personally involved. . . . Aleman said he was given the distinct
impression that Hoffa was to be principally involved* in the elimination of Kennedy."[1] Traficante does not know that Aleman is, and
has been for some time, an FBI informant. In keeping with this role
he promptly reports word of the plan to assassinate President Kennedy to his Miami FBI contacts. *"Aleman . . . personally repeated
everything to . . . [FBI agents] . . . George Davis and Paul Scranton. . . ."* "Aleman. 'I talked . . . to . . . [them] about what was
going on in the conversation, . . . Like I previously had been informing the FBI. . . ." "Both [Davis and Scranton] . . . acknowledge their frequent contacts with Aleman but *both declined to
comment on Aleman's conversations with Traficante. Scranton explained he would have to have clearance. 'I wouldn't want to do
anything to embarrass the Bureau.' " ". . . Davis remarked, 'He's a
reliable individual' "* (emphasis added).[2] Pursuant to standard FBI
procedure, the two agents report the assassination plan to their
superior, Miami SAC, Wesley G. Grapp.[3] The information is then
sent by AIRTEL to Hoover. The Director, Clyde Tolson, and very
probably Courtney Evans analyze this plan. Dramatically different
from previous death threats, this one speaks of a specific contract to
assassinate the President prior to 11/8/64.

Unlike his SACs and field agents, Hoover has access to all information available regarding various Mafia leaders. He undoubtedly
orders Traficante's, Hoffa's, and any close associate's files brought
to him. Logically those nearest to Traficante, with motive to assassinate Kennedy, are prime suspects. He already knows that Marcello
is Traficante's and Hoffa's closest confidant and business associate.
An examination of Traficante's file reveals that in the last few weeks
he has been in contact with Marcello. Hoover also knows that an
associate of Gilbert Beckely, Marcello's gambling liaison in Miami,
has in recent months, like Hoffa, expressed a desire to assassinate
Robert Kennedy, the "brother who has been hitting Hoffa." Recall
that Beckley operates out of a house in Miami owned by the Teamsters. Any official familiar with the powers of the Executive would
know that the assassination of a presidential subordinate by a group
opposing presidential policy (i.e., JFK's dedication to the destruc-

tion of the Mafia) would only increase pressure on that group. Marcello understands this, as does Hoover. Hoover knows, too, that Marcello associate David Ferrie had publicly attacked JFK so vehemently, in a mid-1961 New Orleans speech, that he had to be forcibly removed from the podium. Other threats received from more removed Mafia figures, although spontaneous and angry, have been less focused. In fact, consensus among northern and eastern families, such as those in Philadelphia and Chicago, implies fear, a sense of helplessness. There is talk of the need for commission approval before any action can be taken. No doubt Hoover is by now aware that as head of the oldest Mafia family in the U.S., Marcello occupies a special position. He has the power to act without commission approval. He is also the only Mafia leader who has been subjected to personal humiliation and near-fatal experience by the Kennedys. As Director, Hoover has firsthand knowledge of other factors now placing tremendous pressure on Marcello (see 8/31/62). To one in control of all the data, involvement of this man would seem highly probable. To Hoover and Tolson, men who have survived at the highest levels of power for decades by their ability to detect crime and subterfuge, it is undoubtedly obvious.

Just as obvious to Hoover is the opportunity this contract presents. His prior concealment of other, less focused threats proves his awareness of the potential. His own situation is now very nearly as desperate as Marcello's. As chief investigator in the Billie Sol Estes case, Hoover has firsthand knowledge of Johnson's complicity in the matter. In addition, the Bobby Baker case (i.e., Levinson, Teamsters) has begun to assume ominous proportions. Because of data obtained in those cases and Johnson's status as a longtime friend, the Director knows that he would be considerably more vulnerable as President than Kennedy has proven to be. LBJ has stated, in personal correspondence with Hoover on numerous occasions, how much he is looking forward to working with the Director in the "years" to come. Johnson's dislike for both Kennedys is well known to him. The question that obviously occurs to the Director then is, quite simply, whether Johnson as President would concern himself with Kennedy's assassination were it to occur. At this point, with JFK Hoover has no other cards to play. His attempts at sexual blackmail have failed. To go public with rumors of presidential impropriety would only ensure his replacement. Nor can any deal with regard to the 1964 election be wrangled. No matter what Kennedy agreed to, even publicly, prior to the election, there are no guarantees he would hold to it after reelection. With no third campaign possible, any data Hoover held at that point would become useless. The President has already indicated that the Director will be retired by federal statute. Congress has sided with the President, asking only for advice and consent regarding the Director's replacement. The aging ultrarightist has realized that only the removal of Kennedy from office *prior* to 1/1/65 will save him. Through social conversation with Johnson, Hoover has probably already learned that President Kennedy plans to campaign in Texas, an area of Marcello influence, during the 1964 reelection bid.

But there is something more. Aside from the above is the question of morality. Hoover finds Kennedy's immorality very offensive, particularly in view of his position as President. Hoover has dwelled upon the fact that JFK has repeatedly committed adultery. When one considers the Director's lifelong, monogamous (although homosexual) relationship with Clyde, this theory is actually quite logical. Hoover has often used terms like "adulterer" and "adulteress," to describe the President and his wife. Phrases like "another man's wife" have been used to describe JFK's married partners.

Hoover is also well aware of the source of Kennedy's money, much of it having been derived from illegal trade in scotch whiskey during Prohibition days. The elder Kennedy had used East Coast organized-crime networks to distribute his imported product. Add to this JFK's associations with people like Frank Sinatra and Judith Campbell. To a man of Hoover's mental orientation, the ethical line between President Kennedy and the Mafia may well have ceased to exist. Undoubtedly the Director's sense of moral outrage, need for self-perpetuation, and political conservatism have formed the basis of his rationalization in deciding to allow the President's assassination. Like the previous threats, the Aleman revelation is stored either in his personal-confidential files or the Special File Room, withheld from the Secret Service.

Prior to this point, Hoover and Tolson have only attempted blackmail in their efforts to obtain a retirement waiver for the former and eliminate the power the President holds over them. With this act they, like Marcello, commit a number of profoundly serious federal offenses (see page 184–185 for definitions of the first four applicable statutes).

18 USC 2381. Treason.

18 USC 2384. Seditious conspiracy.

18 USC 2385. Advocating overthrow of Government.

18 USC 372. Conspiracy to impede or injure officer.

18 USC 2. Principals. (*a*) Whoever commits an offense against the United States or aids, abets, counsels, commends, induces or procures its commission, is punishable as a principal.

The key terms are legally defined as follows:

Conspiracy. A combination or confederacy between two or more persons formed for the purpose of committing, by their joint efforts, some unlawful or criminal act.

Aid. To support, help, assist or strengthen. Act in cooperation with; supplement the efforts of others.

Abet. To encourage, incite, or set another on to commit a crime.

Some will suggest that Hoover withheld Mafia death threats from the Secret Service because they were the product of *illegal electronic surveillance* (i.e., ELSUR). With the Marcello contract the argument is clearly not a defense.

9/11/62—TUESDAY: By sheer coincidence, Marcello is asked during a business meeting in New Orleans with a close relative, and another man named Edward Becker, about his war with the Kennedys. He has been drinking. "It was then that Carlos' voice lost its softness, and his words were bitten off and spit out when mention was made of U.S. Attorney General Robert Kennedy. . . . 'Livarsi na petra di la scarpa!' Carlos shrilled the Mafia cry of revenge: 'Take the stone out of my shoe!' *'Don't worry about that little Bobby son of a bitch,'* he shouted. *'He's going to be taken care of!'* Ever since Robert Kennedy had arranged for his deportation to Guatemala, Carlos had wanted revenge. But as *the* subsequent *conversation, which was reported to two top government investigators by one of the participants . . . showed, he knew that to rid himself of Robert Kennedy he would first have to remove the President. Any killer of the Attorney General would be hunted down by his brother; the death of the President would seal the fate of his Attorney*

General. No one at the meeting had any doubt about Marcello's intentions when he abruptly rose from the table. Moreover, *the conversation at Churchill Farms also made clear that Marcello had begun to plan a move.* He had, for example, already thought of using a 'nut' to do the job" (emphasis added).[4]

Becker is in fact an informant, working with an ex-FBI agent (Julian Blodgett) who, in turn works for a private investigative agency in Los Angeles doing contract work with the Los Angeles FBI field office. He had arranged the meeting through a nephew of Marcello's named Carl Roppolo. Ostensibly the purpose of this meeting was to obtain investment capital from Marcello for an oil venture. Within a week Becker will meet with his ex-FBI contact. Although Becker will later state he told the *FBI* nothing of Marcello's threat, there is this qualification found in the HSCA hearings at p. 83 of vol. 9: "Becker further stated that the only person other than [Ed] Reid [author of the *Grim Reapers,* who will interview Becker in 1967] whom he *might* have informed of Marcello's remarks was his close associate Julian Blodgett, who employed him during that period as an investigator" (emphasis added).[5] Such a revelation to Blodgett, a man also making his living by supplying sensitive data to groups like the FBI, may explain the intense level of interest Hoover and the Bureau show in Becker during the fall of 1962.

Press: "A . . . Brooklyn salesman who has served as a Government informant within the Communist party pointed out William Albertson today as one who had a big voice in party affairs in New York. The Justice Department . . . contends he is a member of the party's national committee. At a meeting in October 1961, Mr. Prince said, Mr. Albertson advised party members to invoke the Fifth Amendment's privilege against self-incrimination if arrested by the FBI."[6]

9/13/62—THURSDAY: Press: "The French police announced the arrest today of a sixth person accused of participating in the attempt to kill President de Gaulle Aug. 22."[7]

9/14/62—FRIDAY: Press reports regarding Estes. "At the end of today's session, Senator McClellan recessed the hearings until after Mr. Estes has undergone trial for theft in Tyler, Tex. The trial begins Sept. 24."[8]

Press: "Attorney General Robert F. Kennedy announced here that a United States District Court grand jury at Tyler, Tex., had returned a 109-count indictment against J. C. Stroud and W. V. Stroud of Henderson, Tex. They were charged with the interstate shipment of oil from a slanted well in Rusk County, Tex. The indictment is expected to be the forerunner of many state and Federal actions against oil piracy in the world's largest oil fields. The case came to light last June. The Federal Bureau of Investigation subsequently joined in the investigation at the request of the Interior Department."[9]

9/17/62—MONDAY: Press: "A French Air Force engineer has admitted to being the leader of the plot to assassinate President de Gaulle Aug. 22, the police announced tonight. The assassination of the general, he said, would be for the good of France."[10]

9/18/62—TUESDAY: "Becker . . . first met with [Blodgett] in Brownwood, Tex., . . ." They return together to Shreveport, Louisiana.[11] Becker will meet yet again with Marcello.

Press: "The first proceeding to require a member of the Communist Party to register with the Attorney General ended today. *Mr. Albertson's attorney, John J. Abt of New York . . .* called no witnesses to the stand. The final Government witness, Albert Jackson, who observed party activities for the Federal Bureau of Investigation for four years, testified that he had attended many Communist meetings with Mr. Albertson. *Mr. Abt brought out that Mr. Jackson had received varying sums from the FBI. He asked the witness whether he expected to be paid in the future.* 'After this is finished I guess I'm finished,' Mr. Jackson replied. 'And I'm finished,' Mr. Abt said, ending his cross-examination" (emphasis added).[12] Lee Harvey Oswald undoubtedly follows this story, for Abt is the attorney he will try so desperately to reach by phone the weekend of 11/22–11/24/63, to no avail. What is critical here is the fact that Abt defends alleged communists against the accusations of FBI informants. Oswald, already under pressure from the FBI to inform should he come into contact with any communist spies, readily identifies with this situation. As will be seen, by the time of President Kennedy's assassination, he will have need of such an attorney. This because he, too, will become a paid informant, albeit unwillingly.

9/21/62—FRIDAY: Becker and Blodgett ". . . travel . . . to Shreveport, La. . . ." where the former meets again with Roppolo, arranging a second meeting with Marcello.[13]

French press reports: "President de Gaulle refused to duck when assassins fired on his car last month. 'After the first round of shots I shouted, "Get down," but General de Gaulle and his wife remained upright.' "[14]

8/62—9/62:   LBJ associate Morris Jaffe purchases Estes's bankruptcy estate in Texas for $7 million.[15] With his trial set to begin in a few days, Estes's assets and legal fate are now in the hands of men close to Vice President Johnson.

9/22/62—SATURDAY: Press reports: "A House committee urged the Defense Department today to penalize officials who wrongly withhold Government documents from the public on alleged security grounds. *A security system which carries no penalties for using secrecy stamps to hide errors in judgment, waste, inefficiency or worse is a perversion of true security'* " (emphasis added).[16]

9/24/62—MONDAY: Press reports: "The Senate committee's version of the postal rate bill would revive a controversial program, ended by President Kennedy last year, of intercepting Communist propaganda in mail from abroad."[17] Hoover no doubt rejoices at the prospect.

9/29/62—SATURDAY: Hoffa aide Partin informs RFK aide and ex-FBI agent Sheridan that Jimmy Hoffa is considering a plan to assassinate the Attorney General (see 6/62). "Kennedy's aides were skeptical at first, but Partin's veracity was soon borne out by a meticulous FBI polygraph examination."[18] This probably does not surprise Kennedy very much, however, given the longstanding bitterness between the two men.

10/62—THIS MONTH: FBI is now given full control of Mafia informant Joseph Valachi.[19]

". . . A Bureau of Narcotics report described Marcello as 'one of the Nation's leading racketeers' and noted that he was 'currently under intensive investigation by the Internal Revenue Service Intelligence Division for tax fraud.' The report also noted that Marcello was then instituting a further legal step to forestall deportation. Marcello's attorneys had filed a legal writ in an effort to set aside his Federal conviction on narcotics charges from 24 years earlier. This conviction was one of the key factors in the ongoing deportation proceedings against him."[20] The report is circulated among the twenty-seven-agency task force, adding to Hoover's knowledge on the mobster.

The Nation runs an article by ex-FBI agent Jack Levine, in which he attempts to further expose the minimal nature of the CPUSA threat. The article enrages Hoover.

10/1/62—MONDAY: *FBI Law Enforcement Bulletin* is released. Hoover, aware that it is National Newspaper Week (October 14–20), and hoping for favorable review of his new book, writes "As guardians of American liberty, the press . . . [is] . . . charged with a sacred trust. [The] . . . press is morally obligated to promote the furtherance of justice and the perpetuation of law and order." This is at once masterful media manipulation and brazen self-promotion (both politically and monetarily). Note how Hoover interlaces the morality theme with patriotism, completing the foundation laid in his "Monitor" speech. In effect he is stating that morality is the essence of patriotism while immorality is the essence of communism.

Press: "DALLAS . . . A 22-year-old man has been arrested for trying to transport a small arsenal to Mississippi, the police said today. They said the man, Ashland Burchwell of Dallas, told them he had worked for Edwin A. Walker in the latter's unsuccessful campaign for Governor. Four pistols, a rifle and more than 3,000 rounds of ammunition were seized."[21] In the coming months, this propensity for the use of firearms for political gain will become more apparent among people supporting Walker.

General Walker is arrested in Mississippi and charged with insurrection. The arresting officer states, "I didn't feel like I was talking to a rational man, . . . There was a wild, dazed look in his eyes. He was unable really to speak too well."[22]

10/2/62—TUESDAY: Press: "Former Maj. Gen. Edwin A. Walker . . . was ordered placed under psychiatric examination in a Federal prison today. His attorneys announced immediately that they would fight the order tomorrow. . . . They instructed Mr.

Walker to refuse to cooperate with prison physicians."[23] As is increasingly apparent, Walker is now becoming to aides and supporters less an individual and more a media image. He must be used by
them correctly so as to accomplish their goals. As a public speaker,
he appears incoherent, useless. But as a symbol of opposition to
liberals and even moderate Republicans, he has value to the ultraright.

Dallas press reports: "Dr. Robert Morris, a Dallas lawyer and
former president of the University of Dallas, said today that he was
considering representing Mr. Walker. . . . He said he was also
helping with plans to raise $100,000 to meet the bond. Dr. Morris
was an unsuccessful candidate for Republican nomination for Senator from New Jersey in 1960."[24]

10/7/62—SUNDAY: Press reports: ". . . Walker returned to
Texas today. . . . 'I am happy to be back in Texas'. . . . About
200 supporters welcomed Mr. Walker. Many carried signs saying,
'Welcome home, General Walker.' In a brief news conference, he
said, 'The issue at Oxford was an issue for the good of many states
and millions of people.' During the news conference Mr. Walker's
attorneys repeatedly refused to allow him to answer questions concerning his actions at Oxford. . . . His supporters sang, 'For he's a
jolly good fellow.' At a press conference last night *after his release
he declared that he was 'happy to be on the move to the next phase or
step after a week of some legal and judicial mistakes.' Asked what
instructions he had received from his attorneys he said: 'My attorneys
left it up to me to be my usual self, which is friendly, and to limit my
answers to certain things' "* (emphasis added).[25]

". . . [A] group of Russians, including the de Mohrenschildts
with their daughter and son-in-law, visited the Oswalds at their
. . . apartment in Ft. Worth." De Mohrenschildt, a petroleum engineer, is a man whose complete background may never be known.[26]
At any rate, he evidently has some influence over Oswald, quite
possibly motivating him to change jobs. The weekend's developments concerning General Walker may be discussed during this social gathering, perhaps as a subject of humor. De Mohrenschildt
may also be encouraging Oswald's interest in Cuba.

10/8/62—MONDAY: ". . . One of [Baker's] friends, W. A.
Jernigan, . . . sign[s] the papers for . . ." the purchase of a D.C.

condominium that the Senate aide will use to house a number of women in the coming months.[27]

". . . Oswald quit his job with the Leslie Welding Company, having decided to look for work in Dallas. . . . So . . . the Oswalds were separated. Marina spent nearly a month with Elena Hall, a Russian-American who had befriended her. She saw her husband only on weekends."[28]

10/9/62—TUESDAY: Hoover, in *Las Vegas,* Nevada, to address the American Legion national convention, presents his first speech since learning of the Marcello contract. Entitled, "An American's Challenge," he states:

Two years ago, in 1960, it was my duty to urgently warn your delegates at Miami that communism had gained already a strategic beachhead in nearby Cuba. . . . Today, we stand at the same crossroads and are faced with threats identical to those which confronted us 16 years ago [10/9/46]. *These threats are accepted in some quarters as the normal climate of life, to be met with appeasement or accommodation.* . . . "The only thing necessary for the triumph of evil is for good men to do nothing." . . . *Have our national pride, our moral conscience, our sensitivity to filth and degradation, grown so weak that they no longer react to assaults upon our proud heritage of freedom?*

Crime and subversion are formidable problems in the United States today because there is a dangerous flaw in our Nation's moral armor. Self-indulgence—the principle of pleasure before duty—is practiced across the length and breadth of the land. It is undermining those attributes of personal responsibility and self-discipline which are essential to our national survival. It is creating citizens who reach maturity with a warped sense of values and an undeveloped conscience. Crime is a parasite, feeding upon . . . moral lethargy. . . . Nowhere has this increase been more pronounced than among America's youth. . . . There is a moral breakdown among young people in the United States. . . . There is a quest for status at the expense of morality. The heavy toll of crime, both juvenile and adult, is a direct product of self-indulgence and irresponsibility. *There is a pattern of flight from responsibility.* . . . *Disrespect for law and order is a tragic moral illness.* . . . Too often, our parole boards are being influenced by impractical theorists—conference from "experts" who are without experience in the arena of action against crime. Too often, a cloak of special privilege is thrown around the enemies of society . . . by poorly conceived and maladministered programs intended to promote their rehabilitation. . . . *The public, by its submissive attitude and its lethargic acceptance of infractions of the law, has helped create an atmosphere conducive to the insidious growth of underworld activity.* . . . *Crime has a sinister partner in promoting the breakdown of our moral standards. This partner is international communism.* . . . The barbaric Communist empire now stretches from the wall of *Berlin* to the China Sea. . . . The Communist Party today may be smaller in the United States, but it is a hard-core group of fanatics operating a massive and impressive propaganda machine. We have but to look at the shameful riots in San Francisco in 1960 when college youth in that area, encouraged by Communists, acted like common hoodlums in demonstrating against a committee of the U.S. Congress engaged in public business. *A soft approach toward the menace of communism can lead only to national disaster.* Our Nation's efforts to deal effectively with this menace are not enhanced by those . . . of the extreme left who endeavor to minimize the real danger of communism. This . . . group includes grossly irresponsible elements. . . . We have heard them shout "sententious poppycock" at well-founded and documented warnings against the capacity of the Communists to pervert our thinking and destroy the spiritual supports which form the foundation of our freedom. Inane statements such as these add nothing to the American people's understanding of the true menace of communism at home and abroad. They are a rank disservice to the cause of freedom.

I repeat, a soft attitude toward communism can destroy us. . . . *We should unite as a people around [a]* . . . *very hard attitude against Communism everywhere.* . . . Whenever we have stood firm, communism has retreated. . . . *We must assemble our strength—the moral strength endowed upon us by our Creator. There is a vast difference between Americanism and communism. One teaches morality; the other, expediency.* . . . *But in luxury there is the danger of physical weakening*

*and moral softness. Self-indulgence can prove fatal. It can ac-
complish from within what our most deadly enemies have been
unable to do from without.*

The fight against crime and communism can be won, and it
will be won with, but only with, *the help of every decent American* citizen. . . .

America has accepted the challenge and we must and will
meet it successfully (emphasis added).[29]

In his first speech since learning of the Marcello contract, Hoover
begins with a pointed reference to the late fall of 1946. "Sixteen
years ago" Harry Truman, the only President Hoover ever publicly
denounced as a communist, and the one who had come closest to
firing him prior to Kennedy, had been in office eighteen months. On
10/9/62 John Kennedy has been President less than twenty-one.
Hoover uses this backdrop to imply that the nation is again besieged
on all fronts (internationally and domestically). It was in October
1946 that Russia began its open aggression against *Berlin* by vetoing
the results of that city's first postwar mayoral election. Also by late
1946, as stated in Power's sympathetic biography of Hoover, *Secrecy and Power* (pp. 276–278), "Truman himself had made it clear
that he regarded Hoover and the FBI as enemies of civil liberties.
. . . Hoover watched over the events of 1945, 1946, and 1947 that
would unleash the Cold War. . . . There was the danger of a foreign attack aided and abetted by domestic . . . espionage and subversion." The Director's reference to Cuba, also at the outset of his
speech, is no idle comment. October 9, 1962, is eighteen months
after Kennedy's naval disaster at the Bay of Pigs. In essence then,
Hoover's premise is that Kennedy, like Truman, is soft on communism, suspect. As in the case of Truman, the argument is fallacious.
The Cuban Missile Crisis, and JFK's successful stand against Soviet
aggression, is, intriguingly, less than two weeks away. The Director,
of course, cannot know this.

Using the threat of communism as a springboard, Hoover continues to build and expand on his morality theme as a vehicle for
personal and national salvation. Note how he correlates adult immorality with the growth of underworld activity. He speaks for the
first time of "a dangerous flaw in our Nation's moral armor," simultaneously making reference to such dangers as "self-indulgence,"
"pleasure before duty," and "citizens who reach maturity with a

warped sense of values and an undeveloped conscience." He refers to international communism as the "sinister partner" of immorality. Near the conclusion of his address, he informs the group what will come of all this, stating, "But in luxury there is the danger of physical weakening and moral softness. *Self-indulgence can prove fatal."* Contrast JFK's 11/18/61 statement on the threat of communism, "We know that it comes from *without, not within,"* with Hoover's warning as to the "fatal" effects of self-indulgence: "It can accomplish from *within* what our most deadly enemies have been unable to do from *without."* Read in the context of his struggle with President Kennedy, and considering his knowledge of JFK's personal life, can there be any question but that he has in fact made a moral condemnation of Kennedy? In effect Hoover has rationalized his decision to allow the assassination of the President by concluding, in his mind, that the man is immoral, symptomatic. Kennedy has become merely part of the "challenge," to be swept away in a tide of "Americanism." To Hoover, President Kennedy is now part of a "dangerous flaw in our Nation's moral armor."

In this same context Hoover states "Disrespect for law and order is a tragic moral illness." The "tragic" results that will come of such "disrespect" will, from this point forward, become a recurring theme. On 11/16/63, in an address on personal morality just days before Kennedy leaves for Dallas, Hoover will refer to the "tragic" consequences of immorality. On the afternoon of 11/22/63, in his terse eulogy of the President, he will speak in terms of JFK's "tragic death." In his 12/1/63 *FBI Law Enforcement Bulletin* message, couched exclusively in terms of immorality, he will call for a return to "decency and morality" in America. And on 12/4/63, in his first address after the assassination, he states "Disrespect for law and order is a tragic moral sickness."

There can be no doubt that Hoover is also attempting to accomplish a number of other goals with this speech. In classic manner, he creates the enemy, then points the way to salvation, once again, indispensable. As the most prominent representative of law enforcement, the use of phrases such as "Disrespect for law and order is a tragic moral illness" is blatantly self-serving, if not bizarre. Again, he appeals to his constituency. He responds to recent criticism (e.g., Ferry et al.) by stating that such comments "are a rank disservice to the cause of freedom." Consider this statement. He is equating *himself* with the "cause of freedom." Once again he sends a message to

President Kennedy, subtly, yet publicly, defying him—emboldened by the realization that Kennedy will be assassinated.

Indirectly, he is also conditioning the American people for the coming loss. He knows that the killing will occur sometime prior to November 1964, so he must operate under the assumption it may well happen in the short term. The people must understand that, as an immoral, liberal man, who was also "soft" on communism, Kennedy simply paid the ultimate price: "Self-indulgence can prove fatal." To Hoover, a logical result.

And what must Marcello's people think? They are now hearing Hoover talk of the immorality of those who oppose him, describing them as mortal enemies of "Americanism." Consider that in light of the 5/3/62 death threat against RFK from Marcello's gambling network. That threat was couched in terms of the immorality of JFK. In early September 1962 Marcello associate Traficante attacked President Kennedy by describing him as corrupt, a man who did not keep his bargains. Rhetoric of the type now coming from Hoover can only encourage such men.

But in all this there is also the morality of Hoover himself. Considered in his time, is he any better? As a homosexual, a man harboring an inordinate interest in pornography of all types, a gambler, a daily drinker, a man who habitually allows others to pay his and Clyde's way, a man given to blackmail, can he logically, rationally condemn President Kennedy? He cannot. As a desperate man, he has merely grasped the opportunity presented by the Marcello contract in an attempt to save himself. Tragically it will be at the cost of the President's life, the integrity of constitutional process, and ultimately, the credibility of the FBI.

One final aspect, oddly enough, is the question of Hoover's accommodations while in Las Vegas. "Hoover was less exclusive in his personal relationships. He often stayed for free at the Las Vegas hotels of construction tycoon Del E. Webb, whose holdings were permeated with organized-crime entanglements. Hoover and Webb also met frequently on vacations in Del Mar, California." Webb, for example, was the ". . . builder of the Flamingo and the Sahara. . . ." The latter ". . . had its backing in [a] . . . gambling-horsebook organization. . . ." Shortly after its construction, "Levinson had acquired interests in the Flamingo . . ." as had Lansky.[30] It is not known where Hoover is staying while in Las Vegas this day, but the close association with Webb cannot be ignored. It is quite possible Hoover meets with and/or speaks to the construction tycoon while there. Their relationship is simply one of a number of avenues by which Hoover's, like Johnson's, dissatisfaction with President Kennedy can be conveyed to the wrong people.

Oswald ". . . rented a post-office box [2915], a system which—assuming no official surveillance—ensured the receipt of mail with absolute privacy. Oswald used a post-office box wherever he went from now on." In part this is due to his increasing interest in leftist publications and the fact that he moves every few months. It may be for the purpose of receiving informant payments from the FBI (see 4/15/63).[31]

10/10/62—WEDNESDAY: Press: "President Kennedy said today that one of his Administration's 'most effective though least known' efforts was its drive against organized crime. *'One Las Vegas gambler,' the President said with a smile, 'is supposed to have said he hoped we'd be as tough on Berlin as we've been on Las Vegas. Well, we intend to be.'* From January through June this year there were 83 convictions, he said" (emphasis added).[32] Obviously Kennedy is attempting, with humor, to rebut Hoover's Las Vegas speech of the previous night. Consider the following: It is common knowledge that Hoover is a man who gambles for money every week; Kennedy, as Chief Executive, knows Hoover is in Las Vegas; Hoover had, in his speech, specifically referred to *Berlin* in the context of the threat of communism, and had called for a "very hard attitude against Communism everywhere." Significant portions of Hoover's address had also warned of the dangers of "organized crime." By implication, in referring to Hoover as a "Las Vegas gambler" JFK is also showing his contempt. Kennedy is effectively telling the Director he will eliminate him along with the Mafia. It is Hoover who has the last laugh here, however, for only he and two assistants know what Marcello has in store for the President. Kennedy's attempt at humor only reveals the degree to which he is underestimating the Director.

Beckley defendants Bagneris, Brouphy, and Perez withdraw their not guilty pleas without warning and plead guilty to Count 1, the primary conspiracy count. Perez and Brouphy are part of the main group of defendants.[33] Such a move is highly unusual at this stage of trial, particularly after fighting the charges so vigorously for the last year. They do so on the condition that their sentencing not be imposed until prosecution of the remaining defendants is complete. This effectively frees them from further trial participation. Likewise, Marcello associate di Piazza is planning shortly to request severance from the trial on grounds of extremely ill health.

Press: "Informants planted in the Communist party by the Federal Bureau of Investigation testified here yesterday on their findings and pay. . . . A foundry worker, said he received . . . $75 monthly this year."[34]

10/12/62—FRIDAY: Oswald obtains a new job in Dallas at Jagger-Chiles-Stovall, a graphic arts plant. The job is of an uncomplicated nature, developing negative prints. He will later be fired from this position for incompetence. "He just couldn't seem to do things right," according to his employer. "Oswald seemed to have trouble in producing the exact sizes called for."[35] ". . . When Lee began working more independently 'he began to make . . . mistakes on sizing. . . . My impression of his mistakes was that he just couldn't manage to avoid them. It wasn't that he lacked industry or didn't try.' "[36]Remember also that Oswald has never learned to drive a car. During his time as a Marine he handled firearms poorly, once dropping a loaded pistol, causing it to discharge inside a barracks. In addition, his marksmanship skills deteriorated during that time, to the point where he barely qualified for the lowest rating the Corps allowed.[37] Marine Corps instructors, under intense pressure to produce continuous supplies of quality fighting men, sometimes manipulated the scores of borderline recruits in order to meet minimum quotas. Within a few months, he will sign up for a typing course, only to drop out after a few lessons. Typically, when physically confronted, he makes no attempt to fight, opting to block punches thrown at him.

Oswald's low performance levels clearly imply he has poorly developed hand-eye coordination, thus explaining the fact that he is a poor shot, reacts passively when physically confronted, cannot drive, and is unable to master simple tasks requiring manual dexterity. Mastoid problems and accompanying surgery as a youth, apparently affecting his hearing in one ear, may be a factor.[38]

10/16/62—TUESDAY: Press reports: "Secret Service protection was extended to the Vice President . . . under a bill signed today by President Kennedy."[39]

10/17/62—WEDNESDAY: Press: "President Kennedy has signed a bill repealing the controversial non-Communist disclaimer affidavit that had been required of college students and scientists seeking Federal loans and grants. . . . capping a three-year effort by liberals . . . to abolish the affidavit requirement."[40]

10/18/62—THURSDAY: Press: "The Federal Bureau of Investigation has nearly 1500 informants in the 8500-member Communist party, according to a former agent who also made public a report criticizing the 'autocratic' way the bureau is run. The former agent is Jack Levine. Neither the department nor the FBI would comment last night on an article by Mr. Levine in the current issue of The Nation ["Hoover and the Red Scare"], describing the 'amazingly successful' Communist inquiries. They also withheld comment on a tape he made for radio station WBAI-FM (Pacifica network), to be broadcast at 8:15 tonight containing his report to Mr. Miller. The bureau, Mr. Levine said, had found that the informants payroll had become a 'severe drain,' and that 'through its dues-paying FBI contingent it had become the largest single financial contributor to the coffers of the Communist party.' He cited other agents who . . . could give specific cases of 'the authoritarian, over-demanding perfectionist policies' of Mr. Hoover and of the anti-liberal, anti-Negro and anti-Semitic attitudes of bureau officials and agents. He said agents had conducted many unauthorized telephone wiretaps, occasionally opened others' mail and searched without warrants under policies that would disclaim them if caught." Hoover's arrest and conviction statistics are also revealed to consist, in many cases, of ". . . misdemeanors, not felonies."[41] Clearly both Levine and Turner have sensed that the end is approaching for the Director. Knowing nothing of the Marcello contract, they presume 1/1/65 will be his last day in power. Unfortunately for Pacifica, it will soon come under attack. Hoover, using his influence with HUAC, will attempt to prevent FCC licensing. He will also accuse its officers of being communists. Levine's charge of anti-Semitism is paradoxical, for Hoover has a number of close acquaintances who are Jewish. It is noteworthy here, however, that these "acquaintances," men such as Roy Cohn (the HUAC ultrarightist) and Jesse Weiss (Miami restaurateur) tend to be people Hoover can use to his benefit, be it political or monetary.

Note also Hoover's apparent invulnerability to the attacks of both Levine and Turner. With regard to Bureau rank and file it merely strengthens his basis of control. This control will be demonstrated during the Dallas field office "massacre," now just over one year away.

10/20/62—SATURDAY: FBI (Los Angeles) SAC sends an AIRTEL to Hoover. "The first Bureau reference to Becker appeared in a report of November 20, [*sic*, the source note for this report is dated October 20]1962. . . . The report noted that Becker [was] then associated with an investigator [i.e., Blodgett] being employed by one of the oil service companies that had allegedly been swindled by [Billie Sol] Estes. . . . Becker was associated with an oil geologist in Shreveport, Carl Roppolo, who was alleged to be a close acquaintance of Carlos Marcello. The report noted that one person had told the Bureau that 'Roppolo had said that his mother is Carlos Marcello's sister, and that Roppolo is the favorite nephew.' . . . Roppolo . . . was the man who . . . set up the September [11,] 1962 meeting with Marcello and attended the meeting along with Becker for the purpose of seeking Marcello's support for a proposed business venture of theirs."[42] As stated, it is unclear whether Becker somehow disclosed the September death threat by Marcello to Bureau officials. As a paid informant it would seem plausible that he at least informed his contact, ex-agent Blodgett. Though both Becker and the Bureau will deny he informed them directly prior to the assassination, Blodgett's position will be vague. He will confirm Becker's reliability, stating he believes Becker attended the meeting in question, but will apparently say little else, for the record at least.[43] In 1967, the Bureau and Hoover himself will go to great pains to discredit Becker as a source.[44] The intense level of interest shown prior to the assassination by Hoover, when taken in conjunction with other data, will further betray his foreknowledge of the impending assassination.

Press: "Gus Hall, the American Communist leader, acknowledged . . . that 'some' Federal Bureau of Investigation agents had infiltrated the party. But he contended that the identity of many was known."[45]

President Kennedy, in Chicago, receives word of American U-2 spy plane photos showing advanced state of readiness of Cuban missile bases. He immediately returns to Washington.[46]

10/22/62—MONDAY: Press: "Billie Sol Estes . . . must be tried immediately on state charges of theft and swindling. . . . Defense attorneys had demanded a postponement. . . . Judge Dunagan overruled the motion. . . . The chief defense attorney, John D. Cofer . . . called for a continuance. . . ."[47]

10/23/62—TUESDAY: FBI (Chicago) ELSUR records mafiosi ". . . John D'Arco and Congressman Roland Libonati. . . . Libonati thinks that John Kennedy is a sweetheart, but Robert F. Kennedy is cruel. Libonati describes how he opposed a Robert Kennedy bill and then got a call from Mayor Daley. Libonati told John F. Kennedy to stop Robert Kennedy from calling Daley on such matters. Bobby said on TV that his brother wants him to stay out of politics because he is the Attorney General. Libonati takes credit for this, saying 'That was me.' "[48] The implication here is that some members of the Chicago Mafia see JFK as politically cooperative. It is difficult to know if this official actually did as he claimed.

10/25/62—THURSDAY: Tolson writes a letter to the managing editor of the *Chicago Daily News* reiterating Hoover's views on Levine. ". . . Mr. Levine suddenly—and obviously as a disgruntled former employee—launched a campaign of vilification against Mr. Hoover and the FBI; and in pursuing his vindictive course, he has utterly disregarded the security of the Nation. . . . Assistant Attorney General Herbert J. Miller, Jr., publicly stated that his allegations 'were found to be baseless.' Unfortunately the irresponsible and unsubstantiated charges made by this former employee have received far greater circulation than Mr. Miller's factual appraisal of them. A copy of Mr. Miller's reply to the radio station is attached. Knowing your newspaper's reputation for fairness and accuracy, I felt certain you would want me to bring these facts to your attention so that they could be passed along to your readers." In effect, this is both a thinly veiled warning to the newspaper not to run further stories critical of the Director, and a directive to publish Miller's rebuttal.

10/62: Vice President Johnson makes a second public appearance "at the Carousel Motel in North Ocean City, Maryland . . . (Johnson's former aide Bobby Baker used the Carousel to entertain prominent businessmen and congressmen, together with call girls)."

One, ". . . Ellen Rometsch[,] . . . was seen at parties throughout Washington and at the Carousel Motel. . . . Furthermore, she was said to have organized a ring of Government girls to provide party fun . . . at get-togethers in lobbyists' hotel suites. . . ." This information is reported to Hoover. "In response to this report, alleging *immoral* activities and *'hoodlum interests,'* Hoover demanded that the Bureau's source be contacted to ascertain the accuracy of the allegations. Thereupon 'appropriate discreet inquiries through logical sources' were conducted by the Baltimore field office, and Hoover was 'promptly advised' of information it had learned" (emphasis added). The report is apparently still classified as of 1991.[49] While it is difficult to know what Hoover thinks of LBJ personally, it is obvious that he realizes the Vice President will be easily controlled as President. Johnson has continually sought Hoover's protection for his misdeeds. It is unlikely this latest episode particularly surprises him.

10/31/62—WEDNESDAY: ". . . A Federal court ruled against Marcello's attempt to have the 1938 drug conviction nullified. The court said that his claim that he had not had counsel present when he pled guilty to the narcotics charge on October 29, 1938, was false, as was his claim that he had not known of his rights and could not afford an attorney."[50] This is an ominous turn of events for the Mafia leader. If such a ruling stands on appeal, he will be unable to undercut the basis for his status as an undesirable. This decision must have seriously diminished what little faith he may have had in the legal system, supplying one more reason to take matters into his own hands.

President Kennedy attends the FBI National Academy's seventieth graduation ceremonies, addressing the group as keynote speaker. Hoover presents him with an honorary gold FBI badge. JFK commends the group and law enforcement in general, saying of Hoover, "Mr. Hoover . . . is one of the most distinguished public servants who have occupied positions of high responsibility. . . ." Hoover's friend Benjamin M. McKelway, President of the Associated Press, also speaks in tribute. "The FBI could become a dangerous thing and be used to public disadvantage should the supervision of the FBI ever fall into unscrupulous or merely irresponsible hands."[51] A more perfect forum in which Kennedy could announce the intention to retain Hoover beyond age seventy does not exist. He remains silent on the subject. Hoover appears impassive, confident throughout the ceremony. In his mind, the President is undoubtedly already dead. Interestingly, the story covering this ceremony is withheld from the *FBI Law Enforcement Bulletin* until the January 1963 issue. The November 1962 issue highlights instead Hoover's 10/9/62 speech, "An American's Challenge," containing his thinly veiled admission of scienter (guilty knowledge) concerning the impending contract on the President's life. The December issue contains no articles of consequence.

11/62—THIS MONTH: Within the next sixty days, Hoover issues a directive to Marcello case officer Regis Kennedy in New Orleans, instructing him to report back on the association between the Mafia leader and Roppolo.[52]

Marcello attorney Gill obtains effective dismissal of various criminal charges against David Ferrie. This is accomplished by getting the prosecutor to enter "nolle prosequi" for the record, meaning simply that the case is dropped for want of prosecution.[53] Ferrie now owes Marcello a great deal, both figuratively and monetarily.

11/3/62—SATURDAY: Press: "In a dramatic and surprising action, the defense in the Billie Sol Estes theft and swindling trial rested its case today without putting a witness on the stand. John Cofer . . . spent 22 minutes reviewing the case. He contended that the state had failed to prove any criminal act. . . . Mr. Estes, smiling and apparently relaxed, told newsmen: 'We will stand on our record. Naturally, we hope the jury will find with us.' He lauded Mr. Cofer by saying: 'You know, I've learned something. All great men are simple. We took the state's own evidence and told the jury about it so simply that anyone could understand.' "[54]

11/4/62—SUNDAY: "Oswald found an apartment at 604 Elsbeth Street in the Oak Cliff section of Dallas. . . ." He and Marina are reunited, but ". . . within a day or two . . ." they begin fighting again.[55]

11/7/62—WEDNESDAY: Press: "A jury of 11 men and one woman found . . . Estes guilty today of swindling a Pecos, Tex., farmer . . . on a mortgage deal. They set a sentence . . . of eight years in state prison. . . . Cofer said he would file a motion for a new trial. . . . Estes' attorneys did not ask the jury for a suspended sentence. The case went to the panel with a passionate plea for acquittal. The defendant was impassive during the reading of the verdict, [then] he sagged momentarily. . . ."[56]

Press: "The President emerged with increased prestige and political strength from [the midterm congressional] election[s]. . . ."[57]

11/8/62—THURSDAY: Socialist Workers Party rejects Oswald's membership application.[58]

Press: "Conservatives were disheartened yesterday by the defeat of such right-wing stalwarts as Senator . . . Capehart, . . . and Representative Walter H. Judd . . . ; and by the victories of such liberals as Senator Wayne Morse, . . . and Senator Joseph S. Clark. . . . The ultra-right suffered a spectacular loss. Voters liquidated the John Birch Society's beachhead in Congress. The only avowed members . . . in Congress . . . were unseated by Democrats. Two other Birchers seeking House seats were also rejected."[59]

11/9/62—FRIDAY: Press: "A Senate subcommittee said today it still planned to question . . . Estes despite his conviction . . . on swindling charges. . . . McClellan . . . said that no date had been set for Estes' appearance."[60]

11/10/62—SATURDAY: Tolson sends another letter, nearly identical to his 10/25/62 complaint, to the *Washington Post,* contending ex-agent Levine had attempted to rejoin the FBI one month after his resignation, but was rejected because his record was "substandard." He again implies that this rejection was the impetus for Levine's current vendetta. He also claimes that in taking such actions Levine has ". . . utterly disregarded the security of the nation." Once again Hoover is wrapped in a cloak of patriotism while the public is sidetracked with irrelevant arguments.

A letter to the editor of the *New York Times* from a Jewish FBI agent attacks Levine for charging Hoover with anti-Semitism.

11/12/62—MONDAY: FBI (Los Angeles) SAC reports to Hoover, verifying ". . . that Becker had in fact traveled through Louisiana during . . . [September] and had also traveled to Dallas."[61] The Becker data raises some questions concerning SOG and field office communication: What is Hoover telling New Orleans about what Los Angeles is reporting, and vice versa? Is there any cross-communication between Los Angeles and New Orleans on this matter?

11/13/62—TUESDAY: "Baker executed a subscription agreement . . ." for his D.C. townhouse ". . . listing his salary as $19,263 per year. . . . He gave his net worth as $1,003,587."[62]

Press: "Governor Rockefeller's [New York] office said today he had signed extradition papers clearing the way for Texas authorities to return Maynard Wheeler [of Commercial Solvents] to that state to stand trial on anti-trust charges stemming from the . . . Estes case."[63]

11/14/62—WEDNESDAY: Press reports: "President Kennedy and his brother, Attorney General . . . Kennedy both donate their Government salaries to charity. . . . . . . President Kennedy had donated his . . . to charity ever since entering Congress in 1947."[64]

Press: "The power of committee chairmen and the committee system in Congress is reflected in the fate of President Kennedy's 298 specific legislative requests in 1962. Only 44.3 per cent of them were granted. Nevertheless . . . later in the session, important parts of Mr. Kennedy's program began to move."[65]

11/15/62—THURSDAY: RFK compiles notes on the Cuban Missile Crisis. About LBJ he states, ". . . After the meetings were finished, he would circulate and whine and complain about our being weak, but he never made . . . any suggestions or recommendations."[66]

11/16/62—FRIDAY: Johnson sends a get-well card to Hoover, who is now in the hospital (George Washington University). The nature of his illness remains unknown to this day. Some researchers have speculated that Hoover underwent a prostatectomy. ". . . This note is to tell you I am sorry you are ailing and wish you well."[67]

11/20/62—TUESDAY: Hoover sends a memo to RFK, referring to a hospital stay and his health.[68] If still in George Washington at this date (five days later), his reasons for being there may be more serious than a routine prostatectomy. Perhaps, like Tolson in mid-

1963, Hoover is now suffering from hypertension or angina. Fore-knowledge of a plan to assassinate the President of the United States would presumably cause a certain level of anxiety. Hoover will remain out of the office until at least the end of the month.

11/21/62—WEDNESDAY: "Becker was referred to in a second FBI report . . . which dealt with an alleged counterfeiting ring and a Dallas lawyer who reportedly had knowledge of it. This report noted that Becker was being used as an 'informant' by a private investigator in the investigation and was assisting to the extent that he began receiving expense money."[69] Becker apparently works with Blodgett on a variety of cases.

11/22/62—THURSDAY: Press: ". . . Walker directed two fire-fighting units today and was credited with a major effort in keeping a farm home from being destroyed by fire. Loys R. Dugger said Mr. Walker, driving alone along U.S. 77, 14 miles south of Gainesville, noted the woodshed in the rear of the Dugger farm home ablaze. . . . Mr. Walker then took charge of the fire-fighting and assisted in carrying out furniture and personal belongings from the home."[70] Once again, perceiving an opportunity for publicity, Walker injects himself into dramatic circumstances, taking "charge of the fire fighting. . . ."

11/26/62—MONDAY: On this date ". . . Becker was interviewed by the [Los Angeles] FBI in connection with its investigation of the Billie Sol Estes case on which Becker was then also working as a private investigator [with Blodgett]. Becker told the Bureau of his recent trips to Dallas, Tex., and Louisiana, and informed them of the information he had heard about counterfeiting in Dallas. At that point, Becker also briefly discussed Carlos Marcello. . . ."[71] Becker's demeanor during his interview remains unknown. This man apparently has learned of a contract to assassinate the President, and yet he makes no mention of it, maintains an outward calm that betrays no hint that he may be withholding vital information about the meetings? "He [Becker] advised that on two occasions he has accompanied Roppolo to New Orleans, where they met with one Carlos Marcello. He advised that Roppolo was to obtain the financing for their [oil additive] promotional business from Marcello. *He advised that he knew nothing further about Mar-*

cello" (emphasis added).[72] The Los Angeles field office presumably knows nothing of the McGrath/Hoffa/Beckley and Aleman/Traficante revelations. The interest shown in this meeting by Hoover must make them wonder.

FBI (Los Angeles) SAC sends a report regarding the above interview to Hoover. Shortly after receiving the data, he will issue a directive to Regis Kennedy in New Orleans instructing him to verify Becker's connections with Roppolo, and Roppolo's with Marcello.[73]

11/27/62—TUESDAY: "Becker was briefly mentioned in another Bureau report . . . which again stated that he allegedly made up 'stories' and invented rumors to derive 'possible gain' from such false information."[74] This directly contradicts what Blodgett had said of him at the time, and will say later. It also contradicts what Hoover will learn from New Orleans case officer Regis Kennedy. The Los Angeles Bureau will go to great pains to attempt to discredit Becker, while spending little time trying to verify his information on Roppolo/Marcello.

11/30/62—FRIDAY: Press reports: "A former special agent of the Federal Bureau of Investigation asserted in a radio broadcast last night that he had been dismissed for writing to members of Congress about the bureau's personnel policies. The former agent, William W. Turner . . . filed suit in Federal court in Washington last Oct. 5 for reinstatement. In Washington, the FBI said the Civil Service Commission had twice rejected Mr. Turner's complaints, but declined other comment. The Government has not yet filed its answer to the suit. . . ."[75] Turner, like others, is anticipating Hoover's retirement.

"Three days later . . . another Bureau report on the Billie Sol Estes case made reference to Becker's trip to Dallas in September and his work on the case. The report noted that Becker was apparently associated with various show-business personalities in Las Vegas. Further, a man who had been acquainted with Becker had referred to him as a 'small-time con man.' "[76] Other people the FBI will rely upon to attempt to discredit Becker after the assassination will prove to have Mafia connections. Again, the intense interest in, and effort to defeat, Becker's data begs the question. What has he told Blodgett, and what has Blodgett told the Bureau?

12/62—THIS MONTH: Hoover orders increased surveillance of Judith Campbell.[77]
Oswald subscribes to *The Militant.*[78]

12/5/62—WEDNESDAY: Press: "The Government order
for the deportation of Frank Costello was unanimously upheld yesterday by the United States Court of Appeals. [Deportation of the]
. . . 71-year-old gambler . . . was ordered because after Costello's entry into the United States from Italy in 1895 he was convicted
of two crimes involving moral turpitude, not arising out of a single
scheme of criminal misconduct."[79] Hoover's longtime Mafia contact
appears headed for certain deportation. Undoubtedly he follows
this case. Ironically, Marcello, as a close friend of Costello's, is
doubly interested, for this man's case is nearly analogous to his
own.

12/6/62—THURSDAY: Press: "Attorney   General . . .
Kennedy asked the Subversive Activities Control Board today to
order three men and one woman to register as members of the
Communist party. This brought to 14 the number of persons whose
registration Mr. Kennedy has asked the board to order."[80]

12/11/62—TUESDAY: Estes is ordered to stand trial on fourteen of twenty-nine counts of fraud. The trial is moved from Pecos
to El Paso because a jury could not be obtained in the former.[81]
     Washington, D.C., HUAC subcommittee holds hearings. The
group interrogates members of the Women Strike for Peace organization. Levine, sitting in the gallery, leaps to his feet and launches a
verbal attack upon the subcommittee. "I am a patriotic citizen and
a former FBI Agent. I petition you to end these hearings before you
heap further disgrace upon the American people." He is removed
by Capitol police. "Outside, he [told reporters] he is not a Communist and denounced the hearing as [a smear upon the group.]"[82]

12/12/62—WEDNESDAY: FBI agents testify all day in a
Fort Smith, Arkansas, prosecution of local gamblers. The defendants had been arrested in a crackdown related to off-track betting
in Hot Springs.[83] It is not known whether this group is a part of
Marcello's gambling operation, although Beckley's wire service did
extend to this city.[84]

Press: "An estimated 80 to 250 American college students are preparing to defy the U.S. government ban on travel to Cuba and accept a Fidel Castro offer of an all-expense-paid Christmas vacation there, it was learned here Wednesday."[85] Oswald no doubt follows this story closely.

12/13/62—THURSDAY: Press reports: "The State Department warned . . . that U.S. students who go to Cuba over the Christmas holidays without specially validated passports will face fine and imprisonment. *The State department said it validates passports for citizens to travel to Cuba only when this 'may be . . . in the best interests of the United States, such as newsmen* or businessmen with previously established business interest.' . . . Student passports would not be validated" (emphasis added).[86] Oswald notes that reporters and the like are permitted to travel to Cuba.

Press: ". . . Governor . . . Wallace . . . accused Atty. Gen. . . . Kennedy of using police state methods to obtain tape recordings of one of his prosegregation speeches. 'I am entirely satisfied that J. Edgar Hoover, FBI director, is either unaware of this or inwardly fumes to see the noble role of the FBI thus shamed and debauched by the pugnacious wildling who happens to be the president's brother and hence attorney general.' Wallace pointed out that in approaching [his aide], the FBI agent had asked whether he could simply purchase the tapes or whether he would have to obtain a court order to get them."[87] Note the governor's perception that the FBI, as in Louisiana, is disinterested or unwilling to challenge Southern power structures.

12/17/62—MONDAY: ". . . The Communist Party [USA], as an organization, was convicted . . . and fined $120,000 for failure to register with the Attorney General under the Internal Security Act of 1950."[88]

Beckley court severs di Piazza from further prosecution due to a supposedly critical heart condition.[89] Oddly, he will recover sufficiently during the coming year to become even more closely associated with Marcello. This working relationship will last for the remainder of the decade. In 1967 ". . . Sam di Piazza was a major gambler and bookmaker associated with . . . Marcello. . . ."[90] The line of work is hardly low stress.

Press: "A young graduate student said Monday he expected from

30 to 100 American students to defy a State Department ban and travel to Cuba late this month."[91]

12/18/62—TUESDAY: Today is SOG's biannual reporting deadline for field offices. Accordingly case officers Regis Kennedy (New Orleans) and George Davis and Paul Scranton (Miami) file reports regarding Marcello and Traficante respectively. In addition, the ominously successful efforts to prosecute Beckley et al., are made all the more apparent. Hoover, Tolson, and Evans will again review the information concerning the Marcello contract, only this time in updated, more detailed form. Bear in mind that Hoover is desperately seeking to prevent retirement. Accordingly he is looking for any opportunity that will aid this goal. His top assistants are well aware of this.

Press: "The government . . . followed up its court victory over the Communist Party of the United States by pressing for an early trial of top party leaders, Gus Hall and Benjamin Davis. If an organization is found by the subversive activities control board to be dominated by the worldwide Communist movement, it must register with the Justice Department. *If it fails to register, responsibility to do so reverts first to its officers and then to its members.* Besides these two, the department is seeking to force 14 alleged party members to register and is preparing registration petitions against additional members" (emphasis added).[92]

12/19/62—WEDNESDAY: FAA prepares yet another report on Marcello associate David Ferrie, ultimately providing a copy to the FBI.[93]

Press reports: "The Subversive Activities Control Board . . . ordered two additional persons to register with the attorney general as members of the Communist party in the United States."[94]

12/21/62—FRIDAY: RFK tells a JFK speechwriter that Hoover is vehemently opposed to the commutation of communist Junius Scales's sentence by President Kennedy. "The release of Scales, he told the Attorney General, would make it impossible for the FBI to insist that Communists or ex-Communists name names in the future." Apparently Hoover considered the case precedent, as Scales had always refused to do so.[95]

12/22/62—SATURDAY: Press: "The Canadian government . . . refused to allow a group of American students to use Toronto as the departure point for a Christmas trip to Cuba."[96]

12/24/62—MONDAY: Press: "President Kennedy . . . commuted the sentence of Junius . . . Scales . . . who has served almost 15 months of a six-year term for being a member of the Communist party in violation of the Smith Act. He was tried, convicted and sentenced twice. The first conviction . . . was set aside by the Supreme Court . . . after it ruled that a defendant was entitled to see FBI reports used in his trial. The Smith Act prohibits membership in an organization advocating violent overthrow of the government." Hoover is reported to be furious.[97]

12/26/62—WEDNESDAY: Press: "Bernard L. Boutin, general services administrator, announced . . . selection of a Pennsylvania Avenue site for a new $60-million building to house the Federal Bureau of Investigation."[98]

12/28/62—FRIDAY: FBI SOG Evans sends memo to Belmont regarding Hoover's approval of a plan for Washington, D.C., field office personnel to plant a bug in hotel room and office of lobbyist (and close Bobby Baker associate) Fred Black. ". . . If considered feasible and secure, to install a misur (microphone surveillance) at one or both of these locations."[99] Hoover moves behind the scenes in the Baker case much the same as he had in the Estes case, at once protecting LBJ while continuing to gain incriminating data on him.

Oswald and wife attend a party in Dallas/Fort Worth area given by the local White Russian community (i.e., anti-communist Soviets).[100]

12/31/62—MONDAY: President Kennedy's drive against the Mafia ". . . went on to convict 101 in 1962."[101] Hundreds more are on trial. He is making good on his 10/10/62 threat to destroy the organization.

1/63—THIS MONTH: Based upon Regis Kennedy's biannual report, the overall Mafia Summary Report prepared by SOG lists only one member in New Orleans, Carlos Marcello. In reality it is estimated that there are at least fifty, and another twenty-five in Dallas.[102]

FBI informant Aleman continues meeting with Traficante, reporting the contents of their discussions to Davis and Scranton. "For the next [nine months] . . . Aleman met with [Traficante] frequently to discuss the Teamsters loan. . . . Traficante soon . . . introduce[d] him to . . . Angelo Bruno of Philadelphia. Aleman, like his FBI contacts, . . . played along, hoping the loan would come through. . . . The FBI considered his information valuable and he was pleased to be of service."[103]

New Orleans FBI now has an ongoing relationship with Guy Banister and Cubans within the exile community.

"In January 1963, Bobby [Baker] arranged for Serve-U to purchase the Carousel." This has been done because the resort has cash-flow problems. Lansky/Marcello Las Vegas front man and gambler Edward Levinson is now directly involved with the same resort Lyndon Johnson is frequenting, a resort catering to "immoral activities and hoodlum interests" (see 10/25—10/31/62).[104]

FBI (Las Vegas) ELSUR reveals ". . . in January 1963 . . . $280,000 was skimmed from the Fremont [Levinson's casino], Sands, Flamingo and Horseshoe."[105]

FBI (D.C. field office) ELSUR ". . . eavesdropped on conversations in [Fred] Black's suite at the Carleton Hotel in Washington during 1963."[106]

1/1/63—TUESDAY: Hoover turns sixty-eight. He is now twenty-four months away from compulsory retirement.

"In 1963, Jack Ruby was in dire financial straits. At the start of the year he borrowed more than a thousand dollars from the bank."[107]

1/6/63—SUNDAY: Press reports: "District Attorney Jim Garrison, in office for less than a year, wants to sweep out the trashy and the downright criminal on the street. What will it do to the legitimate business? He now has five strip joints under padlock. Several club owners admit they know of no way to stop him from closing every 'joint' on the street if that is his intention. *Frank Carracci, [sic] who owns three strip clubs* and the famed Court of the Two Sisters restaurant . . . said organizations have canceled convention on top of convention. . . . 'They tell me . . . that all we have to offer now is old buildings, and they want more than that.' "[108] Note that Caracci is a close associate of Marcello.[109] Between June and November 1963 Caracci will act as Marcello liaison to Jack Ruby.[110]

1/13/63—SUNDAY: Press: "The Justice Department is investigating alleged corruption of public officials in 22 states . . . the White House announced today. The disclosures came with the release of Attorney General . . . Kennedy's report to the President on the 1962 activities of the Criminal Division of the Justice Department. . . . The Division . . . increased racketeering prosecutions last year by about 300 percent over 1961 and 700 percent over 1960. Convictions were up by more than 350 percent over 1961 and almost 400 percent over 1960, it said. The FBI investigated 852 cases under new laws prohibiting interstate shipment or transmission of gambling information or equipment. Internal Revenue Service figures indicate a sharp decline in betting 'action,' with gamblers reporting a . . . 20 per cent drop from 1961 and the lowest total since 1952, the first year such reports were required."[111]

1/15/63—TUESDAY: FBI (Chicago) ELSUR AIRTEL to Hoover regarding Giancana aide Chuck English. ". . . He bemoans the fact that the Federal government is closing in on the organization and apparently nothing can be done about it. Makes various and sundry inflammatory remarks about the Kennedy Administration."[112] Note that, like Northeastern Mafia crime families, this anti-Kennedy rhetoric is wild, unfocused. This in marked contrast to the Beckley/Aleman/Marcello contract data. Like other such statements, this one is secretly withheld from the Justice Department and Secret Service by Hoover.

Ruby is now ". . . being pursued for an even greater sum in rent arrears for his club premises."[113]

1/16/63—WEDNESDAY: D.C. press reports on preliminary plans for the new FBI building: "The FBI doesn't want to lease ground-floor commercial space to private shops and cafés in its proposed 60-million-dollar building. The new FBI building, to be built on the Avenue between 9th and 10th Sts. NW, across from the Justice Department. . . . Justice and the FBI do not oppose the idea of an arcaded, open-space first level. But, . . . they think the space should be used for something like an FBI museum. . . ."[114]

1/17/63—THURSDAY: FBI ELSUR AIRTEL to Hoover regarding Mafia figure Raymond Patriarca. "Raymond states that things are not too good as long as Attorney General Kennedy is in Washington, D.C."[115] Again, Hoover withholds this information from the proper agencies.

1/19/63—SATURDAY: Press: "Attorney General . . . Kennedy will make a luncheon address Tuesday in New York at a convocation of the Fund for the Republic, whose vice president has sharply criticized FBI Director J. Edgar Hoover. In a speech last summer the Fund official, W. H. Ferry, said Hoover had distorted out of all proportions the menace of communism in the United States. Kennedy came to Hoover's defense, saying Ferry's remarks were inaccurate. *The Attorney General's office said Kennedy didn't realize Ferry was an officer of the Fund when he accepted the speaking engagement.* Kennedy's subject will be 'The Bill of Rights and the Cold War' " (emphasis added).[116] That RFK would not be aware of the connection, given the political uproar of the previous summer over Ferry's remarks and the Attorney General's comments before the same organization at that time, is absurd. Without a doubt, Hoover is highly offended.

1/20/63—SUNDAY: Press reports: "Mr. Kennedy's popularity at the end of his second year is above that recorded for both . . . Eisenhower and . . . Truman at a comparable point in their first terms."[117] Kennedy had scored an approval rating of 76 percent. Another article states: "In his first two years in office, President Kennedy has spent 215 days away from Washington. . . . In his first two years in office . . . Eisenhower spent 196 days away from the Capital City. . . . The figures . . . included the times both Presidents took off for weekends of rest at their nearby retreats. With Mr. Kennedy it has been Palm Beach, Fla.; Hyannis Port, Mass.; Newport, R.I.; and Glen Ora, a leased estate near Middleburg."[118] Statistical analysis such as this hardly supports rightists of Hoover's ilk in their conclusion that JFK is a "detached," or lesser, leader than conservatives of his day.

1/21/63—MONDAY: Press: "NEW ORLEANS . . . Judge Malcolm V. O'Hara denied today that he had ever been influenced by racketeers or anyone else to quit approving money for vice investigations in the French Quarter. O'Hara testified in the opening-day trial of District Attorney Jim Garrison. . . . The charge revolves around Garrison's statement that a crackdown by the judges against his vice-investigating fund raised 'interesting questions about possible racketeering influences on our eight vacation-minded judges.' . . . Reports circulated that impeachment proceedings may be started if he is convicted."[119]

The Gilbert Beckley trial continues, minus di Piazza, Brouphy, Bagneris, and Perez.[120]

1/26/63—SATURDAY: FBI (New Orleans). A case agent notes in Banister's file that the ex-SAC has supplied information to the Bureau concerning ". . . Gerard F. Tujague, owner of Gerard F. Tujague, Inc. Forwarding Co. . . . a member and officer (vice president) of Friends of Democratic Cuba a Cuban exile group (FDC) in New Orleans." Recall that this is the same group that attempted to purchase trucks for the Bay of Pigs invasion using Oswald's name in early 1961, a group Banister is closely aligned with. ". . . Tujague . . . had employed Oswald as a messenger from November 1955 to January 1956. . . ."[121] It is not known whether Oswald, then a minor with no driver's license, supplied his birth certificate to Tujague in order to obtain employment.

1/27/63—SUNDAY: Oswald fills out an order form for a pistol (SW.38, 2-inch barrel) from a West Coast company, Sea Port Traders, Inc. For some reason, probably a lack of funds, he waits to place the order until 3/12/63.[122]

Press: "The President's Advisory Council on Pennsylvania Ave. will 'blow its top' if the new FBI headquarters is designed as a 'huge monolithic building,' the chairman of the group said yesterday. . . . The Council has been assured by the General Services Administration that the new FBI quarters . . . would be 'an open, free building and not a limestone or granite monolith.' "[123] The personalities of Hoover and JFK are clearly at work here. Not surprisingly, the building finally created will be, under Hoover's guidance, a "granite monolith."

1/28/63—MONDAY: Ex-agent Levine sends a letter to the House Committee on Appropriations. "In his letter, Mr. Levine, a former special agent, criticizes the . . . procedures of the FBI."[124]

1/29/63—TUESDAY: ". . . Oswald finished making his repayment of the State Department loan that brought him back to the United States."[125]

Dallas News and *Texas Observer* publish articles examining LBJ's television and cable interests. In conjunction with this, "Congressman . . . Gross, of Iowa, had been raising persistent and pointed questions about the propriety, the ethics and the legality of Johnson's Radio-TV operations. . . ."

1/31/63—THURSDAY: "FBI La Cosa Nostra Summary . . ." prepared, reviewed, and sent to Hoover by Evans, states "Permission is being sought for retaliation against Federal . . . politicians who expose La Cosa Nostra."[126] Evans is here referring to permission from the mob's National Commission.

Senator Everett Dirksen reintroduces legislation (S.603) that will provide for replacement of Hoover. He also reinserts in the *Congressional Record* the July article "Who Will Fill Hoover's Shoes?" The bill is again referred to committee by Johnson.[127]

2/63—THIS MONTH: Marina Oswald, like many emigres, apparently becomes disillusioned with life in the U.S. "Marina actually wrote to the Soviet Embassy asking for assistance to return to Russia."[128] This could also be part of an Oswald plan to return her and the child temporarily, make his way to Cuba, and then send for them, via direct flight to Havana from Moscow (i.e., Aeroflot).

FBI (New Orleans), via ELSUR ". . . did attempt to institute electronic surveillance [on Marcello] during the period of 1963 and 1964. Two unsuccessful attempts were made to effect such surveillance, failures attributable in all likelihood to the security system employed by Marcello at the various locations from which he operated."[129] The transparency, even absurdity, of this excuse is obvious, especially so in light of Regis Kennedy's status as Marcello case officer. This is not to say, however, that attempts to do the same with Marcello associates also failed. Plainly they had succeeded regarding the Beckley group as early as 5/3/62. And they will shortly obtain a live informant, a man who had worked in a Marcello restaurant during 1962. The Bureau may also have had a tap on Nofio Pecora's phone.[130]

Baker begins a series of "deals" that cause great concern and confusion among Senate Democratic leaders.[131]

2/1/63—FRIDAY: *FBI Law Enforcement Bulletin* is released. Hoover's message deals with recruitment for the Bureau, which is faltering. He speaks of the need for quality personnel. "The probability of their attainment is nil in an atmosphere of . . . predatory political interference, or entrenched corruption." Hoover has publicly stated that the Kennedys have not interfered with him or the Bureau. Yet one is left with the impression that the Director is insinuating just the opposite here. RFK, in agreeing to speak before the Fund for the Republic, is implicitly endorsing the remarks of arch Hoover foe W. H. Ferry. The efforts of ex-agents Levine and Turner have hardly been discouraged by the war of rhetoric between both Kennedys and the Director.

Hoover, Tolson, John P. Mohr, and the Attorney General's assistant Salvatore A. Andretta appear before the House Appropriations committee for annual testimony. Hoover testifies on a variety of subjects, committing perjury on at least two occasions. Excerpts from these proceedings are as follows:

Objectives. Communist Party—USA. "It devolves upon the FBI to furnish the Department with the data to support the prosecutorial moves."

Criminal operations. "[With regard to the] . . . Drive against organized crime . . . we must make every effort to be aware on a current basis of the many and varied activities of the criminal element."

Fugitive Felon Act. "The amendment extended our jurisdiction to cover all state felonies."

Major criminal violations and special type investigations. "The Billie Sol Estes investigation . . . extended to 46 of our 55 field divisions and a peak of 452 special agents participated."

General Statement—Major Factors Affecting Needs. "The Government's drive on organized crime which was accelerated in January of 1961 requires and will continue to require a broad coverage of the criminal element." Mr. Rooney: "Will you tell us how many cases the FBI has handled as a result of this new legislation enacted since the submission of the 1963 budget request?" Mr. Hoover: "6843 cases."

Equipment. Mr. Hoover: "We have need for special equipment requiring an additional $444,106." . . . Technical investigative equipment for use in field . . . $182,306.

Assistance of Confidential Informants. Mr. Hoover: "In addition to aiding us in many of our accomplishments, information made available by our confidential informants greatly assisted other law-enforcement agencies in their fight against crime. *Information received from our informants concerning matters within the investigative jurisdiction of . . . other Federal law enforcement agencies were promptly relayed to those agencies* and these resulted in 2371 arrests . . ." (emphasis added).[132]

Hoover unquestionably perjures himself here, having withheld all information regarding the Aleman/Marcello contract, as well as other illegal ELSUR product, from the Secret Service. His omission of critical data such as this is undoubtedly a violation of statutory duty. The relevant statute governing this crime is as follows:

18 USCA 1621 Perjury. Whoever having taken an oath before a competent . . . [hearing] in which a law of the United States authorizes an oath to be administered, that he will testify . . . that any written testimony [or] declaration . . . by him subscribed, is true, *willfully and contrary to such oath states or subscribes any material matter which he does not believe to be true is guilty of perjury* and shall . . . be fined not more than $2,000 or imprisoned not more than five years, or both [emphasis added].

Hoover's testimony continues:

Dissemination of Criminal Information. Mr. Hoover: "The tremendous volume of criminal information which the FBI disseminates to Federal . . . sources having an interest in it includes, of course, far more than just items from confidential informants. Through our regular investigative activity we develop a vast amount of data of interest to other agencies. This is real cooperation in law enforcement. . . ."

Field Operations. "The strategic location of our field offices and resident agencies enables the FBI to provide prompt and efficient attention to all investigations. . . ."

Cuba. "Our work in this area is . . . complicated by the thousands of Cuban refugees in this country, as well as the activities of both pro- and anti-Castro groups and organizations."

Criminal and Civil Investigative Operations. Mr. Hoover: ". . . Our responsibilities in connection with the Attorney General's drive against organized crime, has [*sic*] increased materially during the past few years."

Organized Crime. "At the present time we are conducting approximately 3000 investigations into the activities of organized crime, including intensified investigation on 80 of the most notorious racketeers and hoodlums in the country. *The drive against organized crime has been marked by close cooperation and the exchange of information between law-enforcement agencies at all levels*" (emphasis added).[133]

Hoover again perjures himself. He then launches into a lengthy exchange with committee members in which he denounces ex-agent Levine personally, openly suggesting the former is a communist.

Proposed New Building. Mr. Hoover: "They have just concluded a survey of the space now occupied by the Bureau in Washington. We are in six different locations here. The next step is for GSA to let the contract for the architects to design the building."[134]

Can a man so actively involved with the initial phase of such a project possibly be thinking of retirement? The massive undertaking will not be completed until the early 1970s, Hoover closely monitoring every aspect.

2/2/63—SATURDAY: American Bar Foundation holds seventh annual dinner in New Orleans. The group passes a resolution regarding Hoover, commending him with a citation and honorary membership in the ABA. ". . . You epitomize the highest type of service that we can expect of anyone in government."[135]

2/5/63—TUESDAY: Press: "NEW ORLEANS . . . The defense and prosecution today presented final arguments in the defamation trial of . . . vice-busting district attorney. . . . [Jim Garrison]."[136]

Washington Evening Star runs an article on Hoover: "Money Making G-Men." "So among all the other reasons for being appreciative of Mr. Hoover's operatives, one must also not forget their spectacular solvency."

2/6/63—WEDNESDAY: Press: "A specially appointed court today convicted crusading District Attorney Jim Garrison of deliberately besmirching eight judges in his drive to end vice and close striptease joints on naughty Bourbon Street. 'I intend to continue my investigation of organized crime without any letup,' Garrison said after the verdict."[137]

2/9/63—SATURDAY: Press: "Thomas L. Fallon, 71, an auditor in the Office of Alien Property of the Department of Justice who was kept on after the compulsory retirement age because of his knowledge and experience died Thursday . . . following major surgery."[138] Contrast this with Hoover's position.

New Orleans press runs a story on Garrison and the Mafia. Apparently A.G. Kennedy reads the article, as well as one appearing on 2/11/63. "When it comes to favoritism, judges in this city have one unique power. There is no procedure for releasing people on bond after they are arrested and before they appear in court. But judges . . . have power to order anyone released 'on parole' in the interim. The records of the 'paroles' made by some of the judges show that they have acted at the request of know [sic] leaders of organized vice. . . . One man was well known here as a partner of *Frank Costello* . . ." (emphasis added).[139]

2/11/63—MONDAY: A second article in the New Orleans press names Marcello personally. "Graft and corruption have become deeply rooted in this city. They are an accepted part of life. . . . The tie between crime and politics comes to the surface with monotonous regularity, but nobody seems to care very much about it. . . . The Kefauver committee spotlighted the political power organized crime has here. Two years after that, in 1954, a special citizens' investigating committee pointed out widespread graft in the Police Department. . . . The only major figure to go to jail was the committee's top investigator Aaron Kohn. Kohn, a former FBI agent, was convicted of contempt for refusing to reveal his sources of information. *Always hanging over the scene is Carlos Marcello, one of the nation's biggest racketeers. Aaron Kohn, managing director of the crime commission, has said Marcello is the real boss of rackets here. . . . the Frank Costello-Phil Kastel group . . . brought big-time gambling here.* Kohn . . . said in an interview last week, 'Many people here never understood what it meant to be governed properly. They had grown up under this kind of government and thought it had to be that way' " (emphasis added).[140] Note the disclosure that it was Hoover confidant Frank Costello who provided original opportunity to Marcello.

2/13/63—WEDNESDAY: The Oswalds again dine with the de Mohrenschildts. Cuba is probably discussed once more in light of JFK's recent Miami address promising a free Havana.[141]

Press reports: "A man came calling on FBI Director J. Edgar Hoover . . . drove right up the front steps of the Justice Department Building, crawled under his car and threw the whole city into a bomb scare. . . . Wise . . . told police he had evidence enough to 'impeach President Kennedy'. . . . Wise told police he had come to see the only man he trusted—Hoover. 'I won't come out, . . . I'll die right here. I'll never leave here alive.' [He] . . . said he had evidence on 'Government operations and on rackets' that he wanted to give to Hoover. . . . He kept insisting, 'Hoover knows what I'm here for.' "[142] The incident occurs during Hoover and Tolson's lunch hour, but the Director is surely informed. Both are probably embarrassed by the man's zeal. He is soon arrested and placed in a local mental ward.

Press reports: "The Navy will offer . . . [Admiral] Rickover an opportunity to stay in service after retirement next year. . . . Anticipating this, several powerful members of Congress have started pressing for his retention on duty, possibly by special law."[143]

2/15/63—FRIDAY: ". . . In an apparent response to Attorney General Kennedy's request for continuing action against Mar-

cello, . . . Hoover directed the New Orleans FBI office to intensify
its coverage of Marcello and his organization. He ordered that a
'special effort' be made to upgrade the level of the investigation
. . . and suggested increased use of informants as well as the possible initiation of electronic surveillance."[144] Of course, Hoover well
knows that, at least officially, the agent has developed almost nothing on Marcello since his assignment began in the 1950s. The Attorney General's frustration is obvious. He has been following both the
Garrison criminal defamation trial and the slowly moving Beckley
case, as well as the recent exposé on the Marcello organization. And
in all this, he sees Marcello still free, in control of his territory.
Hoover, who is now simply awaiting the execution of the contract,
has no incentive to move against the Mafia leader or his organization in any decisive manner.

Press: "PARIS . . . Police said today they had foiled a plot apparently organized by military officers to kill President Charles de
Gaulle by shooting him from a rooftop with a rifle equipped with
telescopic sights. At least five persons and possibly seven were arrested in the plot. . . . De Gaulle wore his uniform and showed no
trace of nervousness, although he was said to have known about the
plot."[145]

2/16/63—SATURDAY: *The Nation* publishes an editorial on
Hoover entitled "The Next Mr. Hoover." "One of the Nation's
objections to Mr. Hoover is that he has allowed and encouraged his
elevation to the status of a national deity, so that he speaks, especially to American youth, with an authority second only to that of
the President. . . . . . . The head of the FBI should not have
such a high place in the American educational system. . . . It will
be a relief when we have a director . . . who . . . does not see
himself in the role of mentor of a national and international morality."

D.C. press reports: "Two private detectives . . . pleaded innocent yesterday to charges that they were involved in the 'bugging' of
a San Francisco attorney's Mayflower Hotel suite [in Washington,
D.C.]. . . . Judge . . . McGuire . . . accepted the pleas from
John J. Frank, an attorney and *former FBI agent* . . ." (emphasis
added).[146]

2/17/63—SUNDAY: Marina Oswald writes letter to Soviet embassy. "I beg your assistance to help me return to Homeland in the USSR."[147]

Hoover essay appears in the *Sunday Visitor,* entitled, "The Indispensable Supports." "Above all, *note these significant statements in the final words of advice which George Washington gave the people whom he had served so faithfully for 45 years: 'Of all the dispositions and habits which lead to political prosperity, religion and morality are indispensable supports. In vain would that man claim the tributes of patriotism, who should labor to subvert these great pillars of human happiness, these firmest props of the duties of men and citizens. . . .' It is . . . easy to understand why the proponents of absolute materialism . . . 'labor to subvert these great pillars of human happiness, these firmest props* of the duties of men and citizens.'—religion and morality. ADULATION OF THE MATERIAL. *Today subtle forces seek to secularize whole bodies of citizens—to substitute adulation of the material for worship of the spiritual. The men promoting such forces are hopeful that time is on their side. . . .* They know that the human creature who is without . . . moral scruples . . . can, with great ease be led into the arid desert of communism. . . . communism . . . outlaws traditional morality. It teaches that existing moral codes . . . are false. Absolute principles of right and wrong are thrown into the discard. *Unfortunately, many generous-minded persons have drifted from their religious moorings and are blind to the moral guideposts by which they once found the way. . . .* They lean toward the exaltation of man—and too many of them seem unaware of the fact that it is but a short step to man's degradation in the name of his glorification. *Our Nation . . . has . . . never before . . . faced an enemy which sought to attack it by secularizing its citizens in order to stultify their will to stand against encroaching communism. . . . It is visible in instance after instance of the sellout of honor and integrity to a vicious, totalitarian enemy.* Today, as then, religion and morality are our stoutest weapons against the enemy."[148]

2/20/63—WEDNESDAY: Press reports: "White House police have taken over responsibility for guarding the entire Executive Office Building previously policed with the assistance of General Services Administration guards. Congressional action last year increased the White House force from 170 to a 250 legal limit."[149]

2/21/63—THURSDAY: The Freedoms Foundation, based in *Valley Forge,* awards Hoover an "honor medal for public address," recognizing his efforts at promoting the "American way of life" during 1962.[150]

2/22/63—FRIDAY: Today is Washington's birthday, a federal holiday. Both Hoover and RFK work this day, Hoover dictating a memo to RFK. "After observing your car in the Department garage, I would like to thank you for coming to work on February 22nd; a national holiday. . . . . . . The spirit you demonstrated —the spirit of *Valley Forge* . . . will, we hope spread through the entire Department of Justice. Keep up the good work" (emphasis added).[151] Note Hoover's obvious reference to Valley Forge. More importantly, notice the demeanor projected by his words. He speaks down to the Attorney General, confident in the knowledge that President Kennedy will be assassinated, thereby bringing an end to the former's tenure. Hoover projects with the ease of a man now holding all the cards. The Attorney General must be mystified by this change in attitude.

The Oswalds attend another de Mohrenschildt party where they meet Ruth Paine. She has been described as "strong, tall, thin, attractive, not a glamorous dresser." She maintains an amicable separation from her husband. Somewhat older than Marina, they soon become close friends.[152]

2/63:   After receiving ". . . an invitation to the Bosch inauguration [in the Dominican Republic] . . . [Baker] flew down to the ceremony in February with Johnson. . . ."[153] Around this same time, Baker apparently meets with Mafia functionary Sigelbaum in Miami, Florida, at the International Hotel.[154] The Dominican trip will be the subject of intense inquiry during the Senate's 1964 Baker hearings. Levinson will be asked whether he accompanied Baker and LBJ.

2/28/63—THURSDAY: Press: "PARIS . . . A band of nine right-wing terrorists whose reported aim was to kill Premier Georges Pompidou has been rounded up by the police. According to informed sources the Government is now in possession of documents indicating that the terrorist movement has its back against the wall and is now preparing a last desperate campaign. Consequently guards have been reinforced around key buildings and around members of the Government. The attack was to take place on a Sunday when Mr. Pompidou was coming out of church. . . ."[155]

Press reports: "Dist. Atty. Jim Garrison was fined $1,000 . . . for defaming the eight New Orleans criminal district judges in a quarrel over a vice investigation."[156]

3/63—THIS MONTH: Hoover and RFK clash head-on over an article the Director intended to publish in *Reader's Digest*. Hoover had planned to take credit for successes in the war on the Mafia, stating he had known about it for some time. RFK forces him to withdraw the false claims (in actuality, less false than the A.G. realizes) and Hoover decides against publishing the article until later in the year. He is, however, reported to be furious.[157]

A New Orleans FBI informant named Eugene De Lapparra overhears three individuals in a Marcello-controlled restaurant talking of the impending contract. "Three men—one reportedly a close associate of Vincent Marcello and another a certain 'professor' of unknown name—were talking of assassinating President Kennedy. As the three were looking at an advertisement . . . for a foreign-made rifle that sold for $12.98, Marcello's friend observed, 'This would be a nice rifle to buy to get the President. . . .' He then went on to tell his friends that there was 'a price on the President's head . . .' adding that 'somebody will get Kennedy when he comes South.' "[158] Marcello's associate David Ferrie is known locally as "the professor," in fact, representing himself as a Ph.D. in psychology.[159] De Lappara apparently flees New Orleans, reporting this information in September to the *Philadelphia* field office.[160] That office presumably sends an AIRTEL detailing the threat to Hoover at that time. There will be some suggestion that they withheld the report from SOG until after the assassination. Considering the subject matter and its specificity, such an assertion seems implausible. At any rate, it will not be news to Hoover.

"In March the Internal Revenue Service was after [Ruby] for nearly twenty-one thousand dollars in unpaid taxes."[161] A sum such as this in 1963 is obviously beyond the means of a man running two sleazy, marginally profitable strip clubs.

3/1/63—FRIDAY: "Release of John A. McCone statement . . . February 19 in which CIA Chief testified that at least one thousand revolutionaries had now gone to Cuba for training. . . ."[162] Castro is reportedly 100 percent behind them. Oswald reads this article, as he probably read all such press reports on this subject. This day ". . . Oswald laid out $3.82 on a thirty-nine-week subscription to *Time.*"[163]

3/3/63—SUNDAY: Ruth Paine sends her first letter to Oswald's wife, asking if she can come visit. Marina promptly approves.[164] The same day the "Oswalds move a block north and half a block west to 214 West Neely Street, the top floor of a rickety wooden two-story duplex."[165]

3/4/63—MONDAY: *Newsweek* publishes an article commending Hoover, entitled "The Faith of the FBI." "As long as Hoover or the Hoover tradition is on guard, Americans need not fear the perils of a police state."

3/5/63—TUESDAY: Cuba's Foreign Minister releases a letter to the U.N. complaining that the U.S., Congress, President Kennedy, and the Cuban exiles have engaged in hostile actions and statements. He claims Guantanamo base is a "den of spies, saboteurs and counterrevolutionaries."[166]
    Press reports: "The Castro regime . . . issued formal denunciations . . . protesting alleged aggressive acts of U.S. warships and Marines. Marine guards . . . were accused of throwing stones and hurling insults at Cuban sentries. . . . U.S. destroyers were accused of three acts of 'harassment' against Cuban fishing boats."[167]

3/6/63—WEDNESDAY: Press reports: "Cuba's leaders are predicting that all Latin America will fall under the Red banner of communism before long. As Prime Minister Fidel Castro's newspaper *Revolución* put it: 'The situation . . . is not for sitting to ruminate brilliant concepts, but to make revolutions.' He also asked his admirers to 'create subjective conditions' which would trigger the upheavals in Latin America."[168]

3/8/63—FRIDAY: The Soviet embassy (Washington, D.C.) writes a letter to Marina. "In reply to your letter we inform you that for purposes of examining your request concerning your return to the homeland it is necessary for you to [detailed requirements stated]. . . . Time of processing requires 5 to 6 months."[169] FBI very likely reads all correspondence to and from the Soviet embassy involving American citizens and their dependents.

3/9/63—SATURDAY: Press reports D.C. group's musical parody of LBJ's increasingly obvious situation. "Oh, bury me not on the New Frontier where you seldom hear any Texas cheer; gimmie back my spread on the Senate floor, lemme wrangle votes as I did before."[170]

3/10/63—SUNDAY: Press reports: "Scores of Soviet merchant ships have been 'buzzed' by U.S. Air Force planes and shadowed by ships of the U.S. Navy, Radio Moscow said. . . ."[171]

3/11/63—MONDAY: "Agent . . . [James] Hosty of the Dallas FBI calls at 602–604 Elsbeth to interview Marina Oswald. Finding that the Oswalds have moved . . . he takes no further action at the time beyond ascertaining [erroneously] from Mrs. Tobias [presumably the landlady] that Oswald was drinking and beating his wife."[172] Oswald rarely, if ever, drank.[173] Hosty closes his file. At this point the FBI may well be under the impression that the marriage is on the rocks, with Marina seeking to return to the Soviet Union.

Press reports: ". . . Estes went on trial in Federal Court today. . . . His lawyer . . . Cofer, moved immediately to postpone the trial, or transfer it to San Antonio."[174]

3/12/63—TUESDAY: Press: "Secretary of State Dean Rusk said . . . the continued presence of Soviet forces in Cuba leaves open possibilities that a 'highly dangerous' situation could still arise. . . . No U.S. commitment has been made to the Russians against an invasion."[175]

". . . Oswald orders 6.5mm Mannlicher-Carcano rifle from mail-order firm in Chicago, sending money order in name of A. Hidell for $21.45. . . . He has it shipped to Hidell at Dallas box 2915." In using the name Hidell, Oswald inadvertently triggers Army Intelligence.[176] Hidell had been the nickname of a fellow Marine. Prior to the assassination then, at least Military Intelligence is aware that Oswald has obtained a weapon, cheap though it is. It is very possible that the FBI is made aware of this development. As an ex-serviceman and defector, Oswald is undoubtedly of interest to the intelligence community. As stated, he has previously

come to the personal attention of Hoover. The Director is himself a
retired Army lieutenant colonel. Army Intelligence will destroy its
file on Oswald, providing no insight in this area.[177] The simple reality, however, is that his purchase of the weapon is insignificant.
Tens of thousands of Americans are doing the same thing. The rifle
he purchased is basically junk. Most such items are in fact purchased as World War II souvenirs. Oswald will never be shown to
have even fired the weapon.[178] The Carcano has a defective, or
worn-out, firing pin.[179] In all likelihood he realizes this, given his
basic training in weaponry. Apparently just days before placing this
order, he also orders ". . . a '.38 S and W Special two-inch Commando . . .' " pistol. "The invoice was prepared on March 13,
1963, the revolver was actually shipped on March 20. . . ."[180] This
purchase is also basically junk, having a worn-out barrel that has
been shortened and rebored.[181] The pictures he poses for shortly
after obtaining the firearms, while holding copies of the *Militant*
and *Worker,* will betray his purpose. In effect Oswald is assembling
his credentials for the role of Cuban revolutionary.[182]

3/13/63—WEDNESDAY: Press reports: "Congressional Republican leaders urged President Kennedy . . . to take the lead in
organizing a solid phalanx of Latin American nations against the
export of communism from Cuba. The OAS group urged tighter
control in travel across national borders, a ban on all travel to and
from Cuba. . . ."[183]

3/14/63—THURSDAY: Press: "An 'alliance for violence' is
brewing in Fidel Castro's Cuba to send 'agents trained in sabotage,
espionage and revolutionary techniques throughout Latin America,'
a House subcommittee reported. . . . . . . *Mexico 'remains a
neutral ground' . . . for Castro Communist traffic and travel in the
Americas.' . . .* Rep. . . . Cramer . . . went into that subject
with a charge that *the Cuban embassy in Mexico 'is the open door
through which Communist subversives throughout the Americas'
enter Cuba* and return home 'for purposes of subversion and sabotage. . . . *Within a short four-month period in 1962, 73 United
States citizens—two of whom are known to have Communist back-
grounds—took the established route of the Communist subversive
and entered Cuba through the Cuban embassy in Mexico.' Cramer
criticized the Justice and State Departments* for not prosecuting

American citizens who . . . are violating the law in this manner and *for 'not closing this open door to Cuba and Communism.' The process, he said, consists of issuing visas which do not become part of the traveler's passport, so that he can go to Cuba and come back by way of Mexico with no record of the trip to be found"* (emphasis added).[184] The intent of Oswald's coming trip to Mexico City and the Cuban embassy, considered in light of the above, becomes obvious. Short of an instruction booklet from the State Department, this article provides the next-best thing.

3/15/63—FRIDAY: Press reports numerous stories regarding Cuba this day: "An 85-year-old veteran of Teddy Roosevelt's charge up San Juan Hill arrived from Cuba . . . and said 'another American invasion of Cuba is the only solution to Castro.' The . . . veteran . . . arrived on a special American Red Cross flight from Havana. . . ."[185]

"The Castro regime charged . . . two U.S. warships sailed into Cuban territorial waters on a 'spy mission' and implied they were visible on the horizon from Havana."[186]

"The administration kept tight secrecy on Cuban developments . . . as the deadline neared on Moscow's promise to withdraw several thousand Soviet troops."[187]

"President Kennedy . . . ordered the selective service deferment of all fathers. . . . The Senate . . . approved a four-year extension of the military draft law. . . . The House had passed the bill earlier this week."[188]

"The Defense Department said . . . it is investigating a Cuban exile leader's report that Soviet combat troops are being used to quell internal Cuban uprisings. The administration has said it would not tolerate a Hungarian-type Soviet action in Cuba."[189] The impression is being conveyed that the U.S. may be preparing for another invasion of Cuba once the Soviet presence is eliminated. Part of Cuba's appeal for Oswald may be its imminent ideological break with the Soviets. As stated previously, he had left Russia out of dissatisfaction with work and living conditions. But it was the failure of the Soviet system to adhere to Marxist theory that created the low quality of life for the worker.

Press: *"FBI Director J. Edgar Hoover has 'no intention whatever' to resign after nearly 40 years as the nation's top law-enforcement officer. Hoover assured Rep. Carl Elliot, D-Ala., of his plans to stay on the job* at a meeting requested by the congressman because he was alarmed about reports the FBI chief planned to retire. *Hoover told Elliot that there has been no political interference by the Kennedy administration.* 'There has never been any political interference, or misuse of the bureau, by any administration since I came here in 1924. . . . There is none now. *I plan to stay and get the job done*' " (emphasis added).[190] Hoover is now publicly stating, for the record, that he will not allow himself to be retired. Given that he can technically be fired by either Kennedy, will at any rate be retired by operation of Federal statute on 1/1/65, cannot look to the Senate for legislative help, and has failed at attempts to blackmail the President, one can only assume that he is now operating under the assumption that with the assassination of President Kennedy he will in fact be able to "stay and get the job done." Both Kennedys are undoubtedly mystified and antagonized by Hoover's pronouncement—bewildered because of their ignorance of ELSUR and the Marcello contract, angered because of the Director's denial of the obvious.

"MEXICO CITY . . . Moralia University students were organized into Castro-type militias by leftist leaders, including one trained in Cuba, for Friday's clashes with federal troops which left one dead and 12 wounded. . . ."[191]

3/17/63—SUNDAY: Press continues its Cuban-related focus: ". . . The Navy's newest amphibious assault ship was launched and christened Saturday at the naval shipyard. . . ."[192]

"Costa Rican Foreign Minister Daniel Oduber said Saturday the Alliance for Progress cannot prosper in an America infected by Cuba-sponsored Communist subversion. Mr. Kennedy's Central American colleagues have made clear they want action, not words. . . . Oduber . . . said nothing can be done about this situation as long as Mexico continues to serve as a gateway for Fidel Castro's Communist Cuba *(Cubana Airlines maintains two flights weekly to and from Mexico City)*" (emphasis added).[193]

"Sen. . . . Ellander, D.-La., cautioned Saturday against a United States invasion of Cuba."[194]

"The Cuban foreign relations ministry has demanded that the Uruguayan embassy disarm asylumed refugees who threatened militiamen in a shooting incident Thursday."[195]

". . . Russians said . . . a Soviet ship in the Caribbean was pursued by an American . . . ship and . . . buzzed several times by low-flying . . . planes."[196]

3/18/63—MONDAY: "At a press conference in Washington, representatives of Alpha 66 and the Second National Front of the Escambray boast that their 'commando groups' in two high-speed boats armed with machine guns and cannon . . . had . . . penetrated the north-coast Cuban port of Isabela de Sagua and shot up a Soviet army camp and a freighter, the *Lwow*."[197] This event could well trigger Oswald's decision to attempt to go to Cuba, explaining his forthcoming letter to Marina.

Press: "Castro said [Saturday night] 'The Yankees cannot win a single battle against us.' "[198]

3/20/63—WEDNESDAY: Press reports: ". . . The presidents of Panama, Nicaragua, Guatemala, Costa Rica, El Salvador and Honduras summoned a meeting of interior ministers for early April to 'put into immediate effect measures to restrict the movement of their nationals to and from Cuba. . . .' "[199]

Press: "The Federal Government today rested its case against . . . Estes."[200]

Press: "Nearly 200 Americans have visited Cuba illegally in the last two years, U.S. sources said Wednesday. . . . Most of the violators have gone by way of Mexico, where they can catch a Cubana Airlines flight to Cuba."[201]

". . . Klein's [Sporting Goods in Chicago] . . . shipped [Oswald's rifle] . . . on March 20, 1963."[202]

3/21/63—THURSDAY: *Congressional Record* insertion of Hoover's 2/17/63 essay, "The Indispensable Supports."[203] Unrelated but also this day, apparently with the acquiescence of JFK and Bureau of Prisons Director Bennett, Alcatraz, the infamous island prison off California, is permanently closed. In Hoover's mind this may be yet another indication of the administration's attitude toward the growing problem of crime.

3/23/63—SATURDAY: Press reports comments of a Miami, Florida, Cuban exile leader. " 'We are going to attack again and again and again.' This was announced Friday by a leader of action

groups that made hit and run forays against . . . northern Cuba
. . . Sunday night."[204]

3/24/63—SUNDAY: Press: "There are frequent power failures in Cuba because of sabotage, an underground report said today."[205] In another article, "Three bands of anti-Castro rebels were
wiped out Friday by government troops . . . the Cuban revolutionary government announced. . . ."[206]

3/25/63—MONDAY: Press: "Dr. Carlos Marquez Sterling, a
former candidate for president of Cuba, Sunday conditionally accepted the provisional presidency of an anti-Castro government reportedly constituted inside Cuba. '. . . For when we have rescued
Cuba, which will be a matter of a few months. . . .' "[207]
". . . Hosty applied for the reopening of the Oswald case. On
March 25 his request was granted."[208] This may be due to Oswald's
acquisition of weapons, his subscriptions to *The Worker* and *The
Militant,* his joining the FPCC, or all of the above.

3/26/63—TUESDAY: Press: "Ex-President . . . Urrutia of
Cuba declared Monday 90 percent of Cubans sullenly resent . . .
Castro for turning their island into . . . a Soviet puppet state. Despite widespread resentment, Urrutia said, there is no other Cuban
capable of taking over the reins with any popular backing. If anything happens to Castro, there will be trouble, he added."[209]
Press: ". . . On the night of March 26, a raiding party of Commando L, a schismatic offshoot of Alpha 66, shot up the Soviet
freighter *Baku* in the Cuban port of Caibarien."[210]
D.C. Press reports: ". . . Johnson refused to say tonight whether
he would seek renomination with President Kennedy next year.
Reminded that President Kennedy has strongly indicated he would
be a candidate for reelection and that he would be happy to have
Mr. Johnson run with him, the Vice-President replied that the decision 'will depend upon the delegates, who have not yet been selected.' "[211] Clearly LBJ sees the writing on the wall. Word has been
circulating for months that he will be dumped, the Estes and Baker
scandals threatening to consume him. It is common knowledge in
Washington that he and the Kennedys have nothing but contempt
for each other. Hoover, as well as Marcello, is mindful of this reality.

3/28/63—THURSDAY: Press: "A Republican publication said . . . President Kennedy has swung support to a Texas liberal faction and touched off a fight among state party Democrats that could knock Vice President . . . Johnson off the 1964 ticket. '. . . By rekindling the factional feud in Texas, the Kennedys are digging his political grave.' "[212]

Press: "Eleven deported missionaries . . . arrived from Cuba Wednesday. . . . The plane returned with 74 passengers, including the missionaries, one Red Cross worker. . . ."[213]

Castro threatens to "arm Cuba with long-range bombers and convoy Cuban shipping" if the U.S. doesn't stop raids by the exiles.[214]

Press reports: ". . . Estes was convicted today of mail fraud involving . . . mortgage deals involving $24,000,000."[215]

Press: "OKLAHOMA CITY—About a dozen pickets marched outside Municipal Auditorium here Wednesday night, protesting the appearance of Evangelist Billy James Hargis and former Maj. Gen. Edwin Walker. . . . *Police received a telephone call predicting trouble if the meeting was picketed.* Walker criticized the Kennedy administration, saying it wants to destroy the U.S. Constitution and the Monroe Doctrine."[216] Note the threat of violence from Walker supporters.

3/29/63—FRIDAY: Press: "Anti-Castro raiders were reported Thursday to be preparing for another strike at Cuba. . . ."[217]

Press: "Sen. . . . McClellan . . . said . . . he will call . . . Estes soon for questioning about the convicted Texas promoter's deals. . . ."[218]

3/30/63—SATURDAY: Press: ". . . Urrutia . . . arrived here [Miami] Friday to a cheering welcome. He promised to fight by every means 'legal and illegal' to topple Castro."[219]

3/31/63—SUNDAY: A former New Orleans Immigration inspector ". . . is absolutely certain that he interviewed . . . Oswald in a New Orleans jail cell sometime shortly before April 1, 1963. Although the inspector is not now certain whether Oswald was using that particular name at that time, *he is certain that Oswald was claiming to be a Cuban alien.* He quickly ascertained that Oswald was not . . . . at which point he would have left Os-

wald in his jail cell" (emphasis added).[220] Obviously the real Oswald
is in Dallas, still attempting to learn how to develop negatives. Considering the fact that Oswald's identity has been in use by Banister
and associates since 1961, a reappearance of this concept (again in
the context of Cuba) is not unusual.

Oswald poses, in black, in the backyard of his Dallas apartment
with pistol and rifle, holding copies of *The Militant* and *The
Worker*. Marina: ". . . I was hanging up diapers, and he came up
to me with the rifle . . . and he gave me the camera and asked me
to press a certain button. . . ."[221] By depicting himself as a revolutionary Oswald can, in his mind, obtain the credentials necessary to
obtain an entrance visa to Cuba.

Press reports: "An attempt to kill . . . Castro at a spot where he
often plays baseball . . . was reported in a letter received by an
exiled Cuban newspaper man. A gun battle resulted and several
persons were killed. . . ."[222]

4/63—THIS MONTH: ". . . Nixon . . . in April twice
made speeches urging . . . reversal [of JFK's policy of accommodation with Cuba]. He called for decisive action to force the Communist regime out of power and open support for the exile mili-
tants."[223]

Baker and his wife purchase and occupy a home in the Spring
Valley area near D.C. "On one side was his friend and business
partner Fred Black. On the other side was his longtime mentor,
Lyndon B. Johnson."[224] Black also belongs to Baker's exclusive
Quorum Club in D.C.[225]

"Baker took time . . . in April . . . to charter a plane . . . to
fly . . . eighty Washington lobbyists and congressional employees
to Las Vegas to attend a $100-a-plate dinner at the *Flamingo Ho-
tel*. . . ." Baker aide "Bromley . . . went to the Las Vegas testi-
monial dinner honoring Nevada Senator Howard Cannon. . . .
While in Las Vegas . . . he met with Baker and Clifford Jones.
. . . Jones 'came right to the point.' He wanted to send Baker
$1,000 a month from his company (the First Western Finance
Corp.). . . . The checks from First Western ($8,000 worth in 1963
and $6,000 in 1964) went directly to Baker's office . . . in Wash-
ington" (emphasis added).[226]

"In April 1963 [an individual named] Kater wrote to Hoover,

with copies to the major newspapers and magazines, claiming to have 'personal knowledge and proof that Miss Pamela Turnure, press secretary to Mrs. John F. Kennedy, had had an illicit sexual relationship with President Kennedy.' Kater's allegation, and photographs supposedly showing Kennedy leaving Turnure's house at 1 A.M., were given front-page publicity in the *Thunderbolt,* the official publication of the segregationist National States' Rights Party. The Birmingham field office immediately forwarded copies of the article and accompanying photographs to Hoover for his attention. After studying Kater's letter, Hoover decided not to share this material with Attorney General Kennedy and the Kennedy White House."[227] He no longer has to. An obvious point here is that the allegation is already public information. It has no value as blackmail. There is also the fact that at this point Hoover needs only to avoid directly antagonizing the President, and let the Marcello contract "get the job done." Another possibility, though more remote, is that the Director himself is the original source of the Kater allegation.

4/1/63—MONDAY: ". . . Oswald was fired by Jaggers-Chiles-Stovall for poor job performance." He is given until April 6 to leave.[228]

4/2/63—TUESDAY: Marina and child are now staying with Ruth Paine. Either Oswald has informed Marina he intends to go to Cuba, or they have had another fight (perhaps over his firing). Oswald rides with Michael Paine to Paine's residence for dinner.[229]

Press: "A petition bearing thousands of signatures was filed with the Senate Judiciary Committee today requesting an investigation of former Maj. Gen. Edwin A. Walker's arrest and imprisonment. The petition, filed by a group called the Citizens Congressional Committee, asked an inquiry on the treatment of 'America's fearless patriot on the occasion of his incarceration at the instigation of the Department of Justice.' "[230] Note how groups surrounding Walker consistently attempt to paint him as a martyr.

4/3/63—WEDNESDAY: ". . . Carmelo Lombardozzi, the father of Carmine Lombardozzi, a capo regime in the family of Carlo Gambino, was buried . . . in Brooklyn. Law-enforcement officers covered the wake and requiem mass for intelligence purposes. As the funeral cortege entered the church, several young men from the mourners assaulted Special FBI Agent John P. Foley, who had a camera. Foley was badly beaten, and his service revolver was stolen"[231] This causes great concern at SOG. For the first time, the Mafia has shown a willingness to publicly assault federal officals. The four responsible are promptly arrested.[232] There is no public response from Hoover, which is very odd, for he took even minor slights very seriously. His silence remains unexplained.

4/3—4/24/63:   Oswald, as a result of the recent hostility toward Cuba, the imminent threat of another U.S. invasion, the loss of his job, the possible urging of de Mohrenschildt, and marital discord, makes the decision to go either to Cuba or Miami to join the cause as a revolutionary. Apparently temporarily separated, he drafts the following note to his wife:

1. *This is the key to the mail box which is located in the main post office in the city on Ervay Street.* This is the same street where the drug store, in which you always waited is located. You will find the mail box in the post office which is located 4 blocks from the drug store on that street. *I paid for the box last month so don't worry about it.*
2. *Send the information as to what has happened to me to the Embassy and include newspaper clippings (should there be anything about me in the newspapers). I believe that the Embassy will come quickly to your assistance on learning everything.*
3. *I paid the house rent on the 2nd* so don't worry about it.
4. Recently *I also paid for water and gas.*
5. The *money from work will possibly be coming. The money will be sent to our post office box.* Go to the bank and cash the check.
6. *You can either throw out or give my clothing etc. away.* Do not keep these. However, *I prefer that you hold on to my personal papers (military, civil etc.).*
7. Certain of my documents are in the small blue valise.
8. The address book can be found on my table in the study should you need same.
9. We have friends here. *The Red Cross also will help you.*
10. *I left you as much money as I could, $60.00 on the second*

of the month. You and the baby [apparently] can live for
another 2 months using $10.00 per week.

11. *If I am alive and taken prisoner, the city jail is located at the
end of the bridge through which we always passed on going to
the city (right in the beginning of the city after crossing the
bridge)* (emphasis added).[233]

This document, produced sometime between April 3 and April 24,
1963, has obviously been written as if Oswald is going away to war.
The post office box he refers to is in downtown Dallas. It is also
obvious that he has just lost his job. "The money from work will
possibly be coming." Most probably he is referring to unemployment. Note that he implies he will not need civilian clothing anymore, and tells her what to do if he is "taken prisoner." His reference to the Red Cross is telling. Upon his return to the U.S. from
Russia he instructed his mother to contact the Red Cross for assistance. In recent weeks, the newspapers have repeatedly stated that
the Red Cross is assisting in regard to Cuban refugees and their
dependents, apparently operating inside Cuba. His reference to the
"Embassy" is significant. He means either the Cuban or Russian,
most likely the latter. Acts in furtherance of the Cuban cause will
surely elicit favorable action from the Soviet embassy, the more so
because his wife is Russian. He apparently plans to be gone at least
two months and is taking some money with him. For some reason, he
is under the impression he may end up in the Dallas jail. This raises
two possibilities. One, he may be planning to commit some local
crime in order to get to Cuba (e.g., hijacking a plane, as Marina will
later confess).[234] Or, two, he may think that if he is "taken prisoner,"
wherever, he will be returned to Dallas to face charges.

For whatever reason, he does not act on this plan. Perhaps because he soon makes the decision to move to New Orleans. Perhaps
he and his wife discuss the idea and she dissuades him. It is not
known whether she even sees this note prior to December 1963. At
any rate, from an evidentiary standpoint, it suggests nothing more.

4/7/63—SUNDAY: Ruth Paine writes, but never mails, a letter
to Marina offering her the opportunity of sharing her house.[235]

4/7—4/24/63:   "Oswald stages brief, one-man 'Hands Off
Cuba' demonstration in downtown Dallas, [and] distributes copies

of *The Crime Against Cuba* as well as other pamphlets he has accumulated in six months' communication with [FPCC]." . . . When approached by police, "[Oswald] . . . removed the Viva Castro sign and ran into H. L. Green Company. . . . [saying] . . . 'Oh, hell, here comes the cops.' "[236]

4/8–4/24/63:   Oswald writes a letter to the FPCC in New York, asking for help:

P.O. Box 2915, Dallas, Tex.

Dear Sirs:

I do not like to ask for something for nothing but I am unemployed.

Since I am unemployed I stood yesterday for the first time in my life, with a placard around my neck, passing out fair play for Cuba pamphlets, etc. I only had 15 or so. In 40 minutes they were all gone. I was cursed as well as praised by some. My home-make [sic] placard said "Hands off Cuba, Viva Fidel." I now ask for 40 or 50 more of the fine basic pamphlets.
——14

> Sincerely.
> Lee H. Oswald[237]

As the FBI is monitoring correspondence to and from this organization, they soon become aware of Oswald's activism. During this general time period, he, according to Marina, is also taking typing lessons. Marketable proficiency requiring considerable manual dexterity, he apparently abandons the course after a few lessons. Lack of funds may also be a factor.[238]

4/8/63—MONDAY: Oswald files a claim for unemployment compensation with the Texas Employment Commission.[239]

Press: "Vice Admiral . . . Rickover will be retained in the Navy's nuclear propulsion program after his compulsory retirement from active duty next year. This was announced today by Secretary of the Navy Fred Korth (a Johnson appointee). Admiral Rickover has indicated his desire to continue in his present job. . . ."[240]

Walker aide, Robert "Boy" Surrey, sees two men prowling around the general's home this night. " 'I saw two men around the house peeking in windows.' Surrey spotted their car, a dark-colored new Ford sedan without license plates. . . . When the two men returned to this car, Surrey tailed them in his own vehicle, but [lost them]. He repeated the incident to General Walker . . . the following morning. Walker reported the matter to the [Dallas] police on April 9, without result."[241] Surrey, apparently one of a number of ultraright followers of the general, is also the individual who will distribute JFK "Wanted for Treason" leaflets in Dallas on 11/22/63.[242]

4/9/63—TUESDAY: Walker aide Max Claunch observes a suspicious-looking dark-complected man driving around the home in a 1957 Chevy.[243]

Press: "MIAMI . . . Nine American adventurers and a missionary from California were flown to Florida today after having been cleared of suspicion as agents of the United States Central Intelligence Agency. . . . The minister's wife and two children and some other missionaries were deported by the Cuban Government and reached Miami last week aboard *a Red Cross flight"* (emphasis added).[244] Note the correlation between this event and Oswald's note to his wife. The common threads of Cuba, adventurism, family dependents, and the Red Cross are intriguing.

4/10/63—WEDNESDAY: This evening, a shot is fired at General Walker's home, reportedly about 9:30 P.M. A fourteen-year-old neighbor, Walter Kirk Coleman, observes three individuals. Two speed away from the scene down an alley in a light-colored 1959 or 1960 Ford. The other man puts something on the floorboard of a white 1958 Chevy in an adjacent church parking lot, jumps in the car, and hurriedly leaves the scene. Walker's ever-present security apparently is elsewhere this evening, for he reportedly investigates the shooting unaided.[245] The news account of this bizarre event is illuminating. The accompanying photo, taken shortly after the shooting, shows Walker appearing relaxed, smiling, drinking a cup of coffee. "DALLAS . . . an unseen rifleman fired through a window and missed former . . . Gen. . . . Walker by a scant inch in his home last night. *Mr. Walker brushed fragments of glass from his hair as reporters arrived shortly after the incident,*

which he described as an attempted assassination. It happened about
9:30 o'clock. *The police said that a slight movement by Mr. Walker,
at a desk working on his income tax report, presumably saved his life.
'Somebody had a perfect bead on him,' Detective Ira Van Cleave
said. 'Whoever it was certainly wanted to kill him.' The bullet,* from
a 30.06 rifle, was fired from an alley behind the Walker home. It
went through wood framing the glass window.''[246] Note that Walker
is the only source of information for what transpired inside the
house. Both the police and reporters, called to his home shortly
after the incident, are relying on Walker's rhetoric to conclude, 1)
he was even in the same room when it occurred; 2) "someone had a
perfect bead on him"; and 3) "Whoever it was certainly wanted to
kill him." Walker's demeanor is highly contradictory. He has supposedly, only a few hours before, survived, à la de Gaulle, being
murdered by a high-velocity, large-caliber bullet, and yet he appears
relaxed, smiling, drinking a cup of coffee. The retired general even
brushes glass from his hair, as if to convince the reporters. The
words of the investigating detectives have an odd ring. Despite the
scanty evidence, Van Cleave does not hesitate to expound on the
purpose and meaning of the event for the media.

When placed in the context of prior occurrences surrounding
Walker, the true nature of this event becomes apparent. Only days
before, Walker had returned from a nationwide speaking tour with
evangelist Billy James Hargis, during which violence had been
anonymously threatened. Supporters have just delivered a petition
to Congress denouncing Walker's martyrdom at the hands of the
administration, and he is scheduled to appear before a women's
group in New York on April 25.[247] As shown by this chronicle,
Walker and his supporters have repeatedly injected him into public
controversy, engineering news to raise support. Almost without fail,
every event has cloaked him in martyr's robes. Walker himself attempts, whenever possible, to project in this fashion. The obvious
question here is why would anyone bother to take a shot at Walker?
The previous year he had been soundly rejected by the voters in a
preliminary Democratic Party vote, his charisma is nonexistent, his
public speaking ability nil, and his views on current issues fundamentally incoherent.[248] Obviously there is the need for staged media
events to bolster the fragile façade.

The strong possibility of complicity on the part of Dallas police
officers cannot be ignored. Their willingness to openly side with,

and reinforce before reporters, the uncorroborated facts recounted by Walker without first investigating the case, flies in the face of accepted police practice. Immediately after the attempt, the Dallas P.D. has fairly detailed descriptions of the three suspects and their cars, and the slug fired from the weapon. Days before the event, they had been put on notice that suspicious characters had been seen near the house. Yet for some reason they will be unable to locate any suspects. The fact that the case remains unsolved until immediately after the Kennedy assassination, when the Dallas P.D. and FBI offer a solution implicating Oswald, is also suspicious.

Interestingly the one piece of evidence (a photograph of Walker's home and driveway) seeming to put Oswald in the vicinity of the general's home will, at some point shortly after the assassination, be mutilated by either the Dallas police or the FBI. This has been conclusively proven. Given that the mutilation obliterated the license plate, and thus ownership, of a car parked in Walker's driveway, and the fact that the car bore a resemblance to one of the vehicles seen prowling the scene of the attempt just days before, one can only assume vested interest or duplicity on the part of local police officials or the FBI.[249] Otherwise, why protect the identity of the owner of the car? Presumably the Dallas P.D. places Walker's home under surveillance immediately after the shooting attempt, simply as a matter of standard procedure. This alone would provide the opportunity to photograph people coming and going, as well as their cars. Not surprisingly, the person who observed the individuals shooting at Walker's home, a neighborhood boy, will when shown a picture of Oswald, fail to identify him as one of the men. The fact that Oswald cannot drive is critical here, for, even presuming he was involved, it necessitates an accomplice. This will, however, prove no obstacle to Hoover and the Warren Commission. The note left by Oswald (April 4), and the mutilated photo of Walker's house, supposedly found by Dallas police along with a camera among his possessions after the assassination, will be deemed sufficient to implicate him.[250] And the 30.06 slug will become a 6.5mm (much smaller) projectile from Oswald's rifle. If the attempt to implicate Oswald in this shooting after the assassination seems desperate, it is because it is. Hoover, the Dallas P.D., and the Warren Commission will realize early on that an examination of Oswald's past reveals only a pacifist engaged in leftist activism. Simply put, he is nonviolent.

In sum then, the Walker shooting is an event unrelated to Oswald and the assassination, and like other media events defining the Walker myth, would have faded into total obscurity (like the man) but for this fiction that will be created on the afternoon of 11/22/63.

Press reports: "MIAMI . . . The infiltration of Cuban agents . . . through Miami has increased in the last year. . . . Waiver visas are issued . . . at the request of the numerous Cuban exile organizations here. These organizations, almost without exception, have been infiltrated by Castro agents. One aim of the Castro agents is to create disunity and promote agitation among the . . . exiles against the United States. . . ."[251] The value of someone like Oswald, or his image, to the FBI becomes obvious in light of revelations such as this.

4/11/63—THURSDAY: FBI (New Orleans) AIRTEL from Regis Kennedy to Hoover. ". . . Becker and his friend Roppolo were referred to once again. . . . The New Orleans office had been instructed to determine if Roppolo was in fact acquainted with Marcello, as advised by Becker. The . . . report concluded that Roppolo did in all likelihood know the . . . Mafia leader. A source had informed the New Orleans office that the Marcello and Roppolo 'families were quite close at one time as they came from the "old country" at approximately the same time and lived as neighbors in New Orleans.' This report further stated that the same source doubted whether Roppolo himself could secure financial backing from Marcello for a business venture, due to Roppolo's alleged reputation as someone 'rather shiftless.' Roppolo was regarded as 'a problem,' a person who 'is always trying to promote something.' "[252] Note the similarities in the Bureau assaults on the credibility of both Becker and Roppolo. Roppolo's mother is actually a courier for Marcello, a fact known to the New Orleans Crime Commission for years. Its director being an ex-FBI agent, presumably the information is known to Hoover as well.

4/13/63—SATURDAY: "Immediately after the [Walker event] press reports quoted the police as having identified the bullet as 30.06 caliber . . . *steel* jacketed'. . . ."[253] Note, the Italian army surplus ammunition and bullet fragments that will be found in connection with Oswald's rifle on 11/22/63 are all *copper* jacketed.

4/15/63—MONDAY: Press reports: "Mrs. . . . King said tonight President Kennedy had told her he hoped the change of government in Birmingham might speed her husband's release from jail. Mr. Kennedy had agents of the Federal Bureau of Investigation visit Dr. King in prison and arranged for him to call her, she added."[254]

Oswald's 1962 federal income tax return is due. The only full-year return he ever files, the original remains classified to this day.[255] The obvious question is why? Only in the U.S. for the latter half of 1962, he has had two menial jobs. His wife does not work. Here the possibility of his recruitment during the fall of 1962 by the FBI as a paid informant arises. Given his ties to Russia and his fascination with Cuba, would he not have been of interest to the Bureau? Hoover considers this type of confidential informant the best that can be had. The fact that his wife can potentially be deported as a "spy" only adds to their power over him. Typically, informants for the Bureau earn from seventy-five to two hundred dollars per month for their cooperation.

The *Internal Revenue Code* (as it then existed) strongly implies that this type of income is not tax exempt. "For Federal tax purposes, 'gross income' means all income from whatever source derived. . . ." [256] Also, "All Federal . . . employees are subject to Federal income tax on their compensation."[257] As such, it would be reported in some disguised manner (e.g., "wages," Form W-2 or "other income," Form 1099, from a fictitious company) by him on his federal tax return. A present-day front company is that of the *Midwest Holding Corporation,* a tax-exempt corporation used by the FBI in the Southern U.S. to handle payments for various services rendered. Presumably Oswald attached all Forms W-2 to his return when he filed it.

An examination of relevant sections of the *Internal Revenue Code* (e.g., 55, 6041, 6103) reveals that informant income is *not* generally reported on Form 1099 (also used to report independent-contractor and other forms of income). Sect. 6041: "Payments of the following character need not be reported on Form . . . 1099. . . . A payment of a type . . . paid as an award to an informer . . . by the United States. . . ." However, this is only true for payments made directly by the government. Certain tax-exempt corporations (e.g., those "lessening the burdens of government . . . [by providing] funds to law-enforcement agencies to help them in offering rewards for information. . . ."[258] are in fact required to report informant pay on that form. Given that all a tax return does is provide a cash-basis record of one's income for a given calendar year, and the obviously innocent nature of the jobs Oswald held, why else would his return remain classified?

The primary reason for return nondisclosure is to preserve confidentiality of the "nature and source" of a taxpayer's income.[259] Another reason, as stated in *Federal Tax Coordinator 2d,* is "if such disclosure would identify a confidential informant. . . ."[260] Note that the Warren Commission, in its *Hearings* and *Report* volumes, will in fact disclose the "nature and source" of Oswald's net wages (Leslie Welding and Jaggers-Chiles), marital status (married), personal exemptions (three), 1962 tax refund amount ($57.40), as well as other pertinent information. At least on the surface, Oswald's tax picture appears very straightforward. Why then, given the gravity of the situation, is the IRS still refusing to release the original return to the public? What is left to disclose? One can only conclude at this late date that releasing the original will in some way identify Oswald as a "confidential informant."

It could be that in filing his 1040 Oswald inadvertently disclosed his informant status in some manner that was not called for by the return. His extended absence from the country, and thus unfamiliarity with IRS forms, inexperience, youth, and lack of education make this a distinct possibility. Taxpayers of considerably greater sophistication sometimes volunteer information not required.

The point of this discussion is that it reveals the intent of Hoover and the Warren Commission to hide from the American public Oswald's relationship with the U.S. government. In all likelihood he did inform for the Bureau, for however short a period of time. This, taken alone, is not necessarily relevant to the assassination. Ruby was also an informant during the late 1950s. But just as Hoover and the Commission will agree not to disclose Ruby's relationship with the government, so, too, they will agree not to release Oswald's original tax return. The concern is that if the public ever learns of both men's relationship to the FBI, questions will be raised. Specifically, people will wonder why Hoover did not learn of the two's intentions before the fact. Worse yet, why had the Bureau hired people associated with the Mafia? In using the two men, Marcello may contemplate these very questions.

For an in-depth analysis of Oswald's income and tax liability during 1962, see Appendix B. This includes a purported copy of the 1962 tax return, published for the first time.

Press reports: ". . . Estes was sentenced today to 15 years in prison for mail fraud and conspiracy."[261]

4/16/63—TUESDAY: Oswald's unemployment claim is rejected.[262]

4/17/63—WEDNESDAY: "Attorney General Kennedy's personal interest in the continuing Justice Department investigation of Marcello was further evidenced in April 1963. He had received a letter which he in turn ordered the chief of the Criminal Division, Jack Miller, to forward to Hoover for his personal attention. The letter was from a citizen claiming to have knowledge of a severe beating inflicted upon a friend by lieutenants of Marcello. The Attorney General requested immediate Bureau attention to the matter." Hoover, in turn, forwarded it to a subordinate who prepares a report this date.[263] There is no indication anything comes of it. Again, it is not in Hoover's interest to intimidate or discourage Marcello at this stage. RFK appears desperate, willing to consider anything to bring Marcello to justice. Note the fundamentally different planes the Director and the Attorney General are operating on. Hoover, with access to the critical data, is in complete control while Kennedy is left uninformed. Note that Hoover, this fall, will have Philadelphia Mafia leader Angelo Bruno arrested for an incident much like this. In that case, Bruno will also appear far removed from the specific acts complained of. But there, Hoover will have reason to act.

Charleston Gazette publishes an article ridiculing Hoover's claim that two of every five hitchhikers had been fingerprinted by the Bureau. "Loose contentions, absurd on their face, hardly enhance the agency's credibility ratings." This type of criticism is becoming commonplace. In part, this is due to the growing perception that the Director will soon be retired. Obviously more and more people are feeling free to voice their opinions about the once sacrosanct activities and pronouncements of the Bureau.

4/20/63—SATURDAY: "Ruth Paine and children come to Neely Street for picnic with Oswalds. . . . [Oswald] spent most of his time fishing. . . . He caught a fish . . . and took it home to be cleaned."[264]

Press reports: ". . . Castro said today that the United States had abandoned plans for a second invasion of Cuba in favor of a plot to assassinate Cuban leaders."[265]

4/21/63—SUNDAY: Oswald's letter to FPCC-NY, informing them he plans to move to New Orleans is opened by ". . . the FBI, which was clearly reading Fair Play For Cuba Committee mail. . . . [The Bureau] . . . knew the contents of [his] letter . . . three days before he left for New Orleans."[266]

4/23/63—TUESDAY: Vice President Johnson meets in Dallas with *Dallas Times Herald* and *KRCD* AM/FM/TV executives, who ". . . quoted [him] as saying that President Kennedy might visit Dallas and other major Texas cities [that] summer." *"Johnson also commented on* widespread criticism of *President Kennedy* in Texas: 'He's the only pilot you have, and if the plane goes down, you go with it. At least wait until November before you shoot him down' "* (emphasis added).[267] Presumably Johnson's offhand comment is not based on anything more than dislike for the Chief Executive.

4/24/63—WEDNESDAY: Oswald moves to New Orleans in furtherance of his plan to become a revolutionary.[268] New Orleans has the second largest Cuban exile population in the country. Marina and the child remain with Ruth Paine, who reportedly was not aware of Oswald's intention to move until this day. "He said, he had not been able to find work in Dallas, around Dallas, and Marina suggested going to New Orleans, which is where he had been born. . . ."[269]

Dallas Times Herald reports President Kennedy will visit Dallas in November. (As a local resident, Marcello functionary Jack Ruby undoubtedly read this.) Vice President Johnson is quoted as stating, "President Kennedy's schedule would permit him to attend a breakfast in Ft. Worth, a luncheon in Dallas and an afternoon in San Antonio. [He] . . . might visit Dallas and other major Texas cities that . . . summer."

Ruby, although not a formal member of the Mafia, is extremely valuable to the Marcello organization as a liaison with the Dallas Police Department, former FBI informant, and bookmaker.

"Charles W. Flynn, a special agent of the FBI, reported that he was contacted on March 11, 1959, by Jack Ruby, who said he wished to assist the FBI by supplying criminal information on a confidential basis. Flynn opened a 'potential criminal informant' file, or PCI, on Ruby, and he met with him eight times between April and October 1959, which covered the period of Ruby's trips to Cuba. . . ."[270] Also on a first-name basis with hundreds of Dallas police officers, the Mafia functionary has provided many favors in exchange for information. That he maintains such a close working relationship with the force is well known. For example:

> Jack Hardee, Jr., an acquaintance of Ruby, told the FBI that [Officer J.D.] Tippit "was a frequent visitor to Ruby's night club" and that "there appeared to be a very close relationship" between Ruby, Tippit, and another officer.[271]

And:

> Hubert: What was the particular group—who did it consist of?
> Rich: The Police Department.
> Hubert: Are you saying that Jack Ruby told you that when any member of the Police Department came in, that there was a standing order that you could serve them hard liquor?
> Rich: That is correct.
> Hubert: Did they pay?
> Rich: Oh, no: of course not.[272]

4/25/63—THURSDAY: A Paul Harvey Commentary, "God Help the United States without John Edgar Hoover" runs on various radio stations. Harvey, an ultrarightist and admirer of Hoover, had just obtained a private interview with the Director. The subject of Hoover's retirement came up, and Hoover again stated for the public record that he will not retire. *"Director Hoover is not retiring. If you have heard otherwise, somebody's sinister wish was the father of that thought. It is not so.* As we face the unpleasant inevitability that Mr. Hoover must someday vacate that command post, those of us who live close to the making of history are chilled by the realization that his successor will likely be a 'political appointee' " (emphasis added).[273] This is Hoover's second pronouncement on the subject within the last five weeks. Consider the fact he has also learned in the last few days that JFK will be traveling, within months, into cities controlled by Marcello. It is known that the purpose of the trip is to campaign for the 1964 election. By definition this will necessitate close contact with the public, including motorcades, public addresses, etc. Through official briefing and conversation with Vice President Johnson, undoubtedly Hoover will soon learn more details of the impending, well-publicized trip.

Oswald arrives in New Orleans, moving in with his Uncle "Dutz" Murret and wife while he hunts for a job. Dutz is a gambler who, like other bookmakers in New Orleans, subscribes to Marcello's wire service.[274] This is, of course, the same wire service operated by Beckley et al. Currently the group is still in trial. Repeated attempts to delay prosecution or obtain dismissal have failed.

4/26/63—FRIDAY: After denying a flurry of motions by the defendants, the Beckley court states, "Now, with respect to all of the other counts in the indictment, I find that there is substantial evidence, which, if believed by the Jury, to support a verdict of guilty, of each of said counts."[275]

General Walker, in New York, again makes the press: "Both parties are dominated by 'liberals voting for each other, whether Republicans or Democrats,' he told a meeting of the New York Colony of the National Society of New England Women."[276] A third-party campaign, via the John Birch Society, would in fact appear to be his only alternative at this point.

Oswald registers with the New Orleans office of Louisiana's Employment Security Division in hopes of finding a job.[277]

4/27/63—SATURDAY: Press: "JOHNSON CITY . . . Vice President and Mrs. Johnson were hosts to 30 United Nations delegates today at the LBJ Ranch. The early settlers moved to the area to 'escape war and find peace,' Mr. Johnson said. They represented 10 languages, he said. Then he quipped: 'Democratic, Republican and Texan.' Mrs. Johnson, wearing a bright orange dress, took the other delegates on a tour of the ranch in a bus. . . . Mrs. Johnson gave a running commentary about the area. She pointed out the house where 'Lyndon was born' and the cemetery where Mr. Johnson's forebears [sic] are buried. A Western band played, and there were demonstrations of sheep-herding, pistol-shooting and whip-cracking."[278]

4/29/63—MONDAY: Oswald contests, in writing, the rejection of his Texas unemployment claim.[279] Note that he is now simply struggling to survive economically. He has a wife and child to support, and no job. His only income at this point could well be a small monthly stipend from the FBI.

4/30/63—TUESDAY: D.C. press reports: "WASHINGTON . . . James R. Hoffa . . . gave the Boy Scouts $336,000 on behalf of his union today for construction of a new Scout center here. 'The teamsters union has a strong interest in the Boy Scouts of America. . . . Many teamsters union members were Boy Scouts. Many Boy Scouts one day will be the teamster union members.' "[280] Such a gift, by a man known to Hoover to be deeply involved with the Mafia, is paradoxical. Hoffa, as many other people, knows of Hoover's keen interest in the Boy Scouts. The gift is local in nature and undoubtedly catches his attention. Hoffa is under investigation by the Justice Department, of which Hoover is a part. The attempt to curry favor is obvious. How enthusiastic will Hoover now be in providing data on this man to the Attorney General, a man he already loaths? Neither can Hoffa's close association with Richard Nixon, a longtime friend of the Director's, be ignored.

"The [Foley] assault caused deep concern at the FBI. On April 30 . . . Evans wrote to Assistant [to the] Director Alan Belmont that, in his opinion, general permission to retaliate against law enforcement officers, although it had been requested, had not yet been given by the [Mafia] leadership. . . . As for FBI agents at the street level, they initiated a series of interviews designed . . . to intimidate members of the Gambino organization, and there was evidence that on at least one occasion a Lombardozzi associate was beaten up and dumped in an ash can. . . ." In addition agents begin leaking data to the Mafia about their criminal enterprise. The depth of Bureau knowledge about the New York families and their activities shocks the organization. News of this spreads very quickly throughout the northeastern families, causing much fear and concern.[281]

5/63—THIS MONTH: Edward Levinson is called to testify over the next few months in a Las Vegas tax case against fellow Mafia functionary Doc Stacher. Levinson, along with "... six other casino executives, flatly refused to answer any question relating to Stacher's income . . . and . . . [was] held in contempt. . . . Brought to trial before U.S. Judge Thurmond Clark they were promptly released. . . . Clark pointed out he had been apprised that the witnesses were interviewed recently by FBI . . . agents. 'Electronic listening devices were recently discovered in the Sands Hotel . . .' the Judge announced."[282] Note Stacher is ". . . a longtime associate of Costello, as well as . . . Meyer Lansky . . ." He also knows of Joseph Kennedy's involvement in illegal importation of scotch whiskey, and thus association with the Mafia, during Prohibition.[283]

Marcello lieutenant Nofio Pecora begins a liaison with Jack Ruby via a neighbor's (Harold Tannenbaum) telephone, which continues into November. "Tannenbaum was a 'friend and colleague' of Marcello lieutenant Nofio Pecora. . . . [He] . . . lived at lot 32 of Pecora's Tropical Tourist Court. . . ." " '. . . In the early 1950s, Jack Ruby held [an] interest in the Colonial Inn' in Hallandale, Florida. A famous . . . gambling house, the . . . principals were Meyer and Jake Lansky. . . . At that time, [FBI informant] Johnson told the FBI, Ruby 'was active in arranging illegal flights of weapons from Miami to Castro. . . . According to a [5/31/58] FBI report . . .' Ruby was associated with a gun runner named James Woodard." Ruby travels to Houston this month, presumably in furtherance of contract goals.[284]

Sometime this month Hoover's ELSUR program monitoring Las Vegas casinos is uncovered by the Mafia. ". . . In May of 1963 when the FBI turned over to the Justice Department a two-volume document called 'The Skimming Report,' which detailed the illegal siphoning off of gambling profits by Las Vegas casinos to avoid taxes, it was obvious from the report that the FBI had gained much of its information from bugging devices, though bugging was explicitly outlawed by Nevada statute. . . . Three days after turning over the report the FBI learned that the racketeers under surveillance had gotten a verbatim copy and they accused the Department of careless security policy. 'But,' recalls Hundley [Justice Department Organized Crime section chief] 'there was only one copy and it went straight . . . to me and I gave it to Jack Miller [Assistant

A.G., in charge of Criminal Division at Justice Department] who took it home over the weekend. We couldn't have leaked it. My personal suspicion has always been that the Bureau knew their bugs had been discovered and they turned the report over to us so that we would be the fall guys.' The report caused a great flap within the Department and three days after receipt [Deputy Attorney General Nicholas de B.] Katzenbach brought the matter to [Robert] Kennedy's attention. Kennedy instructed him to 'make sure they're not doing any more of this.' "[285] Coincidentally, since the fifties Hundley has maintained a friendship with Mafia defense attorney Edward Bennett Williams.[286]

FBI (New York) ELSUR overhears two Mafia figures (Peter Ferrara and another) discussing the beating incident (4/3/63) involving FBI Agent Foley. Apparently one of the two mobsters has been approached by the FBI and has a daughter who is a nun. "In other words they are telling you they don't want to embarrass you. In other words they won't go to the convent. Well I would say right now they are giving you the zing. You want us to go to the convent? You want us to embarrass you? Well then, see that the right thing is done."[287] The East Coast element of the mob appears increasingly intimidated, giving ground.

". . . Baker made a special trip to California . . . [in] . . . May in an effort to protect a race track monopoly in San Diego. . . . [He] had spoken to [Governor Brown] in opposition to legislation requiring competitive bidding for a lease at the Del Mar race track. . . . Baker had [told Brown] . . . the appointment was set up by Vice President Johnson."[288] This is, of course, the same track Texas oil millionaire Clint Murchison, Sr., had acquired partly as a favor to Hoover, and the one that Hoover annually frequents.

Oswald's FBI file in New Orleans is now classified under "anti-Castro activities" (e.g., "105–1095–129").[289]

Cuban exiles are using 544 Camp St., the same building Banister uses, by the time of Oswald's arrival and throughout the summer of 1963. "The new information now available suggests Banister drew Oswald into an American intelligence scheme, perhaps aimed at compromising the FPCC organization."[290]

". . . Delphina Roberts [Guy Banister's secretary] remembers Ferrie as . . . one of the *agents*. Many times when he came into the office he used the private office behind Banister's and I was told he was doing private work. *I believed his work was somehow con-*

nected with the CIA rather than the FBI. . . ." (emphasis added).[291]
Roberts's assertion that Ferrie worked for the CIA "rather than the
FBI" is revealing. For it implies that working for Banister, an ex-
SAC, can be the equivalent of working for the FBI. Note her use of
the term "agents" to describe those working for him. Recall that as
early as January, the local field office has been receiving information
from Banister regarding the exile community. His office is located
only a few doors from the Bureau's. Obviously then, Banister and
local FBI special agents are working together in the case of Oswald,
who ultimately becomes aware of this connection.

Banister is a sinister character in his own right. A member of the
John Birch Society, Louisiana's Committee on Un-American Activities, and the Minutemen, he hates the U.N. and feels that racial
integration is a communist plot.[292] Soon to perform investigative
work in defense of Marcello, he later says of this assignment,
"There are principles being violated, and if this [apparently Marcello's prosecution] goes on it could affect every citizen in the U.S."[293]
In June 1964, he will die of a heart attack, never testifying before
the Warren Commission.[294] Shortly after his death, New Orleans
FBI agents will remove extensive files from his office.[295]

5/1/63—WEDNESDAY: *FBI Law Enforcement Bulletin* is
released. Hoover's topic is Law Day (May 1), Police Week (12–18),
and Peace Officers' Memorial Day (May 15):

> In recent years we have seen an accelerated trend in some
> quarters to overrun rights of society. This is particularly true
> in the realm of organized crime and the underworld. More and
> more our judicial-legal system is being circumvented by the
> criminal elite. Communists, too, are an undermining force
> bent on destroying our rule of law while basking in the light of
> freedom which it provides. They spew the germs of a godless
> ideology which seeks the destruction of our free Government;
> however, they show no qualms in scurrying to the shelter of
> our Constitution when it serves their cause. It was Lincoln
> who stated, *"Let reverence of the law . . . become the political
> religion of the Nation"* [emphasis added].

5/3/63—FRIDAY: Johnson accepts Hoover's invitation to appear as keynote speaker at the June 19 FBI National Academy graduation exercises:

Dear Edgar:

. . . I can't let this pleasant opportunity pass by. I'm delighted to be able to say "yes" to your invitation. Because of my high regard for you and my great respect for the service, I hope you know that *I share in the complete and utter devotion* that all the men in the FBI have *for J. Edgar Hoover. I am so grateful to you and Deke DeLoach for all* the many favors *you both have done* for us . . . [emphasis added].[296]

5/6/63—MONDAY: Press: "President Kennedy appointed Adm. David L. McDonald today as Chief of Naval Operations. The appointment put a surprising end to Adm. George W. Anderson's one-term tenure."[297]

5/7/63—TUESDAY: Press: "A witness refused today to answer more than 40 questions put to him by a House panel investigating illegal travel to Cuba and pro-Castro propaganda. Representative *Edwin E. Willis,* Democrat *of Louisiana,* chairman of the panel, told the subcommittee staff to refer the testimony of the witness, Edward Walter Shaw, to the Department of Justice 'for consideration for prosecution' "(emphasis added).[298] This panel is a part of the HUAC, which Willis will soon head (see 6/5/63). He is currently the number-two man. Hoover of course works with and strongly supports the HUAC. This event illustrates the potential for inadvertent dissemination to the wrong people of Hoover's viewpoint regarding President Kennedy. Accordingly his views on President Kennedy, political and personal, are undoubtedly made known to Willis. The *Operation Abolition* incident is a perfect example. There, Hoover and Willis (number-two man on the HUAC at that time also) would have had a common enemy, President Kennedy. Like any other Congressman in D.C., Willis is undoubtedly aware that Hoover is going to be retired. Hoover has publicly stated his opposition to the plan. Surely Willis communicates with his Louisiana constituency (Banister's Committee on Un-American Activities, for instance) regarding his work on the HUAC, a committee popular in the South. The work of the FBI in Louisiana, albeit reluctant, is a topic of considerable concern. Through interaction with Willis then, it is obvious that Hoover's personal views on the Kennedys can easily be communicated to politically powerful men in that state. Marcello is such a man, as powerful as any in Louisiana. This scenario is more than plausible. Unfortunately for President Kennedy, it is only one of several avenues by which Marcello or his functionaries can easily verify the intense hatred and contempt Hoover feels for the President.

". . . as shown by telephone records, Ruby placed a call to the [Marcello-owned] Sho-Bar on Bourbon Street, beginning a long series of contacts with parties in New Orleans."[299]

5/9/63—THURSDAY: After many years of relentless pursuit, RFK at last corners Teamster leader Jimmy Hoffa. "The grand jury investigation resulted in Hoffa . . . being indicted in Nashville . . . for [jury tampering]. . . ." Hoffa's short circuiting of the system had occurred during the Teamster leader's last trial, which resulted in a hung jury. His attorneys will shortly obtain a change of venue and delay until January 1964.[300] But JFK's assassination, and the Attorney General's fall from power in the coming months, will not save him. The case ultimately destroys the powerful Mafia associate.

Mrs. "Dutz" Murret: ". . . One morning [May 9] [Oswald] saw this job with the Reily Coffee Co., and he went down and applied and he got the job. . . . [He] . . . came home waving the newspaper, and he grabbed me around the neck and he even kissed me and he said 'I got it; I got it!' " This same day he apparently ". . . finds a ground floor apartment. . . ." on 4907 Magazine Street and calls his wife with the good news.[301] To rent an apartment on the same day he obtains a job implies he has savings or has borrowed some money. His relatives, the Murrets, are an obvious source.

Sometime after this date Oswald attempts unsuccessfully to get a union job at the regional offices of the AFL/CIO. " 'He sat around a long time,' said Mr. [E. H.] Williams. 'He talked like a mixed-up kid who seemed to feel the whole world was against him. . . .' "[302]

5/10/63—FRIDAY: Today is Hoover's thirty-ninth anniversary as Director.

Oswald puts in a change-of-address card after obtaining a P.O. box in New Orleans.[303]

Jack Ruby mails a .38 caliber revolver to longtime Mafia gambler Lewis McWillie in Las Vegas, Nevada. Over the course of the next four months, he calls him at least eight times at the *Thunderbird Hotel*. "McWillie [is] closely associated with Meyer Lansky's . . . empire and was installed . . . as pit boss at the Thunderbird casino."[304] This hotel is one of eleven major establishments on the strip.[305] Given McWillie's intimate connections with the mob, it hardly seems likely he needs to rely on Ruby to obtain a weapon. More likely the action is symbolic, or done for the latter's benefit. Its meaning remains unclear. Interestingly, during this time period the chief of police in Las Vegas is Leo Kuykendall, an ex-FBI agent.[306]

In a stunning setback for the Attorney General, all defendants in the Marcello gambling case, Beckley et al., are found not guilty by a New Orleans jury.[307] It will be proven that Marcello successfully bribed at least one juror in his own trial (acquittal 11/22/63).[308] It is not known if such an effort was made in this case. Given that these men are key people in the most powerful segment of his overall organization, a bribery attempt would not have been surprising. The crux of their defense had focused on incriminating wiretap data compiled by the IRS during the late 1950s. At any rate, introduction into evidence was hotly contested. Federal officials will continue to pursue Beckley in the months and years ahead. Between now and 1965 he will retain the legal services of Hundley (Justice Department Organized Crime chief) friend Edward Bennett Williams to defend him in the matter.[309] Note that by 12/4/63 Williams will also be counsel for Bobby Baker.[310]

5/11/63—SATURDAY: "Ruth and Marina arrive at the Murrets' house, . . . Marina somehow gets the impression . . . that 'the Murrets' home was the apartment they were going to.' . . . On seeing the Magazine Street premises, '[she] was not as pleased as . . . [Oswald] had hoped. . . . They argued most of the weekend.' "[311] Mrs. Paine shortly returns to Fort Worth.

Hoover pens letter to Policemen's Association (D.C.): *"America's menacing crime problem threatens* our heritage of freedom and justice. It is a matter of great concern to *all citizens, and they look to our profession for protection and guidance"* (emphasis added).[312]

5/12/63—SUNDAY: "Ruby placed a 6-minute call to the mob-owned Thunderbird Hotel in Las Vegas . . . to McWillie. . . ."[313]

5/14/63—TUESDAY: ". . . Nina Garner, Oswald's landlady in New Orleans, said FBI agent Milton Kaack questioned her about Oswald within three weeks of his arrival in New Orleans. She later learned that her lodger was under heavy surveillance by 'FBI' men in 'a car which used to park there at night and watch him and the house, round the corner by the drugstore.' "[314] This is done, no doubt, as part of a standard investigation of his background. FBI surveillance and his undesirable discharge begin, in combination, to dog Oswald. In the fall he will attempt to deal with the problem by renting rooms under assumed names, convinced that his past, and the Bureau, are causing him serious trouble with landlords and employers.

5/15/63—WEDNESDAY: Hoover speaks before the seventy-first session of the FBI National Academy. "I know the president feels strongly about the magnificent work and the sacrifices that have been made by law enforcement. Just recently I had the occasion to visit with him for a while and during the course of this time he spoke about the great success that has been achieved by the law enforcement profession. . . . *I often wish that the bleeding hearts who are ever so solicitous for the criminal had to face the deadly bullets, the guns . . . of the criminal*" (emphasis added).[315]

5/63: Agent ". . . Hosty . . . having . . . obtained the Oswalds' Neely Street address, visits there to interview Marina Oswald, but 'I found that they had moved . . . and left no forwarding address.' "[316]

5/16/63—THURSDAY: "Tannenbaum . . . calls . . . Ruby on May 16 and June 5." New Orleans FBI learns of this shortly after the assassination.[317]

5/18/63—SATURDAY: Press reports: "NASHVILLE . . . Some 2,000 persons turned out at the Municipal Airport to watch the arrival of the President's silver-and-white Air Force jet. About 150,000 more lined the eight-mile route from the airport to Vanderbilt University, where Mr. Kennedy spoke. . . . Mr. Kennedy walked toward his open limousine . . . but changed his mind and strode over to the fence to shake hands with people in the crowd. There were shrieks of delight from the girl students. The President then stepped into the limousine, which moved off in a 10-car motorcade. The President smiled and waved and the people applauded."[318]

Press: "Louisiana's state law sanctioning segregated hotels was ruled unconstitutional by a special three-judge Federal District Court today."[319]

5/20/63—MONDAY: D.C. press reports: ". . . This week. . . . the District of Columbia Licensing Bureau issued the low-numbered prestige tags of 1, 2, and 3 to the White House for the President's three dogs. Charlie, the Welsh Terrier, has been No. 1 for more than a year. This year Pushinka, the 'non-breed' gift from Premier Khrushchev, was raised to No. 2 and Clipper, the German shepherd, to No. 3. They had been 9 and 10. All this meant that Vice President Johnson's beagle, Little Beagle Johnson, slipped to 4 and J. Edgar Hoover's cairn terriers to 5 and 6 from 3 and 4."[320] Although trivial in nature, Kennedy has once again, rather symbolically, antagonized Hoover.

This day Hoover reluctantly poses for the Associated Press. The photographer, in filing the print with AP offices, states, "Please file carefully, as he will probably never pose again. It took a lot of talking to get this appointment."[321] What he most probably means, of course, is pose *as Director*.

FBI (Philadelphia) ELSUR records Bruno once again. He discusses the Foley incident, reiterating what the New York FBI allegedly told a Lombardozzi family member: "Did you change the laws in your family, that you could hit FBI men, punch and kick them? Well, this is the test, that if you change the laws and now you are going to hit FBI men, every time we pick up one of your people we are going to break their head for them. . . . They almost killed him, the FBI. They don't do that, you know. They said, 'This is an example. Now the next time anybody lays a hand on an FBI man, . . .' "[322] Note the obvious fear in Bruno, fear of challenging the established order. Given the subject matter, this data is undoubtedly sent by AIRTEL to Hoover very shortly.

5/21/63—TUESDAY: Oswald and family go to the public library (six blocks away from their apartment) to obtain a library card. Over the course of the summer, Oswald borrows many books, covering a wide range of subjects.[323]

5/22/63—WEDNESDAY: Evans sends a memo to Belmont regarding an article in the *Saturday Evening Post* about Valachi. "The foregoing clearly indicates that the [Justice] Department is motivated strictly by political considerations. While they have apparently yielded to our view that Valachi should not be interviewed by the magazine writer, they are, nevertheless, exploiting this whole situation for their own benefit. Under the circumstances, we should not get involved, but you will be advised of any further information we can develop as to Department action." Hoover reads this memo and comments in the margin: "I concur. I never saw so much skullduggery, the sanctity of Department files, including Bureau reports is a thing of the past."[324] Note the increasingly adversarial attitude expressed by both the Director and Evans. When considered from the public's perspective (i.e., its right to be kept informed), Hoover's complex motivations become apparent. The informant knows that Marcello and Traficante control the southern Mafia, but his area of experience and expertise appears to be New York. Given this, the obvious question is whether he knows of the longtime liaison between New York Mafia boss Frank Costello and Hoover. Recall that a close connection between Costello and Marcello had been made public earlier in the year. The disclosure of a Hoover/Costello liaison to the American people, in view of current efforts to destroy the organization and deport the mafioso, would prove highly damaging to the Director. Containment of Valachi becomes all the more necessary when one considers that Marcello, in implementing the assassination, may well be apprehended after the fact. Thus, Hoover has both personal and pragmatic reasons for protecting the Mafia.

It is also interesting to note the increasingly compromised position of Evans. With this type of hostile rhetoric on the record, even internally, he will hardly be able to question Hoover's refusal to cooperate with the Warren Commission once the President is assassinated. Memos such as these will work to ensure his loyalty after the fact. Hoover, in command of all the relevant facts, knows this. By agreeing with Evans, he only encourages this hostility. Such rhetoric from the assistant director is paradoxical in light of rumors President Kennedy may be considering his appointment as director upon Hoover's retirement—all the more so because Hoover is himself aware of such rumors.

5/23/63—THURSDAY: Press: "President Kennedy was named father of the year . . . by the National Father's Day Committee. . . ."[325] To Hoover, an award such as this to JFK would have seemed an outrage.

5/24—6/11/63: During this time, Tolson begins experiencing severe angina. This will worsen, and necessitate open heart surgery by September.[326] He is five years Hoover's *junior.* Several factors and events kaleidoscoping by, and/or during, this time very possibly contribute to this condition in Hoover's "right arm:" 1) White House announcement on 4/25/63 that the President will, in November, tour a number of southern cities, including key strongholds of both Marcello and Traficante; 2) Culmination of the Beckley trial in New Orleans; 3) Hoover's public defiance of President Kennedy, twice in recent months, in declaring he will *not* retire; 4) U.S. Supreme Court's denial of certiorari (5/27/63) in Marcello's deportation case, effectively ending all legal recourse previously available to prevent deportation, and leaving him with nothing to lose; 5) President Kennedy, LBJ, and Governor Connally's secret meeting in El Paso (6/5/63) to finalize plans for the fall Texas tour; and 6) ELSUR recording on 6/6/63, wherein New York Mafia figure Stefano Magaddino tells family members, "We got to resist. Today. You got to do something material."

5/25/63—SATURDAY: Marina Oswald writes a letter to Ruth Paine. "It is hard for you and me to live without a return of our love—interesting, how will it all end?"[327]

5/26/63—SUNDAY: "Oswald writes to FPCC headquarters in New York. . . . 'I am requesting formal membership in your organization. . . . Offices down here rent for $30 a month and if I had a steady flow of literature I would be glad to take the expense. . . . Could you give me some advice or recommendations? I am not saying this project would be a roaring success, but I am willing to try.' "[328] The FBI, either in New York or New Orleans, reads this letter.

5/27/63—MONDAY: ". . . The U.S. Supreme Court, in response to an appeal filed by Marcello's attorneys, declined to review [i.e., denied writ of certiorari] the Marcello deportation action and upheld the earlier decision of the U.S. Circuit Court of Appeals."[329] His legal recourse has now ended, leaving his status as an undesirable virtually unassailable. Only a change in administration can save him. Once a host country has been found by the Attorney General or the Immigration and Naturalization Service, he can again be deported.

By this time, Hoover and Tolson must have deduced that Marcello will likely move to assassinate the President when 1) he has exhausted all legal/political recourse to solve his problems; and 2) Kennedy comes within striking distance (i.e., Marcello's or Traficante's territory). Because of ELSUR product, both know that the Mafia's national commission will, in all probability, be unable to reach consensus on an assassination contract. Surveillance has shown that heads of the eastern families are very intimidated by the government. The Director and his two assistants may also have deduced that the South is the logical place for the hit. There are many groups there that hate Kennedy, including elements within the Cuban exile population. The availability of any number of scapegoats is obvious.

Press: "The Supreme Court upheld today the use as evidence of secret recordings a Federal tax agent made of his conversations with a suspected tax evader. The tax agent used an electronic device hidden on his person."[330] Surely rulings such as this serve to heighten fear and concern among mafiosi like Marcello, a man under intense scrutinization by the IRS for tax evasion.

5/29/63—WEDNESDAY: D.C. Press reports: "Indictments that have been outstanding fifteen years against eight convicted top Communist party leaders were dropped yesterday by the Government. . . ."[331]

FPCC responds to Oswald. " 'Enclosed are your card and receipt, along with our thanks and welcome. . . . Louisiana seems somewhat restricted for Fair Play activities. . . . You must realize that you will come under tremendous pressures with any attempt to do FPCC work in that area and you will not be able to operate in the manner which is conventional. . . . I definitely would not recommend an office, at least not one that will be identifyable [sic] to the lunatic fringe in your community.' . . . Oswald . . . visits the Jones Printing Co. opposite the side entrance of the Reily Co. and, under the name Osborne, orders one thousand copies of a handbill. . . . [His] real objective was to establish himself publicly as a vocal and active friend of Cuba."[332] This event alone may activate Banister's interest in Oswald.

5/30/63—THURSDAY: Press: "Bitter-enders from the South say that Lyndon is a traitor to the 'cause,' and therefore, politically, is finished in his homeland. Three years ago, when . . . he surprisingly stepped into the position on the Democratic ticket, there were dire predictions that the volatile and temperamental Texan could not long tolerate being 'second fiddle' in any ensemble. Much gossip and speculation . . . has arisen in recent months. People have asked, 'What's become of Lyndon?' implying that he has been sidetracked by the White House. . . ."[333]

6/63—THIS MONTH: "In early June a number of Chicago racketeers gathered in Dallas for a series of meetings aimed at coordinating syndicate control of local prostitution and gambling. . . . Within days of this Mafia mini-convention, police intelligence noted that the gangsters were meeting in the Carousel Club, one of Ruby's two dives. Telephone company records show that Ruby twice called a restaurant near Dallas where the hoods also held meetings."[334]

"Two months after his Vegas charter junket. . . . Baker began to concern himself with a chain of resort hotels that had three casino operations in the Caribbean. . . . He aimed his influence, and the know-how of [Levinson, et al.], at Intercontinental Hotels Corporation. . . . a . . . subsidiary of Pan American World Airways."[335]

FBI (Miami) installs ELSUR ". . . in the Miami Beach office of attorney Alvin Ira Malnik. The bug was planted in June . . . after . . . a special agent of IRS intelligence, tipped the FBI that young Malnik was deeply involved with organized-crime figures in the Bahamas and Las Vegas. . . . Malnik [had become] a shareholder in and a director of the Bank of World Commerce in Nassau. Officers and stockholders included such [Mafia] figures as . . . [Ed-

ward] Levinson and . . . John Pullman, *Lansky's* international money mover" (emphasis added).[336] Malnik, in turn, is closely associated with Hoover acquaintance Jesse Weiss, living in Miami. The field office is apparently unaware of the connection between Weiss and Malnik.[337] A "Jay Weiss," also living in Miami, is both a close friend of Hoover crony Roy Cohn and Malnik. Cohn and Jay Weiss are mutual investors in Schenley Industries.[338] It is not known whether the two Weisses are related.

FBI (Dallas) learns of Oswald joining the FPCC, probably from SOG.[339] As previously shown, Banister, who keeps extensive files on communists and fellow travelers, has maintained a file on Oswald since at least 1961. Between now and July probably, he becomes interested in the ex-Marine. "Lee Oswald walked into [Banister's] office . . . in [summer] 1963 and asked to fill in the forms for accreditation as one of [his] agents. [Delphina Roberts, Banister's secretary, recalls] 'I gained the impression that he and Guy Banister already knew each other. . . . After Oswald filled out the application form Guy . . . called him into the office [and] . . . a lengthy conversation took place. . . . I presumed then, and now am certain, that the reason for Oswald being there was that he was required to act undercover.' " Banister definitely becomes cognizant of Oswald's activity with the FPCC. "Oswald came back a number of times. . . ." "Mrs. Roberts firmly believes that Banister's 'interest' in Oswald concerned anti-Castro schemes, plans which she feels certain had the support and encouragement of government intelligence agencies." *"Mr. Banister had been a special agent for the FBI and was still working for them. There were quite a number of connections which he kept with the FBI. . . . I know he and the FBI traded information . . ."* (emphasis added).[340]

"Ivan Nitschke, a business associate of Banister and a fellow former FBI agent, recalls that Banister became 'interested in Oswald' in the summer of 1963."[341]

"Adrian Alba . . . testified . . . that he often saw Oswald in the restaurant on the ground floor of 544 Camp St. That restaurant had a rear exit leading up to the office section of the building, and Banister was a regular patron." "Alba . . . had a contract to look after a number of unmarked cars belonging to the . . . FBI. One day in early summer 1963 . . . a man he thought was an 'FBI agent visiting New Orleans from Washington' came to the garage. He showed credentials and was supplied with a green Studebaker from the car pool. A day later [as] Alba . . . watched from his garage he noticed the same green car drive past and stop outside Oswald's place of work—just thirty yards away. . . . says Alba, 'Lee Oswald went across the sidewalk. He bent down as if to look in the window and was handed what appeared to be a good-sized envelope, a white envelope. He turned and bent as if to hold the envelope to his abdomen, and I think he put it under his shirt. Oswald then went back into the building, and the car drove off.' According to Alba, Oswald met the car again a couple of days later and talked briefly with the driver. The 'agent . . .' returned the car to the garage a few days later."[342]

Apparently Oswald is being utilized by the New Orleans field office through Banister's agency to help them infiltrate the Cuban exile community as a way of ferreting out pro-Castroites. As with the FDC and Banister on 1/20/61 (Bolton Ford incident), Oswald's pro-Marxist image, although real to him, again becomes merely a cover from FBI perspective. Because they hold potential leverage over him through his wife, he is forced to cooperate. He does in fact, however, need the money.

Oswald will also play the Mafia side of the fence unknowingly, not realizing that Banister associate David Ferrie is a Marcello functionary. Nor does he realize that Banister also works for, and has accepted money from, the mob leader. He may perceive Ferrie as CIA, assuming funds coming through him and given to exile groups are federal. He would very likely have no way of knowing that Marcello is also a major, if not the primary, source. As one of Banister's agents then, Ferrie soon becomes aware of Oswald's presence. Presumably privy to the assassination contract, he perceives the potential value of Oswald as a "lone nut," as well as shield against federal investigation after the assassination.

6/1/63—SATURDAY: Ruth Paine writes a letter to Marina. "Everything you do and think is interesting to me. . . . Michael and I don't fight, it's just he doesn't want me."[343]

6/2/63—SUNDAY: Oswald goes again to the library, returning books and checking out *Portrait of a President, The Huey Long Murder Case,* and *The Berlin Wall.*[344]

6/3/63—MONDAY: Oswald orders an additional five hundred membership forms for FPCC from a local printing company.[345]

6/4/63—TUESDAY: Oswald picks up the previously ordered one thousand FPCC handbills.[346]

Press: "The Louisiana Supreme Court upheld today the conviction of District Attorney Jim Garrison of New Orleans on a charge that he defamed the city's eight criminal district judges."[347]

6/5/63—WEDNESDAY: "Ruby placed a 28-minute call to the Old French Opera House, a New Orleans bar owned by Marcello associate Caracci."[348]

Tannenbaum makes a call from the Sho Bar to Ruby, in Dallas.[349] An obvious question here is whether Ruby is on the Justice Department's priority list of twenty-three hundred Mafia associates/members slated for prosecution. Well before the assassination he is assessed with a tax deficiency in excess of forty thousand dollars by the IRS and is known, at least to the FBI, as liaison between the Mafia and the Dallas police force. A second question stemming from this is whether he has, by now, been recorded by ELSUR as a result of his numerous calls to various mob figures around the country. Calls to McWillie at the Thunderbird Hotel are an obvious possibility, given the Bureau's only recently ended surveillance of Las Vegas casinos.

"During the next few days, Ruby visited New Orleans, where he was seen by several persons in the Bourbon Street night club district. Among them . . . [was] . . . Caracci. . . ."[350]

This day there is a "memorandum from [Hoover] to Robert Kennedy . . . containing assertions that . . . [John] Kennedy in 1960 had settled out of court a breach-of-promise suit, going back to 1951, for $500,000. The story was improbable on the face. . . ."[351] A story this old is hardly likely to be news to, or taken seriously by, RFK. Hoover may have other motivations.

Press reports Hoover friend "Representative Edwin E. Willis, Democrat of Louisiana, was elected chairman of the House Committee on Un-American Activities today."[352]

Oswald picks up five hundred FPCC application forms from the printer. Surely Banister at some point perceives that through completed FPCC membership forms he can determine the identities of local pro-Castroites, all the more reason to let Oswald promote the organization unhindered.[353]

". . . The Navy Discharge Review Board . . . wrote to . . . Oswald that [his] request to have his undesirable discharge from the Marine Corps changed was under review."[354]

Marina writes letter to Ruth. "Lee . . . has made it plain he doesn't want to live with me."[355]

6/6/63—THURSDAY: FBI (New York) ELSUR records Mafia chief Magaddino: "Here we are situated with this administration. . . . We got from the President down against us. . . . But we got to resist. Today. You see this table? (hits table) You have got to do something material."[356] Like other sensitive ELSUR product, this recording is soon sent by AIRTEL to Hoover, who again does nothing. Note how the eastern Mafia families are still grappling with the question of what to do.

Ruby's attorney, Graham R. E. Koch, tells the IRS he will settle the mobster's accounts due, now $39,129, "as soon as arrangements can be made to borrow money. . . . and will contact this office not later than June 14."[357]

Press: "The Senate Judiciary Committee approved today a bill providing that future directors of the Federal Bureau of Investigation shall be appointed by the President, subject to Senate approval, for 15-year terms. The directorship is not now a statutory office. The director is appointed by and serves at the pleasure of the Attorney General. J. Edgar Hoover, who would not be affected by the bill, has held the post since it was created in 1924. *The bill,* introduced by Senator Everett McKinley Dirksen, . . . *would provide that future directors shall not be eligible for reappointment"* (emphasis added).[358] One cannot escape the feeling that history is catching up with Hoover. The tone of press coverage clearly implies that time is running out. He would have read such an article with growing trepidation. Note the awareness in Congress that an overly long tenure in such a position is no longer acceptable.

6/8/63—SATURDAY: On June 5 "Ruby got in his car—left Dallas . . . [and] turn[ed] up in New Orleans . . . [on] June 8" contacting Tannenbaum that night. He remains in town three days.[359] There can be little doubt his role, in large part, is to provide logistical support for the plan to assassinate President Kennedy. As

Dallas P.D. liaison, he can obtain valuable information about local preparations for the coming visit, as well as data about Secret Service plans. Obviously details about the motorcade route and its timing, building searches, etc., are essential.

6/10/63—MONDAY: Press reports: "President Kennedy has sold the television rights to his Pulitzer Prize–winning book of biographies, *Profiles in Courage*. The buyer . . . will film 26 hour-long dramatizations for the National Broadcasting Company. . . . It was learned that his royalties would total $351,000. . . . The President will donate his royalties to charity."[360] Contrast this move by Kennedy with the freeloading style of Hoover.

Oswald writes to *The Worker* for literature to supplement his FPCC handbills.[361]

6/13/63—THURSDAY: Senate Bill 603, governing Hoover's replacement, is passed by the Senate, but there is apparently no corresponding bill in the House.[362] This is logical in light of Hoover's power with the latter body. His annual refusal to testify before the Senate may well have cut against him in the passage of this bill. The Senate has now clearly sided with the President regarding the Director's impending retirement.

6/14/63—FRIDAY: "Ruby placed a 7-minute call to the Old French Opera House, owned by Caracci. [He] also placed 8-minute and 4-minute calls on June 19 and an 11-minute call on June 21 to that same number."[363]

6/15/63—SATURDAY: Today is the return date for Oswald's books, including *Portrait of a President*. Apparently he indulges in a protest against administration policies by stamping "Fair Play For Cuba Committee, New Orleans, La." on the flyleaf.[364] This is typical of Oswald's style (i.e., nonviolent protest).

6/16/63—SUNDAY: ". . . Oswald was seen on the dock at the port of New Orleans, handing out pro-Castro leaflets to sailors from an aircraft carrier, the USS *Wasp*. Like the last propaganda distribution in Dallas, this . . . effort quickly fizzled. Alerted by a passing naval officer, a policeman ordered Oswald to leave at once."[365] He immediately flees.

6/17/63—MONDAY: ". . . Hosty . . . receiving word that Oswald has written to *The Worker* [from] New Orleans, asks New Orleans FBI to verify Oswald's presence in the Crescent City."[366]

U.S. Senate refers S.603 to the *House Judiciary Committee* for consideration.[367]

6/18/63—TUESDAY: RFK, attending an Equal Employment Opportunity meeting, begins openly arguing with LBJ, ostensibly over minority opportunity. "Johnson, obviously angry, slumped grimly in his chair, his eyes half closed. 'It was . . . pretty brutal . . . very sharp. It brought tensions between [the two] right out on the table and very hard. . . . After making the Vice President look like a fraud . . . [Kennedy left].' "[368] From this point on, the two are bitter enemies. President Kennedy's opinion of Johnson also deteriorates.

6/19/63—WEDNESDAY: Vice President Johnson attends the seventy-first graduation ceremony of the FBI National Academy, where he addresses the group. "I welcomed the opportunity to . . . express appreciation to . . . my friend and for many years my good neighbor, J. Edgar Hoover . . . [and] . . . this great organization headed by this great American. . . ."[369]

New York Beckley associate A. Reyn is again indicted. Press: "The Government . . . described him as a $1,000,000-a-year bookmaker and . . . charged [him] with failing to have the $50 Federal gambling stamp. . . . *Reyn . . . was once employed as a race-horse clerk in Reno, Nevada, and has a prior criminal record for gambling in New Orleans . . .*" (emphasis added).[370]

Ruby calls Caracci-controlled Old French Opera House twice this day.[371]

6/20/63—THURSDAY: Johnson writes Hoover, thanking him for praising his speech the day before. "I deeply appreciate your much-too-kind comments. . . . It was wonderful to be with you. I shall look forward to when time and circumstances will allow us another opportunity to get together."[372]

Baker and Levinson meet with Intercontinental officials in New York in furtherance of obtaining an interest in the corporation's Caribbean casinos. Levinson is introduced as "owner of the Fremont Hotel in Las Vegas. . . ."[373] Associated with Levinson in the venture is Clifford A. Jones, former lieutenant governor of Nevada, Democratic National Committeeman, and part owner of the *Thunderbird Hotel.* Baker is aware of the connection.[374] Hoover has known since 1954 that Jones is closely tied to the Mafia.[375]

6/21/63—FRIDAY: Ruby again calls the Old French Opera House.[376]

Press reports: "The Navy ended uncertainty over the future of Vice Admiral . . . Rickover today by announcing that he would be recalled to active duty after retiring next winter. He has made no secret . . . of his desire to remain on active duty."[377]

6/22/63—SATURDAY: President Kennedy meets with black civil rights leaders, including Martin Luther King, Jr., in the Rose Garden. ". . . [He] . . . invited King to stroll in the Rose Garden. . . . The FBI, Kennedy said, was greatly concerned; 'I assume you know you're under very close surveillance.' He warned King against discussing significant matters over the phone with [Stanley] Levison, whom Hoover regarded, Kennedy said, as a 'conscious agent of the Soviet conspiracy.' (King, noting that Kennedy had walked him out into the garden, reflected, 'The President is afraid of Hoover himself . . . I guess Hoover must be buggin' him too.') . . . He named Levison and [Jack] O'Dell. 'They're Communists. You've got to get rid of them . . . If they [the opponents of civil rights] shoot you down, they'll shoot us down too—so we're asking you to be careful.' "[378]

6/23/63—SUNDAY: Hoover personally announces the arrest of the suspected murderer of civil-rights leader Medgar Evers to the press. "J. Edgar Hoover . . . said that following his arraignment on the Federal charge, Mr. Beckwith 'will be made available to Jackson Police Department authorities for questioning in the event they wish to consider filing local murder charges against him. All information developed by the FBI investigation is being turned over to the Jackson Police Department, and the full facilities of the FBI laboratories and identification division, including testimony of laboratory and fingerprint experts and FBI investigating agents, will be available to them. . . .' Mr. Hoover said FBI agents had traced to

Mr. Beckwith a 'golden hawk' telescopic sight similar to the sight found on a rifle recovered at the murder scene."[379]

6/24/63—MONDAY: ". . . Pecora received a telephone call from Marcello . . . at the very same Tropical Court phone from which Pecora called Ruby a month earlier."[380] Unless this is a long-distance call, one or both of the men's telephones has to be tapped.

"Oswald visits passport office, fills out application on which he lists photographer as occupation, gives countries to be visited as 'England, France, Holland, USSR, France, Findland [sic], Poland,' and his tentative time of departure as 'Oct—Jan.' "[381] Note that his wife's second child is due in October. FBI would have been informed of his application.

6/25/63—TUESDAY: Press: "Up to 70 college students from various parts of the United States were reported . . . to be planning to slip out of the country to take a sightseeing trip to Cuba. *The Federal Government* requires specially validated passports for Cuba, and *has been barring travel to Cuba generally except for newsmen* or businessmen. One version was that they might go to Canada in small groups, to fly from Toronto to Havana by special Cuban airliner, tentatively this Friday. One such student trip was blocked last Christmas . . ." (emphasis added).[382]

Oswald receives his passport.[383]

French press reports: "Two men who participated in a nearly successful ambush of President de Gaulle . . . last year were given prison terms today after a two day trial. . . ."[384]

6/28/63—FRIDAY: Press: "AUSTIN, Texas. . . . It seems safe to say that the Administration is in trouble here as it is throughout the South. Some Democrats . . . are wondering about Vice President Johnson's value to a national Democratic ticket in 1964. If the solid South is to be written off in 1964, the question is whether Mr. Johnson will be retained on the ticket. . . . Mr. Johnson is opening an office this summer in Austin, the center of his old Congressional district. Ostensibly this is routine, although this is not normally done until after Congress adjourns. Cliff Carter, a Washington assistant who is relocating his family here and will have charge of the Austin office while still spending some time in Washington, said Mr. Johnson would be traveling this fall, in Texas and elsewhere. One Democratic professional politician even suggested that *the Vice President may be getting into position to run for the Senate in case he is pushed from the national ticket or decides to leave it"* (emphasis added).[385] Interestingly, Texas Senator Lloyd Bentsen, in the 1988 presidential election, will use precisely this peculiarity (in opposite fashion) in state law to safeguard his Senate seat.

6/30/63—SUNDAY: Press reports: "HAVANA . . . Fifty-nine United States college students arrived here today as guests of the Castro Government. They came in defiance of warnings by the United States State Department that they faced possible prison sentences and $5,000 fines. Travel to Cuba without a specially validated passport is against the law. . . ."[386]

Ex-CIA director Dulles comments in an interview on recent sex scandals in British government. "As for the morality of United States intelligence, he said: 'We don't want people in our security services who do not have high moral ethics. We wouldn't hire them in the first place if we knew it.' "[387]

7/63—THIS MONTH: Hoover, in an internal directive, effectively instructs the New Orleans, Dallas, and Miami field offices to start producing meaningful reports on the Mafia, stating those offices are denying the existence of the organization. ". . . Some cities have blind spots about La Cosa Nostra. It is well to note that we have experienced situations in which certain offices took the position that Cosa Nostra did not exist in their respective territories, only to learn at a later date that this organization, with its typical family structure, is in fact in existence in the area and has been for many years."[388] This very likely was generated either just before or after the biannual filing deadline (latter half of June) with SOG. The timing of this directive is unusual in a number of ways. Hoover has known for years that both New Orleans and Dallas have provided him with little information on the Mafia. Why the sudden interest on his part? Such a directive will, at best, only produce evidentiary results by the *next* biannual deadline, 12/18/63. This order, coming just a few months prior to the President's trip south, is obviously a form of self-protection. Hoover can now go on record, if he is forced to, as saying that he tried to get information before the fact, but the mob was a step ahead of him. The Miami field office must be mystified, considering the fact that *they* have produced the Aleman data providing the basic outline to the plan to assassinate the President of the United States. They, hopefully, do not know that Hoover has withheld the evidence generated from Secret Service.

There is also the simple, and brutal, reality that details about the assassination contract are valuable planning tools. Hoover has always controlled his environment and future by having exclusive knowledge about people and future events. The impending assassination is, in this sense, no different from past opportunities. Knowing the timing of the killing, for example, is crucial. Hoover must have positive results prior to 1/1/65 in order to be in position to obtain a retirement waiver from Johnson. In this regard it is to the Director's benefit to encourage the assassination of President Kennedy in the short term.

Press reports that the Italian government has begun a national-level inquiry into the Mafia in hopes of "propos[ing] measures to repress it."[389]

"A second meeting [with Intercontinental officials] was held . . . with . . . Baker . . . [and] . . . Levinson . . . [present]. . . ."[390]

FBI's semiannual summary reports are now complete. These would of course, via ELSUR, detail recent developments regarding the Mafia, reaffirming the existence of the Marcello contract. Given the pervasiveness of the Bureau's electronic surveillance and informant programs, it is entirely possible that between December 1962 and June 1963 Hoover obtains still more data on the coming hit.

"By midsummer [Ruby's] debt to the [IRS] had risen to nearly [forty-two thousand dollars]."[391] From this, it is obvious that he is subject to manipulation by Mafiosi willing to provide the money to salvage his business. It is a control opportunity for Civello and Marcello.

Oswald makes a trip to the library to return two books. This same day "Marina . . . answers . . . letters . . . from the Russian embassy, Washington . . ." in which she requests return visas for her and Lee. Oswald includes a separate note with her letter, stating, "Please rush the entrance visa for . . . Marina. . . . She is going to have a baby in October, therefore you must grant the entrance visa . . . before then. As for my return entrance visa please consider it separtaby [*sic*]."[392] She will later assert that he had been pressuring her to make the request since mid-May. FBI monitors this latest communication to the embassy.

Press: "The Cuban Government has invited '15 to 20' Americans to attend the 10th anniversary celebration this month of Premier Fidel Castro's 26th of July Movement, and has offered to set up a Mexico-Havana trip for them. *The Cuban move could raise* in another form *the issue of the United States ban on travel to Cuba, for which exceptions have been made for reporters. . . ."* (emphasis added).[393]

Press: "Members of the House Committee on Un-American Activities opened hearings . . . today on unauthorized travel to Cuba."[394]

7/2/63—TUESDAY: Press reports: "Attorney General . . . Kennedy announced tonight that agents of the Federal Bureau of Investigation had arrested four persons in New York and Washington today on charges of conspiracy to spy for the Soviet Union. In New York, according to a supplementary announcement by J. Edgar Hoover . . . a United Nations personnel officer and his wife were arrested today. The man took the name of Robert Keistutis Baltch, a Roman Catholic priest, and the woman took the name of Joy Ann Garber. The priest and Joy Ann Garber, a housewife in Norwalk, Conn., were not aware that their identities had been assumed."[395] Note the parallel to Banister's use of Oswald's identity, without his knowledge, over the last three years.

7/3/63—WEDNESDAY: Press reports again on travel to Cuba: ". . . An administrative ruling making United States passports invalid if used for travel to Cuba without special authorization. United States officials acknowledge that these measures are 'too vague' to provide a case for firm legal action against persons violating them. . . . The Senate internal security subcommittee released today testimony by Robert Taber, former executive secretary of the Fair Play For Cuba Committee, at closed hearings held in April 1962. In Dec., 1961, he said, he made a two-week trip to Czechoslovakia on a Cuban passport before returning to the United States. Senator . . . Dodd . . . said in a separate statement today that he thought it 'noteworthy' that in light of his record 'Mr. Taber was able to walk into the American consulate in Hamburg in March of 1962 and have his passport renewed without difficulty.' . . .

The new regulations would make special allowance for newsmen or persons wishing to travel to the island for 'humanitarian' reasons. . . . . . . A department official hinted that the Administration would not stand in the way of any of the writers or newspapermen who might wish to accept a Cuban Government invitation to attend the 10th anniversary celebrations of the 26th of July Movement in Havana."[396] This article demonstrates both the means and motivation for Oswald's planned trip to Cuba and the apparent ease with which it might be accomplished. Oswald will attempt to use his membership in the FPCC, as well as his status as a "newsman" to gain an entrance visa from the Cuban embassy in Mexico City in the fall. In this context, his high-profile involvement in FPCC over the course of the summer is a potentially vital component of his résumé.

Press: ". . . McClellan said today that he would ask his Subcommittee on Investigations 'most any day now' to set a date for the questioning of Billie Sol Estes about his dealings with the Agriculture Department."[397]

7/4/63—THURSDAY: Hoover's holiday essay is released. The subject is, of course, liberty. ". . . The very wellsprings of our being as a nation are spiritual and idealistic. It is against these sources of our freedom that the regimented forces of materialism currently are directing their most concentrated attacks. *The forward march of materialism* is apparent in changing attitudes and standards. It *is to be seen in the incidence of crime, in the bartering of moral integrity* for the cynicism of getting by, and in the refusal of growing numbers of citizens to accept personal responsibility" (emphasis added).[398]

Press reports: "Three Negro writers decided yesterday to take up the Cuban Government's invitations for expense-paid trips to attend the celebration this month of the anniversary of Premier Fidel Castro's revolution. Issued by the Cuban Institute of Friendship with the Peoples, the invitations provided for a '20-day stay, including visits and interviews,' in which the 'Mexico-Havana round-trip fare as well as your stay will be on our account.' "[399]

7/6/63—SATURDAY: On July 6 and 24 "Ruby placed 12-minute and 1-minute calls, respectively, to the Old French Opera House [in New Orleans]."[400]

7/7/63—SUNDAY: "Marina writes . . . Russian embassy, Washington . . . 'I beg you to inform us of the result of my appeals with regard to the departure of our family to the U.S.S.R.. . . . I urgently beg you to facilitate the expediting of this letter for the reason stated in a previous letter.' "[401]

7/9/63—TUESDAY: Press: "C. Sumner Stone, Jr., a Washington editor, and Charles Howard, a correspondent at the United Nations, both of *The Baltimore Afro-American,* said yesterday they would accept invitations for an expense-paid visit to Cuba. Such trips would require State Department validation of passports."[402]

7/11/63—THURSDAY: Ruth Paine sends a letter to Marina. ". . . Think about the possibility of living with me. Marina, come to my home the last part of September without fail, either for two months or two years. And don't be worried about money." Marina responds to this invitation by writing that she and Oswald were now getting along better.[403]

At the library Oswald checks out *Russia Under Khrushchev.* This summer he also reads *Ape and Essence, Brave New World, Goldfinger, Thunderball, Moonraker, From Russia With Love* (a JFK favorite), and several historical novels.[404]

7/15/63—MONDAY: *New York Post* runs an article alleging that the " 'debilitated' CPUSA is kept alive by the work which FBI undercover agents do for it in the course of maintaining their 'masquerade' . . . [and] . . . demand[s] that Hoover be required to explain his use of public funds to strengthen a subversive body that he claims to oppose."[405]

Banister and Marcello's associate Ferrie, as well as Marcello's attorney, Gill, are in Miami attempting to clear Ferrie's name with Eastern Airlines.[406]

Between now and the assassination, FBI (Miami) ELSUR records, four times, conversations between Traficante and other Mafia associates. These apparently occur in a restaurant he frequents.

1963 ELSUR on Santos Traficante in a Miami restaurant.
Traficante: "Let me tell you this. This is what happens to me.

Now, I don't give a (obscene) about the S(urveillance?) and Government. I know when I'm beat, you understand?

I got a numbers office in Orlando. They grab everybody, forty or fifty people. Forty or fifty thousand in bond. They have no evidence, but when they get through it costs thousands.

I got another office in St. Cloud, Florida. You can't even find St. Cloud on the (obscene) map, but the (obscene) "G" found it.

Kennedy's right-hand man, he goes through the (obscene) nigger town. Must have been 2,000 niggers, and makes a (obscene) big raid over there.

Just a start, any (obscene) place that they found a phone connection in there from Tampa. . . ."[407]

This conversation, like the others, is sent by AIRTEL to Hoover. In monitoring Traficante, Hoover is, no doubt, also hoping to obtain more details about the contract on the President, a subject he knows the Miami mafioso is privy to. The feeling one gets from reading this recording is that Traficante is personally, and bitterly, admitting defeat. Oddly, the specific dates of the Traficante recordings are not released with the transcripts. Note the topic is gambling, a common thread running throughout many significant ELSUR recordings involving Miami, New Orleans, Las Vegas, and New York.

7/17/63—WEDNESDAY: President Kennedy holds a press conference, stating that there is no evidence to show any civil-rights leaders are communists. "I think it is a convenient scapegoat to suggest that all the difficulties are communist and if the communist movement would only disappear we would end this."[408]

". . . Hoover wrote to Senators Mike Monroney and Warren Magnuson that a response to their inquiries [about communist influence within King's organization] would soon be forthcoming, but from the Attorney General, not the Bureau. Hoover sent the senators' letters to Kennedy. . . ."[409]

7/18/63—THURSDAY: Press reports: "The State Department issued *special permits* today to allow several writers and newsmen to accept invitations from Premier Fidel Castro to visit Cuba for the July 26 celebrations. *It has been the department's policy to allow newsmen to travel to Cuba if they are accredited to newspapers, magazines, or radio stations"* (emphasis added).[410] Oswald does not miss this point, and will attempt prior to his trip to Mexico City to obtain, in writing, a commitment from eastern magazines for a job as a journalist or photographer. In reality, without such an accreditation, he has little hope of obtaining a "special permit" from the State Department.

7/19/63—FRIDAY: "Oswald is fired from the . . . Reily Coffee Co. for flagrant dereliction of his duties as oiler and maintenance man."[411]

7/22/63—MONDAY: "Oswald visits Louisiana Division of Employment Security office to seek employment and file interstate claim on Texas for unemployment benefits. . . . He collect[s] and live[s] on $33 a week unemployment benefits from Texas" until he leaves for Cuba.[412]

7/23/63—TUESDAY: RFK responds to Senator Monroney and others regarding communism in the black civil-rights movement. "Based on all available information from the FBI . . . we have no evidence that any of the top leaders are communists or communist controlled. This is true as to Dr. Martin Luther King, Jr., about whom particular accusations were made, as well as other leaders."[413] Here RFK attempts to counter yet another round of allegations designed to discredit King. Hoover is quite possibly the source.

7/24/63—WEDNESDAY: Ruby calls the Old French Opera House.[414]

7/25/63—THURSDAY: RFK sends a memo to JFK speechwriter Schlesinger. "I hope you are working on a schedule for our seminars starting in mid-September. You said you would, and if you don't I'll tell J. Edgar————."[415] Such levity from the A.G. at this late date reveals the degree to which he, like the President, is underestimating the Director.

"Oswald is notified that in response to his 1962 demand for a review of his undesirable discharge from the Marine reserve, the decision had been affirmed. . . . 'Careful consideration was given to the evidence presented in your behalf . . . It is the decision that no change, correction, or modification is warranted in your discharge.' " [416] Given Oswald's previous and ongoing leftist activities, it is difficult to say whether this surprises him in any way.

FBI (Miami) ELSUR records Lansky functionary Alvin Malnik and friend Jay Weiss, who have just discovered that his, Malnik's, office has been bugged:

> 11:57 [P.M.]—[Alvin Malnik]—"As I was walking in someone ran out with a bunch of wires . . . I would like to get it checked out . . . If it is bugged I want to find it . . . A guy came walking out of the next office but I didn't question him. . . ." JW [presumably the same Jay Weiss associated with Roy Cohn] states he followed one guy down the street but he had not seen him up in the office. . . .
> 12:16 A.M.—[Malnik] and [Jay Weiss] discussed what a break they had returned to the office.
> 12:22 [A.M.]—Unit shorted.

For no known reason, by morning the tap was working again. . . . Malnik made the mistake of assuming he had permanently interrupted an effort to bug his office.[417]

7/27/63—SATURDAY: "On invitation of cousin Gene Murret . . . Oswald journeys to Mobile [Alabama] with uncle, aunt, and Marina. In evening he gives thirty-minute talk, followed by question period of similar length, to a small group of students and faculty of Jesuit House of Studies on the practice of communism in present-day Russia. . . . 'When he saw what Russia was lacking, he wanted to come back to the United States, which is much better off materially. (He . . . did not like the widespread lack of goods the Russians had to endure.)' "[418]

7/30/63—TUESDAY: Hoover talks in his Washington office with longtime friend Jesse Weiss, a Miami Beach restaurateur, complaining to him that RFK is now in control, and effectively running the Bureau (see 8/12/63).[419]

7/31/63—WEDNESDAY: CPUSA approves Oswald's request, stating in a letter, ". . . We are sending you some litera-

ture." Pamphlets are sent in a separate mailing.[420] Undoubtedly the
FBI learns of this correspondence, possibly even handling the mailing of circulars.

Los Angeles press reports: "A New England newspaper publisher
joined southern segregationists . . . in leveling new charges of
communism in the civil rights controversy. . . . William Loeb,
publisher of the *Manchester* [New Hampshire] *Union Leader,* . . .
[testified] against President Kennedy's public accommodations bill
. . . in the wake of a charge by State Sen. John C. McLaurin of
Mississippi that Atty. Gen. Kennedy is guilty of 'the most brazen
coverup job ever perpetrated on the American people.' McLaurin
challenged the Senate Commerce Committee to call FBI Director J.
Edgar Hoover to testify. 'I am sure he could present ample evidence
that the Communists were and are now using the self-styled Negro
leaders as part of the Communist conspiracy,' he said, adding: 'I
don't think you will get it from Atty. Gen. Robert Kennedy.' "[421]

8/1/63—THURSDAY: *FBI Law Enforcement Bulletin* is released. Hoover's message is civil rights. "There is a pressing need
for communities to face up to the realization that adequate salaries,
training, equipment and respect for the [law-enforcement] profession are essential to the protection of civil liberties. *It is a . . .
moral responsibility"* (emphasis added).[422]

Oswald writes another letter to the FPCC. "In regards to my
efforts to start a branch office in New Orleans. I rented an office as I
planned and was promptly closed three days later for some obsure
[*sic*] reason by the renters [*sic*], they said something about remodel-
ing, etc., [*sic*] I'm sure you understand. After that I worked out of a
post office box and by useing [*sic*] street demonstrations and some
circular work has substained [*sic*] a great deal of interest but no new
members. Through the efforts of some Cuban-exial [*sic*] 'gusanos' a
street demonstration was attacked and we were officially cautioned
by police. This incident robbed me of what support I had leaving
me alone. . . . We also managed to picket the fleet when it came in
and I was surprised at the number of officers who were interested in
our literature."[423] Obviously Oswald's chapter is a failure in the
ordinary sense, but he has succeeded in the sense that he is now
president of an FPCC chapter in the second largest exile community in the U.S. His credentials have seemingly been established for
purposes of obtaining entrance to Cuba.

The "street demonstration" does not actually occur until August 9, presuming he has not been involved in another unreported incident by this date. It raises the possibility he is already planning the incident. If so, the timing of his letter is important, effectively demonstrating to FPCC his ability to plan or stage demonstrations. The Bureau monitors this exchange.

Press reports: "A sweeping desegregation order by three New Orleans Federal judges highlighted the integration battle Thursday. . . . All the city's public parks, playgrounds, community centers and cultural facilities must be desegregated."[424]

"The subject of immunity first came up about a week later . . . when Malnik conferred with Jay Weiss and Jake Kossman, the noted criminal attorney who had defended such men as James Hoffa. . . ."[425]

8/4/63—SUNDAY: Press: "For the first time in the federal war on organized crime, a figure once fairly high in the mob hierarchy is telling all he knows about crime in America. . . . He has verified uncorroborated information previously developed by the FBI as to the existence of a secret, nationwide organization that dominates a network of mobs in more than a dozen American cities. FBI agents had been collecting information indicating the existence of a close-knit criminal syndicate. He is expected to be produced publicly some time this month to testify. . . ."[426] The Justice Department terms the Valachi case, "an extraordinarily important intelligence breakthrough."[427]

"Ruby placed a 5-minute call to the Thunderbird Hotel in Las Vegas, presumably to McWillie. The same day, a call was placed to one of Ruby's phones from the Tropical Court office phone of . . . Nofio Pecora. Pecora later admitted that he had exclusive access to that New Orleans phone." Ruby then flies to New York (American Airlines flight #186), arriving at the New York Hilton at 10:59 P.M. He calls the Old French Opera House in New Orleans.[428]

8/5/63—MONDAY: FBI (New Orleans) becomes the office of Chief Responsibility for Oswald.[429] This in all likelihood is nothing more than an administrative event. Logically an individual would have to remain in a given locality for a certain period before he would be considered a resident. Recall that the local field office has known of his presence since the beginning of May.

Ferrie, Banister, and Gill attend EAL (Eastern Airlines) hearing in Miami where further testimony is taken.[430]

Oswald goes to Cuban exile leader Carlos Bringuier's clothing store posing as an anti-Castroite in an attempt to infiltrate his organization but is not taken seriously. He vows to return with a Marine Corps training manual as a way of demonstrating his sincerity.[431]

Johnson again corresponds with Hoover, thanking him for the feature article in the August edition of the *FBI Law Enforcement Bulletin.* "I appreciated the opportunity to be with you and I enjoyed the occasion thoroughly."[432]

8/6/63—TUESDAY: "Ruby checked out of the Hilton at 4:40 P.M. . . . On the return to Dallas he went via Chicago. . . . While [there] he stopped at Henrici's Restaurant. . . . Across the street . . . was the Sherman Hotel, a Mafia hangout. . . ."[433] This summer Ruby also speaks with Chicago mobster Lenny Patrick, supposedly about union problems at his Dallas nightclubs.[434] FBI (Chicago) has by now credited Mafia contract killer Lenny Patrick, a friend of Marcello/Traficante liaison man Dave Yaras, with the 2/28/63 execution of Benjamin F. Lewis (a Mayor Daley protégé).[435] Likewise, Yaras is a suspect in the August 1961 torture slaying of "Action" Jackson.

"Oswald returns to Casa Roca, [and] leaves [his] *Marine Guidebook* with Bringuier's brother-in-law."[436]

Press: "The underworld has set a price of $100,000 on the head of Joseph Valachi. . . . . . . The Justice Department's increasing pressure on organized crime is being credited here for a sudden increase in the number of talkative hoodlums. . . . One informant said . . . 'When the man at the top wants a job done . . . he has no trouble letting out the contract. There's always someone who will do it—and for peanuts, too.' Investigators also expressed some surprise over the size and complex structure of Cosa Nostra."[437]

8/8/63—THURSDAY: Oswald is reportedly seen in Orst Pena's bar (Pena is an FBI informant) with an Hispanic individual. "Pena claimed after the assassination that Oswald had been in his bar—one night just before the fracas in the street with Bringuier and the anti-Castro Cubans." He is also supposedly seen various times this summer in the company of FBI agent Warren Debrueys, the local case officer in charge of political groups. Debrueys will

deny ever being with Oswald.[438] The ex-Marine *is,* however, classified by the local field office in the political/subversive groups file. At
the least, Debrueys is aware of him and has undoubtedly read his
file.

8/9/63—FRIDAY: Seeing Oswald handing out FPCC leaflets
on a New Orleans street corner, Bringuier and other exiles assault
the young Marxist. Lee attempts to block their blows rather than
fight. His circulars have Banister's 544 Camp Street address
stamped on them. He is also carrying a "Viva Fidel" placard.[439]
"Shortly after 4:00 P.M. Oswald, along with Bringuier and two
other Cubans, is arrested by New Orleans police for disturbing the
peace in the 700 block of Canal Street. The three Cubans raise bail
of $25 each; Oswald spends the night in jail." Bringuier: " 'And I
was more angry, and I went near Oswald to hit him. . . . But
when he sensed my intention, he put his arm down as an X . . .' Q:
'He crossed his arms in front of him?' A: 'That is right, put his
face. . . .' "[440] The local press becomes aware of the incident. Bringuier's release is secured by Orst Pena, who will later claim Oswald was somehow connected with intelligence agencies that summer.[441] Banister's ". . . reaction was casual, 'Don't worry about
him. He's a nervous fellow, he's confused. He's with us, he's associated with the office.' "[442] It is not known whether Banister is aware
of the 544 Camp Street address on Oswald's leaflets, but "When
somebody in the office mentioned the pro-Castro demonstration,
Banister . . . merely laughed."[443]

   The effect of this incident is that local Cuban exiles now possibly
perceive Oswald and Banister as pro-Castroites, not really friends of
the resistance. This is to Oswald's gain, as he has now lost his value
to Banister and the FBI as an "anti-Castroite" in New Orleans.
However, the Bureau still has potential power over him through his
wife. Oswald has undoubtedly staged this event to bolster his credentials as a Marxist and avoid informing further for the New Orleans FBI through Banister.

   Press: "A Federal judge sentenced a gambler to a year in prison
yesterday for refusing to answer questions about a Florida dice
game that authorities said was attended by a 'who's who of organized crime.' . . . The dice game, described by a Federal investigator as 'possibly the largest floating crap game in the United States,'
was in operation for a month last winter at Ojus, Fla. The dice game

took place in a private house with blacked-out windows, it was learned. Limousines transported participants from Miami Beach hotels."[444]

8/10/63—SATURDAY: ". . . In custody at the New Orleans police station, Oswald asked to see somebody from the FBI. . . . [Special Agent John] Quigley reports being contacted by a police intelligence officer who 'said that Oswald was desirous of seeing an agent and supplying to him information with regard to his activities with the FPCC [Fair Play For Cuba Committee] in New Orleans.' Just what 'information' Oswald discussed with Quigley and what his real relationship was with the Bureau . . . remains a fuzzy area. The performance of the New Orleans FBI office is, moreover, singularly patchy. . . ." . . . "For an hour and a half . . . Quigley sat talking with [him]. . . ."[445] Oswald gives him copies of the leaflets and information, some of it false.[446] Obviously he is aware that Banister's agency serves as independent contractor for the New Orleans FBI. By staging the street demonstration and then dealing directly with the power behind Banister, he can step out of the intelligence loop. Quigley is the same agent who had reviewed Oswald's Navy file when he defected to Russia.[447]

 After the interview, Oswald calls his Uncle Dutz for bail money but reaches Dutz's daughter, who in turn calls "Emile Bruno. . . . an associate of two Syndicate deputies of Carlo Marcello." This includes Nofio Pecora.[448] Bruno posts bond for Oswald who then proceeds to the city editor of the *States-Item,* asking him for more coverage regarding FPCC.[449]

7/63—8/63:   Banister this summer hires Allen and Daniel Campbell as agents. They are former Marines. ". . . When [Daniel] Campbell returned to his office, a young man 'with a marine haircut' came in and used his desk phone for a few minutes. . . . It was . . . Lee Oswald."[450]

 Press reports: "Billie Sol Estes and his family left Pecos today. A shot had been fired into their home last night. The bullet hit a livingroom window, but no one was injured. The police said it apparently had come from a .22 caliber pistol."[451]

8/11/63—SUNDAY: Uncle Dutz ". . . went right out to their apartment to talk to Lee, and . . . asked [him] in a fatherly way, what he was doing, . . . 'You be sure you show up at that courthouse for the trial. . . .' "[452]

Marina mails a letter to Ruth informing her it is all right to come visit in September. "Until we meet in New Orleans."[453] The note is in response to the latter's prior offer to let Marina live with her for "two months or two years."

Press reports: "Sen. . . . McClellan . . . said . . . he plans to call mobster Joseph Valachi out of hiding soon to tell senators publicly what he knows about Cosa Nostra. . . ."[454]

8/12/63—MONDAY: "Oswald appears in court, pleads guilty to 'disturbing the peace by creating a scene,' [and] pays a fine of $10. Charges against his Cuban adversaries are dismissed. . . . In the court was at that moment [a] cameraman from WDSU, and . . . he did an interview with Oswald. . . ."[455] Actually, Uncle Dutz pays the fine.[456] Ominously, with him is an associate of Marcello lieutenant Nofio Pecora.[457] Undoubtedly the individual is there to observe Oswald and report back to the Marcello lieutenant.

FBI (Miami) ELSUR records Hoover's friend Jesse Weiss (JW), who is visiting with Lansky functionary Malnik (AM). ". . . Weiss . . . operated a stone-crab restaurant on Miami Beach and whose friendship with John Edgar Hoover was such that a word to the Director about the off-duty cop at the restaurant door was enough to get that officer into the FBI Police Academy." Weiss is also a friend of Meyer Lansky's. Hoover may well be aware of the relationship as he no doubt maintains files on people he associates with. The transcript is as follows:

AM and JW begin discussion of law enforcement and methods used . . . then AM mentions FBI and Dir. Hoover—

JW: But Al, you don't see anything in the paper about him; it's all BOBBY KENNEDY.
AM: That's all; nothing about him.
JW: They are taking the play away from him.
AM: Hoover is a lost . . .
JW: Cause.
AM: A lost cause, that's all: a lost cause.
AM: Well, does HOOVER realize this great transformation that's happening within his own organization?

JW: I spoke to him two weeks ago—I was in Washington
       before he went to California—he goes out to California
       every year—*he goes to Scripps Clinic* in LA JOLLA—
       couple—goes out there every year —*6 weeks ago* . . .
       [inaud] . . . it's like he . . . he told me the same
       thing . . . shucks, the Bureau is shot, what the hell, he
       says, *but what can I do, he says;* the Attorney General is
       the boss of the Bureau, he runs it . . . dare you to defy
       it (emphasis added).[458]

Once again Hoover is in close interaction with people tied to
Mafia associates of Marcello. The revelation Weiss provides here is
undoubtedly disseminated to other mob figures. Within a week
Malnik will meet with *Hoffa* associate Jake Kossman and *Levinson*
associate Benjamin Sigelbaum. Even if retold only casually, Weiss's
revelation would be taken quite seriously by such men, and would
get back to Levinson and Hoffa within a short time. Bear in mind
that Hoffa and Levinson have in recent months come under increasing pressure from the federal government.

The recording may also be a confirmation of Tolson's worsening
heart condition. The phrase ". . . 6-weeks ago . . . [inaud] . . ."
is intriguing. Recall that it was very likely in June, just over six weeks
earlier, that Clyde began experiencing heart trouble. Mention of this
time frame in the context of "Scripps Clinic," Hoover's, and presumably Tolson's, private physicians, lends support to the possibility.
Information such as this may lead people like Marcello and Traficante to believe Hoover's fall is imminent.

"At a third meeting . . . [with Intercontinental officials] . . .
again arranged by 'Baker's office' but unattended by him, Levinson
showed up . . . with [Clifford Jones]."[459]

Oswald writes a letter to FPCC president, Mr. Lee. "Continuing
my efforts on behalf of the F.P.C.C. I find that I have incurred the
displeasure of the Cuban exile 'worms' here. I was attacked by three
of them as the copy of the enclosed summons indicates. I was fined
$10 and the three Cubans were not fined because of 'lack of evi-
dence' as the judge said. I am very glad I am stirring things up and
shall continue to do so. The incident was given considerable coverage in the press and local TV news broadcasts. I am sure it will be to
the good of the Fair Play for Cuba Committee."[460]

8/13/63—TUESDAY: *Times-Picayune* notes: "Pamphlet Case Sentence Given."

Oswald ". . . went so far as to telephone a prominent New York radio reporter, Long John Nebel, offering to appear on Nebel's radio show at his own expense."[461] He also writes a letter, including clipping and summons copies, to CPUSA.[462] Of course the FBI monitors this latest action.

"On August 13 Hoover's office sent a two-page memo to Deputy Attorney General Katzenbach that dealt only with King's personal life and sexual activities. Copies of that memo went to Marshall and the Attorney General as well. On August 20 Robert Kennedy sent a copy to his brother at the White House, with a cover note stating, 'I thought you would be interested in the attached memorandum.' "[463]

FBI (Miami) ELSUR again records Malnik. Discussing money for a business deal, he states he is not worried about having large sums in his office because ". . . *the best protection I got . . . better than President Kennedy has . . .*" (emphasis added).[464]

8/14/63—11/22/63: FBI (Miami) ELSUR. ". . . Surveillance on Johnny 'Dee' Palmisano in Florida. He is in conversation with an associate, Ralph Petillo, discussing the FBI and Attorney General's fight against organized crime. Johnny Dee says *Hoover is not heard of anymore because of the Kennedys"* (emphasis added).[465] Consider this in light of Weiss's revelation to Malnik and the immediately preceding recording. Palmisano is probably a Traficante functionary.

8/14/63—WEDNESDAY: "An air of international intrigue was added to the [Baker] case by Ellen Rometsch. . . . While her husband, Rolf, worked . . . in . . . the German Embassy, Ellen . . . [worked] . . . as a Washington call girl." Hoover ". . . began [an] investigation. . . . The German Ambassador was advised that the sergeant's wife was persona non grata. 'Then on August 14th, my superior told me that my wife had been indulging in . . . [affairs]. Seven days later Ellen and I were on our way back to Germany.' "[466] On September 27, the serviceman will obtain a preliminary divorce decree.[467]

FBI (Miami) ELSUR on Malnik continues. "[Jake] Kossman came to Malnik's office . . . and there was a review of Malnik's continuing investigation of the FBI. Victor Powell. . . . identified as the FBI agent who had entered Malnik's office, was mentioned in a whisper. The FBI log notes . . . It's possible that JK advises AM to [murder] Powell.

> JK: 'You're not going to kill him are you?'
> AM: 'I'm going to have the Causa *[sic]* Nostra . . . [laughing].' "[468]

Press: "The U.S. Army is guarding Mafia canary Joe Valachi behind barbed wire at Ft. Monmouth, N.J., the New York News learned exclusively Tuesday night. The mobster who squealed on the infamous 'Cosa Nostra' apparatus was turned over to the Army by the FBI after it was discovered that the gangs had offered $100,000 to have him killed."[469]

8/16/63—FRIDAY: ". . . Oswald contrived another scene in the street. . . . He went to the waiting room of a state employment office, offering money to anyone who would help him hand out leaflets 'for a few minutes at noon.' . . . At noon Oswald—accompanied by [two men]—arrived outside the International Trade Mart. They passed out pro-Castro leaflets for just a few minutes. . . . Oswald's demonstration was filmed by a unit from WDSU—the local TV station. . . ."[470]

Bringuier sent his "friend . . . to Oswald's house . . . Oswald was defending Fidel Castro, and he advised to my friend that . . . he will fight defending Castro. . . ." After he leaves, Lee tells Marina, "[It] is probably some . . . FBI agent. . . . Lee did not believe him."[471]

Press: "The latest Harris survey of a cross-section of American voters shows Mr. Kennedy running an average of 57–43% over Govs. Nelson A. Rockefeller, George W. Romney and William W. Scranton and Sen. Barry Goldwater. This would be a landslide victory approximating that of ex-President Dwight D. Eisenhower over Adlai Stevenson in 1958 (58%–42%)."[472]

8/17/63—SATURDAY: "William Stuckey of WDSU radio makes early morning call at Oswald's apartment with offer to do broadcast interview that evening. . . . He finds Oswald eager to appear on his weekly 'Latin Listening Post,' . . . 'He appeared to be a very logical, intelligent fellow. . . .' " In his appearance

Oswald discusses a wide range of political ideas, including: " '. . . government agencies, particularly certain covert, under cover agencies like the now-defunct CIA— . . . its leadership is now defunct. Allen Dulles is now defunct. . . . With a little bit different, humanitarian, handling of the situation, Cuba would not be the problem it is today.' Stuckey: 'I have heard . . . Castro turned left because he could not get . . . aid for industrialization . . . from the U.S.' Oswald: '. . . That was a factor . . . But the current of history is not running to that extreme. . . .' "[473] Unknown to Oswald is the fact that Stuckey is being briefed by the local FBI (probably Agents Quigley or Debrueys) regarding his background. After the event Oswald writes the FPCC, telling of his media appearance.[474]

Stuckey has apparently made a tape recording of his interview with Oswald while at his home. He will paraphrase the tape for reporters after the assassination, stating a number of Oswald's views on various topics, including Cuba. *"That democracy, in his opinion, meant the right to be a member of a minority and not to be suppressed—a right that is lacking in the United States, he said, for persons who want to see Cuba for themselves"* (emphasis added).[475] The interview reaffirms the fact that Oswald has read the articles detailing the attempts of various groups to go to Cuba. Accordingly he is undoubtedly aware that newspapermen and writers can gain visas and expense-paid travel to Cuba via the Cuban embassy in Mexico City.

"When Oswald made news in August with his New Orleans street activities, FBI headquarters did ask the New Orleans office to investigate and report in full. Even so, no report was sent until more than two months later, and it was oddly uninformative considering the furor Oswald had been causing. It hardly reflected the intense attention the FBI was, in fact, paying to Oswald. . . ."[476] Very likely, one or more reports are sent to Hoover prior to November 18, but in the attempt to conceal his duplicity after the fact he may well order portions restructured or destroyed. There is also the fact that Oswald is not particularly sophisticated as leftists go. Simply put, there may not be a great deal to report. For that matter Banister may have the bulk of the information.

8/19/63—MONDAY: WDSU arranges with Oswald for another appearance. "I arranged a debate show . . . called 'Conversation Carte Blanche' . . . a 25-minute public affairs program that runs daily . . . Oswald called me . . . and he said yes, . . . and then he said, 'How many of you am I going to have to fight?' " The station gives a copy of Saturday's tape to the New Orleans FBI.[477]

"Ruby placed a 1-minute call to the Thunderbird Hotel in Las Vegas, followed by a 2-minute call on August 20 and a 7-minute call on August 22 to that phone. . . . McWillie acknowledged calls from Ruby at the Thunderbird in August . . ." after the assassination.[478]

FBI (Miami) ELSUR records Levinson/Baker/Lansky associate Ben Sigelbaum meeting with Malnik:

Sigelbaum:	. . . it's counterintelligence information. I was supposed to drop a copy to you. . . .
Malnik:	What is this a copy of?
Sigelbaum:	This is the information they got from the Justice Department, from somebody, highly intelligence *[sic]*, somebody the boys know. Ya know, they can be informed. Just like you have your contacts, they have their few friends. This is from Justice.[479]

"Other FBI agents listening to recordings [previously made] in Las Vegas casinos were equally startled to learn that Lansky's men there also obtained FBI reports. . . ."[480] The obvious source here is, ultimately, Hoover himself. By way of Johnson, Baker may have obtained information that he in turn made available to Levinson or Sigelbaum, or both. Similar allegations have been made with regard to Roy Cohn and the Director.[481] Also, in the past Hoover has provided Johnson with Bureau reports on prospective employees.

CORE (Congress of Racial Equality) begins intensifying demonstrations in Plaquemine, Louisiana (a suburb of Baton Rouge). Its national director, James Farmer, arrives on August 18 and is arrested on August 19. Protests continue through at least 8/29/63.[482]

8/20/63—TUESDAY: Ruby calls McWillie in Las Vegas.[483]

8/21/63—WEDNESDAY: A district judge in Baton Rouge grants an injunction to stop the CORE protests.[484]

At 5:30 P.M. Oswald appears on WDSU to debate, defending FPCC and himself:

Stuckey:	Are you a Marxist?
Oswald:	Yes, I am a Marxist. . . .
Bringuier:	Do you agree with . . . Castro when . . . he qualified President John F. Kennedy . . . as a ruffian and a thief?
Oswald:	I would not agree with that particular wording. . . . I . . . think that . . . certain agencies, mainly the State Department and the CIA, has made monumental mistakes in its relations with Cuba. . . .[485]

"Oswald was unusually invisible between 8/21/63 and 9/17/63."[486] Much of this time is apparently spent preparing his résumé for the trip to Cuba.

8/22/63—THURSDAY: Ruby calls McWillie in Las Vegas.[487]

8/23 to 8/31/63:   Tolson enters the hospital, undergoing open heart surgery (probably a bypass).[488] He will return to work in some capacity by September 18 but apparently is never the same. He will not attend the annual Bureau budgetary hearings in early 1964.[489] During the course of the Warren Commission hearings, he will suffer debilitating strokes.[490] Prior knowledge of the Marcello contract, as well as Hoover's manipulation of Johnson, may have contributed to his deteriorating condition. Although the record indicates that Tolson has nothing but contempt for the President, sheer knowledge of the impending assassination is undoubtedly highly stressful. Hoover, however, may blame President Kennedy for Clyde's failing health.

8/24/63—SATURDAY: New York Journal American releases a Hoover interview entitled, "Hoover Warns—Beware of Red Deception."

To say that communism is not a danger in the United States today, is to help this party strategy. Part of the Communist strategy today is to make it appear that the party is weak and

is being harassed by the FBI. . . . There is nothing the Communists would like more than to be accepted as respected citizens who are considered thoroughly loyal and working in the
best interests of America. As long as 10,000 hardcore Communists exist in the United States, they represent a "soft spot" in
our national security. . . . Claims that the party is composed
chiefly of FBI informants and supported by FBI funds are
absolutely wrong. The Bureau, of course, cannot, for obvious
reasons, identify the exact number of informants. However, it
is proportionately small to the total party membership. . . .

Texas Chapter of FBI National Academy passes a resolution
commending Hoover, who, they state, ". . . has . . . made a contribution of inestimable value in elevating the ethics and standards
of law enforcement. . . . . . We . . . pledge our complete confidence and wholehearted assistance to Mr. Hoover. . . . Resolved,
That copies of this resolution be forwarded to His Excellency the
Honorable John F. Kennedy. . . ."[491]

8/25/63—SUNDAY: Ruth Paine writes back to Marina, stating she will ". . . arrive in New Orleans on the [20th of Septem-
ber]."[492]
   Press: "Talkative mobster Joseph Valachi is reported to have
given federal agents tips linking big shots of an American 'crime
syndicate' with the dread Mafia in Italy."[493] Revelations such as this
further confirm the inherently foreign nature of the Mafia. Truly the
nation is at war with this criminal organization.

8/28/63—WEDNESDAY: The freedom march on D.C. takes
place, led by King and others. Hoover is reportedly furious.[494]
   Oswald again writes CPUSA, asking advice about how to proceed with his efforts on behalf of Marxism. "Should I dissociate [sic]
myself from all progressive activities? . . . I feel that I may have
compromised the F.P.C.C., so you can see that I need the advise of
trusted, long time fighters for progress. Please advise."[495]

8/31/63—SATURDAY: In an apparent attempt to create an
image of himself as a photographer, presumably with an eye toward
building his résumé, Oswald drafts a letter to *The Worker*'s managing editor, stating, "As a commercial photographer I have, in the

past, made blow-ups, reverses and other types of photo work for the 'Worker.' Mr. Weinstock, in December 1962, expressed thanks for my modest work. . . . Mr. Tormey of the Gus Hall-Ben Davis defense committee also commended some photos I did. . . . I am familiar with most forms of Photo . . . work, and . . . the greatest desire imaginable is to work directly for the 'Worker.' . . . My family and I shall, in a few weeks, be relocating into your area."[496] Consider this letter against the comments of past employers such as Jaggers-Chiles (i.e., Oswald's inability to learn how to even size a photographic print).

9/63—THIS MONTH: FBI (Philadelphia) AIRTEL to Hoover regarding Marcello informant's report on the New Orleans incident (three men, including the "professor," discussing a rifle ad, and President's coming south). ". . . A September 1963 FBI teletype reported that a discussion of such a plot had been overheard in March 1963." Supposedly this information is also sent by AIRTEL to the Dallas and Miami SACs.[497] And yet, no such threat will be found in the Secret Service's PRS file for Dallas prior to the President's ill-fated trip.

"In an FBI interview in September 1963 [Ruby associate James] Woodard admitted having 'furnished ammunition and dynamite to both Castro and Cuban exile forces.' "[498]

Hoover has by now learned of Oswald's joining FPCC in April 1963, in New Orleans, as well as of his possible prior efforts to do so in Dallas. Again, this suggests that Hoover has received an updated report on Oswald. Does this not imply that he is also probably aware of Oswald's dealings with Banister and Ferrie? Both are now actively engaged in investigative work for Gill in the context of Marcello's federal criminal prosecution.[499] Like Ruby, Ferrie is probably involved with the contract in some logistical manner. Hoover also knows that Banister and Ferrie are virulently anti-Castro and anti-Kennedy; Ferrie is associated with Marcello and the exile organizations; and Oswald has worked for the Bureau as an informant through Banister, appearing publicly as a strong pro-Castroite. Do not forget that Hoover has known for years that Banister is probably the individual behind the use of Oswald's name and identity.

"Ferrie's ties to the Marcello . . . family continued through his association with . . . Gill. . . . Ferrie told the FBI [after the assassination] that he had begun work on Marcello's case after his last Eastern grievance hearing. In telling the Bureau about his work for Marcello, however, he mentioned only activities in October and November."[500]

"Talks between the Cuban delegate to the United Nations, Charles Lechuga, and a U.S. delegate, William Attwood, are proposed by the Cubans."[501]

One morning fairly early in the month, "Sometime after ten o'clock . . . a black Cadillac parked near the registrar's office [in Clinton, Louisiana] . . . almost everyone noticed it. . . . There were three men in the car, and one, a slim young white, got out and joined the blacks waiting to register. . . . After the assassination, witnesses were unanimous in saying this had been Lee Oswald. . . . Registrar, Henry Palmer . . . remembered dealing . . . with [him]. . . . 'I asked him for his identification, and he pulled out a U.S. Navy I.D. card . . . it was Lee H. Oswald with a New Orleans address. . . .' Oswald . . . [said] . . . he wanted a job at the nearby East Louisiana State Hospital; . . . [Palmer] told Oswald he had not been in the area long enough to qualify for registration. Oswald thanked him and departed. Meanwhile, out in the street, the black Cadillac had been attracting considerable interest. . . . [a] policeman, [and] other witnesses, later remembered the driver as 'a big man, gray haired, with a ruddy complexion.' Two witnesses . . . remembered the second man . . . for one feature in particular. As CORE chairman Collins put it, 'The most outstanding thing about him was his eyebrows and hair. They didn't seem . . . as if they were real hair.' . . . The town barber . . . remembers Oswald asking for advice on getting a job. . . . He sent him to the State Representative, Reeves Morgan, who confirms that a Lee Oswald did come to see him. Two secretaries at the hospital recall Oswald . . . [but] it seems highly unlikely that Oswald really wanted either to live or work in Clinton. [There is the] possible presence of Banister and Ferrie. . . . The incident was connected with . . . the FBI's . . . Counterintelligence Program . . . COINTELPRO."[502]

"Come the autumn, [Ruby] was advertising a nightclub for sale in a local paper."[503] This month he makes only three out-of-state phone calls, all to relatives. There are no known trips.[504]

9/1/63—SUNDAY: *FBI Law Enforcement Bulletin* is released. The theme of Hoover's message is the Mafia.

> In recent weeks, nationwide attention has been focused on the inner workings of a sinister criminal syndicate known as "La Cosa Nostra." . . . The relentless determination of cooperative law enforcement is beginning to close the circle of secrecy protecting this unholy alliance. . . . As stated in my message here in January 1962, a successful penetration at that time was being made into "the innermost sanctums of the criminal deity," an action which was "creating an uneasy stir among professional vice lords." Information furnished to the FBI since June 1962, by a Federal prisoner, a member of "La Cosa Nostra" since 1930, has corroborated and embellished the facts developed by the FBI as early as 1961 which disclosed the makeup of this gangland horde. . . . Through . . . murder —underworld kings have grown into a dominating force on the national scene. Most have amassed great wealth and accumulated major holdings in widespread business enterprises. Some unions are controlled and exploited by hoodlums. Criminal influence in some areas is even felt in . . . law enforcement agencies. Recent disclosures in the fight against organized crime serve, in a larger degree, to magnify the enormous task which lies ahead. To know the identities of underworld "bosses" and the intricate composition and operations of their "families" and "regimes" is, of course, not enough. The concerted drive by Federal and local authorities must be accelerated. . . .[505]

Hoover attempts to preempt the coming testimony/revelations of Mafia informant Valachi by implying that he, Hoover, is already destroying the organization.

"Oswald writes to the Socialist Workers Party as follows: 'Please advise me as to how I can get into direct contact with S.W.P. representatives in the Washington-Baltimore area. I and my family are moving to that area in October.' "[506]

9/3/63—TUESDAY: CORE demonstrations: 330 people have now been arrested. Farmer is convicted and freed on bail pending appeal.[507]

9/5/63—THURSDAY: Press: "President Kennedy accepted today the resignation of Ambassador deLesseps S. Morrison, former Mayor of New Orleans, who will seek the Democratic nomination for Governor of Louisiana."[508]

9/6/63—FRIDAY: *Las Vegas Review Courier* publishes a column attacking Hoover for FBI methods used in a local case. The article accuses him of being a demagogue. This may be the result of ELSUR operations discontinued in May 1963, and/or prosecution involving Levinson associates.

FBI (SOG) sends the first of three reports this month to CIA regarding Oswald's latest activities. "CIA was sent FBI reports (on Oswald's latest activities) on September 7, 10 and 24, 1963."[509] This implies that the New Orleans field office has by now complied with Hoover's demand for an updated, comprehensive report on this individual.

Press reports: "BATON ROUGE . . . Segregationist-conservative forces scored a 53–42 victory today in the State Democratic Central Committee in their fight to block President Kennedy from getting Louisiana's 10 Presidential electors in 1964."[510]

9/9/63—MONDAY: This day a reporter's recent interview with Fidel Castro, in which he had stated that American leaders "aiding terrorist plans to eliminate Cuban leaders will themselves not be safe," is published in the *New Orleans Times-Picayune.* Were Castro planning to assassinate JFK, a prior, public admission of the intent to do so would hardly enhance its chances of success. Rather, this statement sounds like the bluff of a frightened man who has survived numerous assassination attempts by agents of a foreign government and has now become frustrated and angry. Taken in context, he is also attempting to make the public aware of the CIA's covert program. Perhaps he hopes that by doing so he can force cessation. This rhetoric, however, only plays into the hands of Marcello.

9/10/63—TUESDAY: Second FBI (SOG) report to CIA on Oswald's activities.[511]

Mafia functionary Jim ". . . Braden . . . changed his name from Eugene Hale Brading. A month later he divorced his wife, the widow of a Chicago Teamster official. Braden had been arrested some thirty times and had served several prison sentences." *"Braden [was connected] to a number of underworld figures, including Meyer Lansky, for whom Braden had worked as a 'personal courier.'* "[512] "During [Braden's] several trips to New Orleans in the fall of 1963, he used the office of an oil geologist in room 1701 of the Marquette Building, receiving mail at that address. On one occasion, Brad[en] informed parole authorities that he could be contacted at room 1706 of that building. The office of . . . Gill, Marcello's attorney, which David Ferrie frequented in the fall of 1963, was room 1707" (emphasis added).[513]

Press: "The State Department has banned attendance by United States citizens at *an international congress in Havana* because it believes the Cubans intend to make it an anti-U.S. propaganda circus. *The Congress is that of the International Union of Architects scheduled to be held from September 29 to Oct. 3.* Premier Fidel Castro's regime had claimed strong United States support for the congress which, it said, would draw 2,000 delegates from 80 countries. The United States blocked American participation by notifying would-be delegates that their passports would not be validated for the trip. Fifty-nine Americans who visited Cuba in July in defiance of a United States travel ban now face prosecution involving cancellation of their passports and possible jail and fine penalties" (emphasis added).[514]

9/12/63—THURSDAY: *Washington Post* reports on a breach-of-contract suit against Baker. As stated in *The Bobby Baker Story,* "The key allegation was the charge that Baker had received payoffs totaling $5600 from April 1962 until July 1963. . . . The defendants—Baker [and] Fred Black . . . , had 'conspired maliciously' to take away Capitol's contract with Melpar for their own vending company." This development presumably makes Johnson nervous. The Bobby Baker scandal is about to break.

9/13/63—FRIDAY: *New Orleans Times-Picayune* publishes a story stating that President Kennedy will be in Dallas on November 21 or 22. Undoubtedly Marcello and his people, as well as Oswald, read this article. This establishes a basis for drawing the young leftist into the contract without making him suspicious (i.e., merely involving him in another protest on that day). In other words, he can now be approached and solicited in a simple, straightforward manner.

Dallas Times Herald ". . . printed the first unofficial report . . . that President Kennedy would include Dallas in his November Texas itinerary. That same day federal parole officer Sam Barrett approved Eugene Brading's request to go to Texas."[515] He leaves via plane this day for Houston where he supposedly spends the next ten days, possibly meeting with Marcello people.[516] He may also travel to New Orleans. Note the fact that both Ferrie and Ruby will also appear in Houston in the coming months.

9/16/63—MONDAY: Press: "The Cuban Federation of University Students has again invited American students to travel to the island to see Fidel Castro's regime in operation. . . . Luce . . . said his group would try to send 200 Americans on such a trip in January. He said 'we assume' the invitation provided for all expenses to be paid once again by the Cuban federation."[517]

CIA memo to FBI (SOG) regarding FPCC, stating the agency is ". . . giving some consideration to countering the activities of the FPCC in foreign countries. . . . CIA is also giving some thought to planting deceptive information which might embarrass the committee in areas where it does have some support."[518] In 1961 Hoover had implemented the same for the SWP (Socialist Workers Party).[519] Coordination with the FBI here is obvious.

Press: "SAN ANTONIO . . . 'Revolution' is the word on countless lips in Texas today. What they are talking about is a bloodless, but acrimonious, upheaval in politics—with important implications for the 1964 Presidential campaign. . . . The 'revolution' has two aspects. One is the emphatic burgeoning of Texas . . . into a two-party state. The other aspect is a clearly defined threat by long eclipsed 'minority' groups—liberals, labor, Negroes and Mexican-Americans—to play a decisive, if not dominant, role in a radically revamped Texas Democratic party."[520] This would play into the hands of President Kennedy were he to make the decision to dump LBJ in 1964.

9/17/63—TUESDAY: "Oswald visits Mexican consulate general in the Whitney Building, New Orleans, fills out application for tourist card. On it he describes himself as a . . . 'photographer' with a business address of 640 Rampart Street . . ." in hopes of enhancing his chance of gaining entrance to Cuba. He plans to time his trip so as to arrive in Havana for the month-end "international congress." He reportedly spends the next few days completing a summary of his Marxist activities.[521]

"[Ambassador William Attwood, Special Advisor to the United States delegation at the U.N.] and an African met over coffee at United Nations headquarters in New York. The African was a little-known diplomat. . . . Ambassador . . . Diallo, Guinean envoy to Cuba, brought word from Havana. . . . Attwood listened while the African ambassador talked. . . . The burden of his message was that . . . Castro wanted to reach some sort of understanding with the United States."[522]

9/18/63—WEDNESDAY: Press reports: "Senate hearings that will bring Joseph Valachi from a hidden informer's role into a national spotlight will open here next Tuesday. For more than a year, Valachi has been telling agents of the Federal Bureau of Investigation about the activities of Cosa Nostra. . . ."[523]

Attwood writes a memo seeking permission to travel to Cuba to talk with Castro's people. "[I] would travel 'as an individual but would of course report to the President before and after the visit. . . . For the moment, all I would like is the authority to make contact with Lechuga. We'll see what happens then.' "[524]

9/19/63—THURSDAY: CPUSA answers Oswald's letters with encouragement. ". . . I suggest that when you move [to Baltimore] that you get in touch with us here and we will find some way of getting in touch with you in that city."[525]

9/20/63—FRIDAY: "Ruth Paine arrives in New Orleans, [finding Oswald] 'very outgoing and warm and friendly. . . . He seemed distinctly relieved to consider the possibility of [Marina's] going to Dallas. . . .' "[526] This will clear the way for his trip to Havana via Mexico City. Accordingly he is apparently on his best behavior.

Press reports: "A key witness in the hearings will be Joseph Valachi. . . . The first witness on Tuesday will be Attorney General Robert F. Kennedy."[527]

9/21/63—SATURDAY: A Hoover essay, "What I Would Tell a Son" appears in the *Christian Science Monitor:*

If I had a son, I believe I could help him most by providing him with these . . . indispensables: a personal example to follow, an understanding of the importance of restraint and ideals, a sense of discipline . . . . *Truth telling, I have found, is the key to responsible citizenship. . . . I would also teach a son the importance of restraints and ideals. . . .* Today our youth must cope with the specter of an adult world rife with inconsistency. . . . *But teenagers who have a strong set of standards . . . have developed . . . the moral restraint . . . to turn their backs on the "smart set," and to remain true to their ideals. . . . Theodore Roosevelt, a man of great strength and discipline, had boundless love for his country and her ideals. "Americanism" he said, "means the virtues of courage, honor, justice, truth, sincerity, and hardihood. . . . The things that will destroy America are prosperity at any price, peace at any price . . . the love of soft living, and the get-rich-quick theory of life."* He knew also that softness—mental, physical, or spiritual—is the mortal enemy of all who cherish freedom. Has a "softening process" begun to set in for this generation and its elders? . . . The danger signs are clear. . . . This disease . . . eats from within. *Above all, our youth need our help to insulate them against the negative forces—immorality, overindulgence. . . .* [emphasis added].

Consider the following press report in view of the above essay: "President and Mrs. Kennedy spent the afternoon today aboard the White House yacht *Honey Fitz.* At the end of the cruise, Under Secretary of the Navy Paul B. Fay, Jr., stretched prone on the dock . . . clowning with Mr. Kennedy. . . . Mr. Fay . . . smiled up at the President. Mr. Kennedy laughingly put his foot on Mr. Fay's stomach. . . . The President walked over Mr. Fay and into a convertible. . . . Mr. Kennedy . . . bothered recently by a recurrence of his back trouble, showed no signs of discomfort today. There was also no sign of the limp. . . ."[528]

9/23/63—MONDAY: Diplomatic efforts to resolve the administration's standoff with Cuba continue. "The next morning saw him [Attwood, who is Kennedy's representative] on an early air shuttle to Washington and a meeting with the President's brother. Two days later Attwood met Lechuga again at the United Nations."[529]

"Ruth and Marina leave . . . for Irving." Mrs. Paine later says Oswald told her he was also leaving for either Houston or Philadelphia to look for work.[530] His rifle, disassembled, is taken with their household goods. Marina will later assert that Oswald told her of his impending trip to Mexico, admonishing her to tell no one.[531]

9/24/63—TUESDAY: FBI (SOG) sends yet another report to CIA on the latest activities of Oswald.[532]

Oswald leaves his apartment either this evening or the following evening. He puts in a change-of-address card, forwarding all mail to the Paines in Irving.[533]

Press: "THE PRESIDENT Announced Lieut. Gen. Wallace M. Greene, Jr., would replace retiring Gen. David M. Shoup as Marine Corps commandant."[534]

"A check of Ferrie's telephone records reveals that eight weeks [before the assassination] he made a call to Chicago number WH4-4970. This, it turns out, was the number of an apartment building which in 1963 housed one *Jean West*. On the night before the President's murder, Jean West was staying at the Cabana Motel as the companion of Lawrence Meyers, the friend Jack Ruby visited that midnight" (emphasis added).[535] It is not known whether this woman is the same "Jeane" Beckley gambling associate Eddie McGrath was speaking to on 5/3/62 when he expressed the desire to assassinate RFK with explosives.

Between now and September 29, the "Odio incident" takes place. A man apparently resembling Oswald is introduced as such to an exile named Sylvia Odio at her apartment in the Dallas/Fort Worth area by two other Cubans. He is also described as an ex-Marine and an excellent shot, "kind of loco." "The American says we Cubans don't have any guts. He says we should have shot President Kennedy after the Bay of Pigs. He says we should do something like that."[536] With the real Oswald on his way to Mexico City, this incident is obviously staged. These exiles are probably hard-liners hoping to associate the name Oswald with a more moderate exile faction (which Odio is associated with) in hopes it can possibly be tied to Oswald after the fact. The incident sounds like an aside, something done purely for factional reasons. "A few months earlier, in Puerto Rico, Sylvia had helped form . . . JURE. This group, although against Castro and Communism, was well to the left in exile politics. Its members thought of themselves as social democrats, while many in the exile movement considered them dangerously left wing, offering 'Castroism without Castro.' The men who called on Sylvia Odio in late September said they were fellow members of JURE. . . ."[537] Note that while at the Cuban embassy in Mexico City Oswald will sign his name. That signature will be authenticated by experts, precluding the possibility that he is in Dallas at this moment.[538]

Note also, between now and the assassination Oswald, or someone resembling him, will be seen a number of times in the company of a Latin man (see 11/8, 11/9, 11/16, 11/17, 11/20). There are three possible explanations: 1) The "Oswald" is simply a look-alike appearing in public with a "Cuban," so as to deflect blame on Cuba after the fact as part of the Marcello plan; 2) David Ferrie, through the use of Cuban exiles, has gained the confidence of the real Oswald, tricking him into participating in what he believes will be a pro-Cuba protest in Dealey Plaza on 11/22/63; or 3) the association is a product of after-the-fact CIA disinformation and/or civilian misinterpretation (i.e., innocent zeal), designed to help "convict" the "kill-crazy-communist" and implicate Cuba. Considered on balance, it is most probably a combination of 1 and 2.

9/25/63—WEDNESDAY: RFK testifies before the Senate Government Operations Committee. Per press: "[The Mafia is a] . . . private government of organized crime, resting on a base of human suffering and moral corrosion. . . . . . . [A racketeer is no longer] someone dressed in a black shirt, white tie and diamond stickpin, whose activities affect only a remote underworld circle. He is more likely to be outfitted in a grey flannel suit and his influence is more likely to be as far reaching as that of an important industrialist." The A.G. asks Congress for more legislation, telling them he is expanding his war on the mob. He states that the department's efforts have also caused the Mafia to call off Apalachian-style meetings three times in the last two years. "We had uncovered their well-concealed plans and meeting places."[539] This can only strengthen the resolve of Marcello—a man who can operate outside the will of the Commission—to stop the A.G.

"Sometime between eight in the morning and noon, [Oswald] cashs . . . [a Texas unemployment check] . . . at a Winn-Dixie store at 4303 Magazine Street. . . . Oswald takes Continental Trailways bus 5120 for Houston at 12:20 P.M., with a scheduled arrival time of 10:50 P.M. that night."[540]

Another Oswald impostor appears in Austin, Texas, at the Selective Service System office. "He introduced himself to Mrs. Lee Dannelly, the assistant chief of the administrative division, [as Harvey Oswald]. . . . He had, he said, been discharged from the Marine Corps under 'other than honorable conditions,' and this was making it hard to get a job. He now hoped to get the discharge upgraded on the basis of two years' subsequent good conduct. Could Mrs. Dannelly help? . . . She could not, because there was no 'Harvey Oswald' in her files. Since the visitor said he was living in Fort Worth, Mrs. Dannelly suggested he check with the offices there. 'Oswald' thanked her politely and left. . . . Mrs. Dannelly . . . recalled that her 'Oswald' responded to an awkward question by saying he was registered as a serviceman in Florida. While the real Oswald registered as a Marine in California and had no reason to lie on this point, Florida was the state where the vast majority of anti-Castro activity took place."[541] Note the woman does not say the individual actually looked like Oswald. ". . . Two others . . . believed they had seen Oswald in Austin that day."[542] Apparently it is the same individual described by Sylvia Odio, as the real Oswald is in New Orleans preparing to board a bus for Mexico. He may already be on his way. And the real Oswald has already received final word on his appeal, a rejection of his plea for a change in status. Therefore, this entire scenario would be completely illogical for him. Apparently the impostor and his backers are unaware of that development. This event also implies that the Marcello people have no idea Oswald is on his way to Mexico.

Overall, the plan appears to be to implicate Oswald by: 1) "placing" him in Texas; 2) using his Marine status as a way of pointing out his military background; 3) having him make public statements about being an ex-Marine, practice in public with the assassination rifle in the Dallas area, get work done on the weapon, inquire about a job in a tall downtown Dallas building while asking about its view; and 4) tying him to pro-Castro fanatics and communism in general.

By late this month, "Many of Oswald's possessions had been

stored in the Paine garage, and it was there that Marina said she had last seen the rifle, wrapped in a blanket."[543] This is more than plausible, as she undoubtedly helped unload family possessions from the station wagon upon arriving in Irving around September 25.

9/26/63—THURSDAY: The White House announces JFK will tour Texas in mid-November, visiting Dallas, Houston, Fort Worth, and San Antonio. ". . . the *Dallas Morning News* . . . reported that President . . . Kennedy was planning to make a trip to Texas November 21 or 22."[544]

"Oswald is seen at 6:00 A.M. . . . aboard Continental Trailways bus 5133 bound from Houston to Laredo. . . . 'We observed him conversing . . . with two young Australian women who boarded the bus on the evening of September 26th at Monterrey, Mexico. . . .' "[545] According to reports after the assassination, while in Laredo he may have purchased some clothes (see 11/29/63).[546]

Between now and November 22, substantial gaps appear in the record regarding Ruby's whereabouts and routine.[547]

9/27/63—FRIDAY: Oswald arrives in Mexico City, checking into room 18 of the Hotel Commercio.[548] He then proceeds to the Cuban embassy. According to ". . . Sylvia Duran, a young Mexican woman working in the . . . consul's office [he] . . . explained he was Lee Harvey Oswald, an American citizen, and . . . wanted a Cuban transit visa. His final destination was the Soviet Union, but he wanted to travel via Cuba. . . . Credentials were no problem. . . . Duran was shown passports, old Soviet documents and correspondence with the American Communist Party . . . membership cards for the Fair Play for Cuba Committee, identification as its president in New Orleans, and a newspaper clipping about the demonstration which ended in Oswald's arrest. . . . [She] emphasized . . . her office could not issue a transit visa for Cuba without first knowing the traveler had Soviet clearance for travel to Russia . . . [Oswald] departed, promising to come back with the photographs needed for a visa application. . . . [Upon his return] Duran accepted his visa application and asked him to call in about a week. 'Impossible,' said the young man. 'I can only stay in Mexico three days.' . . . That evening . . . he turned up once more . . . and rushed into the office visibly agitated. . . . He said he had been to

the Soviet Embassy and knew the Soviet visa would be granted.
. . . He insisted . . . the Cubans should issue him a visa at once.
. . . Duran . . . checked by telephone with the Soviet Embassy.
. . . They knew about Oswald but said Moscow could take as long
as four months to decide on his application to go to Russia. At this
news the young stranger caused a scene. . . . He didn't want to
listen. His face reddened, his eyes flashed, and he shouted, 'Impossible, I can't wait that long!' The American visitor was now literally
raging. . . . . . . The   consul   himself . . . intervened. . . .
There was yet another visit and another row with the consul. [Os-
wald] . . . mocked him and Sylvia Duran as mere 'bureaucrats.'
. . . The consul ordered him out of the building."[549] Oswald spends
the remainder of the weekend much the same as a tourist.[550] Both
FBI (LEGAT) and CIA quickly learn of this episode.

RFK puts Valachi on national television for shock effect. Hoover
is reportedly angered by this, having opposed public exposure of the
mobster (see 5/22/63).[551] He may be upset because he fears Valachi
might know of, and thus disclose, the Director's longtime liaison
with Costello, or other specific information that might dissuade
Marcello from carrying out the contract. Note, it is not that Valachi
might reveal the long-term existence of the mob. Hoover has recently been doing that in his own articles.

9/29/63—SUNDAY: Press: "Senator . . . McClellan said
today his crime investigators would work with the Justice Department to draft legislation making it a Federal crime to belong to
Cosa Nostra. . . . . . . The legislation might be based on the fact
that Cosa Nostra members take an oath of allegiance 'that assumes
a disloyalty—pledges a disloyalty to the Constitution of the United
States.' " [552] Considering the fact that some members are foreign
born, or resident aliens like Marcello, such a proposal is not illogical.

Press reports: "Mr. Kennedy was quartered at Bing Crosby's secluded house in the Palm Desert community. He spent the day
relaxing beside the movie star's spacious pool. . . . Thus ended a
trip, labeled nonpolitical, that nevertheless constituted the President's first, tentative foray into the country in search of re-election.
The . . . swing around the Western circuit left at least three important impressions. . . . Another was the conclusion that the impact in the West of far-right organizations like the John Birch Soci-

ety might have been overrated. And finally, the size and enthusiasm of the crowds . . . confirmed . . . the high personal popularity of John F. Kennedy. . . . Mr. Kennedy's glamorous aura. . . . . . . The modern Presidency, with its gleaming Presidential jet, its howling, jet-powered helicopters. . . . The President's personal performances were vigorous and effective, the crowds caught his new intensity and responded to it. . . ."[553]

9/30/63—MONDAY: EAL issues its final ruling against Ferrie, upholding his discharge.[554] This effectively ends his career as a commercial pilot.

10/63—THIS MONTH: ". . . In the second week of October, somebody in New Orleans filed a second change-of-address card, duplicating Oswald's original request. The handwriting on the card was not Oswald's. . . ."[555] This could be for any of several purposes: his landlord for rent arrears, the Marcello people in furtherance of the contract, the FBI or Banister's people for continuance of payments commensurate with informant status, or simply by a friend at his behest to make sure his mail is in fact forwarded.
". . . Hoover briefed Attorney General Kennedy on the matter of Ellen Rometsch, an East German alien resident and one of six women who were 'involved [with] and all tie[d] in with Bobby Baker.' Rometsch and these five alleged prostitutes, Hoover reported, frequented Baker's house in Washington, visited the Quorum Club (which Hoover described as having been 'formed by Bobby Baker, who was secretary of it, and . . . a kind of place where Senators and Congressmen go'), and had appeared at Baker's office numerous times. Hoover's briefing worried the attorney general, who expressed concern that should Senator John Williams (R.-Del.) learn of Rometsch's role and East German origin, he could exploit the 'security angle.' Hoover accordingly recommended that Rometsch be denied a visa to re-enter the United States. Kennedy agreed with this containment strategy and promised to brief the President. The accompanying FBI reports on the Rometsch case and its relationship to Johnson . . . have been withheld in their entirety on claimed personal privacy grounds."[556] Of course, Hoover had already arranged the woman's deportation in mid-August. At this point he is merely protecting Johnson, ensuring that he will be available to step into the presidency once JFK is assassinated.

Hoover delivers no public speeches this month, his next address occurs on November 16. Clyde's deteriorating health is presumably requiring part of his time.

". . . In early October [Ruby] was still engaged in painful negotiations with the IRS."[557]

10/1/63—TUESDAY: Press: "A Government witness told the Subversive Activities Control Board yesterday that she had received payments of $30 to $205 a month from the Federal Bureau of Investigation for reporting to the bureau the names of persons who attended Communist party meetings."[558]

Somewhat disillusioned, and armed only with the Cuban embassy's phone number, Oswald prepares to leave Mexico City.[559]

FBI (Florida, probably Miami) ELSUR again records Palmisano. "Robert F. Kennedy will never get ALL the bookmakers."[560] Here Palmisano echoes the sentiments of men such as Beckely, McGrath, di Piazza, Saia, Levinson, and Sigelbaum.

"New Orleans Police Intelligence unit Detective O'Sullivan . . . felt fairly certain he had seen Ruby in the French Quarter in the company of Frank Caracci. . . ."[561] Very possibly they are discussing the fact of Oswald's disappearance.

"In New Orleans, Jesse Garner [Oswald's landlord] informs the local FBI that the Oswalds have left . . . , Marina and child in [a] stationwagon with Texas license plate[s]."[562]

10/2/63—WEDNESDAY: Press reports: ". . . Valachi is not telling the Senate Permanent Subcommittee on Investigations everything he knows about organized crime in public sessions. A man is sitting close behind him to make sure he does not. He is William G. Hundley, chief of the Justice Department's organized crime section, who keeps close watch on the testimony. Mr. Hundley . . . is responsible for seeing that Valachi doesn't say anything that might jeopardize any one of several investigations going on around the country."[563] As previously stated, there is the obvious danger that someone will ask a question that might relate to the Hoover/Costello relationship. There is also the Cohn/Hoover/Mafia liaison, or even Prohibition era activities of Joseph Kennedy. Information regarding corrupt senators and other officials may also be a concern.

"Oswald departs Mexico City at 8:30 A.M. in Transportes del Norte bus 332. . . . He crosses the border between 1:00 and 2:00

A.M., October 3, as the date stamp imprinted on his tourist card
. . . attests."[564]

"In October, when the real Oswald had just returned from Mexico, three men were disturbed while firing a rifle on private property
just outside Dallas. The owner . . . Mrs. Lovell Penn, asked them
to leave. After the assassination she . . . remembered that one of
the men had looked like Oswald. . . . Mrs. Penn reportedly found
a 6.5mm Mannlicher-Carcano cartridge case on her land and
handed it over to the FBI. Lab tests showed it had not been fired
from the Carcano found in the Book Depository."[565] At most, this is
the look-alike posturing. More likely it is an unrelated incident.

10/3/63—THURSDAY: "Oswald arrives in downtown Dallas shortly after 2:00 P.M., goes directly to Texas Unemployment
Commission, . . . files claim for unemployment . . . and registers . . . for work. . . . In late afternoon, *[He] registers at downtown YMCA,* [and] pays $2.25 for [a] room" (emphasis added).[566]

FBI (Dallas). ". . . Hosty . . . notified of the disappearance of
the Oswalds from New Orleans . . . begins check of Oswald's former neighborhoods in Dallas and Fort Worth, but with negative
results."[567]

Ruby attempts to call a friend, Russell Mathews, ". . . an associate of . . . Traficante and . . . Campisi." ". . . A call was
placed from the Carousel Club to a number in Shreveport, Louisiana, listed to Elizabeth Mathews, Russell's former wife."[568]

10/3—10/7/63:   Dallas Western Union employees, Mr. Ham-
blen and Aubrey Lewis, will recall after the assassination that
*". . . Oswald was a customer who had collected money orders sev-
eral times. . . . He said that one of the money orders had been
delivered to the YMCA and that the customer had identified himself
with a Navy ID card and a library card"* (emphasis added).[569] This
money is very likely coming from the Banister/Ferrie group in the
guise of FBI informant payments. Oswald, in need of cash after the
Mexican trip, may assume it is simply payment in continuation of
his status with the Bureau. If coming from Ferrie, Banister may
well know nothing of it. At this point then, Oswald is in position to
be approached by Ferrie et al. (in the guise of agents) with the idea
of a Dallas political protest (by which Oswald can be framed)
against Kennedy on November 22, maneuvering him either with

Hoover and his Assistants, with the notable exception of Mafia division chief Courtney Evans, as they appeared at the outset of Kennedy's administration. Molded and handpicked by the Director, they were unquestioningly loyal to a man. The shot was taken in Hoover's outer "official" office. Doorway to the left leads to personal secretary Gandy's office.

UPI/Bettmann Newsphotos

2/61. Johnson poses before the wreckage of his personal plane. Against the advice of air traffic controllers and his own pilots, he ordered the plane flown to his ranch on a fog shrouded night. All aboard were killed.

Attorney General Kennedy grills hamburgers in the fireplace of his office. Hoover, his own office just a few doors down the hall, considered him an "adolescent horse's ass."

AP/Wide World Photos

2/61. Hoover confronts President Kennedy unexpectedly at a White House event, hoping to intimidate him and regain the offensive. JFK refused to listen, determined to retire the director by 1/1/65.

4/61. JFK is confronted by ex-V.P. Nixon shortly after the Bay of Pigs fiasco. Hoover used the naval disaster to belittle Kennedy in the media in June.

4/61. An anxious Carlos Marcello shortly before deportation from Guatemala to parts unknown after initial deportation from U.S. by Kennedy. Publicly humiliated by the official, he returned illegally in June 1961 to exact revenge.

7/61. U.E. Baughman, head of Secret Service, retired by JFK after thirteen years as chief. Like Hoover he espoused the opinion that "there is no Mafia in this country...." Here, he takes in the view from Kennedy's future death seat. Baughman was replaced by an ex-FBI agent who had "defected" from the Bureau after serving only a year. Hoover loathed agents who rejected career opportunity with his agency.

7/61. JFK retires CIA director Allen Dulles as the first step in bureaucratic restructuring of the agency after the Bay of Pigs disaster.

9/61. Marcello as he appeared before the U.S. Senate three months after illegal reentry to the U.S. Lost in thought and beseiged by federal agencies, he contemplates his next course of action. His mentor was long time Hoover confidant and New York Mafioso, Frank Costello.

9/61. President Kennedy signs powerful and sweeping anti-Mafia legislation as RFK looks on. Hoover, smiling smugly, stands in the background. His covert mob surveillance program (ELSUR) in full swing and unknown to either Kennedy, he had already begun to gather data with an eye toward regaining "control" of the presidency.

12/61. Kennedy and his wife leave Palm Beach hospital after visiting his father. Felled by a massive stroke after confrontation with Hoover's knowledge of his relationship to Chicago Mafioso Sam Giancana (i.e., campaign contributions to JFK's 1960 fund), the family patriarch never recovered. By the following month word had reached Hoover's desk that the President had no intention of waiving federal statute governing the director's compulsory retirement.

3/62. White-collar criminal Billie Sol Estes at the time of his arrest by the FBI. A man shrouded in mystery to this day, Bureau files detailing his relationship to Johnson and East Coast "organized crime" remain closed to the public at Hoover's directive.

Federal Bureau of Investigation
United States Department of Justice
Washington, D. C.

November 9, 1960

Honorable Lyndon B. Johnson
LBJ Ranch
Johnson City, Texas

Dear Lyndon:

I would like to take this opportunity
to extend my heartiest congratulations to you on
your election as Vice President of the United States.
This is indeed a well-deserved tribute to your many
outstanding accomplishments and your years of
devoted service to our country. This high honor is
an expression of supreme confidence in your ability,
and I am certain you must be very proud of it.

All of your friends in the FBI join
me in wishing you every success in carrying out
the heavy responsibilities of your office, and we
want you to know that we stand ready to be of aid
whenever possible.

With assurance of my highest esteem,

Sincerely,

Edgar

November 19, 1960

Dear Edgar:

I appreciated very much your kind note, and I treasure your good wishes.

You know how delighted I am by the news that you will continue in your present position in the new Administration. This is a recognition not only of your dedicated service during the past, but of the continuing need for your service during the years which lie ahead.

With warmest personal regards, I am

Sincerely,

Lyndon B. Johnson

Hon. J. Edgar Hoover
Director
Federal Bureau of Investigation
United States Department of
    Justice
Washington 25, D. C.

September 1, 1961

Dear Edgar:

It was with great pleasure that I received your thoughtful and heart-warming letter on my birthday. Thank you for your good wishes.

I am grateful that I have good friends as you, upon whom I and our Nation may rely, to represent our best interests in the years ahead.

With many thanks, and warm personal regards.

Sincerely,

Lyndon B. Johnson

The Honorable John Edgar Hoover
Director
Federal Bureau of Investigation
United States Department of Justice
Washington, D. C.

LBJ:WFJ:cjf

September 10, 1962

Dear Edgar:

Just a note to send you my heart-felt
thanks for your thoughtful birthday greetings.
Such kind expressions of friendship will be
a great source of strength and happiness to
me in the days ahead, and I am very grateful
to you.

Sincerely yours,

Lyndon B. Johnson

Honorable John Edgar Hoover, Director
Federal Bureau of Investigation
United States Department of Justice
Washington, D. C.

LBJ:RFS:vws
No. X-4

May 3, 1963   ACCEPT
              Speak
              June 19, 1963
              Washington, D. C.

Dear Edgar:

I'm so happy that you gave me the chance
to speak at the graduation exercises of the
FBI National Academy, and I can't let this
pleasant opportunity pass by. I'm delighted
to be able to say "yes" to your invitation.

Because of my high regard for you and my
great respect for the service, I hope you
know that I share in the complete and utter
devotion that all the men in the FBI have
for J. Edgar Hoover. I am so grateful to
you and to Deke DeLoach for all the many
favors you both have done for us -- and I'm
looking forward to June 19.

My best wishes.

Sincerely,

Lyndon B. Johnson

Mr. John Edgar Hoover
Director
Federal Bureau of Investigation
United States Department of Justice
Washington, D. C.

LBJ:MF

JOHN EDGAR HOOVER
DIRECTOR

Federal Bureau of Investigation
United States Department of Justice
Washington, D. C.

December 17, 1963

My dear Mr. President:

      I cannot tell you how much our time together yesterday means to me. Your very real appreciation of the matters I was privileged to discuss with you and your complete understanding of our problems smooth the way to our mutual desire to serve our country in fullest capacity.

      I shall treasure your photograph and your autographed message as I do your friendship and trust.

                          Sincerely yours,

                          Edgar

The President
The White House
Washington, D. C.

JOHN EDGAR HOOVER
DIRECTOR

Federal Bureau of Investigation
United States Department of Justice
Washington, D. C.

EXECUTIVE
PE 14/H
FG/35-C

May 8, 1964

The President
The White House
Washington, D. C.

Dear Mr. President:

      The great privilege bestowed upon me this afternoon by you in the Rose Garden at the White House is certainly very much appreciated. Your remarks, in the presence of so many old and dear friends, touched me very deeply.

      Your Executive Order waiving the mandatory retirement age provision and your request that I continue as Director of the FBI fill me with gratitude. I know you understand there is no greater happiness than the knowledge that one is free to go on doing, day by day, the best work possible in the job he likes best.

      Words are but empty thanks for the wonderful opportunity you have given me to continue to serve you and my country. One thing I know--there is no such thing as forgetting the most important events in life, and today will always remain one of my most memorable.

                          Sincerely,

                          Edgar

Miami SAC Wesley G. Grapp processed the Aleman data from agents Scranton and Davis to Hoover et al in D.C. in 9/62. Pictured here in late 1966, he had by then become Los Angeles SAC. Early in 1967, he, undoubtedly at Hoover's directive, apparently attempted to supress public disclosure of the Marcello/Kennedy death threat. If still alive, he may well hold unique knowledge of the contract on JFK's life, although waiver of federal secrecy statutes would be required to enable him to make any disclosure.

10/31/62. President Kennedy attends FBI National Academy graduation ceremonies as keynote speaker. The tension between the two men is obvious here. Only weeks before, Hoover and top aides Tolson and Evans had learned of Marcello's plan to assassinate the Chief Executive. Hoover looks at an uninformed Kennedy as if he were already dead.

10/31/62. JFK on stage with Hoover at the same event. Note presence of long-time Hoover companion and number two FBI man, Clyde Tolson, in background.

4/63. Former Maj. Gen. Edwin A. Walker poses for reporters in Dallas just hours after a staged attempt on his life by supporters. It is not known whether he knew of the plan in advance. Dallas PD attempted to frame Oswald with the event within hours of Kennedy's assassination.

11/22/63. Endgame. RFK and Jackie look on as President Kennedy is loaded into a hearse. The individual in the center, bottom foreground, may be Hoover. The similarity is striking, although nothing else in media coverage suggests he was there. In notifying RFK by phone of Kennedy's death earlier in the day, Hoover had simply said, "The President's dead," and hung up. The aging rightist never walked the short distance to the A.G.'s office to offer even the simplest condolences. By April 1964, RFK was saying of Hoover, publicly, "I think [he's]...senile and rather frightening... dangerous...rather a psycho."

AP/Wide World Photos

Dallas District Attorney, and ex-FBI agent, Henry Wade speaks with reporters the morning after the assassination. Although quickly brought under the control of Texas Attorney General Waggoner Carr (himself an ex-FBI agent) and Hoover, he managed, on 11/27/63, one revealing comment for the press: "It...may have involved something far deeper....Our law enforcement agencies are still checking to determine if links exist between Oswald and Ruby...."

12/63. Johnson makes the obligatory visit to JFK's grave. Described by Kennedy only days before the assassination as a man "incapable of telling the truth," he had developed an intimate political liaison with Hoover during his time as Vice President.

UPI/Bettmann Newsphotos

2/64. Mafia functionary and Johnson associate Bobby Baker (rt.) held leverage over the Vice President and undoubtedly conveyed critical data to Lansky/Traficante functionaries Edward Levinson and Benjamin Sigelbaum concerning Johnson's vulnerability and intense dissatisfaction with the vice presidency. Seated with him is Mafia counsel Edward Bennett Williams—attorney for Levinson, Marcello bookmaker Gilbert Beckley, and Jimmy Hoffa. He also defended Hoover intimate, Joe McCarthy and was close to RFK's Justice Department Mafia chief, William Hundley.

3/64. Bookmaker and Las Vegas casino front man, Edward Levinson worked closely with Mafia bosses Meyer Lansky and Santos Traficante. Simultaneously in business partnership with Johnson intimate Bobby Baker, he served as a conduit for information between the two groups.

money or his wife's potential status as a spy. Currently unemployed, Oswald as yet has no job to protect. To him, the idea of enhancing his status in such a way may be appealing. After all, they undoubtedly convey only the impression that his role will be that of an innocent citizen voicing his views on foreign policy, something perfectly legitimate. Like Ferrie, he is aware that President Kennedy will be in Dallas on November 22.

The point is that Oswald probably perceives those influencing him to be acting at the behest of the FBI, hence the continuing payments. After the assassination, the Bureau will seize the records of these money orders from Western Union, as tracing is a simple matter. To allow such would obviously reveal that they came from someone tied to the FBI, such as Ferrie or possibly even Banister.

Ferrie either already knows or will soon learn, via the ex-SAC and the New Orleans FBI, about Oswald's trip to Mexico City and return to Dallas. Through the Marcello people he informs Ruby in the next week or two that the real Oswald is actually in the Irving area. From there, Ruby locates both Oswald and the Irving address and perhaps arranges to have the ex-Marine's rifle stolen. In the coming weeks he will also keep Nofio Pecora, Caracci, and Campisi informed regarding police preparations and other fine points concerning the motorcade route. In monitoring Oswald he will learn of his chance position at the Depository.

10/4/63—FRIDAY: "In Dallas, Oswald goes to JOBCO, an employment agency. . . . [He then] . . . applies for work at Padgett Printing Corp. . . . 'Oswald was well dressed and neat. He made a favorable impression on the foreman of the department.' However, on Oswald's application at Padgett . . . he gives Jaggers-Chiles-Stovall as his place of former employment . . . [which] does not recommend [him]."[570]

"In early afternoon . . . Oswald phones Marina, asks her to send Ruth Paine . . . to pick him up. Marina refuses because Ruth has local grocery shopping to do, and has this morning donated a pint of blood at Parkland Hospital against Marina's admission to have her baby later in the month."[571] "Oswald . . . then hitchhiked to the Paine home in Irving. There he spent the . . . weekend. . . ."[572] According to Marina, ". . . he was disappointed in not being able to get to Cuba. . . . . . . He changed for the better. He began to treat me better."[573]

Press: "President Kennedy, just back from a one-day trip to Arkansas, has at least five out-of-town trips scheduled before the end of November. The next one, the White House announced today, is a visit Oct. 19 to Boston . . . Another political expedition will take Mr. Kennedy to Texas Nov. 21 and 22. Gov. John Connally of Texas visited the President today. He said he had told Mr. Kennedy that the Chief Executive would face a difficult race in the state next year 'but I think he'll carry it.' On Nov. 18, the President has a date to address the Florida Chamber of Commerce . . . at Tampa in the afternoon and the Inter-American Press Association in Miami that night."[574] In the same meeting Connally expresses reservations about the idea of a motorcade, claiming "it would overly fatigue the President. . . ." Associates and aides feel it will be politically divisive and apparently fear the possibility of embarrassing protests by the ultraright.[575]

Press reports Senator Mike Mansfield as saying that Bobby Baker is doing a fine job.[576]

10/6/63—SUNDAY: "FBI [SOG] . . . learns of Oswald contacts in Mexico City."[577]

10/7/63—MONDAY: Rather than meet with Senate leaders ". . . Bobby Baker resigned as Secretary for the Majority amidst swarms of charges [and] denials. . . . . . . Lyndon Johnson's reaction . . . was a terse 'no comment.' He knew his own political life might be on the line. . . ."[578] The Senate is stunned. Johnson is terrified.

Oswald spends the day in Dallas looking for an apartment. He rents one from a Mrs. Bledsoe in Oakcliff, under his own name. "[He] pays [her] $7 for a week's room rent. . . . He stays in his room from 4:00 P.M. onward."[579]

". . . According to the manager of the garage across the street, Oswald made at least two long-distance calls from the pay phone at the garage. The manager, Jerry Duncan, remembered Oswald twice asking for change for the calls, about six weeks before the assassination."[580] The calls may be related to getting a job back East, the Cuban visa, or his continuing role as an informant.

10/9/63—WEDNESDAY: Press: ". . . Valachi gave Senate investigators today the names of 12 cities besides New York that he

said had Cosa Nostra crime syndicate 'families.' He identified them as Philadelphia, Boston, Chicago, Cleveland, Los Angeles, San Francisco, Tampa, Newark, Detroit, Buffalo, Utica and *New Orleans.* He said the syndicate operated also in *Miami* and *Las Vegas* but that these were 'open' cities without families" (emphasis added).[581]

President Kennedy is asked during a news conference about the Mafia and the Valachi hearings. ". . . I wonder whether you feel they are serving any useful purpose? A: No, I would not—I would not want to—oh, I have not commented on the Senate procedures and I would not now, on this hearing or other hearings—that is the judgment for Senator McClellan and the committee. These difficulties occur in a good many different racial groups and I think that they ought to feel a good deal of pride in what they have done and not be concerned because a Valachi or an Irish name or some other name may occasionally get in trouble."[582] Contrast this response regarding the Mafia to a year ago (10/10/62) when he spoke in very tough terms about the elimination of the organization. Clearly he has trouble with the question.

FBI (Chicago) ELSUR records, ". . . Giancana . . . is extremely apprehensive of being subpoenaed before the McClellan Committee hearings on organized crime."[583]

". . . Billie Sol Estes—'jobless, penniless and bankrupt,' to quote the Federal Court—is driving a 1964 Cadillac and is still living 'in style' in a new $50,000 home in Abilene, Texas. Understandably the public wonders, 'How?' One of his lawyers, Jack Bryant, answers that he bought the place for Billie Sol. Then who is financing him?"[584]

"According to Mrs. Bledsoe . . . Oswald leaves rooming house at 9:00 A.M., returns at 1:30 P.M. He has applied for a job, fruitlessly, at Burton-Dixie, on a referral from the Texas Employment Commission. Mrs. Bledsoe: '. . . Then he talked to [Marina] on the phone, and talked in a foreign language . . . and I didn't like that.' "[585]

Ruby flies to New Orleans on American Airlines Flight 985 (11 to 11:30 A.M.). ". . . Ruby made another visit to the nightclub district of New Orleans. He was seen there with Frank Caracci. . . ."[586] He probably remains there until October 12.

10/10/63—THURSDAY: "Central Intelligence Agency circulates to FBI . . . a release classified 'Secret' containing information that Oswald has been . . . identified as individual seen at Soviet embassy in Mexico City."[587] Oddly, the agency had only noted one visit by Oswald to the embassies. He went at least twice to each.

RFK sends a memo to FBI liaison Evans. "Courtney, speak to me, RFK."[588] Obviously, something has happened. Evans is distancing himself from the man who has worked quite closely with him, apparently even considering him for Hoover's replacement. The fact that he is an assistant director, in charge of the organized crime division within the FBI, is critical. Does he sense that RFK will soon become powerless? Worse yet, does he, like Hoover and Tolson, know of the contract? Recall his increasingly hostile rhetoric toward the administration in internal Bureau memo in previous months. It would be almost impossible to believe that he has not seen the Aleman data or ominously threatening ELSUR product generated for his division over the last thirteen months.

"Oswald leaves rooming house at 10:00 A.M., looks for job at the De Vilbiss Co. on referral from JOBCO . . . returns between two and two-thirty in the afternoon. . . ." as yet without employment.[589]

10/11/63—FRIDAY: Shortly after President ". . . Kennedy authorized the sale of wheat to the Soviet Union[,]" he was confronted by "Lyndon Johnson . . . [who] was . . . unhappy." JFK confides in aide Schlesinger: "The Vice President thinks that this is the worst foreign policy mistake we have made in this administration."[590] Undoubtedly Hoover shares Johnson's views on this issue.

10/12/63—SATURDAY: Press reports: "The Senate Permanent Subcommittee on Investigations will focus on Tampa and Orlando, Fla., Tuesday when it resumes its hearings on organized crime."[591] The ever-increasing attention being focused on Traficante is made evident by releases such as this. In rising desperation he in turn undoubtedly looks to the Marcello contract for salvation.

Apparently as a result of a personality clash, Oswald's landlady tells him ". . . you are going to move." He does so, spending the weekend with Marina and Ruth.[592] He begins to suspect, perhaps rightly so, that the FBI is undercutting his efforts to get a job and a room. His past is haunting him, making him realize he must conform. Resentment toward the Bureau grows.

10/13/63—SUNDAY: "Taking advantage of the store's Sunday shutdown, Ruth Paine gives Oswald a driving lesson in a deserted shopping-center parking lot. '. . . It became clear to me in that lesson that he was very unskilled in driving. . . . I noticed when we got to the parking lot when he attempted to turn in a right angle he made the usual mistake of a beginner of turning too much and then having to correct it.' "[593] His hand/eye coordination problems and lack of confidence are apparently still plaguing him in this respect.

In the ". . . latest Gallup Poll on (the) question: 'Do you approve of the way Kennedy is handling his job as President?' . . . 57 percent approve, only 28 percent disapprove."[594]

10/14/63—MONDAY: "Ruth Paine drives to downtown Dallas to get her Russian typewriter fixed, taking Marina and Lee and the three children. Lee gets out at a certain intersection, remarking that it is near the Texas Employment Commission." "[He] applied for a position at the Weiner Lumber Company at Inwood Road and Maple Avenue (which was [coincidentally] on the route a motorcade would take from Love Field to downtown Dallas). But Oswald was unable to satisfy Sam Weiner that he had been honorably discharged from the Marine Corps, and he was not hired." ". . . Quite by chance, Lee stops by at 1026 [North Beckley], where he has been one week earlier, and finds that Mrs. A. C. Johnson has a tiny cubicle of a room . . . for rent at eight dollars a week, refrigerator and television privileges included. He takes the room, pays for the first week, then registers . . ." under the name O. H. Lee.[595] Obviously he is fearful of being kicked out once again, and perhaps of the FBI. In the coming weeks he continues to receive *The Worker* and *The Militant*.[596]

"In the afternoon, Ruth and Marina go to the home of an Irving neighbor for coffee. According to the former's testimony: '. . . This was . . . at my immediate neighbors, Mrs. Ed Roberts, and also present was Mrs. Bill Randle. . . . And the subject of [Oswald's] looking for work came up . . . [during conversation among] the four young mothers at Mrs. Roberts's house, and Mrs. Randle mentions that her younger brother, Wesley Frazier, thought they needed another person at the Texas School Book Depository where Wesley worked." Marina telephones Oswald and he applies the next day.[597] As this event demonstrates, the laws of chance or random occurrence are not suspended during the last weeks of Oswald's life—as many will indirectly suggest in the attempt to implicate him in this crime.

FBI (Chicago) ELSUR: Giancana and "Chuck" English "discuss the Bobby Baker scandal. He just resigned his job; they didn't do anything to him. He must have come out with a ton of money. . . . They discuss golf. Someone asks if Bobby Kennedy plays golf, they know that John Kennedy does. Suggest putting a bomb in his golf bag (they all laugh)."[598]

Press: "Secretary of the Navy Fred Korth's resignation, abruptly tendered, was announced by the White House today. In addition, Mr. Korth has been a controversial figure in a Senate investigation of the Defense Department's award of [aerospace] contracts for the TFX fighter plane. Charges of conflict of interest have been raised against him, but these have been dismissed by the Department of Justice. . . . There was general agreement in the Administration that Mr. Korth would 'fit better' in private life than in Washington. Mr. [Paul H.] Nitze's appointment to the Navy post means that for the first time in the Kennedy Administration it has passed out of the hands of a Texan and out of the direct influence of Vice President Johnson. Mr. Kennedy's first Secretary of the Navy was John B. Connally, Jr., now Governor of Texas and formerly an aide to Mr. Johnson in the latter's campaign for the Democratic Presidential nomination in 1960."[599] This event, given the abrupt resignation and admitted control by Johnson over the post, raises serious questions of corruption. This can only add to LBJ's fears. It is not known whether he had consulted Hoover (through DeLoach) prior to this point regarding the case against Korth, or whether aerospace lobbyist Fred Black is involved.

10/15/63—TUESDAY: "In the morning Oswald goes to Texas School Book Depository, 411 Elm Street . . . to see Roy S. Truly, Depository superintendent, about a job. According to Truly's testimony: 'He came in, introduced himself to me, and I took him in my office and interviewed him. I gave him an application to fill out, which he did. . . . He stressed he really needed a job to support his family. . . . He seemed to be grateful that I was giving him the chance of a little extra work. . . . *So I told him if he would come to work on the morning of the 16th, it was the beginning of a new [semimonthly] pay period. So he filled out his withholding slip, with the exception of the number of dependents. He asked me if I would hold that for 3 or 4 days, that he is expecting a baby momentarily. . . . His hours were from 8 in the morning until 4:45 in the afternoon. His lunch period was "from 12 to 12:45." His pay was "$1.25 an hour." He worked a "5-day week". . . . We had no record of his missing any days.'* " Time clocks are not used. His employer considers it a temporary position.[600] "Oswald telephones Irving immediately. Ruth Paine answers. According to her testimony 'He asked for Marina. . . .' She said, 'Hurray, he has got a job. . . . We must thank Mrs. Randle.' "[601]

10/16/63—WEDNESDAY: "Oswald's first day at work at the Book Depository. According to Truly's testimony: 'I told him what his duties were to be—would be filling book orders. . . . We put Lee Oswald with another worker who was experienced in filling orders. This boy showed him the location of the various publishers' stock. He worked with him, it seems to me, like only an hour or two, and then he started filling orders by himself. And from then on he worked alone. . . . I would say . . . the work that he did was a bit above average. . . . The boy, from all reports to me and what I have seen, kept working and talked little to anybody else. He just kept moving. And he did a good day's work. . . . He was filling mostly one or two publishers' orders. . . . The main publisher was Scott, Foresman and Co. . . .' Q: 'Where, generally, are Scott, Foresman books kept?' A: 'On the first floor and the sixth floor. We have a large quantity of their books on the sixth floor.' Q: 'And this is the area where Lee Oswald worked?' A: 'That is right.' "[602] Note also that this job requires little manual dexterity. Oswald usually snacks at lunch.[603] He will reportedly express pride to coworkers over the arrival of his second child on October 20.[604]

Press: "Attorney General . . . Kennedy submitted a draft bill to the Senate Permanent Subcommittee on Investigations today to help the Federal Government combat organized crime. The measure would give Federal law-enforcement agencies the power to compel testimony by granting immunity to witnesses in crime investigations. The Administration has also pressed at the crime hearings for a bill allowing limited use of wiretap evidence. In announcing the end of the hearings, Senator McClellan said the testimony had shown that organized crime was getting more powerful and would continue to do so unless adequate steps were taken to contain it on a national basis."[605]

10/14—10/18/63: "According to . . . Ruth . . . , sometime during this period Oswald gives her the telephone number at 1026 North Beckley so that he can be notified when Marina goes into labor, just as he had furnished her with the number at 621 North Marsalis during the week previous against the same contingency. He does not, however, give either Ruth or Marina the address."[606] Most likely he is fearful that they will give it to the FBI.

10/17/63—THURSDAY: Havana consulate sends conditional permission to its Mexico City embassy concerning Oswald's visa application. "Allow me to notify you, in regard to the application for a transit visa by North American citizen LEE HARVEY OSWALD, that in order to accede to his application he must inform us by cable, with prepaid reply, when he has the authorized visa of the Embassy of the USSR."[607] Upon receipt of this news Oswald will write a letter to the Soviet embassy in Washington, D.C., in an attempt to obtain the "authorized visa." This will apparently be followed up with a call on 11/18/63. The Mexico City embassy consul with whom he quarreled has been replaced.[608] This development will undoubtedly encourage him to renew plans of moving to Cuba.

Oswald's routine is now to call Ruth Paine after work (5:30 P.M.) on Thursdays to okay his weekend visit. His landlady (Mrs. Roberts) will maintain that Oswald never goes out nights, watches TV only briefly (news?), then retires to his room. He rarely speaks. She will also confirm that he leaves on Fridays and returns on Sunday evenings, never has visitors, and will not be present Veterans Day (returning on Tuesday of that week). She also will not recall some of the known absences of Oswald, whose actions suggest that he is being very careful not to lose his room or job.[609] Evidently he is beginning to conform. After all, he has failed in his initial attempt to get to Cuba, has a wife and child (with another about to arrive) to support, and has experienced firsthand the consequences of his past mistakes (i.e., undesirable discharge, job and rooming difficulties, etc.).

10/18/63—FRIDAY: "Oswald's twenty-fourth birthday. Having established contact with Wesley Frazier, he rides out to Irving. . . . According to Marina . . . 'On the eve[ning] of October the 18th, we celebrated Lee's birthday at Ruth Paine's house. Lee was in a very good mood, since he had a job and was expecting a son.'"⁶¹⁰

10/19/63—SATURDAY: "Probably sometime this weekend, Oswald and Michael Paine get into a discussion regarding Oswald's reading. . . . 'Well, it made me realize that he would like to be active in some kind of—activist. It made me feel that he wasn't very well connected with a group or he wouldn't have such a tenuous way of communication.' " ⁶¹¹ This is where Oswald's interest in the ACLU begins. Paine is a member.⁶¹²

Press: "PHILADELPHIA . . . *An arrest warrant charging interstate travel to commit extortion was issued tonight for Angelo Bruno,* one of the men named by Joseph Valachi as head of the Cosa Nostra in Philadelphia. The Federal Bureau of Investigation in Washington said the issuing of the warrant was not directly connected with the Valachi testimony before a Senate hearing. Bruno was being sought tonight. *Five other men were taken into custody on similar charges and two men were held as material witnesses.* In Washington, *J. Edgar Hoover,* director of the FBI, *said Bruno and the others had lent money to a group of buyers interested in purchasing a Jewish Community Center in Philadelphia. The money was lent at 'Shylock' rates, he said, and when the repayment was delayed, the Cosa Nostra group threatened several members of the group and actually attacked one man with a lead pipe.* Two of the other men arrested tonight in raids here and in Jersey City, had criminal records. They *were identified as Harold Konisberg . . . and Joseph R. Juliano . . ."* (emphasis added).⁶¹³ At first glance, Hoover appears to be doing nothing more than zealously performing his duty. Note, however, he has been aware since 2/9/62 that a *Jewish* member of this family, William Weisberg, wants to assassinate President Kennedy. Note also Hoover's use of the racial slur "Shylock rates" to describe the criminal acts of the defendants. Shylock, of course, was the relentless *Jewish* moneylender in Shakespeare's *Merchant of Venice.* Weisburg is not one of those arrested (see 10/31/63). Bruno, resigned to defeat some months ago, has been in Italy since September 1963 trying to arrange permanent residence. It is also rather odd that Bruno himself would be indicted for something that underlings probably routinely handle. Hoover has had ELSUR surveillance in place on this Mafia family since at least February 1962, so further, as yet classified recordings on the group may well exist to shed light on the event. Hoover has known for weeks that President Kennedy will shortly be in Philadelphia, to appear in an open motorcade. That Hoover also personally handles the announcement of the arrest seems strange, having foregone the opportunity to do so in other indictments of similar magnitude. Recall that ELSUR had also recorded Bruno discussing Hoover's and Tolson's homosexuality, and the Director's impending retirement.

Hoover's actions seem to suggest the following: knowing that at least one key Jewish member of the group wants to assassinate President Kennedy as a result of a January 1962 FBI raid, the Director has an element of the organization arrested (but not Weisberg), just prior to the visit of the President to their home turf. He does this in hopes it will provoke Weisberg (or his henchmen) to actually attempt the assassination of the President. Hoover takes additional pains to use anti-Semitic slurs in the course of publicly humiliating these people. Doing so also allows him to get even with Bruno for referring to him and Clyde as "fairies." To Hoover, it does not necessarily matter *which* Mafia family performs the assassination, only that the job is done before 1/1/65. Weisberg must be furious. If nothing else, this event demonstrates what Hoover is capable of doing with knowledge of specific plans to assassinate the President.

10/20/63—SUNDAY: Marina has her second child this evening.[614]

10/21/63—MONDAY: "Oswald hitches ride to . . . work with Wesley Frazier. According to Ruth: 'It was agreed when he left that he would return [to Irving] that evening. . . .' " This night he goes to the hospital to see his wife and child.[615]

New York press reports: "A year-long investigation into gambling in this area by the [Federal Bureau of Investigation and IRS] is expected to produce a series of indictments soon against big-time bookmakers. Both the [FBI and IRS] have been concentrating on the upper echelon of illegal betting."[616]

10/21—10/31/63:   *According to Oswald supervisor Truly, "So some 4 days or so later—I don't remember the exact day—he told me that he had this new baby, and he wanted to add one dependent. He finished filling [his W-4] out. And I sent it up to Mr. Campbell who makes out the payroll for the company"* (emphasis added).[617] This delay on the part of Oswald will apparently cause his first paycheck to be calculated on the basis of only two withholding exemptions (i.e., he did not initially fill in that portion of his W-4 pertaining to dependents, leaving the impression that he was claiming only his wife and himself). This becomes critical in early November (see 11/1/63).

10/22/63—TUESDAY: "Oswald rides to work from Irving with Wesley Frazier. In the evening, he returns to 1026 North Beckley on the Beckley bus."[618] Oswald has now settled into an 8 A.M. to 4:45 P.M. work routine. After the assassination, a coworker of Oswald's, "Bonnie Ray" Williams, will state, "I didn't know him personally, but I had seen him working. . . . He just went about his work. He never said anything to me, I never said anything to him. . . . He would come into the lunchroom sometimes and eat a sandwich maybe, and then he would go for a walk. . . ."[619] This evening Radio Havana airs a Castro speech with English translation, to which Oswald possibly listens.[620]

". . . The vice president's problems were driving a wedge between him and senior White House aides, who welcomed this situation as an opportunity to drop Johnson or at least disseminate rumors of a 'dump Johnson' strategy for 1964. The President, however, had not joined this effort and in fact told Ben Bradlee of *Newsweek* on 22 October 1963 that the idea 'was preposterous on the face of it,' as the Democrats needed to carry Texas to win. Such disclaimers, however, failed to convince the vice president, who confided his fears to Hoover."[621]

10/23/63—WEDNESDAY: Press   reports: "The   Dallas United States Day Committee will sponsor a rally at 8 P.M. Wednesday in the Memorial Auditorium Theatre with former Major General Edwin A. Walker giving the address." "Oswald . . . attends the evening meeting on this date."[622] True to form, Walker condemns the U.N. in anticipation of the coming visit of the U.S. representative to the body, Adlai Stevenson. Condemnation of U.S. participation is a cornerstone of Walker's and other ultrarightist groups' political agendas. Had Oswald actually made the attempt on Walker's life earlier in the year, it is extremely unlikely he would now risk exposure by placing himself in such close proximity to not only Walker, but his personal security people. Oswald has no way of knowing who will be in the audience. It is logical to assume that Dallas police detectives working the case might also be in attendance. Clearly, like others in the audience, his interest in Walker is purely political. Walker is a local character of some color despite his ultrarightist image.

Press: "The Senate Rules Committee plans to proceed at once with a full investigation of the business affairs of Robert G. Baker. . . . Senator B. Everett Jordan . . . who heads the committee, said the panel would seek the help of the Federal Bureau of Investigation. . . . 'We'll start with Baker,' he told reporters today. 'Where it will go from there we don't know.' "[623]

Press reports again on the growing Baker scandal: "Mr. Baker has remained silent and out of the reach of newsmen. . . . Mr. Baker, a shrewd, alert and personable man, virtually grew up in the Senate and enjoyed the patronage of Vice President Johnson. . . . He became known as 'Lyndon's boy' . . . an important adjunct to the Establishment. . . . . . In July 1962, he invited two busloads of his Senate friends, including the Vice President and his wife, to the opening of a resort motel on the Maryland coast. The first revelation of the extent and diversity of Mr. Baker's outside activities came last September. A suit was filed . . . here . . . against Mr. Baker [and] Fred Black, Jr. . . . As a result of one complex transaction, he and his family now occupy a stone residence in the Spring Valley section of Washington. Vice President Johnson is a neighbor. It has also been disclosed that Mr. Baker bought last November a more modest house . . . in southwest Washington. He said on his application . . . the house would be occupied by Nancy C. Tyler and Mary A. Martin. . . . Miss Tyler has been identified as . . . his cousin."[624]

10/24/63—THURSDAY: Press: "DALLAS . . . Anti-United Nations demonstrators shoved, booed, beat and spat in the face of Adlai E. Stevenson . . . tonight, following a speech he made here marking United Nations Day. 'It was a concerted action by members of . . . Edwin Walker's following and the John Birchers,' "[625]

This development probably concerns Marcello, the fear being that President Kennedy might cancel his tour of the city for security reasons.

10/25/63—FRIDAY: Press: "DALLAS . . . City leaders, reacting with indignation and shame, apologized today to Adlai E. Stevenson, who was struck and spat upon here yesterday. One hundred civic and business leaders sent a telegram to Mr. Stevenson. . . ."[626]

Press reports: "The diversified business interests of . . . Baker . . . a protégé of Vice President Johnson, were disclosed today to have included a struggling Capitol Hill travel agency. He remained unavailable for comment today about his business ventures, which are under investigation by . . . the Federal Bureau of Investigation."[627]

". . . The New Orleans FBI, which had learned of the Oswalds' departure from Magazine Street on Oct. 1, finally consults postal authorities in regard to post office box 30061 and discovers that Oswald has left a forwarding address of 2515 West Fifth Street, Irving, Texas."[628] Contrast this pace of the official Bureau bureaucracy with that of the private activities of Banister and Ferrie.

"After work, Oswald rides out to Irving with Wesley Frazier to spend the weekend. In the evening, Michael Paine invites Oswald to accompany him to a meeting of the Dallas American Civil Liberties Union on the campus of Southern Methodist. . . ." During a discussion of anti-Semitism and the Birchers, Oswald interjects with some observations of his own. Paine will later state he thought Oswald made a worthwhile contribution. Oswald will soon become a member. He spends the weekend at the Paines' with his family.[629] To help Mrs. Paine defray the costs of boarding Marina and the children, Oswald puts money in a wallet in his wife's room every weekend. She will later assert that she did not know how much was in it at any given time, nor how much was in it on November 21.[630] He apparently keeps a portion for his rent and food, eating sparingly judging by his near emaciated appearance at the time of the assassination.

10/26/63—SATURDAY: "Ruby placed a 12-minute person-to-person call to Irwin S. Weiner at Weiner's Chicago home. Weiner is a prominent Chicago Mafia associate, who has been linked to

. . . gambling . . . and murder. He is instrumental in coordinating the flow of cash between the Teamsters [and] Las Vegas casinos. . . . His close associates . . . included Traficante . . . and Hoffa."[631]

10/27/63—SUNDAY: "In Irving, Ruth gives Oswald another driving lesson in the nearby shopping center's deserted parking lot."[632] He still has no license.

Press reports: "PHILADELPHIA . . . President Kennedy will be the guest of honor at a cocktail party and reception Wednesday just before his appearance at a political rally. . . . Mr. Kennedy is scheduled to address a $100-a-plate dinner in behalf of Mayor . . . Tate. . . ."[633]

10/28/63—MONDAY: Press: "A member of the House of Representatives raised the question today whether a young German woman who has been mentioned regarding the affairs of . . . Baker . . . has been forced to return to Germany because of security violations. The woman . . . is Ellen Rometsch. . . . 'Among other things I want to know, Mr. Speaker, are the circumstances under which a young German woman was hastily deported from this country a few weeks ago following an FBI investigation. A high Government official confirmed today that the recall of the Rometsches had been quietly requested following an investigation of the wife's activities by the Federal Bureau of Investigation."[634] How this information has been leaked is unknown.

This week, Ruth Paine last notices Oswald's disassembled rifle wrapped in a blanket on the floor of the garage.[635]

10/29/63—TUESDAY: Press: "Three spokesmen for the press urged Congress today to pass legislation that they said would force the Government to give legitimate information to the public."[636]

Press reports: "President Kennedy will fly to Philadelphia tomorrow and to Chicago on Saturday. In both cities he will drive through downtown areas when street crowds normally are to be expected. The President . . . will go to the Bellevue-Stratford Hotel in a motorcade before addressing a Democratic fund-raising dinner in the evening. On Saturday, Mr. Kennedy will drive through

Chicago's Loop in late morning before attending the Army-Air Force football game at Soldier Field."[637]

Administration efforts at establishing a dialogue with Castro continue. "On October 29 there was movement. Vallejo tentatively brought up the idea that an American official—it was agreed this would be William Attwood—should fly to meet Castro at Veradero, a resort on Cuba's north coast."[638]

"Having received word four days earlier from the New Orleans office that Oswald had been in contact with the Soviet embassy in Mexico City, agent . . . Hosty . . . places higher priority on tracing his subject. . . . That same day, the agent goes out to Irving and makes 'what we call a pretext interview [with] a woman whose name at the time I didn't know . . . Mrs. Dorothy Roberts' at 2519 West Fifth. Mrs. Roberts tells Hosty that Mrs. Paine, residing at 2515, has a Russian-speaking woman residing with her and that the Russian woman's American husband visits there occasionally. . . ."[639]

Ruby makes an entry in his notebook, "October 29, 1963—John Wilson—bond."[640] This is very probably a reference to an individual, by the same name, who, shortly after the assassination, will contact the CIA in London in the context of Ruby's association with Santos Traficante during the 1950s (see 11/28/63).

Press: ". . . Valachi completed today his testimony before Senate investigators on a nationwide crime syndicate."[641]

10/30/63—WEDNESDAY: "At 9:13 p.m., Ruby placed a 1-minute call to the office phone of . . . Nofio Pecora at the Tropical Court in New Orleans."[642]

Press reports: "President Kennedy got a cool reception tonight as he toured the racially disturbed wards of South Philadelphia. This seemed to be reflected in the sparse crowds that stood . . . to watch the President drive past on his 13-mile route from Philadelphia International Airport to the Bellevue-Stratford Hotel. . . . It was one of the poorest receptions Mr. Kennedy has had in a major city since he became President. Riding with the President in an open White House limousine was Mayor James . . . Tate. . . ."[643]

Press reports: "Thirty-eight former employees of the LBJ Company, of which Mrs. . . . Johnson is a principle stockholder, are suing the company over a profit-sharing and incentive plan. The former employees sued in District Court here today, asserting that the company's profit-sharing and incentive plan owed them at least $49,932. They charge that they were employees of the radio and television station KRGV in Weslaco when it was sold about two years ago, thus causing them to suffer 'involuntary termination of employment' with the LBJ Company."[644]

Press: "NEW ORLEANS . . . A test of second-term opposition to President Kennedy in Louisiana is shaping up in the state's Democratic gubernatorial campaign. The outcome will determine if a Kennedy ticket would face an openly hostile Governor next year or one who would give no help to the Republicans even if he refused to endorse the President. Mr. Kennon's platform in the Governor's race leads off with pledges to 'support state sovereignty and segregation, oppose renomination and reelection of John F. Kennedy for President, or anyone else who condones what his Administration stands for, . . . and . . . fight the Federal power grab and the trend toward Socialism.' "[645]

10/31/63—THURSDAY: Hoover has a private, off-the-record lunch with President Kennedy at the White House. Aide Powers: ". . . Their . . . luncheons were awfully long when they had them. . . . He would have been seventy years old and it would have been time for him to retire. . . . that could have been what he was talking to him about . . . three weeks before the assassination. . . ."[646] Aide O'Donnell: "They discussed civil rights."[647]

The meeting may very easily concern LBJ. At his news conference this afternoon Kennedy will reaffirm LBJ as his 1964 running mate. Perhaps in anticipation of the inevitable questions surrounding the growing scandals, the President has summoned the Director for a briefing on what he, Hoover, knows of Johnson's activities. If called for this reason, it provides the aging demagogue with the perfect opportunity to bargain for an Executive Order waiving his compulsory retirement. That President Kennedy and Hoover have a common interest in protecting LBJ cannot be denied. And JFK is well aware of the longtime close friendship between the two men. But he cannot know the Director's true thoughts. Unfortunately Hoover now has more than enough evidence on Johnson to ensure his cooperation as President, and does not need to bargain with JFK over retirement. It is simply a question of timing.

Press reports: "Vice President Johnson's place on the Democratic ticket . . . was assured today by President Kennedy. A questioner at today's news conference, noting reports that Mr. Johnson would be 'dumped' or 'purged,' asked Mr. Kennedy whether he would be retained. 'Yes, he will, no question he will,' . . . There are a number of reasons. . . . The principle one seems to be that nobody has suggested a more practical substitute. 'Q: . . . Mr. President, just shortly after the Bay of Pigs I asked you how you liked being President and . . . you said you liked it better before the event. Now you've had a chance to appraise your job, why do you like it and why do you want to stay in office four more years? A: Well, I find the work rewarding. . . . I've given before this group the definition of happiness of the Greeks. I'll define it again: the full use of your powers along lines of excellence. I find that, therefore, the Presidency provides some happiness.' "[648]

Press reports formal indictment of mafioso Bruno and henchmen: " PHILADELPHIA . . . Nine men were indicted by a Federal grand jury today on charges of interstate loanshark racketeering. One of them, Angelo Bruno . . . is described by the Federal Bureau of Investigation as a top figure in Philadelphia criminal operations. He has been sought since Oct. 19, when a preliminary complaint was filed here. At least five of the defendants were in custody when the indictments were handed up. . . . The other defendants were identified as Harold Konigsberg . . . Samuel James Roberts . . . Anthony Stassi . . . Joseph Lucignano . . . Edward Skowron . . . Ignazio Denaro . . . Armand Colianni . . . Phillip Charles Testa. . . ."[649]

Press: "The Senate Rules Committee will face a critical decision tomorrow on whether to employ special outside counsel to direct its investigation into the affairs of Robert Baker. By implication, at least, the ramifications of the Baker case threaten to extend beyond the conduct of Mr. Baker, and to touch others . . . in the Executive Branch."[650]

Press reports on the Senator in charge of prosecuting the Baker investigation: "If Benjamin Everett Jordan appeared slightly nervous when he took his seat in the Senate in 1958, there was good reason. . . . Senator Jordan may wish that he had not moved up so rapidly to the chairmanship of the Senate Rules Committee. For Mr. Baker . . . has been considered a protégé of one of the men Senator Jordan most admires, Vice President Johnson. *Mr. Jordan was a strong Johnson for President supporter in 1960*" (emphasis added).[651]

11/1/63—FRIDAY: ". . . A young man drew attention to himself while buying rifle ammunition at Morgan's Gunshop in Fort Worth. He was 'rude and impertinent' and boasted about having been in the Marines. Three witnesses . . . remembered the incident and thought the man had looked like Oswald. The real Oswald was busily occupied in Dallas on the day mentioned."[652]

"At noon, Oswald walks . . . to . . . the Terminal Annex Post office and pays $3 for the rental of box 6225. . . . While at the post office, [he] posts a change-of-address card to . . . the Russian embassy, Washington, shifting '4907 Magazine Street and P.O. Box 30061, New Orleans, La.' to 'P.O. Box 6225, Dallas.' . . . Almost surely at the same time, Oswald mails a membership form to the ACLU's headquarters in New York giving . . . 'photographer' as occupation. . . . 'Please enroll me as an associate member at $2.00. Also please notifie [sic] as to how I may contact ACLU groups in my area.' "[653]

Oswald receives his first paycheck, in cash, from the Texas School Book Depository in the amount of $104.41. As made apparent from Truly's comments at the time Oswald was hired, payroll at the Depository is handled in a relatively casual manner. An analysis of his pay from this company also strongly suggests that an effort has been made by the FBI to hide certain facts from the public. Basically put, his *net* pay does not follow from the facts provided by the Bureau and TSBD (Texas School Book Depository). The following data will be given to the Warren Commission by Hoover in this regard:

> 11/28/63 O. V. Campbell, vice president, Texas School Book Depository . . . furnished the following information: LEE HARVEY OSWALD, while employed . . . from October 16 to November 22, 1963, was paid semimonthly in cash. He received two payments of $104.41 each on October 31, 1963, and November 15, 1963. In addition, he now has pay due him of $43.37 which is unclaimed.[654]

Why no pay stubs or internal company records will apparently be made available for purposes of including them as exhibits (as is the case with other sources of income) is unknown. At any rate, the problem is that given a gross wage of $120 for twelve work days, a

Social Security withholding rate of 3 percent, four personal exemptions (and thus $2 federal withholding), and no other deductions (Texas had no state income tax), his net pay should be $114.40, not $104.41.[655]

Recall that Oswald did not complete the dependents portion of the personal exemption section of his W-4 when he started work with the Depository. Truly is not sure when he did. The ex-Marine is also considered only temporary help. From this, it may well be that Oswald's first paycheck is calculated on the erroneous assumption that he has only two personal exemptions, himself and his wife. When computations are run on this basis (resulting in federal withholding of $12), and assuming an even 3 percent for Social Security, one arrives at a net pay figure of $104.40, within one cent of the above reported amount.[656] The point of this is that it reduces to a near certainty the probability that Oswald's employer, innocently in all likelihood, overwithheld on his first check. This becomes extremely important in view of the fact that Oswald will write a letter to the IRS the weekend of November 2–3, 1963.[657] That correspondence then, may well be due in part to a withholding error. Undoubtedly the addition of a dependent will also be a factor. An examination of income tax withholding tables for 1963 reveals that when one went from three to four personal exemptions, federal withholding was all but eliminated.[658] The married individual with two children at Oswald's income level became, practically speaking, exempt from FIT (federal income tax) withholding.

The *U.S. Master Tax Guide,* an annually published layman's guide to taxes, and readily available in most big-city libraries during 1963 (certainly Dallas), makes obvious Oswald's intentions. To quote: "An exemption certificate cannot be given retroactive effect. . . . An employee may file an amended certificate, increasing the number of exemptions at any time . . . *when a child is born to . . . the employee. . . . The employer may make the amended certificate effective with the next payment of wages but is permitted to postpone the effective date until . . . January 1 [1964]"* (emphasis added).[659] Another tax publication of the same year states: "If the overcollection is not returned to the employee, *the employee* cannot thereafter obtain a refund from the employer, but his *remedy lies with the government, through a credit against his tax liability, or if the amounts withheld exceed the credit, through a refund from the government"* (emphasis added).[660] Oswald's tax liability for 1963, given four exemptions, the nontaxability of unemployment benefits (at that time), and low pay scale, was $0. A credit therefore is useless, necessitating contact by him with the IRS in order to obtain adjustment and refund.

The *Master Tax Guide* explains the concept of a "Short Period Return." *". . . Individual returns for periods of less than 12 months must often be filed—for example: An individual voluntarily changes his basis of computing income from fiscal to calendar year, or vice versa, with the Commissioner's approval . . ."* (emphasis added).[661] Oswald was generally familiar with the concept of short period returns simply by virtue of the fact that he returned to the U.S. in June 1962, *six months* before the end of that year. Examination of Oswald's correspondence with the IRS suggests an attempt at this.

His letter, FBI exhibit 274, later placed in the hands of the National Archives, will not be made available to the Warren Commission during its deliberations. The first portion of the document will also be obliterated, perhaps deliberately. As revealed by the *Dallas Morning News* on May 1, 1977:

> Oswald stated . . . that he had "worked only six months in the fiscal year of 1963." The short note was written after Oct. 20, 1963, because it notes he then had two children and thus four dependents for tax purposes. . . . The date of the letter can be further pinpointed to Nov. 1, 1963, because by then Oswald had accumulated exactly six months of work in 1963. Although Oswald's letter referred to having worked only six months in *fiscal 1963,* he previously . . . referred to *"fiscal 1962"* in a letter to the IRS seeking a refund for income taxes withheld on his 1962 earnings. . . . Some of the words in the first part of the letter, where Oswald apparently discusses the birth of his daughter, are blurred beyond recognition as though someone had performed tests on the script or ink. . . .
> The Warren Commission gave no indication it probed for an explanation of the strange letter, or even knew it existed.

From all of this arises the possibility that Oswald, in the coming weeks, is planning to cease working and prepare and file an income tax return for the "fiscal" year 1963. Perhaps he does. His tax file, as stated, remains closed. The obvious question here is simply this: Would a man who is supposedly about to assassinate the President of the United States, either alone or as part of a conspiracy, initiate a protracted interaction with the IRS designed to obtain either a downward adjustment in his withholding rate and/or an early refund of all income taxes paid to date this year? In effect looking beyond the assassination, to year's end? It is hardly likely. And yet, Oswald is doing just that.

During this same time period Oswald is in contact with the Cuban embassy in Mexico City regarding his visa application for passage to Havana. That may be an additional impetus for the above letter. Armed with the knowledge (his 1962 refund of $57.40 had taken several weeks to obtain) that he may well be leaving the country by the end of the year, he is probably trying to set in motion the procedure for obtaining a refund before his departure. For further discussion of Oswald's taxes, see Appendix B.

"According to Hosty's testimony: '. . . at approximately 2:30 P.M., I stopped at the residence of Mrs. Ruth Paine. . . . She was very cordial and friendly, invited me into the house. At this time she was the only one in the living room. . . . I then told her the purpose of my visit, that I was interested in locating the whereabouts of Lee Oswald. . . . She said [he] was living somewhere in Dallas. She didn't know where. She said it was in Oak Cliff but she didn't have his address. I asked her if she knew where he worked. After a moment's hesitation, she told me he worked at the Texas School Book Depository near the downtown area of Dallas. She didn't have the exact address, and it is my recollection that we went to the phone book and looked it up, found it to be 411 Elm Street. . . . . . . She remarked that he came out . . . periodically to visit his wife and children on weekends. . . . Towards the conclusion of the interview, Marina . . . entered the living room. . . . Mrs. Paine then told her in the Russian language who I was, I was an agent with the FBI. I could tell . . . she became quite alarmed. . . . I told Mrs. Paine to relate to her in the Russian language that I was not there for the purpose of harming her. . . . . . . She seemed to calm down a little bit, and when I left she was smiling. . . . Mrs. Paine . . . said that . . . Oswald had alleged that the FBI had had him fired from every job he ever had. I told her this was not true. . . . . . . I reassured her that I wanted to know his place of employment for the purpose of determining if he was employed in a sensitive industry, and when I found out he was working in a warehouse as a laborer, I realized this was not a sensitive industry.' Sometime during Hosty's stay, Marina sees and jots down for transmission to her husband (with one error) Hosty's license number."[662] This evening, Oswald arrives and Ruth tells him of Hosty's visit, giving him the agent's phone number. Mrs. Paine will later state that she felt that Oswald was very worried about losing his job, fearing people would find out about his past. She will say she never made any attempt to get Oswald's address for the agent because she "assumed FBI had it all along." Also, Marina tells her she does not want her to provide the information.[663]

Press reports again on Baker: ". . . A partisan split in the Senate rules committee over the hiring of independent counsel to conduct the investigation into Mr. Baker's affairs, broke into the open today. . . . Senator . . . Jordan announced that a decision on the hiring of independent counsel to conduct the investigation had again been postponed—until Wednesday."[664]

"Baker couldn't peddle much influence on his own; his influence came from his close association with Senators and with officials who knew he was close to Vice President Johnson. . . ." FBI (SOG?) interviews Baker associate Wayne L. Bromley regarding Baker's financial deals. He apparently cooperates.[665]

11/2/63—SATURDAY: "In Irving, Oswald posts three change-of-address cards. . . . They are to furnish his post office box 6225 location to the Fair Play for Cuba Committee; to *The Militant;* and to *The Worker.*"[666]

11/2—11/3/63: Oswald, Marina, and children are in Irving shopping. They apparently enter a store displaying a sign indicating guns are sold. ". . . The manager recalled an early November visit by a man she thought looked exactly like Oswald. He had been accompanied by a wife and two children, one of them an infant. The wife had not uttered a word, although the husband spoke to her in a foreign language. The manager, whose account was corroborated in detail by a second witness, said this 'Oswald' asked where he could get the firing pin on his rifle repaired. She thought she had directed him to the nearby Irving Sports Shop. . . ."[667] Since there is also no record of the real Oswald ever firing his rifle, the obvious implication is that, as army surplus, it came to him in an inoperative condition. Here he may simply be anticipating need of the rifle once his visa to Cuba is approved.

11/3/63—SUNDAY: Texas press reports: "Only three speakers will be on the program for the 'Texas Welcomes' $100-a-plate dinner here Nov. 22 for President Kennedy. . . . . . . the President's Texas visit . . . will begin Nov. 21 with attendance at a dinner in Houston honoring U.S. Rep. Albert Thomas. The President will visit other cities during the tour. . . ."668

"It is probable that on this date Oswald takes a third driving lesson (of three testified to by Ruth Paine), which consists of parallel parking practice in front of the West Fifth Street residence."669 He is now going on twenty-five, and yet has never had a driver's license nor owned a car. In a car-crazy American society, this is unusual. Would a man planning to assassinate the President, either alone or as part of a conspiracy, be spending his time just before the hit learning to drive? Would a group of conspirators rely on such a man to pull the trigger?

11/4/63—MONDAY: FBI (Dallas) Agent Hosty: "On Monday morning I made a pretext call to the Texas SBD. I called up and asked for the personnel department, asked if a Lee Oswald was employed there. They said yes, he was. I said what address does he show. They said 2515 West Fifth Street, Irving, Tex., which I knew not to be the correct address. I then sent a communication, airmail communication, [AIRTEL] to the New Orleans office advising them—and to the headquarters of the FBI advising them—and then instructing the New Orleans office to make the Dallas office the office of origin. We are now assuming control, because he had now been verified in our division."670

"Secret Service agent . . . [Winston] Lawson in Washington and . . . [Forrest] Sorrels, the latter agent in charge of the Secret Service Dallas office, receive first official notification of the President's coming trip. Lawson is to act as the White House detail's advance man in Dallas. . . . Sorrels was instructed to make a preliminary survey of two possible luncheon sites: the new Trade Mart north of the downtown section on Stemmons Freeway and the Women's

Building at Fair Park, east of the business district."[671] Hoover is presumably also notified of the coming trip.

"Marcello went on trial in New Orleans on criminal charges in connection with his false Guatemalan birth certificate. . . ."[672] He remains confident knowing that at least one juror has been bribed. Additionally, with the assassination prosecutorial pressure will almost certainly alleviate.

After the assassination, "Dial Ryder, an employee in the [Irving Sports Shop], found a customer's ticket for work on a rifle between November 4 and 8. It bore the name the customer had given, just 'Oswald.' Intensive inquiry turned up no other Oswald in the area who had had a gun repaired. While neither Ryder nor his boss could remember much about their mysterious client, both did remember something about the gun. According to the ticket, the work done involved drilling three holes for a telescopic sight mounting. The weapon found in the Book Depository required only two holes. There were other technical differences, and the sum of the evidence pointed in one direction. Somebody who was not Oswald had commissioned alterations for a gun—not Oswald's—in Oswald's name." Ryder will be emphatic on this last point.[673] Note also there is no mention of repair to a firing pin. Besides all this, the real Oswald is working all day in downtown Dallas during the period November 4–8.

11/1—11/6/63:   At this time Oswald, according to Marina, begins discussing the idea of quitting his job at the Depository. He reportedly states that ". . . there was another job open, more interesting work . . . related to photography."[674] He may be alluding to the possibility of yet obtaining the visa to Cuba, perhaps hoping to work for the revolutionary government as a photographer. Oswald could well have phoned the embassy by now. It has, or is about to, move ahead with a conditional approval of his application.

Dallas papers report: "The blue-ribbon Dallas Citizen's Council tentatively is scheduled to host President Kennedy's visit to Dallas Nov. 21 or 22, *The News* learned Sunday."[675]

11/5/63—TUESDAY: David Ferrie purchases a .38 caliber revolver.[676]

FBI (Dallas) Agent Hosty and a rookie pay a second, shorter

visit to Mrs. Paine. "I . . . stopped at Mrs. Paine's very briefly. . . . [She] told me she would attempt to locate where he . . . was living. . . . She also made the remark that she considered him to be a very illogical person, that he had told her that weekend that he was a Trotskyite Communist. . . . She was a little more amused than anything else. . . ." Hosty leaves, intending to let the matter drop until preparation of his December 18 biannual report. He does not communicate with either New Orleans or SOG, because "There was nothing new that they didn't already know that would aid them. . . ."[677]

Press reports: "Senator . . . Jordan . . . said today that he now favored employing outside counsel to direct the committee's investigation into activities of . . . Baker. . . . The North Carolina Democrat's switch appeared to remove the last obstacle to getting the inquiry, approved almost a month ago, under way. *The committee has already employed a chief investigator. He is William Ellis Meehan, a former agent of the Federal Bureau of Investigation,* who retired last December after 22 years of service" (emphasis added).[678] The facts that the investigation is now controlled by ex-FBI agents, relies heavily on the FBI for logistical support, and involves Johnson (a man terrified by the hearings and increasingly subject to manipulation by Hoover), can only lead one to the conclusion that the Director is now in position to make or break the Vice President.

11/5—11/14/63: This evening at Ruby's Carousel Club in Dallas an individual named Wilbur Waldon Litchfield waits to speak with the mobster. "The next to see Ruby, Litchfield reported, was a man in a V-neck sweater who had been sitting four tables in front of Litchfield. [He] had paid particular attention to that man, he explained, 'because of his sloppy dress'; the man's 'hair was not combed,' and he stood out from the other men in suits or sport jackets. . . . Fifteen or twenty minutes after entering Ruby's office, the man . . . came out with Ruby. . . . As the man left, he passed within two feet of Litchfield underneath a bright light. [He] observed that the man was 'in his middle 20's, 5'7"–5'9"; and very slender. . . . After President Kennedy was assassinated' . . . Litchfield positively identified the man as Oswald. . . . The Dallas Police immediately took the highly unusual step of giving Litchfield a polygraph exam. The police's curt conclusion was that Litchfield 'ha[d] been untruthful.' . . . Officials attempted to shake his testimony through a questionable means of pressure, again highly irregular. . . . '. . . When the Federal agents talked to me, they said, "You know, if you say you are positive and it wasn't him," it's a Federal charge. . . .' "[679] Because there is no solid evidence to suggest that the real Oswald ever met Ruby, who this individual sees in all likelihood is the look-alike.

11/6/63—WEDNESDAY: The FBI National Academy holds graduation ceremonies for its seventy-second session. Speaker of the House McCormack of Massachusetts, a bitter political foe of President Kennedy, is the keynote speaker. Hoover provides introductory and closing commentary to the speech. "I now have the truly unusual privilege and the distinct honor of introducing our next speaker. He is a distinguished New Englander and a champion of law enforcement, a truly great statesman, and *a close personal friend of mine for nearly 34 years. Born in . . . Boston . . . he has earned his present position of prominence* through personal dedication, tireless energy, and the help of a dear and lovely wife. *In January of 1962, he was elected Speaker of the U.S. House of Representatives, the third highest office in our land. . . . He has proved himself to be a particularly staunch friend of effective law enforcement on all levels"* (emphasis added). **McCormack** replies ". . . There are few institutions whose names are indelibly associated with the integrity, the strength, and the devotion of one man. The Federal Bureau of Investigation is certainly one of these: and the man, Director J. Edgar Hoover, is entirely worthy of the honor. To praise J. Edgar Hoover and the FBI is to heap more icing on an elaborately decorated cake." **Hoover:** "We are thrilled at the remarks of Speaker McCormack. You have heard a man here this morning who I believe has done more than any other man in this country . . . to bring about the enactment of legislation that enabled the agencies of Government to proceed against . . . the criminal underworld. That took a great deal of courage. He . . . has alined [*sic*] himself very forcefully with the legislation being sought by the various Attorneys General over the recent years to combat the underworld activities and, particularly now, the activities of the Cosa Nostra."[680] Hoover knows full well that in the event both President Kennedy and Johnson become unable to serve, Mc-Cormack, next in line to the presidency, will undoubtedly prevent his retirement.

Press reports: "Investigators for the Senate Rules Committee have begun sifting through a mass of charges and reports concerning the outside business activities of . . . Baker."[681]

Oswald's landlady finds him to be a good boarder, later describing him as neat and cordial. "He was nice enough, I'd say, as a roomer because he always kept his room nice and he was well behaved. He didn't-uh-talk to anyone. He might speak to you when he came in and he might not. I suppose it was according to the mood he was in, or something. . . ."[682]

"[I]n the early evening, Oswald visits the public library where he borrows *The Shark and the Sardines* by Juan Jose Arevalo, left-wing former president of Guatemala, a book highly critical of the United States' economic and political record in Latin America. . . ." During early 1964 someone will anonymously return the book.[683]

Press reports: "*. . . Baker has acted as an intermediary in behalf of a prominent Las Vegas gambler [Ed Levinson] who has extensive associations with notorious underworld figures. . . . A retired agent of the Federal Bureau of Investigation, William E. Meehan, will direct the investigative staff, Senator Jordan said.* For weeks officials not directly connected with the Baker investigation have said privately that he had been involved in the entry of Las Vegas gamblers into other business activities that, unlike gambling, are legal in all states. . . . An executive of one of the nation's major and most respected business concerns—Pan American World Airways—complained that Mr. Baker had involved him and his company with three Nevada gamblers [Levinson, Jones, and Kozloff], and that now Pan American was connected with the Baker case. *The man Mr. Baker brought to see Mr. Gates was Edward Levinson, manager of the Hotel Fremont casino in downtown Las Vegas and its largest stockholder. . . . Mr. Levinson also holds a 27½ per cent interest in the Horseshoe Club, another casino in Las Vegas. . . .* Mr. Baker and Mr. Levinson have had close business relationships. These reports asserted that Las Vegas gambling money might be involved in some of Mr. Baker's operations. *Mr. Levinson is one of three brothers whose prominence in gambling was first established in Newport*

. . . *Ky.* One brother, Mike Levinson, has been associated with Edward Levinson . . . and . . . with a third brother, Louis Levinson, *in the Flamingo Club* in Newport. *The Flamingo Club was closed as an illegal gambling club after a reform sheriff . . . was elected in 1961. Observers of the Kentucky gambling operations said the Levinson brothers had been dominant figures there for more than 15 years.* Two weeks ago, in Las Vegas, Edward Levinson was asked . . . if he had a financial holding in . . . Baker's Serve-U Corporation. 'I don't want to discuss that,' Mr. Levinson said. He also declined to discuss his relationship . . . with Mr. Baker" (emphasis added).[684] Note that the Newport operation Levinson is involved in is the same as that assailed by RFK in late 1961. Levinson, much like Weisberg in Philadelphia, is obviously deeply involved with the Mafia. It is entirely probable that he (and those he represents) is using Baker as an intermediary, attempting to gain leverage over Johnson, and thus immunity from prosecution. The real possibility is that money received by Baker from the Levinson/Sigelbaum group at some prior point may by now have found its way into the pockets of Johnson in the form of bribes or kickbacks. By early February 1964 LBJ will be known to be living in fear of criminal indictment and impeachment over the Baker scandal.[685]

"Press reports Senator . . . Jordan said today that the newly recruited investigative staff—William E. Meehan, the former FBI agent, and two auditors . . . from the General Accounting Office —had been studying material in the committee's files, and would shortly start interrogating possible witnesses. This phase of the work is getting under way immediately, he said, without awaiting the choice of a counsel to take overall charge of the inquiry. The employment of such a counsel from outside the ranks of Government was voted unanimously by the committee. . . ."[686]

11/7/63—THURSDAY: "Oswald was plunged into a black mood by news of the Hosty visits. He . . . reacted . . . by making a personal appearance at the FBI's Dallas office. According to a receptionist who talked to him, Oswald's purpose was to see Agent Hosty. When told Hosty was out for lunch, Oswald gave [her] an envelope. He said curtly, 'Get this to him' and departed. . . . The receptionist . . . said she . . . caught a glimpse of the note and that it read:

Let this be warning. I will blow up the FBI and the Dallas Police Department if you don't stop bothering my wife. Lee Harvey Oswald.

Agent Hosty . . . maintained the message read roughly as follows:

If you have anything you want to learn about me, come talk to me directly. If you don't cease bothering my wife, I will take appropriate action and report this to the proper authorities.

He insists that the note was nothing out of the ordinary, that he simply placed it in his work tray and forgot about it until after the assassination. [The receptionist's] . . . version of the note rings false: it is wholly out of character with Oswald's usual actions or words. It is difficult, on the other hand, to take Hosty's account as gospel."[687]

Hosty's may well be the more accurate of the two. As pointed out to me by Dallas researcher Mary Ferrell, the page in Oswald's notebook containing Hosty's name, phone number, and license plate number, a page the FBI will remove and attempt to withhold from the Warren Commission, also contains the name "Gandy." Never explained, it probably refers to Helen Gandy, Hoover's personal secretary. As the person who screens all of Hoover's calls, during this time she probably takes a call from Oswald when he attempts to "take appropriate action and report [Hosty's harassment] to the proper authorities" (i.e., J. Edgar Hoover). Having interacted at least indirectly with the Bureau over the last year, Oswald is more than familiar with the basic bureaucratic structure. Hoover, as the ultimate "authority," would be the logical person to call. The phone number for SOG is public information. It would be almost impossible to believe that Oswald, if he does make such a call, ever gets past Miss Gandy. As a leftist closely monitored by the Bureau and known personally to Hoover, he in all likelihood encounters the same negative response that any other "communist" attempting to dress down the Bureau would receive. Couple this with the fact that when Hosty attempts to interrogate Oswald the afternoon of the assassination, he will be met with an immediate, apparently very unflattering, verbal assault upon none other than Hoover himself.

From the above, an intriguing and startling question arises. Would Oswald, a man long suffering the effects of Hoover's machinations, well aware that "certain agencies . . . [have] . . . made monumental mistakes in . . . relations with Cuba" (recall Oswald's 8/21/63 radio interview in New Orleans), and also aware, like anyone who has been reading newspapers, that President Kennedy is planning to retire the Director, participate in or plan the assassination of the one man who can restrain/reform the Bureau? Recall that in the same August interview Oswald had shown his awareness of the fact that Kennedy had removed top officials from the CIA, an agency now, in his words, "defunct."

Dallas press reports: "The President will speak in Houston Nov. 21 at the first stop in his tour. . . . The White House said second day plans tentatively call for stops at Fort Worth, Dallas, and Austin. Arrangements and formats for these events are still being worked out."[688]

Press reports: "The Internal Revenue Service has also been looking into Mr. Baker's income tax returns."[689]

"Ruby received a collect call from 'Barney Baker, Chicago, Illinois,' and spoke for seven minutes. Baker . . . was a Hoffa aide described by federal sources as 'a reported muscle and bagman' for Hoffa and 'a hoodlum with organized crime and Teamster connections.' "[690]

11/8/63—FRIDAY: Press reports: "Gov. . . . Brown disclosed today that . . . Baker made a special trip to California last May in an effort to protect a race track monopoly in San Diego. Governor Brown said Mr. Baker had spoken to him in opposition to legislation requiring competitive bidding for a lease at the Del Mar race track. The track . . . since 1936 has been leased to a charitable organization headed by the wealthy Murchison family of Texas. The Governor said Mr. Baker had been accompanied on the trip by Clint Murchison, Jr. . . . Mr. Baker was intervening on behalf of the Murchisons because of the financial support the family had given the Democratic Party. Governor Brown noted that Mr. Baker had said the appointment was set up by Vice President Johnson. The Governor said this was not true, and that Mr. Baker had acted independently."[691] The fact that Hoover and Murchison originated the idea of the charitable organization, and the fact that Hoover spends his annual vacation at this track cannot be overlooked. The interconnections here between Hoover and Johnson are intriguing. Baker's specific motivations in this regard remain unexplained.

11/8—11/15/63:   "One of the witnesses at the Western Union
Office, where an ex-Navy 'Oswald' drew attention to himself, described his visitor as being accompanied by a second man who
looked 'Spanish.' A witness at the Sports Drome [rifle] range made a
similar comment."⁶⁹²

It is during this "second week in November" that Oswald reportedly sends a telegram via Western Union.⁶⁹³ He is most likely either
checking with the Cuban embassy on his visa application or attempting to meet their requirements regarding a Russian visa.

FBI surveillance records a Cuban exile prior to the assassination,
talking with others in his group. "He confided to his audience, 'We
are waiting for Kennedy the 22nd [November], buddy. We are going
to see him, in one way or the other. We're going to give him the
works when he gets to Dallas.' "⁶⁹⁴ This individual may be connected
to the contract via Ferrie et al., or the Walker people in the context
of a protest against government policy on Cuba. It may be mere
bravado.

"At the White House, *Secret Service agent Lawson . . . is briefed
on his assignment:* 'Mr. Roy Kellerman, who is an assistant special
agent in charge of the detail, gave myself and other members of the
advance teams going out what information they had up to that time
on their respective stops. . . . Mr. Kellerman gave me the name of
a car contact in the Dallas area so that we would be able to obtain
cars for the motorcade, which is normal.' Immediately after this
meeting: *'I went . . . . to the office in the Executive Office Building
where our agents of the Protective Research Section are, and notified
agents at that location that I was being assigned the advance for the
Dallas, Tex., trip, the date of this trip, and that I requested them to check
their files and determine as to whether I should have the name of any
individual in the Dallas area who was on record to us as an active
subject. . . . I was told after waiting there a little while that there were
no subjects of record in the Dallas area, of active PRS individuals that
we would expect to harm the President'* " (emphasis added).⁶⁹⁵ Because of Hoover, the D.C. Secret Service advance agent learns
nothing of Marcello's plan to assassinate President Kennedy. The
Chief Executive's fate is now sealed. The Sicilian mobster cannot
have imagined that the Director would prove to be so close an ally at
this point.

Dallas press reports the details of the November 22 visit. There is
to be a noon luncheon at either the Trade Mart or Women's Build-

ing. "No parades are planned in any one of the cities but the President's routes in leaving and returning to airports will be announced in advance."[696]

"After work, Oswald rides to Irving with Wesley Frazier. According to Ruth Paine . . . : '. . . Marina . . . told him [about Hosty's visit] and then Lee inquired of me about that meeting, and he said . . . the FBI was inhibiting his activities. . . . I said to him, "Don't be worried about it. You have your rights to your views, whether they are popular or not." But I could see that he didn't take that view but rather was seriously bothered by their having come out and inquired about him. . . . *He told me that he had stopped at the downtown office of the FBI and tried to see the agents and left a note. . . . I learned only a few weeks ago that he never did go to the FBI office. . . . It appears to have been another lie . . .*' " (emphasis added).[697] Of course, during the 1970s his trip to the field office, as well as the note, will in fact be verified. This testimony, taken in 1964, makes apparent Bureau efforts to hide the fact after the assassination, undoubtedly at Hoover's directive. Mrs. Paine is apparently given disinformation in an attempt to contain the matter.

"Ruby placed a 4-minute call to the Eden Roc Hotel in Miami, person to person to Dusty Miller. . . . [He] was the head of the Southern Conference of Teamsters. . . . . . . Miller 'was associated with numerous underworld figures.' Also on November 8, Ruby placed a 14-minute call to Barney Baker . . . at Baker's Chicago residence."[698]

11/9/63—SATURDAY: Press reports: "Senate investigators plan to call Billie Sol Estes next week for a long-awaited inquiry. . . . . . . McClellan . . . wound up almost four months of hearings centered on the cotton acreage manipulations in September of last year, but kept the record open for Estes to testify personally."[699]

Miami police informant William Somerset has a conversation with Joseph Milteer (a wealthy ultrarightist active in the Cuban exile community), who tells him President Kennedy is going to be assassinated.

Somerset: I think Kennedy is coming here on the 18th, or
                 something like that to make some kind of
                 speech. . . .

Milteer:	You can bet your bottom dollar *he is going to have a lot to say about the Cubans.*
Somerset:	Yeah. Well, he will have a thousand body-guards, don't worry about that.
Milteer:	The more bodyguards he has, the easier it is to get him.
Somerset:	Well, how in the hell do you figure would be the best way to get him?
Milteer:	From an office building with a high-powered rifle. . . . *He knows he's a marked man.* . . .
Somerset:	*They are really going to try to kill him?*
Milteer:	*Oh, yeah, it is in the working.* . . . *They will pick somebody up within hours afterwards.* . . . *Just to throw the public off* (emphasis added).[700]

Somerset informs his police contact, who informs Captain Charles Sapp. Sapp reports to his chief of police, the local Secret Service, and FBI, "noting especially Milteer's remark that the President's assassination was 'in the working.' The Secret Service did check on Milteer's whereabouts, but he was not . . . questioned. . . ."[701] The obvious implication here is that Milteer, active in the Cuban exile community, has somehow became privy to the Marcello contract, yet is misinterpreting who is behind it. He is assuming the exiles are responsible. In the sense that via Ferrie a few may be contributing to the creation of the Oswald look-alike in Dallas, that much could be true.

"Perhaps most interesting, however, were meetings on November 9 and 16 between Ferrie and Marcello at the Mobster's Churchill Farms estate, Ferrie claimed they were there 'mapping strategy in connection with Marcello's trial.' "[702]

Oswald spends the weekend with Marina in Irving. Saturday morning he uses Ruth's typewriter to compose a letter to the Soviet embassy in furtherance of his goal of obtaining a Russian visa, and thus entrance to Cuba. Ruth Paine: " 'He typed it early in the morning . . . because after he typed it we went to the place where you get the test for drivers.' . . . The driver's license place was closed. . . . Despite the minor disappointment, Lee is ebullient. . . . '. . . We shopped at a dime store immediately adjacent, or in the same shopping center as the driver's license bureau. . . . . . .

Lee was as gay as I have seen him in the car riding back to the house. He sang, he joked, he made puns. . . .' . . . that afternoon '. . . He . . . looked at [college football on] television.' "[703]

This day the Oswald look-alike appears in several areas, including the downtown Dallas Southland Hotel where he applies for a job. Reportedly he asks whether the building commands a view of Dallas, as well as its height. "Then there was Hubert Morow, the manager of Allright Parking Systems. . . . He recalled that a man, identifying himself as Oswald, inquired about a job as a parking attendant. . . . When Morow at first wrote the man's name down as 'Lee Harvey Osborn,' the applicant corrected it to 'Oswald'. . . . The real Oswald did not usually spell out his full name but called himself simply 'Lee Oswald.' "[704] The impostor also makes an appearance at a downtown Dallas Lincoln Mercury dealership, where he draws attention to himself by recklessly driving a car and saying such things as "I might have to go back to Russia to get a car." He also states he has a new job and will be expecting money in two to three weeks, specifically identifying himself as Lee Oswald. Two salesmen speak to "Oswald," although one will be unable to positively identify him later. The impostor's request for credit is refused.[705]

"The sightings at the Sports Drome Rifle Range began on November 9, the day after the rifle was probably retrieved from the Irving Shop. A number of witnesses later described a man who had drawn attention to himself by being loud and obnoxious. He was variously described as being both an excellent shot and yet a man who infuriated another sportsman by shooting at his neighbor's target." Also, he is usually described as being in the company of at least one other man, who often acts as a driver.[706]

Press reports: "Texans voted today to keep their 61-year-old poll tax, a decision that might bear significantly on next year's Presidential race in this state. Both advocates and opponents of the repeal proposal were certain that it would have added thousands of liberal voters to the registration rolls, thus reinforcing a Kennedy-Johnson ticket in 1964. Gov. . . . Connally, . . . gave nominal support to the repeal plan, but did little to muster the necessary votes."[707]

Press: "Here in Texas's capital, home territory of Vice President Johnson, the television fare has been dubbed LBJ-TV [KTBC-TV]. This fall competition is being offered for the first time. But whether it will be as effective as it might be rests with a decision expected

soon from the Federal Communications Commission. TV Cable of
Austin . . . plans to relay programs to sets in Austin. . . . A ri-
val, Capital Cable Company, has granted the LBJ Company an
option to buy 50 per cent of its stock and has arranged to attach its
master antennas to the KTBC-TV tower. . . . Mrs. Johnson's station is affiliated with all three television networks, and so can force
TV Cable to 'black out' any program. Capital Cable, on the other
hand, is under no such restriction, because it is not operating with
an F.C.C. microwave permit. . . . Capital is advertising that sub-
scribers to its service will incur no blackouts or delays. TV Cable
cried 'foul' when Capital's plans became apparent and petitioned
the commission for a waiver of the 30-day restriction. The petition
contends that the Johnston [sic] station 'cannot openly aid and abet
a cable television system in which it has an interest and at the same
time reasonably expect the commission to impose substantial restrictions upon the operation of a competitor cable system' . . .
TV Cable spokesmen charge that influence 'from the top' may be
delaying their waiver petition."[708]

11/10/63—SUNDAY: Ruby's tax picture deteriorates further. ". . . He owed the federal government excise taxes going
back six years and totaling almost $40,000: and . . . owed 'an ad-
ditional $20,000' in other federal taxes."[709]

   "According to Ruth Paine: '. . . I was the first . . . up. I took a
closer look at [Oswald's letter to the Soviet Embassy].' " It reads as
follows:

   This is to inform you of recent events since my meetings with
   comrade Kostin in the Embassy of the Soviet Union, Mexico
   City, Mexico. I was unable to remain in Mexico indefinily [sic]
   because of my Mexican visa restrictions which was for 15 days
   only. I could not take a chance on requesting a new visa unless
   I used my real name, so I returned to the United States. I had
   not planned to contact the Soviet Embassy in Mexico, so they
   were unprepared, had I been able to reach the Soviet Embassy
   in Havana as planned, the Embassy there would have had time
   to complete our business. Of course the Soviet Embassy was
   not at fault, they were, as I say unprepared, the *Cuban consulate was guilty of a gross breach of regulations, I am glad he has
   since been replaced.* The Federal Bureau of Investigation is not

now interested in my activities in the progressive organization
"Fair Play for Cuba Committee," of which I was secretary in
New Orleans (state Louisiana) since I no longer reside in that
state. However the FBI has visited us here in Dallas, Texas, on
November 1st. Agent James F. Hasty [*sic*] warned me that if I
engaged in F.P.C.C. activities in Texas the F.B.I. will again take
an "interest" in me. This agent also "suggested" to Marina
Nichilayeva that she could remain in the United States under
F.B.I. "protection," that is, she could defect from the Soviet
Union, of course, I and my wife strongly protested these tactics
by the notorious F.B.I. Please advise us of the arrival of our
Soviet entrance visas as soon as they come. Also, this is to
inform you of the birth, on October 20, 1963 of daughter,
AUDREY MARINA OSWALD IN DALLAS TEXAS to my
wife [emphasis added].[710]

Ruth Paine continues: "[In the] . . . early evening . . . Michael
Paine was also at the home. . . . 'I asked the gentlemen . . . to
. . . help me move the furniture around.' " Afterward Oswald
watches the late show.[711]

11/11/63—MONDAY: Press reports: "Another Federal
agency joined today the widening investigation of . . . Baker's
business activities. Joseph P. McMurray, chairman of the Federal
Home Loan Bank Board, said his agency would investigate possible
conflicts of interest in the spectacular rise of the Mortgage Guaranty
Insurance Corporation. The stock . . . in which Mr. Baker was an
investor, rose substantially in price following a favorable tax ruling
in Washington. The Senate Rules Committee and the Federal Bureau of Investigation are already investigating whether he used
influence and inside information for his own profit . . . while serving in the strategic Senate Post."[712]

"Veterans Day. Oswald is off work and stays in Irving with Marina. . . . Marina's testimony . . . is as follows: '. . . He played
with June and helped me a little with the preparations of lunch, and
he sat around, watched television. . . . It seems to me that on that
day he was typing. . . . It seems to me it was *the envelope.* . . .
. . . A letter which mentioned Mexico and Kostin, it was that envelope. . . . You see *the date* [of the cancellation] *is the 12th* ' "

(emphasis added).[713] Ruth Paine takes the car to Dallas to see a divorce attorney.[714]

Ruby visits his physician. "Dr. Ulevitch prescribes pills to calm Ruby's nerves. Ruby fills the prescription immediately."[715]

11/12/63—TUESDAY: Press reports: "The Justice Department is investigating a connection between . . . Baker and an American-owned packing plant in Haiti that was seeking approval in 1961 to export meat to the United States and Puerto Rico. State Department officials . . . said today it was understood that Clinton W. Murchison, Jr., the Texas industrialist, who has an interest in a flour monopoly in Haiti, also had an interest in the slaughter house and packing plant."[716]

"In the evening, Secret Service agent Lawson . . . arrives at Love Field [Dallas] from Washington."[717]

"Oswald rides to work from Irving with Wesley Frazier, returns to his roominghouse on the Beckley bus later. . . . He posted his letter to the Russian embassy this day."[718]

"Ex-convicts Paul R. Jones and Alex Gruber hold meetings with Ruby. They have come from out-of-town points after not visiting with Ruby in years." Jones is a Mafia functionary from Chicago.[719] These men and the look-alike would see little harm in meeting in public with Ruby, as his involvement is never meant to be anything more than logistical in nature. The killing of Oswald via Ruby will be a last-minute solution to an otherwise desperate situation.

This day "Ruby placed a 10-minute call person-to-person to Frank Goldstein . . . a 'professional gambler.' Mob killers Russell Mathews, Lewis McWillie and Lenny Patrick were similarly described in the assassination evidence."[720]

Marcello's trial reopens in New Orleans and runs until November 22.[721]

Press: ". . . Estes declined today to tell Congressional investigators anything. . . . He invoked the Fifth Amendment's protection . . . 26 times before the Senate Permanent Subcommittee on Investigations. After a 45-minute public session . . . McClellan indicated that the case was closed. . . . But, he said, there are some areas 'where law enforcement officers may want to examine the . . . record carefully.' He did not elaborate."[722] After a year and a half of delay, Estes finally appears in D.C., only to plead the Fifth.

With all that has come before, McClellan's failure to "elaborate" is, sadly, not surprising.

11/13/63—WEDNESDAY: Press reports: "The Murchison family . . . 'are the money partners' in the Haitian-American Meat and Provision Company. Questioned about Mr. Baker's commission, Mr. Dancy declined to comment. . . . 'This is something they [in Dallas] told me specifically not to talk about,' he said. . . . Mr. Baker had to share the commission with several other persons. They declined to give the names of these persons."[723]

"Agent Lawson reports to Sorrels at Dallas office of Secret Service. . . . The two take note of the Stevenson incident of October 24. According to Lawson . . . 'we talked about it. We talked about these extremist groups off and on . . . all the time I was there. . . . I specifically talked about right-wing groups. . . . I asked . . . perhaps we had better at least try to find out if they were going to do anything, which is what I did.' " This day Lawson makes an inspection tour of potential luncheon sites in Dallas.[724]

Dallas press reports: "Groups which make up 'a cross section of the community' will decide who gets invitations to the Dallas luncheon for President Kennedy, The News was told Tuesday. Its source was a businessman who is helping arrange details of the President's visit to Dallas Nov. 22. He said Secret Service agents are checking potential sites for the luncheon."[725] This, of course, focuses attention on possible motorcade routes and the Stemmons Freeway. Ruby is following this closely, obtaining inside information from the Dallas P.D.

Ruby continues meeting with Jones and Gruber.

11/14/63—THURSDAY: Press reports: "Two Democratic Senators disclosed today what they regarded as deception by . . . Baker . . . on appointments to a Senate committee. The liberal Senators told how they were apparently kept by Mr. Baker from getting seats in 1961 on the Judiciary Committee despite the fact that they had greater seniority than their rivals."[726]

President Kennedy, at a press conference, is asked about Baker and Korth. "I think it's always—firstly, you don't lump the two cases together. I think there are differences between the two cases. I want to make clear. There are differences between the cases. Now, if you are talking about—there are always bound to be in the government, newspaper business, labor, and so on, farmers—there are always going to be people who can't stand the pressure of opportunity so that—but the important point is what action is taken against them and I think that this Administration has been very vigorous in its action and I think that you try to accept responsible standards. There's always going to be people that fail to meet that standard and we attempt to take appropriate action dealing with each case. But Mr. Baker is now being investigated and I think we will know a good deal more about Mr. Baker before we're through. Other people may be investigated as time goes on. We just try to do the best we can and I think that—the governmental standards, let me say, on the whole, I think compare favorably with those—in Washington —with those in some other parts of America."[727] Kennedy's growing difficulties with Johnson are made apparent by his attempt to minimize the two cases. Note his comment about "governmental standards." No doubt RFK has already briefed him on the seriousness of the Baker case. JFK, while serving in the Senate, had of course observed Johnson and Baker firsthand.

President Kennedy travels to New York City for an address. In doing so, he drops his regular security and escort. "The President does not wish a motorcade and wishes to go about without fuss or feathers. . . . We will, however, provide details of police at the Carlyle and wherever else the President goes so that he will have all necessary security."[728]

Press: "Last night, not long after he arrived at the Carlyle, the President stepped out of the hotel by way of the Madison Avenue doors and leisurely strolled a block west to the home of his brother-in-law and sister, Mr. and Mrs. Stephen Smith. An elaborate police guard had been set up in the main lobby of the Carlyle, and police officials appeared surprised when they learned that the President had left by the side exit instead of the main doors on 76th Street. He left the Smiths' home at 12:38 A.M. and returned to the Carlyle by limousine."[729]

Secret Service agent Winston Lawson decides upon the motorcade route. ". . . Lawson and Sorrels . . . drove the route which Sorrels believed best suited for the proposed motorcade." . . . The two ". . . met with Dallas Chief of Police . . . Curry, Assistant Chief . . . Batchelor, Deputy Chief . . . N. T. Fisher, and several other command officers to discuss details of the motorcade . . . routes. . . . The route was further reviewed . . . on November 15.''[730] He details in essence the route to be taken, including the obvious pass through Dealey Plaza.

"When Oswald makes his usual 5:30 P.M. call to Irving, Marina asks him not to visit on the coming weekend. . . ." Marina: "He had wanted to come, he had telephoned. . . . He said, 'As you wish. If you don't want me to come, I won't.' " Ruth Paine: "She felt that he had overstayed his welcome the previous weekend, which had been 3 days. . . . I did tell her that I was planning a birthday for my little girl, and I heard her tell Lee not to come out because I was having a birthday party." "Evidently, Lee . . . objects that he wants his learner's permit. . . . 'I . . . said I couldn't possibly take him again to this place so he could take a test. But that he didn't need a car. This was news to him. He thought he needed a car for his initial test. . . . I said he could go himself from Dallas.' ''[731]

11/15/63—FRIDAY: Press reports again on Kennedy's New York trip: "A group of teenagers surrounded the limousine in which President Kennedy was riding . . . and it took a small band of uniformed patrolmen—their clubs raised as a precaution—to free the car. Mr. Kennedy didn't seem to mind. But the police did, for they and the Secret Service are not happy with the President's ban on motorcycle escorts. . . . *The teenagers* who crushed in on the President's car while it was stopped for a red light at the Avenue of the Americas and 54th Street *were members of the Catholic Youth Organization. They were attending a C.Y.O. convention* at the nearby New York Hilton Hotel, *and had just heard a short talk by Mr. Kennedy.* One police inspector, standing in the Carlyle Hotel lobby, where the President was staying, said, 'As far as I'm concerned he can walk into the city the next time he visits' " (emphasis added).[732] Within hours, Hoover will deliver a major speech, his first in months, before the same group. A fairly long one, its focus, of course, will be morality. The scheduling of these two speeches seems odd. Is one attempting to counter the other? JFK's seems the more spontaneous. Note that he was ostensibly in New York to deliver a speech before the AFL-CIO.[733] He may be attempting, while there, to preempt or dilute Hoover's coming address. It is possible the near simultaneous appearances are mere chance.

Dallas press reports: "A decision is expected Friday on whether the luncheon will be held in the Women's Building at Fair Park or the Trade Mart beside Stemmons Freeway. Secret Service agents have inspected both." "In the course of this morning the decision on the luncheon site comes through from Washington in time to be announced in the afternoon *Times Herald:* it is to be the Trade Mart on Stemmons Freeway."[734] It is apparently common knowledge to locals that any downtown motorcade to such a destination will surely pass through Dealey Plaza on its way to the freeway.

". . . Ruby began behaving as though he expected his financial affairs to take a dramatic change for the better. [He] . . . began using a safe and discussed plans to embed it in concrete in his office. This was a change for Ruby, who had long lived out of his hip pocket or left his money littered around his apartment."[735] He also "refilled the prescription to calm his nerves."[736] Obviously he cannot possibly know he will soon be required to murder Oswald.

The Oswald look-alike is seen again in the Carousel Club with Ruby. "Entertainer Bill DeMar . . . told the Associated Press by telephone [on 11/24/63] that he was positive that Lee Harvey Oswald was a patron about nine days ago in the Dallas night club of Jack Ruby. . . . And Carousel stripper Karen Carlin also 'vaguely remembered Oswald being at the club' when questioned by the Secret Service on November 24."[737]

Per request, Oswald stays in Dallas this weekend. He apparently spends his days out, for his landlords will claim he is absent Saturday and Sunday. ". . . His whereabouts from the evening of Friday, November 15, to the morning of Monday, November 18, are not [completely] established. Mrs. Johnson had the impression that Oswald visited the local laundromat Saturday morning. . . ."[738] This weekend the ex-Marine may be approached a second time by Ferrie et al. If anything, he will participate unwillingly, perhaps maneuvered once again on the basis of his informant status (i.e., money orders received via Western Union, wife's status as potential spy). He really has no reason to risk involvement in such a business, as he is well on his way to obtaining his entrance visa to Cuba. Manipulation of Oswald through his history of public protest is the obvious avenue by which to frame him—convincing him to bring pro-Cuba material of some form into the Depository.

Press: "Senate investigators hinted today that the Murchison brothers of Texas might be called to testify in the investigation of the business activities of . . . Baker. Today, William Kentor, president of Packer's Provision, said . . . he had 'voluntarily and at my own expense' come to Washington last week to confer with the Federal Bureau of Investigation. . . . Mr. Kentor gave as the reason for his 'hedge' a suggestion of these officials that he not discuss the matter with reporters."[739]

11/16/63—SATURDAY: The look-alike again appears at local rifle ranges. "Witnesses at the rifle range say the marksman there carefully collected his cartridge cases before leaving. The schoolteacher also added one last clue: she remembered that at least one of the threesome . . . was 'Latin, perhaps Cuban.' "[740]

"Dr. Homer Wood . . . [stated] . . . 'On November 22, in the afternoon I was watching the television at home. As soon as I saw Oswald on TV I said to my wife, "He looks like the man who was sitting in the next booth to our son, out at the rifle range." ' . . . Dr. Wood . . . called the FBI. Wood's thirteen-year-old son . . . well remembered talking to the man in the next booth, who was an excellent shot. The man volunteered that the gun he was using was a 6.5mm Italian rifle with a four-power scope. It emitted a 'ball of fire' when fired. The FBI later tried persistently to get young Wood to change his very specific story. . . . [The son] remembered a gun with a scope different from the one on the weapon linked to the assassination. And he recalled that when the marksman left, he was accompanied by 'a man in a newer model car.' "[741]

"Other witnesses also remembered 'Oswald' but thought him only similar in appearance, not Oswald."[742]

"[The] . . . man was better than average shot, took all shell casings with him when he left the range."[743]

Press reports on President Kennedy's speech before the national convention of the Catholic Youth Organization in New York City only hours before. "I am glad to be here today. . . . In any case I am glad to see you and I want to congratulate you on the effort that you are making. . . . *I can't imagine a greater cause in which to be engaged, to give the best that you have . . . for the United States. . . . Whatever we are able to do in this country. . . . whatever leadership we are able to give, whatever demonstration we can make that a free society can function and move ahead and provide a better life for its people—all these things that we do here have their effect all around the globe. . . . It is our responsibility not merely to denounce our enemies and those who make themselves our enemies but to make this system work, to demonstrate what freedom can do. . . .*

It requires more of you—discipline, character, self-restraint, a will-ingness to serve the public interest as well as our own private interests.
. . . I come here today. Not just because you are doing well and because you are outstanding students, but because we expect something of you. And *unless in this free country of ours we are able to demonstrate that we are able to make this society work and progress . . . then, quite obviously, all the hopes of all of us that freedom will not only endure but prevail, of course, will be disappointed.* So we ask the best of you . . . *I hope that in a long life that you will recognize your obligations to the Great Republic . . ."* (emphasis added).[744]

Dallas press reports that the motorcade is definitely on. "President and Mrs. Kennedy are expected to drive west on Main St. at noon while in route to a luncheon at the Dallas Trade Mart beside Stemmons Freeway. The President is expected to travel over Lemmon Ave. or Cedar Springs Road to the downtown area, then west on Main St. before turning north after driving through the triple underpass. If he stays on schedule he would pass through the downtown area about noon."[745] At this point the Marcello contract killers now know the arrival time of the President, the time of the luncheon, and the motorcade route.

Ferrie is at Marcello's estate ostensibly to help with trial preparation.

"In the afternoon, Oswald calls Marina to tell her he has been to the license bureau. According to Ruth: 'He called us . . . to say he had been and tried to get his driver's permit but that he had arrived before closing time but still [too] late to get in because there was a long line ahead of him. . . . There were a lot of people who wanted to get permits and he was advised that it wouldn't pay him to wait in line. He didn't have time to be tested.' "[746] If anything, it sounds as though he is simply avoiding the test once again.

Hoover, also appearing before the Catholic Youth Organization in New York, delivers a major speech entitled, "Keys to Freedom."

I accept this award with a deep feeling of humility. I shall treasure it because of my great admiration for the outstanding work being performed by the Catholic Youth Organization. . . . To the outstanding young people assembled here tonight, I bring warm greetings. Yours is a generation of great challenge. Through no choice of your own, you have entered the world at a time when deadly forces challenge your right, and the right of every American, to live in freedom under God. *High ideals are the birthright of youth, but the youth of postwar America must face, also, the chaos which present-day society presents, . . . mortal enemies of freedom and deniers of God Himself conspire to undermine the fundamental forces which are the lifeline of our country's vitality and greatness. . . . What are these forces?. . . .*

Faith—faith in supreme being. . . .

Individualism—inherent dignity and worth. . . .

Courage—the courage of a free people. . . .

Integrity—that quality of trustworthiness. . . .

Discipline—and self-discipline. . . .

Vision—such as led our founding fathers. . . .

These . . . great bulwarks . . . are under savage attack today, just as they were so severely tested nearly 200 years ago at . . . Valley Forge. Daniel Webster . . . knew . . . *the disintegrating effect of self-indulgence, neglect of duty. . . . These lethal influences are at work, constantly undermining the sense of personal responsibility and self-discipline so essential* to our Nation's welfare. *They form a common denominator with the aggressive enemies of our Republic in assaulting the cause of decency and justice. . . . Who are these enemies of our Republic? They are the crime syndicates . . . the corrupt politicians . . . the . . . false liberals who would subvert our Constitution* and undermine our democratic processes in furtherance of their selfish ends. This is especially true of the intense civil rights movement. . . . No amount of lies and duplicity can conceal this carefully documented fact. *Americans, in growing numbers, are developing a dangerously indulgent attitude toward crime, filth, and corruption. . . . Our youth do not need weakness: they need strength. They do not need indulgence; they need . . . guidance and . . . discipline. . . . Despite the dedicated efforts of church and civic leaders and others . . . the failures continue to mount. . . . They represent a tragic waste of America's most valuable resource—the moral . . . health of her young citizens. The voices of . . . decency must speak out more effectively and make their influences felt. . . . This country has never run from its enemies.* Challenge, not compromise—bravery, not cowardice—are integral parts of our heritage. *. . . Our greatest patriots have been men . . .*

of deep religious conviction. . . . America remains free be-
cause men of faith . . . individualism . . . courage . . . in-
tegrity . . . discipline, and vision have patrolled her most vital
outposts for 187 years. . . . History, all too often, repeats itself. The freedoms you enjoy today will be lost . . . through
neglect and abuse. *We must never become so accustomed to*
filth or so intimidated by the so-called advocates of worldly
reality that we fail to revolt against corruption and decay" [em-
phasis added].[747]

Consider this speech against Kennedy's before the same group.
Once again, the fundamental differences in personal philosophy are
made obvious.

11/17/63—SUNDAY: Press reports: "L. P. McLendon . . .
said today he was confident that the Rules Committee would make
a full disclosure of any findings concerning Mr. Baker's alleged use
of his Senate influence to further outside business interests. '. . . I
received no indication that there would be any attempt to cover up
anything.' "[748]

FBI (SOG) has by now learned of Oswald's November 12 letter
to the Soviet embassy requesting a return visa to Russia. ". . . A
routine FBI mail intercept turned up a copy Oswald actually mailed
to the Soviet Embassy."[749] Upon arrival in D.C., presumably on
November 14 or 15, it had apparently been routed to the Bureau
where it was copied and then forwarded to the embassy.

"According to witnesses interviewed by the FBI, [Ruby] was seen
in Las Vegas, Nevada, on November 17."[750] Without a doubt, he
meets with McWillie at the Thunderbird. It is unknown whether he
sees other Mafia functionaries while there. At this point, he only
perceives himself as a peripheral part of the conspiracy, perhaps
even feeling somewhat buoyant.

Dallas civic leaders ask the public for no demonstrations. "Inci-
dent-Free Day Urged for JFK Visit." One-hundred extra police will
be on duty on the twenty-second to ensure cooperation.[751]

This evening Marina tries to call Oswald. Ruth Paine: "I said, 'Is
Lee Oswald there?' He said, 'There is no Lee Oswald living here.'
. . . I said, 'Is this a roominghouse?' He said, 'Yes.' I said, 'Is this
WH 3-8993?' and he said, 'Yes.' I then thanked him and hung
up."[752]

JFK spends the weekend in Palm Beach, feeling that the only threat in Dallas is potentially from the ultraright, men like Walker.[753]

The Abilene incident occurs. ". . . A citizen of Abilene, two hundred miles west of Dallas, picked up a note left for one of his neighbors. It was an urgent request to call one of two Dallas telephone numbers, and the signature read 'Lee Oswald.' *After the assassination the citizen, Harold Reynolds, twice tried and failed to arouse FBI interest.* The neighbor, it turns out, was Pedro Gonzalez, president of a local anti-Castro group called the Cuban Liberation Committee. Gonzalez became noticeably nervous when he was handed the note and minutes later was seen phoning from a public telephone. Reynolds says he had previously seen a man who closely resembled Oswald attending a meeting at Gonzalez's apartment along with a second and older American from New Orleans. Gonzalez is remembered for extreme anti-Kennedy sentiments and was known as a friend of Antonio de Varona, leader of the CIA backed Cuban Revolutionary Council. He left Abilene soon after the assassination and was last heard of in Venezuela" (emphasis added).[754]

11/18/63—MONDAY: Dallas press reaffirms the downtown motorcade route. "Most likely the motorcade will move west on Main St. through the downtown area."[755]

As will be revealed by Hoover in his 11/23/63 five-page report to Johnson the morning after the assassination, "A highly confidential source of this Bureau advised that an individual identifying himself as Oswald on November 18, 1963, was in contact with the Soviet Embassy in Washington, D.C. . . ."[756] Hoover's report reads as if Oswald actually called the embassy on November 18. His letter to them having been mailed November 12, a followup call a week later would not be unusual. People often follow letters with phone calls to verify arrival and reiterate or bolster their positions. It is possible Hoover is referring to the date Oswald's letter actually arrived at the Soviet embassy, but the time interval between its mailing and this date seems too long. Also, it would be difficult for Hoover to know exactly what day the letter was delivered to the embassy, presuming once opened and copied it was resealed and then delivered with regular embassy mail by the Post Office. As has been shown, Oswald made long-distance calls during November.

". . . The Chief of the Secret Service unit in Dallas, Forrest Sorrels, made a slight change in the motorcade route . . . that provided for an abrupt dogleg turn to the right in Dealey Plaza. . . . This would bring the presidential motorcade right under the windows of the Book Depository where . . . Oswald worked and almost within spitting distance of the picket fence on the grassy knoll. This . . . route change was then communicated to both Dallas papers . . . which published the amended route on Tuesday, November 19th. . . ."[757] The purpose of the change is to obtain access to Stemmons Freeway.

President Kennedy is in Miami to deliver an address. ". . . It has been reported that there was a last-minute change in the Miami program. Captain Sapp recalls that a planned motorcade was canceled—for fear of trouble from the anti-Castro movement. . . . The President flew by helicopter to and from his speech-making at the Americana Hotel. . . . the Secret Service failed to mention the Miami scare to the agents responsible for advance planning in Texas."[758]

Press reports: "Waggoner Carr, Attorney General of Texas [an ex-FBI agent], said today that he had no choice but to drop attempts to extradite from New York the president of the Commercial Solvents Corporation on a charge stemming from the . . . Estes case."[759]

"Oswald calls Marina. . . . 'When he telephoned me . . . on Monday, I told him that we had telephoned him but he was unknown at that number. Then he said that he had lived there under an assumed name. . . . We had a quarrel. I told him that this was another of his foolishness. . . . He said he did not want his landlady to know his real name because she might read in the paper of the fact that he had been to Russia and that he had been questioned. . . . Also that he did not want the FBI to know where he lived. . . . Their visits were not very pleasant for him and he thought that he loses jobs because the FBI visits the place of his employment.' "[760]

11/19/63—TUESDAY: Press: "The possibility that . . . Johnson had a role in awarding the controversial TFX airplane contract was raised today before the Senate Permanent Subcommittee on Investigations. Senator . . . Curtis, Republican of Ne-

braska, drew attention to the Vice President's possible connection
with the award of the contract to the General Dynamics Corporation. . . . Representative Jim Wright, Democrat of Texas. . . .
said . . . 'You've got to have friends and they've got to stick with
you through thick and thin, even if you do have merit on your
side.' "[761]

Press: "The Dallas City Council unanimously adopted yesterday
an antiharassment ordinance designed to prevent a repetition of the
recent attack on Adlai Stevenson. The ordinance permits peaceful
picketing but makes it unlawful to interfere with anyone entering or
leaving the premises where a public or private meeting is held."[762] In
effect this allows demonstrations *along* the motorcade route. Such
information strengthens the position of those maneuvering Oswald
into a protest in Dealey Plaza.

Ruby gives his attorney power of attorney to deal with the IRS,
probably via Form 2848. ". . . Ruby told his tax lawyer that he
now had a 'connection' who would supply him with money to settle
his tax debts."[763] Clearly, he has either received his payoff, or is
about to.

". . . Ambassador Attwood placed a call from New York to the
White House. He briefed McGeorge Bundy, the President's advisor
on foreign affairs, on the latest contact with Castro. The President
. . . had given 'the go-ahead.' Attwood was to go to Havana and
'see what could be done to effect a normalization of relationship.' "[764]

Press reports on the connection between Baker and the Mafia:
". . . Mr. Jones also was the Lieutenant Governor of Nevada.
Later he ran a casino in Havana and was the central figure in the
state Gaming Control Board's attempt about eight years ago to
prove that *his interest in the Thunderbird Hotel was really a concealed interest of Meyer Lansky, the gambler.* . . . More recently
Mr. Jones was involved in the controversy that followed the resignation of . . . Baker. . . . Mr. Baker arranged a series of meetings last summer for Mr. Jones and two other Nevada gamblers
with John Gates, the president of Intercontinental Hotels, Inc., a
Pan American World Airways subsidiary" (emphasis added).[765]
Note the connection to the Thunderbird Hotel, both a place Ruby
has been calling regularly for months and the employer of McWillie. Through Baker, Johnson has clearly been drawn into association with the Mafia. As a conduit for money to LBJ, Baker may

well by this point have compromised him with the mob via his association with Levinson et al. President Kennedy himself has referred to Johnson as a "riverboat gambler," a man who is ". . . incapable of telling the truth."[766]

11/20/63—WEDNESDAY: Two individuals ". . . believed they saw a person resembling Oswald firing a similar rifle at another range near Irving."[767] The real Oswald is, of course, at work.

Irving postman delivers, along with the Paines' mail, a package for Oswald. " '1 notice of attempt to deliver mail, card dated November 20, 1963, to Mr. Lee Oswald, 2515 West 5th St., Irving, Texas—a parcel to be picked up.' There is no reference to this parcel in the [Warren] Report. The Commission allows it to remain a highly suggestive mystery."[768]

". . . A bruised and battered woman was found lying on a road near Eunice, Louisiana. She was Rose Cheramie. . . . Taken to Louisiana State Hospital near Jackson, Louisiana, [she] spoke of the assassination of President Kennedy, to occur two days later." She will reiterate her beliefs on November 25 to another physician at the same institution. "[Dr. Victor] Weiss questioned [her] about her statements. She told him she had worked for Jack Ruby. She . . . stated the 'word in the underworld' was that Kennedy would be assassinated."[769]

"Wayne January . . . ran a plane rental business at Red Bird Airport [near Dallas]. . . . Two days before the assassination he was approached by two men and a woman, who inquired about renting an aircraft on Friday, November 22, to go to Mexico. He did not like the look of them and did not rent them a plane. After the assassination, when he saw Oswald on television, he thought he strongly resembled one of the men who had been at the airport. He gave this information to the FBI."[770] Could this be the real Oswald, being duped into thinking that as a result of his cooperation in the coming protest he will be given passage to Cuba via Mexico? Or is it the contract people simply arranging for the look-alike's exit?

"Beginning in the late evening . . . Frank T. Tortoriello held an all-night party at his residence in the Tanglewood Apartments in Dallas. According to FBI's first report of this party, Tortoriello's guests were Jada, the Carousel stripper, Jack Ruby. . . . Tortoriello . . . was a partner in a mob-linked construction company and a buddy of Mafioso Joseph Campisi."[771]

Press reports again on Baker's condominium: ". . . The house—reportedly the scene of frequent parties—had been occupied for nearly a year by two Capitol Hill secretaries."[772]

Press: "Senator Ralph Yarborough . . . charged last night that . . . Baker had a hand in keeping him from a choice committee assignment in 1961. . . . Baker had told some people: 'We couldn't afford to let Yarborough have that seat. He would then be in a position to control Texas' judicial patronage, or would be in a position to prevent Lyndon from controlling it.'"[773]

Press reports on Baker's relationship to Las Vegas gamblers: "The relationship of the leading stockholder in another casino to the . . . Baker case is now coming under scrutiny. And there may be other casinos involved in other investigations. . . . *Baker* has been shown to be involved in deals with Edward Levinson, the manager of the Fremont Hotel casino in downtown Las Vegas. . . . Officials have said that *[Sam] Garfield* [a mob associate of long standing] has had relationships with *Meyer Lansky,* the gambler, *Gerardo V. Catena,* who is described as holding things together in New Jersey for the jailed *Vito Genovese,* and with *Edward Levinson. . . .*" (emphasis added).[774] Garfield is also tied to Chicago bookmakers.[775] An examination of other Levinson associates mentioned here is both revealing and ominous. Lansky, as previously mentioned, is in partnership with Marcello via gambling casinos in New Orleans. Catena is a lifelong friend of Doc Stacher, who is currently embroiled in litigation in Las Vegas as a probable result of ELSUR taps on casino phones (see May 1963). "Second-in-command during Genovese's absence is Jerry Catena. . . . Arrests of Catena . . . include pickups . . . for robbery, hijacking, bribing a federal juror and suspicion of murder."[776] Both Catena and Levinson were directly involved with Lansky in the development of the Sands Hotel in Las Vegas.[777]

As revealed in John Davis's *Mafia Kingfish:* "There also lurked the disturbing shadow of Marcello's Texas associate and political fixer Jack Halfen, who . . . had, in the fifties, allegedly siphoned off a percentage of Carlos Marcello's racing wire and slot machine profits in Texas and contributed them to Lyndon Johnson's political campaigns in return for Johnson's efforts in the U.S. Senate, both on the floor and in its back rooms, to protect mob interests. . . . Johnson, because of his dependence on Halfen-Marcello money, had helped kill in committee all antiracketeering legislative propos-

als that could have affected Halfen's and Marcello's activities in
Texas. . . . Halfen . . . kept 800 feet of movie film showing himself and his wife cavorting with the Johnsons on a Texas hunting
trip, and there were plenty of people in Texas willing to talk with
Justice Department officials, including Attorney General . . .
Kennedy, of the Halfen-Marcello-Johnson relationship. . . . In
fact . . . at the time of President Kennedy's assassination, there
was a thick investigative file on Robert Kennedy's desk . . . detailing the Marcello-Halfen-Johnson connection that Kennedy was de-
bating whether to pursue."[778]

11/21/63—THURSDAY: Dallas press states, "A weather bureau forecaster said Wednesday that rain appears likely Friday,
when President Kennedy will fly into Dallas." "Afternoon *Times
Herald* front-pages map of motorcade route."[779]

According to Agent Hosty, "There were some scurrilous pamphlets [actually leaflets] circulated around Dallas on the 21st. . . .
It was a poster of President Kennedy with a front and profile view
saying, 'Wanted for Treason.' I took those pamphlets over to the
Secret Service office the morning of the 21st."[780] These are circulated by Walker's people.

Oswald goes to work as usual. During the 10 A.M. break, he
approaches Frazier. "I was standing there getting the orders in, and
he said, 'Could I ride home with you this afternoon?' And I said,
'Sure. . . . anytime you want to go see your wife, that is all right
with me.' . . . And he said, 'I am going home to get some curtain
rods. . . . You know, put in an apartment.' . . . I said, 'Very
well.' . . . I never thought more about it."[781] In reality, Oswald is
probably more anxious to resolve his argument with Marina.

"By Thursday afternoon . . . Ruby was [in Houston] monitoring President Kennedy's movements in preparation for the next
day's assassination in Dallas."[782]

Press reports: "Mrs. Gertrude Novak, a former business associate
of Robert G. Baker, 'opened up several avenues of information' for
Senate investigators today. [She] was questioned for nearly three
hours at a closed session of the Senate Rules Committee. . . . Mrs.
Novak was not questioned about either the alleged 'sex angles' in
the Baker case or reports that her husband's death last year was a
suicide. . . . In another development today, Senator . . . Moss
. . . said he suspected . . . Baker of responsibility for denying

him choice committee assignments last January. His assertions closely parallel the views of two other Senators, who said last week that Mr. Baker had managed to block their assignments to committees of their choice."[783]

Press: "Robert F. Kennedy said today he planned to remain in his Attorney General's post."[784]

"Dolan [an associate of Nofio Pecora and Marcello] was seen by an FBI agent entering a bookmaking establishment in Dallas. . . . He was said to be connected to . . . Eugene Hale Brading."[785]

Lansky functionaries Eugene Brading (aka Jim Braden) and his associate Morgan H. Brown ". . . arrived in Dallas on November 21 and checked into Suite 301 of the Cabana Hotel . . ." overlooking the Stemmons Freeway near downtown Dallas.[786]

Press reports: "President Kennedy mixed a strong defense of his space program with some old-fashioned, earthbound politics today as he opened a two-day tour of Texas. . . . The President was welcomed by large crowds lining the streets of San Antonio and Houston as he and Mrs. Kennedy drove past in an open car. . . . The Presidential party will return to Washington Saturday."[787] This evening the group flies on to Fort Worth, staying at the Texas Hotel.[788] Ruby returns to Dallas. JFK is reportedly relaxed.[789]

"In the late afternoon, Ruth Paine drives home from her grocery shopping and . . . sees Oswald on the front lawn: 'I was surprised to see him. . . . [He was] playing with June and talking with Marina. . . . . . . As I entered the house and Lee had just come in, I said to him, "Our President is coming to town." And he said, "Ah, yes," and walked on into the kitchen, which was a common reply from him on anything. . . . Nothing more was said about it. . . . He went to bed very early, she stayed up and talked with me some, but there was no coolness that I noticed. He was quite friendly on the lawn. . . . . . . they seemed warm, like a couple making up a small spat. . . .' "[790] Marina: "He said that he was lonely because he hadn't come in the preceding weekend and he was anxious to make his peace with me. . . . He was not angry—he was upset. . . . He tried very hard to please me. He spent a bit of time putting away diapers and played with the children on the street. . . . He suggested that we rent an apartment in Dallas. He said he was tired of living alone. . . . . . . But I refused. . . . I said it would be better if I remained with Ruth until the [Christmas] holidays. . . . . . . While he was living alone and I stayed with

Ruth, we were spending less money. And I told him to buy me a washing machine. . . . He said he would buy me a washing machine." "He said since he was home on Thursday, that it wouldn't make sense to come again on Friday, that he would come for the weekend." ". . . He then stopped talking and sat down and watched television."[791] As usual he leaves money for her and the children. "Ruth 'realized he had gone to bed. . . . I went out to the garage to paint some children's blocks, and . . . I noticed when I [entered the garage] that the light was on. . . . I felt Lee . . . had gone out to the garage, perhaps worked out there or gotten something. Most of their clothing was out there, all their winter things. They were getting things out from time to time, warmer things for the cold weather, so it was not at all remarkable that he went to the garage, but I thought it careless of him to have left the light on. . . .' "[792]

"At about 10 P.M. . . . Ruby stopped in for about 45 minutes at the Egyptian Lounge, a Dallas underworld hangout. One of its owners was Joseph Campisi. . . . On December 7, 1963, Campisi . . . told the FBI of his 'contact with Ruby' that Thursday night, 'when Ruby came to the Egyptian Lounge for a steak.' "[793] "About midnight, Ruby stopped in at a restaurant in the Teamster-financed Dallas Cabana Hotel. With [him] was Larry Meyers, who had checked into the Cabana that day. . . . He was accompanied by Jean West. . . . Meyers [later] said he had picked her up at the 20 East Delaware Lounge in Chicago, which was a hotel with a 'reputation for party girls.' "[794] In the late 1970s the House Select Committee on Assassinations will state: ". . . we were unable to locate West."[795]

11/22/63—FRIDAY: "Mrs. Mary Lawrence was working as head waitress at the Lucas B&B Restaurant in Dallas during the early morning of November 22. At about 1:30 A.M., she told the FBI, a young man came into the restaurant and sat down at a table. When approached, the man 'stated he was waiting for Mr. Ruby.' Mrs. Lawrence knew Jack Ruby, a regular patron, but had never seen that man before. About an hour later, 'Jack Ruby came into the . . . restaurant and, after looking at the young man at the table, sat down at a table behind the cash register. He did not order his usual food, stating he didn't feel good, and ordered a large glass of orange juice. A few minutes later, the young man . . . went over to Ruby's table. Thereafter, Ruby paid the bill for both himself and the young man who had eaten." They leave together.[796]

"As late as 2:30 A.M., according to one of [Ruby's] employees . . . , [Ruby] telephones [his club] from the Cabana [Hotel]."[797]

On the morning of the assassination, as Marina will testify, "I woke up before . . . [Lee]." At 7:10 A.M. ". . . Oswald was still asleep ten minutes after his alarm went off. He was roused by [Marina] and rushed off to meet his ride. . . ."[798]

". . . Mrs. Randle, Wesley Frazier's sister . . . sees Oswald crossing the street carrying a 'package in a sort of a heavy brown bag. . . .' She watches him go to Frazier's car, and 'He opened the right back door and I saw that he was laying the package down so I closed the [kitchen] door. . . . . . . He come back and stood on the driveway.' "[799] Frazier: "I was talking sitting there eating breakfast and talking to the little nieces, it was later than I thought it was."[800] After getting in the car Frazier notices the package. ". . . I said, 'What's the package, Lee?' and he said 'Curtain rods.' " "Frazier describes the trip to Dallas. . . .'. . . I asked him did he have fun playing with them babies and he chuckled and said he did. . . .' "[801] Upon arrival at the Depository, Oswald gets out, takes his package and proceeds toward the building, evidently not wanting to get himself or his bag wet (it is raining this morning). Frazier: "From what I seen walking behind he had it under his arm and you couldn't tell that he had a package from the back."[802] He continues: ". . . It is right as you get out of the grocery store, just more or less out of a package—you have seen some of these brown paper sacks you can obtain from any, most of the stores, some varieties—but it was a package just roughly about two feet long."[803] Note that Oswald's rifle, disassembled, is nearly three feet long.[804]

Another fellow employee, Jack Dougherty, observes Oswald entering the building. "I saw him when he first came in the door. . . . . . . I didn't see anything in his hands. . . ."[805] The testimony of these two men suggests that what Oswald is carrying into the building is easily concealed, something narrow and flexible he holds close to his body (such as rolled cardboard or cloth).

Frazier later observes Oswald:

A: . . . I saw him back and forth, you know, that morning walking around, filling books and so forth, filling orders, had invoices filling orders.

Q: Were you on the sixth floor any that morning?

A: One time, just a few seconds. . . .

Q: Were they doing some work there that day?

A: Yes, sir: they were.[806]

"On the day of the assassination, Milteer telephoned Somerset, saying he was in Dallas and that Kennedy was due there shortly. Milteer commented that Kennedy would never be seen in Miami again."[807] He then joins the crowds gathering near the corner of Elm Street in Dealey Plaza.

Press reports on deep involvement of Hoffa with Baker associates Levinson et al: "Mr. *Hoffa is a trustee of the pension fund. . . . The earliest of the pension fund loans* showing in the records at the [Las Vegas] county courthouse *is $1 million to build Sunrise Hospital* . . . on the edge of Las Vegas near the Strip. *It is owned by a partnership.* The *partners [include]* . . . *Moe Dalitz* . . . *and Sam Garfield.* . . . . . Dalitz and Garfield attended school together in Detroit a half century ago. . . . The Stardust Country Club was built with a $1.2 million loan from the Teamsters. . . . The Stardust and the Desert Inn needed more buildings, so a $6 million loan was negotiated with the pension fund. . . . *The downtown Fremont Hotel also got a pair of pension fund loans,* totaling $4.6 million . . . . *The chief operating officer of the Fremont Hotel is Edward Levinson* . . . *who was a school boy in Detroit at the time Moe Dalitz and Sam Garfield were attending the Bishop school together.* Levinson owns 20 per cent of the Fremont Hotel, as the largest stockholder, and he has 27½ per cent of the Horseshoe Club. . . . He was frequently arrested in his youth in Detroit, where he was a bookmaker, and in Miami, where he lived in the years when gambling ran openly in Dade County. He moved to Las Vegas after the Kefauver committee's disclosures brought an end to gambling activity in Miami Beach. The records show that *Levinson* was first connected with the Flamingo and later with the Sands. He shifted to the Fremont in 1955. He *is a brother of Louis Levinson, a leading gambler in Newport and Covington, Ky.,* when those towns were wide open.

A development in Levinson's recent activities is the suggestion that he may be a part owner with . . . Baker of the Serve-U Corporation, a vending machine concern with aero-space company locations. . . . Levinson has refused to discuss the question of his ownership of part of the company. The pension fund also provided . . . $475,000 to Hank Greenspun, the publisher of *The Las Vegas Sun.* [He] used the money to build a golf course" (emphasis added).808

Prior to this at some point during Kennedy's administration ". . . The FBI without telling anyone had bugged Moe Dalitz's office and recorded Dalitz's half of a phone conversation with Hoffa; [and] had also monitored several Hoffa conversations in Teamster radio cars in Detroit. . . . These tapes contributed nothing to the Hoffa prosecutions."809 RFK aide Sheridan will later state, "There had been a recording of a conversation between . . . Dalitz, one of the owners of the Desert Inn in Las Vegas, and Hoffa in 1962."810

Around 9 A.M. President Kennedy, in his hotel room, jokes with his wife in response to news of the "JFK Wanted" leaflets, stating, "We're really in nut country now."811

Oswald coworker, James Jarman, speaks with him twice this morning. Between 9:30 and 10 A.M. they talk on the first floor. "Well, he was standing up in the window and I went to the window also, and he asked me what were the people gathering around the corner for, and I told him that the President was supposed to pass that morning, and he asked me did I know which way he was coming, and I told him yes, he'd probably come down Main and turn on Houston and then back again on Elm. Then he said, 'Oh, I see.' And that was all."812

Hoover sends two memos to RFK regarding Martin Luther King and CPUSA.813 He also writes a letter to an editor (Mr. Smith): "Your editorial support and confidence in our organization have contributed immeasurably to the success we have obtained in law enforcement. You may be sure we will continually strive to merit the trust you have placed in us."814

"[Secret Service agent] Lawson: It was quite rainy early in the morning . . . and I received a phone call from the Assistant Agent in Charge . . . who was in Fort Worth with the President, asking about weather conditions in Dallas . . . and discussing whether to use the bubble-top on the President's car. . . . I was told the bubble-top was to be on if it was raining, and it was to be off if it was not raining. . . . The weather became quite sunny all of a sudden. . . . . . . So I told them to have it off."[815]

"At about this time the sixth-floor work crew of half a dozen young men knocks off for lunch. According to Williams: 'I believe this day we quit about maybe 5 or 10 minutes [early], because all of us were so anxious to see the President. . . . We took [both] elevators down. . . . We always had a little kid's game we played racing down with the elevators. . . . On the way down I heard Oswald— and I am not sure whether he was on the fifth or the sixth floor. . . . And he said, 'Close the gate on the elevator and send the elevator back up.' "[816] Obviously Oswald needs one in order to get down to the first floor himself.

11:50 A.M.: Coworker Givens ". . . observed Lee reading a newspaper in the domino room where the employees eat lunch. . . . 'The domino room' is on the first floor of the Depository. . . . Bill Shelly, a foreman, said he saw Oswald on the first floor as early as ten or fifteen minutes before noon."[817]

12:00 A.M.: "An employee called Eddie Piper said he actually spoke to Oswald 'just at twelve o'clock, down on the first floor.' The Warren Commission had . . . these statements but omitted them. . . . Piper . . . said Oswald told him: 'I'm going up to eat' " (i.e., the lunch room is on the *second* floor).[818] He does so, buying his lunch from one of the machines.[819]

Between 12:00 and 12:15 P.M.: Another employee eats his lunch on the sixth floor of the Depository. He sees no one, including Oswald.[820] At a quarter past he joins others on a lower floor to view the motorcade, due to pass by at 12:25 P.M.

12:15 to 12:20 P.M.: "Carolyn Arnold was secretary to the vice-president of the Book Depository. An FBI report, omitted altogether from the (Warren) report, said Mrs. Arnold was standing in front of the Depository waiting for the motorcade when she 'thought she caught a fleeting glimpse of . . . Oswald standing in a hallway. . . . She said: 'About a quarter of an hour before the assassination, I went into the lunchroom on the second floor for a moment. . . . Oswald was sitting in one of the booth seats on the right-hand side of the room as you go in. He was alone as usual and appeared to be having lunch. I did not speak to him but I recognized him clearly. . . . It was about 12:15. It may have been slightly later.' "[821]

12:15 P.M.: Across the street from the main entrance to the De-

pository ". . . Arnold Rowland, said he saw two men in sixth-floor
windows, one of them holding a rifle across his chest, at 12:15.
Rowland's wife confirmed that her husband drew her attention to
the man, whom he assumed to be a Secret Service guard. There was,
of course, no such guard, and no other employees were on the sixth
floor at that time. The time detail . . . can be fixed so exactly
because Rowland recalled seeing the man with the rifle just as a
police radio nearby squawked out the news that the approaching
motorcade had reached Cedar Springs Road. The police log shows
that the President passed that point between 12:15 and 12:16. Mrs.
Arnold's given time for leaving her office . . . is corroborated by
contemporary statements made by her and office colleagues. She
told the FBI she finally left the building, after visiting the lunchroom, as late as 12:25 P.M. If Mrs. Arnold saw Oswald in the lunchroom at 12:15 or after, who were the two men, one of them a
gunman, whom Rowland reported in the sixth-floor windows?"[822]

12:25 P.M.: "Had the motorcade been on time, . . . it would
have passed beneath the windows of the Depository at 12:25 P.M.
This fact was evident from the published program, and would
clearly have come into the calculations of any would-be assassin. A
killer who had planned the assassination would hardly have been
sitting around downstairs after 12:15 P.M., as the evidence about
Oswald suggests, if he expected to open fire as early as 12:25."[823]
Gordon Arnold (no relation to Carolyn), a soldier home on leave,
positions himself with others on the grassy knoll area to the right
side of the plaza. "Armed with his movie camera, Arnold walked to
the top of the grassy knoll just before the President arrived, looking
for a good vantage point. He went behind the fence, trying to find a
way to the railroad bridge which crossed the road in front of the
motorcade route. . . . Arnold was moving along the fence—on the
side hidden from the road—when '. . . this guy just walked towards me and said that I shouldn't be up there. He showed me a
badge and said he was with the Secret Service and that he didn't
want anybody up there.' It sounded sensible enough, and Arnold
retreated to the next best spot—beside a tree on the road side of the
fence, high on the grassy slope beyond the colonnade."[824]

12:30 P.M.: The motorcade turns right, ninety degrees, onto
Houston Street. Amateur photographer Hughes films the limousine
as it heads directly for the Depository at the corner of Elm. Simultaneously he catches the sixth floor of the building in the back-

ground. Two figures are seen in the far right windows.[825] Although there is some debate over the film, when considered in light of compelling eyewitness testimony from several sources, its accuracy becomes apparent. Milteer stands near the intersection at Elm, watching the President as he passes. The car turns left in front of the Depository, enters Dealey Plaza, and slowly heads toward the triple underpass leading onto Stemmons Freeway. Over the next few seconds President Kennedy is assassinated. The leading treatise on this moment is *Six Seconds in Dallas,* by Josiah Thompson. Used recently by *Nova* (in conjunction with the actual film of the assassination, the Zapruder Film) to analyze the event, it remains (after twenty-three years) the definitive narrative. Thompson's description of the sequence of shots is as follows:

"**THE FIRST SHOT** [strikes the President in the upper right back, penetrating a depth of one to two inches]. . . .

GOVERNOR CONNALLY: We had—we had gone, I guess, 150 feet, maybe 200 feet, I don't recall how far it was, heading down to get on the freeway . . . when I heard what I thought was a shot.

ROY H. KELLERMAN: [Secret Service agent in the limousine]: As we turned off Houston onto Elm and made the short little dip to the left going down grade . . . and there is (*sic*) a report like a firecracker, pop.

JERRY D. KIVETT: [traveling with the motorcade, fourth car back]: As the motorcade was approximately 1/3 of the way to the underpass, traveling between 10 and 15 miles per hour, I heard a loud noise.

LEE BOWERS: [sitting in an observation tower in the train yard to the right of the motorcade]: At the moment of the first shot, as close as my recollection serves, the car was out of sight behind this decorative masonry wall in the area.

MRS. BILLIE P. CLAY: [standing on the sidewalk immediately to the right of the motorcade as it began passing the grassy knoll]: Just a few seconds after the car . . . passed the location where I was standing, I heard a shot.

JOHN ARTHUR CHISM [standing at the bottom of the grassy knoll, to the right of the motorcade]: And just as he . . . got just about in front of me, he turned and waved at the crowd on this side of the street, the right side; at this point I heard what sounded like one shot.

JEAN NEWMAN: [standing next to Mrs. Clay]: The motorcade had just passed me when I heard something that I thought was a firecracker at first, and the President had just passed me, because after he had just passed there was a loud report, it just scared me.

KAREN WESTBROOK: [standing next to Mr. Chism]: The car he was in was almost directly in front of where I was standing when I heard the first explosion.

GLORIA CALVERY: [standing next to Mrs. Westbrook]: The car he was in was almost directly in front of where I was standing when I heard the first shot.

JOE HENRY RICH: [with the fourth car in the motorcade]: We turned off of Houston Street onto Elm and that was when I heard the first shot.

MRS. EARLE CABELL: [fifth car back in the motorcade]: We were making the turn . . . just on the turn, which put us at the top of the hill you see . . . I heard the shot, and without having to turn my head, I jerked my head up.

MAYOR EARLE CABELL: [fifth car back in the motorcade]: We were just rounding the corner . . . , making the left turn, when the first shot rang out.

. . . Yet perhaps the most graphic description of the impact of the first shot was given by William Newman:

We were looking back up the street to see if the motorcade was coming and the first two shots were fired, and of course the first shot, boom, the President threw his arms up like that, . . . and then it looked like he was looking in the crowd, you know, like he was looking for something, just kind of a wild expression.

. . . Kenneth O'Donnell saw the President waving just before he was hit; we see the President waving until he disappears behind the sign. . . . O'Donnell and Powers saw the force of the shot move the President left from his sitting position on the extreme right-hand side of the seat. . . . Mrs. Connally and Jean Newman saw the President's hands and elbows raised after the first shot. . . . A close study of the Zapruder film . . . reveals that the President's fists are clenched and that the movement carries his hands up above his neck. . . . The President seems to be guarding his face with his clenched fist, his elbows elevated at either side.

". . . With respect to the bullet hole located in the back, pathologist at National Naval Medical Center was of the opinion this bullet worked its way out of the victim's back during cardiac massage performed at Dallas. . . .

". . . During the autopsy news reached Bethesda that a 6.5-millimeter bullet had been found on a stretcher in Parkland Hospital. . . ."[826]

"THE SECOND SHOT [strikes Governor Connally in the back just to the left of his right armpit, traverses his rib cage, destroying a significant portion of one rib, exits his right front chest, pierces and shatters his right wrist, a fragment of the bullet then embedding itself in his left (inside) thigh. This bullet enters the limousine at a much sharper downward trajectory, 27 degrees, than the bullets which strike Kennedy, and is in all likelihood fired from the top of the Records Building located behind and slightly to the left of the motorcade]. . . .

HOLLAND: [standing on the triple underpass directly in front of the approaching motorcade] And the Governor turned to . . . his right . . . ; then he turned like that, and that's when the Governor was shot. . . . He definitely was not hit by the first shot.

THOMPSON: So you believe the Governor was hit by the second shot?

HOLLAND: I know the Governor was hit by the second shot.

"What Holland saw was echoed in the statements of many other witnesses in Dealey Plaza. Not one of these several hundred witnesses saw the assassination as the Warren Commission believed it happened. . . . Nor did any of these witnesses believe the second shot missed.

MRS. HILL: [standing on the opposite side of the street, immediately to the left of the limousine]: . . . It wasn't with the first shot. To me he wasn't hit when the first shot hit.

MRS. JOHN CONNALLY: . . . As the first shot was hit, and I turned to look at the same time, I recall John saying, 'Oh, no, no, no.' Then there was a second shot and it hit John, and as he recoiled to the right, just crumpled like a wounded animal to the right, he said, 'My God, they are going to kill us all. . . .'

GOV. CONNALLY: . . . We had just made the turn, well, when I heard what I thought was a shot. I heard this noise which I immediately took to be a rifle shot. I instinctively turned to my right because the sound appeared to come from over my right shoulder, and I saw nothing unusual except just people in the crowd, but I did not catch the President in the corner of my eye, . . . I was turning to look back over my left shoulder into the back seat, but I never got that far in my turn. I got about in the position I am in now facing you, looking a little bit to the left of center, and then I felt like someone hit me in the back. . . . Any rifle has a velocity that exceeds the speed of sound, and when I heard the sound of that first shot, that bullet had already reached where I was . . . and

after I heard that shot, I had
the time to turn to my right,
and start to turn to my left before I felt anything. . . ."[827]

"THE HEAD SHOTS [the President is struck in the back of the
head by a bullet fired from the sixth floor of the Depository, driving
his head forward at a speed of 69.6 feet per second per second; one-
eighteenth of a second later, a shot fired from behind the picket
fence on the grassy knoll to the right front of the limousine strikes
the President in the area of the right temple, and explodes out the
back of his skull. This snaps his head backward and to the left at the
rate of 100.3 feet per second per second.

HOLLAND: The report of the third shot wasn't nearly as
             loud as the first and second shot or the fourth
             shot. . . . The bullets travel faster than
             sound, but the report that I heard of the third
             one—I heard that before I heard the fourth
             one, the fourth shot. . . . The third and the
             fourth bullets hit the President . . . in the
             head.

". . . With the help of Bill Hoffman, a bright young physicist,
and the use of a dissecting microscope, I was able to measure with
great accuracy the movement of the President's head. After holding
steady for some twelve frames, it is suddenly driven forward between frames 312 and 313. Amazingly, in the very next frame, 314,
it is already moving backward, a movement it continues in suc-
ceeding frames until the President's shoulders strike the seat cush-
ion at Z321. . . . What could cause such a reversal? How could
this violent double movement be explained? [Five] alternatives present themselves. . . ."[828] Thompson eliminated the first three (i.e.,
possibility of the President's head striking some object in the car,
Mrs. Kennedy pulling him backward and to the left, or a sudden
acceleration of the car). Alternatives 4 and 5 are discussed as follows: "(4) There was some neuromuscular reaction to the shot from
behind that arched the President's body in the opposite direction.
The extremely small time factor combined with the relatively large

mass of the President's head would tend to rule out such an explanation. The fastest reflex action known to science—the startle response—takes place over an interval of 40 to 200 milliseconds. Beginning with an eyeblink in 40 milliseconds, the response wave
moves the head forward in 83 milliseconds, and then continues
downward reaching the knees in 200 milliseconds. The change in
direction we observe occurs in 56 milliseconds ($1/18$ second), and
involves not the negligible mass of an eyelid but the considerable
mass of a human head moving forward under an acceleration of
several g's. . . . Were a neuromuscular phenomenon involved, we
would expect the muscles of the neck to keep accelerating the head;
its velocity would not show the constancy it does after Z314. But
since the motor strip (pre-central gyrus) was blown out by the entering bullet, the likelihood of any muscular reaction at all is considerably diminished. Even if this area did excite some nerve im-
pulse before it was torn from the brain, the resultant movement
would be general and random; it would not throw the President's
body in any particular direction. As a neurologist explained it to
me, the expected neurological effect of such a shot to the head
would be for the victim's body to go limp.

"(5) There is some physical principle or law of nature that explains the double movement. The physics of impacting bodies is
quite clear. As Dr. A. J. Riddle, member of the Brain Research
Institute and Assistant Professor of Physics at the University of
California at Los Angeles, has pointed out . . . the effects of such
impacts are governed by Newton's second law of motion:

> Newton's second law of motion [namely, that the rate of
> change of momentum is proportional to the impressed force,
> and is in the direction in which the force acts] has remained
> inviolate for three centuries. Not even the advent of relativity
> and quantum mechanics has disturbed its validity. No physical
> phenomenon is known that fails to obey it. One of the most
> immediate consequences is the conservation of momentum;
> basically the law says that an object hit by a projectile will be
> given a motion that has the same direction as that of the pro-
> jectile. . . . Thus, if someone is shot, and the shot strikes
> bone, the general direction of recoil will be away from—not
> toward—the marksman.

Applying Newton's second law to the case in question and supposing that a bullet fired from the rear struck the President's head, we would expect to see his head and body driven forward, the force of the impact perhaps forcing him out of the rear seat onto the floor. We see the beginning of such a movement at Z312–313. But then it is suddenly interrupted and replaced by a movement in the opposite direction. If we account for the sudden forward movement as the consequence of a bullet's impact, only a similar hypothesis could account for the equally sudden backward movement. What we see on the Zapruder film are the effects of a double transfer of momentum—one forward, the other backward. At Z313 we witness the effect of a virtually simultaneous double impact on the President's head. One shot was fired from the rear, and the other from the right front."[829]

Other witnesses (e.g., Mrs. Hill, Secret Service Agents Kellerman and Hill) offered testimony that also tended to support this conclusion.[830] The double impact disperses brain matter in two directions. Thompson's analysis continues:

. . . a first umbrella of impact debris dispersed forward over the occupants of the limousine in a pattern that would be the natural outcome of a shot fired from the rear. But there is another pattern of debris, greater in magnitude, that distributed itself over the left rear of the car and over the two motorcyclists riding behind and to the left. . . . Officer B. J. Martin, riding the outboard cycle some 5 feet to the left and 6 to 8 feet to the rear of the presidential car . . . told the Commission . . . there was blood and other material on his uniform and on the windshield and motor of his cycle.

Officer Martin's partner, riding the inboard cycle, was even more spattered. . . . 'I was splattered with blood and brain, and kind of bloody water.' . . . A sizable piece of skull. . . . was found . . . 10 to 15 feet to the left of the car's path. . . . Another piece of bone . . . was found 'approximately 25 feet south of the spot where President Kennedy was shot. . . .' It is difficult to understand how a shot from the rear could drive a piece of the occipital [rear of the skull] bone 25 feet to the left of the vehicle's path. It is not so difficult to understand how a shot from the right front exploding through the rear of the skull could produce precisely that effect.

Marilyn Sitzman was only some 75 feet away looking down into the car when the President's head exploded. . . . 'And the next thing I remembered clearly was the shot that hit . . . him on the side of his face . . . above the ear and to the front . . . between the eye and the ear.'[831]

Other eyewitnesses, the Newman family, standing between the limousine and the grassy knoll, observe the same. "I was looking directly at him when he was hit in the side of the head."[832]

As the majority of witnesses race toward and up the grassy knoll, "J. C. Price saw . . . a person escaping the area. 'I saw one man run towards the passenger cars on the railroad siding after the volley of shots. This man had a white dress shirt, no tie, and khaki colored trousers. His hair appeared to be long and dark and his agility running could be about 25 years of age. He had something in his hand.' "[833]

As stated in Anthony Summer's *Conspiracy:*

. . . Policemen started pouring into the area. One of the first was Patrolman Joe Smith, who rushed into the parking lot behind the fence because a woman said the shots had come 'from the bushes.' It was there . . . that he smelled gunpowder. The patrolman had drawn his pistol as he ran . . . He came across a man standing by a car. The man reacted quickly at sight of Smith and an accompanying deputy. As Smith remembers it, 'The man, this character produced credentials from his hip pocket which showed him to be Secret Service. I have seen those credentials before, and they satisfied me and the deputy sheriff. So I immediately accepted that and let him go and continued our search around the cars.' . . . There were no authentic Secret Service agents on the grassy knoll. . . . None was on foot either before or immediately after the assassination, and those on motorcycle duty stayed with their cars. . . . As Officer Smith puts it, 'He looked like an auto mechanic. He had on sports shirt and sports pants. But he had dirty fingernails, it looked like, and hands that looked like an auto mechanic's hands. And afterwards it didn't ring true for the Secret Service. . . . I should have checked that man

closer, but at the time I didn't snap on it. . . .' Jean Hill, who
had seen smoke on the knoll, . . . just before Officer Smith
. . . [ran] impetuously across the road, dodging between the
cars while the motorcade was still going by. She was ahead of
the field in the parking lot, and there . . . she met a 'tall and
slender man.' . . . A man who whipped out Secret Service
identification. . . . Jean Hill . . . says that beyond and behind him she caught sight of a man running. . . . she lost
sight of him by the railway lines some twenty yards away.
. . . Officer John Tilson was off duty on the day of the assassination but . . . happened to be driving with his daughter on
the road beyond the railway tracks . . . when he saw a man
'slipping and sliding' down the railway embankment. 'He
came down that grassy slope on the west side of the triple
underpass. He had a car parked there, a black car. He threw
something in the back seat and went around the front hurriedly and got in the car and took off.' . . . Tilson [gave]
chase. After a while he lost his quarry, but—as his daughter
confirms—he managed to take the license number of the car.
Tilson reported the incident, and the number, to Dallas Police
Homicide that afternoon, but heard no more about the matter.[834]

Thompson pieced together reports of individuals seen fleeing the
Depository.

A second man besides the gunman was seen at a window by
Carolyn Walther, who was standing on Houston Street. This
second man . . . had on a brown sport or suit jacket. A man
answering the same description was seen by James Worrell
leaving a rear door of the Depository a few minutes after the
assassination. Richard . . . Carr (watching from a building
under construction on Commerce Street) saw a man in a tan
jacket on the top floor of the Depository shortly before the
assassination. Carr saw the same man a few minutes afterward
walk "very fast" down Houston Street, turn the corner onto
Commerce Street, and get into a light-colored Rambler station
wagon (driven by a Negro) on Record Street. Deputy Sheriff
Roger Craig and motorist Richard Robinson both saw a man
run down across a grassy incline in front of the Depository

and get into a light-colored Rambler station wagon. Craig said the driver of the station wagon was either a Negro or "a dark-complected white man." The station wagon then proceeded through the triple underpass.[835]

12:31–32 P.M.: Oswald is confronted in the second-floor lunch room, finishing a Coke, by the building superintendent (Mr. Truly) and Dallas P.D. officer Marrion L. Baker:

TRULY: [Immediately after the shooting] I saw a young motorcycle policeman run up to the building, up the steps to the entrance of our building. He ran right by me. And he was pushing people out of the way. . . . I ran up and . . . caught up with him inside the lobby of the building. . . . I ran in front of him . . . I went up on a run up the stairway. . . . This officer was right behind me and coming up the stairway. By the time I reached the second floor, the officer was a little further behind me than he was on the first floor . . . a few feet. . . . I ran right on around to my left, started to continue on up the stairway to the third floor, and on up. . . . I suppose I was two or three steps before I realized the officer wasn't following me. . . . I came back to the second-floor landing. . . . I heard . . . a voice, coming from the area of the lunchroom. . . . I ran over and looked in this door . . . I saw the officer almost directly in the doorway of the lunchroom facing Lee Harvey Oswald. . . . He was just inside the . . . door . . . two or three feet possibly. . . . The officer had his gun pointing at Oswald.

BAKER: As I came out to the second floor there . . . I caught a glimpse of this man walking away from this—I happened to see him through this window in this door. . . . He was walking away from me about 20 feet away

	. . . in the lunchroom [. . . drinking a Coke]. I hollered at him at that time and said, 'Come here.' He turned and walked right straight back to me. . . .
REP. BOGGS:	Were you suspicious of this man?
BAKER:	No, sir; I wasn't.
REP. BOGGS:	. . . Was he out of breath, did he appear to be running or what?
BAKER:	It didn't appear that to me. He appeared normal, you know.
REP. BOGGS:	Was he calm and collected?
BAKER:	Yes, sir. He never did say a word or nothing. In fact, he didn't change his expression one bit.
TRULY:	The officer turned this way and said, 'This man work here?' And I said, 'Yes.' . . . [Oswald] didn't seem to be excited or overly afraid or anything. He might have been a bit startled, like I might have been if somebody confronted me. But I cannot recall any change in expression of any kind on his face. . . . Then we left . . . Oswald immediately and continued to run up the stairways. . . .[836]

". . . Oswald was seen next by Mrs. Robert Reid, a clerical supervisor whose office was on the second floor. . . . She had been watching the motorcade from the street. . . . When she heard the shots:

Mrs. Reid: . . . I ran into the building. . . . I ran up to our office . . . up . . . the front stairs. . . . I went into the office. . . . I kept walking and I looked up and Oswald was coming in the back door of the office. I met him by the time I passed my desk several feet. . . . I had no thoughts of anything of him having any connection with it at all because he was very calm. He had gotten a Coke and was holding it in his hands and I guess the reason it impressed me seeing him in there I thought it was a little strange that one of the warehouse boys would be up in the office at that time, not that he had

done anything wrong. . . . [He was] . . . just calm. . . .
He was moving at a very slow pace. I never did see him moving fast at any time."[837]

Oswald is initially under the impression that a protest has just
taken place, nothing more. However, when he goes downstairs he
quickly perceives the reality of the situation. Panic begins to set in.
"Outside the Depository he encountered a crew-cut young man
whom he believed to be a Secret Service agent because he had
flashed an identity card. Oswald had directed the 'agent' to a telephone, and then traveled home to his lodgings by bus and taxi. . . .
The 'Secret Service agent' was probably Robert MacNeil [later of
"MacNeil/Lehrer News Hour"], a reporter for the National Broadcasting Company, who had abandoned the motorcade after hearing
the shots. Oswald's story of how he got home is corroborated by the
bus ticket found in his pocket when he was arrested, and by a
Dallas taxi driver."[838] "A few moments later [Lansky functionary
Eugene Hale] Brading was noticed by the elevator man in the Dal
Tex building, an edifice in Dealey Plaza. [The Dal Tex building is
directly across the street from the Records building.] The observant
elevator man noticed Brading as a stranger and ran to fetch a policeman. Out on the sidewalk, Brading was detained for 'acting
suspiciously' and escorted to the sheriff's office for questioning."[839]
"At the moment of the assassination [Brading] says he was with his
probation officer in an office two blocks away. . . . The U.S. Parole Officer, Roger Carroll, denies that this meeting ever took
place."[840] When questioned at the police station, his alias, "Jim Braden," fools the authorities and he is released.[841]
    Ruby sits in a nearby newspaper office with a view of Dealey
Plaza. "As people gathered around a television in reaction to news
of the shooting, Ruby appeared 'obviously shaken and an ashen
color—just very pale . . . and sat for a while with a dazed expression in his eyes.' "[842]

Scienter*

11/22/63 to 5/8/64

*. . . the defendant's . . .
previous knowledge of . . .
a state of facts which
it was his duty to
guard against, and his
ommission to do which
has led to the injury. . . .

—*Black's Law Dictionary*

Overview

The time period 11/22/63 to 5/8/64 constitutes an unprecedented challenge for J. Edgar Hoover, undoubtedly taxing his capabilities to the limit. Though the effort to aid the Marcello contract had been successful, he has now to turn the opportunity to his advantage by containing the matter and obtaining a retirement waiver from Johnson. The growing Baker/Mafia scandal complicates his task by threatening to dethrone LBJ at the outset. Hoover, quite simply, has to save Lyndon once again in order to save himself. No fool, LBJ soon perceives the reality of the situation. In this regard, his not inconsiderable political skills are quickly brought to bear in aid of the two's mutual goals.

Hoover's first priority is to contain news of Oswald's relationship to the FBI. Initially this seems an almost impossible task, for Oswald is in police custody, steadfastly maintaining his innocence, and loudly voicing his hatred of the FBI, including Hoover. An initial examination of his file reveals his connection to Banister, Ferrie, and thus Marcello. Moving quickly, the Director seeks a basis for jurisdiction, and finds it in the area of civil-rights violations. Before JFK's casket reaches Andrews Air Force Base and Oswald is charged with anything, Hoover is asserting in writing that Oswald is guilty. By Friday night he is in control of most of the important physical evidence, but realizes, just as had Marcello, that the ex-Marine is basically nonviolent and has no motive to assassinate the President. This, however, proves no deterrent. On Saturday morning he submits a five-page report to Johnson implicating Oswald, depicting him as both a communist and lone nut, but excluding any reference to his relationship to the Bureau. The aging icon is given control of the case and immediately sets about gaining control of the Dallas P.D., no small task. In the ensuing chaos, Marcello functionary and Dallas P.D. liaison Jack Ruby murders Oswald.

This is an incredible stroke of luck for Hoover, who wastes no time capitalizing on the new situation. Sunday afternoon the Director instructs Dallas SAC Shanklin to sanitize Oswald's file. The official quickly complies. This amounts to wholesale destruction of evidence and nothing less than obstruction of justice.

Almost from the moment Oswald is arrested, the Dallas P.D. attempts to set its own course. After a search of Oswald's room and the Paines' residence Friday afternoon, members tell the Dallas press that Oswald is a suspect in the Walker shooting, something no one to that point had even remotely considered. The press is also given a false story alleging the ex-Marine had a map hidden with his possessions detailing the actual trajectory of the bullet that felled the President, a patent absurdity. This piece of "evidence" will quickly disappear in the coming days. Newsmen are effectively given access to the young defendant, who frantically proclaims his innocence. By Saturday morning Chief Jesse Curry and others are telling the press of the FBI's prior knowledge of Oswald. After obtaining authority from Johnson, Hoover intercedes, and by late that afternoon forces retractions of morning statements by the same authorities. Incredible as it sounds, stenographic or tape recordings of Oswald's interrogation sessions are not made. By Sunday morning Dallas P.D. is telling the press that Oswald is the sole assassin. Within a few hours after he is killed, Assistant Attorney General Miller delivers Hoover's directives to ex-agent and district attorney Henry Wade, who promptly calls a press conference and makes the case against Oswald. Dallas police Captain Will Fritz tells the media the case is closed. At day's end on November 25 two of Hoover's top aides are in Dallas, in control of the investigation. Local authorities openly admit FBI is in charge. By December 4 the Director has contained the Oswald/Banister/Bolton Ford incident as well as prevented Marina from obtaining access to the press. This latter feat is critical, for she undoubtedly knows of Oswald's relationship to the Bureau. On December 24, she is forced to distance herself from the Paines.

In the midst of all this, Dallas P.D. Chief Curry quietly conducts an internal investigation, and on December 23 he fires one officer. Publicly, however, he asserts there is no connection between Ruby and the Dallas P.D. A basically decent man, Curry will, in the years to come, essentially admit his belief in a second gunman.

On 1/24/64 Wade and Texas A.G. Carr, in response to press reports suggesting Oswald was in fact an FBI informant, meet secretly in D.C. with Warren Commission members Rankin and Warren to discuss their fears. In response to this, the commissioners hold a closed-door session in an attempt to decide what to do. Of the group, only Cooper suggests an independent investigation to resolve the matter. The Commission appears fearful of the development. The following day Rankin asks Hoover about it directly, the latter immediately asserting there is no truth to it. By the end of the first week in February, Hoover has submitted a sworn affidavit denying any Bureau relationship with Oswald. On February 13, ten agents do the same. This, of course, is standard procedure and basically meaningless. There the matter essentially dies.

Hoover's next, and near simultaneous, objective is to attempt to prevent the public, and Warren Commission, from learning of the Marcello contract, as well as his, Clyde's, and Evans's involvement in it. Fortunately for the Director, he has an ally in the Dallas P.D., which is not anxious for the American people to learn that Ruby was Marcello's liaison to the department. But as far as internal awareness at the Bureau is concerned, containment soon proves a near impossible goal. This is due to the sheer magnitude and complexity of the situation. Presumably at Hoover's directive, general or specific, Miami, Florida, Jose Aleman FBI contacts George Davis and/or Paul Scranton meet with the Cuban exile the afternoon of the assassination. After obtaining all they can from him, the two agents order him not to discuss the matter with anyone, all in the national interest. They leave, and probably within hours AIRTEL a report to Hoover. In their defense, it could well be they have done nothing improper to this point. The two may not realize that Hoover had in fact withheld their original data from the Secret Service.

The following day there is a general call on the public for evidence and eyewitness reports. This is done by Hoover to gain control of all meaningful information. Examination of the affidavits of the majority of Dealey Plaza eyewitnesses, in conjunction with photographic evidence, makes apparent the conspiratorial nature of Kennedy's assassination. In the hours after Oswald's murder, Hoover is briefed on Ruby, whose connections with the Mafia were previously known. While making no direct reference to conspiracy, Hoover admits as much in an afternoon memo the same day. This day Hoover also approaches Johnson directly, trying to convince him of the need to tell the public Oswald was just a lone nut. This, in the context of the dizzying pace of events and Hoover's initial boldness, must make LBJ deeply suspicious. Given the devious orientation of his own mind he may begin to suspect complicity on the part of Hoover. With the arrest of Ferrie the following day, in part due to the fact that his library card has been found in Oswald's possessions, the connections to Marcello become obvious. The week of November 25, Hoover makes direct attempts to prevent Bureau personnel from examining the Marcello organization, with only limited success. Ruby's ties to Civello and McWillie also become apparent. It may well be that the connection between Ruby and Levinson via the Thunderbird Motel has, by this point, led Hoover to consider some form of complicity on Johnson's part via Baker. If such were the case, LBJ's assistance in containing the Warren Commission would not be difficult to obtain. On November 30 Hoover obtains the Hughes Film, strongly suggesting the presence of two gunmen on the sixth floor, just as numerous eyewitnesses's testimony had predicted. After suppressing the Las Vegas/McWillie/Ruby connection on December 3, he learns of the nightclub owner's ties to gambling in the Dallas area. This in turn connects him to Campisi, Saia, and Beckley. Through the previously revealed connection between Levinson and Beckley, the circle is now complete.

In an attempt to stop the spiraling accumulation of data pointing to the Mafia, Hoover uses his power as Director to administratively assault the various Dallas and New Orleans personnel investigating Marcello organization leads. Ostensibly it is done because of their "mishandling" of Oswald prior to the assassination. In reality, the move is purely self-serving. The attack has the desired effect, and the intensity of the investigation slows. On December 12 Hoover pressures the Mexico City LEGAT to conclude its work, and on December 18 directs the New Orleans field office to cease its investigation of the Ferrie/Marcello link.

With the death of Oswald, Hoover launches a disinformation campaign designed to prevent the media from gaining a clear picture of the assassination, and thus Marcello's and his involvement. It begins in Dallas with directives to SAC J. Gordon Shanklin on November 24. The SAC publicly states that the Bureau had had no contact with Oswald before the assassination and claims the Dallas P.D.–administered paraffin test on Oswald, results of which strongly suggest his innocence, in fact implicate him. Both assertions are complete fabrications. On the national level, Hoover leaks stories to the press attempting to counter eyewitness statements revealing the presence of a gunman on the grassy knoll. Oswald is painted as a mentally deranged communist. Statements of doctors who had attended Kennedy in Dallas are clouded, and in some instances simply stated to be completely incorrect. The week of November 25 media people are given off-the-record briefings demanding their cooperation, all "for the good of the country." Somehow, *Life* magazine is recruited in this effort. After paying $150,000 for rights to the Zapruder Film (to date the most studied film in history) it is convinced to supress it, allowing the public to see only a few, basically irrelevant frames, mostly of Jackie Kennedy in her moment of terror. Understanding the power of first impressions, particularly visual ones, the American people are thus given a profoundly distorted perception of the assassination. This week Hoover also begins a film "reconstruction" of the assassination in an attempt to counter the growing body of physical evidence pointing to conspiracy. This technique is old hat to the Director, who has reduced the procedure to a science. This reconstruction will be forced on the Warren Commission in the coming months to aid further in obscuring the truth from the public. Before turning over the Bureau's report on the assassination to Johnson and the Warren Commission, Hoover leaks its conclusion to the press in an attempt to preempt any official disagreement with his position. Around the same time he bolsters the Dallas P.D.'s false assertion that it was Oswald who attempted to kill General Walker. He accomplishes this by tying together bits of unrelated evidence, misrepresenting them as data stemming from the April 1963 event. The Dallas P.D. silently cooperates. Oswald's Marxist activism is played up, with an eye toward tying him to the specter of "godless communism."

Taking advantage of an effort by National Security entities to prevent the public from learning the true results of Kennedy's autopsy by releasing a near totally false report, Hoover preempts its conclusions by claiming the report will merely agree with his own.

Using his well-established propaganda machine, the Director as early as December 1, publicly implies that JFK was merely symptomatic, part of a larger problem with American society: "moral cowardice." Building on his 10/9/62 attack on JFK, in which he had stated, "Disrespect for law and order is a *tragic* moral illness," in a December 4 speech he equates disrespect for law and order with that of a *"tragic* moral sickness." His terse November 22 eulogy of Kennedy only hours after the assassination had specifically categorized the death as a *tragedy.* During March 1964 he publishes an essay on the history of the Mafia, in which he draws a parallel between the Mafia and Irish immigrants such as the Kennedys.

During the winter of 1963 and spring of 1964, Hoover's most formidable foe is undoubtedly the Warren Commission. Not because of any meaningful hostility on the part of individual members, but because of its access to Bureau files. The sheer size of the group makes it difficult to contend with. With so many people examining Bureau reports, someone would be bound to learn his secret, or worse yet, leak it to the press. Accordingly, from its inception the Director seeks its demise. The assistance of Johnson is evident early on. At its first meeting Warren makes it plain he does not want to antagonize Hoover. Dulles, as previously stated, passes out books in an attempt to convince the others that only lone nuts kill American presidents. Their initial goal is to contain the avalanche of data suggesting conspiracy. Here, their prior knowledge of Hoover's bitter hostility toward JFK cannot be ignored. These men did not exist in a vacuum. They, like others during the Kennedy administration, were aware of the struggle. While it may not have been openly discussed, it has to be on their minds. Johnson's increasing reliance on Hoover to shield him from exposure and prosecution would also have been apparent to members of the group by this point. It is perhaps a reason Warren was so reluctant to even consider the appointment. When pressed for data the following day, he reveals that the Commission does not even have a copy of the FBI's report. At their first meeting, December 5, any doubts about Hoover's intentions are dispelled when he refuses to send any representatives. The Director only supplies a copy of his report on December 9, simultaneously demanding that members of the Commission publicly agree with his conclusions. While not doing so, the group the previous day had effectively signaled its collective acquiescence by appointing a chief counsel who is not known for his knowledge about, or aggressiveness toward, the Mafia.

Chief Counsel Rankin appears to be the least political member of the Commission. The day of his appointment he effectively reveals to the press that LBJ has pressured Warren to conclude the investigation by February, a practical impossibility. On December 12 Rankin meets with staff members. A tremendous debate begins, apparently with regard to the Commission's focus and goals, and the session degenerates into a political standoff. No further staff meetings are held. At some point early on, Rankin, perhaps at this same meeting, tells members that Hoover cannot be trusted. This same day, Gerald Ford becomes an informant for the FBI, supplying Hoover with details regarding Commission activities and plans. Dulles presumably does the same with the CIA

Completely stymied by Hoover's lack of cooperation, the group quickly realizes that it cannot pursue its purpose at all without data from the Bureau. On December 16 it makes a public demand for raw FBI files from Hoover. In response to this, Hoover meets privately with Johnson the same day for an off-the-record luncheon in an obvious effort to deflect the Commission's demand. He is apparently unsuccessful, but he does manage to delay compliance for almost one month.

Senator Richard B. Russell also meets secretly with the Bureau, disclosing the fact that he does not want to be on the Commission, as well as his intense dislike for Warren. This day Johnson is in contact with Russell on four separate occasions, speaking also with Hoover and Ford. One month later to the day, the Commission receives a copy of JFK's autopsy report. By early January 64, the majority of the staff does not want Marina to take a lie detector test. Two days into the new year Hoover tells the press that the Bureau's investigation of the assassination is complete. On the seventh, he leaks news that Marina is now convinced that Oswald killed President Kennedy. She has yet to testify before the Commission. Shortly after this "Marina" writes the ACLU, instructing them to stay away. On January 11 Rankin publicly admits the Commission will rely on Hoover for data. Two days later Hoover turns over a supplemental FBI report to the group in a further attempt to promote his position. Rankin acts on his previously stated intention to rely on Bureau reports by attacking the idea of a defense counsel for Oswald. Hoover reluctantly begins turning over FBI reports to the Commission. He does this in such a way as to obscure reality once again. Mafia reports are interlaced with stacks of hundreds of irrelevant and crackpot allegations, the effect of which is to bury the important data. Some reports are simply withheld from the Commission.

On January 17, a Friday, Rankin requests access to photographic evidence of the assassination from Hoover, who complies. On January 27 the chief counsel and other members apparently view the Zapruder, Hughes, and Nix films. On January 22 and 27 they meet in secret session, openly discussing the reality of the situation. Hoover is essentially charged with obstruction of justice. The seriousness of the situation appears to overwhelm some members of the group.

In February, Marina finally testifies and "verifies" her new position on Oswald's guilt. Perhaps in relation to Rankin's questions concerning Oswald's informant status, on February 27 Hoover reveals to him the fact that Ruby had been an FBI informant during the late 1950s. Simultaneously, however, he demands that the chief counsel conceal the fact from the public, raising the specter of "national security." He makes the mistake of revealing that Ruby had originally been recruited because of his knowledge of the Dallas "criminal element." March and April, according to staff, become the Commission's "busiest months."

Hoover's attempt to inundate the Commission staff with irrelevant data apparently fails, as evidenced by fifty-two written interrogatories sent to him on March 26. In Hoover's own words, they are a "cross-examination" of the Bureau. Rankin becomes more aggressive. On April 20 he, and staff assistants Norman Redlich and Howard Willens (the liaison to the Bureau and one in position to read Mafia reports), set a trap for Hoover. Anticipating his May appearance before the Commission, at which time he will be placed under oath, they ask him outright in a letter whether he knows if Oswald had connections to the Mafia. On April 30 Hoover responds in the only way he can by denying there is any link. He can hardly do otherwise. Failure to answer at all would also have been tantamount to admission of complicity. The Director is outraged by the use of such an obviously hostile trial tactic, and on May 5 leaks derogatory information on Redlich to the press. Hoover's supporters immediately call for suspension of the Commission's proceedings until all staff members can be subjected to "full security investigations" by the Bureau. The ferocity of Hoover's attack stuns the Commission, which in turn apparently makes the decision to force Rankin to abandon his obvious plan of confronting the Director under oath with both his April 30 denial and Bureau reports suggesting Mafia complicity in the assassination. The following day, Warren refuses Assistant FBI Director Alen Belmont's offer to even look at Oswald's now sanitized file. Rankin suggests Commission members be allowed to examine the documents, but not the staff. He is overruled. Finally, on May 14, *after* he has obtained public endorsement and retirement waiver from Johnson, Hoover appears before the Commission. Rankin sets the stage by introducing both his April 20 letter and Hoover's April 30 denial, asks him point blank whether he still denies any role by the Mafia, then, tragically, does not follow through with questioning and evidence that could expose Hoover as a liar. Commission chairman Warren and members Ford and Dulles repeatedly intervene by interjection and redirection whenever Rankin even approaches the subject. The Director may have been informed in advance that Rankin would not be allowed to pursue the matter, for he willingly perjures himself by asserting that the Bureau had withheld no data from the Secret Service regarding threats against the President. It remains unclear whether Rankin himself knew beforehand that he would not be allowed to fully explore the issue.

From 11/22/63 onward, the symbiotic nature of the Hoover/Johnson relationship becomes evermore apparent. From the beginning, Johnson is deeply indebted to the Director. Having contained the Estes scandal and blunted the initial investigation into the Baker/Johnson/Mafia connection, Hoover is now in position to demand much. LBJ, with his ill-gotten power, is in position to comply. As stated, from the morning of November 23 onward Johnson gives Hoover complete control of the investigation. Justice Department access to Bureau files on Baker/Levinson et al., is cut off. The following day Johnson meets privately with Texas A.G. Waggoner Carr, undoubtedly suggesting that the official give Hoover his full cooperation. By November 25, LBJ is telling everyone concerned that Hoover is in charge of the investigation. That same day Hoover tells Johnson the investigation is winding down, and that he has succeeded in "killing" a *Washington Post* story suggesting there will be a full presidential report on the assassination. Also on this day Hoover briefs Johnson by memo on Ruby. It is not known whether he discloses Ruby's Mafia connections, but the issue becomes academic when the same is revealed by the Chicago press a few days later. The following day LBJ appoints Baker's attorney, Abe Fortas, to act as overall White House coordinator of the investigation. His job is to oversee the collection of data and orchestrate all aspects of the inquiry for Johnson.

Public pressure, however, soon forces Johnson to set up a presidential commission. This may have been done as much to contain the matter as meet congressional demands. Now, with only hand-picked appointees to contend with, he will be in position to at least attempt to control their findings. It focuses power in his direction. Preliminary congressional calls for full-scale inquiry are silenced. Hoover is apparently an integral part of Johnson's decision to set up the new commission. On the day Johnson makes his announcement they speak on three separate occasions. The Director dictates a memo revealing that while LBJ did not want an independent investigation any more than he did, public pressure had forced their hand. The intimate nature of their relationship is made obvious in this same document.

After a November 26 announcement by the state of Texas of its intention to conduct an independent inquiry, Carr meets with Justice Department officials, who are now simply following orders from Hoover. On December 3, Carr effectively announces that there will be no inquiry. This becomes a virtual reality on December 6 through the joint efforts of Johnson and Hoover. Texas state statute requiring investigation is simply overidden. The day after the Commission makes its demand for raw FBI reports, December 17, Hoover pens an effusive note to Johnson, revealing the pair's "mutual desire to serve [the] country in fullest capacity." Discussion of an Executive Order waiving Hoover's retirement has probably taken place. Curiously, late that night, Johnson calls Hoover companion Clyde Tolson at his apartment. The subject of their conversation is not known.

Apparently the Christmas holidays and preoccupation with the Baker scandal in January take Johnson's attention, for there appears to be little interaction with Hoover during this time period. As an apparent result of Warren Commission frustration/conclusions in late January, however, rumors begin to circulate in D.C. to the effect that the Director is about to be removed from power. The latter part of February 1964, Johnson and Hoover begin a series of communications. These apparently deal both with Hoover's increasingly precarious position and Republican charges of corruption against Johnson. On March 1, the press openly asserts that Hoover has given FBI reports to Johnson for use against political foes, including those testifying against him in the Baker proceedings. By March 10, LBJ is publicly stating that he intends to waive Hoover's retirement. To members of the Warren Commission, the message must be clear. Over the course of the next week there are numerous conversations between Johnson and the Director. By April 21, LBJ is directly pressuring Warren to conclude the proceedings. Making good on his March announcement, Johnson waives Hoover's retirement on May 8, just two days prior to his fortieth anniversary as FBI director. The Director is overcome with emotion, returning to his office and penning a profusely ingratiating letter to LBJ within hours.

Almost from the moment Johnson is sworn in, he begins to capitalize on his newly acquired power. The night of November 22, after leaving the executive offices, he meets privately with aides at his residence until 3 A.M. (EST) planning strategy. On November 28 he presents his first speech. Like Hoover has done in years past, Johnson equates his own fate with that of the nation's. He invokes God, simultaneously calling upon the American people to support him. The burgeoning Baker scandal is everpresent on his mind and he does not miss the opportunity to distract the electorate. On December 1 he makes a formal visit to JFK's grave, in part for purposes of gaining further sympathy from the public. By December 5, however, the press begins to complain that he is avoiding them. This is nothing more than a continuation of vice-presidential policy. Johnson had always avoided noncontroled press situations, in part for fear reporters would ask questions that might expose his dealings with men like Estes and Baker. He retreats to his Texas ranch for an extended Christmas vacation, at times appearing elated, at others the buffoon. In early January he begins, with the aid of Hoover, to move against RFK. On 1/11/64, in what has to be one of the American presidency's more bizarre moments, LBJ publicly thanks Robert Kennedy for waging so successful a campaign against the Mafia. The cruelty and sadism of Lyndon Johnson is never made more obvious.

With the assassination, Robert Kennedy is effectively removed from power. By November 30 his hotline to Hoover is disconnected. On December 5 he informs Schlesinger that the Director has reverted to his old ways. During the same time he tells the JFK aide that it is an open question whether the Mafia is responsible for his brother's murder. By the time RFK returns to work in early January, Hoover is no longer speaking to him.

The Baker/Levinson investigation is temporarily delayed by the assassination, but resumes the following week. It receives its first shock when Fortas resigns as Baker's counsel. Change in counsel automatically warrants a delay. The Mafia functionary retains, a few days later, new counsel; none other than renowned Mafia defense attorney Edward Bennett Williams (also counsel to Levinson and Beckley). The day closed hearings resume, December 6, Johnson telephones committee chairman Jordan. This day the longtime Johnson supporter deadlocks the committee on issues of morality by asserting that aspects involving sexual impropriety are irrelevant. On December 8 Jordan announces there will be no public hearings for months. Republican committee members rebel, causing Jordan to suspend further hearings until January. In mid January 1964 the press reveals Levinson's and Baker's close connections to Hoffa. Loans to Baker during March 1962, possibly associated with his Carousel resort, become known.

On January 17 Baker opponent Don B. Reynolds threatens to expose Johnson when he reveals a kickback scam engineered by the Senate aide for LBJ's benefit. In an attempt to protect his position Johnson appears to confront the issue at a news conference, but then dodges charges by refusing to elaborate on his statement. Apparently after this encounter with the press, Johnson turns once again to Hoover, obtaining derogatory data on Reynolds, which, through aides, he then attempts to use. On February 4 Johnson panics, telling Speaker McCormack in a private meeting he will pay Baker one million dollars if he agrees to remain silent about LBJ's past.

Near the end of February, Baker finally appears before the committee with Williams at his side. Calling the proceedings a "legislative trial," Williams effectively denies the U.S. Senate has the authority to challenge Baker. The attorney shocks the committee by revealing that the FBI has conducted ELSUR on Levinson through his Las Vegas casinos. Baker repeatedly takes the Fifth, throughout his appearance a look of amusement on his face. His secretary also claims the Bureau has her under surveillance. On February 28, Johnson, when confronted, again refuses to discuss the Baker case. The first week in March, Levinson also appears. Like Baker he refuses to testify, raising FBI's ELSUR coverage as a defense. The following day Jordan basically announces his intention to discontinue proceedings in the near future. One week later Sigelbaum appears, taking the Fifth 136 times. Despite Republican efforts, the committee goes out of existence by April.

The actions of the press in the time between the assassination and Hoover's May 1964 triumph are, despite the circumstances, largely commendable. Initial reports in the first few days after Kennedy's murder are quite accurate. Doctors are quoted in such a way as to make apparent the true nature of the wounds. Descriptions of the small entry wound in JFK's right temple are detailed for the public. Oswald's denials of guilt are repeatedly aired. The negative evidentiary result of the paraffin test on his face and hands is also reported. Despite *Life*'s best efforts, there are even accurate descriptions of the Zapruder footage. The violent backward snap of Kennedy's head in response to the shot from the right front is graphically revealed.

With the murder of Oswald, however, and the advent of Hoover's disinformation campaign, the overall quality of reporting suffers. Clearly the press becomes confused, not knowing whom to believe. The European press, viewing the events from a position of greater objectivity, is, however, not fooled. By November 27 they openly accuse Hoover of complicity, and suggest the Mafia is behind Ruby. Domestically, disinformation releases regarding Oswald intensify. To the media's credit, on November 30 his connections to the Bureau as an informant begin to surface. The Western Union money orders are disclosed. Starting December 1 Ruby is described by some as nothing less than Chicago Mafia. The same day Oswald's mediocre capabilities with a rifle are made apparent. The press also manages to reveal the fact that JFK's autopsy physicians have been instructed not to talk to the public. Look-alike stories from local rifle ranges surface. On December 10 news of in-fighting between Hoover and the Secret Service is revealed. The absence of Oswald from the Secret Service's Dallas PRS file is made public. This issue is overblown, as there never was any real reason for him to be considered a presidential threat. The true issue is, of course, the absence of the Aleman/Traficante data. By mid-December the presence of the gunman and backup man behind the fence on the grassy knoll is confirmed. On December 16, D.C. press flatly states that feuding between Hoover and the Secret Service led to the death of JFK. From late December well into January, members of the press continue to attack Johnson for refusing to meet with them.

With Johnson and Hoover at center stage, Marcello enjoys the fruits of victory. Other than an initial flurry of activity surrounding buffers Ferrie and Banister, something the mobster had anticipated, there is little immediate threat. He may even have watched the machinations of Hoover with a certain degree of amusement, sensing that while the Director is undoubtedly aware of his role in the matter, he clearly had not anticipated that the New Orleans mobster would use a Bureau informant as a scapegoat. Ruby, despite his reluctance, had performed well. On November 30 Marcello sends associate Campisi to meet with the ex-club owner in the Dallas jail, undoubtedly impressing upon him the importance of remaining silent. He cooperates. When he finally appears in court in late January, he stumbles only momentarily, admitting deep feelings of remorse in the hours after JFK's death. He is quickly cut off by his everpresent phalanx of attorneys and makes only oblique references to the Mafia in the coming months and years. Religion becomes a near "hysterical" obsession.

Oswald, in reality only a minor figure in the assassination of JFK, spends most of his remaining hours after the event trying to extract himself from what he perceives to be the clutches of the FBI. Despite the fact that the overwhelming body of evidence points toward his innocence, something Hoover himself admits in a November 24 memo, he senses that he is effectively being railroaded by the Bureau. He is denied access to legal counsel, and subjected to gross violation of his civil rights. The Banister connection is nearly revealed on November 23 when Cuban exile foe Bringuier publicly states in New Orleans that he had believed Oswald was an FBI informant early on. Sensing objectivity and interest from the Secret Service, Oswald expresses, just hours before his death, a willingness to tell his story to them once he obtains anti-FBI counsel John Abt as counsel. In the weeks after Oswald's death, legal authorities nationwide begin to express the opinion that he was basically the victim of a lynching.

Other groups with different agendas attempt to profit from the assassination. The CIA, unable to force Kennedy to invade Cuba during life, attempt to use his death to accomplish the same. A protracted disinformation campaign designed to paint Oswald as nothing more than a paid pro-Castroite contract killer is launched even before his murder by Ruby. This effort backfires, however, leading some to conclude in the coming years that Oswald himself was in fact a CIA agent, or that CIA directly ordered Kennedy's assassination. There can be no doubt the CIA benefited from the killing. Unfortunately, their willingness to attempt to misuse the assassination of an American president for political gain proves, ultimately, to be merely symptomatic of larger problems within the agency. Domestically, ultrarightists such as the Walker people use

Oswald's leftist affiliations as a basis for an assault upon liberal groups. The ex-Marine is labeled as a "kill-crazy-communist."

In a final irony, Las Vegas casinos fall silent from 7 A.M. to midnight the day of Kennedy's funeral, a parting "tribute" to the man who had tried so hard to destroy the very men who controlled the gambling network.

12:35 P.M.: Hoover, receiving word of the assassination via the UPI ticker in his building, calls Attorney General Kennedy at home. "The President's been shot, I think it is serious, I'll call you back . . . when I find out more."[1]

"Hoover . . . telephoned the Dallas FBI office and ordered [SAC Shanklin to initiate] an all-out investigation of the [assassination]. . . ."[2]

The limousine arrives at Parkland Hospital. Secret Service Agents Hill, Kellerman, and Greer observe Kennedy's head wounds. Beginning with the exit wound caused by the shot from the right front, Kellerman: "He had a large wound [diameter of 5 inches] . . . on [the right rear portion of the head]. . . . To the left of the ear . . . and a little high . . ."; Greer: "His head . . . [the right rear side] . . . was all blown off"; Hill: "The right rear portion of his head was missing . . . one large gaping wound in the right rear portion of the head." The point of entry by the same shot is also detected. Kellerman: "Entry [hole the size of the little finger] into this man's head was . . . the bottom of the hairline immediately to the right of the ear about the lower third of the ear."[3]

As the press will soon quote a bystander outside Parkland: "I could see a hole in the President's left [from viewer's perspective] temple and his head and hair were bathed in blood."[4]

" '. . . It appeared that the bullet had struck him above the right ear or near the temple.' Seth Kantor, a Scripps-Howard reporter, jotted down in his notebook at Parkland hospital the phrase 'entered . . . right temple. . . .' Only an hour and half after the assassination [NBC] reported that 'the President was struck in the right temple by the bullet' . . ."[5]

Per *Washington Post*: "He was shot at 12:30 P.M. CST . . . by an assassin, who sent a rifle bullet crashing into his right temple."[6]

Seattle Post Intelligencer: "President Kennedy was shot in the right temple."[7] Note, the *entry* point of the shot fired from the

Depository and striking Kennedy in the back of the head (i.e., the first head shot) may have been obliterated by the exiting blast of the shot fired from the right front. As made apparent from Thompson's book, the shot fired from the rear evidently fragmented inside the head and damaged the area directly behind the President's upper facial bones.

1 P.M.: President Kennedy is pronounced dead. Doctor's at Parkland soon issue statements. " 'Dr. Ronald Coy Jones described . . . an exit wound in the posterior portion of the skull.' Dr. Malcolm Perry noted 'a large avulsive [exploded] injury of the right occipitoparietal area,' while Dr. Charles Baxter recalled 'a large gaping wound in the back of the skull . . . literally the right side of his head had been blown off.' . . . Dr. Robert N. McClelland: '. . . the right posterior portion of the skull had been blasted. . . . A third or so, at least of the posterior cerebral tissue and some of the cerebellar tissue had been blasted out.' "[8]

Hoover again calls RFK. "His terse words were, 'The President is dead.' He hung up. . . ."[9] Kennedy notes that the Director's voice appears very calm, as if he were reporting some minor incident.[10] ". . . From that time on, [the Director] rarely spoke to the attorney general while he was in office."[11]

Press: "J. Edgar Hoover issued a statement, saying: 'The assassination of President Kennedy is a blow to all mankind. He is mourned as the leader of free men everywhere and his *tragic* death is a blow to the hopes and aspirations of all of us" (emphasis added).[12] Thus, the Director officially categorizes Kennedy's murder as a tragedy (i.e., a serious drama with an unhappy ending).

Within the next hour, Dallas police officer J. D. Tippit is killed and Oswald is arrested. Any connection between the two remains extremely dubious. Tippit's death is very probably totally unrelated. A reading of Mark Lane's *Rush to Judgment* makes clear that Tippit's assailant(s) do not match Oswald's description, slugs taken from the officer's body are ballistically unrelated to Oswald's pistol (even FBI will admit this), and Dallas P.D. has mishandled/altered other evidence to such a degree, it would be inadmissible in a court of law.[13] Revelations in the 1970s and 1980s (see Hurt's *Reasonable Doubt*) very strongly suggest that Tippit may have been killed by some unknown third party as a result of extramarital activities.[14] Dallas P.D. undoubtedly knows a great deal about this event. Investigations (if only internal) of officer killings are always given high priority, for obvious reasons. But, as with other aspects of Kennedy's murder, the department chooses to remain silent on the subject.

1:45 P.M. (CST): The Marcello jury goes into deliberation in New Orleans.[15] The mobster is already aware of the success of the contract and appears unmoved.

Individuals within the Dallas P.D. make the decision to implicate Oswald in the staged attempt to shoot General Walker the previous April. There is a possibility that Oswald, as a leftist, already has politically related data among his possessions that trigger the idea of planting evidence. Perhaps he had, like many people in Dallas, at some point photographed the general's home or collected news clippings. Walker would have been a natural subject. At any rate, Hoover will leap at the opportunity. Given Kennedy's moderate viewpoint on the nature of the internal communist threat, one can only assume that the Director ultimately derives a certain satisfaction in promoting this falsification by the Dallas P.D., especially in light of the fact that Oswald is a self-professed, if somewhat confused, Marxist. Hoover's May 1964 Warren Commission testimony will bear this out.

Press will report: "Police Friday were not overlooking a possibility that President Kennedy's assassin may have been the mystery sniper who shot at . . . Walker last April 10. . . . The sniper attack occurred two nights after Walker had returned from a coast-to-coast anti-Communist crusade which he called 'Midnight Alert.' "[16]

2 P.M.: ". . . Cabana Motel . . . records put [Braden's friend Morgan Brown's] departure time . . . at 2:01 P.M. . . . Braden testified that he had caught a commercial flight to Houston that night."[17]

There is ". . . a 3-minute call from Ruby to [Alex] Gruber in Los Angeles two hours after the assassination."[18]

2:15 to 4:05 P.M.: Oswald is interrogated for the first time. Hoover is suddenly in a very difficult position, for Oswald, in addition to being FBI informant, is now antagonist. In Oswald's mind, men directly associated with the FBI (Banister, Ferrie et al.) have, by framing him, implicated themselves in the assassination. Ferrie's library card has been found in Oswald's wallet.[19] Oswald himself has, over the last year, been manipulated by the Bureau, in all likelihood informing for them for pay. The Dallas FBI, undoubtedly at Hoover's directive, quickly responds.

"Now, according to [police captain] Fritz's testimony, about 2:20 P.M.: 'Just about the time I started talking to [Oswald], . . . I got a phone call from . . . Gordon Shanklin, agent in charge of the FBI calling for Mr. . . . Bookout [FBI liaison to Dallas Police]. . . . Mr. Shanklin asked that Mr. Hosty be in on that questioning because of Mr. Hosty knowing these people and he had been talking to them and he wanted him in there right then. . . . . . . And he said some other things that I don't want to repeat, about what to do if [FBI Agent James Bookout] didn't do it right quick. . . . I walked out there and called them in.' "[20] "Hosty had been introduced because of FBI Dallas Bureau Chief Shanklin's urgent call to Fritz. Hosty was the 'Oswald expert.' "[21] According to Fritz, Oswald ". . . became very upset and arrogant with Agent Hosty when he questioned him and accused him of accosting his wife two different times. When Agent Hosty attempted to talk to this man, he would hit his fist on the desk."[22] Hosty: "I told Oswald my name and he reacted violently. . . . He adopted an extremely hostile attitude towards the FBI. . . . He made the remark to me, 'Oh, so you are Hosty. I've heard about you.' He then started to cuss at us, and so forth, and I tried to talk to him to calm him down. The more I talked to him the worse he got, so I just quit talking to him, just sat back in the corner. . . . He made some derogatory remarks about the Director [J. Edgar Hoover] and some about FBI agents in general. . . ."[23] According to Bookout, "Oswald at this time adopted a very violent attitude toward the FBI and both Agents and made many uncomplimentary remarks about the FBI. . . ."[24] Hosty did not appear at any further interrogations.[25]

"Oswald frantically denied shooting Dallas police officer Tippit or shooting President . . . Kennedy." Agent Bookout noted that ". . . Oswald stated that he would not agree to take a polygraph examination without the advice of counsel."[26]

2:50 P.M.: ". . . Dallas police took a paraffin test of Oswald's hands and right cheek, to determine if there were traces on his skin indicating that he had fired a weapon; the test was positive for the hands, but negative for the cheek."[27] Because no powder and metal particles are found on his face, his use of a rifle in recent hours, particularly one as leaky as the Carcano, is precluded. *Note* that both hands test positive, also effectively eliminating the evidentiary value of the test for purposes of determining whether he had fired a pistol. When a pistol is fired it generally disperses particles only on the hand in which it is held. Note that Oswald handled books and boxes all day at work, many of which were presumably coated with chemical sealants.[28] It is possible such substances could have triggered positive results.

"... A U.S. Army . . . colonel in intelligence was feeding information to the FBI within an hour of Oswald's arrival at the police station."[29]

3:20 P.M. (CST): Marcello is acquitted.[30]

"On the day of the . . . assassination, Aleman arrived home to find that the FBI had telephoned. . . . What they were interested in was Traficante's previous statement that Kennedy was going to be 'hit.' 'The two agents [Aleman is quite certain one of them was Paul Scranton] came out to see me. They wanted to know more and more. I finally had to tell them he didn't say he was going to do it. He just said Kennedy was going to get hit.' The agents stayed until they had explored every possible angle and then told Aleman to keep the conversation confidential."[31] Although their report is undoubtedly sent by AIRTEL to Hoover right away, it is unknown whether these agents contacted Aleman on their own initiative or as the result of a directive.

RFK leaves for Andrews Airforce Base at 4:40 P.M. (EST) from his home.[32]

"Oswald faces identification lineups at 4:05, 6:20, and 7:40 [P.M. CST]."[33] Oswald undergoes further interrogation as well. He becomes increasingly agitated, angry. FBI Agent Manning C. Clements: "Oswald 'stated he thought perhaps interview to obtain descriptive information was too prolonged, that he had declined to be interviewed by any other officers previously, and did not desire to be interviewed by this agent.' "[34]

Ruby is seen at the Carousel Club by one of his employees. As later reported by the press, he informs her the club will be closed until further notice because of the assassination. When pressed, he says, "It's awful, just don't talk about it."[35] Ruby is apparently having second thoughts about his role in the killing and feels guilty. Prior to this he went to Parkland Hospital for reasons that remain unclear. He was seen, and recognized, by a number of people.[36]

Press: "Later in the afternoon, Dr. Malcolm Perry, an attending surgeon, and Dr. Kemp Clark, chief of neurosurgery at Parkland Hospital, gave more details. . . . Mr. Kennedy . . . had a massive, gaping wound in the back [of the head] and one on the right side of the head. However, the doctors said it was impossible to determine immediately whether the wounds had been caused by one bullet or two. . . . A missile had gone in and out of the back of his head causing external lacerations and loss of brain tissue."[37]

"When Jack Miller, the Asst. Attorney General for criminal affairs flew to Dallas the afternoon of the assassination to take charge of the investigation, he was rudely ignored by Hoover's agents."[38]

11/22—11/24/63: Louisiana State Police and mental-health officials report the Cheramie incident/prediction to the FBI, to no avail.[39]

"Reeves Morgan, a member of the Louisiana State Legislature . . . informed the FBI of Oswald's presence in Clinton almost immediately after the assassination. . . . The FBI failed to investigate, and the Warren Commission never learned of the Clinton episode. . . ."[40]

"One of Oswald's former neighbors in New Orleans would later tell investigators that Ferrie visited her after the assassination—asking about Oswald's library card. Oswald's own landlady says the same—and adds a disturbing factor. She recalls Ferrie turning up to ask about the card within hours of the assassination—*before* he set off on his Texas trip."[41]

Before 5:15 P.M. (EST): Hoover states in an internal memo that Oswald is probably JFK's killer, placing him ". . . in the category of a nut and the extreme proCastro crowd . . ." He contacts the Dallas P.D. regarding Oswald's "safety," establishing, of course, a basis for FBI intervention in the area of potential civil-rights violations.[42]

5:59 P.M. (EST): Johnson arrives at Andrews Airforce Base with Kennedy's body. ". . . A large delegation of Administration officials was on hand as the plane taxied to a stop."[43] "There were high officials of the New Frontier. . . . Robert [Kennedy] . . . had somehow gotten onto the plane although he never left Washington. He was holding Mrs. Kennedy by the hand."[44] Hoover may be among the group. One photograph reveals a man bearing a striking resemblance standing next to Kennedy's coffin as it is loaded into the hearse. Unlike the pained, anxious expressions of others, his is distant, almost serene. Associated Press, which took the photograph, has stated in a letter to me that they are not certain, but "it does appear that it is he."[45]

Press: "After a brief ramp-side discussion with the Congressional chieftains, while a bevy of aides from the White House, the Vice-President's office and Federal agencies stood nearby, Johnson boarded an Army helicopter for his flight to the White House lawn."[46] Johnson enters the White House at 6:26 (EST).[47]

"Dallas television reporter Vic Robertson, Jr., another acquaintance of Ruby, was positive that early Friday evening he saw Ruby try to open the door of Captain Fritz's office, where Oswald was being questioned. Robertson then heard a voice say, 'You can't go in there, Jack.' John Rutledge, a *Dallas Morning News* reporter, also saw Ruby directly across from . . . Fritz's office before 6 P.M. that night."[48] Apparently after this he goes to his sister's house. According to Ruby's sister, at around 6:00 P.M. ". . . she said to Ruby, 'I could never conceive of anybody in his right mind who would want this President hurt.' Saying nothing, Ruby went into the bathroom and 'threw up.' Ruby left about 7 P.M."[49]

Hoover has Oswald's rifle and the bullet fragments flown to D.C. aboard an Air Force jet. "FBI laboratory technicians immediately began intensive ballistics and fingerprint tests on the rifle and slugs."[50]

"That evening, [assistant Jack] Martin got into an argument over the matter with Guy Banister in Banister's office. Martin claimed the provoking factor was his remark to Banister, 'What are you going to do—kill me like you all did Kennedy?' What happened next was described in a police report filed that day: Banister severely beat Martin on the head with his revolver. According to Martin, Banister would have killed him but for the intervention of Banister's secretary."[51] ". . . Banister . . . told his secretary not to talk to the FBI about Oswald. . . ."[52]

"At ten past seven . . . Oswald was charged with the killing of police officer Tippit."[53]

"Ferrie began to act very oddly. In the company of two young friends, he drove 350 miles . . . to Houston, Texas. After resting briefly at a motel, Ferrie visited the Winterland Skating Rink, and there, he would later claim, went ice skating. . . . The rink manager remembered . . . Ferrie had not been skating at all but had spent a great deal of time at a pay telephone, making and receiving calls."[54]

9:10 to 9:25 P.M. (EST): Johnson ". . . conferred by phone with FBI Director . . . Hoover about the investigation of the assassination. . . ." After this, LBJ leaves the White House for his private residence, meeting with personal aides until 3:25 A.M. Saturday morning.[55]

9:40 P.M. (EST): The first of two teletypes from SOG to all field offices goes out. "Contact . . . all informants."[56]

11 P.M. (EST): A second, contradictory, SOG teletype is sent to all field offices. "Resolve all allegations."[57]

11:26 P.M. (CST): Oswald is taken from the interrogation room to a courtroom within the building, where he is charged with the assassination. While being led out, he states to reporters, "These people have given me a hearing without legal representation or anything. Q—Did you shoot the president? A—No sir, I didn't shoot anybody."[58] Also, "A—I did not kill the President. I did not kill anyone."[59]

11/23/63—SATURDAY: 12:01 A.M. (CST): Oswald is taken from the third-floor interrogation room down to the basement for a news conference with reporters. Ruby, attempting to blend with reporters, is also in attendance. "Fella's name is Oswald. Oswald: 'I positively know nothing about this situation here, I would like to have re—, legal representation.' Q—unintelligible. A—'Well, I was questioned by a judge. However, I protested at that time that I was not allowed legal representation during that very short and sweet hearing. I really don't know what this situation is about. Nobody has told me anything except that I'm accused of murdering a policeman. I know nothing more than that. I do request someone [note he does not request the FBI as he had when jailed in New Orleans] to come forward to give me legal assistance. Q—Did you kill the president? A—No, I have not been charged with that. In fact, nobody has said that to me yet. The first thing I heard about it was when the newspaper reporters in the hall asked me that question." A policeman standing nearby quickly states, twice, "You have been charged with that." Reporters continue, "Q—What did you do in Russia? How did you hurt your eye? A—A policeman hit me."[60] This night the ACLU attempts to see Oswald but is rebuffed by the Dallas P.D.[61]

In an effort to obtain further inside information regarding Oswald, "[It] appears likely that Ruby never visited KLIF [radio station] on the morning of November 23 [as he would later claim]; rather he met Dallas Policeman Harry Olsen at Simon's garage around 12:30 or 1 A.M. for 'two or three hours,' as Olsen testified in his second version of events."[62]

From dawn to dusk in D.C. there came "The booming of artillery [at Arlington]. . . . Beneath Old Glory at half staff, the guns sounded every half hour."[63]

The press reports a variety of stories concerning the previous day's events. Articles discussing shots from both the grassy knoll and the Book Depository appear. Senator Long (Louisiana), a powerful Marcello supporter, states that Kennedy's death was "an act of God."[64] Chief Justice Warren, like most other key officials, eulogizes the President.[65] The existence of various movies and photos of the killing is pointed out.[66] Johnson's decreased accessibility is mentioned.[67] Senator B. Everett Jordan announces that the Baker hearings will be delayed until early December, becoming defensive when reporters press him for reasons.[68] The White House announces that Kennedy was struck by two bullets, one in the throat, the other in the head.[69] See *Six Seconds in Dallas,* p. 51 for explanation of the throat wound (i.e., caused by exiting bone fragment driven through floor of Kennedy's skull).

Washington Evening Star: "Mr. Kennedy crumpled, with bloody holes in the back of his head and in his throat—whether from one or two bullets doctors were not sure."[70]

Dallas Morning News reports on Kennedy's prior decision to travel to Dallas: "The President made the final decision. Confident that Secret Service agents and other officers could protect him, he approved slow-moving motorcades through both cities."[71]

Washington Post quotes Oswald foe, Bringuier, in New Orleans as saying "I was suspicious of him from the start. . . . I thought he might be an agent from the FBI."[72]

Denver Post: "Oswald was exposed to the press several times during the evening as he was led from one part of the police building to another. In one brief exchange in a crowded hallway, a reporter shouted, 'Did you kill the President?' 'No, I didn't, and I don't know why I am here,' Oswald replied. 'Were you in the building (from where the shots were fired)?' Oswald was asked. 'I work in the building and of course I was there,' he said."[73]

L.A. Times: "Late Friday evening, Mr. Johnson discussed the investigation of his predecessor's assassination by telephone with J. Edgar Hoover. . . . The White House declined to give any details."[74]

New Orleans States Item: "Newsmen had agreed not to ask Oswald any questions as he passed, but as the slim, accused man approached a television microphone, he stopped. Leaning over slightly, he said, 'I want to contact Mr. Apt [*sic*] in New York to defend me as my lawyer.' "[75]

"Robert Kennedy remained attorney general for nine months, but . . . Hoover never walked down the hall to offer his condolences."[76]

CIA begins a disinformation campaign designed to create the public perception that Oswald is a pro-Castroite contract killer with direct links to Cuba. The goal is to implicate Castro formally and trigger another invasion of Cuba. These rumors are circulated among Washington officials, including Hoover, who privately dismisses the notion.[77]

10:01 A.M. (EST): Hoover calls LBJ at the Executive Offices. They speak in the context of Hoover's five-page report (sent over to Johnson by special courier service) on the assassination prepared for Johnson, who may already have received it.[78] The Director apparently informs him he would like to issue a report stating Oswald is a lone nut, since that is the basic thrust of his memo to Johnson. This morning he also orders the conflicting teletypes of the previous day rescinded and instructs Bureau officials to cease communicating with the Justice Department's Organized Crime section.[79] Hoover's motivation here is twofold. Obviously he cannot allow his prior knowledge of the Marcello contract to become known. Just as important, he cannot allow Johnson to be directly implicated (and very probably impeached) over the Baker/Levinson scandal. Hoover will, from this point forward, communicate directly with Johnson. According to Sullivan, Evans is no longer Bureau liaison to the A. G.[80] The five-page report to Johnson is a point-by-point summation of the case against Oswald, and little else. He makes the following conclusions:

Oswald had been employed at the Texas School Book Depository, determined to have been the building from which the shots had been fired.

A fellow employee had observed him to carry to work, on the morning of November 22, a package of sufficient length to contain a rifle.

He had been observed on the fifth floor . . . at about 11:50 A.M.

He had been observed inside the Book Depository shortly after the shooting, but he had then disappeared.

A witness stated he had seen the shots being fired from a sixth-floor window of the Book Depository by a man resembling Oswald. . . .

A 6.5 caliber Italian rifle, found on the sixth floor . . . had been sent from Chicago to one "A. Hidell," the name on a Selective Service card in Oswald's possession at the time of his arrest.

A bullet found on a stretcher at Parkland Hospital and fragments from the presidential car had been identified as having been fired from the rifle found in the . . . Depository.

A latent fingerprint on a brown paper bag found near the window from which the shots had been fired . . . had been identified as the left index finger impression of Lee Harvey Oswald.[81]

There is also this:

A highly confidential source of this Bureau advised that an individual identifying himself as Oswald on November 18, 1963, was in contact with the Soviet Embassy in Washington, D.C., at which time he referred to a recent meeting with Comrade Kostin at the Soviet Embassy in Mexico City. This individual indicated that he originally intended to visit the Embassy in Havana, Cuba, where he would have had time to complete his business, but that he had been unable to do so.[82]

Were Hoover simply an investigative official doing his job, with nothing to hide, would he not be presenting Johnson with a balanced, comprehensive report outlining all the evidence, proconspiracy and con? Hoover's report reads rather like that of a man hiding matters of critical importance. And Johnson, in the coming days, reacts like a man indifferent, unwilling to question his motives.

Hoover effectively violates obstruction-of-justice statutes with this memo. Quoting the standard definition from *Black's Law Dictionary:*

> Impeding or obstructing those who . . . have duties or powers of administering justice. . . . *The act by which one or more persons . . . prevent the execution of lawful process . . . by hindering* witnesses from appearing . . . obstructing court orders or *criminal investigations. Any act . . .* pertaining to pending proceedings, *intended to play on human frailty and to deflect and deter* the court from performance of its duty and drive it into compromise with its own unfettered judgment by placing it, through medium of knowingly false assertion, in wrong position before [the] public. . . . [emphasis added]

". . . As a Justice Department lawyer later . . . told . . . the *New York Times,* John Kennedy was assassinated and 'the next day we stopped getting information from the FBI on the Bobby Baker investigation. Within a month the FBI . . . wouldn't tell us anything.' "[83]

10:25 A.M. to 1 P.M.: Oswald is again interrogated (he spends an hour in his cell during this time as well). "Fritz's report . . . refers to Abt: 'He reminded me that he did not have to answer any questions at all until he talked to his attorney, and I told him again that he could have an attorney any time he wished. He said he didn't have any money to pay for a phone call to Mr. Abt. I told him to call "collect" . . . or that he could have another attorney if he wished. He said he didn't want another attorney. . . .' "[84]

The FBI conducts a search of the Paines' residence. Not surprisingly, both Paines think Oswald is incapable of violence. When the agents arrive, Ruth Paine informs them about Oswald's letter to the Soviet Embassy. ". . . I gave the original to them."[85]

11 A.M.: Dallas Police Chief Curry holds a press conference. "I understand the FBI did know he was in Dallas."[86] He also tells them the FBI had prior knowledge of Oswald based upon surveillance.[87] This type of rhetoric undoubtedly makes Hoover very nervous. Curry also admits to reporters that the paraffin test performed on Oswald had produced negative evidentiary results.[88]

A Dallas County police official announces "We do have this. The Federal Bureau of Investigation has asked us, and we join in with them in requesting that any person who was in the vicinity of the

assassination yesterday who was taking pictures, bring these . . .
to the police department here. Anyone who has any information
concerning this certainly should contact the police department immediately."[89] Within hours, many Dealey Plaza witnesses come forward.

1:10 P.M.: ". . . Oswald is allowed to talk with his wife and with
his mother, whom he has not seen since October 7, 1962."[90]

"At 1:40 P.M., Oswald places an unsuccessful call to New York
for Abt, obtaining from the long-distance operator Abt's number
and the number of *The Worker*."[91] He has no way of knowing that
the lawyer is out of town. Obviously he has now realized that, as
both an FBI informant and unwitting tool of Banister and Ferrie et
al., he needs an attorney experienced in defending leftists framed by
the Bureau. The fact that the FBI now has control over the situation probably terrifies him. At his interrogation sessions he continues to ask for the New York attorney.

Reached by reporters this afternoon, "Abt . . . at his summer
home in Kent, Conn., said he had not been asked to take the case
but added, 'If I were asked, I would in all probability have to decline. It would have to be a very serious decision,' he admitted. . . .
Abt said Oswald probably thought of his name, because 'I have a
reputation for representing the underdog, particularly unpopular
political minorities.' "[92]

11/22—12/63: FBI ELSUR: "And then there was this post assassination reaction by . . . mobsters Anthony Giacalone and his
brother Vito (Billy) . . . Giacalone, who welcomed Lyndon Johnson's elevation. . . . Tony G: 'That Johnson's going to be a good
man in there.' Billy: 'Yeah, real good for the country.' "[93]

4 P.M.: Oswald calls Ruth Paine twice. Ruth: "And he said he
wanted me to call Mr. John Abt in New York for him after six P.M.
He gave me a telephone number of an office in New York and a
residence in New York. . . . He said he was an attorney he wanted
to have. . . . He thanked me for my concern."[94]

Ruby is seen again at the Dallas P.D., apparently attempting to
get to Oswald. "Thayer Waldo, a Fort Worth reporter, ran into
Ruby in the police building at 4 P.M. Saturday. . . . NBC News
Producer/Director Fred Rheinstein testified that Saturday afternoon before 5 P.M., he saw a man in the police building who he was
'reasonably certain was Ruby.' This man entered a police building

office in which District Attorney Henry Wade was reportedly working and from which newsmen had been excluded."[95]

As *Denver Post* will report, "Late Saturday afternoon Chief
Curry called a special conference to deny that he had any knowledge that the FBI had interviewed Oswald."[96] Dallas District Attorney Wade tells the press, including *Washington Evening Star,*
"There is no one else but [Oswald.]"[97]

5:30 P.M.: Oswald is allowed five minutes with the president of
the Dallas Bar Association. ". . . He asked me first did I know a
lawyer in New York named John Abt. . . . I said I didn't know
him, and he said, 'Well, I would like to have him represent
me, . . .' . . . Then he asked me if I knew any lawyers who were
members of the American Civil Liberties Union, and he said, 'Well,
I am a member of that organization, and I would like to have
somebody who is a member of that organization represent me.' "[98]

Seattle press will report: "[Oswald] . . . wheeled on inquiring
reporters enroute to the homicide bureau tonight and [said]: 'Look,
I don't know what you people are talking about. I haven't committed any act of violence. I've got nothing against nobody.' "[99]

6:00 to 7:15 P.M.: Oswald is again interrogated. "According to
Fritz: 'I showed Oswald an enlarged picture of him holding a rifle
and wearing a pistol.' "[100] Agent Bookout: ". . . additionally reported Oswald's denial of shooting the President. . . ." With regard to the photo of Oswald standing in his back yard early in the
year posing with rifle, pistol, and copies of *The Militant* and *Worker*
he notes ". . . Oswald stated he would not discuss this photograph
without advice of an attorney."[101] Note that neither the Dallas P.D.
nor the FBI will ever produce verbatim transcripts of Oswald's
statements. Fritz will lamely claim later that he would have but he
just didn't have a tape recorder.[102] One would assume that the interrogation of a man accused of assassinating the President, wounding
the governor of the state, and murdering a police officer would rate
either a stenographer or tape recorder.

The *Denver Post* will report on November 24: "Oswald, who had
been questioned for almost an hour Saturday morning and then
returned to his cell, was brought down again to the homicide bureau early Saturday evening. As he passed reporters in the hallway
he said: 'I'd like a change of clothing . . . I'd like my basic fundamental rights. . . .' "[103]

As the *L.A. Times* will report, Oswald tells reporters, "I do not know what fantastic stories you've been told but I deny all these charges."[104]

Oswald is obviously becoming increasingly agitated as he is apparently subjected to interrogation sessions without the aid of counsel. There are further, louder protestations to newsmen. At one point as he is being led into another room, he cries out, "I don't know what dispatches you people have been given, but I emphatically deny these charges! I have not committed any acts of violence!" The door is closed behind him.[105]

8 P.M.: "Oswald calls Ruth Paine and . . . asks for Marina. 'I said she was not there, that I had a notion where she might be (apparently in FBI custody), but I wasn't at all certain. . . . He said he thought she should be at my house. He felt irritated. . . .' "[106]

"Ferrie had arrived in Galveston just before the arrival in town of Ruby's friend Breck Wall and just before the phone call to Galveston that Ruby found it so vital to make that night."[107] From Ferrie's hotel "a collect call went to the Town and Country Motel, Marcello's New Orleans headquarters."[108] The day before, only ". . . three hours after the President's death, Ruby visited his bank and talked to an official who regularly dealt with his affairs. According to the official, Ruby was then carrying the huge sum of $7,000. The money was in large bills, stuffed in his pockets."[109] Ruby has apparently received at least a partial payoff. In years to come, Marcello will finance "a lucrative service station franchise in an ideal location in . . . New Orleans . . . " for Ferrie.[110]

By now the FBI and Dallas police have discovered that there are virtually no recorded comments (or recollections of others) suggesting that Oswald had any hostility toward the President. ". . . And barring psychological speculation, his motive for killing President Kennedy was indiscernible."[111] Contrast this with the statements of David Ferrie.

11/24/63—SUNDAY: "During the early hours of November 24, the sheriff's office and FBI officials in Dallas received almost identical warnings that . . . Oswald would be murdered as he was transferred. . . . [Officer] Grammer . . . immediately felt that he recognized the voice . . . but he could not put a face or a name with the voice. . . . The caller began speaking of details of the transfer plans that were not known even to Grammer. . . . 'You're going to have to make some other plans, . . . or we're going to kill Oswald right there in the basement.' " He and another officer file a report, but police officials for some reason do not initiate adequate protective measures.[112] Grammer will later come to the realization that the caller was Jack Ruby. Ruby's attempt to short-circuit the transfer, and thus avoid becoming directly involved through the commission of murder, is understandable. Recall also his reluctance to even discuss the assassination with club employees, as well as nervousness (including vomiting) while at his sister's house on Friday evening. His clumsy attempt to blend as a reporter in the police basement early Saturday morning may also have been designed to draw the attention of Dallas P.D. officers, many of whom knew him by first name.

2:15 A.M.: Dallas FBI SAC Shanklin calls the Dallas P.D. in an attempt to reach Chief Curry with news of the threat.[113]

8:15 A.M.: Shanklin reaches Curry by phone and informs him of the Oswald death threat.[114]

Press reports numerous stories concerning Friday's and Saturday's events. *New York Times:* "The editors [of *Life*] said . . . the [Zapruder] film was developed Friday night. . . . Editors said yesterday that it had been studied by their Dallas representatives, who were authorized to make the purchase. *The film was sent by air to the Chicago laboratories of the magazine.* From a description given by the Life representative in Dallas, the editors said it appeared that the shots had been taken with a telephoto lens. . . . *Life editors here said that they were unable last night to give precise details* as to what the film showed, but that they were assured that it depicted the impact of the bullets that struck Mr. Kennedy" (emphasis added).[115]

L.A. Times: Regarding JFK's head wound, "The occipito parietal, which is a part of the back of the head, had a huge flap."[116]

New York Times: "Dr. Kemp Clark . . . chief of neurology at Parkland Hospital . . . said that there were two wounds, a traumatic wound in the back of the head and a small entrance wound below the Adam's apple. . . . The head wound could have been caused by an emerging bullet, Dr. Clark said, or it could have been a tangential wound. He said that the wound was 'large with a considerable loss of tissue.' "[117] Obviously then, by coupling this description with those detailing the small entrance wound in the right temple, it becomes clear that: a bullet fired from the right front struck him in the "right temple," traveled "tangentially" upward and backward, and exited "the back of the head" in the "occipito parietal" region, creating a "huge flap."

Dallas Morning News: ". . . Reports from Dallas said there were two wounds, one in the neck, one in the back of the head."[118]

Also, ". . . Oswald . . . was interviewed by the FBI here six days before the Friday assassination. But word . . . was not conveyed to the U.S. Secret Service and Dallas police, reliable sources told the Dallas News. . . . However, *in Washington, a spokesman for the FBI said it was 'incorrect' that the FBI had questioned Oswald or had him under surveillance at any time in recent months,* the Associated Press reported. The interview reportedly was held November 16—at a time when the Secret Service and police officials were coordinating security plans. . . . These sources said the . . . interview added more data to an already 'thick file' the FBI has on . . . [him]. Presumably the FBI knew when Oswald obtained a job here several weeks ago. . . . Police Chief . . . Curry added fire to the sources' disclosure by telling the press conference Saturday he 'understood' the FBI had interviewed Oswald a week or so ago and never informed his department. Curry then hurriedly recalled reporters to say he did not have first-hand information on this. He said he had been told by 'someone' Friday night that the FBI recently had interviewed Oswald. But this turned out to be wrong information, he said. . . . *Curry [said] 'I do not want to accuse the FBI of withholding information. They have no obligation to help us.'* . . . Despite Curry's retraction, sources maintained . . . the interview by the FBI did take place with no mention of it to the Secret Service and police" (emphasis added).[119] Obviously someone at the initial interrogation session of Oswald on November 22 has leaked information to the press about his prior run-in with Hosty.

Washington Evening Star: "*The FBI said its agents had interviewed Oswald only once . . . when he got into some trouble in New Orleans. . . . FBI sources* indicated Oswald came to Dallas from Fort Worth about two months ago, but *said the suspect's presence here was not known to them*" (emphasis added).[120]

Also, "The Secret Service wants to know first what combination of circumstances occurred to frustrate the elaborate precautions always taken to guard the President. . . . [Oswald] . . . had been arrested in New Orleans in August and FBI agents had questioned him then, but he was not kept under surveillance and an FBI spokesman said it was not known that he had settled in Dallas two months ago. A White House spokesman said . . . no information in the nature of a warning reached Washington that would have prompted . . . additional precautions. Customarily, the Secret Service has stressed preventive protection. This has included both tracking down anonymous threats and exploring every possibility of danger. . . . Usually the Secret Service advance agents have worked out the details to the point where the local forces can give the maximum protection."[121] Surely Johnson reads this article, or is briefed on it by aides. What must he think, learning this via media reports such as these instead of from Hoover's November 23 morning report?

L.A. Times: ". . . Curry said the FBI had informed him around 6:30 P.M. [Saturday] that the handwriting on the mail order which purchased the rifle believed to be the murder weapon was that of Oswald. . . . Curry said preliminary ballistics tests of the rifle . . . indicated that it was the assassination weapon—and the same rifle that was purchased by Oswald. . . . When . . . asked if he were certain in his own mind that this was the rifle which fired the fatal shots, he replied, 'Yes.' "[122]

Dallas Morning News: "Robert Morris [Walker's backer], the former head of the Defenders of American Liberties, said, 'Dallas and indeed the whole nation should be very grateful to Dallas Police Chief (Jesse) Curry for his subordinates' work. Can you imagine,' he said rhetorically, 'the reign of terror if they had not apprehended an out-of-town suspect?' "[123] Consider this comment in light of Dallas P.D. officers' Friday assertion that Oswald is now a suspect in the Walker shooting, as well as earlier Dallas P.D. comments immediately after the staged attempt on Walker, in which they so eagerly volunteered "evidence" for the media.

Chicago Tribune: "Police said a man who fires a pistol would have gunpowder traces only on the hand used to grip the pistol. . . . The Federal Bureau of Investigation [was] reportedly in agreement with local authorities that Oswald had played a lone hand in the tragedy."[124]

L.A. Times will report that Curry, shortly before Oswald's murder, stated to reporters, "This is the man. We are sure he is the one who killed the President and Officer Tippit. . . . Curry said he did not believe that Oswald had any actual accomplice."[125]

". . . On the morning of Sunday, November 24, Mrs. Oswald

was asked . . . 'Do you know a Mr. David Farry?' [*sic*] Marina replied she did not."[126]

9:30 to 11 A.M.: Oswald is again interrogated. According to Dallas P.D. interrogators, "Oswald at no time appeared confused or in doubt at to whether or not he should answer a question."[127] Allowed to speak privately with the Secret Service for a few minutes, he reacts positively. Agent Kelly: ". . . He asked me whether I was an FBI agent and I said that I was not, that I was a member of the Secret Service. He said when he was standing in front of the Textbook Building and about to leave it, a young crew-cut man [Robert Mac-Neil] rushed up to him and said he was from the Secret Service, showed a book of identification, and asked him where the phone was. Oswald said he pointed toward the pay phone in the building and that he saw the man actually go to the phone before he left. . . . *Out of the hearing of the others except perhaps one of Captain Fritz's men, [I] said that, as a Secret Service agent, we are anxious to talk with him as soon as he had secured counsel; that we were responsible for the safety of the President; that the Dallas police had charged him with the assassination of the President but that he had denied it; we were therefore very anxious to talk with him to make certain that the correct story was developing as it related to the assassination.* He said that he would . . . discuss this proposition with his attorney and that after he talked with one, we could either discuss it with him or discuss it with his attorney, if the attorney thought it was the wise thing to do, but at the present time he had nothing more to say to me" (emphasis added).[128]

Ruby is seen this morning by ". . . three technicians for WBAP-TV [.All] said they believed they saw Ruby in the vicinity of the Police and Courts Building before 11 o'clock."[129]

11:15 A.M.: Oswald, apparently emboldened by support from the Secret Service, blurts out to reporters as he is being transferred, "I'm just a patsy!"[130] Undoubtedly, he means "patsy" in the context of manipulation by Banister and Ferrie, as well as the FBI. He cannot have realized that Ferrie had fooled him into bringing a package into the depository as part of the Marcello contract. Banister himself probably only realized this after the fact. Operating only from the knowledge that Ferrie and Banister work with the FBI, Oswald may well be assuming formal conspiracy on the part of the latter at this point. That something of this nature had occurred probably first became apparent to him shortly after the assassination, explaining his sudden trip home to get his revolver. He was at that point obviously in fear for his life. Oswald's absolute determination to obtain an attorney well versed in FBI tactics becomes entirely understandable in light of the above.

11:20 A.M.: ". . . Ruby . . . entered the basement [possibly] via an elevator and . . . moments later . . . executed Oswald."[131] Ruby's car is searched, revealing ". . . copies of Fort Worth and Dallas newspapers from November 20, showing what President Kennedy's proposed motorcade route . . . would be . . . on November 22."[132] Within a short time ". . . FBI agent C. Ray Hall arrived in the fifth-floor cell block to interview Ruby . . . from 12:40 to 3:15 that Sunday afternoon. . . ."[133] Recall that the latter was himself once an informant for the FBI.

Dr. Hume, one of the JFK autopsy surgeons, this day prepares a fresh draft of his autopsy report. ". . . I personally burned . . . [preliminary draft notes] in the fireplace of my recreation room." He maintains he did this *before* Oswald was murdered.[134]

Oswald's ". . . corpse was taken to a mortuary, where an FBI team photographed [him] and took his fingerprints for the last time."[135] In this context, it is interesting to note that "The bag [that] was firmly linked to Oswald by a fingerprint and a palm print . . . was free from any scratches or oil from the metal parts of a rifle. This is rather strange, because the . . . Carcano was oily when found. . . . The palm print . . . could not be detected on the rifle when it reached the FBI headquarters [Friday night] and was produced [only] days later—by the officer who first processed the rifle in Dallas—as a 'lift' he said he had made on the night of the assassination."[136]

Hoover calls Shanklin and orders Oswald's Dallas file sanitized. The killing is a very fortunate break for the Director, making containment now much easier. ". . . Hosty was summoned once more. He says Shanklin produced the note from a desk drawer, saying, 'Oswald's dead now. There can be no trial. Here—get rid of this.' Hosty then tore up the note in Shanklin's presence, but Shanklin cried, 'No! Get it out of here. I don't even want it in this office. Get rid of it.' Hosty then took the note to the lavatory and—in his words—'flushed it down the drain.' A few days later Shanklin asked Hosty for an assurance that he had done as ordered. . . . Hosty himself has strongly suggested that the original order to destroy the note came from FBI headquarters and perhaps from the top."[137]

The Bureau also deletes Hosty's name, (as well as Miss Gandy's) address, and phone number from Oswald's notebook.[138]

For the sake of protocol, Johnson officially orders Hoover into the case on the grounds that the Dallas P.D. violated Oswald's civil rights.[139]

As *New York Times* will report, "The Justice Department showed its concern by sending the head of its criminal division, Assistant Attorney General Herbert J. Miller, Jr., to Dallas this afternoon. Mr. Miller will talk with FBI men working on the case and with the case and with the United States Attorney in Dallas. . . . He is also expected to confer with state and local prosecutors and police officials."[140] Miller is also carrying Hoover's instructions for Wade and Curry.

3:45 to 4:10 P.M. (EST): Johnson meets, or talks by phone with, Texas Attorney General (and ex-FBI agent), Waggoner Carr.[141]

4 P.M. (EST): Hoover, in response to his sudden good fortune, prepares a memo for the record. In relevant part it is as follows:

There is nothing further on the Oswald case except that he is dead. Last night we received a call in our Dallas office from a man talking in a calm voice and saying he was a member of a committee organized to kill Oswald. We at once notified the Chief of Police and he assured us Oswald would be given sufficient protection. . . . However, this was not done. . . . A man stepped out [of the crowd] and shot him in the stomach. This man was arrested at once. . . . His real name is Rubenstein. He runs two night clubs in Dallas and has the reputation of being a homosexual . . . . *Ruby says no one was associated with him and denies having made the telephone call to our Dallas office last night. He says he . . . guessed his grief over the killing of the President made him insane. That was a pretty smart move on his part because it might lay the foundation for a plea of insanity later. I dispatched to Dallas one of my top assistants in hope that he might stop the Chief of Police and his staff from doing so damned much talking on television.* They really did not have a case against Oswald until we gave them our information. . . . All the Dallas police had was three witnesses who tentatively identified him. . . . Oswald had been saying he wanted John Abt as his lawyer and Abt, with only that kind of evidence, could have turned the case around, I'm afraid. All the talking down there might have required a change of venue. . . . If they keep on talking, perhaps the same will be true of Ruby . . . . *Curry I understand cannot control Captain Fritz* . . . who is giving much information to the press. Since we now think it involves the Criminal Code on a conspiracy charge under Section 2-11, *we want them to shut up.* Furthermore, I have ordered the evidence be secured by the Police Department. . . . *The thing I am most concerned about, and so is Mr. Katzenbach, is having something issued so we can convince the public that Oswald is the real assassin.* Mr. Katzenbach thinks that the President might appoint a Presidential Commission of three outstanding citizens to make a determination. I countered with a suggestion that we make an investigative report to the Attorney General with pictures, laboratory work, etc. Then the Attorney General can make the report to the President and the President can decide whether to make it public. . . . *We have no information on Ruby that is firm, although there are some rumors of underworld activity in Chicago"* (emphasis added).[142]

Hoover calls Johnson aide Walter Jenkins, telling him, "The thing I am most concerned about, and so is Mr. Katzenbach, is having something issued so we can convince the public that Oswald is the real assassin."[143] Note also the fact Hoover's memo makes clear the point that he is aware from the start that some entity is behind Ruby.

Dallas FBI, Shanklin presumably, speaks with District Attorney Wade regarding the evidence against Oswald, all in the context of "having something issued so we can convince the public that Oswald is the real assassin."[144]

"Ryder [of the Irving Sports Shop] had become known to the Dallas Police on Sunday . . . (a few hours after Oswald was shot to death) as the result of an anonymous telephone call to [the FBI and] a television newscaster informing [them] that Oswald had had a rifle sighted . . . at a gun shop . . . in Irving, Texas." ". . . Ryder, 'presented this [repair] tag to agents of the FBI' on November 25. . . ."[145]

Wade, following Assistant A.G. Miller's instruction, calls a news conference and makes his case against Oswald, couching him in the category of a lone nut. "I would say without any doubt [Oswald] was the killer of President Kennedy. . . . There's no doubt in my mind we would have convicted him. I've sent people to the electric chair on less. . . . Q. 'What about the paraffin tests?' A. Yes, I've got paraffin tests that showed he had recently fired a gun—it was on both hands. Q. 'On both hands?' A. Both hands. Q. 'Recently fired a rifle[?]' . . . A. A gun. . . . Q. 'You talked with the FBI this morning. Did you leave the rest with the FBI?' A. I won't go—I'm not at liberty—to go into the FBI report."[146] Note the distinction he makes between a gun (i.e., pistol) and a rifle. The reporters also are obviously bewildered by the statement that the paraffin test showed positive for *both* hands. Wade is obviously fearful of incriminating himself by publicly falsifying the results of the test. Shanklin, however, under direct pressure from Hoover, has no such difficulty. Press: "Gordon Shanklin . . . said today . . . a paraffin test, used to determine whether a person has fired a weapon recently, was administered to Oswald shortly after he was apprehended Friday, one hour after the assassination. It showed that particles of gunpowder from a weapon, probably a rifle, remained on Oswald's cheek and hands."[147] With this knowingly false statement Shanklin undoubtedly commits a number of federal offenses, obstruction of justice to name just one. Hoover will use such disinformation techniques many times in the coming months.

Dallas police captain Fritz states to the press: "[Oswald] . . . said absolutely nothing before or after he was shot. . . . the case is closed. . . ."[148]

"Ferrie spoke with Gill by telephone, on the evening of the day Ruby killed Oswald, but did not immediately report to the authorities. When he finally did so next day, Ferrie turned up accompanied by the Marcello lawyer. He denied knowing anything about Oswald or the assassination."[149] The two discuss an alibi for Ferrie's whereabouts during the actual assassination. Despite his distance from the actual mechanics of the killing, Ferrie must be very much afraid at this point, not realizing that Hoover will not allow him to be implicated.

8:55 P.M. (EST): Johnson calls Hoover from his private residence.[150] The topic of their conversation is not known. However, based upon what LBJ has learned this day, there is every likelihood he now suspects complicity on the part of Hoover. The Director had attempted to keep him from learning of Oswald's relationship to the Bureau, Oswald himself has just been murdered in an extremely suspicious manner, and Hoover has, only hours ago, told him he wanted a statement issued so that the public could be *convinced* that Oswald was "the real assassin." Through Wade, Curry, and the Dallas FBI, this has been done. Add to this Johnson's knowledge, like many people's, of Hoover's bitter hatred of JFK and obvious quest for an Executive Order waiving his retirement, and the implications become obvious. How can Johnson not suspect him? One can only hope that LBJ was no more directly involved in the assassination than aiding Hoover after the fact.

11/25/63—MONDAY: From 7 A.M. to midnight this day Las Vegas casinos are silenced at the order of owners. Today is JFK's funeral.[151]

Press: "Dallas authorities were willing today to make public all their physical evidence connecting . . . Oswald with the murder of President Kennedy, but the revelation was postponed at the suggestion of Federal officials here and in Washington. . . . Curry and . . . Wade, said they would like to place the evidence before the public. Both men added, however, that they would not do so if authorities in Washington wished otherwise."[152]

Denver Post: ". . . Shanklin . . . told the Denver Post Monday the FBI had not questioned Oswald before the assassination. . . . Questions about the matter to local officials of the Secret Service were referred to Washington."[153] Only Johnson can have ordered the Secret Service not to respond.

L.A. Times: Ruby spoke to his sister, apparently on Sunday. Ruby: "Take care of yourself and don't worry. . . . The FBI and the officers are treating me well. I've got friends."[154]

Dallas Morning News: "Officers who searched . . . Oswald's room found a map on which a line marked the path of the bullets which killed President Kennedy and wounded Gov. . . . Connally. . . . This map was apparently the 'major evidence' which . . . Curry reported officers had uncovered. . . . Curry . . . said it definitely linked Oswald to the assassination. . . ."[155]

New York Times: "President Kennedy was a man who exemplified moral leadership, Britain's Chief Rabbi . . . said in London tonight." This statement presumably irks Hoover.[156]

"By Monday, . . . two senior FBI officials had been dispatched to Dallas to supervise the marshaling of evidence for the report to

Johnson that Hoover hoped would stay the mounting clamor for a high tribunal."[157]

10:25 A.M. (EST): Johnson ". . . call[s] [Hoover] regarding editorial in Washington Post regarding Presidential Commission and plans to set up such a commission."[158] This day the White House formally announces Johnson's order for Hoover to investigate the assassination.[159]

This day, whether before or after Johnson's call remains unclear, ". . . Hoover reiterated his views in a memorandum that morning, explaining how he had prevailed upon the editors of *The Washington Post* to kill an editorial calling for a presidential commission: 'we told the *Post* that a . . . full report will be made . . . by either the President or some distinguished jurist. . . .' "[160] A check of the editorial page for November 25 indeed indicates Hoover was successful. This display of power by the Director conveys a double message to Johnson, who is now very much concerned about the growing Baker/Mafia scandal.

The *Washington Daily News* will report the following day: ". . . Johnson talked at least once with . . . Hoover. . . . The FBI chief is said to have told [Johnson] he expects to complete his investigation of both cases this week."[161]

Ferrie, accompanied by Marcello's attorney, turns himself in to local authorities. "When David Ferrie needed an alibi after the assassination, it was Regis Kennedy who lined up with Carlos Marcello himself, and with Marcello's lawyer, to provide the inconsistent alibi."[162] A superficial investigation by the local field office follows, presumably under the direction of both agents Quigley and Regis Kennedy. Ferrie is soon released and the matter dropped. Only Marcello, who had doubtless anticipated the benefits of associating himself with people active in the intelligence community, is not surprised by the Bureau's inaction.

"A report by the chief counsel of the Assassination Committee found that the 'FBI's limited work on the Marcello case may have been attributable to a disturbing attitude on the part of the senior agent who supervised the case, Regis Kennedy.' Regis Kennedy directed much of the New Orleans inquiry after the assassination."[163]

". . . After Ferrie returned to New Orleans and surrendered to the authorities, an agent of the Secret Service asked him: 'Did you loan your library card to Lee Harvey Oswald?' Ferrie replied he had not."[164]

New Orleans FBI interviews Ferrie's boyfriend, Layton Martens. "Gill, the teletype noted, had gone to Ferrie's residence on November 24 and had told Ferrie's roommate, Layton Martens, that when . . . Oswald was arrested by the Dallas Police, Oswald was carrying a library card 'with Ferrie's name on it.' "[165]

As *New York Times* will report: "Oswald appeared at a store in Laredo, Tex., store employees have reported, and bought clothing for $32. Where he got the money is undetermined. Agents of the Federal Bureau of Investigation were in Laredo Monday through Wednesday tracing his activities there because of a receipt from the store dated Sept. 26 that was found among his belongings in Dallas after the assassination."[166]

In New York, a psychiatrist who had examined Oswald as a *child* turns over his files to the FBI. Press will report ". . . a psychiatrist's report in the case had found that Oswald showed schizophrenic tendencies and was 'potentially dangerous.' "[167] Information such as this will be used both by Hoover and the Warren Commission to "convince the public" that Oswald was a "lone nut," and therefore killed the President. Note that in criminal law, without a showing of the requisite intent, a defendant cannot be convicted of a crime such as murder. A person must have the intent to commit the crime. Without it there is no motive. If, however, such a person can be shown to be insane (i.e., "schizophrenic") the need to prove intent is eliminated. He cannot have formulated the intent because he was not sane. But he can still be shown to have committed the offense. The break in the evidentiary chain is ignored by the court. Hence the verdict we are all familiar with, "Not guilty by reason of insanity" (e.g., John Hinkley's attempt on Ronald Reagan). Hoover's and the Commission's logic, by necessity, will become circular. To wit, because Oswald was a communist he was insane. Because he was insane he killed the President. And because he was insane it is not necessary to prove the case against him. In short, the legal basis for not having to prove the crime becomes the proof itself. Of course, courts of law do not allow circular logic as a method by which to convict people. And even diehard Commission member Ford will admit in later years that the group never could find a motive for Oswald's supposed crimes.

Ruby is transferred to the Dallas County Jail. He will remain there until he dies.[168]

"After the assassination the citizen, Harold Reynolds, twice tried and failed to arouse FBI interest [in the Abilene incident, which had occurred on November 17]. [Pedro Gonzalez] left Abilene soon after the assassination and was last heard of in Venezuela."[169]

Rep. Hale Boggs of Louisiana calls for a full-scale congressional inquiry of the assassination.[170]

Wayne January reports the Red Bird Airport incident (see 11/20/63) to the Dallas FBI. "He gave this information to the FBI."[171] Like Reynolds (i.e., Abilene incident), he will be ignored. By this time, Shanklin is known to be very nervous about any information suggesting Oswald was anything more than a lone nut. Given the close communication with Hoover over the last few days (more than at any previous point in his career), such information now would only exacerbate his problems.

FBI prepares a report detailing Ruby's actions prior to shooting Oswald. Hoover sends it to Johnson this day.[172]

New Orleans FBI Agent Wall prepares a report on Arcacha Smith. "The New Orleans FBI . . . obscured Banister's address by referring to it as 531 Lafayette Street. That was, in fact, the side door to 544 Camp Street, an address which just might have sparked interest in Washington."[173] Smith's association with Marcello via Ferrie (i.e., contributions by Marcello) is presumably hidden as well.

11:53 P.M.: RFK and Jackie visit President Kennedy's grave alone. She places a small sprig of lily-of-the-valley on his grave.[174]

11/26/63—TUESDAY: *Washington Daily News* reports three stories. "Three major investigations were developing today into the assassination and the murder of his accused slayer, Lee Harvey Oswald. The inquiries by the FBI, the state of Texas and possibly the Senate Judiciary Committee were expected to reveal all the details surrounding the death of the President to choke off at once any of the inevitable rumors of a 'plot.' As one senator remarked, . . . 'Now is the time to get the whole story (of the Kennedy assassination).' The Justice Department said yesterday it will give whatever aid Texas officials needed in the state's investigation. Texas Atty. General Waggoner Carr announced after President Kennedy's fu-

neral that a 'court of inquiry' would be called to consider the slay-
ings. The court . . . with the power to subpoena witnesses, would
serve to replace the trial of Oswald that never can be held and bring
all the facts to the public. . . . Gov. . . . Connally . . . had no
comment on Mr. Carr's announcement."[175]

Also, "Both . . . Curry and . . . Wade today denied seeing an
'assassination blueprint'—a marked city map showing the President's route and the (bullets') trajectory—reportedly found in Lee
Harvey Oswald's room. . . . Wade said yesterday he understood
the Dallas police department had the map but he had not seen it.
Today, Homicide Lieut. Ted Wells said the map was in . . .
Wade's possession. . . . Wade again denied it. . . . Wells, questioned again, told reporters to refer their questions to . . . Curry.
'I haven't seen the map,' the Chief said. 'In the light of a court of
inquiry, I don't think we should say what we've got at this
time.' "[176]

The third article states, "Two amateur photographers from Dallas . . . have gotten close-up films of the assassination of President
Kennedy. One film . . . bought by Life Magazine for $40,000, is in
color. Of the three copies made by . . . Zapruder . . . one went
to Life, one to the FBI and one to the Secret Service. . . . The FBI
and Secret Service declined comment on the films since they contain
'evidentiary' matter. . . . Persons who saw the color film . . . say
it shows the following sequence: . . . The first of three . . . shots
appears to strike . . . Kennedy in the shoulder or back.
. . . Gov. Connally turns toward the right . . . [and is struck].
. . . Then *a third shot strikes Mr. Kennedy in the head, and he
lurches forward.*"[177] This article may well be disinformation leaked
by the Bureau to precondition the public to the coming release by
Life. Even the most casual viewing of the film immediately reveals
the opposite description of the head shots.

In contrast, the *Boston Record American* runs an article giving
accurate description of the film's content.[178]

The *Chicago Tribune* runs a story today detailing Ruby's Mafia
background from earlier days in that city.[179]

Press: "The investigation of the . . . Baker case is going forward
without interruption despite President Kennedy's assassination,
Senator . . . Jordan said today. 'I see no reason to make any
changes in our plans. . . .' No date has yet been set for the start of

public hearings, but Mr. Jordan has expressed hope they can get under way next month."[180]

Press: "The Senate will make a full investigation of the assassination of President Kennedy. The decision was announced to the Senate tonight by Senator . . . Dirksen . . . the Republican leader. . . . Members of both houses were asking for such an investigation. . . . He said he was speaking out because he wished to give assurance to the country that there would be a Congressional investigation. He said that members of Congress were receiving great numbers of telegrams asking for such an inquiry. . . . There was consultation with the Justice Department before the announcement was made. Mr. Dirksen said that Senate leaders of both parties had approved the move. . . . The first suggestion . . . was made yesterday by Representative Hale Boggs of Louisiana."[181]

Press: "Oswald was in Mexico between Sept. 26 and Oct. 3. While here he applied under his own name for visas both to Cuba and to the Soviet Union. It has been established, however, that his activities in Mexico came to the attention of authorities only after his arrest on Nov. 22 following the shooting of President Kennedy that day in Dallas. . . . All information available indicated that Oswald, after having abandoned his attempts to obtain visas . . . conducted himself more or less as a tourist. He entered the country with a 15-day tourist permit."[182]

New York Times reports: "The continuing investigation into the assassination . . . has cleared up some questions about the number of shots and how many struck the President. Three shots are known to have been fired. Two hit the President. One did not emerge. Dr. . . . Clark, who pronounced Mr. Kennedy dead, said one struck him at about the necktie knot. 'It ranged downward in his chest and did not exit,' the surgeon said. The second he called a 'tangential wound' caused by a bullet that struck the 'right back of his head.' . . . A third bullet was found in fragments in the car and is presumed by official sources to be the one that coursed through . . . Connally. . . . Dallas authorities announced that they were turning over all evidence in the assassination to the Federal Bureau of Investigation. They acted at the request of Federal authorities after the White House said . . . that a broad inquiry was being made into events here during the last few days. . . . Normally, the evidence would be held by District Attorney Henry Wade. An assistant district attorney, Bill Alexander, disclosed that among the books and papers found in Oswald's room Friday afternoon were letters written him from New York on Communist Party of America letterheads. Mr. Alexander said the letters . . . showed a 'working friendly relationship' between Oswald and the party. . . . He said he saw the letters before they were turned over to the FBI along with other personal effects found in Oswald's room. . . . *A strip of color movie film taken by a Dallas clothing manufacturer with an 8-mm camera tends to support [the following] sequence of events.* The film covers about a 15-second period . . . . *The President was struck . . . The President turned toward Mrs. Kennedy as she began to put her hands around his head. At the same time . . . Connally, riding in front of the President, turned to see what had happened. Then the President was struck in the head. His head went forward, then snapped back, as he slumped in his seat. At that time, Governor Connally was wounded.* . . . Police Chief Jesse Curry issued a statement today denying any negligence in Oswald's death. He said he received a telephone call at 7 A.M. Sunday from a police officer advising him that the department had received a tip that Oswald would be killed while being transferred from the city to the Dallas County Jail. . . . A hospital spokesman said the medical record of President Kennedy's assassination, written in longhand by Dr. Clark, chief of neurosurgery at Parkland, had been given to the Secret Service and the hospital had no copy. . . . The Communist Party of the U.S.A., made the following comment. . . . 'We get many letters every week from people who are not Communists including students, faculty members and others. . . . Publishers of The Militant . . . said yesterday that they had found Oswald had been briefly a subscriber. A spokesman said Oswald had sent in $1 for a four-month subscription in December, 1962, and renewed this for another four months at $1, expiring in September, 1963, with no further communication indicated in the records. . . . The American Civil Liberties Union said . . . it had found that Oswald sent it a $2 cash contribution on Nov. 4 along with a filled-out membership application. The newly found paper . . . had been sent to the Department of Justice" (emphasis added).[183]

Press: "A special court of inquiry into the assassination of President Kennedy will be held in Dallas, probably within a month, the Attorney General of Texas said tonight. . . . 'We hope a public hearing will emphasize and demonstrate to the world and the people of Texas that nothing has been covered up or tainted and no effort has been made on behalf of public officials to conspire or mislead or cover up. . . .' Herbert Miller, chief of the Criminal Division of the United States Department of Justice, pledged full cooperation of the Federal Government. Mr. Miller said that the court of inquiry was necessary to 'make sure all the facts are brought into the open and made a public record.' . . . All evidence obtained by the Federal Bureau of Investigation, Mr. Miller said, will be made available to the court. The FBI is still working on the case. . . . Mr. Carr also said: 'No one has said that all the evidence has been made public at this point. . . . We want to find out who did what and when.' "[184]

Press: "The European press, Communist and non-Communist, voiced suspicions today that the entire truth had not been told. . . . There was widespread condemnation of the Dallas Police Department . . . and expressions of indignation at what The London Daily Telegraph called the 'monumental absurdity' of Dallas homicide Capt. Will Fritz's declaration that the Kennedy case was closed with Oswald's death. The Hamburg Die Welt said the police handling of the Kennedy and Oswald cases left a 'forest of question marks.' The Lisbon Diario Popular spoke of 'too many mysterious facets.' The London Daily Mail told of 'whispers' that Oswald was a tool who was liquidated. . . . In Germany The Hamburger Echo said, 'Dallas police had an understandable interest in producing any suspect as quickly as possible, while the rest of the country doubts that Oswald was the only or even the real assassin.' It said Oswald's murder raised suspicions that 'would make Kennedy's assassination a gang plot.' "[185]

Press: "Three brothers and two nephews of Carmine Lombardozzi, an underworld figure, were found guilty . . . of atrocious assault on a special agent of the Federal Bureau of Investigation. . . . The FBI agent, John P. Foley, was beaten while on duty taking photographs outside a Brooklyn church at the requiem mass on April 3 for Carmelo Lombardozzi, father of the brothers."[186]

Press: "Johnson . . . moved into the oval office in the White House today."[187] This same day Johnson and Senator Russell lunch together.[188] Presumably the idea of a commission is discussed. Over the course of the next six months the two will talk almost daily.[189]

". . . Memo by Texas Attorney General Waggoner Carr: Mr. Fortas informed me that he has been assigned to coordinate the

FBI, Department of Justice and Texas Attorney General's efforts regarding the assassination. . . ."[190] Fortas will withdraw as Bobby Baker's defense counsel. He will also be, under Johnson, the only U.S. Supreme Court Justice forced to resign under cloud of corruption.[191]

This day Wade turns all evidence over to the FBI because ". . . he thought it would be good to have the FBI do it and get it out of the hands of the state for the time being."[192]

Ruby is indicted for the murder of Oswald.[193]

As detailed in *Mafia Kingfish*, ". . . Johnson met with CIA Director McCone and told him that the FBI had primary responsibility for the investigation. . . . He . . . gave out word that talk of conspiracy should be discouraged by the media and law-enforcement agencies, . . . Katzenbach sent a message . . . to Presidential Assistant Bill Moyers as follows: It is important that all the facts surrounding President Kennedy's assassination be made public in such a way which will satisfy people in the United States and abroad that all the facts have been told. . . .

1. The public must be satisfied that Oswald was the assassin; that he did not have confederates who are still at large; and that the evidence was such that he would have been convicted at trial.
2. Speculation about Oswald's motivation ought to be cut off, and we should have some basis for rebutting thought that this was a . . . right-wing conspiracy. . . ."

". . . On the 26th Hoover received a long teletype from the New Orleans FBI about the interrogation of David Ferrie. . . . It . . . [told] . . . of Ferrie's association with the violently anti-Castro Cuban Revolutionary Council and of his employment by Carlos Marcello's attorney G. Wray Gill. Gill, the teletype noted, had gone to Ferrie's residence on November 24 and had told Ferrie's roommate, Layton Martens, that when . . . Oswald was arrested by the Dallas Police, Oswald was carrying a library card 'with Ferrie's name on it.' The teletype concluded with a sketchy account of Ferrie's recent trip to Texas, Ferrie's assertions that he did not know Oswald, and his contention that from the 'end of August through November 22 he had been working on the case involving Carlos

Marcello' . . . and was with Marcello in federal court at the moment Kennedy was assassinated.

"Hoover's reaction . . . was to order the . . . investigation of Ferrie continued, then to publicly stand by Katzenbach's morning message to Moyers, which he, Hoover, had drafted. . . ."[194]

This same day Evans states in a memo to Belmont: "Katzenbach noted. . . . There have also been allegations that Oswald and Ruby were known to each other and were part of a conspiracy. It has been further alleged that Oswald was killed to silence him. . . . *It is [Katzenbach's] belief there might have to be some so-called editorial interpretation.* He noted that the report will be subjected to the closest scrutiny by the worldwide press and foreign government representatives, as well as the American people. *He knew that we were keeping this in mind in preparation of the report. . . . The problem is to show motive and this . . . is a condition of Oswald's mind. . . . Oswald has admitted he was an avowed Marxist. . . . While neither the White House nor the Department should be able to contend that our report does not meet the required purpose, we must be factual and recognize that a matter of this magnitude cannot be fully investigated in a week's time"* (emphasis added). Hoover comments in the margin, "Just how long do you estimate it will take? It seems to me we have all the basic facts now."[195] In effect, Evans, a man supposedly cut out of the loop by Hoover, is saying the Department of Justice wants them to falsify their report by denying there was a conspiracy, and at the same time wrongly implicate Oswald as a lone nut. And Hoover, almost comically, pressures the two by telling them to produce a false report in less time than they think they can safely do so.

FBI (Dallas) report is generated regarding Mrs. R. E. Arnold's assertion she had seen Oswald on the first floor of the Depository between 12:15 and 12:20 P.M.[196] This apparently catches Hoover's eye, as he will have different agents obtain a contradictory statement from her on 3/18/64. At that time she will state, "I did not see Lee Harvey Oswald at the time President Kennedy was shot." She will not be called as a Commission witness.[197]

FBI report 44-24016-255 is generated regarding Ruby's meeting with Traficante while the latter was in a Havana jail, per fellow inmate John Wilson. "In one of Ruby's notebooks, seized after he shot Oswald, police found the entry 'October 29, 1963—John Wilson—bond.' "[198]

FBI (Dallas) interviews Robert Moore, a Ruby piano player. "Moore, who had worked . . . in a store owned by Civello . . . said 'Ruby was a frequent visitor [at Civello's store] and [an] associate of Civello. . . .' "[199] Civello/Marcello associate Campisi will visit Ruby in jail on November 30.

11/27/63—WEDNESDAY: Press: "Henry M. Wade . . . said today he did not believe the story of . . . Ruby that he had killed . . . Oswald to avenge the assassination of President Kennedy. 'It . . . may have involved something far deeper. . . . Our law enforcement agencies are still checking to determine if links exist between Oswald and Ruby. . . .' "[200]

Washington Daily News: ". . . Curry is quietly conducting a probe to find out if one or more of his own officers could have been an accomplice in the murder of . . . Oswald. . . . Curry is not discounting the possibility that one or more of his officers could have 'aided Ruby in his scheme.'. . . He said he will not make the report of his findings public, but will turn it over to . . . Wade."[201]

Boston Record American: "In regards to the continuing investigation . . . [Curry] said he wanted to talk to . . . Carr and the FBI before turning over any evidence. 'So far, I haven't talked to either,' he said."[202]

"The French press continued today to show tremendous interest in the details of the assassination. . . . It carried a headline that read 'Oswald cannot have been alone in shooting.' . . . Questions asked in the street were: 'Who was really responsible for the assassination? Is there a secret organization opposing desegregation behind it all?' Paris-Jour said, 'the proofs of the guilt of Oswald divulged by the Dallas, Tex., justice authorities are not convincing.' *A correspondent of the evening newspaper Paris Presse wrote from Dallas that the Federal Bureau of Investigation had said that Oswald had an accomplice beside him at the window who helped him to fire.* . . . 'The behavior of this dubious person [Ruby] at the time of the assassination remains unexplained'. . . . [Tass] The conviction is growing in America proper that it was not Oswald who assassinated the President, but somebody else, carefully protected by the Dallas police. The prominent American lawyer [Emile Zola] Berman, who carefully studied the clues advanced by the police against Oswald, arrived at the conclusion that they do not prove Oswald's implication in the terroristic act. Many people are suspicious of the energy with which the Texas lawyers are coming out in behalf of Oswald's murderer, the gangster Ruby" (emphasis added).[203] Although Soviet reporting during this time period is biased, it is interesting that its basic thrust, like much of the foreign press, is to suggest complicity by the Mafia. Obviously, foreign journalists will have a more objective, less emotional perspective.

"CBS producer Peter Noyes recalls a conversation he once had with . . . a former member of the NBC television camera team that had covered the murders of the President and Oswald. Sometime toward the middle of the week of November 25, as interest in Ferrie was reaching a crescendo in New Orleans and Dallas, *the NBC man had a discussion about Ferrie's links to Oswald and Marcello with a group of FBI agents and newsmen that he remembered everyone found most provocative. However, the FBI soon put a damper on his interest in the subject. For, immediately after the discussion broke up, one of the agents took him aside and told him that he should never discuss what they had just been talking about with anyone, 'for the good of the country' "* (emphasis added).[204]

Press: ". . . Connally . . . gave the nation tonight the story of the three quick rifle shots that spelled assassination for President Kennedy. . . . Shot One struck the President. Shot Two coursed through the Texas Governor's body. Shot Three struck the President. The Governor said the President 'slumped and said nothing.' . . . He went on: 'We heard a shot. I turned to my left and the President had slumped. He said nothing. As I turned I was hit and I knew I was hit badly. I knew the President had been hit and I said: "My God, they're going to kill us all." Then there was a third shot and the President was hit again.' It was then that Mrs. Kennedy cried out. . . . "[205]

A close associate of Gandhi states to the press: "He said he was fearful that the 'enemies of peace' might have used Oswald as a tool and then 'silenced him.' His reasoning was as follows: Jack Ruby, the slayer of Oswald, appears to be the sort of man who might kill for money rather than ideas—a man with a police record. The Dallas police have sought to close the case with 'unseemly haste.' This also suggested to Mr. Rajagopalachari that there might be 'important money in the background.' Neither the 'lunatic left' nor even southern segregationists have the kind of money required to facilitate a shooting like that done by Ruby and give him confidence of subsequent protection. . . . The Patriot, a daily paper . . . published an editorial headed 'Murder Politics.' The editorial said 'it looks now as though Oswald, who was silenced so quickly, was only an agent. . . . The ease with which a nightclub keeper with a criminal record could get access to a prisoner in police custody and shoot him suggests collusion. . . . Obviously the effort of the Dallas authorities . . . was to insinuate that Oswald was connected with Communism and the Soviet Union. . . . This taken together with the Dallas police chief's haste in declaring that the 'case had been closed' with the killing of Oswald points to the existence of influences bent on changing Mr. Kennedy's policies at whatever cost. . . . We cannot but be conscious of the fact that the man who was assassinated a few days ago was able to show men and women everywhere how to proceed along the path that will lead us to peace.' "[206]

". . . The next day brought in a report of an allegation made to the FBI office in Oakland that linked . . . Ruby to an associate of . . . Marcello's. The report . . . told of the interview with Bobby Gene Moore, in which he reported to an FBI agent that . . . Ruby had 'gangster connections' in Dallas, including Joseph Civello. . . . Hoover knew full well that . . . Civello was boss of the Mafia in Dallas, that he had attended the Mafia Summit meeting in Apalachin in 1957, and that he was . . . Marcello's agent. . . . He had already been informed that Oswald had been friendly with one of Marcello's men in New Orleans. Now Ruby, too, was connected to a Marcello associate. What was Hoover's reaction . . . ? Officially, he ordered the FBI in Dallas to conduct a pro forma interview of . . . Civello, and then he ignored the sinister implications of Moore's allegation entirely."[207]

". . . Ruby . . . had been involved with an anti-Castro gunrunner he identified only as 'Davis.' Ruby's first lawyer had asked him to specify anything that might damage his defense. Ruby responded promptly that there would be a problem if Davis's name should come up. The FBI . . . did not locate Davis for the Commission. . . . Ruby's contact, it turns out, was in Texas FBI files all the time. He was a former bank robber named Thomas Davis, an American criminal not unknown to the CIA. Davis, who had met Ruby at one of his Dallas clubs, had friends—not least, apparently, in American intelligence circles. At the time of the Kennedy assassination Davis was in North Africa. Less than a month later he was in jail in Tangier, being held in connection with the President's murder. According to correspondence between . . . Hoover and the State Department, Moroccan security police thought it necessary to detain Davis 'because of a letter in his handwriting which referred in passing to Oswald and the Kennedy assassination.' "[208]

Press reports: "An unskilled occupation from which he was dismissed for incompetence accounted for about five months of . . . Oswald's time in Dallas last fall and winter. . . . A downtown graphics arts concern hired Oswald last October. He had been referred by the State Employment Commission. He was given a discharge notice late last March and his employment ended early in April. . . . *'He didn't show any competence or hope of developing competence,' he said. Oswald's job was to develop photostatic prints, described by the employer as an 'unskilled occupation.' Oswald seemed to have trouble in producing the exact sizes called for, the employer said.* . . . Oswald, he said, came to work on time, returned from lunch on time and was . . . remote. . . . Oswald's job at the . . . Depository paid about the same. The man who hired him there said he had no complaints about his work, which was menial. *Meanwhile, the Secret Service re-enacted today the assassination. . . . The purpose was 'to test whether it could be done the way we believe it was done,' an official source said.* . . . The consensus was that the shooting began after the President's car had made the turn from Houston Street into Elm Street. . . . *No results of the test were announced"* (emphasis added).[209]

Press reports further on Wade: ". . . Rumors in recent days of friction between himself and the Federal Bureau of Investigation in dealing with the case of . . . Oswald . . . and . . . Ruby. . . . *Mr. Wade is an alumnus of the FBI.* As an agent from 1939 to 1943, he served in Boston, Baltimore and Washington, worked . . . in New York and . . . in South America. . . . *One picture on his office wall is a portrait of . . . Johnson. Another is of . . . Hoover"* (emphasis added).[210]

Washington Evening Star: "Dr. . . . Clark, a brain surgeon who was summoned to the emergency room . . . where the President was taken . . . said in Dallas yesterday that a bullet did such massive damage at the right rear of the President's head that attending surgeons could not tell whether it had entered or come out of the head there."[211]

Press: "Dr. Malcolm Perry, who operated on both President

Kennedy and . . . Oswald, said . . . that there had never been a chance to save the President but that Oswald nearly survived. . . . Said bleeding of Oswald had been controlled and blood pressure restored to normal, when his heart suddenly stopped beating. 'Everything was under control when it happened, . . . We were very close to saving him.' . . . He said he had been eating lunch in the hospital when he was called . . . to treat the President. . . . Dr. Perry performed a tracheotomy—he opened the throat and inserted a tube to prevent fluid from keeping air from the lungs. Another surgeon inserted a tube into the President's chest to keep the lung from collapsing. . . . He said a resident—a first-year doctor—had inserted a tube into the President's trachea, or windpipe, before Dr. Perry or other physicians arrived. . . . 'My initial impression was that he had a mortal wound. . . .' He said he believed the President had two wounds—a massive one in the back of the head and a small, circular wound in the neck" (emphasis added).[212]

Press reports: ". . . Federal Bureau of Investigation agents . . . traced some of the library books [Oswald] . . . read during the summer." He borrowed twenty-seven in all.[213]

Johnson presents his first speech to Congress, RFK attending.[214]

Castro states that Ruby killed Oswald to silence him, calling Ruby "that gangster."[215]

FBI (New Orleans) interviews Caracci. He ". . . denied any contact with Ruby."[216]

11/28/63—THURSDAY: *Washington Daily News:* "Movie cameras whirred at a sixth story window of a warehouse-like building and a Lincoln convertible drove slowly below yesterday as [Dallas] police and FBI agents reconstructed the assassination of President Kennedy."[217]

Johnson makes the decision to establish a presidential commission to investigate the assassination.[218]

"The *classified message about Santos [Traficante] was sent* Thanksgiving Day . . . *from CIA headquarters to: McGeorge Bundy,* President Johnson's special assistant for national security affairs . . . *and the FBI.* The message read:

On 26 November 1963 a British journalist named John Wilson . . . gave information to the American Embassy in London which indicated that an 'American gangster-type named

Ruby' visited Cuba around 1959. . . . In prison in Cuba, Wilson says he met an American gangster gambler named Santos. . . . While Santos was in prison, Wilson says, Santos was visited frequently by an American gangster-type named Ruby.

The next day . . . [November 29] the FBI came up with a preliminary report that . . . John Wilson 'likely be psychopath [*sic*]. We gather he gave this impression when testifying before Eastland Committee in 59' " (emphasis added).[219] Johnson knows nothing about the Aleman/Traficante revelation or the presence of the name John Wilson in Ruby's notebook, no doubt, but note how quickly Hoover moves to discredit this allegation. It is the name association that he fears, if nothing else.

Press reports again on Connally's wounds. " 'The bullet passed completely through his chest, fracturing ribs, collapsing his right lung and causing massive bleeding. . . .' The bullet fractured his right forearm and penetrated his thigh. 'He was on the brink of death. . . .' "[220]

FBI (New Orleans) Teletype to Hoover and Dallas SAC detailing the November 25 revelation that Oswald was carrying Ferrie's library card in his wallet when he was arrested. "Gill remarked to Martens that when . . . Oswald was arrested by the Dallas police, Oswald was carrying a library card with Ferrie's name on it. Gill instructed Martens to tell Ferrie to contact him and Gill would represent Ferrie as his attorney."[221]

FBI (Dallas) sends a report to SOG concerning Civello. "He has known . . . RUBY for about ten years. . . . He was never closely associated with RUBY and last saw him sometime in 1957, to the best of his knowledge. . . . He had no knowledge of RUBY's personality, political or philosophical beliefs and could not furnish any information regarding him. He had no knowledge of . . . OSWALD and therefore knew of no association between RUBY and OSWALD."[222]

". . . Still another allegation mentioning an associate of the Marcellos arrived at headquarters. It was Eugene De Laparra's allegation that in March or April he had overheard Vincent Marcello's friend Ben Tregle say that there was 'a price on the President's head,' and that somebody would kill Kennedy when he came south."[223] Hoover had reportedly heard this story in September 1963. He ignores this second report also.

Press: Johnson takes to the airwaves in an appeal to the public. ". . . I come before you to ask your . . . prayers that God may guard this republic and guide my every labor. . . . *So, in these days, the fate of this office is the fate of us all.* I would ask all Americans in reverence to think on these things. *Let all who speak,* and all who preach, and all who *publish, and all who broadcast,* and all who read or listen, let them *reflect upon their responsibilities to bind our wounds,* to heal our sores, to make our society well and whole for the tests ahead of us. . . . And finally, *to you as your President, I ask that you* remember your country and *remember me each day in your prayers . . .*" (emphasis added).[224] Johnson attempts to use the assassination to gain sympathy for his own situation (i.e., Baker/Mafia scandal) while simultaneously calming the nation. Note his veiled threat to the various media entities.

Press reports: "A gunsmith from Irving, Tex., said today he mounted a telescopic sight on a gun for a man named Oswald about a month ago. The gunsmith, Dial D. Ryder, said he could not remember what the gun looked like, nor could he remember the customer. Mr. Ryder found a receipt showing that he had mounted and adjusted a sight on a gun for a customer named Oswald. There was no date on the receipt, he said, but the work was done about a month ago. The customer paid $4.50 for drilling and $1.50 for boresighting the weapon. . . . He said he believed a close examination of the Oswald weapon would show that he had not done the work. The police and agents of the Federal Bureau of Investigation refused to disclose information about another gun Oswald was supposed to have used to kill . . . Tippit. . . . That weapon, a .38-caliber pistol, has been turned over to the FBI with other evidence in the case. . . . Meanwhile, it appeared that Oswald's employment in a building along the parade route that President Kennedy would travel was happenstance. Statements by persons familiar with the circumstances indicated that Oswald had no way of knowing when he took the job . . . that it would provide a vantage point for assassinating the President. . . . Mrs. Paine said that the sports shop where Mr. Ryder, the gunsmith, works is about three miles from her home. She did not recall Oswald's making a trip to the shop."[225]

Press: "Federal investigators today carried on their painstaking task of re-creating the mind of . . . Oswald. . . . What he did during the months preceding the President's assassination . . . is occupying a team of Federal Bureau of Investigation agents. . . . While in custody, he denied taking any part in the deaths . . . according to the Dallas police. The FBI worked during the Thanksgiving holiday. . . . Johnson asked the agency earlier this week to compile a complete report on all aspects of the assassination as quickly as possible. . . . [Oswald] lost his job at the coffee warehouse on July 19. 'He was never there when we looked for him,' one of his superiors said. . . . Mr. Bringuier said he was about to punch Oswald when the younger man dropped his arms in a gesture of nonviolence. . . . *On Sept. 17 Oswald applied at the Mexican consulate here for a 15-day tourist card. He represented himself as a photographer* who wanted to visit Mexico by bus. The card was granted. . . . At about this time, *Oswald described his 'business address' as 640 Rampart Street. . . . The Louisiana Weekly, a newspaper of the Negro community, is published at 640 South Rampart Street"* (emphasis added).[226] Oswald had obviously picked up on the fact that earlier that year black journalists had been invited to travel to Havana via Mexico City—hence his occupation as that of "photographer," and "business address" as that of a black newspaper's. Note also the parallel to Ferrie's and Banister's Clinton/ CORE smear (i.e., again the association between Oswald, communism, and black unrest).

11/29/63—FRIDAY: Press reports: *Johnson ". . . met with . . . Central Intelligence Agency director, John A. McCone and* Presidential assistant for national security affairs, *McGeorge Bundy. . . ."*[227] One can only assume the CIA memo of the previous day is the topic of conversation. At the least, the impression must now be growing in LBJ's mind that Oswald was merely the victim of a gangland slaying, and that, by implication, the Mafia is now a prime suspect.

This day Johnson creates the Warren Commission. The following excerpt from White House phone logs is a fascinating study in the exercise of power:

11:30 A.M. LBJ calls Hale Boggs.
11:40 A.M. LBJ calls Senator Dirksen regarding House and Senate investigations.

1:11 P.M. Boggs calls LBJ.

1:40 P.M. Hoover calls LBJ. They discuss "Proposed Committee for investigating Dallas affair."[228]

After talking with Johnson, Hoover prepares a memo:

[Johnson] called and asked if I am familiar with the proposed group they are trying to get to study my report—two from the House, two from the Senate, two from the courts, and a couple of outsiders. I replied that I had not heard of that but had seen reports from the Senate Investigating Committee. [Johnson] stated he wanted to get by with just my file and my report. I told him I thought it would be very bad to have a rash of investigations. He then indicated the only way to stop it is to appoint a high-level committee to evaluate my report and tell the House and Senate not to go ahead with the investigation. I stated that would be a three-ring circus. [Apparent deletion] I advised [Johnson] that we hope to have the investigation wrapped up today, but probably won't have it before the first of the week as an angle in Mexico is giving trouble—the matter of Oswald's getting $6500 from the Cuban embassy and coming back to this country with it. . . . He was in Mexico on the 28th [of September].[229]

In the same memo "Hoover recorded that Johnson thought of him, the Director, as 'more than head of the FBI—I [Hoover] was his brother and personal friend; that he knew I did not want anything to happen to his family; that he has more confidence in me than anybody in town.' "[230] Note also how Hoover states that it was Johnson who called him. The obvious attempt to scare LBJ with the reference to Cuba must now seem rather transparent to him. Every indication to this point has implied the Mafia. Such an attempt to manipulate a man so adept at manipulation himself would only confirm his suspicions about the Director.

4:05 P.M.: "Johnson calls Senator Russell in Georgia regarding investigative committee."[231]

4:30 P.M.: Johnson calls Warren. "On the afternoon of November 29 . . . Johnson summoned Earl Warren to the White House, realizing that the Chief Justice had already refused a request that he serve as chairman of the presidential commission, which had been

transmitted to him that morning by Katzenbach. . . . A renowned
. . . manipulator, Johnson was at his best."[232] LBJ browbeats Warren into accepting, the chief justice reportedly leaving the Oval Office in tears. ". . . Rankin . . . said that 'Warren accepted, only
with the greatest reluctance. . . .' "[233]

5:32 P.M.: LBJ calls Hoover.

5:40 P.M.: LBJ calls Dulles.

5:41 P.M.: Hoover calls LBJ.

5:45 P.M.: LBJ calls Senator Cooper.

5:55 P.M.: McCloy calls LBJ.

6 P.M.: LBJ calls Cooper again. "I want you on that commission."

6:52 P.M.: LBJ calls Ford.[234]

7:45 P.M.: Johnson signs the formal order establishing the Warren
Commission. As the press will report the following day "[Johnson]
is instructing the special commission to satisfy itself that the truth is
known as far as it can be discovered. . . ."[235]

8:55 P.M.: LBJ calls Senator Russell again.[236]

". . . As soon as Johnson had appointed his seven commissioners, Hoover . . . ordered his aides to compile secret dossiers on
each member of the Commission, so he would have adequate dirt in
his files, if a need arose."[237] More important, he will also intensify
the systematic destruction, alteration, and withholding of evidence
in order to avoid indictment and prosecution for treason. Hoover's
overall plan regarding the Warren Commission is to: prepare dossiers on Commission members and staff; bypass RFK and report
directly to Johnson; withhold from the Commission anything that
might "embarrass the Bureau"; do not let them know anything of
ELSUR; convince the public that Oswald was a "lone nut"; do not
let Commission know of Oswald's role as a Bureau informer; and
persuade Johnson to aid him in this containment policy.

Recall that Hoover is aware of Dulles's knowledge of the CIA/
Mafia plots to kill Castro.[238] Thus, the ex-CIA director's appointment by Johnson may have encouraged the Director's efforts at
containment.

Assistant FBI Director Sullivan will later state: "Hoover was
delighted when Ford was named to the Warren Commission. The
Director wrote in one of his internal memos that the bureau could
expect Ford to 'look after FBI interests,' and he did, keeping us

fully advised of what was going on behind closed doors. He was our . . . informant on the Warren Commission."[239]

Press will report: "The commission, according to the White House statement, will be instructed 'to evaluate all available information concerning the subject of the inquiry.' It said this would include evidence obtained by the Federal Bureau of Investigation in a special inquiry previously ordered by Mr. Johnson. The FBI report on that investigation is expected to be ready next week. The Attorney General of Texas, Waggoner Carr, has 'offered his cooperation,' the White House said. This means, officials explained, that evidence obtained by a state court of inquiry created by the Attorney General will be made available to the Presidential commission."[240]

". . . Marcello received word around November 29 that the [FBI] had been questioning his associate Caracci and either Pete [Marcello] or Pete's night manager, Nick Grafagninni, about . . . Ruby."[241] In all likelihood, having control over case officer Regis Kennedy, and, like the public at large, having observed the controls Hoover and Johnson are now putting in place, this development does not concern him to any great degree.

Press reports: "The County Medical Examiner said today there was nothing physically wrong with . . . Oswald's brain."[242]

Life magazine, in its regular weekly issue, publishes only thirty-one, out of over four hundred, frames of the Zapruder film. Thirteen are of Jackie *after* the shots are fired (and include the largest photos), and another three are of the motorcade *before* shooting begins, leaving only fifteen for the time span in between. None of these depict the head shots, almost all dealing with Kennedy and Connally reacting to the first and second shots, respectively.[243] Prior to this release *Life*'s photographic experts had repeatedly analyzed the film. They obviously realize what they are doing. Deliberate elimination of the frames revealing the double head shot so as to hide the fact of *frontal* assault will not be made apparent until the Warren Commission prints the entire sequence the following fall. Even then, the two key frames will be reversed so as to obscure their meaning. The hand of Hoover is apparent on this day.

This day Marina is quoted by *Life* magazine. She says, "I love Lee. Lee good man. He didn't do anything."[244] Note that she has not yet been subjected to the totality of FBI pressure, some forty-six interrogation/conditioning sessions in all.[245] Note also the curious role of *Life.* It controls, and has already suppressed (undoubtedly at Hoover's insistence), the key frames of the Zapruder film. It has also been given some form of access to Oswald's wife. Soon it will provide exclusive, impressive photos of the Johnson family's new look.

Press reports: Ruby "visited his sister, Mrs. Eva Grant, at her apartment several times. She described him as very upset over the assassination."[246] And in another article, "[one of Ruby's dancers] had nothing but praise for Ruby, a former associate of gangsters in Chicago. . . ."[247]

Press: "In Austin, State Attorney General Waggoner Carr indicated he would seek testimony of Oswald's widow in a Court of Inquiry. . . . The FBI was checking today to determine whether Oswald practiced firing his rifle before the President was killed. Agents were reported to be investigating several places in Dallas County where bullet-riddled tin cans and silhouette targets were found."[248]

Press: "The Justice Department had planned to make public the FBI's report on its investigation as soon as it was ready. The department said today that it had not received any instructions to the contrary from the White House. It is possible, these officials suggested, that . . . Johnson will order the report turned over to the new Warren Commission. The commission could either make it public or use it as a basis for its own inquiry."[249]

Press reports on the withdrawal of the JFK movie, *PT-109.* It also discusses *The Manchurian Candidate.* ". . . a melodrama about an expert marksman's attempt to shoot a presidential nominee at a national convention. The film was released in October of 1962."[250]

11/30/63—SATURDAY: *New York Times* unwittingly disseminates and gives great credibility to *Life*'s surrealistic falsification of the Zapruder film by publishing six of the frames released: Z233 (JFK after first shot but before Connally hit); Z269 (Connally after hit); Z323 (JFK well after double head shot, in his wife's arms); Z343 (Jackie Kennedy starting to climb out back of car); Z361 (Jackie partially onto trunk of car); and Z371 (Jackie on trunk with Secret Service agent on rear bumper). The last three of the six frames are totally irrelevant as evidence. Z233 and Z269 are of marginal significance, and Z323 is relevant only in conjunction with the immediately preceding frames, which are not shown. The following caption accompanies the frames: "The President's hand moves convulsively as he is shot (1). Gov. John B. Connally Jr. of Texas, on jump seat, turns toward back and is also hit (2). The President falls toward Mrs. Kennedy (3). Mrs. Kennedy cries out as she sees blood flowing from the President's head (4). She scrambles onto the seat searching for help (5). A Secret Service man leaps upon the bumper to protect her and to get her back into the limousine (6)."[251] As late as 1990, *Life* will be touting Hoover as one of the one hundred most important men of the twentieth century.

Life photographer Karsch takes photos of LBJ in the Oval Office.[252]

Dallas Times Herald runs an article alleging that the FBI was the party sending Western Union money to Oswald after his return from Mexico City, thereby asserting that he was a paid informant. "Someone telegraphed small amounts of money to . . . Oswald for several months before the assassination of President Kennedy, it was reported today. The unidentified sender telegraphed Oswald $10 to $20 at a time." They do not realize that it was most likely Ferrie, operating in the guise of a Banister (i.e., FBI) agent, who did this. The article also states that Oswald sent a telegram as well, and that the Bureau will not discuss the matter.[253]

Hoover has by now ordered RFK's hotline returned to Miss Gandy's desk, reportedly stating at the time, "Put that damn thing back on Miss Gandy's desk where it belongs!"[254]

Marcello gambling functionary Campisi visits Ruby in jail. "In December 1963, Campisi told the FBI that he had visited Ruby on November 30, 1963, in the Dallas County Jail, as confirmed by police records."[255] Note this in the context of the FBI interview of Civello only days before. Undoubtedly this day he tells Ruby to keep quiet about the Marcello contract. That this individual meets with Ruby is unquestionably almost immediately relayed to SOG, where his relationship to Civello and Marcello is known. One would presume that Dallas P.D. is recording all of Ruby's conversations at this point, if for no other reason than self-protection.

FBI (Dallas) Agent Barrett files a report telling of the receipt of the Hughes film on November 26.[256] This film, capturing almost the entire sixth floor of the Depository only seconds before Kennedy is shot, clearly reveals the presence of two men in the far right windows. But this is something already known to the Bureau through

affidavits of citizens standing across the street from the building in
the moments before the assassination.

Press: ". . . Oswald . . . underwent a court-ordered psychiatric examination here in 1953, when he was 13 years old. . . .
Judge . . . Kelly, presiding judge of the Family Court, said she
had turned the records over to the Federal Bureau of Investigation.
. . . The report had recommended that Oswald be committed to an
institution for unruly youths, but that the court had rejected the
recommendation. . . . In this period, Oswald is reported to have
suffered some difficulty with his hearing, following a mastoid operation some months earlier. Later this difficulty disappeared."[257]

Press reports on cooperation from the Soviet Union, which
". . . turned over to the State Department today documents that it
believed might be of help in the assassination of President Kennedy.
The documents included official Soviet files concerning the visit of
. . . Oswald . . . to the Soviet Union. The files also include information on Oswald's attempts to obtain visas to the Soviet Union,
both successful and unsuccessful. . . . Judicial silence was swiftly
imposed on the plans of the seven-man investigating commission
appointed by . . . Johnson last night. . . . Warren . . . sought
to reduce the flow of speculation regarding the manner in which the
investigation would be conducted. He did not even inform other
members of the commission of his plans for the preliminary, organization meetings. There was no indication of the identity of the investigative staff members. The only public announcement today
concerning the inquiry was the release of the text of the Executive
Order signed by . . . Johnson at 7:45 o'clock last night."[258]

Press: "There has been speculation as to how Oswald, who always seemed to be in financial straits, could afford to support his
wife and daughters, buy weapons and ammunition, and travel from
New Orleans to Mexico City and then to Dallas. . . . Mrs. . . .
Paine . . . pointed out several ways. . . . He contributed no
money to her for feeding and sheltering his family. . . . . . . He
had continuous income through Texas unemployment compensation. . . . He habitually hitchhiked or traveled by bus. . . . He
incurred little medical expense for his wife and children while they
were at Mrs. Paine's home. . . . Mrs. Paine noted that Oswald
could not drive and had none of the expenses of owning an automobile. She also pointed out that he seldom bought new clothes for
himself or his family and that he left New Orleans without paying

his rent. A report that Oswald purchased $32 worth of clothing in Laredo on Sept. 26 is not true, the Federal Bureau of Investigation said today."[259] Note FBI's assertion, in the face of previously reported facts to the contrary, that Oswald *did not* purchase thirty-two dollars' worth of clothes in Laredo. The press has already picked up on the fact that Oswald was receiving payments through Western Union, and seemed to have unexplained income. Here, the Bureau appears to be scrambling to contain the issue. Otherwise, why would it possibly matter if Oswald had spent money on clothing while on his way to a foreign country?

Press: "It was also learned today that the Louisiana Department of Labor, which administers the unemployment compensation program here, turned over certain files to FBI agents."[260]

12/1/63—SUNDAY: *FBI Law Enforcement Bulletin is released.* Hoover's message, apparently written shortly after President Kennedy's assassination, deals entirely with immorality. This message is in stark contrast to the previous thirty-four.

ARE WE AMERICANS ASHAMED to be identified today with decency and morality? Are we forsaking the time-tested principles upon which our great country was founded for a substandard, more accommodating code of conduct?. . . . It is high time righteous, freedom-loving people take a closer look at what is happening to our moral standards. Morality is one of the more perplexing and controversial problems facing our Nation. Why? Primarily, it is because of . . . moral cowardice. . . . We do not have the courage to stand in conflict with the mad rush for material wealth, indulgence, and social prestige. . . . The lack of morality and integrity stems from a false sense of values. Many persons are so preoccupied with selfishness and greed they no longer know—nor care for that matter—where honor stops and dishonor commences. . . . *Rationalization and double standards have so clouded some moral principles that right and wrong are no longer clearly distinguishable. . . . Immorality . . . is . . . reflected . . . in payoffs to politicians . . . in voting frauds.* . . . Some theorists suggest our moral standards be scrapped for a less restrictive code by which our moral derelictions can be justified. Such thinking is a flight from responsibility and an accelerant to further moral decadence. If the destruction of our great Nation itself were the goal of these advocates, they could not devise a better means to achieve it. . . . Let us as God-loving people shoulder our moral responsibilities, not flee from them. . . . Let us assure that it may always be said of our country, "America is great because she is good" (emphasis added).[261]

Consider that Hoover's last public statement prior to the assassination (November 16 before the Catholic Youth Organization), and his first after, both deal almost exclusively with the subject of "immorality" as he defines it. He speaks of Kennedy here as if he had been merely symptomatic, part of a larger problem. Hoover's 10/9/62 speech and brief eulogy of JFK on November 22, as will shortly be seen, correlate with this theme (see 12/4/63).

Press: ". . . Hoffa declared last night that Attorney General . . . Kennedy would no longer be able to crusade against him. 'Bobby Kennedy is out. . . .' "[262]

Dallas Morning News continues its story on the Oswald-Western Union incident.[263]

Regarding the New Orleans Bolton Ford incident, dealer: "[Oscar] Deslatte found a docket showing that a prospective purchaser named Oswald had negotiated to buy Ford trucks two years previously. The FBI expressed an interest and took possession of the old docket, carefully enclosed in a fingerprint cover."[264] Of course, Hoover has known of this incident since 1/20/61, as well as of Banister's probable involvement in the affair.

Press: ". . . Johnson paid a visit to John F. Kennedy's grave today. . . ."[265]

Press reports on Oswald's mother: " 'I want another question answered. . . . Why would a known underworld character be allowed within a few feet of a prisoner—of any prisoner.' . . . She insisted that on the night of Nov. 23, about 17 hours before Ruby shot her son, an agent from the Federal Bureau of Investigations [*sic*] showed her Ruby's photograph. . . . The FBI would officially make no comment. . . . It was understood, however, that Federal agencies had acknowledged that she had been shown a photograph that night for identification, but spokesmen would not disclose whether it was that of Ruby. . . . This is Mrs. Oswald's account of the incident. 'About 6:30 P.M., Saturday night, an FBI agent, with another man, presumably another agent, came to our door at the

Executive Inn in Dallas. The agent said, "May I talk to your daughter-in-law?" I said, "Not until we have seen a lawyer." Then he took out a photograph and held it in his cupped hand. "Tell me one thing," he asked me. "Have you ever seen this man before?" . . . [when shown a newspaper photo of Ruby on the following Monday] I said, "This is the man the agent showed me a picture of." Then I was told that that was the man who shot my son. . . . I cannot be mistaken. I will never forget that face. I think it is more likely that the FBI was investigating and heard rumors that he [Ruby] might shoot my son.' . . . She said her son told her, 'Don't worry, Mother. Don't interfere. I can handle this. I know my rights.' "[266] Because Ruby may well have been the subject of ELSUR (through either McWillie or Roselli/Traficante) earlier in 1963, Marguerite Oswald's assertion regarding the photograph cannot be dismissed out of hand.

"Katzenbach and Kennedy never received any of the conspiracy allegations involving associates of the Marcellos. Nor did they receive transcripts of any of the taped conversations the FBI had made of various Mafia bosses threatening the lives of the Kennedy brothers in 1962 and 1963."[267]

Press reports again on Ruby, now routinely referring to him as a ". . . 52-year-old former associate of gangland figures in Chicago. . . ."[268]

Press: "Across the street is a grassy knoll where citizens from Texas and many other states have strewn hundreds of wreaths. It is beside the highway where President Kennedy was shot a week ago Friday. The crowds have never stopped coming."[269]

Press reports: ". . . Oswald was a 'loner' who did not have friends in the Marines, a Milwaukee man who served with him said here today. . . . He remembers Oswald as quiet, serious, and 'trying to find himself,' Mr. Felde said. . . . I didn't know the names of Senators or where they were from, but he could rattle them off and he knew their ideals and what they stood for. . . . *He also said he did not recall that Oswald had been exceptionally good on the rifle range"* (emphasis added).[270] In fact, he had been considered the joke of the platoon in this regard.

Press: "Two nationally known psychiatrists today began examinations of Jack Ruby in the Dallas County Jail. . . . The psychiatric examinations may provide the basis for Ruby's defense at his murder trial, scheduled for Feb. 3. If a jury finds he was insane, he could go free. . . . Agents of the Federal Bureau of Investigation questioned Ruby in the presence of Mr. Belli. On the attorney's instructions, Ruby volunteered to submit to lie-detector or 'truth serum' tests for the FBI."[271] Hoover will, in the coming months, oppose the submission of Ruby to such tests, asserting that they are "unreliable."[272]

12/2/63—MONDAY: ". . . Ruth Paine turned over to the [Dallas] police some of the Oswalds' belongings, including a Russian volume entitled 'Book of Useful Advice.' In this book was an undated note written in Russian."[273] This is Oswald's (April 1963) note about leaving Dallas. As part of the ongoing effort to frame Oswald, in the coming days Marina will "confess" Lee's involvement in the attempt on General Walker.[274] But she will also go on record as stating that Oswald had contemplated hijacking a plane from Dallas to Cuba in early 1963.[275]

FBI (Savannah) files report with SOG on reinterview of informant Sumner regarding Town and Country (a Marcello restaurant) incident in early 1963 involving an Oswald look-alike. "SV T-1 advised this photograph resembles the individual he observed one night at the Town and Country Restaurant in New Orleans between February 15, 1963, and March 15, 1963. The restaurant owner joined the couple at their table and SV T-1 observed the restaurant owner remove a wad of money from his pocket which he passed under the table to the man sitting at the table [who resembled Oswald]."[276] Note that like others who saw Oswald in places and circumstances when he was known to be elsewhere, the man only "resembled" the real Oswald.

Press: "A Houston lawyer with a record as a war crimes prosecutor was named today as special counsel for a state Board of Inquiry that will investigate the assassination of President Kennedy. Mr. Carr said the Board . . . would meet in Austin or Dallas after the Federal Bureau of Investigation has completed its investigation of the assassination, the slaying of . . . Tippit and the subsequent fatal shooting of . . . Oswald. . . . 'The facts are then to be transmitted to the newly appointed Presidential commission for its use in preparing its report,' Mr. Carr said. . . ."[277]

Press: "A spokesman for the Federal Bureau of Investigation denied tonight that Mrs. Marguerite Oswald was shown a picture of Jack Ruby, . . . at any time prior to the shooting."[278]

Press: ". . . Oswald made below-average grades when he was a junior high school student . . . but his instructors saw no evidence of maladjustment. . . . As Oswald . . . prepared to enter senior high school . . . he was asked to fill out a personal history form. . . . He described his general health as good, and recalled only one health condition that would be likely to remain: 'abnormal eardrum in left ear.' " The article quotes individuals who were administrators at the time. "I handled 90 per cent of the routine disciplinary cases. . . . We called the kids who were troublemakers 'characters.' If he had been a 'character,' I would have remembered him. As it was, I didn't remember. His name never came up."[279]

Press: "The Mexican Ministry of the Interior disclosed that the results of its intensive police investigation had indicated that Oswald came here alone. . . . Indeed few mysteries remained as to Oswald's trip here. . . . Sebastian Perez Hernandez, desk clerk, said Oswald had arrived alone and had left early in the mornings and come back late at night. He had no visitors."[280]

Hoover leaks the following investigative "conclusion" to the press: "The Federal Bureau of Investigation hopes to send to . . . Johnson this week its report on the assassination of President Kennedy and the subsequent slaying of the man accused of firing the fatal shots. It will be a narrative account in minute detail of the events surrounding the two deaths. If it follows the pattern of other FBI investigative reports, it will stick to positive statements of what happened, dismissing baseless rumors by not mentioning them. Much of the report will be a repetition of accounts that already have appeared in the press. It is expected to state that . . . Oswald, acting alone, killed Mr. Kennedy, and that . . . Ruby, acting alone, shot Oswald. How the report will be made public is up to Mr. Johnson. He has promised the public every detail."[281]

Press: "Abe Fortas, the Washington lawyer who has been representing . . . Baker, is withdrawing as counsel because of the advisory role he is playing in the Johnson Administration. Mr. Fortas is an old friend of . . . Johnson's. . . . He has been not only a friend but also a lawyer to Mr. Johnson in the past."[282]

"Ten days after the assassination, an FBI listening device picked up Charles 'Chuckie' English . . . , one of . . . Giancana's underbosses, expressing the mob's relief to his boss: 'I will tell you something, in another two months from now, the FBI will be like it was five years ago. They won't be around no more. They say the FBI will get it [the investigation of Kennedy's murder]. They're gonna start running down Fair Play For Cuba, Fair Play For Matsu. They call that more detrimental to the country than us guys.' "[283]

12/3/63—TUESDAY: FBI (Las Vegas) agents Doyle, Barrett, and Holland file separate reports confirming Ruby's presence there on the weekend of 11/16–17/63.[284]

Hoover leaks to press: "An exhaustive FBI report now nearly ready for the White House will indicate that . . . Oswald was the lone and unaided assassin of President Kennedy, Government sources said today."[285]

Secret Service Chief Rowley: "Dec. 3, 1963, at 5 P.M., delivered to Orin Bartlett, FBI, this date [two .38 caliber shells taken from the revolver . . . of Lee Harvey Oswald at time of his arrest by Dallas police. The remaining revolver ammunition (expended) is in the hands of the FBI. The Dallas Police Department have retained one unexpended shell in their Property Room]."[286] Handling of evidence in such piecemeal fashion, by different agencies, is, as stated by researcher Harold Weisberg (*Whitewash* series): "Hardly the best way for bullets of various manufacture to be traced."[287] Standard ballistics tests have by this point precluded the use of Oswald's revolver in the killing of Tippit.[288] The Warren Commission will attempt to rely, instead, on the empty shell casings "recovered" by Dallas P.D. at the scene.[289] As made apparent by this Secret Service report, the evidentiary handling of the ammunition is suspect. Courts will quickly dismiss an otherwise airtight prosecution if breaks in the chain of possession appear with regard to critical evidence. As revealed in Lane's *Rush to Judgment,* the empty shell casings the Warren Commission received from the Dallas P.D. were not the ones collected, and *initialed,* by the officer at the scene of Tippit's killing (i.e., those turned over to the Commission were free of initialing).[290]

Press: "The special commission to investigate the assassination of President Kennedy will hold its first meeting Thursday in the National Archives Building. This was announced today by Chief Justice Earl Warren, chairman. . . . Meanwhile, it was learned officially, the report of the Federal Bureau of Investigation 'probably' will say that . . . Oswald acted alone in firing the three shots that killed Mr. Kennedy and seriously wounded . . . Connally. . . . This has been a crucial point whether Oswald acted without accomplices in planning and executing the assassination. . . . It was learned that several high-ranking department officials, who will review the report before it is transmitted to the White House, had not yet seen it. . . . The Chief Justice . . . said the closed meeting, at 10 A.M., would deal largely with organization and the establishment of procedures. The investigation is expected to last weeks or months. . . . Agents confirmed that the FBI report would 'almost certainly' detail the circumstances of two warnings to the Dallas police that Oswald's life would be threatened. The warnings, received in the Dallas FBI office through anonymous telephone calls, were relayed to the city police and the Dallas County sheriff's office on the morning of Nov. 24, the day Oswald was shot. The FBI said that J. Gordon Shanklin, an agent, phoned the Dallas police at 2:15 A.M. and again at 8:15 that morning, relaying a report on the death threat directly to Police Chief Jesse Curry during the second call. . . . Officials of the Fort Worth Press Club reported . . . that 10 or 12 men who said they were 'in the White House party' visited the club bar early on Nov. 22. They were described as 'drink-nursers' and 'completely sober.' Treasury officials indicated that the agents involved had been on the night shift of the Presidential detail. They had just been relieved and were not expected to go on duty again until the following night, when Mr. Kennedy was scheduled to go to Austin. . . ."[291]

Press: "Attorney General Waggoner Carr slowed plans today for a Texas court of inquiry on the assassination. He said he sought to prevent the inquiry from running into the FBI's and possibly causing 'damage.' . . . Mr. Carr said he wanted to hold the court 'as fast as we can.' "[292]

Press: "The Mexican investigation has so far indicated that Oswald came here alone last September in an unsuccessful quest for Cuban and Soviet visas. . . . He said he was a friend of Cuba and the Soviet Union. The consul general replied that Cuban routine required that Oswald show a visa from the country of destination first, no matter what that destination. Oswald reportedly became violent in language to the point at which the consul was said to have told him that if it were up to the consul, he would not grant a visa to Oswald. As Oswald left, he slammed the consulate door."[293]

Press: "From motion pictures of the President's assassination . . . authorities have concluded that the three shots were fired over a period of five to five and one-half seconds. But that period is calculated from the moment when the first bullet was fired. . . .

Further evidence—which also tends to discount the notion of another assassin—shows that all three bullets came from the same rifle. . . . The ballistics evidence was developed during a test on the weapon at the Federal Bureau of Investigation Laboratory in Washington. The result of the test was announced two days after the assassination on the day Oswald was slain. . . . But some persons have continually expressed skepticism that one man could have fired the three bullets so rapidly."[294] This article, which completes the lone-nut interpretation, shows the degree to which the public and media are being blinded by Hoover early on. Obviously this reporter has been given a summarized *scoop* by the FBI or those sympathetic to Hoover's conclusions. The article says nothing of the dramatic backward head snap of Kennedy or the crowd reaction to activity on the grassy knoll. It is a perfect example of press naïveté during this period.

Press: "The trial of . . . Ruby . . . was postponed today until Feb. 3. Judge . . . Brown . . . ordered the delay after attorneys for Ruby and the state said their cases could not be prepared earlier. . . . Nor is there any indication that Oswald and Ruby . . . had ever met. . . . A former master of ceremonies at Ruby's . . . club, the Carousel, has been quoted as saying he thought he saw Oswald there a week or so before the assassination. . . . Ruby seemed devastated [immediately after the assassination, a club employee] said, and had gone without food and sleep. . . . Ruby has a police record that includes two cases of carrying concealed weapons. . . . He was well known to the police force and seemed to cherish association with policemen. Ruby has also had several scrapes with the Internal Revenue Service. . . . Recently . . . he moved into a new, well-appointed apartment building."[295]

Press: "Oswald was a child of average intelligence and low achievement, who responded to any interest or affection shown him at school, his teachers said today. . . . In class, he was a slow-reader and a poor speller. He joined reluctantly in the games of other children. But he gave no indication of severe emotional problems."[296]

Press: ". . . Johnson will hold no news conference this week the White House said today. There was also no indication when he would. The White House press secretary, Pierre Salinger, said no decision had been made on whether Mr. Johnson would permit live radio and television coverage of news conferences."[297]

12/4/63—WEDNESDAY: Press: "The President's motorcade route was not made firm until Nov. 19, three days before the
fatal ride. However, anyone with a knowledge of Dallas could have
determined from previously published information that the logical
route would take the President past the Texas State School Book
Depository, which provided a perfect vantage point for the rifleman. . . . In fact, quirks of fate and strange coincidences seem to
have contributed far more toward setting the circumstances of the
murder."[298]

Press: "Theodore Voorhees, chancellor-elect of the Philadelphia
Bar Association, said today that Lee H. Oswald had been
'lynched.' "[299]

Press: "Attorney General Robert F. Kennedy returned to his job
today. The 38-year-old brother of President Kennedy had been resting with his wife and friends in Florida since a few days after the
assassination. . . . He was carrying a small framed picture as he
entered his office in the Justice Department. But it could not be
learned immediately what was in the frame."[300] Shortly after the
assassination, he had said to his press secretary, [Edwin O.] Guth-
man, "I thought they might get one of us, but Jack, after all he'd
been through, never worried about it. . . . I thought it would be
me."[301]

"FBI memorandum from Sullivan to Belmont indicates there is
no evidence that Oswald's assassination of the President was in-
spired or directed by (pro-Castro) organizations or by any foreign
country."[302]

"On December 4 . . . an undeliverable package addressed to
'Lee Oswald' was retrieved from the dead-letter section of a post
office in a Dallas suburb. It was wrongly addressed to 601 W. Nas-
saus St., which could approximate to Neches Street, which was near
where Oswald had lived. When opened, it turned out to contain a
'brown paper bag made of fairly heavy brown paper which bag was
open at both ends.' Since no postal worker is likely to have tossed
aside a package addressed to 'Lee Oswald' after the name became
world famous . . . it is reasonable to assume the parcel arrived
before the assassination."[303] This package remains unexplained.
Some will theorize that it was sent to Oswald by the same people
who tricked him into bringing a bag into the Depository on November 22.

Texas A.G. Carr arrives in D.C. for a meeting with Katzenbach.

He will meet "briefly" with Hoover on Friday. Carr is persuaded, undoubtedly by Johnson (through Fortas) and FBI officials, to drop the Texas inquiry.[304]

Marina agrees to an interview with the press, but it is called off by the Dallas FBI.[305]

Press: "Robert G. Baker . . . has a new lawyer. The firm of Edward Bennett Williams, who is one of the country's noted criminal lawyers, said today that Mr. Baker had retained the services of Mr. Williams. . . . Mr. Williams has defended . . . Frank Costello [Hoover's Mafia confidant], the gambler, James R. Hoffa [who in the last year has given several hundred thousand dollars to Hoover's favorite charity] . . . and the late Senator Joseph R. McCarthy [a man very close to Hoover]. . . ."[306] That Williams is also counsel for Levinson and is either already, or soon to become, defense counsel to Marcello associate Gilbert Beckley, reveals another aspect of the close working relationship between members of the gambler's network.[307]

2:30 P.M. LBJ calls lobbyist Thomas Corcoran.[308] Recall that Johnson, on 4/26/62, had used Corcoran in an effort to gain further assistance from Hoover during the Estes scandal.

Press: "Senate investigators will explore in closed hearings Friday the role of . . . Baker in a vending machine business dispute."[309] In the coming weeks Baker's partner, Fred Black, will begin to guardedly discuss his association with Mafia functionary Ed Levinson. Black: " 'I go along as far as Levinson is concerned with gambling, but he is far from being a racketeer.' Black then told the committee that he was a gambler at heart. 'I shoot crap, play the horses, as you know. Being with gamblers gives me a kick.' 'How long have you known Levinson,' asked McClendon. 'I have known Ed Levinson since the day before Jack Kennedy's inauguration.' 'Do you know how Baker met Levinson?' 'Yes,' said Black. 'We both met him in this building in a pre-inauguration party. . . .' "[310]

Press: "Republican members of the House and Senate introduced bills today to provide subpoena power for the commission investigating the assassination. . . ."[311] Warren will immediately oppose this move.

FBI (Dallas) Agent Barrett prepares a memo on the Zapruder film, camera, etc. He states the camera had been turned over to him apparently by December 4. "The original is on 16 mm film, and according to Mr. Zapruder is much clearer than those appearing on

8 mm film. He subsequently turned over two copies to the U.S. Secret Service and sold the original and one copy to Life Magazine."[312]

Hoover receives an award from, and addresses, the Washington Hebrew Congregation in D.C., presenting a speech entitled "Faith in Freedom."

This is a great moment in my life. . . . I am especially honored by . . . the distinguished civic leaders whom you have selected as recipients of other awards. How have these men come to positions of prominence in our community? It is because they have dedicated themselves to service . . . and they are willing to be judged upon their records of positive contributions to the cause of decency and of justice. *Decency and justice—these are the high aims of this brotherhood.* . . . Americans . . . are . . . blessed . . . with a proud heritage of freedom. It is a heritage that was won by the sweat, the blood, and the sacrifices of men. . . . I have said this before and I would like to repeat it here: We are at war with communism and the sooner every red-blooded American realizes this the safer we will be. . . . Today, the Communists are engaged in a vigorous campaign to divide and weaken America from within. . . . *There is unmistakable evidence of divine guidance all through the history of our Nation. We must guard it. We must cherish it. We must work for it.* . . . *Communism* feeds upon . . . sickness of the mind. . . . It *probes relentlessly for weaknesses in America's moral armor.* . . . Invariably, these merchants of hate attempt to drape themselves in a cloak of patriotism. . . . The peddling of their dishonest doctrine to highminded, largely inexperienced, and basically eager-to-believe young people is not unlike the peddling of filth and dope in demoralizing effect. . . . *The God-given ideals which are responsible for this country's greatness are being attacked on many fronts today. Moral lethargy, self-indulgence, neglect of duty—these lethal forces are undermining many facets of . . . government. . . . Disrespect for law and order is a tragic moral sickness. . . . The moral strength of our Nation has slipped alarmingly. . . . We must follow the teachings of God if we hope to cure this moral illness.* Law and order are bulwarks on which successful government must stand. . . .

Fantasy and weakness have too often prevailed in the administration of justice where strength and realism are essential
needs. . . . Justice is needed—stern justice. . . . Wherever
politics and opportunism remain primary considerations in the
appointment of . . . others charged with the administration
of justice, *the public should have more adequate guarantees for
the immediate removal of those who prove by their unjustifiable
actions that they cannot be entrusted with the important responsibilities of their offices.* . . . Let us never forget that religion
has made us what we are. . . . *There must be a moral
reawakening in every home in our land. History shows us the
great accomplishments that can be attained by the . . . efforts
of selfless men . . . who are dedicated to a noble cause.* We
have such a cause in America . . . to preserve the rule of law.
. . . Law and public sanctions help to keep our deeds in line
—only conscience polices our thoughts. It is much easier to
control our actions than our thoughts. For, 'As a man thinketh
in his heart so is he.' . . . *Today, we hold this . . . vision—
the determination that faith, courage, and decency will prevail
over all enemies of freedom.* . . . [emphasis added].[313]

Note Hoover's use of the phrase "Disrespect for law and order is a
tragic moral sickness" in the context of his November 22 categorization of Kennedy's assassination as a *tragedy*. Recall that Hoover,
in a speech aimed directly at JFK on 10/9/62, had used the phrase
"Disrespect for law and order is a *tragic* moral illness," and also
used the term *"tragic* waste" in his 11/16/63 speech to describe the
supposed moral degeneration of America's young people at the
hands of the New Frontier. Here he continues the broader assault
on immorality in general.

12/5/63—THURSDAY: "The FBI report was delivered to
Johnson on December 5." It flatly asserts Oswald was a lone nut,
killed by another lone nut.[314] Hoover having previously leaked the
conclusion of the report to the press, Johnson has little choice now
but to accept the Director's version of the event. This type of dramatic reconstruction is a familiar one for Hoover. One need only
peruse *Look* magazine's *The Story of the FBI* (1947) to understand
his penchant for such simplistic melodrama. He also forwards a
copy of the report to the Justice Department.

RFK tells Schlesinger about Hoover's return to the old ways. Schlesinger: "He spoke to me in early December about the 'revolt of the FBI.' . . ." "In his talk with Johnson after the address to Congress, Kennedy warned that the FBI was operating once again as an independent agency."[315]

Congressional Record insertion, twice, of Hoover's December 4 speech.

The Warren Commission holds its first meeting. "The FBI was upset enough to decline to send a representative to the initial meeting of the Commission on December 5."[316] ". . . Warren announced his belief that the Commission needed neither its own investigators nor the authority to issue subpoenas and grant immunity from prosecution to witnesses if they were compelled to testify, after first having chosen to take the Fifth Amendment on grounds of self-incrimination. The Chief Justice was overruled by the Commission on the subpoena and immunity authority, though immunity was never used; but he held sway on his insistence that evidence that had been developed by the FBI would form a foundation for the Commission's investigation."[317]

"Curiously, at the Commission's first executive session, Dulles gave each of his colleagues a book purporting to show how American assassinations were always perpetrated by lone, demented men."[318]

*". . . Members . . . conceived of the Commission's purpose in terms of the national interest. Allen Dulles said that an atmosphere of rumor and suspicion interferes with the functioning of the government, especially abroad, and one of the main tasks of the Commission was to dispel rumors. . . . McCloy said that it was of paramount importance to 'show the world that America is not a banana republic, where a government can be changed by conspiracy.' . . . Cooper said that one of the Commission's most important purposes was 'to lift the cloud of doubts that had been cast over American institutions.' . . . Ford said that dispelling damaging rumors was a major concern of the Commission, and most members of the Com-*mission agreed" (emphasis added).[319] Warren and Boggs, during the course of proceedings, will appear overwhelmed at times. Chief Counsel Rankin (appointed on 12/8/63) will do his best under the circumstances, but is under the direct control of the Commission as a group.

Press reports: *"The request for subpoena power opens the possibil-*

ity that *the commission will* hold public hearings and otherwise
*make its own detailed search for the facts. The alternative would be
to appraise material gathered by* others; especially *the Federal Bureau of Investigation.* . . . *Warren* . . . *said* after the meeting that
the commission had no official information yet. '*We are deliberating
somewhat in the dark,* . . . *because we have no report as yet* from
any agency of the Government. The information we have now is
little more than what we have learned through the news media.'
. . . Photographers were allowed in before the meeting began.
Then the doors were closed. . . . *The FBI turned over the report to
Mr. Katzenbach this evening.* Justice officials still have much work
to do on it before it is sent to President Johnson and, presumably,
the commission. Part or all of the report may be made public when
it is completed. Meanwhile, a reconstruction of the assassination
was still being carried out in Dallas today by Federal agents. Indications are that the commission will work without publicity. The
members took care not to speak to reporters today. It is believed
that every effort will be made to preserve a judicial atmosphere. For
reasons of legal propriety it is considered likely that the commission
will steer clear of any findings about Jack Ruby until he has been
tried" (emphasis added).[320]

"FBI reports on this highly secret investigation . . . indicate
that Ferrie . . . was reinterviewed by the FBI on December
5. . . ."[321]

FBI (San Francisco) interviews a woman apparently familiar with
Ruby's friend McWillie, who at one time ran illegal gambling establishments to the east and west of Dallas County. She asserts she
often saw him in the company of Ruby and felt Ruby idolized the
man.[322]

Press: ". . . Connally . . . answered a few questions. . . .
[He] . . . was felled by a bullet that pierced his back, chest, right
wrist and thigh. . . . The Governor said he understood his shattered wrist might stay in its cast at least 90 days. 'And it will be at
least six months before it can be determined if I have the full use of
the hand and wrist'. . . ."[323]

Press: "The American Civil Liberties Union charged . . . that
the police and prosecuting officials of Dallas committed gross violations of civil liberties in their handling of . . . Oswald. . . . The
group said . . . he had already been 'tried and convicted' by the
public statements of Dallas law enforcement officials. . . . The

Dallas police would not say whether Oswald had been given access to a telephone, nor would they comment on the duration and intensity of the questioning."[324]

Press: "Thirteen days after the assassination . . . Federal investigators were still reconstructing the crime on film today. . . . An open car with a man and a woman in the back seat simulated again and again today the ride of the President. . . . A motion picture camera in the sixth-floor window that was used by the assassin recorded these trips. . . . Each simulation differed slightly, either in the speed of the car or the gestures of the occupants or in some other detail. On one trip both occupants of the back seat waved. On another the man turned to the right and, moments later, slumped in his seat; then the car's speed picked up. . . . *One question was how the President could have received a bullet in the front of the throat from a rifle in the . . . Depository . . . after his car had passed the building and was turning a gentle curve away from it.* One explanation from a competent source was that the President had turned to his right to wave and was struck at that moment. *The best authority presumably on the exact angle of entry of the bullet is the man who conducted the autopsy. He is Dr. J. J. Humes* of the Naval Medical Center, Bethesda, Md. *Dr. Humes said he had been forbidden to talk. Most private citizens who had cooperated with newsmen reporting the crime have refused to give further help after being interviewed by agents of the Federal Bureau of Investigation.* Dallas city and county police withdrew their help the same way. *One high officer said he wished he could answer questions 'because it would save us a lot of work' "* (emphasis added).[325]

"On December 5 FBI Report DL 89-43, containing Mrs. Walther's [see 11/22] statement, was filed in Dallas. It was submitted to the Commission on December 10 and became part of 'Commission Document No. 7.' . . . Mrs. Walther was not called as a witness. She was never questioned by the staff lawyers, and no requests were made for further FBI investigation of her statement."[326] As she was standing across the street from the Depository immediately before the assassination, the report is worth quoting in relevant part:

> In his hands, this man [on the sixth floor] was holding a rifle with the barrel pointed downward, and the man was looking south on Houston Street [toward the oncoming motorcade].

The man was wearing a white shirt and had blond or light hair. . . . The rifle had a short barrel. . . . She noticed nothing like a telescopic sight on the rifle or a leather strap or a sling on the rifle. . . . She thought the rifle was different from any she had ever seen. This man was standing in or about the middle of the window. In the same window, to the left of this man, she could see a portion of another man standing by the side of this man with a rifle. The other man was standing erect and his head was above the open portion of the window. . . . She could not see the head of the second man. . . . This second man was apparently wearing a brown suit coat, and the only thing she could see was the right side of the man, from about the waist to the shoulders. Almost immediately after noticing this man with the rifle and the other man standing beside him, someone in the crowd said 'Here they come. . . .'327

Press: "Mrs. [Marguerite] Oswald . . . called a news conference for tomorrow at 4 P.M. She has been complaining about what she considers discrepancies and gaps in the official reconstruction of the Nov. 22 crime. . . . Mrs. Oswald suggested to visitors that the assassination had been a plot for which her son had been made a 'scapegoat.' "328

12/6/63—FRIDAY: Hoover and/or Dallas P.D. leaks a fabricated story, connecting Oswald with the Walker shooting, to the press. "DALLAS . . . A rifle shot that narrowly missed former Maj. Gen. . . . Walker in his Dallas home last April 10 was fired by . . . Oswald, *police sources said* today. Oswald . . . told at least one person that he fired the shot at . . . Walker, it was learned. That person was believed to have been . . . Marina. An unconfirmed report said that the name of . . . Walker . . . had been found in a notebook in Oswald's room. The bullet fired at Walker was fragmented. Study of the fragments has not proved conclusively that the bullet was fired by the same rifle that fired three shots into the Kennedy motorcade Nov. 22. It was established, meanwhile, that the Federal Bureau of Investigation knew at least two weeks before the assassination that Oswald worked in the building from which the fatal bullets were fired. . . . Walker was not struck but slivers of glass and metal showered his right forearm. A Dallas

detective said after the shooting that Mr. Walker must have moved
his head just as the sniper was squeezing his trigger. The bullet
missed his head by about an inch. The Dallas Times Herald reported that . . . Walker went to the second floor of his home, got a
pistol, searched for the sniper, and then telephoned the police. *The
newspaper quoted a detective, D. E. McElroy,* as saying, 'Whoever
shot at the general was playing for keeps. The sniper wasn't trying
to scare him. He was shooting to kill.' The possibility that more
than one person was involved in the Walker shooting was suggested
by a 14-year-old boy, Kirk Newman [*sic*], who lived nearby. He was
quoted as saying that he had seen several men jump into an automobile after the shooting and speed away. . . . Boy Surrey, an aide to
Mr. Walker, was quoted after the shooting as saying that suspicious
things had been happening since the general returned from the tour.
On Monday night, April 8, the night Mr. Walker returned home,
two men prowled through the alley, Mr. Surrey said. He said that
he had watched the men leave in an automobile with no license
plates and that he had followed them until they were lost in downtown traffic. . . . Oswald's wife is still in the Dallas-Fort Worth
area but whether she is being held against her will could not be
learned. Two days ago she agreed to talk to a newsman, but the FBI
intervened before the meeting took place. . . . Police reports published locally after the attack on Mr. Walker at first said that the
bullet fired at him had been of .30-.30 caliber. Later reports described it as being .30-.06. . . . However, it was said that the
Walker bullet had been so fragmented as to make conclusive identification impossible" (emphasis added).[329] What would be fascinating
to know at this point is whether Detectives McElroy or Van Cleave
(one of the other detectives quoted at the time of the Walker shooting) took part in the November 22 search of Oswald's room and the
Paine residence, as it was from that group of Dallas P.D. detectives
that came the original suggestion that Oswald was involved in the
Walker incident. Given the similarities between the two events (i.e.,
shooting at a public figure) it is logical to assume they may have
been.

Press quotes Marguerite Oswald as saying, "The gun he had purchased was in a blanket in the garage in Irving, where his wife was
staying. . . . He did not hide it in his Dallas apartment. Anybody
had access to that gun, anybody."[330]

FBI (SOG) internal memo by DeLoach. "Katzenbach mentioned

that Waggoner Carr . . . would like very much to see the Director
. . . on Friday. . . . I asked him what for. He stated that Carr had
no particular motive in mind other than to indicate to the press later
on that he had discussed matters with the Director. I told him I
could see no percentage in the Director's seeing Carr. . . . Katzenbach indicated that the White House might think otherwise. He
stated that the President was most anxious for Carr to be given
attention in Washington inasmuch as Carr was running for office
next year. I told Katzenbach I knew this. However, I still felt that the
Director should not be injected into this matter. Katzenbach stated
he would attempt to dissuade Carr from seeing the Director. However, Carr was quite persistent. . . . In view of the close relationship which Carr obviously has with the President, the Director may
desire to just shake hands with Carr without sitting down and discussing facts concerning our report. . . . Hoover looked at it and
wrote in longhand: 'If he calls I will see him.' Eventually they settled
on posing for a quick picture together and Carr was ushered out
immediately."[331]

Press: "Texas Attorney General . . . Carr announced today the
indefinite postponement of a state inquiry into the assassination.
. . . He said he did not want to interrupt the continuity of the
investigation now being carried on by the Federal Government. The
attorney general's announcement was made simultaneously in
Washington, where Mr. Carr was today, and in the state capitol at
Austin. . . . He said his decision was based on conferences he had
been holding in Washington since Wednesday with . . .
Katzenback [*sic*], Federal Bureau of Investigation Director J. Edgar
Hoover, and Chief Justice Earl Warren. . . . Mr. Carr said: 'We are
convinced that the investigative authority of the Federal Government is being used to the fullest extent. The files and the evidence
. . . are in the hands of the FBI for its use.' He also said, 'A public
inquiry in Texas at this time might be more harmful than help-
ful.' "[332]

Life magazine releases its memorial edition on the Kennedy assassination. The cover is captioned "All of LIFE'S Pictures . . . on
the Most Shocking Event of Our Time." In reality, only an additional nine frames are released, Z183, 226, 232, 258, 277, 309, 347,
371, and one other between 371 and the end of the film. Once again,
key frames are withheld. Three of the nine are again of Jackie trying to escape the limousine. Captions create a near completely

false description of the killing. ". . . The first bullet struck [Kennedy] in the neck. . . . The President slumped forward in his seat and down toward his wife. . . . The second shot struck Governor Connally. . . . Oswald's last bullet . . . struck the President in the rear right part of his head." With a federally appointed investigative body already in place, *Life,* with this fabrication, very probably violates obstruction-of-justice statutes. Further, as ultimately discussed in *Reasonable Doubt,* "Citing the Zapruder film, which *Life* owned and which the public was not allowed to see until 1975, the article reported that the film showed JFK turned completely around so that he was facing the sniper's nest—thus explaining the entry wound in the throat. As any viewer of the Zapruder film can instantly discern, no such turn was made by the President."[333] Not coincidentally, around the time (1975) *Life* returns the film to the Zapruder family for the sum of one dollar, Congress begins to closely scrutinize the activities of the FBI during the 1960s.

Warren Commission holds its second meeting, again in Executive Session.[334] Hoover's refusal to cooperate, combined with press leaks (i.e., Hoover's disinformation campaign) in recent days, must by now have created fundamental questions in the minds of Commission members.

Press: "Congressional Republicans deplored today what they called attempts to blame 'hatred' in this country for the assassination of President Kennedy. . . . 'It was a single kill-crazy Communist who was acting to the dictates of his own unexplainable left-wing dementia.' . . . Government officials who have viewed the available information say there is every reason to think that . . . Oswald acted on his own, not in any conspiracy or on behalf of any movement. . . . Warren . . . told reporters . . . that it was not possible to lay out the inquiry or even the staff in the absence of [the FBI] report. 'We have no idea of the magnitude of the work,' the Chief Justice said."[335]

Press: "The Senate Rules Committee resumed its questioning of witnesses today in preparation for public hearings on the business activities of Robert G. Baker. It was the first such session since the committee began questioning key figures in the Baker affair Nov. 21, the day before the assassination of President Kennedy. . . . Mr. Baker . . . was an influential protégé of . . . Johnson when . . . Johnson was the Senate majority leader, from 1953 to 1960.

. . . Also named . . . is Fred Black, a close friend of Mr. Baker. . . ."³³⁶

5:43 P.M.: LBJ calls Senator Jordan. It is not known whether they discussed the Baker hearings held this day.³³⁷

"William Abadie was sought out by FBI agents and questioned in Los Angeles on December 6, 1963. . . . *Abadie reported that 'while he was making book for Ruby's establishment, he did observe police officers in and out of the gambling establishment on occasion.'* . . . The FBI report of Abadie's interview spans five consecutive pages of Commission Document 86 in the National Archives. Yet the version published in the Warren Commission Hearings and Exhibits . . . contains only four pages. The first page of this report, which describes Abadie's employment in *Ruby's . . . bookmaking establishment,* is missing. . . . Ruby's 'one outstanding characteristic . . . was his own personal intense interest in gambling of any kind,' . . . Abadie told the FBI. A one-time acquaintance reported that *Ruby 'bet heavily, made frequent telephone bets on horse races.'* . . . . . . Ruby once won $5,000 on a telephone bet with a Montreal bookie. . . . *Ruby's* affinity for betting was also demonstrated in the summer of 1957, when he *went to the races in Hot Springs, Arkansas with . . . McWillie."*³³⁸ ". . . Ruby was . . . involved with . . . bookmaking interests. . . . This meant he had to have known Vincent Marcello, . . . for *in 1963 . . . Marcello's . . . racing-wire service was hooked up to most of the [Dallas] bookies."*³³⁹ Ruby was, in effect, a part of the Beckely/Marcello gambling network. As such, would his association not have become known to the Bureau when it and the IRS attempted to break up the wire service on 6/27/61? Further, does it not strengthen the connection between Ruby and Levinson et al.? The latter's background and interests have been shown to be closely interwoven with Newport, Kentucky, wire services and Las Vegas casino gambling networks. Recall Ruby's frequent calls to the Thunderbird prior to the assassination.

7:20 P.M.: LBJ meets with Texas Attorney General Waggoner Carr.³⁴⁰

12/7/63—SATURDAY: Press reports again on Marina. "Her friend said Secret Service agents had suggested to her that it might be safer and easier for her to return to the Soviet Union than to try to live in the United States. This distressed her. . . . Mrs. Oswald spends most of her time in her rooms, where the Federal Bureau of

Investigation still occasionally questions her through an interpreter. . . . She is now secluded from Oswald's relatives as well as from the public."[341]

Press interviews "JFK Wanted" poster author, Weissman: " 'But I was even more shocked by the fact that many people kept blaming the conservatives even when it had been established that a Communist was the assassin.' . . . Until today, Mr. Weissman had told his story to only a few friends and the Federal Bureau of Investigation. . . . 'We knew the President was coming, and we wanted to do something. . . . We knew a protest demonstration was out, after what had happened to Stevenson, so we hit upon the idea of the ad.' "[342]

Press publishes Oswald's six letters to the FPCC. ". . . The texts of letters to the Fair Play for Cuba Committee [were] made available last night by Vincent Theodore Lee, national director of the committee."[343] The correspondence focuses on Oswald's attempt to obtain a local charter for the New Orleans area. Apparently Lee had turned the letters over to the FBI, which had in turn released them to the press. Of course the Bureau had obtained copies of the correspondence long before this, as a result of mail intercepts and illegal break-ins at the New York FPCC offices in New York. "Asked about the exchange of letters between Mr. Lee and Oswald, the FBI said it had no comment."[344]

LBJ talks with Senator Russell three times today.[345]

10:07 and 11:50 P.M.: LBJ again calls lobbyist Thomas Corcoran.[346]

12/8/63—SUNDAY: ". . . Philadelphia *Inquirer* . . . flatly stated: 'The FBI attempt to recruit Oswald as an informant, an informed law enforcement official said, was made in September, just after he had moved to Dallas from New Orleans. . . . Oswald's mother said an "agent named Hosty" came to the Irving house and talked to the young man at length in his car. An FBI agent named James Hosty handles investigations of subversives for the Dallas field office. The source said he did not know if the FBI succeeded in hiring Oswald; and the federal agency would not discuss the matter.' "[347]

Press: "The chairman of the Senate committee investigating the business affairs of . . . Baker indicated doubt today that public hearings would be held soon. Public hearings on the vending machine phase of the inquiry will not be held until the damage suit against Mr. Baker . . . has been tried in the Federal District Court here, Senator B. Everett Jordan said. . . . Mr. Baker, 35-year-old protégé of President Johnson. . . . Mr. Jordan's announcement indicated there would be no public hearings for months. Another factor working against an early trial, and therefore against early Senate hearings, is that Mr. Baker changed lawyers last week. Such a step traditionally entitles a litigant to a postponement should he seek it from the court. . . . Senator Jordan commented, 'We wouldn't want to bring out anything that might cause a mistrial or prejudice a law suit.' "[348]

Warren Commission appoints a compromise chief counsel, J. L. Rankin. "Rankin was accepted, not because he was 'more nationally prominent,' but he was safer."[349] "The objection to Olney [a candidate rejected by the Commission as a whole], based . . . to some degree on Hoover's feelings . . . was unfortunate, in light of our conclusions about organized crime's role in the assassination. Olney had been counsel to the Special Study Commission on Organized Crime, which was established by Warren when he was Governor of California, and he was regarded as an authority on the underworld."[350]

12/9/63—MONDAY: Dallas press reports Irving rifle-range sightings of "Oswald" prior to the assassination. "The operator [Mr. Davis] said Mr. Slack and the other customers did not notify the Federal Bureau of Investigation until it became known that investigators were looking for sites where Oswald might have practiced. . . . *Mr. Price declined to answer further questions because he said, the FBI had asked him not to talk. The FBI here denied this. . . . Mr. Slack said that Oswald was accompanied by another man on his first visit to the range. The two men brought three rifles with them, and, when they left, Oswald handed them over a wire fence to the other man in the parking lot,* Mr. Slack recalled. He said one of the weapons was wrapped in a canvas or old quilt. . . . *Mr. Slack said he was watching television after the President's assassination when Oswald was shown on the screen. 'I wasn't quite sure the first time I saw him. . . .'* . . . The customers recalled that *on the first visit the man resembling Oswald came alone in a battered automobile. On the second visit they said he came with another man. Mrs. Michael R. Paine* of Irving . . . *has said that Oswald apparently* *did not know how to drive a car. She said that in late October or early November she tried to teach him how to drive her car in a parking lot, but that Oswald did not even learn how to park it.* Mr. Davis said that after his customers had reported their recollections of Oswald to the FBI, two agents came to the range and picked up about 25 pounds of rifle shells. Mr. Davis said he had sent other shells, fired about the time of the young man's visit, to a Dallas gunshop for reloading. He said he understood that the FBI had obtained those shells, too. . . . Meanwhile, authorities had nothing to say about their theory that it was Oswald who fired into the Dallas home of . . . Walker last April 10. *Federal investigators have said privately that they believe Oswald was the sniper.* . . . The *police doubted* a version of the shooting given them by a 15-year-old neighbor of Mr. Walker. . . . *The boy, Kirk Coleman, said he ran into Mr. Walker's yard after the shooting and saw two men flee in two cars. One of the men, he said, carried an object that looked like a rifle. The boy said the man, whom he described as resembling Oswald, thrust the object into the back seat of his car, a 1958 model, and drove away. He said the first man, driving a 1950 car, left a moment before.* . . . The Dallas Morning News, meantime, reported in a story . . . that a fourth cartridge had been found in Oswald's rifle on the day of the assassination."[351]

". . . Just four days after the Commission held its first meeting, and before there even was a Commission staff, . . . Hoover turned over to . . . Warren a four-volume summary report of the FBI's probe of the Kennedy and Oswald assassinations. That instant report was the basis of the final conclusion the Warren Commission officially would reach nine months later. [FBI liaison] Howard Willens was upset by the superficiality of the FBI report and Rankin agreed. Rankin assembled the staff lawyers and told them not to accept the FBI report as gospel and to request more facts."[352] Undoubtedly at Hoover's request or demand, ". . . Katzenbach wrote each member asking them to issue a press release stating that the FBI report said Oswald was the lone assassin."[353] The report, a fundamental distortion of reality, contains, for example, with regard to the head shots, the following lie: "The President, *who slumped forward* in the car, was rushed to . . . [Parkland Hospital]" (emphasis added).[354] Of course, the Zapruder film, evidence that has been in Hoover's hands for weeks, graphically reveals the opposite. Kennedy's upper body is thrown violently *backward* and to the left.

Consider the Bureau's report against the backdrop of all that has come before. The members of the Commission, as longtime political insiders, know that Hoover hated JFK, opposed his war on the Mafia, and had publicly stated his intention to avoid compulsory retirement. What must they think, now confronted with the fact that this same man, in charge of the investigation of Kennedy's death, is refusing to cooperate with them? These men, and their motivations in the coming months, must be considered in this light. To do otherwise is to deny reality.

And what of Johnson? Commission members have seen Hoover repeatedly come to his aid prior to the assassination, and well know of the close relationship between the two men.

10:32 A.M.: Boggs calls LBJ.[355]

Kennedy speechwriter Schlesinger has a conversation with RFK concerning the assassination. "I asked him, perhaps tactlessly, about Oswald. He said that there . . . was still argument if he had done it by himself or as part of a larger plot . . . by gangsters."[356]

Press: "A Federal Bureau of Investigation report went to a special Presidential commission today and named . . . Oswald as the assassin. . . . . . . The Department of Justice, declining all comment on the content of the report, announced only that on instructions of . . . Johnson the report was sent directly to the special commission. . . . The commission asked that the report not be made public until it had had an opportunity to review it and had taken 'whatever action it may feel appropriate.' "[357]

Press: ". . . Oswald . . . got in trouble for unauthorized possession of a pistol while serving in Japan with the Marines. . . . The fact that Oswald had the pistol was discovered when he dropped it on the floor of his barracks and it went off. . . ."[358]

Press: "The Federal Bureau of Investigation gave the Secret Service a 'risk' list of Dallas individuals in advance of President Kennedy's fatal trip, but the list did not include the name of . . . Oswald. An official source explained . . . the FBI found nothing in Oswald's background to mark him as a potential assassin. The provision by the FBI . . . a routine matter of cooperation between the agencies, followed normally when the President visits a city. 'But,' an official source in behalf of the FBI said, 'you can't pass everything.' Oswald was not under surveillance by the FBI at the time of President Kennedy's visit to Dallas . . . the FBI noted. Months of checking by the FBI had indicated that Oswald was neither a spy nor a saboteur. That, it was said, covered the statutory area of FBI responsibility. . . . 'There was nothing in the world in his background to indicate he was going to do anything like this,' the FBI spokesman went on. 'There was information on individuals in Dallas that was passed along because there was something in their record. . . . This has gone on for years.' For the FBI to have kept Oswald under surveillance, this source said, 'there would have to be some reason, and the only reason in his case, was he a spy or saboteur? In Oswald's case there was absolutely no indication whatsoever he was an agent.' . . . 'In the practical realm, there was no reason at all.' . . . There had been, it was learned, no suspicion of a link between Oswald and the rifle shot into the Dallas home of . . . Walker on April 10. In fact, one well-placed source said he understood that Oswald's name was not in the Dallas police files at all. . . . *There have long been rumors of rivalry and jealousy among* the Federal investigative agencies, particularly *the FBI and the Secret Service. . . . An information man at the FBI snorted at rivalry reports, saying: '. . . We report information on anybody who has threatened the President' "* (emphasis added).[359]

"On December 9, . . . [Representative H. R.] Gross put his finger upon the vital spot: 'I submit . . . that every member of the Federal Communications Commission is going to be aware of the interests of the Johnson family in the field of radio and television. And I further submit that in the case of the FCC the chairman holds office at the pleasure of [Lyndon Johnson].' "[360]

Press reports on Oswald and his wife's relationship with the Dallas Russian exile community: "A Fort Worth engineer . . . said today that Oswald spoke Russian fluently but not grammatically. . . . They said Oswald did not seem enthusiastic about life in the Soviet Union, although he did not complain about it."[361]

12/10/63—TUESDAY: Hoover sends a memo to Belmont about damage control, protecting the FBI's image during the Commission proceedings.[362] Then, both furious and terrified by the previous day's leak to the press, possibly by Sullivan, responds by ". . . secretly censuring five field investigative agents, one field supervisor, three special agents in charge [Dallas, New Orleans, and Miami?] four headquarters [SOG] supervisors, two headquarters section chiefs, one inspector and William Sullivan, the assistant director of the FBI."[363] This is done against the advice of his assistants, who fail to see where the office has erred.[364] Of course, it has not. Hoover has simply sensed the situation is deteriorating and has decided to send a message to the Dallas, New Orleans, and Miami field offices. The message undoubtedly is that if they value their careers, they will not reveal any more about the assassination or related information they have uncovered. Above all, they should avoid making apparent Oswald's innocence.

"Shortly after his appointment to the Commission, Dulles told New York Post columnist Murray Kempton that he was certain no evidence of a conspiracy would be found. . . ."[365] This belief is logical. Dulles, schooled in intelligence work, has been placed on the Commission for the very purpose of containment. More important, having realized that Hoover is not going to cooperate (and is, in fact, obviously hiding evidence from the Commission), Dulles has simply deduced that the Commission is not *supposed* to look for conspiracies.[366] Hoover's near insistance that the Commission immediately agree with his-lone nut thesis only confirms his suspicions.

Press: "Senators investigating the dealings of . . . Baker . . . have reached an impasse on procedure that threatens to stall the inquiry. . . . The outcome of the dispute will determine whether the investigation will have a wide scope or will be limited strictly to Mr. Baker's business affairs. . . . The committee chairman, Senator . . . Jordan . . . ruled last week that questioning on alleged moral improprieties was not germane to the purpose of the investigation. . . . L. P. McLendon, who has been engaged as chief counsel for the Baker inquiry, in effect supported the chairman's ruling over the objection of Republican members of the committee."[367]

Press interviews Rankin: "He said today that . . . Warren had asked him to keep February in mind as a possible target date for a report. 'It would be very dangerous . . . for the commission to come out with a report before it has all the facts. *The President and the Chief Justice want to get it resolved as soon as possible. . . .*' . . . There is a possibility that the Commission will soon release part of the long report prepared by the Federal Bureau of Investigation" (emphasis added).[368] Note that Johnson, through Warren, is already exerting pressure on the other Commissioners to agree with Hoover and bring the matter to a speedy close.

Press: ". . . Ford . . . predicted today that the panel's report would not be made until after the trial of . . . Ruby in February."[369]

Press: ". . . Walker confirmed today that he was flying flags in front of his home at full staff despite the half-staff mourning period for President Kennedy. He declined to say why. 'My flags are always from full staff now. . . .' "[370] Walker obviously relishes the moment, as well as the publicity surrounding allegations that it was Oswald who had attempted to kill him.

Press: ". . . Oswald attended a big right-wing rally a month before President Kennedy was assassinated. Two days later, at a meeting of the Dallas Civil Liberties Union, he spoke out in criticism of the rightists. . . . On Oct. 25, a Friday, Mr. Paine attended a meeting of the Civil Liberties Union, of which he was a member. He took Oswald along. . . . Oswald rose to say that he had heard both anti-Catholic and anti-Semitic statements at the rally two nights before. . . . Robert A. Surrey, a Walker aide, rented the theatre for the rally. . . . Oswald . . . joined ACLU on Nov. 4, three weeks before President Kennedy was killed."[371]

Press: "Mr. Spahr was Oswald's non-commissioned officer who tried to get him a hardship discharge when his mother . . . was ill in September 1959. . . . Although he gave a lengthy statement to the Federal Bureau of Investigation about Oswald, he declined to give specifics to a reporter. 'I don't want to condemn the dead.' . . . But his reticence was also dictated in large part by the FBI and, he said, by his concern for his own future."[372]

Press: "Two prominent California attorneys, Melvin Belli of San Francisco and Sam Brody of Los Angeles, said today they would defend Jack Ruby. . . . . . . They planned to argue that their client was the victim of temporary insanity when he killed . . . Oswald. . . ."[373]

12/11/63—WEDNESDAY: Press reports on the Baker scandal: "The boycott would protest what the Republicans believe is a Democratic cover-up in the investigation of . . . Baker's business dealings. . . . Other Republicans on the committee are . . . Curtis of Nebraska and *John Sherman Cooper* of Kentucky. . . . Mr. Baker reportedly acquired a $2 million fortune while serving in his influential $19,600-a-year Senate post" (emphasis added).[374] Johnson's choice of Cooper is intriguing. He knew, of course, that Cooper was on the Baker committee when he appointed him to the

Commission. How much time will the Senator be able to give either investigation, considering the magnitude of each? Despite this, Cooper will come to oppose both the early demise of the Baker/ Mafia hearings and the Warren Commission's ultimate conclusion that Oswald acted alone.

5:06 P.M.: LBJ meets with Ford.[375]

Peace Justice David L. Johnston reports to Dallas FBI agents Hardin and Wilkison that "Ruby . . . [had] . . . co-signed Dallas bank loans for certain police."[376]

12/12/63—THURSDAY: Hoover is putting pressure on the Mexico City LEGAT to conclude its investigation of Oswald.[377]

". . . At the next staff meeting, the lawyers began to quarrel loudly among themselves. One threatened to quit, Rankin lost control of the proceedings and from that point on there were no more regular staff meetings. . . . The Commission itself didn't have anyone on its staff designated as an investigator—and would be vulnerable because it had to depend on such agencies as the FBI . . . and Dallas police to investigate themselves. 'It was a mistake that we never had any investigative staff of our own,' Griffin [a staff member] believes. 'Rankin himself indicated to us that the FBI couldn't be trusted.' "[378] Rankin is simultaneously fearful that Hoover will discover their mistrust.

FBI (SOG) DeLoach memo to Hoover regarding a meeting with Ford. "He asked that I come up to see him. . . . Upon arriving he told me he wanted to talk in the strictest of confidence. This was agreed to."[379] "Ford indicated he would keep me thoroughly advised as to the activities of the Commission."[380] Ford apparently discusses the fact that he, Dulles, and Boggs had successfully opposed Warren's choice for General Counsel (Olney). He states he is "disturbed about the manner in which Chief Justice Warren is carrying on his chairmanship of the Presidential Commission."[381] Warren's defeat on this issue, in conjunction with other data he possesses, may well have convinced him that he should do nothing more than go along with Hoover and Johnson. Ford's data is very good news to Hoover as he had, of course, also opposed Olney. Ford is fundamentally at odds with Warren from the outset, presumably believing he is trying to deflect attention from the fact that Oswald was a "kill-crazy-communist." He feels that Warren is dangerously liberal, a belief that is undoubtedly reinforced by the FBI. Hoover loathes Warren.[382] Ford also tells DeLoach that CIA Director McCone has informed him of an Oswald/Cuban contact in Mexico City, during which Oswald had accepted money. DeLoach informs Ford that the report is baseless, no doubt being fully aware of the CIA's ongoing effort to implicate Cuba in any way it can.[383] By this point Ford is unknowingly eating out of Hoover's hand, providing considerable aid to a traitor.

FBI (Dallas) agent Charles T. Brown files another report regarding the Moorman photos (taken at critical moments in the assassination).[384]

Press: "Members of the Senate Rules Committee reached a *gentleman's [sic] agreement* . . . to talk about call girls if they are mentioned during the committee's special investigation of impropriety on Capitol Hill. . . . A discussion of 'party girls' had already occupied some of the committee's time. Their statements were shrouded in delicacy. . . . *There were indications that the Democratic majority had been put under considerable pressure to hasten the pace of the inquiry.* . . . Senator B. Everett Jordan . . . opened a brief conference with newsmen with an announcement that the committee . . . would hold its first public hearings in two months at 10 A.M. next Tuesday. Only three meetings with witnesses have been held since the inquiry was authorized last Oct. 10, and they were in executive session" (emphasis added).[385]

12/13/63—FRIDAY: Press: "The Senate Rules Committee is seeking Presidential authority to inspect income tax returns filed by Robert Baker. . . . . . . The request to examine Federal income tax returns . . . was submitted before President Kennedy's assassination. Mr. Jordan said Mr. Baker's income tax return was 'the only one we're interested in as of now.' He said an Executive Order by . . . Johnson would be necessary to make the tax returns available. . . . Jordan's comments were made after the Committee had devoted a four-hour closed session to questioning Eugene A. Hancock, president of a *Miami vending machine company*" (emphasis added).[386]

Press: "BOSTON . . . Angelo Bruno . . . the head of the Philadelphia . . . Cosa Nostra . . . stepped from a trans-Atlantic plane into the hands of five Federal agents today. . . . He said he had been in Italy since September and was returning to Philadelphia to give himself up on a charge that he contended he knew nothing about."[387]

Public Law 88-202 (joint resolution, SJ 137) is introduced to give the Warren Commission the power to "compel the attendance and testimony of witnesses and the production of evidence."[388]

". . . The Secret Service . . . release[d] its final report on [Ferrie] . . . December 13. . . ."[389]

Texas Observer publishes the story of officer Joe Smith's encounter on November 22 with the "Secret Service" agent behind the picket fence moments after the assassination.[390]

12/14/63—SATURDAY: Press: "The National Broadcasting Company will televise live on Tuesday the opening day of the . . . investigation of . . . Baker. . . . . . . A protégé of . . . Johnson when the latter was Senate Democratic leader, Mr. Baker reportedly acquired a $2 million fortune while serving in his influential $19,000-a-year Senate post."[391]

Press: "A sixth attorney was added today to the team that will defend Jack Ruby. . . . The first attorney . . . described him today as 'the best appellate lawyer in the state.' . . . The attorneys would shed no light on who would be paying their fees and other expenses of the case. . . . Mr. Belli said that he had arranged to post a $100,000 bond if Judge . . . Brown would allow Ruby to go free on bail while awaiting trial. . . . . . . The chief defense attorney has also said he was arranging for a nationally known psychiatrist, 'the very best available,' to examine Ruby. A temporary insanity plea is planned."[392]

"The White House announced today it would permit Senate investigators to examine the tax returns of . . . Baker. . . ."[393] Johnson can just as easily do the same with Oswald's 1962 return, although it remains unknown whether the Commission requested it. The record so far only reveals that the IRS was requested to audit Oswald's income.

12/16/63—MONDAY: "At first Hoover saw no need to transmit the raw data on [Mafia] allegations to the . . . Commission, as he had not seen fit to transmit raw data on other matters relating to the assassination, preferring to issue general summary reports instead. By December 16, this practice had begun to bother certain members of the Commission. On that date, the commissioners adopted a resolution designed to force Hoover to release his raw files:

RESOLVED, that the Commission request promptly from all government agencies and Departments of the government the raw materials upon which any reports given to the Commission are based. . . .

This resolution was sent to . . . Hoover, by letter, on December 17, and it made him furious." He will avoid large-scale compliance until mid-January, 1964.[394]

Press: "[Johnson] . . . lunched with FBI director J. Edgar Hoover."[395] He also presented (at 1:45 P.M.) Hoover with an autographed photo which included the inscription "Than whom there is no greater from his friend of 30 years."[396] The two meet at the Executive Building at 1:45 P.M., then go over to the White House where they eat and talk privately until 3:20 P.M.[397] Evidently Hoover is meeting with Johnson in an attempt to derail the Commission's resolution.

Press: "The Commission investigating the assassination of President Kennedy made clear today that it plans a searching inquiry going beyond existing Government reports. . . . *Warren . . . announced after a two-and-a-half hour meeting that the group was calling on the Federal Bureau of Investigation for all the materials underlying the report it submitted a week ago. The Chief Justice also said the Commission had no plans now to release any part of the FBI report or summary of it. . . . These developments reflected the fact that the FBI report did not answer all the questions about the assassination.* The Commission evidently believes it would stir up more doubts to release a document that did not settle the disputes raised in the press and elsewhere. Officials of the Justice Department . . . agree. They recognize that the bureau's report was by no means complete and say it could not conceivably have been, given the time and the circumstances. What the report does not do is demonstrate that various theories advanced are untrue. To prove such negatives is always difficult. For example, *it has been theorized that there may have been a second person shooting at Mr. Kennedy in addition to . . . Oswald. . . . The bureau did not address itself to the problem in the report submitted to the Commission last week.* Another major question is whether there was any connection at all between Oswald and the man charged with his murder, Jack Ruby. Had they ever met? . . . *The report takes a firm position against various reports that at least one of the bullets that hit Mr. Kennedy had come from in front of him. Such a theory would conflict with the fact that Oswald was allegedly firing from a window above and behind the President.* The FBI report said the shots came from that window. It said Mr. Kennedy was hit by two bullets, one where the right shoulder joins the neck and the other in the right temple. . . . The . . . bullet, which hit . . . Connally . . . was said to have been too smashed for accurate ballistic appraisal. *The report itself did not spell out the evidence and trajectory-plotting by which bureau agents came to the conclusion that the shots were fired from that window. That is the sort of material that the . . . Commission wants to see.* . . . The Chief Justice told reporters after today's meeting that the seven Commission members regarded it as 'essential to have the materials on which the reports we are receiving are based.' *What the group had so far, he said, was 'summaries . . . and in more or less skeleton form' "* (emphasis added).[398]

Washington Post alleges that a lack of cooperation between the FBI and the Secret Service ". . . may have contributed to the tragedy in Dallas. . . ."[399]

Sullivan: "Both the Dallas police and the Secret Service began accusing us of not cooperating with them."[400]

Press: ". . . Johnson said today he would do his utmost to maintain 'the high quality and character of the career service in the Government and to advance its usefulness through improvement.' "[401]

12/17/63—TUESDAY: Hoover writes a letter to Johnson in regard to their meeting the previous day.

My dear Mr. President:

I cannot tell you how much our time together yesterday means to me. *Your very real appreciation of the matters I was privileged to discuss with you and your complete understanding of our problems smooth the way to our mutual desire to serve our country in fullest capacity* [emphasis added].

I shall treasure your photograph and your autographed message as I do your friendship and trust.

Sincerely yours,
Edgar [402]

Obviously Johnson and Hoover have come to some sort of under-standing. Johnson cannot survive the growing scandal surrounding Baker without Hoover's help; nor can Hoover stave off retirement without Johnson's Executive Order. LBJ is soon to say of Hoover, "I'd rather have him inside the tent pissing out, than outside the tent pissing in."[403] Hoover may well have guaranteed his coopera-tion on 12/16/63. Johnson is, after all, the only man who can con-trol the Warren Commission.

Press: "The conviction of the Communist party for failing to register under the Internal Security Act was reversed today by the United States Court of Appeals. . . . One effect that today's deci-sion seems likely to have is to halt the Government's effort to make individual Communist party members register because of the same point of self-incrimination."[404]

Hoover attempts to counter the revelations of the prior day with regard to the nature of Kennedy's wounds by leaking the following distortion to the press: "The first shot fired by President Kennedy's assassin struck Mr. Kennedy in the back and did not hit any vital organ, a reliable source familiar with the autopsy findings reported tonight. The second bullet to hit Mr. Kennedy—after another had struck . . . Connally . . . hit the President in the back of the skull and proved fatal."[405] In reality, of course, one of the two fatal head shots hit Kennedy in the right temple and *exited* the "back of the skull."

Press reports on Baker's Caribbean interests: "Among those cul-tivated by Trujillo officials and business associates in Washington was Robert G. Baker. . . . *Mr. Baker himself displayed an interest in other gambling concessions* in the Dominican Republic *this year*" (emphasis added).[406]

Press also reports on the testimony of a female associate of Baker, a Mrs. Novak: "A number of times, she said, he gave her large sums of cash to be deposited in the bank account of the motel. The sums varied from $1,000 to $13,000, usually in $100 bills. She would pick the money up in Mr. Baker's Senate office and take it to the bank, she said." This session is broadcast live by NBC.[407]

Press: ". . . Johnson started today the mechanics for making permanent the three-star rank of Vice Adm. . . . Rickover and keeping him on active duty after the mandatory retirement age of 64. . . . Mr. Johnson's nomination of . . . Rickover to hold the higher rank permanently in retirement is subject to Senate ratification."[408]

9:18 P.M.: Johnson calls Clyde Tolson, apparently at his apartment, from the White House.[409] The subject of their conversation is probably the Commission's resolution, although at this point Clyde may no longer be an active participant in Hoover's machinations.

12/18/63—WEDNESDAY: Hoover again leaks selective information regarding the nature of Kennedy's wounds to make it appear as if the FBI report is correct. This is accomplished by asserting that the autopsy report will show only shots from behind. The second head wound, inflicted from the right front, is omitted from the discussion. *"Officials declined all comment today* on reports of what pathologists found in an autopsy on President Kennedy's body. *The reports gave detailed support to the Federal Bureau of Investigation's finding that two bullets had hit Mr. Kennedy from the rear. The FBI came to this conclusion in its report on the assassination.* The *pathologists were said to have found* that a first bullet hit the President in the back. The bullet lodged in the body. It assertedly did not hit any vital organs. The second shot, it said, hit the right rear of Mr. Kennedy's head and caused fatal injury. A fragment of this bullet, according to the reports, passed out the front of the throat. This presumably would account for various reports suggesting—on the basis of the hurried observations of doctors in Dallas after the shooting . . . that there was an 'entry wound' in the front of the throat. . . . The talk of a front 'entry wound' had caused wide speculation about a second assassin's firing at Mr. Kennedy from in front of his car. The man who was accused of the killing, . . . Oswald, was said to have shot from a window above and behind the car. *The FBI, in its report to the special Commission . . . stated flatly that both bullets had come from the window where Oswald assertedly was.* But the report did not mention the autopsy" (emphasis added).[410] Note that this story is not based on any "official" statement, and that both the FBI and autopsy reports have not been released to the public. The FBI, of course, attended the autopsy. Through articles such as this, Hoover is scrambling to fix his conclusions in the public's mind, to preempt the Commission. What must the commissioners think? To see Hoover broadcasting such misinformation, coupled with his refusal to cooperate in general, must add to the Commission's concerns.

Press: "Dr. Malcolm O. Perry, a surgeon at Parkland Hospital who attended President Kennedy shortly after he was shot, said today that physicians seeking to save the President's life noted that he had been wounded in the throat and head but did not seek to trace the course of the bullets."[411]

Washington Post prints an article regarding the autopsy findings. A bullet "was found deep in his shoulder, . . . [It] . . . hit the President in the back shoulder five to seven inches below the collar line."[412]

New York Times: "The first bullet made what was described as a small, neat wound in the back and penetrated two or three inches."[413]

The Senate Judiciary Committee reports that S.603, which governs Hoover's replacement, is still pending in the House, apparently stalled.

Johnson holds a surprise press conference.[414]

Press: "DALLAS . . . A group of judges here has proposed a statement of policy that would bar photography in the courtrooms of Dallas County after Jan. 1. This would eliminate both television and still photography at the murder trial of . . . Ruby, now scheduled for Feb. 3. . . . Some civic leaders have privately expressed the fear that a televised trial might take on aspects of a 'circus' that would further damage the public impression of Dallas."[415]

Press: "Michael Levine, attorney for Ruby's family, said that the Vegas and Carousel clubs would be sold as soon as possible. He emphasized that the clubs were not owned by Ruby, but by other members of his family. Ruby only managed the night spots, Mr. Levine said."[416]

". . . Hoover had his agents in New Orleans and in Texas drop their investigation of Ferrie after December 18 and make no mention of him, or of Carlos Marcello, in the FBI supplemental report of January 13, 1964. . . ."[417]

12/19/63—THURSDAY: "In his interview with the FBI on the subject of Jack Ruby, December 19, 1963, at Birmingham, Alabama, [Paul Roland] Jones said he first met Ruby in the fall of 1946. . . ."[418] "The 37-year-old Jones . . . had been convicted in Kansas in the murder of a state's witness. . . ."[419] Through "his people," "there would be the horse-race wire for Dallas bookie shops. . . ."[420]

Press: "Mark Lane . . . submitted a 10,000-word brief to the Warren Commission by mail Tuesday night. . . . *Mr. Lane also cited what he said he knew were Federal Bureau of Investigation 'off-the-record briefings' to newsmen.* One of his contentions was that a wound in the front of President Kennedy's throat could not have been made by a shot from the Texas School Book Depository Building which was behind the Presidential car when the shot was fired. . . . Three physicians who examined the President at the hospital said the throat injury was an 'entry through the throat'. . . . In rebuttal to . . . Wade, Mr. Lane put forward the following arguments: Only one witness said he saw Oswald at the sixth-floor warehouse window, and his testimony would be 'speculative' and inadmissible because he said, according to Newsweek magazine, 'I can't identify him but if I see a man who looks like him I'll point him out.' A palm print—such as the one . . . on the murder rifle and a nearby cardboard box—'unlike a fingerprint is not always uniquely identifiable.' The asserted off-the-record FBI briefings said 'no palm prints were found on the rifle.' No Oswald prints were found on immovable fixtures. The prosecutor's statement on paraffin tests on both of Oswald's hands showing that Oswald had recently 'fired a gun' referred specifically twice to a 'gun.' This could have been a pistol, and The Washington Evening Star has said the tests found no gunpowder traces on Oswald's face, such as might have come from a rifle. There are questions whether Oswald would have . . . within moments after the shooting . . . stopped first for a soda in the lunchroom."[421]

Press: "Although . . . Johnson has not yet offered the networks an opportunity to televise his press conferences, he is not ignoring them completely. High officials of the three national networks were invited to lunch with the President at the White House on three successive days this week. . . . The networks . . . do not yet know what policy Mr. Johnson will adopt. At another of his informal surprise meetings with the press on Wednesday he said that he wanted to maintain a flexibility—maybe 'a meeting of this kind today, maybe a televised meeting tomorrow, with maybe a coffee session the next day.' "[422] Note that Johnson has not changed significantly in his attitude toward the press, still fearful, perhaps the more so because of the Baker hearings.

Press: "The Senate Rules Committee . . . has subpoenaed bank records of [Baker's] borrowings. . . . No further hearings will be held by the Committee until January."[423]

12/20/63—FRIDAY: Press reports on the FBI's control over Marina: "Curiously, neither the Secret Service nor the Department of Justice is willing to take responsibility for holding Mrs. Oswald or for silencing her. . . . Her seclusion may continue for months, at the insistence of the Department of Justice, until the Government's investigation of the case is completed. . . . Few persons besides agents of the Federal Bureau of Investigation have been allowed to see her. . . . Mr. Martin repeated today that Mrs. Oswald would not now be permitted to cast more light on the unanswered questions raised by the assassination. . . . Meanwhile, it has been disclosed that ballistics tests conducted by the FBI have failed to establish that a bullet fired at . . . Walker last April was from the type of rifle used to kill President Kennedy."[424]

LBJ is in communication with Russell four times today.[425]

3:35 P.M.: Hoover calls LBJ.[426]

4:08 P.M.: Ford calls LBJ.[427]

Deloach sends a memo (presumably to Hoover) concerning a meeting with Commission member Russell. "Russell confided to [DeLoach] that he had tried to talk . . . [Johnson] out of naming him to the panel because it was 'a nasty job [and] very distasteful to him . . . to serve on the same Commission as Chief Justice Warren, inasmuch as he had no respect for Warren.' "[428] Note that this makes three Commission members, Ford, Dulles, and Russell, who dislike Warren. Hoover then, through DeLoach, is now communicating with Ford and Russell.

12/21/63—SATURDAY: Press: "An agent of the Federal Bureau of Investigation waited in vain beside mortally wounded Lee H. Oswald . . . for a deathbed confession. . . . . . . An agent, wearing the robe and face mask of a doctor, stood at Oswald's side until Oswald was pronounced dead."[429]

"Ruby filled in . . . specifics on December 21, when the FBI interviewed him again." He discloses the fact that ". . . he had carried a handgun into the Dallas police station on Friday night, November 22, when he first viewed Oswald in the station." He also states that he always carried a gun.[430] He denies having gone to Parkland Hospital shortly after the assassination. He refers to Oswald as "smirky, smug, *vindictive*" (emphasis added).[431] Ruby's choice of the last descriptive is odd. Why would he describe Oswald as "vindictive"? This may imply that he thought Oswald, by his denials of guilt, was somehow getting revenge. Against whom? The fact that Ruby had undoubtedly helped engineer Oswald's frameup may help explain his choice of words. He had perhaps taken Oswald's denials and arrogant demeanor personally. Ruby may see him in this light because he was maneuvered into killing him, becoming a murderer.

5:45 P.M.: LBJ calls Russell.

8:07 P.M.: Hale Boggs calls LBJ.[432]

12/22/63—SUNDAY: Ruby again meets with his psychiatrist. He speaks of McWillie and his admiration for the man. "He sent me tickets to Cuba—think of it, a man like that sending me tickets."[433]

12/23/63—MONDAY: Press: ". . . Melvin M. Belli, the chief defense attorney, said he would ask that Ruby's murder trial be moved out of Dallas. 'It is utterly and completely impossible to have a fair trial in Dallas due to the statements that have been made by The Dallas News.' "[434]

Ruby employee Karen Bennett and his roommate George Senator testify at a hearing in Dallas. Bennett, who within months will be found shot to death in a Houston hotel, is carrying a gun in her purse, wearing sunglasses, and appears frightened. She testifies that the morning Ruby murdered Oswald he had wired money to her for rent, prior to entering the police station basement. "Mr. Senator . . . said that Ruby woke him up at 3 o'clock on the morning of Nov. 23. The first thing Ruby asked him was whether Mr. Senator had seen Ruby's advertisement announcing that his night club would be closed that Friday, Saturday and Sunday. . . . 'He had a look in his eye I've never seen before—a stary look—a stony look. He looked like he was out in space.' "[435]

"When [Dallas P.D. officer] Olsen was questioned by the FBI, he acknowledged that the [meeting with Ruby] had taken place but denied encouraging Ruby to murder Oswald, and told the FBI he 'never liked Ruby.' A month after the shooting of Oswald, Olsen abruptly left the police force under unclear circumstances, and left Dallas."[436]

Johnson sends yet another autographed photo to Hoover. This one apparently is of him and the director together. It is inscribed "To J. Edgar the best, LBJ"[437]

"An autopsy report signed on Sunday, November 24, had gone from Bethesda Naval Hospital to the White House the next day."[438] "The FBI and the Warren Commission each received a copy of the official autopsy report on December 23. . . ."[439]

12:35 P.M.: LBJ calls Boggs.[440]

Press: "Oswald . . . tried to enter a military language school by taking a test in Russian, a Marine Corps officer disclosed today. 'I don't know the official result, . . . but he said when he came back that he'd flunked the test.' "[441]

12/26/63—THURSDAY: Press: "Marina Oswald . . . will go to Washington to testify before the Federal Commission. . . ."[442]

FBI (Alabama) interviews another Ruby associate, Jack Hardee, Jr., in a federal prison. "He stated that this individual . . . told him that Ruby had the 'fix' with the [Dallas] county authorities, and that any other fix being placed would have to be done through Ruby. . . . Hardee also stated that the police officer . . . Oswald allegedly killed . . . was a frequent visitor to Ruby's night club along with another officer who was a motorcycle patrol in the Oaklawn section of Dallas. Hardee stated from his observation there appeared to be a very close relationship between these three individuals."[443]

Hoover letter to Johnson.

My dear Mr. President:

Thank you so much for the beautiful leather-bound copy of "The White House" which you autographed to me. I shall treasure this book as I do your friendship. Thank you especially, also, for the autographed photograph which was taken on the day I had luncheon with you. This will always remain in my mind as a most memorable occasion.

With every good wish for the New Year,

Sincerely yours,
Edgar[444]

12/27/63—FRIDAY: Ruth Paine responds to Marina's letter of December 24. "You closed your face to me. Is it true, have I offended you?"[445]

Press: "SANTA BARBARA . . . The sheriff's office investigated today the hanging in effigy of Chief Justice Earl Warren from the county courthouse flagpole, as well as a sign describing him as 'Head of the Oswald Whitewash Committee.' "[446]

Press reports on a Johnson party at his ranch. "The President's question-and-answer session, labeled by the White House as Mr. Johnson's 'Press Conference No. 3,' took many of the 200 reporters and photographers by surprise. . . . While a press briefing by Mr. Salinger had been announced, there was no hint that Mr. Johnson would take it over and answer questions. The reporters were herded into three buses for the tour of the ranch and its neighboring countryside. Acting as tour guide in one was Mrs. Johnson. . . . The President also had on low-heeled Western boots and wore a zippered windbreaker. The portly Mr. Salinger was wearing a similar windbreaker and the President, standing a full head taller than his press secretary, quipped: 'I gave Pierre that jacket he has on today because it is too large for me to wear.' "[447] Both Johnson's wariness of the press and cruelty toward aides is here apparent.

Press: "A member of the Warren Commission and . . . [general counsel] Rankin . . . intend to come to Dallas early next year to question . . . Marina . . . Mr. Rankin said today. He said the commission had tentatively decided to hold the hearing with the widow of President Kennedy's accused assassin here, rather than in Washington. . . . Commission members have announced that the hearings would be closed and that the reports from the Federal Bureau of Investigation submitted to the commission would not be made public until after the murder trial of Jack L. Ruby. . . . Mrs. Oswald . . . preferred to testify in Dallas, a spokesman said."[448]

12/28/63—SATURDAY: Ruth writes another letter to Marina. "They say that it is your choice to speak with someone or not to speak. . . . But I do not believe this, while I have not heard it from your lips."[449] The distancing of Marina from Ruth and her husband may well have occurred because of the Paines' association with the ACLU.

12/29/63—SUNDAY: Press: ". . . Johnson perched a ten-gallon Texas hat on the head of Chancellor Ludwig Erhard today after this German-speaking area had tendered the West German leader a 'herzlich wilkommen.' . . . Mr. Johnson said he would have to call it a 'forty-liter hat.' In high good humor . . . Johnson acted as his own master of ceremonies in handing out more than 30 of the broad-brimmed felt hats. For some of the recipients he even 'creased' the hats, a ritual taken seriously by Texans. The President . . . at one point called upon . . . Salinger, to play the piano. . . . Salinger . . . got a forty-liter hat as a reward."[450]

12/30/63—MONDAY: Press: "At the LBJ Ranch today . . . Johnson posed with the defense chiefs for pictures. There was an air of jollity, and the President reported: . . . 'I'm sorry these Joint Chiefs came down here, these warmongers, and cooled things off, . . .' Johnson suddenly seized General Shoup's arm. 'It's his birthday . . . let's all sing "Happy Birthday" to him.' . . . The generals, Admiral McDonald, the Secretary of Defense, the photographers, six freezing reporters and the President of the United States raised their voices in the howling wind and sang General Shoup a happy birthday."[451] Note Johnson's curious ebullience in both this article and the one directly preceding it. The rest of the nation is still in shock, the Baker hearings may not as yet have been contained, and yet LBJ appears as lighthearted as ever.

Press: Apparently calling for legal representation for the deceased Oswald, "Percy Foreman . . . president of the National Association of Defense Attorneys, said: 'There's no other way, in my opinion, that the evidence in this case can be properly evaluated.' He participated in a CBS-television panel show, 'The Law and Lee Oswald.' . . . Marina, will go to Washington next month to testify before the commission, according to a source close to her in Fort Worth. She remained in seclusion today. . . ."[452]

Press: "The night before . . . Walker was shot at . . . Oswald left his wife instructions on what to do if he were arrested, The Houston Chronicle said today. . . . Information on the instructions . . . was turned over to the Presidential commission. . . . The notes from Oswald told his wife . . . that something about to happen might get him arrested."[453]

12/31/63—TUESDAY: Press: "LOS ANGELES . . . Boys, Inc., a California charitable organization of which Clint Murchison, Sr., . . . is president, is planning to sue the Federal Government for nearly a million dollars. . . . The state-owned track facilities at Del Mar are indirectly under a seasonal lease to Boys Incorporated of America. . . . Boys, Inc., now has a board of directors that includes . . . Gov. John B. Connally, Jr., of Texas and others. . . . The conflict has attracted attention because of the peripheral involvement of . . . Baker. . . . Gov. . . . Brown of California has confirmed that Mr. Baker acted as an intermediary in a discussion Mr. Brown held last spring with Clint Murchison, Jr., . . . The discussion, it was stated, was concerned with avoiding any interruption of Del Mar's annual fall race meeting, regardless of who was conducting it. . . . The Murchison claim for charitable exemption rests on an unusual philanthropic undertaking and a complicated financial arrangement. . . . In effect it is trying to combat juvenile delinquency by facilitating adult gambling. He is channeling revenue from race track gambling into work against juvenile delinquency. Boys, Inc., developed . . . from a conversation Mr. Murchison had with J. Edgar Hoover . . . a decade ago, during the racing season at Del Mar. Mr. Hoover, who often visits race tracks, is said to have remarked: 'If I had the money that's spent at race tracks, I could do a wonderful job building character among the nation's young people.' "[454]

Press: "New information linking . . . Oswald with an attempt on the life of . . . Walker was disclosed today by a spokesman for Oswald's widow. . . . Marina . . . has told agents investigating the assassination . . . that her husband confessed to her that he had fired a rifle bullet at . . . Walker last spring. . . . The disclosures . . . came today from Jim Martin, speaking for Mrs. Oswald. . . . Mr. Martin said that after the Walker episode, Mrs. Oswald warned her husband that if he were to shoot at anyone else she would turn his note over to the police as evidence against him. . . . Ballistics tests conducted by the Federal Bureau of Investigation failed to prove that the bullet fired at Mr. Walker was the same type that killed the President."[455] Note that in the coming months the now overly cooperative Marina will also say that Oswald planned to kill Richard Nixon during the time period leading up to the assassination.[456]

1/64—THIS MONTH: Johnson's ". . . conversation . . . with . . . DeLoach . . . [concerned] the 'continued employment' of individuals associated with Robert Kennedy. . . . Hoover both catered to and sustained Johnson's fears—for his own reasons. The Director first learned of this opportunity in January 1964, following DeLoach's briefing on a recent meeting with Walter Jenkins concerning an individual described by Jenkins as 'strictly Bobby Kennedy's boy and [one] that Kennedy had been protecting . . . all along.' As a matter of 'strict confidence,' Jenkins advised, Johnson 'was not yet quite ready to take on Bobby, however, [name deleted but apparently Paul Corbin] would definitely be eased out in the near future when the time was right.' Hoover unhesitatingly queried: 'Have we furnished Jenkins a memo on [name deleted]?' On Hoover's order DeLoach furnished the memo to Jenkins that same day."[457] Note that in the fall of this year Jenkins will be arrested by local police for attempting to sodomize another man in a D.C. bathroom, resulting in his resignation from Johnson's staff. Hoover will personally intervene on Johnson's behalf in this investigation as well.[458]

"Johnson did not hesitate to turn to Hoover for information about his administration's critics (which information, for ideological as well as strategic reasons, Hoover generously gave); for another, Johnson, like Hoover, harbored an inordinate interest in derogatory personal information. . . . The two men were made for each other."[459]

". . . In January, . . . the staff got into a heated argument over whether . . . Marina should be asked to submit to [a lie detector examination] . . . as a backup to her regular testimony. Assistant Counsel David Belin felt there were many . . . facts about what the widow knew and had seen, and led the fight to have the test made available to her. . . . Belin failed to convince superiors . . . at the Commission."[460]

1/1/64—WEDNESDAY: Press: ". . . Marina . . . will testify this month . . . before the Presidential commission. . . . Mrs. Oswald was watching television when President Kennedy was slain, Mr. Thorn said. 'Like millions of Americans she was shocked. . . . She told me she never dreamed at the time that officers would arrest her husband and charge him with the assassination.' Mrs. Oswald knows of the evidence against her husband . . . 'but I don't know whether she is convinced in her mind that he pulled the trigger.' "[461]

Hoover turns sixty-nine, entering his final allowable year as director under federal statute.

FBI Law Enforcement Bulletin is released. Hoover's message is about the citizen's duty to combat crime. "It is most disheartening to note the increasing abuse and ridicule inflicted on officers throughout the country. . . . These contemptible incidents are shocking incidents of a civilized society. They are a disgrace to a privileged people who choose to live under a government of law, but in many instances flout and attack those charged with administering and enforcing the law." This issue of the *Bulletin* also carries Hoover's 11/16/63 speech.[462]

The Houston Post publishes an article entitled "Oswald Rumored as Informant for U.S." Wade is quoted as saying, "It may be true, but I don't think it will ever be made public."[463]

Press: "The ACLU urged the Federal Communications Commission to withdraw a questionnaire sent to [Pacifica] foundation directors on possible Communist affiliations. . . . The Pacifica Foundation decided against filling out the form. The FCC move was called 'a serious threat to freedom of speech and diversity of opinion on the air'. . . . One particular program that aroused Washington's attention included a former agent for the Federal Bureau of Investigation who criticized J. Edgar Hoover, the FBI director."[464]

8:32 P.M.: LBJ calls Russell.[465]

1/2/64—THURSDAY: Press: ". . . Hoover . . . reported today that the Communist party was striving to exploit what it termed a 'drift toward the left' among the nation's youth. . . . He also said that an investigation of the assassination of President Kennedy and the slaying of Lee Oswald . . . had been completed."[466]

FBI agents Kaiser and Miller interview journalist Seth Kantor regarding his claim of having seen Ruby at Parkland Hospital. They tell him Ruby has denied it. Kaiser's report reads, "He was asked what he would say if under oath and on the witness stand in a court of law. . . ."[467] For the definitive analysis of Ruby, see Kantor's *Who Was Jack Ruby?*

1/3/64—FRIDAY: Press: "DALLAS . . . Judge . . . Brown delayed today a bond hearing for Jack Ruby until Jan. 24."[468]

Press: "Herbert A. Philbrick, who . . . lived three lives as a counter-spy for the Federal Bureau of Investigation, said today that the American Civil Liberties Union was used effectively as a Communist front. . . . Mr. Philbrick said that today on all major issues, the position taken by the Communist party and by the ACLU was identical."[469]

1/5/64—SUNDAY: Press: ". . . Johnson returned to Washington. . . ." Speaking of Johnson's Texas environment, the article states, "Now, when the President and his family take their nightly walk a mile down the road to visit Cousin Oriole Bailey, the silent presence of watchful men is sensed. . . . There is even a white phone in Cousin Oriole's house. 'Don't you pick that thing up Cousin Oriole,' the President said jokingly the other night, 'Khrushchev might answer.' . . . The sound of Muzak, piped in from Austin, 65 miles away, fills the main house, the guest house, the foreman's house, and even the yard and swimming pool terrace. . . . Mr. Johnson, for instance, rides over his acres in a glittering Lincoln Continental. . . . He sounds a specially fitted horn that moans like a sad bull. Not far from one end of the paved landing strip, hogs fatten for the winter kill. Chickens flutter in a coop near where the President's personal plane, a $90,000 twin-engined craft, waits in a hangar. . . . The car . . . paused, the horn moaning, beside a pen where Herefords are fattened for slaughter and eating on the ranch. . . . Around the ranch house Mr. Johnson is a relaxed, talkative, entertaining host. An excellent mimic, he accompanies his tales with good-natured imitations of acquaintances. . . ."[470]

1/6/64—MONDAY: Press: "District Attorney Henry Wade said today that an intensive investigation showed 'no evidence whatever' of any collusion between Jack Ruby and Dallas police officers in the slaying of . . . Oswald. . . . He received a report prepared by an investigating board that had been appointed by Police Chief Jesse Curry. He said a copy . . . had been sent to the Warren Commission. . . ."[471]

Press: "Nancy Carol Tyler is back in Washington, working as secretary for . . . Baker. . . . She is reported to be living in the town house that she occupied for several months before leaving the

Senate position. The house, owned by Mr. Baker, was said to have been used by him for entertaining."[472]

Johnson writes a letter to Edward F. Ryan, President of the Radio Television News Directors' Association: "You may be sure that we will make full use of television in the months ahead, and television will be permitted to cover some of our press conferences. We would be most interested in any suggestions you have in making more effective use of television and radio."[473]

Press: "Daniel Garcia . . . appeared last night on the television panel show 'I've Got a Secret.' He told Garry Moore . . . that he had been spanked by a teacher when he was thirteen years old. It developed that the teacher was . . . Johnson. While the program was still on live, [LBJ], who had been watching it, called the Columbia Broadcasting System studio here and asked to speak to Mr. Garcia. The invitation to the White House and acceptance followed."[474]

1/7/64—TUESDAY: Press: "Mrs. Lee H. Oswald is convinced that her husband assassinated President Kennedy, her business advisor said today. James H. Martin . . . said her conviction was so strong that even if a jury could find Oswald not guilty her opinion would be unchanged. . . . 'She has this feeling that her husband killed the President,' Mr. Martin said. 'When the lawsuits are proposed to her she says that we should let sleeping dogs lie.' . . . *'Secret Service agents are guarding her, at the direct order of . . . Johnson,* because there had been some crank letters threatening her life.' . . . She now lives in a private residence in the Dallas area. Both Mrs. Marguerite Oswald . . . and Mrs. Rugh [*sic*] Paine . . . have protested that they have not been able to see her for the last six weeks. Mr. Martin said it was Marina Oswald's decision not to speak with them" (emphasis added).[475]

Press: ". . . Ruby's defense attorney said today that he would go to court if necessary to obtain copies of the Federal reports on President Kennedy's assassination. Joe Tonahill . . . said Ruby . . . would be offered to the Warren Commission as a witness."[476] Another article states "The Warren Commission has promised to give 'appropriate consideration' to a New York lawyer's brief raising points in behalf of . . . Oswald . . ."[477]

Press: "The Senate Rules Committee will resume Thursday its inquiry into . . . Baker. . . . The closed session will deal with

Mr. Baker's insurance interests. Mr. Baker . . . was once a silent partner in an insurance company here. The company . . . later wrote a $200,000 policy on the life of . . . Johnson, then the Senate Democratic leader. . . . Representative . . . Gross, Republican of Iowa, told the House last month that the Rules Committee 'is now in possession of information that the L.B.J. Company . . . was spending $7,000 to $12,000 a year for a "key man" insurance policy for $200,000 on the life of Lyndon B. Johnson.' "[478]

1/8/64—WEDNESDAY: Press reports on the return of RFK to work: "He had no heart for his work for weeks after the assassination. . . . Pale, subdued almost to the point of numbness."[479]

"When Kennedy returned to his office . . . , Hoover stopped reporting to him in favor of reporting directly to the White House. Courtney Evans was removed from his liaison job and was replaced by . . . DeLoach, who was a good friend of . . . Johnson's aide Walter Jenkins. The FBI ceased sending an official car to pick up Kennedy during his travels. . . ."[480]

6:05 P.M.: LBJ calls Russell.

7:45 P.M.: LBJ calls lobbyist Corcoran.[481]

1/10/64—FRIDAY: Press: "Mrs. Lee H. Oswald has written to the Dallas Civil Liberties Union that she is satisfied with her seclusion and with the protection of the Secret Service. She also said that she was continuing to meet with agents from the Federal Bureau of Investigation. 'I am in as good a position as one can expect me to be after what has happened,' her letter said. Officials of the civil-liberties group had requested an interview with her to assure themselves that Oswald's widow was not being held by the Government against her will. The organization received instead a letter in Russian. . . . Greg L. Olds, president of the group, said that its officers would continue to seek an interview with Mrs. Oswald. . . . The Secret Service will probably continue to guard her until the Presidential commission that is studying the assassination makes its report, her advisors have said. . . . 'We will not know all the circumstances unless we can talk with her firsthand,' he said. . . . 'Let me thank you,' the note began, 'for the attention you are giving me. I don't think you have anything to worry about. . . . What you read in the newspapers—everything is correct. I don't object to the Secret Service guarding me. I am only grateful for their time. . . . I am free to go where I want and see whom I please. I myself don't want to see anybody to remind me of what has happened. I hope you understand. . . . When I feel I'm ready, I would see with pleasure Mrs. Ruth Paine, who is a very nice person. I hope you also understand that I lived in a strange house. I wouldn't want to inconvenience anyone as kind as Mrs. Paine with the visitors I would be sure to receive. . . . *I also give much time to visits with the FBI'* " (emphasis added).[482] In all, Marina, according to her count, is interrogated by the FBI forty-six times during this period.[483]

Johnson calls Russell twice this day.[484]

Press reports Mrs. Kennedy had an inscription carved on the mantel of the presidential bedroom two days prior to leaving the White House. It read, "In this room lived John Fitzgerald Kennedy with his wife Jacqueline during the two years, ten months and two days he was President of the United States."[485]

1/11/64—SATURDAY: Press: "The staff of the commission investigating President Kennedy's assassination has divided its job into six broad areas of inquiry. One covers every detail of Lee Oswald's activities on the day of the assassination. . . . A second topic is the life and background of Oswald. . . . Oswald's career in the Marine Corps and his stay in the Soviet Union will be handled separately as a third. His murder in the Dallas police station will be the fourth subject. . . . Fifth will be the story of Jack Ruby. . . . Finally, the staff will inquire exhaustively into the procedures used to protect President Kennedy. This will involve a scrutiny of the performances of the Secret Service, the Federal Bureau of Investigation, and the Dallas police. . . . Rankin said there was no intention to appoint a lawyer to act in Oswald's behalf as a kind of defense counsel. 'The commission is not engaged in determining the guilt of anybody,' Mr. Rankin said. 'It is a fact-finding body.' . . . These hearings will be closed to the public. A first hearing is expected to be held later this month to take the testimony of Oswald's Russian-born wife, Marina, who has not talked to the press since the tragedy. *Mr. Rankin said there was no present intention to hire private investigators. Instead the commission will rely primarily on Government investigative agencies for any further checking needed. But Mr. Rankin said there would be no shying away from investigative scrutiny of these same agencies' performance"* (emphasis added).[486] The logic of Rankin's reasoning in this last regard is profoundly flawed. In relying on Hoover for the bulk of the raw data he will, ultimately, only arrive at the conclusion the Director dictates. Here the general counsel effectively reveals the schizophrenic nature of his unenviable position. Simply put, he is being subjected to two powerful opposing forces—historical versus political truth.

1:05 P.M.: LBJ calls Russell.[487]

Ruby's psychiatrist, Bromberg, forwards a seventeen-page memo to Belli. "Ruby [is] . . . basically an extremely unstable man. This is an aggressive psychopath with definite antisocial feelings." He also notes that Ruby has a "kind of hysterical interest in religion."[488] Considering the nature of his crimes, it is small wonder Ruby has turned to religion.

Press: "The Justice Department's fight against organized crime is beginning to show substantial results in terms of actual cases. Figures released by the White House this week disclosed. . . . The Federal Bureau of Investigation, which had not been deeply involved in the crime problem, has become much more so. . . . Johnson, in releasing the figures, paid a particular tribute to Mr. Kennedy. He *said 'it should be recognized that the intensified Federal effort against organized crime stems in large part from the deep interest and leadership of the Attorney General. His efforts deserve our appreciation' "* (emphasis added).[489] Ironically, were it not for the efforts of the Kennedys in this area, Johnson would not have obtained power. LBJ is famous for his psychological cruelty. Given that he and RFK have long been bitter enemies, one can only wonder in what context, at this point, Johnson is expressing his appreciation.

LBJ and Russell talk twice, then watch a movie together this evening at the White House.[490] Given their almost daily interaction, one would assume that the deliberations of the Commission are a recurring topic of conversation. Although he will personally attend few hearings in the coming months, Russell, through aides, can easily be Johnson's eyes and ears on the Commission. If so, the former's ultimate opposition to the conclusions of the Warren Report, like Cooper's, becomes all the more paradoxical.

1/13/64—MONDAY: Baker press coverage continues: "In other testimony, a *Nevada gambler, Edward Levinson, was identified as a major stockholder in the Serve-U Corporation, the vending ma-*

chine concern that is the nucleus of Mr. Baker's financial interests. Today's hearing also produced the first public corroboration of statements by the Capitol Vending Company that its president had made substantial payments to Mr. Baker in return for the latter's influence in arranging for a profitable contract at a Virginia defense plant. . . . Mr. Hill told the Committee that he 'had heard' that Mr. Baker had negotiated a $100,000 loan from 'a union.' He did not elaborate. However, Mr. Hill [later] told a reporter that he had been told by 'an insurance man' about a loan and that the money had come from the teamsters' union's Western Conference pension fund. . . . *Testimony that* . . . *Levinson, a Las Vegas casino operator who long has been a figure in Newport Kentucky gambling, was linked with Mr. Baker was the first tentative substantiation of reports that gambling money might be involved in Mr. Baker's activities.* Mr. Levinson has declined to discuss any relationship with Mr. Baker" (emphasis added).[491]

Hoover turns over a second, supplemental report to the Warren Commission, summarizing additional investigative conclusions of the FBI. ". . . A fifth volume . . . was sent to the Commission on January 13, 1964."[492]

1/14/64—TUESDAY: Press: "An assertion that . . . *Baker* . . . *was linked to Las Vegas gambling interests* was put into the public record *today.* . . . *Mr. Baker was co-signer on a $175,000 bank loan in March, 1962, with Edward Levinson, Benny Sigelbaum and Fred A. Black.* The four men used the money in a financial venture, it was stated. Mr. *Levinson and* Mr. *Sigelbaum are operators of gambling casinos in Las Vegas,* Nev." (emphasis added).[493]

"In an FBI interview on January 14, . . . Civello acknowledged having known Ruby for 'about ten years.' "[494]

Mark Lane writes a letter to Chief Justice Warren. "I have been retained by Mrs. Marguerite C. Oswald . . . to represent the interests of the deceased Lee Harvey Oswald before your Commission."[495]

Press: "Mrs. Marguerite Oswald told a news conference at her home that Mark Lane, a former New York Assemblyman, had agreed to present a defense for Oswald before the Commission. . . . "[496]

Press will report: ". . . Rankin . . . has said the group had no intention of appointing a lawyer to act in Oswald's behalf. 'The

Commission is not engaged in determining the guilt of anybody,'
Mr. Rankin said over the weekend."[497]

Press: "A New York House member asked today why . . .
Johnson had held no televised news conferences. . . . Representative . . . Horton . . . said he was concerned by what he called a
'news lockout at the White House.' This cannot be corrected, he
said, by an occasional kaffee klatsch, barbecue or guided tour."[498]

1/15/64—WEDNESDAY: Press: "The Texas Court of Criminal Appeals upheld today the conviction of . . . Estes on swindling charges and ruled that he must serve an eight year prison
sentence. . . . His attorney, Hume Cofer, also refused comment.
. . . Estes still has pending against him four more Federal and state
indictments containing more than 30 counts of theft, swindling,
mail fraud, false statements and criminal antitrust violations."[499]

4:30 P.M.: LBJ calls Russell.[500]

1/16/64—THURSDAY: Press: "Attorneys for . . . Ruby
charged today that 'a hostile press of much power and influence in
Dallas' wanted the nightclub owner to die in the electric chair. . . .
They asked Judge . . . Brown to transfer the trial to some other
area. . . . Meanwhile, defense attorneys subpoenaed 21 witnesses
for the resumption of Ruby's bond hearing. . . . The witnesses include Police Chief Jesse Curry, Federal Bureau of Investigation
agents. . . ."[501]

4:15 P.M.: LBJ calls Russell.[502]

1/17/64—FRIDAY: Press: "The Internal Revenue Service has
found that . . . Estes . . . owes the Government more than $18.2
million in back taxes and fraud penalties."[503]

Rankin contacts Hoover, requesting information regarding the
films and photos of the assassination so that he can arrange a viewing.[504]

Baker associate Don Reynolds (no relation to the Harold Reynolds discussed at 11/17/63) again testifies before the Rules Committee in closed-door session. "Reynolds then told the details of his
dealings with Jenkins on . . . Johnson's life insurance. . . . Senator . . . Cooper asked Reynolds if he had talked with Johnson
about the insurance. Reynolds replied that he personally delivered
the . . . policy to the then Majority Leader. . . . Senator . . .

Curtis asked about the $1,208 purchase of advertising time on LBJ's station. Curtis: 'Why did you buy it?' Reynolds: 'Because it was expected of me, sir.' Curtis: 'Who conveyed that thought to you?' Reynolds: 'Mr. Walter Jenkins, sir.' "[505] Unfortunately for Johnson, this is only the tip of the iceberg. Baker himself undoubtedly knows the intricacies of many, much larger scale instances of bribes and kickbacks to LBJ during the 1950s and early 1960s.

1/18/64—SATURDAY: Press: ". . . Johnson . . . has invited newsmen to suggest ways for more effective use of the medium. . . . Johnson has held no formal news conference in Washington since taking office last Nov. 22, but he has met informally with newsmen a number of times both here and at his Texas ranch. These sessions have not been broadcast."[506]
   LBJ and Russell meet for a private lunch.[507]

1/19/64—SUNDAY: Press: "Attorneys for . . . Ruby will base their defense on a psychiatrist's report that he suffers from organic brain damage. They will attempt to prove that damage to Ruby's brain has produced a form of epilepsy."[508]
   LBJ calls Russell.[509]

1/20/64—MONDAY: Hoover responds to Rankin's request. ". . . Set forth herein-after is a list of the films that can be shown at any time at the office of the President's Commission: . . . Hughes . . . Zapruder . . . Nix. . . ."[510] At this point Hoover is still asserting that two shots hit Kennedy, a third hit Connally, and that there were no misses.
   Press releases a story quoting defense psychiatrist Bromberg as saying of Ruby that he didn't remember the Oswald shooting because he was experiencing severe emotional shock after the Kennedy assassination.[511]
   Press: "The Senate Rules Committee will release tomorrow testimony about an insurance man's purchase of a $465 stereophonic set for . . . Johnson when he was majority leader of the Senate. . . . Mr. Reynolds, a business associate of Mr. Baker, is said to have sold . . . Johnson a $200,000 life insurance policy. It is understood that the policy was purchased by the L.B.J. Company, a family holding company that was controlled by Mrs. Johnson until she placed her stock in trust after Mr. Johnson succeeded to the Presidency. An-

drew Hatcher, assistant White House press secretary, had no comment when asked about the reports."[512]

LBJ calls Russell.[513]

1/21/64—TUESDAY: Press: "An aide to . . . Johnson and a Maryland insurance man have given conflicting testimony about an alleged advertising kickback to a Texas television station owned by the President's family. . . . He testified that, with Mr. Baker's help, he sold . . . Johnson $200,000 worth of life insurance from 1957 to 1961. He told the Committee under oath that a Johnson aide, Walter Jenkins, had induced him to buy $1,200 worth of advertising on station KTBO of Austin, Tex., owned by the LBJ Company. . . . In an affidavit . . . Mr. Jenkins denied that he had ever talked to Mr. Reynolds about buying advertising time. The testimony also showed that, at Mr. Baker's insistence, Mr. Reynolds gave . . . Johnson a $542 [a several-thousand-dollar system in today's dollars] stereophonic phonograph in 1959 and paid $42.5 for its installation in the Senator's Spring Valley home. '. . . The invoice was billed from the Magnavox Company directly to Senator Johnson. . . .' . . . In his sworn statement, Mr. Jenkins said he had been informed that 'the alleged gift of the record player to Mr. and Mrs. Johnson was a present from . . . Baker.' . . . Mr. Reynolds was recently 'threatened' by Mr. Baker's law partner, Ernest C. Tucker, because of his testimony before the Committee. . . . *The Democratic members are believed to be wary about looking too deeply into areas that impinge upon the relationship between Mr. Baker and [Johnson].* For the decade while . . . Johnson was Senate Democratic leader and Vice President, Mr. Baker was regarded as his protégé. . . . Mr. *Baker* also *put [Reynolds] in touch with Mr. Webb, a Washington lawyer who* represented Clint Murchison . . . and *had close connections with . . . Hoffa.* . . . Through Mr. Webb, the group obtained a $100,000 mortgage loan from the teamsters' union welfare and retirement fund. . . . Later the group got a commitment from the fund for an additional loan of $400,000. . . . In 1961, Mr. Johnson, then Vice President, bought another $100,000 policy through the same company, making his daughters the beneficiaries. Mr. Reynolds said that sometime before the second policy was placed he was called to Mr. Jenkins's office. He was shown a letter from a rival Texas insurance man saying that if he, the rival, could write insurance on Mr. Johnson, he would be will-

ing to buy advertising time on station KTBC, Mr. Reynolds said"
(emphasis added).[514] Note the connections between Baker and Hoffa
via Teamster loans.

10:45 A.M.: LBJ meets with McCloy.[515]

". . . Hoover, in response to the Warren Commission's [Decem-
ber 16] demand for raw FBI data, began sending hundreds of FBI
investigative reports to the Warren Commission. At this time, . . .
Katzenbach designated Howard Willens to serve as liaison between
the Warren Commission and the Justice Department in the handling of all FBI documents sent to the commission. Soon he became
an assistant to . . . Rankin. . . . Since . . . Willens had been
working in the division of the Justice Department that was directly
concerned with Attorney General Kennedy's . . . war on organized crime, . . . Willens would have been familiar with the Marcello organization. . . . [He] should have immediately recognized
the names David Ferrie, Carlos Marcello . . . Joseph Marcello
. . . if he had managed to pluck the allegations in which these
names were mentioned from the huge piles of crank allegations
Hoover had sent over to satisfy the commission's request for the
FBI's 'raw files.' . . . We are left then, with the . . . conclusion
that either Howard Willens saw fit not to bring the allegations involving the Marcellos to the attention of . . . the commission or,
. . . the commission chose to ignore them."[516]

Ruby gives a press conference while at his bail hearing, in which
he denies ever knowing Oswald. "Ruby spoke distraughtly as he
appeared at a bail hearing, which ended when his attorneys withdrew their request that he be released on bond. . . . The attorney
at his side, Joe H. Tonahill, made no attempt to stop him. . . .
Pale and agitated, Ruby recalled that . . . he had gone to Cuba by
way of New Orleans. In Havana, he said, he stayed at the apartment of a friend, L. J. McWillie. . . . 'I never spoke to Lee Oswald
in my life, I never saw him or knew of him.' . . . *Ruby, . . . became more nervous and excited as he spoke. Unexpectedly, he said:
'The word angry is not in my vocabulary. I was more remorseful than
angry.' Asked what he had meant, he said that after the assassination
. . . he had often been described as angry. Ruby was swallowing
repeatedly; he had become pale and was trembling; tears came to his
eyes. He replied in a high, choked voice: 'I can't understand how a
great man like that can be lost.' Mr. Tonahill cut off further questions. . . .* William Alexander, who is prosecuting the case with

Mr. Wade, was called by the defense. He testified that he knew
Ruby 12 years" (emphasis added).[517] Ruby's admission that he feels
"remorseful" (i.e., deep and painful sense of guilt for wrongdoing)
immediately after the assassination is telling. Given his role in facilitating the assassination, such a remark is also quite logical. It undoubtedly makes the reporters around him uneasy—small wonder
his attorney cuts off further questions at this point.

Press reports: "[Mark Lane] said he wrote to . . . Chief Justice
Earl Warren . . . 'to determine the nature of [Marina Oswald's]
confinement and to discover if unfair and inappropriate methods
have been utilized to tamper with or influence her testimony.' "[518]

Press reports on Commission staff appointments. "Leon D. Hubert, Jr., a New Orleans lawyer, was appointed a senior attorney on
the staff. . . . The commission scheduled its next meeting for next
week."[519] The influence of Hale Boggs (R-La.) in this appointment
is apparent. It is logical to assume all Commission members had
such input in staff selection.

1/22/64—WEDNESDAY: Press: "Republicans were sharply
critical today over an allegation that . . . Johnson's family received a kickback on an insurance policy bought from an associate
of . . . Baker. They also decried a gift of a stereo phonograph to
the Johnsons from the associate of Mr. Baker. . . . Representative
. . . Gross . . . asked in the House: 'Was pressure put on . . .
Reynolds . . . to force him to rebate or kickback things of value to
Lyndon B. Johnson and the LBJ Company?' . . . Efforts to reach
Mr. Jenkins at the White House for comment on the matter were
unavailing. . . . 'Whenever anyone gives a public official an article
of such value, he is expecting something in return and any public
official who accepts such gifts is not so naïve as to be unable to
recognize the point. . . .' 'It is time for the committee investigators
of the other body to quit toying with Mr. Walter Jenkins and engage
in serious questioning of this man as to his involvement in the gift of
a stereophonic set to Lyndon B. Johnson. It is clear favoritism to
permit the type of statement he did. It would seem to me that even
if the White House version is correct, Mr. Johnson should have
raised some questions if his $19,600-a-year protégé suddenly be-
stowed a stereo set, with an $800 or $900 retail value, on him as a
gift.' "[520]

Ex-FBI agents Carr and Wade contact Rankin to inform him of

specific allegations that Oswald had been a paid FBI informant during the time from September 1962 to the day of the assassination, reinforcing recent press stories to that effect. The chief counsel calls an emergency session of the Commission. "Each [commissioner] received an urgent message to come at 5:30 P.M. to the Commission's offices in the Veterans of Foreign Wars Building. . . . The session . . . lasted until after seven. . . . The Commission made the decision to ask [Carr and] Wade . . . to come at once to Washington and secretly present what they had heard."[521] Possibly after the others leave, Rankin, Dulles, and Boggs have the following discussion, which, although apparently sparked by Carr's and Wade's revelation, deals with the broader problem of Hoover's non-cooperation. ". . . Commissioners Allen Dulles and Hale Boggs, and . . . Rankin, held a secret executive session, the minutes of which do not appear in the final record but were discovered later among a stenotypist's notes.

DULLES: Why would it be in [the FBI's] interest to say he [Oswald] is clearly the only guilty one?

RANKIN: They would like us to fold up and quit.

BOGGS: This closes the case, you see. Don't you see?

RANKIN: They found the man. There is nothing more to do. The Commission supports their conclusions, and we can go home and that is the end of it.

BOGGS: I don't even like to see this being taken down.

DULLES: Yes. I think this record ought to be destroyed. . . .

RANKIN: There is this factor too that . . . is somewhat of an issue in this case, and I suppose you are all aware of it. That is that the FBI is very explicit that Oswald is the assassin . . . and they are very explicit that there was no conspiracy, and they are also saying they are continuing their investigation. Now in my experience of almost nine years, in the first place it is hard to get them to say when you think you have got a case tight enough to convict somebody, that this is the person who committed the crime. In my experience with the FBI they don't do that. They claim that they don't evaluate [come to conclusions] and it is my uniform experience that they don't do that.

DULLES: Secondly, they have not run out all kinds of leads in Mexico or in Russia and so forth which they could probably—It is not our business, it is the very . . .

DULLES: What is that?

RANKIN: They haven't run out all the leads on the information and they could probably say . . . that isn't our business.

DULLES: Yes.

RANKIN: But they are concluding that there can't be a conspiracy without those being run out. Now that is not from my experience with the FBI.

DULLES: It is not. You are quite right. I have seen a great many reports."[522]

Obviously, at least these three commissioners are now coming to the realization that Hoover may somehow have been directly involved in the assassination. Their perception may well be that Hoover provided direct support to the Mafia in the form of Oswald, for by now Ruby's association with that organization has been made apparent. They cannot know that Hoover himself had been duped by Marcello in this respect. Recall that Dulles is aware that his own agency had associated directly with the Mafia for the purpose of killing Castro. Boggs of course, being from Louisiana (and thus aware of Marcello) and knowing of Oswald's New Orleans background, may already have perceived the Marcello connection. By the end of the decade the Louisiana representative will begin to openly, and bitterly, denounce Hoover in the press, calling for his resignation.[523] And what of press reports linking Johnson with the Mafia via Baker/Levinson? And Estes's purported mob ties to Hoffa through attempts at Teamster loans, as well as his involvement with Commercial Solvents?

1/17—1/22/64:   "The publisher of another major publication received a phone call from a White House aide, who deprecated Reynolds. *The caller read excerpts from what purported to be an FBI dossier"* (emphasis added).[524] "Senator Hugh Scott demanded an investigation of the 'leak' of 'the raw FBI files,' (which) could only have occurred at the instance of some person . . . higher than the FBI in government.' . . . Hoover denied a leak to any unauthorized source. . . . Newsmen pin-pointed it directly on the White

House— . . . [Johnson] himself. This . . . use of power pro-
voked . . . Ted Lewis, of the *New York Daily News,* to put the
question. . . . 'Does the White House have the authority . . . to
order . . . Hoover to turn over its secret files anytime the Administration wants to crack down on an embarrassing witness . . . ?' "525

1/23/64—THURSDAY: Press: "President Johnson pictured
as innocent today his receipt of an expensive stereophonic phonograph from . . . Baker. . . . But he did not comment on charges
that have been made in the Baker investigation that the agent who
sold the insurance was forced to buy advertising on the Johnson
family television station. Mr. Johnson, . . . surprised White House
reporters with his remarks. He left the room . . . before they
could question him. Mr. Johnson's unexpected remarks were the
first that he has made on the Baker case. . . . Mr. Johnson appeared at 5:04 P.M. in the White House Fish Room near his office,
ostensibly to make a policy statement on the situation in Panama.
Television and newsreel cameras were present but Mr. Johnson was
not being televised 'live.' . . . To many reporters it seemed that he
had been waiting for a suitable opportunity. 'You are also writing
some other stories,' he said. 'I think about an insurance policy that
was written on my life some seven years ago. . . . The company in
which Mrs. Johnson and my daughters have a majority interest
. . . were somewhat concerned when I had a heart attack in 1955
and in 1957 they purchased insurance on my life made payable to
the company. . . . That insurance was purchased here in Washington and on a portion of the premiums paid Mr. Don Reynolds got a
small commission.' . . . Mr. Johnson made no mention of the
charge made by Mr. Reynolds concerning advertising. . . . 'There
is a question . . . about a gift of a stereo set that an employee of
mine made to me and Mrs. Johnson. . . . He was an employee of
the public and had no business pending before me and was asking
for nothing and so far as I knew expected nothing in return any
more than I did when I had presented him with gifts.' Thus, Mr.
Johnson referred to Mr. Baker both as an 'employee of mine' and as
an 'employee of the public.' . . . After concluding his remarks
. . . Mr. Johnson smiled broadly and said: 'I think that that is
about all I know that is going on the Hill.' . . . Mr. Johnson
laughed. . . . Then he added, just before he left the Fish Room: 'I

hope that covers it rather fully. That is all I have to say about it and all I know about it.' "[526] Johnson's reluctance to elaborate on the matter betrays his concern over the development.

Press: "Also introduced as evidence in today's hearing was a series of financial statements by Mr. Baker, which showed a rise in his claimed net worth from $11,025 in 1954 to $2,266,865 as of Feb. 1, 1963. . . . Some Democrats are voicing concern that the ramifications of the Baker investigation could endanger the party's prospects in an election year."[527]

Rankin sends a letter to Hoover: "Thank you for your letter of January 20, 1964 regarding various films of the assassination which are available for the use of the Commission. Members of my staff have arranged for a showing of these films at the office of the Commission next Monday, January 27, 1964, at 10 A.M."[528]

6:55 P.M.: LBJ calls Russell.

9 P.M.: LBJ and Warren meet at a D.C. dedication ceremony.[529]

1/24/64—FRIDAY: ". . . Warren and . . . Rankin . . . met secretly with . . . Carr and . . . Wade. The Texas officials related a story alleging that Oswald had been working for the FBI as an informant since September 1962: that Oswald was on the FBI payroll at $200 a month on the day he was arrested; and that Oswald had been assigned an informant number, 179. The source of the story seemed to be Alonzo Hudkins, a Houston newspaper reporter. . . . Wade, a former FBI agent, had some reason to believe that there might have been a connection between Oswald and the FBI. Wade had . . . heard that Oswald's address book contained the telephone number and license-plate number of Dallas FBI agent James Hosty. The Commission had received the list of names in Oswald's address book in a December 21, 1963, FBI report, but Agent Hosty's name had been omitted from that list by the FBI. Wade also had heard that a government voucher for $200 was found in Oswald's possession. In addition, a Western Union employee had claimed that Oswald was periodically telegraphed small sums of money. Also, Wade thought that Oswald's practice of setting up postal-box 'covers' each time he moved—a practice Wade himself had used as an FBI agent—was an 'ideal way' to handle undercover transactions."[530]

"Wade . . . told Rankin about his wartime experiences as a former FBI man. 'He did say he had considerable experience with the

FBI and knew their practices, that he handled as much as $2,000 a month during the war period in which he paid off informers and undercover agents in South America, and he knew that it wasn't revealed on any records he ever handled who he was paying it to and he never got any receipts; that he would have a list of numbers in his office—that was one of the most closely guarded records that he had—and he would put down the amount he paid off.' "[531]

"The officials returned to Dallas. . . . Their presence in Washington . . . unknown to the press or the public."[532]

"On January 24, three days prior to the [January 27] Commission meeting, the Secret Service submitted about thirty investigative reports to the Commission. One of these reports, carrying the control number 767, contained a Secret Service interview with [Alonzo] Hudkins [a Houston newspaper reporter]. Hudkins told the Secret Service agents that his information came from Allen Sweatt, the chief of the criminal division of the Dallas sheriff's office. According to Hudkins, Sweatt stated:

Oswald was being paid two hundred dollars per month by the FBI in connection with their subversive investigation [and] that Oswald had informant number S-172.

Allen Sweatt was never questioned by the Commission or its staff."[533]

1/25/64—SATURDAY: LBJ calls Russell.[534]

1/22—1/28/64: "The FBI denied any possible connection with Oswald."[535]

1/26/64—SUNDAY: LBJ calls Russell.[536]

1/27/64—MONDAY: This day, at 10 A.M., all or part of the Commission and staff view the various films and photographs of the assassination, including the Zapruder, Hughes, and Nix films.

11:20 A.M.: LBJ calls Russell.[537]

"The Commission heard the full allegation [that Oswald had been an FBI informant] at its January 27 meeting. . . . Ford observed: 'The Commission itself had not grounds at the moment for rejecting or accepting [the rumor]. *Members simply knew that the*

whole business was a most delicate and sensitive matter involving the
nation's faith in its own institutions and one of the most respected
federal agencies.' . . . Rankin presented the problem to the Commission in no uncertain terms, stating,

> *We do have a dirty rumor* that is very bad for the Commission,
> the problem, and *it is very damaging to the agencies that are*
> *involved in it and it must be wiped out insofar as it is possible to*
> *do by this Commission.*

. . . The problem was the 'dirty rumor.' It was considered 'dirty'
. . . because it was known to be 'damaging' to the government.
. . . *If the rumor was true, making the truth known might very well*
result in irreparable damage to the FBI and might heighten suspicions . . . about the assassination itself. On the other hand, dispelling the rumor, even if it was true, would protect the national interest. Ford stated aptly that 'the dilemma of the Commission' was
how to approach this problem. . . . Dulles observed that the allegation was 'a terribly hard thing to disprove,' because written
records were not always kept on undercover agents. 'If this be true,'
. . . Boggs responded, '[it makes] our problem utterly impossible,
because you say this rumor can't be dissipated under any circumstances' " (emphasis added).[538]
  "The Commission's approach to the problem had to be consistent
with the national interest. . . . Rankin proposed that the Commis-
sion permit the FBI to investigate the matter and 'clear its own skirts'
before the Commission investigated it. He suggested that he personally should speak to . . . Hoover and

> tell him this problem and that he should have as much interest
> as the Commission in trying to put an end to any such specula-
> tions, not only by his statement . . . but also if it were possi-
> ble to demonstrate by whatever records and materials they
> have that it just couldn't be true.

Rankin said that he would also tell Hoover that the Commission
would reserve the right to investigate the matter further 'if it found
it necessary, in order to satisfy the American people that this question of an undercover agent was out of the picture.' . . . Two
Commissioners were not entirely satisfied by it. . . . Cooper sug-

gested an alternate approach in which the Commission would apprise Hoover of the facts but at the same time pursue its own independent investigation into the rumor. Cooper said that the Commission was 'under a duty to see what Hudkins . . . says about it, where he got that information.' "⁵³⁹ *"Russell: 'There is no man in the employ of the Federal Government who stands higher in the opinion of the American people than . . . Hoover.' . . . Dulles: 'That is right.'* . . . Russell: 'Of course, we can get an affidavit from . . . Hoover and put it in this record and go on and act on that, but if we didn't go any further than that, and we don't pursue it down to Hudkins or whoever it is, there still would be thousands of doubting Thomases who would believe this man was an FBI agent and you just didn't try to clear it up and you just took Hoover's word. Personally, I would believe . . . Hoover. I have a great deal of confidence in him.' . . . Dulles: 'I do, too' " (emphasis added).⁵⁴⁰

"The Chief Justice then concluded: 'We must go into this thing from both ends, from the end of the rumor . . . and *from the end of the FBI,* and *if we come into a cul-de-sac—well, there we are,* but we can report on it.' " "Whatever you want me to do I am willing to approach it in that manner." *". . . McCloy observed, 'If we got a statement from* the Department that the Attorney General and perhaps from [*sic*] . . . *Hoover,* or from . . . Hoover himself, which said, "I am telling you that this man was not in any way employed by the FBI," . . . *I think that probably stops us,* unless we run into something . . .' " (emphasis added).⁵⁴¹

This same day, apparently at some other point in the session, the obvious problems with the autopsy report are discussed.

RANKIN: "There is a great range of material in regard to the wounds, and the autopsy and this point of exit or entrance of the bullet in front of the neck, and that all has to be developed much more than we have at the present time. We have an explanation there in the autopsy that probably a fragment came out the front of the neck, but with the elevation the shot must have come from, and the angle, *it seems quite apparent now, since we have the picture of where the bullet entered in the back, that the bullet entered below the shoulder blade to the right of the backbone, which is below the place where the picture shows the bullet came out in the neckband of the shirt in front,* and the bullet, according to the autopsy, didn't strike any bone at all, that particular bullet, and go through—

. . . BOGGS: *I thought I read that bullet just went in a finger's length—*

. . . RANKIN: *That is what they first said.* They reached in and they could feel where it came, it didn't go any further than that . . . and *then they proceeded to reconstruct where they thought the bullet went, the path of it, and which is [why] we have to go into considerable items and try to find out* how they could reconstruct that when they first said that they couldn't even feel the path beyond the first part of a finger. And then *how it could become elevated;* even so it raised *rather than coming out at a sharp angle that it entered,* all of that, we have to go into, too, and we are asking for help from the ballistics experts on that. We will have to probably get help from the doctors about it, and find out, we have asked for the original notes of the autopsy on that question, too" (emphasis added).[542]

The overall situation regarding Hoover has now become a topic of grave concern:

MCCLOY: . . . *the time is almost overdue for us to have a better perspective of the FBI* investigation than we now have . . . We are so dependent on them for our facts. . . .

RANKIN: *Part of our difficulty* in regard to it *is that they have* no problem. They have *decided that no one else is involved.* . . .

RUSSELL: They have tried the case and reached a verdict
                       on every aspect.
BOGGS: You have put your finger on it [emphasis
                       added].[543]

1/28/64—TUESDAY: "Rankin discussed the rumor with
Hoover . . . and was told flatly, 'Oswald had never been an informant of the FBI.' "[544]

1/29/64—WEDNESDAY: Hoover, for the first time, testifies
without Clyde before the Appropriations Committee concerning the
Bureau's annual budgetary request. Apparently Tolson's rapidly deteriorating physical and psychological condition is the reason. Only
Mohr accompanies him.[545]
    ". . . the FBI interviewed 'Braden' . . . in Beverly Hills, con-
cerning his arrest in Dallas . . . on November 22."[546]

1/31/63—FRIDAY: 5:45 P.M.: LBJ meets with Cooper.[547]

2/3/64—MONDAY: Marina appears before the Commission
in D.C. Apparently at some point prior to testifying she is introduced to Hoover. Marina: "When I went to Washington to testify
. . . seven or more men met me; apparently they were all FBI. But
when I shook hands with Mr. Hoover, who was with them, I was
chilled from top to bottom. It was as if you met a dead person; he
had a coldness like someone from the grave."[548]

2/4/64—TUESDAY: Johnson finally panics over the growing
Baker scandal.
    "On February 4, 1964, [Washington lobbyist] Winter-Berger was
discussing public relations with [Speaker of the House] McCormack
in McCormack's Washington office. . . . Johnson then barged in
and began ranting hysterically, . . . oblivious to the lobbyist's
presence. . . . Johnson said:

    John, that son of a bitch [Bobby Baker] is going to ruin me. If
    that cocksucker talks, I'm gonna land in jail. . . . I practi-
    cally raised that motherfucker, and now he's gonna make me
    the first President of the United States to spend the last days of
    his life behind bars.

When Johnson finally noticed Winter-Berger's presence, McCormack explained that the visiting lobbyist was a close friend of Nat Voloshen. Johnson then became enthusiastic, exclaiming, 'Nat can get to Bobby. They're friends. Have Nat get to Bobby.' When Winter-Berger volunteered that he had an appointment with Voloshen the next day, Johnson told Winter-Berger,

> Tell Nat that I want him to get in touch with Bobby Baker as soon as possible—tomorrow if he can. Tell Nat to tell Bobby that I will give him a million dollars if he takes this rap. Bobby must not talk. I'll see to it that he gets a million-dollar settlement."[549]

Hoover responds in writing to Commission staff request for detailed information about the speed at which the Nix film runs. Hoover: ". . . the FBI Laboratory has made a study of the film speed of the camera used by Mr. . . . Nix . . . [highly technical description follows]."[550] As stated in *High Treason* by renowned assassination photographic expert Robert Groden, "The Nix film was taken across the street from Zapruder. This . . . film makes very clear that the President has been hit from the front and is being driven . . . backwards."[551]

"On February 4 a reporter asked [Warren] if the full report was to be made public; Warren replied: 'Yes, there will come a time. But it might not be in your lifetime. . . . There may be some things that would involve security."[552]

6:30 P.M.: Russell calls LBJ. This night Johnson holds a reception for members of Congress. According to White House daily logs, seating is as follows: "Senator Russell will be seated on your right with Senator John Sherman Cooper on your left."[553] It is indeed odd that two men so obviously close to Johnson will disagree with the basic findings of the Commission. History may ultimately conclude that it is *because* of their close association with him.

2/6/64—THURSDAY: *Congressional Record* insertion of an editorial by an ex-FBI man (Claude N. Swanson) in the *Fairmont* (Minn. *Sentinel*). ". . . Swanson . . . is disturbed by rumors about the possible replacement of the famous FBI Chief. . . . 'There's a rumble emanating from the Nation's Capital. It is ominous in sound and portent. It concerns the possible replacement of J. Edgar Hoover.*

. . . Whether there actually is a move on to oust Hoover we don't know. . . . We have heard only one person named as a possible successor. That person, it is said, is the descendant of a long line of Communists; obviously for security reasons alone, not a prime replacement for one of Hoover's unquestioned loyalty and capabilities. . . . Hoover . . . would pick the best man for the job . . . a man who could probably come closest to giving this Nation and our people the service we have had for *four decades.* . . . In the tested ranks of the FBI, there are several people who could qualify and who would be willing to serve. Let Hoover pick one. . . . Let Hoover make the selection' " (emphasis added).[554] At this point, there is only one group in Washington with the potential power and motivation to "oust" Hoover: the Warren Commission.

"Hoover submitted an affidavit to the Commission, stating a search of FBI records had shown that Oswald had never been an informant. . . ."[555]

2/7/64—FRIDAY: LBJ is in contact with Russell on four separate occasions today.[556]

2/13/64—THURSDAY: ". . . Affidavits were filed [with the Commission] by each of the ten FBI agents who had been in contact with Oswald, all of whom denied he had been an informant."[557]

2/19/64—WEDNESDAY: Baker at last appears before Senator Jordan's investigating Rules Committee, but refuses to talk, claiming Fifth Amendment privileges. His attorney, Edward Bennett Willams, states: " 'We do not recognize that your committee or any other committee of the Senate had the right to conduct a legislative trial.' . . . Williams's most spectacular comment . . . was that Baker had been the victim of a government phone tapping operation. The attorney brandished a device in the hearing room. He said it had been attached to the phone of Baker's business partner, Ed Levinson, president of the Fremont Hotel. 'Mr. Baker and Mr. Levinson talked over this telephone on numerous occasions in 1963.' "[558] Williams is, of course, talking of the Bureau's ELSUR program regarding Las Vegas casinos. It is unknown whether Baker in fact ever receives one million dollars from Johnson.

3:40 P.M.: Johnson calls Russell.[559]

2/25/64—TUESDAY: Baker again appears before Committee, again takes the Fifth.[560] Apparently Johnson has now, with the aid of Hoover and Baker, weathered the worst of the scandal.

5:33 P.M.: LBJ meets with friend Robert Kerr, Jr.[561] Interestingly, when Baker spoke of needing capital for his storm-damaged Carousel in 1962, he claimed that Johnson had sent him to Senator Kerr, an oil millionaire, for help.[562]

2/26/64—WEDNESDAY: Baker's secretary, Nancy Carol Tyler, one of the occupants of his D.C. condo, testifies. "She complained that she was being investigated by the FBI. . . ."[563]

Hoover calls Johnson at the White House.

9:45 A.M.: Johnson calls Hoover from the Executive Office Building.

Johnson is in contact with Russell three times today.[564]

2/27/64—THURSDAY: 9:30 A.M.: Johnson calls Boggs.[565]

Hoover memo to Rankin confiding that "Ruby had been contacted nine times by the FBI in 1959, from March 11 to October 2, 'to furnish information' on criminal matters."[566] "The letter said in part, that Ruby was contacted . . . in 'view of his position as a night club operator who might have knowledge of the criminal element in Dallas. . . .' "[567] Hoover requests, presumably in the name of national security, that the fact be kept from the public. The Commission agrees to do so.[568]

"On February 27 Special Agent Robert Gemberling submitted an affidavit explaining why the FBI, in its December 23 report, had deleted the name of FBI agent James P. Hosty from the list of names in Oswald's address book. According to Hoover, this was done because 'the circumstances under which Hosty's name, et cetera, appeared in Oswald's notebook were fully known to the FBI.' "[569] The transparency of this excuse is obvious to the Commission. Consider also the "Gandy" notation. Again Hoover appears to stonewall the group.

2/28/64—FRIDAY: Boggs calls LBJ from New Orleans.[570]

3/64—THIS MONTH: According to at least one Warren Commission staff member, "That period, March and April 1964, was really our busiest period."[571]

3/1/64—SUNDAY: Hoover writes a piece for the spring issue of *DePaul Law Review* entitled, "The War on Organized Crime" in which he attempts to set out the historical record on the subject. *"Organized crime as we know it today can best be traced to the Prohibition Era* which started in January, 1920, with the enactment of the Eighteenth Amendment to the Constitution and ended thirteen bloody years later when the Volstead Act was repealed in 1933. *Bootlegging—the illegal importation . . . of whiskey—became the pot of gold at the end of the rainbow for most hoodlums and racketeers in the United States. Many common criminals suddenly became men of great wealth* as some Americans' desire for whiskey seemed quenchless. *This wealth begot power and greed and signaled certain conflict"* (emphasis added).[572] Hoover's use of Joseph Kennedy, an Irishman who found his "pot of gold" by way of importation of scotch whiskey during Prohibition, is revealing. By analogy, he is equating Kennedy with the Mafia, further rationalizing his, Hoover's, act of treason. In effect he is taking the position that Kennedy's assassination was nothing more than the resolution of an internal conflict by the Mafia.

Press reports: ". . . Johnson has said his piece on the . . . Baker affair and yesterday he backed away from a question about its possible political whiplash. The case is still in the hands of a Senate committee, he told his news conference. 'I am sure they will take proper action. . . . We will have to see what the consequences are following their recommendations after all the evidence is in.' . . . The Republicans and even the Communist Chinese kept the matter alive yesterday. The Peking regime . . . commented: *'The image of honesty which he tries so hard to create is coming apart. It is useless for Johnson to hide his real self behind his false guise.'* Also yesterday, Sen. . . . Scott . . . accused the Defense Department of 'evasion' in his attempt to find out who leaked derogatory information about . . . Reynolds. . . . One prospective witness . . . was expected to tell the Senators on Monday whether he will appear for questioning. He is Edward Levinson of Las Vegas, Nev., a gambler and hotel operator who was an early stockholder in Serve-U Corp., vending machine enterprise in which Baker has a major interest."[573]

3/2/64—MONDAY: ". . . Hoover speaks on the telephone to Senator John McClellan. Tells him that the Valachi hearings, 'shook them all up.' "[574]

Levinson appears before the Rules Committee with an attorney from Williams's firm. He is both aggressive and arrogant. While the mobster answers no questions, some of the questions themselves are illuminating.

> Levinson: I . . . refuse to answer the questions for the following reasons. No. 1., the constitutional rights guaranteed to me . . . have been invaded by *agents of the executive branch of the Government. . . . acting in concert with the Central Telephone Co. of Nevada, during 1963 placed an electronic eavesdropping device in the telephone in my office at the Fremont Hotel.*
>
> *. . . Agents monitored all the conversations in my office whether held over the telephone or not.* The device used was a small radio transmitter hidden in the base of my telephone. It was discovered only by chance after *it had been there for an undetermined length of time. . . .* I do not yet know how extensively this invasion of my rights to privacy was carried on with respect to other telephones I used in other places where I held conversations. But I am now having an investigation conducted to determine this. In the meantime, I shall refuse to provide any additional information to any agents of government.
>
> 2. Against this background . . . I specifically refuse to answer because of the privilege against self-incrimination.

> McLendon: Did you ever visit the North American Aviation Corp. in connection with negotiating a contract between that corporation and the Serve-U for Serve-U to render vending machine services in North American plants?

> What, if anything, did you have to do with obtaining vending machine contracts with North American Aviation Co. or the Northrop Aviation Co.?

> Sen. Curtis: *Have you made any trips to the Dominican Republic with anyone else when Robert Baker was also along?*
>
> *Has Mr. Baker visited you in Las Vegas?*

> Did Mr. Baker visit Las Vegas in June 1963 and attend a prize fight with you and one Jack Cooper and Nick Popich?

> Do you know Mr. Fred Black?

Have you ever given Mr. Robert Baker any money?

Have you ever had any business dealings with Robert Baker and Fred Black?

Did you go to the Dominican Republic in February 1963 with Baker on any business in connection with any cigarette vending rights?

Senator Pell: I think the record should also show that this is the first witness who . . . has resorted to . . . constitutional protection. . . . When witnesses themselves come in, who are not under investigation by the Committee, and adopt this line of questioning [*sic*], I think it is most regrettable.

Senator Cooper: *I have no questions.*

McClendon: . . . Can you help this committee . . . determine . . . why . . . Baker, together with Fred Black, owned 57 percent of the stock in Serve-U Corp., but it was never recorded in the name of either one of them? [emphasis added][575]

Obviously Levinson and the Committee do not know that Hoover had had the bug in place from early 1962 on. The Bureau no doubt has a large number of recordings on this man. There is no telling what he and Baker discussed. Note that the Committee is keenly interested in knowing whether there has been direct association between Levinson and Johnson. Did the former accompany Baker and Johnson on their trip to the Dominican Republic in February 1963? The line between Johnson and the Mafia again appears to disappear, just as it did with his endorsement of the Carousel. A central question is whether ELSUR recorded any conversations in which Baker conveyed Johnson's dissatisfaction with the Kennedys to Levinson.

3/3/64—TUESDAY: Press reports on Levinson's appearance: "Levinson, a slight man with a short answer, declined to reply to more than five dozen questions. . . . There was also testimony that Baker set up appointments for Levinson for obtaining gambling concession in . . . the Dominican Republic. . . . Today the Committee will go further into Baker's Caribbean dealings when it questions two Dominican businessmen, former Dominican Minister of Industry and Finance Diego Bordas and Gary E. Mazza. . . ."[576]

3/4/64—WEDNESDAY: Hoover sends a thank-you letter to
Johnson.

My dear Mr. President:

   I was indeed surprised and most pleased to receive the photographs which you sent me this morning. With the tremendous demands on your time and the many difficult burdens
facing you each and every day, it meant a great deal to me to
have you do this. It is typical of you to be so thoughtful and
kind, and I do appreciate this wonderful gesture of friendship.
*Thank you so very much for this memento of my recent visit
with you!* [emphasis added]
   With expressions of my highest esteem and best regards, I
am

                                            Sincerely,
                                            Edgar[577]

Prior to this date, Johnson has "recently" called Hoover to the
White House. Undoubtedly their discussion was related to containment of the Baker/Mafia investigation and the Executive Order
waiving Hoover's retirement.
   Press reports on the Baker scandal: ". . . A cabinet member in
the government of former Dominican president Juan Bosch testified
that he was a close personal friend of Baker. . . . Bordas . . . testified that he retained Baker . . . when American cement producers complained that he was importing cement at dumping prices.
. . . Committee members hammered questions at Bordas . . . on
whether he had intervened for Baker in . . . gambling concessions
in the Dominican Republic. . . . At the conclusion of the hearing,
. . . McClendon said the Senate panel will reach a decision this
week on closing the four-month-old inquiry into Baker's financial
affairs."[578] The implication here is that Baker worked in concert
with Johnson to arrange gambling concessions in the Dominican
Republic under its new and short-lived leader, Juan Bosch. As
Baker had accompanied Johnson to the inauguration of Bosch in
February 1963, his influence would have been apparent. Otherwise,
why would the minister of finance and industry look to a mere
Senate aide for help in controlling complaints from powerful elements of American industry? With Cuba's casinos out of reach, the

Mafia was obviously looking to other Caribbean nations. Traficante himself, in reapproaching Aleman in 1963, had sought such an introduction. "Q: . . . Traficante . . . wanted . . . to see if there was a possibility of you achieving some introduction with President Juan Bosch? ALEMAN: That is correct."[579] It is possible then that Levinson, acting in concert with Baker and Johnson, was attempting to facilitate introduction of casino gambling into the Dominican Republic at the behest of Traficante, Lansky, and others, including presumably Carlos Marcello.

3/6/64—FRIDAY: Hoover states in a letter to Senator McClellan regarding Valachi's testimony, "Public opinion has moved against the forces of evil."[580]

Press: ". . . Jordan . . . [has] . . . indicated that the Baker probe is nearing an end. But Sen. Hugh Scott . . . said that 'to close the investigation arbitrarily without calling a number of key witnesses would be in violation of the mandate of the Senate.'"[581]

3/9/64—MONDAY: Hoover moves quickly after Jordan's public announcement that the Baker investigation is basically over:

1:35 P.M.: Johnson "Departs for pool [with] J. Edgar Hoover, Deke DeLoach, Walter Jenkins."

1:37 P.M.: "To mansion for lunch w/J. Edgar Hoover, Deke Deloach, and WJ."

3:04 P.M.: "Return to office w/J. Edgar Hoover." After a short discussion Hoover evidently returns to his own office.

4:31 P.M.: Hoover calls LBJ.

4:35 P.M.: LBJ and Bill Moyers discuss the call from Hoover.[582]

Apparently Hoover's retirement waiver is the topic of conversation, for Johnson will, the following day, disclose the fact that he intends to issue the long-sought Executive Order.

3/10/64—TUESDAY: Press discloses the fact that Johnson has already made the decision to issue an Executive Order waiving Hoover's retirement.[583]

Press: "At least three of the Democratic members [of the Baker committee] have asserted publicly that they consider the inquiry to be at an end. Another has let it be known that he is 'bored' and considers the Baker case a 'second-rate scandal.' Still another has regularly failed to show up for public hearings. High on the list of prospective witnesses being drafted by the GOP members is Walter Jenkins. . . ."[584] Although Cooper's involvement in the questioning of Levinson (and Sigelbaum shortly) has been minimal at best, he is apparently one of the GOP members (the minority) who votes to keep the committee alive.

3/11/64—WEDNESDAY: Baker and Levinson associate Sigelbaum appears before the committee. Asked basically the same questions as Levinson, he takes the Fifth 136 times. Senator Cooper asks two questions of substance.

> Senator Cooper: Did you visit the offices of the North American Aviation Corp. and the Northrop Co. seeking a vending contract for Serve-U?
> Did you talk to Mr. Attwood, president of North American, about a vending contract for Serve-U?[585]

The hearings show, if nothing else, that Sigelbaum and Levinson are frightened men. As probable conduits (via Baker) for private, even if only inadvertent, rhetoric from Johnson to very powerful elements of the Mafia over the past two and one-half years, they may well have reason to be.

3/12/64—THURSDAY: 3:05 P.M.: Hoover calls LBJ.
5:32 P.M.: FBI liaison Cartha DeLoach calls LBJ.[586]

3/13/64—FRIDAY: 9:10 A.M.: Hoover calls LBJ at the "Mansion."[587]

3/19/64—THURSDAY: 12:15 P.M.: Johnson calls De-Loach.[588]

3/26/64—THURSDAY: Rankin, apparently, ". . . requests the FBI respond to [written interrogatories, fifty-two in all]."[589] This is classic adversarial approach. One can only assume that something he and staff members have learned since Hoover began providing raw FBI reports has caused this change. The issue of Oswald's status with the Bureau has already been resolved. The line of questioning Rankin, Willens, and Redlich now begin to pursue would seem to indicate that they may have deduced that the Mafia engineered the assassination, and that Hoover was somehow involved.

4/64—THIS MONTH: Baker hearings are permanently discontinued.[590]

4/1/64—WEDNESDAY: 3:35 P.M.: LBJ calls Russell.
5:22 P.M.: Boggs calls LBJ.[591]

4/3/64—FRIDAY: Hoover, having perceived the change in stance from Rankin, and apparently after having reviewed the hostile interrogatories, writes in a memo to Sullivan: "Their so-called compliments of the Bureau's work are empty and have no sincerity. . . . The questions are those of a cross-examination of the FBI. . . ."[592]

4/7/64—TUESDAY: LBJ speaks with Boggs three times today.[593]

4/9/64—THURSDAY: Johnson calls Russell.[594]

4/14/64—TUESDAY: 10:12 A.M.: Waggoner Carr meets with LBJ at the White House.[595]

4/18/64—SATURDAY: 10:42 A.M.: LBJ calls Russell.[596]

4/20/64—MONDAY: General counsel Rankin, *Howard Willens,* and Norman Redlich send a letter to Hoover which states in part: *"The Commission would like to know whether your Bureau possesses any information not hitherto disclosed* to this Commission *concerning the association of* Lee Harvey *Oswald with any . . . criminals or criminal groups either in the United States or abroad.* The *Commission is most anxious to be assured* that it possesses the full extent of your Bureau's knowledge and information concerning the aforementioned associations of Lee Harvey Oswald" (emphasis added).[597] This is nothing less than a point-blank question. Was the Mafia behind the assassination? It is also a textbook trial tactic. Hoover will have no choice but to respond in the negative, something they no doubt anticipate. With a written denial on the record,

Hoover can be confronted with evidence to the contrary when he testifies under oath on May 14. The Director realizes his position.

4/21/64—TUESDAY: "On April 21 . . . Johnson was meeting . . . with a group of out-of-town editors and broadcasters, when he was asked if he could tell 'when we might expect a complete report from the Warren Commission.' 'No,' [Johnson] answered indifferently. 'I don't think that they have a particular deadline. It is a very thorough commission, made up of the most able men in this country. A very patriotic group. They're taking testimony today.' They were taking testimony that day from . . . Connally, who told Commission members it was 'inconceivable' that he had been hit by the same bullet that had gone through John Kennedy. . . . Johnson did not like the portent of . . . Connally's dissent, since without substantiation of the single-bullet hypothesis the Warren Commission's case against . . . Oswald . . . would collapse . . . the White House had begun to exert private pressure on Earl Warren to wind up everything. A June 1 deadline was expected."[598]

4/29/64—WEDNESDAY: 6:26 P.M.: LBJ calls Fortas.[599]

4/30/64—THURSDAY: Hoover responds to Rankin. ". . . Concerning the association of . . . Oswald with any . . . criminals or criminal groups either in the United States or abroad. . . . You may be assured the Commission has been furnished all information developed by this Bureau concerning . . . Oswald. . . ."[600] In making such a statement, Hoover has, at the least, again engaged in obstruction of justice. He is now in a highly vulnerable position should Rankin and the others confront him under oath.

5/5/64—TUESDAY: Hoover launches a covert attack against Rankin and his assistants ". . . by seeing to it that derogatory information on . . . Redlich reached a group of reactionary Congressmen." These individuals allege that Rankin's assistant is a communist seeking to undermine the goals of the Commission (i.e., which are to prove to the American people that a single "kill-crazy-communist" had assassinated the President). *"[Senator] . . . Mundt demanded that the Warren Commission suspend the taking of all further testimony* and hold up on all writing of its report to the American public until Redlich and others on the Commission staff faced the challenge of obtaining 'complete security clearances' " (emphasis added).[601] Note Hoover's obvious bid to prevent being confronted with evidence of the Mafia's involvement in the assassination. By forcing the Commission to "suspend the taking of all further testimony" he can avoid further confrontation, as well as perjuring himself.

His efforts to stop the proceedings fail. But in the coming days he will be in extremely close contact with Johnson, the only man, other than Warren, who can control Rankin.

This same day Rankin retaliates with another letter to Hoover asking him point blank whether the Bureau knows of any connection between Oswald and Ruby in the context of the Walker incident. He apparently includes a copy of a recent *National Enquirer* article alleging the same.[602] This article is clearly in the category of a crank allegation, yet Rankin treats it seriously. One can sense his growing hostility and distrust of the Director.

5:22 P.M.: LBJ "To Cabinet Room to tape a message for J. Edgar Hoover."[603]

5/6/64—WEDNESDAY: "On May 6 Alan H. Belmont, assistant director of the FBI, appeared before the Commission and offered to leave Oswald's file with the Commission. Rankin advised the Commission to retain the file, although the staff would *not* be permitted to examine it. . . . Warren, however, refused to accept the file, saying: 'Well, the same people who would demand that we see everything of this kind would also demand that they be entitled to see it, and if it is a security matter we can't let them see it.' The file thus was returned to the FBI, and . . . no independent check was ever made of it."[604] Hoover may have already gotten to Warren via Johnson. The Commission chairman's intervention here obviously cuts against Rankin's efforts to get at the truth. Oswald's file, previously sanitized, undoubtedly contains nothing at this point that would "embarrass the Bureau." It is the intervention of Warren that is significant here.

6:44 P.M.: Boggs calls LBJ.[605]

5/8/64—FRIDAY: Hoover responds to Rankin's 5/5/64 letter:

[Dallas Police Chief] Curry was interviewed on May 7 . . . at which time [the *National Enquirer*] article was exhibited to him. . . . Curry read the entire article after which he advised as follows: Prior to the assassination of President Kennedy neither he nor his Department had ever heard of . . . Oswald. . . . Curry had no information linking Oswald and Ruby to the plot to shoot General Walker. . . . Curry emphatically stated he . . . had never been requested by any official of the FBI not to arrest Oswald or Ruby. . . . The files of this Bureau do not contain any reference that an FBI official was asked to request the Dallas Police not to arrest Oswald or Ruby.[606]

Hoover will testify on May 14. The opportunity to confront Hoover with what Rankin and others must now suspect thus presents itself. Bear in mind however, that Hoover's testimony does not occur until *after* Johnson has publicly endorsed him through the retirement waiver, hailing him as a "hero to millions of citizens." The exchange on May 14 will be as follows:

WARREN:	Mr. Hoover will be asked to testify in regard to whether . . . Oswald was ever an agent, directly or indirectly, or an informer or acting on behalf of the Federal Bureau of Investigation in any capacity at any time, and whether he knows of any credible evidence of any conspiracy, either domestic or foreign, involved in the assassination of President Kennedy.
HOOVER:	I can most emphatically say that at no time was he ever an employee of the Bureau in any capacity, either as an agent or as a special employee, or as an informant.
RANKIN:	From your study of this entire matter of the assassination and work in connection with it, do you know of any credible evidence that has ever come

to your attention that there was a conspiracy either foreign or domestic involved in the assassination?

HOOVER: I know of no substantial evidence of any type that would support any contention of that character. . . . I have been unable to find any scintilla of evidence showing any foreign conspiracy or any domestic conspiracy that culminated in the assassination of President Kennedy. . . . All the [assassination] reports that come in from the field are, of course, reviewed at Washington by the supervisor in charge of the case, and then in turn by the assistant director of the division, and then in turn by Mr. Belmont, who is the assistant to the Director. . . . Recently the *National Enquirer* had a fantastic article in it. . . . Chief Curry . . . branded it as an entire lie. . . . Prior to [the assassination] we reported to the Secret Service all information that dealt with individuals who were potential killers or by whom acts of violence might be anticipated. And I also am further convinced that there is absolutely no association between Oswald or Ruby. There was no such evidence ever established.

DULLES: Or Oswald and anybody else? Would you go that far?

HOOVER: Anybody else who might be—

DULLES: In connection with the assassination?

HOOVER: Yes; I would certainly go that far. . . . So far as we have been able to establish there was no relationship or contact between Oswald and Ruby or anyone else allegedly involved in this assassination. . . . We found no indication at all that Oswald was a man addicted to violence. . . . I think in the *Enquirer* article there is reference to the fact that the Dallas Police knew or suspected Oswald of possibly being a party to the shooting into the house of General Walker. . . . There was no connection of that kind and there was no evidence that Oswald had any streak of violence.

BOGGS: You have spent your life studying criminology and violence and subversion. Would you care to speculate on what may have motivated the man? I know it would just be speculation.

HOOVER: My speculation, Mr. Boggs, is that this man was no doubt a dedicated Communist. . . . I personally believe it was . . . the twisted mentality the man had.

BOGGS: Now we have some people, including this man's mother, talk about Oswald having been an agent of the Government of the United States.

HOOVER: . . . The first indication of [Marguerite Oswald's] emotional instability was the retaining of a lawyer [Mark Lane] that anyone would not have retained if they were really serious in trying to get down to the facts.

BOGGS: And the allegations she has made about this man being an agent . . . of the . . . FBI are false?

HOOVER: Well, I can certainly speak for the FBI that it is false. . . . No one can work for the FBI without the approval being given at Washington and a record kept of it, even of the confidential informants. That is very tightly controlled. . . . So there has to be a voucher and specific details of payment. And I know at no time was he an informant or agent or special employee or working in any capacity for the FBI. . . . We have also checked the administrative records where vouchers or payments would have been made and there is no indication that any money was ever paid to Oswald.

SENATOR COOPER: May I just ask one question there? I think you have answered it, but in your examination of this aspect as to whether or not Oswald . . . held any relationship to the FBI, you, yourself, have looked into all of the means you have of determining that fact when you make the statement to us?

HOOVER: I have personally looked into that. . . . It must be done by voucher, and those vouchers are examined by the General Accounting Office every year or so. . . . The next incident was the difficulty he had at New Orleans. We were concerned there as to whether he was functioning officially for the Fair Play for Cuba Committee which was financed and supported by Castro and Castro's government, and if he was, where he obtained money and with whom he had dealt.

Rankin shifts the line of questioning to the Mafia.

RANKIN: I call your attention to Exhibits 864 and 865, and ask you if you have seen those before or, you have seen the original of 864 and 865 is a photostatic copy of your letter to us in answer to 864, is that correct?

HOOVER: That is correct; yes. I recall very distinctly.

RANKIN: Do you recall those letters involved an inquiry as to any connections of . . . Oswald with . . . any criminal groups or others that might be conspiratorial?

HOOVER: That is correct; and my letter of April 30 states the facts as they are. . . .

RANKIN: Mr. Chairman, we offer in evidence Exhibits 864 and 865.

WARREN: They may be admitted.

RANKIN: *Mr. Hoover, do you have any suggestions that you would like to tell the Commission about of your ideas that might improve the security of the President, and you might comment upon information the Commission has received. You have a special appropriation that is related to that area.*

HOOVER: *Well, I, at the request of—*

WARREN: *Director, before you get into that question, and may I ask something that I would like to hear you discuss in this same connection?*

HOOVER: *Yes.*

WARREN: You have told us that you had no jurisdiction down there in Dallas over this crime.

HOOVER: That is correct.

WARREN: Because there is no Federal crime committed. And I assume that that caused you some embarrassment and some confusion in doing your work?

HOOVER: It most certainly did.

WARREN: Because of the likelihood of your being in conflict with other authorities. Do you believe there should be a Federal law?

HOOVER: I am very strongly in favor of that. . . . Almost as soon as [an FBI report] would reach the Dallas Police Department, the chief of police or one of the representatives of the department would go on TV or radio and relate findings of the FBI. . . . I was so concerned that I asked my agent in charge at Dallas, Mr. Shanklin, to personally go to Chief Curry and tell him that I insisted that he

not go on the air any more until this case was
resolved. . . . The Chief concurred in my request. . . . If the case had been in the hands of
the FBI none of that information would have
been given out.

RANKIN: *Mr. Hoover, to remind you of my question, any
suggestions that you may have concerning the protection of the President, and the information that
the Commission has that you have a special appropriation in that connection for the Bureau?*

HOOVER: *We do not have a special appropriation for the
protection of the President. The Secret Service, of
course, has that responsibility. On December 2, I
prepared this memorandum . . .* outlining suggestions that I felt should be considered to
tighten up on the security of the President. . . .
I will be glad to read it to the Commission.

BOGGS: *Why don't you ask the Director just to summarize
it.*

RANKIN: *Will you summarize it?*

DULLES: *Can we have a copy?*

HOOVER: Oh, yes.

FORD: *Could the copy be [read into] the record as an
exhibit?*

HOOVER: *Yes, sir;* that is all right with me. [proceeds to read
lengthy memo into the record] (emphasis
added).[607]

Rankin, cut off twice by members of the Commission does not
make a third attempt to continue his line of questioning. His original
plan was undoubtedly to build on the two letters he entered in
evidence by getting Hoover to admit that he had a statutory duty to
protect President Kennedy. Once done, he would have been able to
confront Hoover with contradicting physical evidence (e.g., FBI
reports, eyewitness statements, photographs) of conspiracy which it
had been his duty to guard against. He could at once have shown
Hoover had lied in his letter to the Commission, and exposed
conspiratorial aspects of the assassination. That Rankin was allowed
only to lay the foundation and not follow through with evidence of
complicity must have been demoralizing to both him and the staff.
The message was apparently made clear. The opportunity to expose

the lies of the last six months passes. Rankin will, like the others, agree with Hoover's lone-nut thesis in the fall. Through control of Johnson and the fears of the dominant faction (Warren, Dulles, Ford, McCloy) on the Commission, Hoover's position has become unassailable. In his own words, he is, once again, "not gettable." In the late 1970s, Rankin will voice his frustration with the situation by stating to the HSCA, "Who could protest against what Mr. Hoover did back in those days?"

5/8/64—FRIDAY: 5:35—5:45 P.M.: "[Johnson] went to the Rose Garden and participated in ceremony honoring J. Edgar Hoover['s] . . . 40th Anniversary as Director of the FBI. Present were: Clyde Tolson, Cartha D. DeLoach, Speaker John McCormack, Sen. Everett Dirksen. . . . Remarks by [Johnson]."[608]

As the press will report the following day, ". . . Johnson cleared the way today for J. Edgar Hoover to remain as director of the Federal Bureau of Investigation. Mr. Hoover will reach the compulsory retirement age, 70, on Jan. 1. Minutes before meeting with Mr. Hoover in the White House Rose Garden late this afternoon, . . . Johnson signed an Executive Order exempting him from the Federal retirement law for 'an indefinite period of time.' . . . Johnson said he signed the order because the nation needed Mr. Hoover. 'I know you wouldn't think of breaking the law,' the President told Mr. Hoover, who stood ramrod straight beside him. . . . The President described Mr. Hoover as a 'household word, a hero to millions of citizens and an anathema to evil men.' He also praised him as a 'quiet, humble and magnificent public servant.' "[609]

Immediately after leaving the Rose Garden, an emotional Hoover returns to his office and writes Johnson a final letter.

Dear Mr. President:

The great privilege bestowed upon me this afternoon by you in the Rose Garden at the White House is certainly very much appreciated. Your remarks, in the presence of so many old and dear friends, touched me very deeply.

Your Executive Order waiving the mandatory retirement age provision and your request that I continue as Director of the FBI fill me with gratitude. I know you understand there is no greater happiness than the knowledge that one is free to go on doing, day by day, the best work possible in the job he likes best.

Words are but empty thanks for the wonderful opportunity you have given me to continue to serve you and my country. . . .

Sincerely,
Edgar [emphasis added][610]

VII

Epilogue: Crisis in Government

Through the correlation of facts gleaned from many previous works with the new data presented in this chronicle, a comprehensive explanation of the assassination of John F. Kennedy has herein been provided. This historical truth has been revealed despite the fact that various entities of government, primarily the FBI, have destroyed critical evidence and continue to withhold vital data on the event.

By mid-1961, FBI Director J. Edgar Hoover had come to despise John F. Kennedy, considering him an immoral, indecisive liberal. Kennedy, under whose watch Hoover would be retired by federal statute, felt that the Director's time had passed, and fully intended to let statute take effect. To the Director, the idea of "forced" retirement by such a man as JFK was utterly unacceptable. A political standoff quickly developed. In the middle of the ensuing, rather personal political struggle, there arose for Hoover the opportunity presented by the Marcello contract. Hoover, up to that point stymied by Kennedy, but in exclusive control of the data concerning the conspiracy, realized that simply by withholding word of the plot from the Secret Service, he could multiply the likelihood of its success ten-fold. Simply put, he directly aided Marcello by allowing the assassination to happen. With Lyndon Johnson long ready, even anxious to obtain power, and at the same time wholly compromised by the Director through the Billie Sol Estes and Bobby Baker/ Mafia scandals, the stage was set. At midday on 11/22/63 President John F. Kennedy was horribly murdered by Marcello contract killers in the streets of Dallas, Texas. For Hoover, the assassination brought a multitude of blessings. Within a few months, he obtained the long-sought retirement waiver. In his mind, the Bureau was saved from the irreparable damage sure to occur under a Kennedy-appointed director, and the country was basically back on track, although still suffering the residual effects of Kennedy's "tragic moral illness." And all of this had occurred with minimum personal risk or involvement on his part. True, there had been a period of intense effort, after the fact, in order to contain the Warren Commission, but with Johnson under his control, and the Commission dependent upon LBJ for its very existence, there was never any real doubt about the Director's ultimate triumph. The Commission itself aided in this goal by making the decision to keep the reality of the event from the American people.

Just as Hoover used Lyndon Johnson, so, too, Carlos Marcello used the Director and his Bureau. Marcello and his organization were under heavy prosecutorial pressure from the Kennedy brothers by the fall of 1962 as a result of illegal gambling (i.e., bookmaking) and other criminal activities. Through indirect political liaisons and thus informal communication with Johnson and Hoover, the mafioso perceived a way by which he could at once prevent his own destruction and ensure a safe future for his organization. Marcello astutely realized that the two officials who would be most able to prevent his prosecution after the fact, Hoover and Johnson, would personally benefit in very real ways from the assassination of President Kennedy—Hoover through perpetuation as director, and Johnson through the acquisition of power as well as containment of the Estes scandal and Baker/Levinson connection. Marcello well knew of Hoover's and Johnson's apathy toward the ongoing prosecution of the Mafia. Accordingly, realization of the above factors triggered his decision to put out a contract on the life of JFK. By the clever use of buffers with connections to the FBI, men like Ferrie, Banister, Ruby, and Oswald, Marcello succeeded in his plan, while simultaneously insulating himself from exposure and prosecution. In all likelihood the actual assassins of John Kennedy were contract killers brought in from other parts of the country in typical gangland fashion. These people may have been supplied through the cooperation of gambling network functionaries like Saia, Campisi, di Piazza, Nolan, Beckley, Ruby, McWillie, and McGrath, who were the common thread between men like Marcello, Traficante, Giancana, and Lansky.

With JFK's murder, the presidency fell to a man Hoover could easily manipulate. The Attorney General once again became irrelevant. The cost of this victory, however, had been great. Clyde Tolson, Hoover's one companion in life, was now in failing health, wracked by a stress-induced heart condition and strokes. Both men had become traitors. Constitutional safeguards concerning presidential succession had been violated. The man he had placed in power was himself compromised by the Mafia.

Johnson, like Hoover, no doubt aided the assassination plan by making known to those around him how dissatisfied he was with his status as Vice President and how much he disliked both Kennedys. In many respects, he was, like Hoover, amoral, a consummate opportunist. We will probably never know if he, through his own sources and relationship with Hoover, also knew beforehand of the plan to assassinate the President. But by way of Mafia functionaries like Bobby Baker and others, an obvious two-way channel of communication existed between LBJ and the mob. Johnson's unquestioning loyalty to Hoover after the fact cannot be ignored. His indifferent attitude toward the Mafia in general is a matter of record.

As Lyndon Johnson would soon prove, the ability to enrich oneself at public expense requires neither leadership skills nor personal integrity. After the remainder of John Kennedy's administrative agenda had been passed by Congress, Johnson's administration began to experience serious difficulty. In an attempt to stave off disaster, his wholesale use of the FBI to manipulate the Constitution and legislative process became routine. Unchecked by the presidency, Hoover, in turn, ran wild, exacerbating the social unrest of the 1960s and effectively operating as an independent fourth branch of government.

The Warren Commission, the reluctant invention of both Johnson and Hoover, failed in its primary purpose. Suspicious of the Director from the beginning, and mystified by LBJ's brazen promotion of the man, the immensity of their task soon became all too apparent. Perhaps as a consequence of this, the Commission split along ideological lines, some wanting only to prove the guilt of a deceased "kill-crazy-communist," others to obtain the truth. In effectuating the first line of thought, the controlling faction within the group (Warren, Dulles, Ford, and McCloy) was ultimately forced to prevent its general counsel, Rankin, from exposing the Director. To the same end, members Russell and Cooper were forced to sign a report they did not agree with. Boggs, with his special perspective (i.e., being a U.S. Representative from Louisiana) acquiesced in signing the report, but in the coming years became bitter, and openly challenged the Director, calling for his removal.

With the Commission members' knowledge of Hoover's complicity and Johnson's unquestioning support of him (because of his own associations), the question of institutional integrity became paramount. Their problem was threefold. They knew that if they scrutinized and revealed the Mafia's role, that in itself would alarm the general population. Exposure of Oswald's and Ruby's relationship to Marcello and the Bureau would then greatly exacerbate the crisis by focusing attention on Hoover. While the Commission did not know of the September 1962 Jose Aleman/Traficante surveillance data revealing the existence of the Marcello contract, other information that was available to them, taken as a whole, clearly raised the disturbing issue of foreknowledge on the part of the Director. His initial refusal to supply data had only strengthened those concerns. From this arose the third, and most unsettling issue, that of Johnson's own relationship to the Mafia. To expose the mob and the Director to prosecution might ultimately lead to the downfall of the President himself.

Because of the basic issues raised by the crisis, the controlling faction within the Commission made the decision to withhold the truth from the public. John Kennedy was dead. In their minds, the integrity of the presidency and the FBI could not be allowed to follow him. Tragically this decision had the disastrous effect of ensuring both Hoover and Johnson's positions in power, not to mention the general chilling effect on the efforts of others to prosecute the Mafia.

Some members of the Commission benefited politically and monetarily from the decision. Gerald Ford, with his covert status as a Bureau liaison, had gleaned special insight and soon made considerable sums of money promoting the myth of the "kill-crazy-communist" to conservatives everywhere. Some staff members went on to national prominence. Arlen Specter, the author of the single-bullet thesis, is now a U.S. Senator.

The logic behind the decision of the Commission was fundamentally flawed. The long-term consequences of their failure to pursue and reveal the truth were *not* considered. The resilience of the American system and people was seriously underestimated. Had the Commission so chosen, it could have seized the initiative and found a way to make the truth known. A contemporaneous model of sorts had just been provided by France. Its own President, de Gaulle, had barely survived a conspiratorial attack by elements of his own government, consisting of forces within the French military. Although motivated no doubt in part by the opportunity for political gain, the realities of the attempted coup were disclosed to the French public as they became known. The Republic was strengthened. Institutional credibility survived. The people of that country were allowed to put the disastrous event behind them. We were not given such an opportunity.

And who were JFK and LBJ? Though married, Kennedy was apparently an unrepentant philanderer. Johnson was clearly a corrupt man who, through his associations, was directly involved in white-collar crime. Both had at least indirect connections to the Mafia. Johnson, perhaps more like Joseph Kennedy than many would care to think, was doubtlessly motivated in his associations by money and the quest for power. He was not a man of personal integrity.

Kennedy, his fortune previously assured in part by his father's past association with the mob, was a generation removed from this corruption. It is to his credit that he not only perceived the danger that the Mafia represented, but also sought, some would say heroically, to destroy it. In a social context, his fatal flaw was perhaps his inability to distance himself, until it was too late, from women supplied by mobsters. He was, evidently, acutely aware of the corrupt source of some of his fortune, for he consistently gave substantial sums to charity. This concern also expressed itself in his work. His donation of all moneys received as an elected official, as well as the proceeds ($351,000) from the sale of screen rights to his bestselling book, *Profiles in Courage,* are but two examples.

Also to his credit was the attempt to restructure the bureaucratic power elite in Washington, D.C., into a more moderate, progressive leadership force. Had he not retained Hoover as FBI Director at the outset of his administration, he could well have essentially succeeded by the end of his second term.

The long-term effects of both Hoover's and the Warren Commission's actions are with us today. The primary, and most damaging consequence of this watershed event was, and is, a crisis in government. As anyone who examines the evidence can plainly see, the mishandling of the event has substantially contributed to the current state of decay in government institutions. The effectiveness of a governmental system is no better than its credibility. Without this basic ingredient, people will not obey the laws it legislates. In refusing to investigate and apprehend those responsible, the Justice Department has damaged the concept of rule of law in this nation as it is perceived by the public. People no longer have the guarantee that the Department will always act in the public interest. By its refusal to address the issue, it only perpetuates and worsens this crisis. The FBI and the Department of Justice simply cannot bring themselves to confront the truth. The idea of Hoover's place in history being destroyed by revelations of his involvement in the assassination of a President such as John F. Kennedy is perceived as a threat to the Department's existence. Treason in leadership is indeed a hard truth. Having officially attempted to convince the public that the President was killed by a "lone, ultra-left-wing nut" over the last twenty-seven years, can the Department of Justice now voluntarily admit that the party primarily responsible was in fact a right-wing lunatic? It is not likely.

The continuing cost to the Department of Justice and the FBI of holding to their position on the assassination has been the substantial loss of trust of the American people. This perception was reinforced in 1979 when the Justice Department refused to act on the *House Select Committee*'s 1979 findings of conspiracy. The presidency and the FBI have been stonewalling ever since. Undoubtedly this loss of respect has contributed significantly to the lawlessness that now grips the nation. To the average citizen, the attitude of the Justice Department and FBI was, and is, one of indifference. Our criminal justice system is on the verge of collapse. Lawyers are seen, despite the efforts of television script writers, as little more than criminals themselves.

Perhaps almost as important, there remains the sense of loss that comes with the unexpected annihilation of a popular, charismatic leader. The very real psychic damage caused by Kennedy's assassination is an ongoing topic in our contemporary literature, as discussed in lecturer Robert Bly's *Iron John,* released only last year.

> Many men of the generation now forty-five or so projected their undeveloped inner king on Jack Kennedy. . . . When forces in the United States opposed to any spiritual kingship killed [him] . . . in mid-career, it was a catastrophe for the men of that generation. Some men have told me in tears that

they lost something then, and have never regained it; they have never gotten back on track.

And so, what must be done to finally resolve this crisis? To restore the faith of the American people in our system of justice? There are four decisive steps that can be taken. First, the President, Attorney General, Director of the FBI, and surviving members of the Warren Commission (including relevant staff members) should make a formal, public statement in recognition of Hoover's treason and the Commission's decision to withhold that reality from the American people. The basis for such a statement can be found in the *Warren Report* itself. As stated in chapter 8:

> The Commission believes that . . . the FBI [has] too narrowly construed [its] . . . responsibilities. The Commission has the impression that too much emphasis is placed . . . on the investigation of specific threats by individuals and not enough on dangers from other sources. . . . *The FBI . . . carr[ies] the major responsibility for supplying information about potential threats, particularly those arising from organized groups, within their special jurisdiction. . . . They should be responsible for advising the Secret Service if information develops indicating the existence of an assassination plot.* . . . In the appropriations of the FBI there has recurred annually an item for the "protection of the person of the President." . . . The FBI . . . does have an assignment . . . in the field of preventive investigation in regard to the President's security [emphasis added].

Not surprisingly, when read by Hoover, he stated angrily to his assistants, "Chapter 8 [of the report] tears us to pieces. . . ." The point should also be made, publicly, that Hoover's actions do not in any way reflect on the great majority of Bureau employees, past and present. These people should not be held responsible for the treasonous acts of a handful of Bureau officials. The basic structural integrity of the FBI, as it exists today, should be made apparent as well.

Second, they should call upon the public, conservative and liberal alike, to make a conscious distinction between Hoover's rhetoric and his act of treason. Much of what he espoused over the decades is mere common sense. Few would argue with the need for solid family structure, personal morality, belief in God, and loyalty to country. None should say espousal of such rhetoric is justification for treason. Disagreement with elected officials should rather be expressed in words, acts of civil disobedience (revolution in the extreme case), and in votes cast at the ballot box.

Third, these same officials should compel the Justice Department to prosecute the surviving members of the Marcello organization for treason and murder. Identities of actual triggermen should be determined. If still alive, they should be prosecuted. Under grant of immunity from prosecution, former FBI officials and associates of Johnson should be compelled to testify.

Lastly, and symbolically, J. Edgar Hoover's name should be taken *off* the FBI building in Washington, D.C. Its presence is, and should be, considering what is now known, an affront to the American people and all who visit the facility.

If these steps are taken, this disgraceful episode in our history can be morally resolved. The historical lessons provided by the disintegration of ancient Rome and the more recent collapse in the Soviet Union prove that when governments lose credibility, lawlessness becomes rampant. These same governments either collapse or become brutally authoritarian. Is either alternative worth preserving our memory of J. Edgar Hoover? We can afford nothing less than the truth, for the hour grows late.

> Prudence, indeed, will dictate that Governments long established should not be changed for light and transient causes; and accordingly all experience hath shown, that mankind are more disposed to suffer, while evils are sufferable, than to right themselves by abolishing the forms to which they are accustomed. But when a long train of abuses and usurpations, pursuing invariably the same Object, evinces a design to reduce them under absolute Despotism, it is their right, it is their duty, to throw off such Government, and to provide new Guards for their future security.*

* Declaration of Independence

VIII

Appendix A

Correspondence between J. Edgar Hoover and Lyndon B. Johnson: July 1960 to May 1964.

These letters, and those reproduced in the photographic inset, were gleaned from various LBJ Library files and may represent only a portion of the correspondence between the two during the described time period. Organization and declassification of Johnson's vice-presidential files is ongoing. Most noticeably, there is a possibly critical gap between September and December 1963, as well as one between December 1960 and September 1961. Undoubtedly there were other writings between the two during the Kennedy administration, but with Hoover's personal files destroyed by the FBI, much may be lost for all time. At any rate, this selection does make apparent the closeness between the two, as well as their increasing interdependence.

July 25, 1960

Dear Edgar:

I very deeply appreciated your wonderful
letter. Just to know that a distinguished
public servant and a very dear friend like
you feels as you do, is richly rewarding
to me personally. I only hope that I can
live up to the trust of the people who have
nominated me for this office -- and to the
confidence of J. Edgar Hoover.

Warmest regards.

                 Sincerely,

                 Lyndon B. Johnson

The Honorable J. Edgar Hoover
Federal Bureau of Investigation
United States Department of Justice
Washington, D. C.

LBJ:BDM:bc

September 6, 1960

Dear Edgar:

Many thanks for your thought
on my birthday. It's good to be remembered
by your friends -- and your neighbors!!

With warm regards.

Sincerely,

Lyndon B. Johnson

Honorable J. Edgar Hoover
Federal Bureau of Investigation
United States Department of Justice
Washington, D. C.
LBJ:AT

Condolences
sister

January 4, 1962

Dear Edgar:

I appreciate so much your thoughtfulness and kindness and thank you for your
telegram of sympathy. It is a comfort to
know that others understand; others care.

Sincerely,

Lyndon B. Johnson

The Honorable
J. Edgar Hoover
Director
Federal Bureau of Investigation
Department of Justice
Washington, D. C.
LBJ:MJDR:vws

COMMUNISM

February 28, 1962

Dear Mr. Hoover:

Thank you very much for sending me a
copy of The Party Line. It reflects clearly
the relentless aspects of the Communist menace.
Nevertheless, it is indeed a very interesting
document.

Sincerely,

Lyndon B. Johnson

Honorable J. Edgar Hoover
Director
Federal Bureau of Investigation
United States Department of Justice
Washington 25, D. C.

LBJ:HLB:mds

COMMUNISM

August 2, 1962

Dear Mr. Hoover:

I deeply appreciate your sending me the monograph on the Communist Party Line.

As always, you are serving your country by maintaining the high degree of objectivity for which you have so rightly earned the respect of all Americans.

Sincerely

Lyndon B. Johnson

Honorable J. Edgar Hoover, Director
Federal Bureau of Investigation
Washington 25, D. C.

LBJ:GRR:dj

COPY

August 29, 1962

Dear Mr. Director:

Your birthday message to the Vice
President has been placed on his desk awaiting
his return from his assignments abroad.

I have told him about your greeting
and he asked me to be sure to hold it so he
could see it on his return.

Sincerely

Walter Jenkins
Administrative Assistant to
The Vice President

Honorable John Edgar Hoover, Director
Federal Bureau of Investigation
United States Department of Justice
Washington, D. C.

WJ CKB dj

return file to geraldine

PUBLIC ACTIVITIES
condolence

November 16, 1962

Dear Edgar:

     I wanted to come by to see you but am being called to Texas today for the funeral of an old friend. Hence, this note is to tell you I am sorry you are ailing and wish you well.

     Best personal regards.

        Sincerely,

        Lyndon B. Johnson

Honorable J. Edgar Hoover
c/o George Washington University Hospital
Washington, D. C.

LBJ:WJ:ms

February 4, 1963

Dear Mr. Director:

Thank you for sending to me Copy 4
of the monograph entitled "The Communist Party
Line, July 1962 -- December 1962."

I am glad to have it, and I am grateful
for your thoughtfulness.

Sincerely

Lyndon B. Johnson

Honorable J. Edgar Hoover, Director
Federal Bureau of Investigation
Washington 25, D. C.

LBJ GER dj

June 20, 1963

Dear Edgar:

I deeply appreciate your much-too-kind comments about my address yesterday at the FBI National Academy's graduation exercises.

Quite frankly, I was not sure what to say to the graduates. I knew the rigorous, demanding training they had endured to master so many skills. But, I also knew the immeasurably difficult tasks they had volunteered to face, to strive to overcome and -- with characteristic aplomb -- uphold the distinguished tradition of the Federal Bureau of Investigation. They had my unstinted respect, my admiration and my encouragement.

It was wonderful to be with you. I shall look forward to when time and circumstance will allow us another opportunity to get together.

Sincerely,

Lyndon B. Johnson

The Honorable J. Edgar Hoover
Director, Federal Bureau of Investigation
Washington, D. C.

LBJ:IS

COPY

July 10, 1963

Dear Edgar:

Thanks much for sending the pictures.
I'm proud to have them in my library.

My best wishes.

       Sincerely,

       Lyndon B. Johnson

Mr. John Edgar Hoover
Director
Federal Bureau of Investigation
Washington, D. C.

LBJ:MF

Pictures sent to archives.

August 5, 1963

Dear Edgar:

Thank you very much for the excellent display you gave my speech in the Law Enforcement Bulletin.

I appreciated the opportunity to be with you and I enjoyed the occasion thoroughly. Best regards.

Sincerely

Lyndon B. Johnson

Honorable John Edgar Hoover, Director
Federal Bureau of Investigation
Washington, D. C.

LBJ GER dj

August 28, 1963

Dear Edgar:

 I was real pleased to receive
your good wishes on my birthday.   It
is wonderful to be remembered by such
old and good friends.

  With warmest personal regards.

   Sincerely,

   Lyndon B. Johnson

The Honorable
John Edgar Hoover
Director, Federal Bureau of
 Investigation
Washington, D. C.

EXECUTIVE

PR6-1/H ✱

December 16, 1963

Autographed photograph (telephone picture)
TO:
        ✱
J. Edgar Hoover

"Than whom there is no greater
from his friend of 30 years

                    Lyndon B. Johnson

                    personally handed photograph
                    to Mr. Hoover at 1:45 p. m.
                    Dec. 16, 1963

PRESIDENT'S PERSONAL AUTOGRAPH FILE RECORD

EXECUTIVE
PR6-1/H*

Date Mailed: Sent to Mr. Hopkins, dtd 12/23/63

Item Autographed:

( ) White House Card
( ) Autograph Album
( ) Book
( ) First Day Cover
( ) Souvenir Program

( ) Photograph of the President, furnished by office
( ) Photograph of the President, furnished by party being autographed for
(X) Photograph of President with someone else
( ) Magazine Cover
( ) Newspaper Picture
Further description of photograph if necessary:

( ) Other

Inscription:

"To J. Edgar the best, LBJ"

For party other than one to whom addressed or delivered:

Sent or delivered to: Honorable J. Edgar Hoover
Federal Bureau of Investigation

JOHN EDGAR HOOVER
DIRECTOR

Federal Bureau of Investigation
United States Department of Justice
    Washington, D. C.

December 26, 1963

My dear Mr. President:

     Thank you so much for the beautiful leather-bound copy of "The White House" which you autographed to me. I shall treasure this book as I do your friendship.

     Thank you especially, also, for the autographed photograph which was taken on the day I had luncheon with you. This will always remain in my mind as a most memorable occasion.

     With every good wish for the New Year,

             Sincerely yours,

               Edgar

The President
The White House
Washington, D. C.

RECEIVED
JAN 7 1964
CENTRAL FILES

JOHN EDGAR HOOVER
DIRECTOR

Federal Bureau of Investigation
United States Department of Justice
Washington, D. C.

March 4, 1964

EXECUTIVE
PR6-1/H*
FC 135-6

My dear Mr. President:

I was indeed surprised and most
pleased to receive the photographs which you
sent me this morning. With the tremendous
demands on your time and the many difficult
burdens facing you each and every day, it
meant a great deal to me to have you do this.
It is typical of you to be so thoughtful and kind,
and I do appreciate this wonderful gesture of
friendship. Thank you so very much for this
memento of my recent visit with you!

With expressions of my highest
esteem and best regards, I am

Sincerely,

Edgar

The President
The White House
Washington, D. C.

Nothing else sent to 3/11/64
Central Files as of _____

Appendix B
Analysis of Lee H. Oswald's 1962 income and tax return; and interaction with IRS.

The Oswalds signed and filed their 1962 1040-A return on January 29, 1963, the same day they completed repayment of their loan from the U.S. State Department. The date would indicate that Oswald filled out the return after receiving his W-2's, apparently waiting for one or both employers to process the paperwork. Then, as now, sizable companies often utilized most of January to produce the reports. How many of us have received our W-2's on or near the 31st? The return and its preparation were straightforward. By using the short form and the two W-2's, the task would have taken about five minutes, involving the addition of only two sets of numbers. What was finally released on June 8, 1982, to Marina suggests the above, but also deliberate alteration, presumably by either the FBI, Warren Commission, or IRS. A brief history of the struggle to obtain the seemingly innocuous document will assist here.

Pursuant to presidential powers and internal IRS regulations, the return was "audited" by Internal Revenue as part of its analysis of Oswald's finances during 1962 and 1963 for the Warren Commission.

According to Warren Commission staff member Liebler, there were ". . . Internal Revenue Service people that worked for the Commission. . . ." (See HSCA vol. 11, p. 258). And at page 41 of the same volume, HSCA revealed ". . . the Commission had the Internal Revenue Service do an audit of Oswald's income. . . ." Whether this means IRS provided the Warren Commission staff or FBI personnel with the original return or a copy, or neither, is unclear. After the Commission released its report attempts were made to obtain public disclosure, to no avail. As stated by Anthony Summers at p. 587 of *Conspiracy* in 1980, "IRS records closed: refusal sent to Dallas researcher, June 22, 1968, on grounds that, being dead, Oswald could not give permission to make his returns public (sections 6103 and 7213 of Internal Revenue Code and 18 U.S.C. 1905, cited by Archivist of U.S.A.)." And at p. 550, ". . . IRS record for 1962 most recently denied to two private researchers who in 1978 asked to see the record under the Freedom of Information Act."

Ultimately, Marina, in conjunction with preeminent assassination researcher Mary Ferrell, filed a FOIA action on April 16, 1982, to obtain the return. On May 18, 1982, they were notified by the chief of the Judicial Branch of the National Archives that Oswald's ". . . return was not a joint return. It was headed only by the name of Lee Harvey Oswald and was signed only by him." It is true that the return was headed only by the name "Lee H. Oswald," but even the most casual perusal also instantly reveals the fact that Marina did indeed sign and date the return, and that it *was* filed as a joint return. Bear in mind the National Archives copy the official had available to him is undoubtedly of much higher quality than the one ultimately released to Marina. His statement is telling, for the return, or copy, must have been pulled and examined in order to "conclude" it was "headed only by the name of Lee Harvey Oswald." As if to avoid further involvement of the National Archives in the issue, the notification went on to state, "We have requested the opinion of the Internal Revenue Service concerning the release of the income tax return to you." On June 2, 1982, IRS wrote to Marina, "We regret we are unable to provide you with a copy of the 1962 return which you filed with your husband. The return has been destroyed in accordance with the regular retention and destruction schedule for individual tax returns." As will be seen, this claim is almost certainly mere subterfuge. IRS concluded by stating, "We have been in contact with the National Archives and Records Service concerning your request. . . . We have provided the Archives with our disclosure recommendation. The Archives will respond to you directly concerning disclosure of the document." IRS was apparently equally unwilling to take direct action in the matter. Finally, on June 8, 1982, the National Archives agreed to send Marina a copy of a copy (at best), stating "The Internal Revenue Service has . . . recommended that it be disclosed to you. . . ." The only explanation for its earlier, hostile position was this incredible statement: "We regret that we failed to note that you signed the return."

By agreement with Marina Oswald, the return is published in this Appendix for the first time. As stated, it is a copy several generations removed from the original. Despite this, there are strong indications of alteration. To aid in analysis, I have provided a typed/ written facsimile which more clearly shows the obvious data.

I began my analysis by examining Oswald's paychecks from both employers (Leslie Welding and Jaggers-Chiles). The accompanying schedules for those companies illustrate my methodology. In short, his net pay was "grossed up," using 1962 Internal Revenue Service federal income tax withholding tables, and applicable rates for social security withholding (Texas had no state income tax). This approach revealed the data, within a few cents, which would have appeared on Oswald's W-2's, and upon which his return would have been based.

Oswald showed $727.81 for "wages" from Jaggers-Chiles and either $55.10, $55.40, or $55.70 in federal withholding. My calculations, following standard tax and bookkeeping procedures (in my work experience I have prepared both W-2's and payroll by manual means), resulted in amounts of $727.50 and $55.10. The difference between my calculations and the figures on the return is undoubtedly due to cumulative rounding error during the preparation of Oswald's eleven paychecks and W-2. What this proves is that Oswald was in all likelihood working from W-2's when he prepared his return. It is extremely unlikely he did otherwise for three reasons: 1) he did not file until the end of January, suggesting he waited for the exact figures from his employers; 2) without adequate alternative explanation and supporting documentation IRS would not have mailed him a refund; and 3) reconstructing income from paycheck stubs can be tedious. The paychecks themselves were simply cashed as they were issued and then returned to the issuing companies. I could find no data to suggest that Oswald retained or used paycheck stubs to calculate his 1962 income.

He next reported what *appears* to be $626.25 in "wages" from Leslie Welding Co. but no federal withholding. I calculated $627.31 and $28.60 respectively. As pointed out by Henry Hurt in *Reasonable Doubt,* the apparent omission of withholding is very odd. Oswald was a man who pinched every penny. With W-2's before him it is impossible to believe that he would not claim the $28.60 due him. As also revealed by Hurt, when Oswald filed his return he took pains to point out in a note he sent along with it the fact that IRS should refund his withholdings. "I believe if you check your records to substaniate *[sic]* these figures you will find I should get a substantial refund" (this could also have served as an oblique reference to withholdings on informant pay).

Examination of the line on which the Leslie Welding data appears strongly suggests alteration. The space for "Federal Income Tax Withheld" appears to have been erased or blotted out. The "2" in the $626.25 appears to have been overwritten. My own calculation, $627.31, is close enough to suggest that the $626.25 figure was probably copied from the W-2. Why then the apparent overwrite to some greater sum? The total for "wages" then, $1354.06, may be a forgery. Such alteration is not difficult. Simply by copying the original, altering the copy, then copying the copy one can accomplish and hide any range of changes.

The possibility of alteration is compounded by the total shown for "Total Federal Income Tax Withheld," $57.40. The source and accuracy of the $55 plus change figure proven, why would Oswald, three lines directly below, enter a total figure distinctly higher? Higher and yet nowhere near the sum of $84 (give or take a few cents), which would have been shown had the $28.60 withheld by Leslie Welding been included? The amount of Oswald's refund from the IRS, on April 2, 1963, was, according to the FBI and IRS, $57.40 (see Warren Report, p. 744).

To make matters worse, Line 12, the all important "Refund" line of the return, has either been left blank or erased. Who does not enter the amount due him when that opportunity arises? Failure to do so would invite confusion and retention of amounts owed the taxpayer. In this regard it is possible Oswald wrote a letter to IRS concerning his 1962 withholdings. An oblique reference to this effect can be found in a May 1, 1977, article in the *Dallas Morning News,* which stated Oswald ". . . referred to 'fiscal 1962' in a letter to the IRS seeking a refund for income taxes withheld on his 1962 earnings." Due to a shortage of time I was not able to learn the date Oswald apparently wrote to the IRS.

It appears that Oswald's original entries somehow included the amount withheld by Leslie Welding, while simultaneously including a third, much smaller amount. Consider the range of differences between the $55-plus-change figure and $57.40: $2.30, $2.00, and $1.70. That range of withholding, given Oswald's number of exemptions, three, and assuming weekly pay, requires additional income of $48–52. Interestingly, at the time Oswald was arrested, allegations arose that he was receiving informant pay of $200 per month from the FBI. This, in turn, breaks down to pay of $50 per week.

That Oswald was approached by the Dallas FBI soon after his return from Russia is documented. At that time he was asked to "notify" the Bureau if he came into contact with any subversives in the Dallas area. It is then very possible that Oswald was, however briefly, recruited in the fall of 1962 and received a small amount of informant pay.

Such income was apparently required to be reported on one's return, thereby subjecting it to taxation. As revealed by an FBI report obtained by Seth Kantor (see p. 128 of *Who Was Jack Ruby?*), Ruby was himself instructed on the matter of informant pay when he was recruited in 1959. "He was further advised of the fact that such money was considered as income—reported on his income tax return." The reportability of informant pay on the federal level was standardized between agencies—by statute undoubtedly. One need only examine IRS Form 211, "Application for Reward for Original Information," to verify this point. That form states, "We use the information to record the claimant's reward as taxable income. . . ." Here, "claimant" is IRS's euphemism for criminal informant.

Given reportability, the question arises, *how* was it reported on the return? As discussed in the text of this book, (see 4/15/63), it is possible the typical informant received a W-2 from a "front company," to all appearances no different from any other wage statement. As revealed by Hoover himself in his May 1964 testimony before the Warren Commission, the IRS was updated annually by federal agencies with regard to informants. It is also very possible that such income was disguised and the IRS had a way of flagging such returns or otherwise verifying that informants in fact reported their pay. That being the case, the income could have been reported on the return in any one of a number of ways. It could easily, for instance, have been included or "buried" in other, unrelated, reported amounts of income; in this case, Leslie Welding Company figures.

What *is* certain from all this is that Oswald's 1040-A should appear very straightforward, when in fact it does not. The indications of alteration are strong. IRS and the National Archives struggled long and mightily to prevent its disclosure, apparently well aware that the document in its present state raises many unpleasant questions. Clearly more research and data is needed to resolve this issue.

IRS has since its inception carefully guarded tax returns against unauthorized disclosure. As early as 1919, federal statute stated:

> Section 3167. It shall be unlawful for any collector, deputy collector, agent, clerk, or other officer or employee of the United States to divulge or to make known in any manner whatever . . . to any person . . . the amount or source of income . . . or any particular thereof, set forth or disclosed in any income return, or to permit any income return or copy thereof . . . to be seen or examined by any person except as provided by law. . . .

From this undoubtedly evolved a policy of isolating sensitive returns from general files. By this method the temptation of copying a well-known celebrity's or official's return, or a large corporation's sensitive tax file and selling it to the highest bidder could be avoided. Competitors and political enemies would obviously pay a great deal for such information. In all likelihood Oswald's return was isolated in a category governing sensitive criminal defendants or political investigations. From this it can be assumed that it was, or should have been, spared routine shredding procedure.

An indication that IRS has long maintained methods of retaining tax file data is seen in the following excerpt from *Federal Tax Coordinator 2d:* "In a 1965 case, IRS said that it kept individual . . . returns for 7 years. . . . In addition to the returns, tax account information is kept on magnetic tape for three years after which it's transferred to microfilm, which is kept for 30 years." So, even if Oswald's paper return has been destroyed, the data is apparently being kept on microfilm, at least until 1996.

That IRS would use physical destruction as an excuse for not providing Marina a copy of the 1962 return is highly suspect in light of Oswald's "crimes." Here was a man who supposedly assassinated the President of the United States, very nearly killed the governor of a large, economically powerful, and strategic state, murdered a police officer, became the subject of an unprecedented national inquiry including audit of his tax return, and yet the IRS has the individual's return, a document of intense controversy, "destroyed in accordance with the regular retention and destruction schedule for individual tax returns." Patently absurd! Unless, of course, the government has something to hide.

Lee Harvey Oswald's
1962 1040-A

Facsimile

Form 1040A	U. S. INDIVIDUAL INCOME TAX RETURN (Less than $10,000 total income)	1962

Please print →

1. Name (If a joint return of husband and wife use first names and middle initials of both)
LEE H   OSWAld

2. Your Social Security Number
433 : 54 : 3937

3. Wife's Social Security Number
-- : -- : --

Home address (Number and street or rural route)
602   ELSBeTh   Apt 2   texAs

City, town, or post office
DALLAS   Zone   State

4. Check one:
☐ Single; ☑ Married filing joint return (even if only one had income);
☐ Married filing separate return—If wife or husband also filing separately,
give name ....

5. WAGES SHOWN ON FORMS W-2 AND OTHER INCOME		FEDERAL INCOME TAX WITHHELD		EMPLOYER'S NAME. Where employed. Write (W) before name of each of wife's employers
If Item 9 is $10,000 or more, or if Item 6 is over $200, use Form 1040.	727	81	55	70	① JAGGeRS-CHiLes-STOVAL INC. 1522BROWNER
	626	25			② LeLie Welding Co. FT. WORTh

6. INTEREST, DIVIDENDS, AND OTHER WAGES — Yours / Wife's

7. Total Federal income tax withheld

8. If you had an expense allowance or charged expenses to your employer, see instruction 8 and check here ☐ if appropriate.

9. TOTAL INCOME → 1354 | 06   57 | 40

Enclose Forms W-2, Copy B. If your income was $5,000 or more, you must compute your tax. However, if your income was less than $5,000, you may have the Internal Revenue Service compute your tax by omitting items 10, 11, and 12. If you compute your own tax, ← pay balance (item 11) in full with return to your District Director.

10. Enter tax from Tax Table or from tax computation schedule ►

11. If Item 10 is larger than Item 7, enter balance due ►

12. If Item 7 is larger than Item 10, enter refund ►

● Check here ☐, if you want refund applied to U.S. Savings Bonds.

U.S. TREASURY DEPARTMENT ● INTERNAL REVENUE SERVICE   (OVER)   LIST YOUR EXEMPTIONS AND SIGN ON OTHER SIDE.

---

13. EXEMPTIONS FOR YOURSELF—AND WIFE (only if all her income is included in this return, or she had no income)

Check boxes which apply.
(a) Regular $600 exemption .... ☑ Yourself ☑ Wife
(b) Additional $600 exemption if 65 or over at end of 1962 .... ☐ Yourself ☐ Wife
(c) Additional $600 exemption if blind at end of 1962 .... ☐ Yourself ☐ Wife

Enter number of boxes checked → 2

14. EXEMPTIONS FOR YOUR CHILDREN AND OTHER DEPENDENTS (List below)

NAME ► Enter figure 1 in the last column to right for each name listed (Give address if different from yours)	Relationship	ANSWER ONLY FOR DEPENDENTS OTHER THAN YOUR CHILDREN			
		Months lived in your home. If born or died during year also write "B" or "D"	Did dependent have income of $600 or more?	Amount YOU furnished for dependent's support. If 100% write "ALL"	Amount furnished by OTHERS including dependent. See instruction 14
JUNE LEE OswAld	DAUGHTeR			$	$

→ 1

15. Total exemptions from items 13 and 14 above .... → 3

SIGN HERE

I declare under the penalties of perjury that to the best of my knowledge and belief this is a true, correct, and complete return.

Lee H. Oswald   Jan. 29   M. Oswald   Jan. 29
(Your signature)   (Date)   (If joint return, wife's signature)   (Date)

● If joint return, BOTH HUSBAND AND WIFE MUST SIGN even if only one had income.

TC●

Oswald's 1962 income from Leslie Welding Company

Hours Worked	Pay Day	Gross Pay		Social Security		Fed. W/H		Net Pay
40.48	7/21/62	$50.60	—	$1.58	—	$2.20	=	$46.82
46.75	7/28	58.44	—	1.83	—	3.60	=	53.01
50.93	8/4	63.66	—	1.99	—	4.40	=	57.27
44.50	8/11	55.63	—	1.74	—	3.10	=	50.79
40.00	8/18	50.00	—	1.56	—	2.20	=	46.24
40.75	8/25	50.94	—	1.59	—	2.20	=	47.15
41.50	9/1	51.88	—	1.62	—	2.30	=	47.96
40.00	9/8	50.00	—	1.56	—	2.20	=	46.24
40.00	9/15	50.00	—	1.56	—	2.20	=	46.24
40.00	9/22	50.00	—	1.56	—	2.20	=	46.24
29.46	9/29	36.83	—	1.15	—	0.00	=	35.68
39.48	10/6	49.35	—	1.54	—	2.00	=	45.81
7.98	10/13	9.98	—	.31	—	0.00	=	9.67
		$627.31	—	$19.59	—	$28.60	=	$579.12

Payroll data: $1.25 pr. hr; forty hr. wk.; married filing joint, three exemptions; social security rate .03125.

Oswald's 1962 income from Jaggers-Chiles-Stovall Co.

Hours Worked	Pay Day	Gross Pay	Social Security	Fed. W/H	Net Pay
32.20	10/18/62	$43.47 —	$1.36 —	$ .90 =	$41.21
40.15	10/24	54.20 —	1.69 —	2.90 =	49.61
40.00	10/31	54.00 —	1.69 —	2.90 =	49.41
52.00	11/7	70.20 —	2.19 —	5.90 =	62.11
56.87	11/14	76.77 —	2.40 —	6.90 =	67.47
58.75	11/21	79.31 —	2.48 —	7.30 =	69.53
56.65	11/28	76.48 —	2.39 —	6.90 =	67.19
60.62	12/5	81.84 —	2.56 —	7.70 =	71.58
55.00	12/12	74.25 —	2.32 —	6.60 =	65.33
46.90	12/19	63.32 —	1.98 —	4.40 =	56.94
39.75	12/26	53.66 —	1.68 —	2.70 =	49.28
		$727.50 —	$22.74 —	$55.10 =	$649.66

Payroll data: $1.35 pr. hr.; forty hour work week plus overtime; married filing joint, three exemptions; social security rate .03125; net pay figures for this and Leslie Welding schedule taken from canceled checks, vol.22 of Warren Commission Hearings and Exhibits.

IX

Note on Sources

Much of the data in this book regarding J. Edgar Hoover is the result of years of painstaking original research on my part. My intent has been to focus primarily on his activities during the Kennedy administration and just after, particularly where they had a personal impact upon the President and Lyndon Johnson. In doing so, I also felt it was necessary to paint as complete a picture as possible of the Director and the times in which he lived. Accordingly, heavy use was made of a wide range of media material, government documents, writings, and editorial comment. The aspect of the book detailing the Mafia contract on the life of JFK is based upon testimony and exhibits from the *Warren Commission Hearings* (1964) and *House Select Committee on Assassinations Hearings* (1979), as well as the mountain of material that developed from those investigations in the form of books, newspaper and magazine articles, and film. There are obviously hundreds and hundreds of books on the Kennedy assassination, with theories running to all extremes. To locate, read, and analyze them all is a practical impossibility. I have, therefore, drawn from the best and most available works to piece together an historically balanced and accurate interpretation of the Marcello contract. When assembled into chronicle form, as done here, the data generated from all of the above sources makes clear the horrific nature of Hoover's deed. These sources, then, tell a terrible but necessary historical truth.

Notes

The Man

1. Jacob Hay and Robert F. Sisson, "The FBI, Public Friend Number One," *National Geographic,* June 1961, p. 862.
2. Richard Gid Powers, *Secrecy and Power: The Life of J. Edgar Hoover* (New York: The Free Press, 1987), pp. 7, 8, 11, 28, 381; "J. Edgar Hoover and the FBI," *Newsweek,* December 7, 1964, p. 21; J. Edgar Hoover, *A Study of Communism* (New York: Holt, Rinehart and Winston, Inc., 1962), see back cover.
3. *Newsweek,* December 7, 1964, p. 21; Ovid Demaris, *The Director: An Oral Biography of J. Edgar Hoover* (New York: Harper's Magazine Press, 1975), p. 3, 79; Joseph Angier and Blaine Baggett, *Secret Intelligence: The Only Rule Is Win* (Community Television of Southern California, 1988—PBS Video).
4. Hoover, *A Study of Communism,* back cover; *Newsweek,* December 7, 1964, p. 21; Joseph L. Schott, *No Left Turns* (New York: Praeger Publishers, 1975), p. 165.
5. Hoover, *A Study of Communism,* back cover.
6. Neil J. Welch and David W. Marston, *Inside Hoover's FBI* (Garden City, New York: Doubleday & Company, Inc., 1984), p. 43; *National Geographic,* June 1961, p. 886.
7. Robert J. Nash, *Citizen Hoover* (Chicago: Nelson-Hall, 1972), p. 234, 235; *FBI Law Enforcement Bulletin,* May 1962, p. 11; Demaris, *The Director,* pp. 383–387.
8. *Newsweek,* December 7, 1964, p. 21; Welch, *Inside Hoover's FBI,* p. 159.
9. Ralph de Toledano, *J. Edgar Hoover: The Man in His Time* (New Rochelle, New York: Arlington House, 1973), p. 42; Welch, *Inside Hoover's FBI,* pp. 40, 48; *Newsweek,* December 7, 1964, p. 24.
10. *Newsweek,* December 7, 1964, pp. 24–25.
11. Welch, *Inside Hoover's FBI,* pp. 5, 275.
12. Schott, *No Left Turns,* p. 3.
13. Fred J. Cook, *The FBI Nobody Knows* (New York: The Macmillan

Company, 1964), pp. 4–5; William C. Sullivan with Bill Brown, *The Bureau: My Thirty Years in Hoover's FBI* (New York: W.W. Norton & Company, 1979), p. 184.

14. Welch, *Inside Hoover's FBI,* p. 27.
15. Demaris, *The Director,* pp. 23, 140.
16. Ibid., p. 171.
17. Welch, *Inside Hoover's FBI,* p. 25.
18. Demaris, *The Director,* pp. 35, 39.
19. Ibid., pp. 37, 42–44.
20. Ibid., p. 44.
21. Ibid., pp. 41, 44, 339–382.
22. Ibid., p. 47.
23. Ibid., pp. 38, 46.
24. Ibid., p. 44.
25. Ibid., p. 46.
26. Ibid., p. 43.
27. Welch, *Inside Hoover's FBI,* pp. 221–222.
28. Demaris, *The Director,* pp. 40–41, 49.
29. Nash, *Citizen Hoover,* p. 4.
30. *Washington Post,* 7/23/61; Demaris, *The Director,* p. 34.
31. Welch, *Inside Hoover's FBI,* p. 74.
32. Demaris, *The Director,* pp. 34, 45.
33. Sullivan, *The Bureau,* p. 39.
34. Demaris, *The Director,* p. 41.
35. Ibid., p. 39.
36. Sullivan, *The Bureau,* p. 87.
37. de Toledano, *J. Edgar Hoover,* p. 34.
38. Demaris, *The Director,* p. 12.
39. de Toledano, *J. Edgar Hoover,* p. 30.
40. Demaris, *The Director,* p. 80; Sullivan, *The Bureau,* p. 101.
41. Powers, *Secrecy and Power,* p. 356.
42. Demaris, *The Director,* pp. 41, 43.
43. *Washington Post,* 1/29/61, p. C1; *New York Times,* 2/18/62.
44. *Newsweek,* December 7, 1964, p. 25.
45. *Washington Post,* 4/21/61.
46. *Newsweek,* December 7, 1964, p. 25.
47. Nash, *Citizen Hoover,* p. 5; Demaris, *The Director,* p. 12.
48. Schott, *No Left Turns,* p. 162; Demaris, *The Director,* pp. 77, 80.
49. *Esquire,* September 1974.
50. Demaris, *The Director,* p. 83.
51. Sullivan, *The Bureau,* p. 102.
52. Ibid., p. 123.
53. Demaris, *The Director,* p. 83.
54. Welch, *Inside Hoover's FBI,* p. 27.
55. Ibid., p. 182.

56. Powers, *Secrecy and Power,* p. 6.
57. Ibid., p. 171.
58. Ibid.
59. *Esquire,* September 1974; Powers, *Secrecy and Power,* p. 314.
60. Demaris, *The Director,* p. 36.
61. Schott, *No Left Turns,* p. 140.
62. Leigh W. Rutledge, *The Gay Book of Lists* (Boston: Alyson Publications, 1987), pp. 48–49; Dennis Altman, *The Homosexualization of America* (Boston: Beacon Press, 1982), p. 130; Vern L. Bullough, *Homosexuality: A History* (New York: Garland STPM Press, 1979), p. 139; *Austin American Stateman,* September 24, 1989, p. A6; Powers, *Secrecy and Power,* 172.
63. Schott, *No Left Turns,* p. 162; Rutledge, *The Gay Book of Lists,* p. 49.
64. *Austin American Statesman,* 9/24/89, p. A6.
65. *Washington Post,* 6/24/61, sect. A: "Defended Slayers of 'Cider' Brown, All Found Guilty," 7/7/61, p. 1.
66. Sidney Zion, *The Autobiography of Roy Cohn* (Secaucus, N.J.: Lyle Stuart, Inc.), pp. 9, 11–12; Demaris, *The Director,* p. 159.
67. John H. Davis, *The Kennedys: Dynasty and Disaster 1848–1984* (New York: McGraw-Hill Book Company, 1984), pp. 400–401, 517.
68. Demaris, *The Director,* pp. 11, 88.
69. Ibid., p. 200.
70. Welch, *Inside Hoover's FBI,* pp. 40, 41.
71. Ibid., pp. 57, 140.
72. G. Robert Blakey and Richard N. Billings, *The Plot to Kill the President* (New York: New York Times Book Company, 1981), p. 257.
73. de Toledano, *J. Edgar Hoover,* p. 38; Demaris, *The Director,* p. 4.
74. Welch, *Inside Hoover's FBI,* p. 180.
75. Powers, *Secrecy and Power,* p. 483.
76. *Holy Bible* (Revised standard version), Micah 6:8; de Toledano, *J. Edgar Hoover,* p. 32.
77. Athan G. Theoharis and John Stuart Cox, *The Boss* (Philadelphia: Temple University Press, 1988), p. 328; *New York Times,* 3/20/61, p. 1; *Washington Post,* 6/2/61.
78. Schott, *No Left Turns,* p. 6.
79. J. Edgar Hoover, *Masters of Deceit* (New York: Holt, Rinehart and Winston, 1958), p. 113; Hoover, *A Study of Communism,* pp. 8–9.
80. Schott, *No Left Turns,* p. 211.
81. William W. Turner, *Hoover's FBI, The Men and the Myth* (New York: Dell, 1971), pp. 251, 253.
82. *New York Times,* 3/20/61, p. 1.
83. Schott, *No Left Turns,* p. 213.

84. Ibid.
85. J. Edgar Hoover, "To All Law Enforcement Officials," *FBI Law Enforcement Bulletin,* January 1961.
86. Arthur M. Schlesinger, Jr., *Robert Kennedy and His Times* (Boston: Houghton Mifflin Company, 1978), p. 258.
87. Sullivan, *The Bureau,* pp. 72, 125; Powers, *Secrecy and Power,* pp. 313, 314.
88. Demaris, *The Director,* p. 197.
89. Welch, *Inside Hoover's FBI,* pp. 46, 159.
90. Ibid., pp. 84, 86.
91. Powers, *Secrecy and Power,* pp. 152, 153; Demaris, *The Director,* pp. 31, 96.
92. Demaris, *The Director,* p. 202.
93. Ibid., p. 203.
94. "The Truth About Hoover," *Time,* December 22, 1975, p. 16.
95. Schott, *No Left Turns,* generally throughout book; Welch, *Inside Hoover's FBI,* p. 13.
96. Welch, *Inside Hoover's FBI,* p. 181.
97. Schott, *No Left Turns,* p. 4.
98. Sullivan, *The Bureau,* p. 127; Schott, *No Left Turns,* p. 213.
99. Sullivan, *The Bureau,* p. 86; Demaris, *The Director,* p. 77.
100. Demaris, *The Director,* p. 83.
101. Victor S. Navasky, *Kennedy Justice* (New York: Atheneum, 1971), p. 6.
102. Demaris, *The Director,* pp. 81–82.
103. *Washington Post,* 2/24/61; Powers, *Secrecy and Power,* p. 290.
104. Demaris, *The Director,* p. 84.
105. *Newsweek,* December 7, 1964, p. 23; Turner, *Hoover's FBI,* p. 49.
106. Demaris, *The Director,* p. 198.
107. David J. Garrow, *The FBI and Martin Luther King, Jr.* (New York: W.W. Norton & Company, 1981), p. 293, n. 23.
108. Ovid Demaris, "The Office Politics of J. Edgar Hoover," *Esquire,* November 1974, p. 146.
109. Navasky, *Kennedy Justice,* p. 104.
110. Sullivan, *The Bureau,* p. 88.
111. Demaris, *The Director,* p. 76.
112. Ibid., p. 77; de Toledano, *J. Edgar Hoover,* p. 34.
113. *Newsweek,* December 7, 1964, p. 23.
114. Ibid., p. 23; Sullivan, *The Bureau,* p. 116.
115. Sullivan, *The Bureau,* p. 115.
116. *New York Times,* 12/14/63, p. 30; 12/15, p. 66; Sullivan, *The Bureau,* pp. 30, 52.
117. Davis, *The Kennedys,* pp. 400–402; Powers, *Secrecy and Power,* pp. 265–266.
118. *Hearings: Subcommittee of the Committee on Appropriations,*

House of Representatives, Eighty-Eighth Congress, First Session, Department of Justice, February 1, 1963. See "Allegations of Mr. Jack Levine."

119. Sullivan, *The Bureau,* p. 85.
120. Demaris, *The Director,* p. 84.
121. *FBI Law Enforcement Bulletin,* January 1962, p. 14; July 1963, p. 11; Demaris, *The Director,* p. 16.
122. Powers, *Secrecy and Power,* p. 219.
123. *Washington Post,* 3/25/61, 4/20/61, 4/25/61, 12/2/61.
124. *San Francisco Chronicle,* 5/3/61.
125. Demaris, *The Director,* p. 118.
126. Ibid., p. 14.
127. Turner, *Hoover's FBI,* p. 83; Schott, *No Left Turns,* p. 178.
128. Sullivan, *The Bureau,* p. 16.
129. Ibid., p. 84.
130. Ibid., p. 85; Welch, *Inside Hoover's FBI,* p. 77.
131. *National Geographic,* June 1961, p. 870.
132. See *FBI Law Enforcement Bulletin* generally, inside cover.
133. Demaris, *The Director,* p. 190.
134. See Chronicle generally.
135. Demaris, *The Director,* pp. 67, 90.
136. *NBC Monitor Program,* July 15, 1962.
137. *Washington Post,* 11/8/61, see "Washington Scene."
138. *Newsweek,* December 7, 1964, p. 23; Demaris, *The Director,* pp. 128, 167.
139. Welch, *Inside Hoover's FBI,* p. 4.
140. Demaris, *The Director,* p. 340. Wake-up time is inferred from departure time to office, 7:30 A.M., allowance for shower, breakfast, and advanced age.
141. de Toledano, *J. Edgar Hoover,* p. 25.
142. Powers, *Secrecy and Power,* p. 314.
143. Ibid., p. 314; de Toledano, *J. Edgar Hoover,* p. 25.
144. Turner, *Hoover's FBI,* p. 87.
145. Ibid.
146. Demaris, *The Director,* pp. 26, 96.
147. *Newsweek,* December 7, 1964, p. 25.
148. Sanford J. Ungar, *FBI* (Boston: Little, Brown & Co., 1975), p. 255.
149. Sullivan, *The Bureau,* pp. 58, 61.
150. de Toledano, *J. Edgar Hoover,* p. 21; See *Congressional Record Index,* 1961, p. 433; 1962, p. 362; 1963, p. 472.
151. *New York Times,* 11/10/62, p. 13.
152. *FBI Law Enforcement Bulletin,* January 1962, p. 14, January 1964, p. 29.
153. Schlesinger, *RFK and His Times,* pp. 409, 1005.

154. *Report of the Select Committee on Assassinations, U.S. House of Representatives,* Vol. 9, p. 59; Blakey, *The Plot to Kill the President,* p. 215.
155. Welch, *Inside Hoover's FBI,* p. 57.
156. de Toledano, *J. Edgar Hoover,* pp. 29, 34.
157. *Newsweek,* December 7, 1964, p. 25.
158. Powers, *Secrecy and Power,* p. 314.
159. Demaris, *The Director,* pp. 36, 38.
160. Ibid., p. 203; Turner, *Hoover's FBI,* p. 87.
161. Demaris, *The Director,* pp. 15, 36; Schott, *No Left Turns,* p. 197.
162. Demaris, *The Director,* p. 36.
163. Ibid.
164. Schott, *No Left Turns,* p. 197.
165. Demaris, *The Director,* p. 38.
166. *Hearing: Subcommittee of the Committee on Government Operations, House of Representatives, Ninety-Fourth Congress, First Session,* December 1, 1975—*Inquiry into the Destruction of Former FBI Director J. Edgar Hoover's Files and FBI Record Keeping,* p. 202; Sullivan, *The Bureau,* p. 101.
167. de Toledano, *J. Edgar Hoover,* p. 25.
168. Ibid.; Welch, *Inside Hoover's FBI,* pp. 19, 28.
169. Richard Lovegrove and Tom Orwig, *The FBI* (New York: Exeter Books, 1989), p. 143.
170. *Newsweek,* December 7, 1964, p. 21.
171. Ibid.
172. Welch, *Inside Hoover's FBI,* p. 115.
173. *FBI Law Enforcement Bulletin,* March 1962, p. 5; Lovegrove, *The FBI,* p. 143.
174. Ibid.
175. *Hearing: Subcommittee of the Committee on Government Operations,* p. 202.
176. *National Geographic,* June 1961, pp. 862–863.
177. Ibid.; Demaris, *The Director,* p. 75.
178. Angier, *Secret Intelligence: The Only Rule Is Win;* Sullivan, *The Bureau,* p. 101.
179. *National Geographic,* June 1961, pp. 862–863.
180. Ibid.
181. *FBI Law Enforcement Bulletin,* March 1962, p. 5; Lovegrove, *The FBI,* p. 77.
182. *Hearing: Subcommittee of the Committee on Government Operations,* p. 202; Lovegrove, *The FBI,* p. 77.
183. Ibid, p. 36; Lovegrove, *The FBI,* p. 77.
184. Lovegrove, *The FBI,* p. 77, 143.
185. Schott, *No Left Turns,* p. 201.
186. *Time,* December 22, 1975, p. 20.

187. Demaris, *The Director,* pp. 26, 94.
188. *New York Times,* 4/10/61, p. 21.

The Bureaucracy

1. Jacob Hay and Robert F. Sisson, "The FBI, Public Friend Number One," *National Geographic,* June 1961, p. 861; *Hearings: Subcommittee of the Committee on Appropriations—House of Representatives, Eighty-Seventh Congress, Second Session, Department of Justice,* January 24, 1962, p. 338; Sanford J. Ungar, *FBI* (Little Brown Company: Boston, 1975), p. 224.
2. *Hearings,* p. 338.
3. Neil J. Welch and David W. Marston, *Inside Hoover's FBI* (Garden City, New York: Doubleday & Company, Inc., 1984), pp. 95, 134.
4. *National Geographic,* p. 860; William W. Turner, *Hoover's FBI, The Men and the Myth* (New York: Dell, 1971), pp. 197–198.
5. Welch, *Inside Hoover's FBI,* p. 124.
6. Joseph L. Schott, *No Left Turns* (New York: Praeger Publishers, 1975), p. 4; Ungar, *FBI,* p. 179; Turner, *Hoover's FBI,* p. 174; Welch, *Inside Hoover's FBI,* p. 213; 18 USC 1 *(United States Code),* Act of June 25, 1948.
7. *Hearings,* p. 312; *Hearings, Subcommittee of the Committee on Appropriations—House of Representatives, Eighty-Eighth Congress, First Session, Department of Justice,* February 1, 1963. See "Tenure of Service."
8. Turner, *Hoover's FBI,* p. 71; Schott, *No Left Turns,* p. 3; Welch, *Inside Hoover's FBI,* pp. 5, 13.
9. Welch, *Inside Hoover's FBI,* p. 86.
10. Schott, *No Left Turns,* p. 210; Welch, *Inside Hoover's FBI,* p. 167.
11. David J. Garrow, *The FBI and Martin Luther King, Jr.* (New York: W. W. Norton & Company, 1981), see footnotes, pp. 233–311, "SAC to Director" memos; Welch, *Inside Hoover's FBI,* p. 137.
12. *Report of the Select Committee on Assassinations, U.S. House of Representatives,* vol. 9, p. 18 (fn. 2.), p. 59.
13. Welch, *Inside Hoover's FBI,* p. 181.
14. *Hearings: Subcommittee of the Committee on Appropriations, House of Representatives, Eighty-Sixth Congress, Second Session, Department of Justice,* February 8, 1960. See "Inspection Program"; William C. Sullivan with Bill Brown, *The Bureau: My Thirty Years in Hoover's FBI* (New York: W.W. Norton & Company, 1979), p. 107; Welch, *Inside Hoover's FBI,* p. 69; Schott, *No Left Turns,* p. 107.
15. Welch, *Inside Hoover's FBI,* p. 69.

16. Ibid., p. 70.
17. Ibid., p. 49.
18. Ibid., p. 168.
19. Ibid., p. 83.
20. Ibid., p. 5; Fred J. Cook, *The FBI Nobody Knows* (New York: The Macmillan Company, 1964), pp. 11–13.
21. Welch, *Inside Hoover's FBI*, p. 24; Cook, *The FBI Nobody Knows*, p. 30.
22. Edited by Pat Watter and Stephen Gillers, *Investigating the FBI* (Garden City, New York: Doubleday & Company, Inc., 1973), p. 10; Eugene Lewis, *Public Entrepreneurship: Toward a Theory of Bureaucratic Political Power* (Bloomington, Ind.: Indiana University Press, 1980), p. 142; "J. Edgar Hoover and the FBI," *Newsweek,* December 7, 1964, p. 23.
23. Welch, *Inside Hoover's FBI*, p. 76.
24. Ibid., pp. 24, 76–77; Schott, *No Left Turns,* pp. 3–4.
25. Welch, *Inside Hoover's FBI*, pp. 64, 134, 139.
26. Ibid., p. 48.
27. Ibid., p. 64.
28. *Newsweek,* December 7, 1964, p. 24.
29. *National Geographic,* June 1961, p. 869; *Hearings,* February 1, 1963, see "Proposed New Building."
30. Welch, *Inside Hoover's FBI*, pp. 66, 74.
31. Ovid Demaris, *The Director: An Oral Biography of J. Edgar Hoover* (New York: Harper's Magazine Press, 1975), p. 203.
32. Ibid.; *Congressional Directory,* April 1961, pp. 468–469.
33. Demaris, *The Director,* p. 203.
34. Ibid.
35. *Hearings,* January 24, 1962, p. 312; Victor S. Navasky, *Kennedy Justice* (New York: Atheneum, 1971), p. 7.
36. *Newsweek,* December 7, 1964, p. 23; Richard Gid Powers, *Secrecy and Power: The Life of J. Edgar Hoover* (New York: The Free Press, 1987), p. 362.
37. "The Truth About Hoover," *Time,* December 22, 1975, p. 16; Demaris, *The Director,* p. 80; Powers, *Secrecy and Power,* p. 379; Turner, *Hoover's FBI,* p. 89.
38. Demaris, *The Director,* p. 32.
39. Sullivan, *The Bureau,* p. 50.
40. Ibid., p. 121; Navasky, *Kennedy Justice,* pp. 5, 25.
41. Sullivan, *The Bureau,* p. 99.
42. G. Robert Blakey and Richard N. Billings, *The Plot to Kill the President* (New York: New York Times Book Company, 1981), pp. 210, 215, 238; See also Chronicle 12/10/63, Hoover memo to Belmont; Belmont testimony before Warren Commission, May 6, 1964.

43. Demaris, *The Director,* pp. 30, 153–154.
44. Ibid., p. 30.

The System

1. *Hearing: Subcommittee of the Committee on Government Operations, House of Representatives, Ninety-Fourth Congress, First Session, Inquiry Into the Destruction of Former FBI Director J. Edgar Hoover's Files and FBI Recordkeeping,* December 1, 1975, pp. 120, 129. Hereafter referred to as "Inquiry."
2. Ibid., p. 116; William C. Sullivan with Bill Brown, *The Bureau: My Thirty Years in Hoover's FBI* (New York: W.W. Norton & Company, 1979), p. 220.
3. *Hearings: Subcommittee on Civil and Constitutional Rights of the Committee on the Judiciary, House of Representatives, Ninety-Fourth Congress, First Session, FBI Oversight,* February 27, 1975, pp. 8–10.
4. *Inquiry,* pp. 129–130, 132–134.
5. Ibid., p. 131; Jacob Hay and Robert F. Sisson, "The FBI, Public Friend Number One," *National Geographic,* June 1961, p. 873.
6. *Inquiry,* p. 130.
7. Ibid.
8. Ibid., pp. 129, 131.
9. Ibid., p. 121.
10. Ibid., p. 132.
11. Ibid.
12. Sullivan, *The Bureau,* p. 118; Richard Gid Powers, *Secrecy and Power: The Life of J. Edgar Hoover* (New York: The Free Press, 1987), p. 157.
13. *Inquiry,* p. 135.
14. Ibid., p. 138.
15. Ibid., p. 130.
16. *Report of the Select Committee on Assassinations, U.S. House of Representatives,* vol. 9, p. 88, fn. 76, notes generally; David J. Garrow, *The FBI and Martin Luther King, Jr.* (New York: W.W. Norton & Company, 1981), pp. 230–231.
17. *Inquiry,* pp. 139–140.
18. *Congressional Directory,* April 1961, p. 469; January 1962, p. 469; March 1963, p. 480; January 1964, p. 493; *National Geographic,* June 1961, p. 862.
19. *Inquiry,* pp. 125–126.
20. Ibid., p. 116.
21. Ibid., pp. 116–117.
22. Ibid., pp. 106, 140.

23. Ibid., pp. 35–36.
24. Ibid., pp. 56, 84.
25. Ibid., pp. 125–126; *Report of the Select Committee on Assassinations, vol. 9,* see footnotes generally for memos to Director; Garrow, *The FBI and Martin Luther King, Jr.,* see footnotes generally for memos to Director.
26. *Inquiry,* pp. 44–46, 106.
27. Ibid., pp. 45, 71.
28. Ibid., p. 126; Sullivan, *The Bureau,* p. 191; Neil J. Welch & David W. Marston, *Inside Hoover's FBI* (Garden City, New York: Doubleday & Company, Inc., 1984), p. 200.
29. Welch, *Inside Hoover's FBI,* pp. 200–201.
30. *Inquiry,* p. 36.
31. *Hearings: FBI Oversight,* p. 10; *Inquiry,* p. 38.
32. *Hearings: FBI Oversight,* p. 11.
33. *Inquiry,* p. 206.
34. *The Official Warren Commission Report on the Assassination of President John F. Kennedy* (Garden City, New York: Doubleday & Company, Inc., 1964), p. 432; Kenneth O'Reilly, *Hoover and the Un-Americans* (Philadelphia: Temple University Press, 1983), p. 206.
35. Welch, *Inside Hoover's FBI,* p. 13.
36. *Hearings Before the President's Commission on the Assassination of President John F. Kennedy, vol. 5,* see testimony of FBI Assistant Director Alan Belmont, May 6, 1964.

Means to an End

1. William W. Turner, *Hoover's FBI: The Men and the Myth* (New York: Dell, 1971), p. 198; Neil J. Welch and David W. Marston, *Inside Hoover's FBI* (Garden City, New York: Doubleday & Company, Inc., 1984), pp. 60–61.
2. *New York Times,* 10/10/62, 10/18/62; *London Sunday Times,* 12/3/61, see interview with RFK; Kenneth O'Reilly, *Hoover and the Un-Americans* (Philadelphia: Temple University Press, 1983), pp. 231–232.
3. Welch, *Inside Hoover's FBI,* pp. 60–61.
4. Ibid., p. 60.
5. Anthony Summers, *Conspiracy* (New York: McGraw-Hill Book Company, 1980), p. 320.
6. *Washington Post,* 2/9/63, p. A3; William C. Sullivan with Bill Brown, *The Bureau: My Thirty Years in Hoover's FBI* (New York: W.W. Norton & Company, 1979), p. 179.
7. Summers, *Conspiracy,* p. 232.

8. Victor S. Navasky, *Kennedy Justice* (New York: Atheneum, 1971), p. 67.
9. Joseph Angier and Blaine Baggett, *Secret Intelligence: The Only Rule Is Win* (Community Television of Southern California, 1988 —PBS Video).
10. Turner, *Hoover's FBI,* p. 332.
11. Summers, *Conspiracy,* pp. 308–312.
12. Ibid., pp. 297, 302, 309.
13. Ibid., pp. 319–321.
14. Ibid., pp. 322–323.
15. Ibid., pp. 333–336.
16. Welch, *Inside Hoover's FBI,* pp. 57, 114.
17. *Los Angeles Times,* 8/18/63, sect. C, p. 1; Turner, *Hoover's FBI,* pp. 175, 181; Ovid Demaris, *The Director: An Oral Biography of J. Edgar Hoover* (New York: Harper's Magazine Press, 1975), p. 150.
18. *Los Angeles Times,* 8/18/63, sect. C, p. 1; Demaris, *The Director,* p. 197.
19. Sullivan, *The Bureau,* p. 226.
20. See Chronicle, 12/12/61, 2/9/62, for ELSUR recordings of mafiosi.
21. *Los Angeles Times,* 8/18/63, sect. C, p. 1.
22. Hank Messick, *John Edgar Hoover* (New York: David McKay Company, Inc., 1972), pp. 213, 215; See also *FBI Oversight,* n. 30, below.
23. Navasky, *Kennedy Justice,* p. 68; Demaris, *The Director,* pp. 150, 151.
24. *Los Angeles Times,* 8/18/63, sect. C, p. 1.
25. Sullivan, *The Bureau,* p. 179.
26. Messick, *John Edgar Hoover,* pp. 207, 210.
27. Ibid., p. 207; Sullivan, *The Bureau,* p. 219; David J. Garrow, *The FBI and Martin Luther King, Jr.* (New York: W.W. Norton & Company, 1981), p. 165; John H. Davis, *The Kennedys: Dynasty and Disaster 1848–1984* (New York: McGraw-Hill Book Company, 1984), p. 111.
28. *Report of the Select Committee on Assassinations, U.S. House of Representatives,* vol. 9, fns. pp. 87–92.
29. Ibid., p. 91, fn. 215, p. 134, fn. 64; Welch, *Inside Hoover's FBI,* p. 75; *Hearing: Subcommittee of the Committee on Government Operations, House of Representatives, Ninety-Fourth Congress, First Session, Inquiry Into the Destruction of Former FBI Director J. Edgar Hoover's Files and FBI Recordkeeping,* December 1, 1975, p. 126.
30. Welch, *Inside Hoover's FBI,* p. 95; *Inquiry,* p. 126; *Hearings: Subcommittee on Civil and Constitutional Rights of the Committee on the Judiciary, House of Representatives, Ninety-Fourth Congress, First Session, FBI Oversight,* February 27, 1975, p. 8.

31. *The Official Warren Commission Report on the Assassination of President John F. Kennedy* (Garden City, New York: Doubleday & Company, Inc., 1964), p. 30.

32. Ibid., pp. 429–432, 445.

33. Davis, *The Kennedys: Dynasty and Disaster,* pp. 373, 419; *Washington Post,* 2/24/61, see photo of Hoover and Kennedys; Jacob Hay and Robert F. Sisson, "The FBI, Public Friend Number One," *National Geographic,* June 1961, p. 862; See also Chronicle 11/18/ 61 and 12/7/61 for opposing rhetoric of both.

34. Davis, *The Kennedys: Dynasty and Disaster,* pp. 401–402, 425; Richard Gid Powers, *Secrecy and Power: The Life of J. Edgar Hoover* (New York: The Free Press, 1987), p. 353; Arthur M. Schlesinger, Jr., *Robert Kennedy and His Times* (Boston: Houghton Mifflin Company, 1978), p. 176.

Cooperation (11/8/60—1/29/61)

1. John H. Davis, *The Kennedys: Dynasty and Disaster 1848–1984* (New York: McGraw-Hill Book Company, 1984), pp. 56–57, 335.

2. Richard Gid Powers, *Secrecy and Power: The Life of J. Edgar Hoover* (New York: The Free Press, 1987), p. 357.

3. Davis, *The Kennedys,* pp. 111–112.

4. Athan G. Theoharis and John Stuart Cox, *The Boss* (Philadelphia: Temple University Press, 1988), pp. 335–336.

5. John H. Davis, *Mafia Kingfish: Carlos Marcello and the Assassination of John F. Kennedy* (New York: McGraw-Hill Book Company, 1989), p. 105; Davis, *The Kennedys,* p. 287.

6. Theoharis, *The Boss,* p. 335.

7. Powers, *Secrecy and Power,* p. 359.

8. Arthur M. Schlesinger, Jr., *Robert Kennedy and His Times,* (Boston: Houghton Mifflin Company, 1978), p. 657.

9. Davis, *Mafia Kingfish,* p. 272.

10. Ed Reid, *The Grim Reapers: The Anatomy of Organized Crime in America* (Chicago: Henry Regnery, 1969), pp. 123, 127.

11. Ibid., p. 152 (photo inset).

12. Theoharis, *The Boss,* pp. 344–345.

13. Robert Rowe, *The Bobby Baker Story* (New York: Parallax Publishing Co., 1967), pp. 22–23.

14. Davis, *Mafia Kingfish,* p. 272.

15. Rowe, *Bobby Baker Story,* p. 28; See Chronicle, early-mid-1962 for Estes/Jenkins/Carter interaction.

16. Joseph L. Schott, *No Left Turns* (New York: Praeger Publishers, 1975), p. 138.

17. Schlesinger, *RFK and His Times,* pp. 218–219, 650–651.

18. *Lyndon B. Johnson Presidential Library,* Austin, Texas, famous names box Johnson to Hoover; see also Johnson's correspondence files generally, vice presidential years; White House Central Files, "H." Hereafter, Johnson/Hoover correspondence cited as "famous names box."

19. William C. Sullivan with Bill Brown, *The Bureau: My Thirty Years in Hoover's FBI* (New York: W.W. Norton & Company, 1979), p. 271; Neil J. Welch and David W. Marston, *Inside Hoover's FBI* (Garden City, New York: Doubleday & Company, Inc., 1984), pp. 81–82.

20. "The Truth About Hoover," *Time,* December 22, 1975, p. 20.

21. Powers, *Secrecy and Power,* p. 199; Hank Messick, *John Edgar Hoover* (New York: David McKay Company, Inc., 1972), p. 50.

22. Messick, *John Edgar Hoover,* pp. 83–84.

23. Sullivan, *The Bureau,* pp. 117–118; Victor S. Navasky, *Kennedy Justice* (New York: Atheneum, 1971), p. 44.

24. Davis, *Mafia Kingfish,* pp. 42, 212; Davis, *The Kennedys,* p. 489.

25. Dan E. Moldea, *The Hoffa Wars* (New York: Paddington Press, Ltd., 1978), p. 132. Note Moldea states Hoover was not *told* of CIA involvement at this point, but given his close, long-term working relationship with the then two-term Republican administration, Vice President Nixon, and considerable familiarity with CIA methods, it is unlikely he had not surmised as much during the closing months of 1960. CIA's predecessor, OSS, had used Mafia contacts during World War II, something commonly known in intelligence circles no doubt; Schlesinger, *RFK and His Times,* p. 504.

26. Ed Reid and Ovid Demaris, *The Green Felt Jungle* (New York: Pocket Books, Inc., 1963), p. 196.

27. G. Robert Blakey and Richard N. Billings, *The Plot to Kill the President* (New York: Times Books, 1981), p. 186.

28. Blakey, *The Plot to Kill the President,* p. 257.

29. *Attorney General's Conference on Organized Crime,* Report of February 15, 1950, p. 20; hearings before the Select Committee to Investigate Organized Crime in Interstate Commerce, U.S. Senate, 82nd Congress, January—February 1951, part 8 (Washington, D.C.: U.S. Government Printing Office) *(Kefauver Committee Hearings and Report);* hearings before the Select Committee on Improper Activities in the Labor and Management Fields, 86th Congress, 2nd Sess., March 1959, part 48 (Washington, D.C.: U.S. Government Printing Office, 1959) *(McClellan Committee);* hearings before the *Permanent Subcommittee on Investigations* of the Committee on Government Operations, U.S. Senate, 87th Congress, Gambling and Organized Crime, August—September 1961,

parts 2 and 3 (Washington, D.C.: U.S. Government Printing Office, 1961;) Davis; *Mafia Kingfish,* pp. 66, 73.
30. Davis, *Mafia Kingfish,* p. 35.
31. *House Select Committee on Assassinations, John F. Kennedy,* vol. 9, pp. 62, 63, *(HSCA,* 1979).
32. Hank Messick, *Lansky* (New York: Berkley Publishing Corporation, 1973 ed.), pp. 196–197.
33. Reid, *Grim Reapers,* pp. 13–14; Reid, *Green Felt Jungle,* pp. 183–184; See also fn. 29; Francis A. J. Ianni and Elizabeth Reuss-Ianni, eds., *The Crime Society* (New York: Meridian, 1976), generally for excerpts from government reports.
34. Davis, *Mafia Kingfish,* p. 57; Moldea, *The Hoffa Wars,* pp. 178–179; Anthony Summers, *Conspiracy* (New York: McGraw-Hill Book Company, 1980), p. 504. Simultaneous use of Gill's firm is presumed from the fact that Marcello and Traficante had interlocking business interests, management of which would necessitate the use of legal counsel.
35. Moldea, *The Hoffa Wars,* p. 179; David E. Scheim, *Contract on America* (Silver Spring, Md: Argyle Press, 1983), pp. 96, 322.
36. Scheim, *Contract on America,* pp. 96, 339; Davis, *Mafia Kingfish,* pp. 58–60, Kohn photo 118–119, 274; See also Kohn testimony, *Permanent Investigations Subcommittee,* 1961.
37. Scheim, *Contract on America,* pp. 49, 50.
38. Davis, *Mafia Kingfish,* pp. 312–313.
39. Theoharis, *The Boss,* p. 339.
40. Moldea, *The Hoffa Wars,* p. 108; see also, *Washington Post* 1/5/61 for "Nixon-Hoffa Alliance Described."
41. Blakey, *The Plot to Kill the President,* p. 202.
42. *The Official Warren Commission Report on the Assassination of President John F. Kennedy* (Garden City, New York: Doubleday, 1964), p. 390; Sullivan, *The Bureau,* p. 51.
43. Summers, *Conspiracy,* p. 410.
44. Davis, *Mafia Kingfish,* p. 238.
45. Sullivan, *The Bureau,* p. 50. After Hoover's death Sullivan also stated, "Never once did I hear anybody, including myself, raise the question, 'Is this course of action which we have agreed upon lawful, is it legal, is it ethical or moral?' " (see *Washington Post,* 11/10/77).
46. Schlesinger, *RFK and His Times,* p. 265.
47. *LBJ Library,* famous names box, Hoover to Johnson.
48. *Washington Post,* 11/11/60, p. A8.
49. Ovid Demaris, *The Director: An Oral Biography of J. Edgar Hoover* (New York: Harper's Magazine Press, 1975), p. 190.
50. *Congressional Record*—Senate, 7/25/62, p. 14669.
51. *Washington Post,* 11/12/60, p. 1.

588 *Notes*

52. Ibid., 11/13/60, p. A15.
53. Ibid., 11/17/60.
54. *New York Times,* 11/20/60.
55. *LBJ Library,* famous names box, Johnson to Hoover.
56. *New York Times,* 11/20/60.
57. *Washington Post,* 11/24/60.
58. Ibid. Interestingly, *Washington Post,* 12/15/60, will report that the *Republican*-dominated Illinois State Electoral Board, in certifying Kennedy's victory concluded ". . . insufficient evidence was offered to justify withholding the Democratic Electoral votes."
59. J. Evetts Haley, *A Texan Looks at Lyndon,* (Canyon, Texas: Palo Duro Press, 1964), pp. 110–111.
60. Robert Sherrill, *The Accidental President* (New York: Pyramid Books, 1967), p. 182.
61. *Washington Post,* 12/4/60.
62. Fred J. Cook, *The FBI Nobody Knows* (New York: The Macmillan Company, 1964), p. 230; *Washington Post,* 1/4/61 will report "Quinn Tamm, an assistant director of the FBI, has retired after 26 years . . . and will take the post of director of the [IACP]." Hoover and this man quickly become bitter enemies.
63. Schlesinger, *RFK and His Times,* p. 242.
64. *Washington Post,* 12/16/60.
65. Sullivan, *The Bureau,* p. 53.
66. *Washington Post,* 12/16/60.
67. Ibid.
68. Ibid., 12/20/60.
69. *Associated Press* release, 12/22/60.
70. Schlesinger, *RFK and His Times,* pp. 293–294.
71. *New York Times,* 6/28/61; *U.S. v. Gilbert Lee Beckley,* 5th Cir., Eastern District of Louisiana, 6/27/61, Crim. No. 28247.
72. Davis, *Mafia Kingfish,* p. 310.
73. Messick, *Lansky,* p. 238.
74. Hoover to RFK, 1/10/61, in *Senate Select Committee to Study Government Operations with Respect to Intelligence Activities, Hearings,* vol. 6 Fed. Bur. of Investigation, 94 Cong., 2 Sess. (1976), p. 822.
75. *HSCA,* vol. 9, p. 70.
76. *Washington Post,* 5/16/76, Cl.
77. *New York Times,* 7/18/62; Note *Washington Post,* 1/19/61 reports previous night The Lone Star State Society held a preinaugural gala at the D.C. Statler Hilton for LBJ. Estes was very likely in attendance.
78. Reid, *Green Felt Jungle,* p. 219.
79. Summers, *Conspiracy,* pp. 407–409.
80. Davis, *The Kennedys,* p. 385, 389.

81. Ibid., p. 390.
82. Demaris, *The Director,* p. 191.
83. Sullivan, *The Bureau,* p. 49; Demaris, *The Director,* p. 220.
84. *HSCA,* vol. 9, p. 70.
85. *New York Times,* 7/12/62.
86. *Washington Post,* 1/27/61.
87. Schott, *No Left Turns,* p. 192; Schlesinger, *RFK and His Times,* p. 988, n. 54.
88. Schott, *No Left Turns,* p. 192.
89. *Washington Post,* 1/28/61.
90. Ibid., 1/29/61.
91. Ibid., 1/30/61. Dulles and his wife were also in attendance. " 'I'm glad they didn't consider [Allen's] job political,' said Mrs. Dulles.' "
92. Ibid., 1/29/61.

Animosity (1/30—2/22/61)

1. Athan G. Theoharis and John Stuart Cox, *The Boss,* (Philadelphia: Temple University Press, 1988), p. 341.
2. Joseph L. Schott, *No Left Turns,* (New York: Praeger Publishers, 1975), p. 193; Ovid Demaris, *The Director: An Oral Biography of J. Edgar Hoover* (New York: Harper's Magazine Press, 1975), p. 185.
3. Ralph de Toledano, *J. Edgar Hoover: The Man in His Time* (New Rochelle, New York: Arlington House, 1973), p. 306; Victor S. Navasky, *Kennedy Justice* (New York: Atheneum, 1971), p. 13.
4. William C. Sullivan with Bill Brown, *The Bureau: My Thirty Years in Hoover's FBI* (New York: W.W. Norton & Company, 1979), p. 53.
5. J. Evetts Haley, *A Texan Looks at Lyndon* (Canyon, Texas: Palo Duro Press, 1964), p. 117.
6. William W. Turner, *Hoover's FBI: The Men and the Myth* (New York: Dell, 1971), p. 100.
7. John H. Davis, *The Kennedys: Dynasty and Disaster 1848–1984* (New York: McGraw-Hill Book Company, 1984), pp. 375–377; *Washington Post,* 3/6/61; Dan E. Moldea, *The Hoffa Wars* (New York: Paddington Press, Ltd, 1978), p. 110.
8. Haley, *A Texan Looks at Lyndon,* p. 116; This same month *Washington Post,* 2/12/61, reports LBJ attended a gala New Orleans style "Mardi Gras" celebration at the Sheraton Park Hotel in D.C. It is not known if Marcello interests were present, although the situation would have obviously lent itself to their purposes.
9. Turner, *Hoover's FBI,* p. 101; Demaris, *The Director,* p. 147.

10. Albert H. Newman, *The Assassination of John F. Kennedy* (New York: Clarkson N. Potter, Inc., 1970), p. 199; Gerald R. Ford with John R. Stiles, *Portrait of the Assassin* (New York: Simon & Schuster, 1965), pp. 48–49; Four weeks prior to this Oswald had also noted ". . . the money I get has nowhere to be spent. . . . I have had enough." See *Warren Report,* p. 394.
11. Anthony Summers, *Conspiracy* (New York: McGraw-Hill Book Company, 1980), p. 410.
12. Neil J. Welch and David W. Marston, *Inside Hoover's FBI* (Garden City, New York: Doubleday & Company, Inc., 1984), p. 4, 90.
13. *Washington Post,* 2/4/61, D17. In his personal life, Kennedy's more casual style was also evident early on, as can be seen by two *Washington Post* reports. 2/4/61, "President Kennedy disregarded 7 inches of snow, sleet and freezing rain last night and took in a movie *(Spartacus).* . . . When he emerged shortly before midnight two news photographers were waiting. He departed quickly in a White House limousine." Also, 2/8/61, ". . . Mr. Kennedy has made [an] unannounced excursion . . . to a . . . Georgetown dinner party. . . ."
14. *HSCA,* vol. 9, p. 70.
15. Theoharis, *The Boss,* p. 326.
16. *Washington Post,* 2/14/61.
17. Haley, *Texan Looks at Lyndon,* pp. 249–251.
18. Ibid., p. 117.

Political Confrontation (2/23/61—9/62)

1. *Washington Post,* 2/24/61.
2. *New York Times,* 2/26/61, p. 1.
3. *Washington Post,* 2/25/61.
4. *Notre Dame Law Review,* March 1961.
5. *Report of The House Select Committee on Assassinations, John F. Kennedy,* 1979, vol. 9, p. 70. Hereafter, *HSCA.*
6. Arthur M. Schlesinger, Jr., *Robert Kennedy and His Times,* (Boston: Houghton Mifflin Company, 1978), p. 270.
7. *Los Angeles Times,* 8/16/62; *New York Times,* 6/11/62.
8. G. Robert Blakey and Richard N. Billings, *The Plot to Kill the President* (New York: Times Books, 1981), p. 243.
9. *New York Times,* 3/9/61.
10. John H. Davis, *The Kennedys: Dynasty and Disaster 1848–1984* (New York: McGraw-Hill Book Company, 1984), pp. 111–112.
11. *Washington Post,* 3/9/61, p. B17.
12. *New York Times,* 3/15/61, p. 34.
13. *Washington Post,* 3/18/61.

14. Anthony Summers, *Goddess* (New York: New American Library, 1986), Onyx paperback ed., p. 497.
15. Ibid.
16. *Washington Post*, 3/24/61.
17. Ibid., 3/25/61.
18. Ibid., 3/26/61.
19. *New York Times*, 6/7/62.
20. *HSCA*, vol. 9, p. 89.
21. David E. Scheim, *Contract on America* (Silver Spring, Md: Argyle Press, 1983), p. 50.
22. William W. Turner, *Hoover's FBI: The Men and the Myth* (New York: Dell, 1971), pp. 44, 49.
23. *HSCA*, vol. 9, p. 71.
24. Blakey, *Plot to Kill the President*, p. 243.
25. *New York Times*, 4/5/61; Blakey, *Plot to Kill the President*, p. 243.
26. *Washington Post*, 4/6/61.
27. *New York Times*, 4/8/61.
28. Ibid.
29. Blakey, *Plot to Kill the President*, p. 244.
30. *New York Times*, 4/10/61.
31. *Washington Post*, 4/10/61, p. B19.
32. Ibid., 4/16/61.
33. Ibid., 4/20/61.
34. Scheim, *Contract on America*, p. 50.
35. *Washington Post*, 4/21/61.
36. Ibid., 4/24/61, p. B19.
37. Ibid., 4/25/61.
38. Ibid.
39. Ibid., 4/26/61.
40. Blakey, *Plot to Kill the President*, pp. 380–381.
41. Fred J. Cook, *The FBI Nobody Knows* (New York: The Macmillan Company, 1964), pp. 404, 412.
42. Blakey, *Plot to Kill the President*, pp. 380–381.
43. Anthony Summers, *Conspiracy* (New York: McGraw-Hill Book Company, 1980), p. 304.
44. Davis, *The Kennedys*, p. 838.
45. *Washington Post*, 5/1/61, p. B19.
46. *New York Times*, 6/7/62.
47. *Washington Post*, 5/4/61.
48. Ibid.
49. Ibid., 5/3/61, p. A19.
50. Ibid., 5/5/61, p. A3.
51. Blakey, *Plot to Kill the President*, p. 243.
52. *Washington Post*, 5/5/61.
53. John H. Davis, *Mafia Kingfish: Carlos Marcello and the Assassina-*

tion of John F. Kennedy (New York: McGraw-Hill Book Company, 1989), p. 99.

54. *Washington Post*, 5/14/61.
55. Ibid., 5/18/61.
56. Ibid., 5/20/61.
57. Ibid.
58. Ibid., 5/22/61, p. B20.
59. *HSCA*, vol. 10, pp. 109, 112.
60. *Washington Post*, 6/2/61.
61. *HSCA*, vol. 9, p. 72.
62. *Washington Post*, 6/3/61.
63. Ibid.
64. *New York Times*, 5/4/62.
65. Athan G. Theoharis and John Stuart Cox, *The Boss*, (Philadelphia: Temple University Press, 1988), p. 386. (See also Bantam paperback.)
66. *Washington Post*, 6/17/61, p. C15. The article only states the incident occurred "the other Sunday morning." I took this to mean not the immediately preceding Sunday, but rather the Sunday before, or 6/4/61.
67. *HSCA*, vol. 9, p. 72.
68. *Washington Post*, 6/6/61.
69. Ibid., 6/8/61, p. A24.
70. *HSCA*, vol. 9, p. 72.
71. Scheim, *Contract On America*, p. 87. Marcello, as reported in the 7/14/61 *Washington Post*, apparently had ties to Louisiana Rep. Jimmy Morrison as well. ". . . Morrison introduced several private bills in Congress to permit Silvestro Carollo (a Louisiana Mafia figure) to remain in the United States despite his record of three convictions for bootlegging, narcotics, and attempted murder."
72. *Washington Post*, 6/20/61. Perhaps not coincidentally, the same day as the acquittal, Hoover announced the arrest of saboteurs. ". . . Hoover said all four were being held for possession of machine guns, hand grenades, pistols and ammunition. . . ." One need only read FBI press releases during this time period to gain insight into the Director's penchant for such sensationalism. Papers like the *Washington Post* and *Evening Star* appeared to revel in it, often playing up dramatic angles. Oddly, the following day, June 20, reporters were told, not by the FBI, but "a well-placed source," that the threat posed by the group was "imaginary."
73. *Washington Post*, 6/23/61, p. B2.
74. Ibid., 6/24/61.
75. *Washington Post*, 6/28/61; *New York Times*, 6/28/61. This case, *U.S. v. Beckley*, is difficult to research. It does not appear in the

Federal Reporter series (a collateral action involving Beckley appears only in the mid-60s) and the file is no longer kept in New Orleans. To access it, one must order it, at a fee, from the Federal Court in Dallas, have it shipped to the court in New Orleans, and then travel to that city to examine it, under supervision.

76. Dan E. Moldea, *The Hoffa Wars* (New York: Paddington Press, Ltd, 1978), p. 156; Blakey, *Plot to Kill the President,* p. 80; Davis, *Mafia Kingfish,* p. 310. The importance of the gambling network to Marcello's overall communication system can easily be discerned from the following description, found in Reid's *Grim Reapers* (p. 156): "Via a complicated series of 'cheesbox' phones—used by bookies to hide their location—Carlos [Marcello] made calls until March 1967, from his office in the Town and Country Motel near New Orleans. . . ."

77. Hank Messick, *Lansky* (New York: Berkley Publishing Corporation, 1973 ed.), p. 39.

78. Ibid., p. 238.

79. *Washington Post,* 7/1/61.

80. Ibid., p. A9.

81. Blakey, *Plot to Kill the President,* p. 168.

82. *Washington Post,* 7/2/61, p. D19.

83. *New York Times,* 6/7/62.

84. *Washington Post,* 7/7/61, p. 1.

85. *Washington Post,* 7/7/61.

86. Ibid.

87. *New York Times,* 7/8/61, p. 20.

88. *HSCA,* vol. 9, p. 72.

89. Blakey, *Plot to Kill the President,* p. 381.

90. Ibid, p. 210; *HSCA,* vol. 9, p. 72.

91. *Congressional Record—Senate,* 7/29/61, p. 14,000.

92. *Washington Post,* 7/21/61.

93. Ibid., 7/23/61.

94. Ibid., 7/25/61. When Baughman's replacement, Rowley, was sworn in on 9/1/61, President Kennedy made a surprise appearance. *Washington Post,* 9/2/61, that day reported: " 'Oh, My!' gasped Mrs. Rowley as the ad libbing bystander sidled over to greet them with easy effusion. It was obvious that President Kennedy's presence at the ceremony was as unexpected as it had been unannounced." Ironically, Kennedy had quipped "He (Rowley) hasn't lost a president in all [his time with the Secret Service]. On a record like that, he deserves a promotion."

95. Schlesinger, *RFK and His Times,* pp. 670, 1034 n. 105.

96. *Washington Post,* 7/26/61.

97. Ibid., 7/27/61.

98. Ibid., 8/1/61.

99. Ibid., 8/2/61.
100. Ibid., 8/3/61.
101. Ibid., 8/4/61. The paper also reports Hoover announcement concerning the hijacker of an airplane in El Paso. "FBI Director Hoover, through his Washington office, said . . . Bearden had arrests dating back to 20 years ago and that he was identified as a man who in January visited the Cuban embassy in Mexico City and indicated a desire to go to Cuba." Hoover often used this technique to reinforce the myth that he was always on the job. Through spokesmen, he could project in this manner, anywhere, at any time, even while on "vacation." Note the almost eerie parallels to Oswald, who in 1963 reportedly considered the same action, and also visited the Cuban embassy under the watchful eye of Hoover.
102. Ibid., 8/3/61, p. 2.
103. *Congressional Record*, 8/4/61, pp. 7791, 12012, 14652.
104. Blakey, *Plot to Kill the President*, p. 381.
105. Ibid., p. 168.
106. *HSCA*, vol. 10, p. 118 n. 96.
107. *New York Times*, 8/22/61.
108. Ed Reid, *The Grim Reapers: The Anatomy of Organized Crime in America* (Chicago: Henry Regnery, 1969), pp. 122–123, 190–191, 248.
109. Blakey, *Plot to Kill the President*, p. 168.
110. *HSCA*, vol. 9, p. 87.
111. *Washington Post*, 9/1/61. Kohn also asserted that ex-New Orleans mayor, DeLesseps S. Morrison, who by 1961 had become U.S. ambassador to the OAS (Organization of American States), had at one time accepted ". . . $25,000 . . . contributed by associates of Carlos Marcello . . . for permission to operate a racing wire." Morrison immediately denied the charge.
112. *Lyndon B. Johnson Presidential Library*, Austin, Texas, famous names box Johnson to Hoover.
113. *Washington Post*, 9/8/61.
114. Reid, *Grim Reapers*, pp. 31–32.
115. *Washington Post*, 9/14/61, p. A2.
116. Ibid., 9/16/61.
117. Ibid., 9/21/61.
118. *Congressional Record*, Appendix 9/21/61, p. A7905.
119. *HSCA*, vol. 10, pp. 109, 115.
120. *Washington Post*, 9/24/61.
121. Ibid., 9/28/61, p. A1.
122. James Phelan, "Hoover of the FBI," *The Saturday Evening Post*, 9/25/65, p. 23; *New York Herald Tribune*, 10/5/61 (approximate date).

123. *Washington Post,* 10/13/61, p. A1.
124. Ibid., 10/13/61, p. D13.
125. Ibid., 10/16/61.
126. Schlesinger, *RFK and His Times,* p. 266.
127. Hank Messick, *John Edgar Hoover* (New York: David McKay Company, 1972), p. 202.
128. *Washington Post,* 10/18/61, p. C4.
129. *New York Times,* 6/28/62, 8/2/62.
130. *Washington Post,* 10/21/61.
131. Ibid., 10/22/61.
132. *New York Times,* 6/8/62.
133. *Washington Post,* 10/29/61, p. A4.
134. *HSCA,* vol. 9, p. 73. The SAC for New Orleans during this general time period was a man named *H. G. Maynor.* Presumably he was aware of the apparently symbiotic relationship between Regis Kennedy and Carlos Marcello. It is not known if he is still living, but he may have valuable knowledge regarding the Ferrie investigation as well. Interestingly, he is not mentioned in leading books on the assassination, nor is he listed in the index (including Meagher's) to the Warren Commission hearings. He is perhaps an unknown variable.
135. *HSCA,* vol. 10, p. 115 n. 20, 119 n. 102; *U.S. Senate Intelligence Reports, Foreign Assassinations,* pp. 75–77.
136. *HSCA,* vol. 10, p. 152; see verbatim conversations, Giancana 12/61, this chronicle. In the context of CIA's use of Giancana and Traficante to engineer the assassination of Castro, note that the go-between used by the agency, ex-FBI agent Maheu, was also an investigator for the law firm of Edward Bennett Williams.
137. *Washington Post,* 11/4/61.
138. Richard Gid Powers, *Secrecy and Power: The Life of J. Edgar Hoover* (New York: The Free Press, 1987), p. 370.
139. Schlesinger, *RFK and His Times,* p. 409.
140. Blakey, *Plot to Kill the President,* p. 379.
141. *Washington Post,* 11/11/61.
142. Blakey, *Plot to Kill the President,* p. 379.
143. *Washington Post,* 11/19/61, p. A1. Three days prior to this speech, the Justice Department ". . . gave up its attempt to convict Claude Lightfoot, veteran American Communist leader, on charges that he had broken the law simply by belonging to the Communist Party. . . . Within an hour after Lightfoot's dismissal, the case of another Communist, Max M. Weiss . . . was postponed. . . . The dismissal stemmed directly from the Supreme Court's ruling last June in the case of Junius Irving Scales. . . ." See *Washington Post* 11/16/61.
144. Summers, *Goddess,* p. 260.

145. *Washington Post,* 11/20/61, p. A1.
146. Ibid., 11/22/61.
147. Ibid.
148. Summers, *Goddess,* p. 293.
149. Blakey, *Plot to Kill the President,* p. 380.
150. *Washington Post,* 11/27/61.
151. Davis, *The Kennedys,* p. 377.
152. *Washington Post,* 12/2/61.
153. Ibid.
154. Ibid., 12/5/61.
155. Ibid., 12/6/61.
156. Ibid., 12/7/61.
157. Ibid., 12/8/61; Neil J. Welch and David W. Marston, *Inside Hoover's FBI* (Garden City, New York: Doubleday & Company, Inc., 1984), p. 97. On 10/28/61 (*Washington Post*) Johnson had also presented a speech on ultraconservatives. ". . . 'Good Americans' are unwittingly aiding the Communists by 'planting seeds of doubt' about the loyalty of the Nation's leaders. . . . [by saying] 'that the Executive branch is loaded with traitors. . . .' " Johnson's public alignment with JFK on this issue apparently had no negative effect on his relationship with Hoover. But then again, people with differing philosophies often unite against a common enemy.
158. *Washington Post,* 12/8/61; *Congressional Record,* Appendix 1/11/62, pp. A94–95.
159. Davis, *The Kennedys,* pp. 485, 839; Summers, *Goddess,* p. 293.
160. Blakey, *Plot to Kill the President,* p. 382. RFK may have fallen out with Sinatra very early on. The previous July, Kennedy had attended a baptism in Santa Monica, Ca. "Singer Frank Sinatra was expected to appear, but didn't. 'I don't know where he is,' [Peter] Lawford said later." See *Washington Post,* 7/10/61.
161. Davis, *The Kennedys,* p. 486.
162. Ibid.
163. *New York Times,* 6/28/62.
164. *Hoover vs. The Kennedys: The Second Civil War,* Sunrise Films, Ltd. video, 1987.
165. *Tulsa Daily World,* 12/18/61.
166. *Washington Post,* 12/21/61.
167. *Tulsa Daily World,* 12/21/61.
168. *HSCA,* vol. 9, p. 73.
169. *Washington Post,* 12/22/61.
170. Victor S. Navasky, *Kennedy Justice* (New York: Atheneum, 1971), p. 81.
171. *New York Times,* 6/28/62.
172. *Washington Post,* 12/25/61, p. B1.
173. Ibid., 12/30/61.

174. Theoharis, *The Boss,* p. 377.
175. Schlesinger, *RFK and His Times,* p. 269; Davis, *The Kennedys,* p. 419; Theoharis, *The Boss,* p. 382.
176. William C. Sullivan with Bill Brown, *The Bureau: My Thirty Years in Hoover's FBI* (New York: W.W. Norton & Company, 1979), p. 55.
177. Ed Reid and Ovid Demaris, *The Green Felt Jungle* (New York: Pocket Books, Inc., 1963), p. 218.
178. Robert Sherrill, *The Accidental President* (New York: Pyramid Books, 1968), p. 195.
179. Blakey, *Plot to Kill the President,* p. 196.
180. Davis, *The Kennedys,* p. 409.
181. *New York Times,* 1/11/62.
182. J. Evetts Haley, *A Texan Looks at Lyndon* (Canyon, Texas: Palo Duro Press, 1964), p. 143.
183. David J. Garrow, *The FBI and Martin Luther King, Jr.* (New York: W.W. Norton & Company, 1981), pp. 26, 41–43.
184. *Washington Post,* 1/9/62.
185. *New York Times,* 5/12/62.
186. Ibid., 5/29/62.
187. Ibid., 8/16/62.
188. Ibid., 5/17/62.
189. Haley, *A Texan Looks at Lyndon,* p. 139.
190. *Washington Post,* 1/21/62.
191. Cook, *The FBI Nobody Knows,* p. 48.
192. *Hearings: Subcommittee of the Committee on Appropriations—House of Representatives, Eighty-Seventh Congress, Second Session, Department of Justice,* January 24, 1962. Hoover also discussed the Beckley indictment. "Considerable information has come to the attention of the FBI indicating the very strong deterrent effect [Kennedy's war on the Mafia] has had on gambling operations. Several wire services which were actually the 'lifeline' of gambling operations suddenly discontinued their activities. . . . Wire services utilized by gamblers in *Hot Springs,* Arkansas, Chicago, . . . *New Orleans,* Cincinnati, [and] *Dallas* . . . promptly discontinued their service" (emphasis added). Here, Hoover explicitly, under oath, admits the fact that the bookmakers serve as an interlocking communication network for the Mafia.
193. Haley, *A Texan Looks at Lyndon,* p. 140.
194. *Washington Post,* 1/28/62.
195. *New York Times,* 8/16/62.
196. *Washington Post,* 1/28/62.
197. Schlesinger, *RFK and His Times,* p. 651.
198. *HSCA,* vol. 10, p. 110.
199. Ibid.

200. Ibid., p. 112.
201. Schlesinger, *RFK and His Times,* p. 384.
202. Summers, *Goddess,* pp. 279–280.
203. *Washington Post,* 2/2/62.
204. Ibid.
205. Theoharis, *The Boss,* p. 371.
206. *HSCA,* vol. 5, p. 448; Blakey, *Plot to Kill the President,* p. 237.
207. *Washington Post,* 2/9/62, p. B11.
208. Theoharis, *The Boss,* p. 346.
209. *New York Times,* 2/18/62.
210. *HSCA,* vol. 5, p. 449.
211. *Washington Post,* 2/17/62, p. B13.
212. *New York Times,* 2/23/62.
213. *Congressional Record,* 3/1/62, p. 3188.
214. Blakey, *Plot to Kill the President,* p. 258; *FBI Crime Condition Report—Dallas,* 3/1/62.
215. Moldea, *The Hoffa Wars,* p. 134.
216. Davis, *The Kennedys,* p. 400.
217. *Washington Post,* 2/28/62.
218. *HSCA,* vol. 10, p. 110.
219. Blakey, *Plot to Kill the President,* p. 251.
220. *New York Times,* 1/15/64.
221. Ibid., 3/3/62.
222. Schlesinger, *RFK and His Times,* p. 989.
223. Summers, *Goddess,* pp. 456, 459.
224. Sullivan, *The Bureau,* p. 56.
225. Schlesinger, *RFK and His Times,* p. 989.
226. *New York Times,* 3/10/62.
227. Schlesinger, *RFK and His Times,* p. 266.
228. Summers, *Goddess,* pp. 300, 498; *New York Times,* 3/14/62, p. 29.
229. *New York Times,* 3/13/62.
230. Ibid., 6/14/62.
231. Ibid., 3/19/62.
232. Ibid., 3/20/62.
233. Ibid., 3/21/62, p. 30.
234. Theoharis, *The Boss,* p. 382.
235. Moldea, *The Hoffa Wars,* p. 135.
236. Summers, *Goddess,* p. 294.
237. Ibid.; *New York Times,* 3/24/62, p. 10.
238. Summers, *Goddess,* p. 294.
239. Ibid., p. 295.
240. *New York Times,* 3/25/62.
241. Ibid.
242. Ibid., 3/27/62.

243. Haley, *A Texan Looks at Lyndon,* p. 128; *New York Times,* 6/24/62.
244. *New York Times,* 5/17/62.
245. Ibid., 3/29/62.
246. Ibid., 5/5/62.
247. Ibid., 3/30/62.
248. Ibid.
249. Haley, *A Texan Looks at Lyndon,* p. 144.
250. *New York Times,* 3/31/62.
251. *HSCA,* vol. 11, p. 509.
252. Robert Rowe, *The Bobby Baker Story* (New York: Parallax Publishing Co., 1967), p. 145.
253. Haley, *A Texan Looks at Lyndon,* p. 26.
254. Ibid., p. 137.
255. *New York Times,* 4/3/62.
256. Ibid.
257. Messick, *John Edgar Hoover,* p. 252–253.
258. *New York Times,* 4/4/62.
259. Haley, *A Texan Looks at Lyndon,* p. 137.
260. *New York Times,* 4/6/62.
261. Ibid., p. 72. Within the general context of scandal surrounding Estes and Johnson, on 4/11 Rep. Heistand charged that Johnson had received "political payola" of $29,265 for "navigational lights and radio instrumentation" on his private field near Johnson City. Apparently the FAA had designated the strip Johnson City Airport. See *Congressional Record,* 4/11/62, p. 5915.
262. Schlesinger, *RFK and His Times,* p. 419.
263. *New York Times,* 4/12/62.
264. Theoharis, *The Boss,* p. 535 n. 13.
265. Schlesinger, *RFK and His Times,* pp. 419–420.
266. *New York Times,* 4/12/62.
267. Schlesinger, *RFK and His Times,* p. 421.
268. *New York Times,* 4/16/62.
269. Theoharis, *The Boss,* p. 364.
270. *New York Times,* 4/17/62.
271. Theoharis, *The Boss,* pp. 346–347 (hardcover ed.).
272. *New York Times,* 4/29/62.
273. Ibid.
274. *FBI Law Enforcement Bulletin,* May, 1962.
275. *New York Times,* 5/2/62.
276. Blakey, *Plot to Kill the President,* p. 238.
277. *New York Times,* 5/3/62.
278. Ibid.
279. Ibid., 5/4/62. Marcello's people undoubtedly observed Kennedy while he was in New Orleans, noting firsthand the mechanics of

Secret Service protection and public interaction. "He was cheered as his motorcade passed along crowd-lined streets. He was applauded as he spoke . . . from the balcony of City Hall. And he was cheered again as he spoke at the Nashville Avenue Wharf. . . ."

280. *Fort Worth Star Telegram,* 10/1/78, p. A12.
281. *U.S. v. Gilbert Lee Beckley,* 5th Cir., Eastern District of Louisiana, 6/27/61, Crim. No. 28247.
282. *New York Times,* 5/8/62.
283. Ibid., 5/10/62.
284. Ibid.
285. Ralph de Toledano, *J. Edgar Hoover: The Man in His Time* (New Rochelle, New York: Arlington House, 1973), p. 294.
286. *New York Times,* 5/11/62.
287. Ibid., 5/12/62.
288. Ibid., 5/17/62.
289. Ibid.
290. Ibid., 5/18/62.
291. Ibid., 5/19/62.
292. Summers, *Goddess,* pp. 308–310.
293. *U.S. v. Beckley.*
294. *New York Times,* 5/23/62.
295. Ibid.
296. Ibid., 5/25/62.
297. Ibid.
298. Ibid., 5/28/62.
299. Ibid., 5/27/62.
300. Ibid., 5/28/62.
301. Ibid.
302. Ibid., 5/29/62.
303. Blakey, *Plot to Kill the President,* p. 344.
304. *New York Times,* 5/29/62.
305. Albert H. Newman, *The Assassination of John F. Kennedy* (New York: Clarkson N. Potter, Inc., 1970), p. 221; *Warren Commission Hearings and Exhibits,* vol. 16, pp. 198, 578.
306. *New York Times,* 6/1/62.
307. Davis, *The Kennedys,* p. 402.
308. Blakey, *Plot to Kill the President,* p. 202.
309. Moldea, *The Hoffa Wars,* p. 148. As reported in *Contract on America* (p. 40), Hoffa, only hours after President Kennedy's assassination stated, RFK was now ". . . just another lawyer. . . ." When Teamster offices around the nation closed and lowered flags to half staff out of respect, the union boss flew into a rage.
310. *New York Times,* 6/2/62.

311. Ibid., 6/6/62.
312. Ibid., 6/7/62.
313. Ibid.
314. Ibid., 6/8/62.
315. Ibid., 6/10/62.
316. Ibid., 6/12/62.
317. Ibid., 6/13/62.
318. Ibid., 6/14/62.
319. Summers, *Goddess,* p. 321.
320. Gerald R. Ford with John R. Stiles, *Portrait of the Assassin* (New York: Simon & Shuster, 1965), p. 118.
321. Ibid., pp. 118, 126.; Blakey, *Plot to Kill the President,* p. 350.
322. Ford, *Portrait of the Assassin,* pp. 156–157.
323. *New York Times,* 6/15/62, p. 1.
324. Schlesinger, *RFK and His Times,* p. 273. The day after this notation, Schlesinger attended a dinner party at RFK's house. As reported by the *New York Times,* 6/21, "Mrs. Robert F. Kennedy, wife of the Attorney General, fell into the family pool during an outdoor dinner dance Saturday night. . . . So did Arthur Schlesinger, Jr., special Presidential advisor, and Mrs. Spencer Davis, a friend of Mrs. Kennedy. . . ." Although trivial, such stories surely enhanced Hoover's negative view of the administration.
325. *New York Times,* 6/16/62.
326. Ibid.
327. Ibid., 6/17/62.
328. Ibid., 11/30/63. Newman, *Assass. of JFK,* pp. 244–245. If the "engineer" Oswald was referring to was George de Mohrenschildt, this would suggest that CIA (de Mohrenschildt was possibly a contract agent), like FBI, took an initial look at Oswald upon his return to the U.S.
329. *New York Times,* 6/19/62.
330. Ibid., 11/30/63.
331. Ibid., 6/21/62.
332. Ibid., 6/22/62.
333. Blakey, *Plot to Kill the President,* p. 240.
334. *New York Times,* 6/23/62.
335. Ibid., 6/24/62.
336. Ibid.
337. Ibid.
338. Ibid.
339. Ibid., 6/26/62, p. 1.
340. Summers, *Goddess,* p. 330.
341. Summers, *Conspiracy,* p. 219.
342. Summers, *Goddess,* p. 333.
343. *New York Times,* 6/28/62.

344. Summers, *Goddess,* pp. 333, 501.
345. *New York Times,* 6/29/62.
346. Ibid., p. 12.
347. Blakey, *Plot to Kill the President,* p. 233. Just prior to this, on 6/22, in its ". . . *Criminal Intelligence Digest,* the FBI ascribed to . . . Lansky the statement that 'organized crime is bigger than United States Steel.' " Lansky was obviously referring to the power of the Mafia verses that of the American steel companies, which in April had effectively kneeled before John Kennedy (See *HSCA* vol. 9, p. 14.)
348. de Toledano, *J. Edgar Hoover,* p. 312.
349. *New York Times,* 10/24/63; Rowe, *Bobby Baker Story,* p. 42.
350. *New York Times,* 7/2/62.
351. Summers, *Goddess,* p. 330.
352. *New York Times,* 7/5/62, p. 1. Interestingly, Freeman, just as with the Estes scandal, ". . . turned the case over to the Federal Bureau of Investigation."
353. Ibid., 7/6/62.
354. *Washington Post,* 7/7/62.
355. *New York Times,* 7/7/62.
356. Ibid., 7/9/62.
357. *Congressional Record—Senate,* 7/10/62, p. 13047.
358. Summers, *Conspiracy,* p. 560.
359. *New York Times,* 7/11/62.
360. Ibid., 7/12/62.
361. *The Manchurian Candidate,* MGM/UA Home Video, 1988. See Sinatra's, director's concluding remarks.
362. *New York Times,* 7/14/62.
363. Summers, *Goddess,* p. 459.
364. *New York Times,* 7/14/62.
365. Summers, *Goddess,* p. 330.
366. Summers, *Conspiracy,* p. 218.
367. Blakey, *Plot to Kill the President,* p. 242.
368. *U.S. v. Beckley.*
369. Summers, *Goddess.* p. 330.
370. *New York Times,* 7/21/62.
371. Ibid.
372. Ibid., 7/23/62.
373. Ibid., p. 12.
374. Summers, *Goddess,* p. 330.
375. *New York Times,* 7/25/62.
376. Summers, *Goddess,* p. 339.
377. *U.S. v. Beckley.*
378. *Washington Post,* 7/26/62.
379. *New York Times,* 7/28/62.

380. Ibid.
381. Ibid., 7/31/62.
382. Summers, *Goddess,* p. 330.
383. *New York Times,* 8/1/62.
384. Theoharis, *The Boss,* p. 381.
385. Peter Maas, *The Valachi Papers* (New York: G.P. Putnam's Son's, 1968), pp. 36–37.
386. Theoharis, *The Boss,* p. 374.
387. *New York Times,* 8/2/62.
388. Blakey, *Plot to Kill the President,* p. 381.
389. Ibid.
390. *Los Angeles Times,* 8/4/62.
391. Summers, *Goddess,* p. 346.
392. Ibid., p. 345; Robert F. Slatzer, *The Curious Death of Marilyn Monroe* (New York: Pinnacle Books, 1974), p. 265.
393. Summers, *Goddess,* pp. 346, 353.
394. *New York Times,* 8/6/62.
395. *Los Angeles Times,* 8/4/62, p. 1.
396. Summers, *Goddess,* p. 346.
397. Ibid., p. 454.
398. Ibid., p. 346.
399. *New York Times,* 8/6/62. This same day, JFK, from the family compound in Hyannis Port, Mass. ". . . asked the Senate . . . to strengthen its pending new drug law to ensure 'safer and better' drugs for the American consumer. . . . to move faster to remove from the prescription market any new drug suspected of being a hazard to public health."
400. Summers, *Goddess.* p. 360.
401. Ibid., p. 448.
402. *Congressional Record—House,* 8/7/62, p. 15802; *New York Times,* 8/7/62.
403. Summers, *Goddess,* p. 502.
404. *New York Times,* 8/8/62, p. 13.
405. *New York Times,* 8/8/62.
406. *U.S. v. Beckley.*
407. Blakey, *Plot to Kill the President,* p. 350.
408. Summers, *Conspiracy,* pp. 133, 298, 572.
409. *Los Angeles Times,* 8/11/62, p. 3.
410. Newman, *Assass. of JFK,* p. 240.
411. *Congressional Record—Senate,* 8/8/62, p. 15996.
412. *Los Angeles Times,* 8/16/62, p. 1.
413. *New York Times,* 8/17/62.
414. *Los Angeles Times,* 8/16/62, p. 32.
415. Newman, *Assass. of JFK,* pp. 241–242.
416. *New York Times,* 8/17/62.

417. *Los Angeles Times,* 8/18/62, p. 12.
418. Ibid., 8/19/62.
419. Ibid.
420. Ibid.
421. Ibid., 8/22/62.
422. *New York Times,* 8/23/62, p. 1.
423. *New York Times,* 8/23/62.
424. Ibid., 8/24/62.
425. Ibid., 8/25/62.
426. Ibid., 8/28/62.
427. Newman, *Assass. of JFK,* p. 248.
428. *New York Times,* 9/1/62.
429. Davis, *Mafia Kingfish,* pp. 337–338.
430. *HSCA, Final Report,* p. 173; Reid, *Grim Reapers,* pp. 158–159.
431. Moldea, *Hoffa Wars,* p. 87.
432. 42 *USC* 1986 (United States Code, 1958 ed.).
433. Seth Kantor, *Who Was Jack Ruby?* (New York: Everest House, 1978), p. 136.
434. Newman, *Assass. of JFK,* p. 249. Note, FBI mail-intercept programs of early 1960s were commonplace.
435. Haley, *A Texan Looks at Lyndon,* p. 125.
436. *New York Times,* 9/7/62.
437. Ibid.
438. Ibid., 9/9/62.
439. Ibid.
440. Ibid., 9/10/62.
441. Ibid., 9/11/62.
442. *LBJ Library,* famous names box Johnson to Hoover.

Treason (9/62—11/22/63)

1. *Washington Post,* 5/16/76, p. C1; *House Select Committee on Assassinations, John F. Kennedy,* vol. 5, pp. 310, 317, 319. Hereafter *HSCA.*
2. *HSCA,* vol. 5, pp. 310–311, 321–322; *Washington Post,* 5/16/76, Cl.
3. *Washington Post,* 2/13/62. Grapp, if still alive, may hold unique knowledge about the Marcello contract. As verified by a 10/31/66 AP wirephoto description accompanying a photo of Grapp, he had by then become SAC for Los Angeles. As revealed by the *HSCA* (vol. 9, pp. 77–85), Becker's interaction with Marcello caused intense interest in both the fall of 1962, and again in 5/67. That May, Reid had shown the Los Angeles field office the manuscript for his book, *The Grim Reapers,* which contained the 9/62 Marcello death threat. Grapp, presumably still SAC, almost im-

mediately notified Hoover, while simultaneously launching a character assault on Becker. Memos were sent to Hoover on 5/17 and 6/5 containing derogatory information about Becker. Efforts were made to prevent Reid from publishing the Becker data. "FBI files clearly indicate a high-level awareness that the Bureau was involved in trying to 'discredit' . . . Edward Becker." Further research should be conducted to determine if Grapp was indeed the Los Angeles SAC during the 5/67—6/67 time period. Another, equally relevant, question would be whether he was SAC during 1968, when RFK was assassinated in that city.

4. Ed Reid, *The Grim Reapers: The Anatomy of Organized Crime in America* (Chicago: Henry Regnery, 1969), p. 158.
5. *HSCA,* vol. 9, pp. 77, 82–83.
6. *New York Times,* 9/12/62.
7. Ibid., 9/14/62, p. 3.
8. Ibid., 9/15/62, p. 11.
9. *New York Times,* 9/15/62.
10. Ibid., 9/18/62.
11. *HSCA,* vol. 9, p. 80.
12. *New York Times,* 9/19/62.
13. *HSCA,* vol. 9, p. 80.
14. *New York Times,* 9/22/62.
15. J. Evetts Haley, *A Texan Looks At Lyndon* (Canyon, Texas: Palo Duro Press, 1964), pp. 149, 151.
16. *New York Times,* 9/23/62.
17. Ibid., 9/25/62.
18. Dan E. Moldea, *The Hoffa Wars* (New York: Paddington Press, Ltd., 1978), p. 149; John H. Davis, *The Kennedys: Dynasty and Disaster 1848–1984* (New York: McGraw-Hill Book Company, 1984), p. 840.
19. Peter Maas, *The Valachi Papers* (New York: G.P. Putnam Sons, 1968), p. 37.
20. *HSCA,* vol. 9, p. 73.
21. *New York Times,* 10/2/62.
22. Ibid.
23. Ibid., 10/3/62.
24. Ibid.
25. Ibid., 10/8/62, p. 14.
26. Anthony Summers, *Conspiracy* (New York: McGraw Hill Book Company, 1980), pp. 229–230.
27. Robert Rowe, *The Bobby Baker Story* (New York: Parallax Publishing Co., 1967), p. 77.
28. G. Robert Blakey and Richard N. Billings, *The Plot to Kill the President* (New York: Times Books, 1981), pp. 350–351.
29. *Congressional Record-Senate,* 10/12/62, p. 23335. Hoover had

loathed Truman, in 1953 publicly denouncing him as a communist. See Power's *Secrecy and Power,* p. 370.
30. David E. Scheim, *Contract on America* (Silver Spring, Md: Argyle Press, 1983), p. 193; Ed Reid and Ovid Demaris, *The Green Felt Jungle* (New York: Pocket Books, Inc., 1963), p. 51; Reid, *Grim Reapers,* pp. 123, 218.
31. Summers, *Conspiracy,* p. 230.
32. *New York Times,* 10/11/62. Approximately three weeks prior to this, and just after Hoover had learned of the Marcello contract, the Director sent Kennedy an inscribed copy of his new book, *A Study of Communism.* Actually written by Sullivan and other FBI employees, it had to be promoted by field offices around the country because of its inability to stand on its own. See Sullivan, *The Bureau,* p. 268. In reviewing the book on 10/21/62, the *New York Times* pulled no punches, referring to

> . . . its weaknesses in organization, its too-frequent fuzziness of thought, and its inadequacies in taking full account of the many recent changes in the . . . Communist world. . . . The lack of intellectual precision creates confusion and difficulty at many points. . . . There is . . . disturbing internal evidence in this volume that suggests that Mr. Hoover is not entirely familiar with all these changes. . . . The worst part of the book is the discussion of the rest of the Communist bloc outside the Soviet Union. . . . Mr. Hoover owes it to his readers and himself to take energetic action to remedy these many needless faults. They prevent it from being an adequate introduction to the study of Communism, even at high-school level.

The book has virtually been forgotten, even die-hard Hoover supporters avoiding its mention. Kennedy, as if anticipating the review, on 9/26 responded sarcastically to Hoover in a thank-you note, "I know that this book is the outcome of many years of reflection and experience. I am sure that this book, as its predecessor, will find a wide and appreciative audience." Like the "Las Vegas gambler" comment, its timing was, unknowingly, very unfortunate. Such mockery from the President, a Pulitzer Prize winner, undoubtedly enraged Hoover, perhaps prompting the 10/31/62 presentation to Kennedy of an honorary, "gold-plated FBI special agent's badge." A hollow gesture.

33. *U.S. v. Gilbert Lee Beckley,* 5th Cir., Eastern District of Louisiana, 6/27/61, Crim. No. 28247.

34. *New York Times,* 10/11/62.
35. Gerald R. Ford with John R. Stiles, *Portrait of the Assassin* (New York: Simon & Shuster, 1965), p. 157; *New York Times,* 11/29/63.
36. Albert H. Newman, *The Assassination of John F. Kennedy* (hereafter *Assass. of JFK)* (New York: Clarkson N. Potter, Inc., 1970), p. 324. Newman's book provides an almost day-by-day chronicle of Oswald's activities for the last several years of his life, a not inconsiderable accomplishment on the former's part.
37. *The Official Warren Commission Report on the Assassination of President John F. Kennedy* (hereafter *Warren Report)* (Garden City, New York: Doubleday, 1964), p. 191; Newman, *Assass. of JFK,* p. 169.
38. *New York Times,* 12/1/63.
39. Ibid., 10/17/62.
40. Ibid., 10/18/62.
41. Ibid.
42. *HSCA,* vol. 9, pp. 79–80.
43. Ibid., p. 83.
44. Ibid., pp. 78–79.
45. *New York Times,* 10/20/62.
46. Arthur M. Schlesinger, Jr., *A Thousand Days* (Boston: Houghton Mifflin Company, 1965), p. 809.
47. *New York Times,* 10/23/62.
48. *HSCA,* vol. 5, p. 446.
49. Athan G. Theoharis and John Stuart Cox, *The Boss,* (Philadelphia: Temple University Press, 1988), p. 386; Rowe, *Bobby Baker Story,* p. 73.
50. *HSCA,* vol. 9, p. 73.
51. *FBI Law Enforcement Bulletin,* January, 1963. Unfortunately, Kennedy's aide O'Donnell, who held a very low opinion of Hoover from the outset of the administration, declined the Director's personal invitation to attend the ceremony. See *JFK Library,* White House Central Files, O'Donnell to Hoover, 10/16/62; for O'Donnell opinion of Hoover, see Demaris, *The Director,* p. 193. The timing of this snub cannot be ignored.
52. *HSCA,* vol. 9, p. 81.
53. *HSCA,* vol. 10, p. 111.
54. *New York Times,* 11/4/62.
55. Blakey, *Plot to Kill the President,* p. 351.
56. *New York Times,* 11/8/62.
57. Ibid., 11/7/62.
58. Newman, *Assass. of JFK,* p. 276.
59. *New York Times,* 11/8/62.
60. Ibid., 11/10/62.
61. *HSCA,* vol. 9, p. 85.

62. Rowe, *Bobby Baker Story*, p. 77.
63. *New York Times,* 11/14/62.
64. Ibid., 11/15/62.
65. Ibid.
66. Arthur M. Schlesinger, *Robert Kennedy and His Times* (Boston: Houghton Mifflin Company, 1978), p. 548.
67. *Lyndon B. Johnson Presidential Library,* Austin, Texas, famous names box Johnson to Hoover.
68. Richard Gid Powers, *Secrecy and Power: The Life of J. Edgar Hoover* (New York: The Free Press, 1987), pp. 363, 571. On 11/29 Hoover responded to a get-well note from JFK, "I am happy to say that I am feeling fine and expect to be back at my desk before too long." See *JFK Library,* JFK Office Files, Hoover to Kennedy, 11/29/62. It is not known whether Hoover was still in the hospital at that point, but a two-week absence from work implies *some* form of serious medical problem. It remains a matter unresolved to this day. As is evident from photos, Hoover aged markedly during the two years and ten months of the Kennedy administration. He ultimately died of a degenerative heart condition, exacerbated by hypertension.
69. *HSCA,* vol. 9, p. 80.
70. *New York Times,* 11/23/62.
71. *HSCA,* vol. 9, p. 80.
72. Ibid.
73. Ibid., p. 81.
74. Ibid., p. 80.
75. *New York Times,* 11/30/62.
76. *HSCA,* vol. 9, p. 81.
77. Davis, *The Kennedys,* p. 841.
78. Newman, *Assass. of JFK,* p. 295.
79. *New York Times,* 12/5/62, p. 53.
80. Ibid., 12/7/62.
81. *Tulsa Daily World,* 12/11/62.
82. *Hearings: Subcommittee of the Committee on Appropriations-House of Representatives, Eighty-Eighth Congress, Second Session, Department of Justice,* February 1, 1963. (FBI Appropriations Hearings).
83. *Tulsa Daily World,* 12/12/62.
84. See Hoover's January 1962 *Appropriations* testimony on wire services. Also see 12/6/63 Abadie statements, this chronicle.
85. *Tulsa Daily World,* 12/13/62.
86. Ibid., 12/14/62.
87. Ibid.
88. *Congressional Record—Senate,* 1/31/63, p. 1430.
89. *U.S. v. Beckley.*

90. John H. Davis, *Mafia Kingfish: Carlos Marcello and the Assassination of John F. Kennedy* (New York: McGraw-Hill Book Company, 1989), pp. 310, 340–341. Note, there have been serious allegations raised, and examined in depth by the *HSCA,* that di Piazza may somehow have been involved in the Martin Luther King assassination.
91. *Tulsa Daily World,* 12/18/62.
92. Ibid., 12/19/62.
93. *HSCA,* vol. 10, p. 116.
94. *Tulsa Daily World,* 12/20/62.
95. Schlesinger, *RFK and His Times,* p. 411.
96. *Tulsa Daily World,* 12/23/62.
97. Ibid., 12/25/62.
98. Ibid., 12/27/62.
99. Theoharis, *The Boss,* p. 368.
100. Newman, *Assass. of JFK,* p. 297.
101. Davis, *Dynasty and Disaster,* p. 377.
102. Blakey, *Plot to Kill the President,* pp. 235–236; *HSCA,* vol. 9, p. 59.
103. *Washington Post,* 5/16/76.
104. Rowe, *Bobby Baker Story,* p. 119.
105. Blakey, *Plot to Kill the President,* pp. 251–252. Anyone doubting the connections and power of Edward Levinson, and thus the ominous nature of his association with Bobby Baker, need only consider the following excerpt from *HSCA,* vol. 9, p. 25, discussing an early 1963 Bureau Las Vegas ELSUR recording: "Ed Levinson . . . discussed . . . a plan to issue dividends to owners of record [of Las Vegas casinos] instead of only 'skimming.' Thus, hidden owners could get profits, and this would reduce the amount that had to be 'stolen' (skimmed) each month. The skim could then be reduced to $60,000 per month instead of $100,000. . . . The report also noted . . . Levinson was to send $100,000 to 'Miami.' . . . On January 21, 1963, $123,500 was skimmed from Las Vegas casino operations 'the same amount of money as last month.' . . . Lansky was to get the money. His share would be $71,000; $42,500 was to go to Gerardo Catena. . . ."
106. Rowe, *Bobby Baker Story,* p. 131.
107. Summers, *Conspiracy,* p. 474.
108. *Tulsa Daily World,* 1/6/63.
109. Scheim, *Contract on America,* pp. 86–87.
110. Ibid., p. 88.
111. *Washington Post,* 1/13/63.
112. *HSCA,* vol. 5, p. 438.
113. Summers, *Conspiracy,* p. 474.
114. *Washington Post,* 1/16/63.

115. *HSCA*, vol. 5, p. 447.
116. *Washington Post*, 1/19/63.
117. Ibid., 1/20/63.
118. Ibid.
119. Ibid., 1/20/63.
120. *U.S. v. Beckley.*
121. *HSCA*, vol. 10, p. 134.
122. *Warren Report*, p. 174.
123. *Washington Post*, 1/27/63.
124. *FBI Appropriations Hearings*, 2/1/63.
125. Ford, *Portrait of the Assassin*, p. 186.
126. *HSCA*, vol. 5, p. 438.
127. *Congressional Record—Senate*, 1/31/63, p. 1430.
128. Summers, *Conspiracy*, p. 234.
129. *HSCA*, vol. 9, p. 74.
130. Summers, *Conspiracy*, p. 472. See also, Chronicle 6/24/63.
131. *New York Times*, 10/23/63.
132. *FBI Appropriations Hearings*, 2/1/63.
133. Ibid.
134. Ibid.
135. *Congressional Record—Senate*, 2/19/63, p. 2522.
136. *Washington Post*, 2/5/63.
137. Ibid., 2/7/63.
138. Ibid., 2/9/63.
139. Ibid., 2/11/63.
140. Ibid., 2/12/63.
141. Blakey, *Plot to Kill the President*, p. 353.
142. *Washington Post*, 2/14/63, p. 1.
143. Ibid., 2/13/63.
144. *HSCA*, vol. 9, p. 73.
145. *Washington Post*, 2/16/63.
146. Ibid.
147. Ford, *Portrait of the Assassin*, p. 177.
148. *Congressional Record*, 3/21/63, Appendix, p. A1613.
149. *Washington Post*, 2/20/63, p. B11.
150. Ibid., 2/22/63, p. B6.
151. Schlesinger, *RFK and His Times*, p. 270.
152. Blakey, *Plot to Kill the President*, p. 353; Ford, *Portrait of the Assassin*, pp. 179–182.
153. Reid, *Grim Reapers*, p. 140.
154. *Hearings before the Committee on Rules and Administration, United States Senate, Eighty-Eighth Congress, First and Second Sessions*, (hereafter, Bobby Baker hearings) Part 17, p. 1592.
155. *New York Times*, 3/1/63.
156. Ibid.

157. Powers, *Secrecy and Power,* p. 366; Schlesinger, *RFK and His Times,* p. 280.
158. Davis, *The Kennedys,* p. 596.
159. Davis, *Mafia Kingfish,* p. 119; *HSCA,* vol. 10, pp. 106–107.
160. Davis, *The Kennedys,* pp. 508, 596.
161. Summers, *Conspiracy,* p. 474.
162. Newman, *Assass. of JFK,* p. 316.
163. Ibid., p. 330.
164. Ibid., p. 317.
165. Ibid., p. 316.
166. Ibid.
167. *Tulsa Daily World,* 3/6/63.
168. Ibid.
169. Ford, *Portrait of the Assassin,* pp. 177–178.
170. *Tulsa Daily World,* 3/9/63.
171. Ibid., 3/11/63.
172. Newman, *Assass. of JFK,* p. 318.
173. Myrna Blyth & Jane Farrell, "Marina Oswald: Twenty-Five Years Later," *Ladies' Home Journal,* November 1988, p. 188.
174. *New York Times,* 3/12/63, p. 4.
175. *Washington Post,* 3/13/63.
176. Newman, *Assass. of JFK,* p. 319.
177. Summers, *Conspiracy,* p. 235; Henry Hurt, *Reasonable Doubt* (New York: Henry Holt and Company, 1985), p. 238.
178. See *Warren Commission Report, Hearings,* and *Exhibits* generally, for *lack* of credible evidence in this regard.
179. Sylvia Meagher, *Accessories after the Fact* (New York: Vintage Books, 1976), pp. 102–103.
180. *Warren Report,* p. 174.
181. Ibid., pp. 172–174.
182. Newman, *Assass. of JFK,* p. 329.
183. *Tulsa Daily World,* 3/14/63.
184. Ibid., 3/15/63.
185. Ibid., 3/16/63.
186. Ibid.
187. Ibid.
188. Ibid.
189. Ibid.
190. Ibid.
191. Ibid.
192. Ibid., 3/17/63.
193. Ibid.
194. Ibid.
195. Ibid.
196. Ibid.

197. Newman, *Assass. of JFK,* pp. 321–322.
198. *Tulsa Daily World,* 3/18/63.
199. Ibid., 3/20/63.
200. *New York Times,* 3/21/63.
201. *Tulsa Daily World,* 3/21/63.
202. *Warren Report,* p. 119; Ford, *Portrait of the Assassin,* p. 187.
203. *Congressional Record,* 3/21/63, Appendix, p. A1613.
204. *Tulsa Daily World,* 3/23/63.
205. Ibid., 3/24/63.
206. Ibid.
207. Ibid., 3/25/63.
208. Newman, *Assass. of JFK,* p. 318.
209. *Tulsa Daily World,* 3/26/63.
210. Newman, *Assass. of JFK,* p. 326.
211. *New York Times,* 3/27/63.
212. *Tulsa Daily World,* 3/28/63.
213. Ibid.
214. Newman, *Assass. of JFK,* p. 326.
215. *New York Times,* 3/29/63.
216. *Tulsa Daily World,* 3/28/63.
217. Ibid., 3/29/63.
218. Ibid., 3/30/63.
219. Ibid.
220. Summers, *Conspiracy,* p. 407.
221. Blakey, *Plot to Kill the President,* p. 354; Newman, *Assass. of JFK,* p. 329.
222. *Tulsa Daily World,* 3/31/63.
223. Summers, *Conspiracy,* p. 263.
224. Rowe, *Bobby Baker Story,* pp. 45, 72.
225. Ibid., p. 72.
226. Rowe, *Bobby Baker Story,* p. 141; Reid, *Grim Reapers,* p. 13.
227. Theoharis, *The Boss,* pp. 379–380.
228. Blakey, *Plot to Kill the President,* p. 355.
229. Ibid., p. 354.
230. *New York Times,* 4/3/63.
231. Blakey, *Plot to Kill the President,* p. 238.
232. Ibid., p. 239; *New York Times,* 4/4/63.
233. Ford, *Portrait of the Assassin,* p. 188.
234. *Warren Report,* p. 413.
235. Ford, *Portrait of the Assassin,* p. 185.
236. Newman, *Assass. of JFK,* p. 327.
237. *New York Times,* 12/8/63.
238. Newman, *Assass. of JFK,* p. 336.
239. Ibid.
240. *New York Times,* 4/9/63.

241. Newman, *Assass. of JFK,* p. 336.
242. Ibid., p. 524; Summers, *Conspiracy,* p. 247.
243. Summers, *Conspiracy,* p. 244.
244. *New York Times,* 4/10/63.
245. Newman, *Assass. of JFK,* pp. 337–338; Summers, *Conspiracy,* p. 243.
246. *New York Times,* 4/11/63.
247. Ibid., 4/3/63, 4/26/63, 12/7/63.
248. Ibid., 4/5/62, 4/6/62, 4/8/62.
249. Summers, *Conspiracy,* pp. 244–245. It is possible that Oswald did own the camera and take the photos of Walker's house. As explained by Newman, *Assass. of JFK,* pp. 292–293, Oswald had sent samples of photos to the SWP (Socialist Workers Party) in 12/62, in an apparent attempt to gain credibility as a photographer. Considering Oswald's interest in politics, in early 1963 Walker would have been a natural subject. Photos of that nature could well have been of interest to the SWP. Doubtless, Oswald would have been only one of many who photographed either Walker or his house during this time period. Walker was given to placing numerous flags, in cryptic positions, in his front yard. The near immediate 11/22/63 association of Oswald to the Walker incident by Dallas police officers who searched the Paine residence would thus be explained, as would the fact that his rifle could never be linked to the 4/10/63 shooting attempt. However, Oswald would have had to have taken the photos without being observed, as nothing in the record suggests he was ever seen at or near the residence. To complicate matters, most of his daytime hours were taken up with work at Jaggars-Chiles.
250. *Warren Report,* pp. 183–187.
251. *New York Times,* 4/11/63.
252. *HSCA,* vol. 9, p. 81.
253. Summers, *Conspiracy,* p. 238.
254. *New York Times,* 4/16/63.
255. Hurt, *Reasonable Doubt,* pp. 406–407.
256. *U.S. Master Tax Guide,* 1963–64, (New York: Commerce Clearing House, Inc.), see "Nature of Gross Income," Chapter VI, p. 203.
257. *CCH-Standard Federal Tax Reports,* 1961, (New York: Commerce Clearing House, Inc.), p. 17079.
258. *Internal Revenue Bulletin,* Cum. Bull. 1959.1, p. 583; *Federal Tax Coordinator 2d,* 1990, D-4135, see "Charitable, Religious, Etc., Organizations," p. 19241.
259. *Internal Revenue Code,* Section 6103.
260. Ibid., subsection (i)(6).
261. *New York Times,* 4/16/63.

262. Newman, *Assass. of JFK,* p. 348.
263. *HSCA,* vol. 9, p. 74.
264. Newman, *Assass. of JFK,* p. 349.
265. *New York Times,* 4/21/63.
266. Summers, *Conspiracy,* pp. 298, 572.
267. Blakey, *Plot to Kill the President,* p. 357.
268. Ibid.
269. Newman, *Assass. of JFK,* p. 350.
270. Blakey, *Plot to Kill the President,* p. 295.
271. *Warren Commission Hearings,* vol. 14, p. 632; *Contract on America,* pp. 247–248.
272. *Warren Commission Hearings,* vol. 14, p. 341.
273. *Congressional Record,* Appendix, 4/30/63, p. A2612.
274. Blakey, *Plot to Kill the President,* pp. 161, 357.
275. *U.S. v. Beckley.*
276. *New York Times,* 4/26/63.
277. Newman, *Assass. of JFK,* p. 352.
278. *New York Times,* 4/28/63.
279. Newman, *Assass. of JFK,* p. 353.
280. *New York Times,* 5/1/63.
281. Blakey, *Plot to Kill the President,* pp. 238–239.
282. Reid, *Green Felt Jungle,* p. 149.
283. Blakey, *Plot to Kill the President,* p. 376.
284. Scheim, *Contract on America,* pp. 201, 213–215; Seth Kantor, *Who Was Jack Ruby?* (New York: Everest House, 1978), p. 139.
285. Victor S. Navasky, *Kennedy Justice,* (New York: Atheneum, 1971), pp. 79–80.
286. Davis, *Mafia Kingfish,* p. 266.
287. Blakey, *Plot to Kill the President,* pp. 238–239.
288. *New York Times,* 11/9/63.
289. Summers, *Conspiracy,* p. 574, n. 316.
290. Ibid., p. 319.
291. Ibid., p. 329.
292. Ibid., p. 320.
293. Ibid., p. 338.
294. Ibid., p. 496.
295. Ibid., p. 321.
296. *LBJ Library,* famous names box Johnson to Hoover.
297. *New York Times,* 5/7/63.
298. Ibid., 5/8/63.
299. Scheim, *Contract on America,* p. 212.
300. Blakey, *Plot to Kill the President,* pp. 201–202. In fact, just ten days before the assassination, "The U.S. Supreme Court declined . . . to examine an appeal by . . . Hoffa and cleared the way for his trial in [Nashville], Tennessee on jury-tampering charges." See

New York Times, 11/13/63. The Mafia associate was also indicted on 6/4/63 ". . . on charges of having fraudulently obtained $20,000,000 in loans from a Teamster union pension fund. . . . The diverted funds included at least $100,000 that . . . Hoffa used . . . in a Florida housing development." See *New York Times,* 6/5/63.

301. Newman, *Assass. of JFK,* p. 353.
302. *New York Times,* 11/30/63.
303. Newman, *Assass. of JFK,* p. 355.
304. Scheim, *Contract on America,* pp. 93, 219; Kantor, *Who Was Jack Ruby?,* p. 24.
305. Reid, *Green Felt Jungle,* p. 2.
306. Ibid., p. 15.
307. *U.S. v. Beckley.*
308. Davis, *Mafia Kingfish,* pp. 299–300.
309. *259 F. Supp. 567* (i.e. Federal Supplement, a legal reporter series).
310. *New York Times,* 12/4/63.
311. Newman, *Assass. of JFK,* p. 355.
312. *Congressional Record—House,* 5/14/63, p. 8538.
313. Scheim, *Contract on America,* p. 219.
314. Summers, *Conspiracy,* p. 310.
315. *FBI Law Enforcement Bulletin,* July, 1963, p. 20.
316. Newman, *Assass. of JFK,* p. 356.
317. Scheim, *Contract on America,* p. 214.
318. *New York Times,* 5/19/63.
319. Ibid.
320. Ibid., 5/20/63.
321. AP wirephoto description 5/20/63, photo of Hoover.
322. Blakey, *Plot to Kill the President,* p. 239.
323. *New York Times,* 11/28/63; Summers, *Conspiracy,* pp. 300, 573 nt. 300.
324. See *HSCA,* JFK Exhibit F—631.
325. *New York Times,* 5/24/63.
326. *Hoover vs. The Kennedys: The Second Civil War,* Sunrise Films, Ltd. video, 1987; Powers, *Secrecy and Power,* p. 363.
327. Ford, *Portrait of the Assassin,* p. 207.
328. Newman, *Assass. of JFK,* p. 357.
329. *HSCA,* vol. 9, p. 74.
330. *New York Times,* 5/28/63.
331. Ibid., 5/30/63.
332. Newman, *Assass. of JFK,* pp. 358–359.
333. *New York Times,* 5/31/63.
334. Summers, *Conspiracy,* p. 469.
335. Reid, *Grim Reapers,* p. 131.

336. Hank Messick, *John Edgar Hoover* (New York: David McKay Company, 1972), p. 210.
337. Ibid.
338. Robert J. Nash, *Citizen Hoover* (Chicago: Nelson-Hall, 1972), p. 109; Messick, *John Edgar Hoover*, p. 211.
339. Newman, *Assass. of JFK*, p. 358.
340. Summers, *Conspiracy*, pp. 324–326.
341. Ibid., p. 325.
342. Ibid., p. 312.
343. Ford, *Portrait of the Assassin*, p. 209.
344. *New York Times*, 11/29/63.
345. Newman, *Assass. of JFK*, p. 360.
346. Ibid., p. 361.
347. *New York Times*, 6/5/63.
348. Scheim, *Contract on America*, p. 220; Kantor, *Who Was Jack Ruby?*, p. 19.
349. Scheim, *Contract on America*, p. 220.
350. Ibid.
351. Schlesinger, *RFK and His Times*, pp. 270–271.
352. *New York Times*, 6/6/63.
353. Newman, *Assass. of JFK*, p. 361.
354. Kantor, *Who Was Jack Ruby?*, p. 19.
355. Ford, *Portrait of the Assassin*, p. 209.
356. Blakey, *Plot to Kill the President*, p. 239.
357. Kantor, *Who Was Jack Ruby?*, p. 20.
358. *New York Times*, 6/7/63. Just days before approval, an article *(New York Times*, 6/15/63) appeared that reveals the power of Hoover in the House, where the bill ultimately stalled. ". . . the House Appropriations . . . committee's cutting drive hit all the big agencies except the Federal Bureau of Investigation. . . . The Bureau's director J. Edgar Hoover, was singled out by the committee for personally backing up all his money requests with the aid of two assistants." Hoover also supplied "staff" to committee chairman Rooney to help him "interpret" FBI's annual requests.
359. Kantor, *Who Was Jack Ruby?*, p. 20.
360. *New York Times*, 6/10/63. Oswald borrowed the book from the library on 7/15/63. See Warren Commission Exhibit CE1117, vol. 22, p. 83. The fact that JFK, on 6/10/63, donated several hundred thousand dollars to charity, resulting from sale of the film rights, is intriguing. It is possible Oswald read this book because of Kennedy's philanthropic act. A *New York Times* article (11/28/63) does not mention the book, but states "Agents of the Federal Bureau of Investigation visited the library . . . and began . . . removing the cards from pockets in hundreds of books." Oddly,

another *New York Times* article the following day also details Oswald's reading, yet makes no mention of *Profiles in Courage.*

361. Newman, *Assass. of JFK,* p. 362.
362. *Congressional Record,* 6/13/63.
363. Scheim, *Contract on America,* p. 220.
364. *New York Times,* 11/29/63.
365. Summers, *Conspiracy,* p. 299.
366. Newman, *Assass. of JFK,* p. 364.
367. *Congressional Record,* 6/17/63.
368. Schlesinger, *RFK and His Times,* p. 350.
369. *FBI Law Enforcement Bulletin,* August, 1963, p. 6.
370. *New York Times,* 6/19/63, p. 34.
371. Scheim, *Contract on America,* p. 220.
372. *LBJ Library,* famous names box Johnson to Hoover.
373. Reid, *Grim Reapers,* p. 132.
374. Ibid., pp. 133, 135; Reid, *Green Felt Jungle,* p. 217.
375. Reid, *Green Felt Jungle,* pp. 112–113, 117, 123.
376. Scheim, *Contract on America,* p. 220.
377. *New York Times,* 6/22/63.
378. Schlesinger, *RFK and His Times,* p. 372.
379. *New York Times,* 6/24/63.
380. Scheim, *Contract on America,* p. 213.
381. Newman, *Assass. of JFK,* p. 365.
382. *New York Times,* 6/25/63.
383. Newman, *Assass. of JFK,* p. 365.
384. *New York Times,* 6/26/63.
385. Ibid., 6/29/63.
386. Ibid., 7/1/63.
387. Ibid.
388. *HSCA,* vol. 9, p. 59. Hoover, in the same directive, stated that compliance was required only ". . . by December 15, 1963."
389. *New York Times,* 7/7/63.
390. Reid, *Grim Reapers,* p. 133.
391. Summers, *Conspiracy,* p. 474.
392. Newman, *Assass. of JFK,* pp. 365–367.
393. *New York Times,* 7/2/63.
394. Ibid. Hoover's philosophical alliance with this committee was near absolute. An internal Justice Department memo, dated 7/12/63, from a Mr. Yeagley to Hoover directed the latter to stop submitting "prospective summary reports" attacking a group (i.e., the NCAHUAC) then seeking the abolishment of the HUAC. Hoover complied, but intensified covert efforts against members. See *Hoover and the UnAmericans,* p. 261.
395. *New York Times,* 7/3/63.
396. Ibid., 7/4/63.

397. Ibid.
398. *Congressional Record,* Appendix, 7/24/63, p. A4660.
399. *New York Times,* 7/4/63.
400. Scheim, *Contract on America,* p. 220.
401. Newman, *Assass. of JFK,* p. 369.
402. *New York Times,* 7/9/63.
403. Ford, *Portrait of the Assassin,* pp. 210–211.
404. *New York Times,* 11/28/63; 11/29/63.
405. Harry & Bonaro Overstreet, *The FBI in Our Open Society* (New York: W.W. Norton & Company, 1969), p. 207.
406. *HSCA,* vol. 10, pp. 111, 136.
407. *HSCA,* vol. 5, p. 441. Interestingly, ELSUR recordings of Traficante were released without specific dates or place of recording. Why in this fashion, remains unknown. Typical captions merely cite the year recorded. On 10/16/63, *New York Times* ran an article focusing on Traficante. "Chief Neil G. Brown of Tampa said that Santo Traficante . . . controlled illegal gambling 'throughout the state of Florida.' . . . Brown described Traficante as a business associate of such notorious criminals as Meyer Lansky . . . the scope of the . . . gambling operations was disclosed a few months ago when a raid on one of his places in Sanford, Fla., showed it had a gross revenue of $250,000 a week."
408. *New York Times,* 7/18/63.
409. David J. Garrow, *The FBI and Martin Luther King, Jr.* (New York: W.W. Norton & Company, 1981), p. 65.
410. *New York Times,* 7/19/63.
411. Newman, *Assass. of JFK,* p. 371.
412. Newman, *Assass. of JFK,* pp. 373–374.
413. Schlesinger, *RFK and His Times,* p. 373.
414. Scheim, *Contract on America,* p. 220.
415. Schlesinger, *RFK and His Times,* p. 619.
416. Newman, *Assass. of JFK,* p. 374.
417. Messick, *John Edgar Hoover,* pp. 215–216.
418. Newman, *Assass. of JFK,* p. 375.
419. Messick, *John Edgar Hoover,* pp. 219–220.
420. Newman, *Assass. of JFK,* p. 376.
421. *Los Angeles Times,* 8/1/63.
422. *FBI Law Enforcement Bulletin,* August 1963.
423. Newman, *Assass. of JFK,* pp. 376–377.
424. *Los Angeles Times,* 8/2/63, p. 18, part 1.
425. Messick, *John Edgar Hoover,* p. 216.
426. *Los Angeles Times,* 8/4/63. McClellan, before whom Valachi testified in the fall, had stated as early as 4/24/63 that the threat posed by the Mafia ". . . transcends and exceeds any immediate danger of infiltration or subversion by the Communist interna-

tional conspiracy." See *New York Times,* 4/25/63. Note McClellan's choice of words. By taking a position less extreme than RFK he carefully avoided antagonizing Hoover. Still, like the Kennedys, he fully realized the gravity of the Mafia's threat to the nation.

427. Blakey, *Plot to Kill the President,* p. 200; *Facts on File—World News Digest,* 9/26/63–10/2/63, p. 341.

428. Scheim, *Contract on America,* pp. 221–222.

429. Newman, *Assass. of JFK,* p. 378.

430. *HSCA,* vol. 10, p. 136.

431. Newman, *Assass. of JFK,* p. 378.

432. *LBJ Library,* famous names file Johnson to Hoover.

433. Scheim, *Contract on America,* pp. 222–223.

434. Summers, *Conspiracy,* p. 599.

435. *New York Times,* 3/1/63; Blakey, *Plot to Kill the President,* p. 288; Scheim, *Contract on America,* p. 96; See HSCA, JFK Exhibit F-627 for Giancana statement on 2/28/63. In part, "That will teach that little fucker Kennedy, who runs Chicago." While HSCA suggested Giancana's remark related to the results of a local election, I believe he was talking about Lewis's murder by his, Giancana's, henchmen. The fact that his comment was made on the same day of Lewis's murder would seem too great a coincidence not to be connected.

436. Newman, *Assass. of JFK,* p. 380.

437. *Los Angeles Times,* 8/7/63.

438. Summers, *Conspiracy,* p. 311.

439. Newman, *Assass. of JFK,* p. 380.

440. Ibid., pp. 380–381.

441. Summers, *Conspiracy,* p. 311.

442. Ibid., p. 324.

443. Ibid., p. 322.

444. *New York Times,* 8/10/63. As Traficante controlled gambling in the state of Florida, an event that significant may have been directly organized by his people. Individuals who attended the game would thus have good reason to remain silent about details. Some of those who attended were Thomas Duchese, ". . . a racketeer . . . who the Justice Department recently concluded was a member of an oligarchy that controls [the Mafia]" and Al Harris, who ". . . had twice been convicted of gambling offenses in Miami and had also operated in New York and Las Vegas." Again, little is known about others who attended or what matters they dealt with.

445. Summers, *Conspiracy,* p. 309.

446. Newman, *Assass. of JFK,* p. 382; Hurt, *Reasonable Doubt,* p. 294.

447. Summers, *Conspiracy,* p. 309.

448. Scheim, *Contract on America,* p. 53.
449. Summers, *Conspiracy,* p. 301.
450. Ibid., p. 322.
451. *New York Times,* 8/11/63.
452. Newman, *Assass. of JFK,* p. 385.
453. Ibid.
454. *Los Angeles Times,* 8/12/63.
455. Newman, *Assass. of JFK,* pp. 386, 387.
456. Davis, *The Kennedys,* p. 509.
457. Ibid.
458. Messick, *John Edgar Hoover,* pp. 219–220.
459. Reid, *Grim Reapers,* p. 133.
460. Newman, *Assass. of JFK,* p. 387.
461. Summers, *Conspiracy,* p. 301.
462. Newman, *Assass. of JFK,* p. 388.
463. Garrow, *FBI and Martin Luther King, Jr.,* p. 67.
464. Messick, *John Edgar Hoover,* pp. 218–219.
465. *HSCA,* vol. 5, p. 442. Like ELSUR recordings of Traficante in 1963, the exact date in 1963 of this recording was not released with the transcript. Presuming Palmisano is a Traficante function-ary, I place this recording within the same general time frame accorded the latter.
466. Rowe, *Bobby Baker Story,* pp. 70–71.
467. Ibid., p. 71; *New York Times,* 10/29/63.
468. Messick, *John Edgar Hoover,* p. 219.
469. *Los Angeles Times,* 8/14/63.
470. Summers, *Conspiracy,* p. 301.
471. Newman, *Assass. of JFK,* p. 389.
472. *Los Angeles Times,* 8/16/63.
473. Newman, *Assass. of JFK,* pp. 389–390, 392–393. Interestingly, a 3/23/62 article quoting a speech JFK had made the same day, had stated "[the] . . . great currents of history are carrying the world 'away from communism and toward national independence and freedom.' " In Oswald's interview with Stuckey he had re-ferred to the Cuban revolution as typifying ". . . a world trend."
474. Ibid, pp. 394–395.
475. *New York Times,* 11/29/63.
476. Summers, *Conspiracy,* p. 310.
477. Newman, *Assass. of JFK,* p. 395.
478. Scheim, *Contract on America,* p. 223.
479. Hank Messick, *Lansky* (New York: Berkley Publishing Corpora-tion, 1973 ed.), pp. 266–267.
480. Ibid., p. 268.
481. Messick, *John Edgar Hoover,* p. 137.
482. *Facts on File-World News Digest,* 9/26/63—10/2/63, p. 343.

483. Scheim, *Contract on America,* p. 223.
484. *Facts on File-World News Digest,* 9/26/63—10/2/63, p. 343.
485. Newman, *Assass. of JFK,* p. 398; Ford, *Portrait of the Assassin,* p. 241.
486. Summers, *Conspiracy,* pp. 357, 366.
487. Scheim, *Contract on America* p. 223.
488. *Hoover vs. the Kennedys;* Powers, *Secrecy and Power,* p. 390.
489. *FBI Appropriations Hearings,* 1/29/64, see first page.
490. Powers, *Secrecy and Power,* p. 363.
491. *Congressional Record—Senate,* 10/3/63, p. 18684.
492. Newman, *Assass. of JFK,* p. 400.
493. *Los Angeles Times,* 8/25/63.
494. *New York Times,* 8/29/63; Schlesinger, *RFK and His Times,* p. 366.
495. Newman, *Assass. of JFK,* pp. 403–404.
496. Ibid., p. 404.
497. Davis, *The Kennedys,* p. 508.
498. Scheim, *Contract on America,* p. 201.
499. Summers, *Conspiracy,* p. 388.
500. *HSCA,* vol. 10, p. 112.
501. Davis, *The Kennedys,* p. 843.
502. Summers, *Conspiracy,* pp. 334–336.
503. Ibid., p. 474.
504. Scheim, *Contract on America,* p. 223.
505. *FBI Law Enforcement Bulletin,* September, 1963.
506. Newman, *Assass. of JFK,* p. 404.
507. *Facts on File—World News Digest,* 9/26/63—10/2/63, p. 343.
508. *New York Times,* 9/6/63. This move by Morrison may well have been part of a plan by JFK to destroy Marcello. As Governor, Morrison would have sweeping powers. His attitude toward the Mafia is revealed by Blakey, pp. 181, 186. "After . . . Morrison was elected mayor of New Orleans in 1946, the Costello operation was moved to the neighboring parishes. . . ." Further, "Law enforcement officials from all over the nation met in Washington in February [1950] . . . to consider the growing, nationwide scope of [the Mafia], particularly professional gambling. De Lesseps S. Morrison, the mayor of New Orleans, spoke for the majority: 'We do not have the whole picture—but each of us present . . . have seen small segments of this national scene of organized . . . crime. These pieces fit together in a pattern of mounting evidence concerning several highly organized . . . syndicates whose wealth, power, scope of operations, and influence have recently grown to . . . alarming proportions.' " A development such as this would have only encouraged Marcello to move against Kennedy more quickly.

509. Summers, *Conspiracy,* pp. 388, 584.
510. *New York Times,* 9/8/63.
511. Summers, *Conspiracy,* pp. 388, 584.
512. Moldea, *The Hoffa Wars,* p. 159; Blakey, *Plot to Kill the President,* p. 396.
513. Scheim, *Contract on America,* p. 56.
514. *New York Times,* 9/10/63. In the same article it was also stated that any who attended the event would be given "a 'full briefing' on the abortive 1961 United States backed [Bay of Pigs] invasion."
515. Kantor, *Who Was Jack Ruby?,* p. 34.
516. Ibid.
517. *New York Times,* 9/17/63.
518. Summers, *Conspiracy,* p. 366.
519. Theoharis, *The Boss,* p. 361.
520. *New York Times,* 9/17/63.
521. Newman, *Assass. of JFK,* p. 410.
522. Summers, *Conspiracy,* p. 419.
523. *New York Times,* 9/19/63.
524. Schlesinger, *RFK and His Times,* p. 576.
525. Newman, *Assass. of JFK,* p. 414.
526. Ibid., p. 415.
527. *New York Times,* 9/20/63.
528. Ibid., 9/22/63.
529. Summers, *Conspiracy,* pp. 421–422.
530. Newman, *Assass. of JFK,* pp. 418, 431.
531. Summers, *Conspiracy,* pp. 581–582 n. 370.
532. Ibid., p. 584 n. 388.
533. Newman, *Assass. of JFK,* p. 418.
534. *New York Times,* 9/25/63.
535. Summers, *Conspiracy,* pp. 477–478.
536. Ibid., pp. 412–413.
537. Ibid., p. 411.
538. Ibid., p. 376.
539. Schlesinger, *RFK and His Times,* p. 273.
540. Newman, *Assass. of JFK,* p. 419.
541. Summers, *Conspiracy,* pp. 401, 406.
542. Ibid., p. 401.
543. Ibid., p. 87.
544. Ford, *Portrait of the Assassin,* p. 303.
545. Newman, *Assass. of JFK,* p. 422.
546. *New York Times,* 11/30/63.
547. Scheim, *Contract on America,* p. 223.
548. Newman, *Assass. of JFK,* p. 425.
549. Summers, *Conspiracy,* pp. 371–372. Oswald's seemingly cryptic statement, "I can only stay in Mexico three days" is explained by

the fact that the press had reported on 9/10/63 that an "international congress in Havana" was to be held "from September 29 to Oct. 3." Counting the 27th, Oswald had exactly three days to make it to Havana. See Chronicle 9/10.

550. *New York Times,* 11/27/63.
551. Ibid., 9/28/63, p. 1
552. Ibid., 9/30/63.
553. Ibid.
554. *HSCA,* vol. 10, p. 111.
555. Summers, *Conspiracy,* p. 400.
556. Theoharis, *The Boss,* p. 388.
557. Summers, *Conspiracy,* p. 474.
558. *New York Times,* 10/2/63.
559. Summers, *Conspiracy,* p. 376.
560. *HSCA,* vol. 5, p. 451.
561. Scheim, *Contract on America,* p. 216.
562. Newman, *Assass. of JFK,* p. 429.
563. *New York Times,* 10/3/63.
564. Newman, *Assass. of JFK,* p. 430.
565. Summers, *Conspiracy,* pp. 405–406.
566. Newman, *Assass. of JFK,* pp. 430, 431.
567. Ibid.
568. Scheim, *Contract on America,* p. 92.
569. Summers, *Conspiracy,* p. 402.
570. Newman, *Assass. of JFK,* pp. 432–433.
571. Ibid., p. 433.
572. Blakey, *Plot to Kill the President,* p. 360.
573. Ford, *Portrait of the Assassin,* p. 271.
574. *New York Times,* 10/5/63.
575. Blakey, *Plot to Kill the President,* p. 5; Davis, *The Kennedys,* p. 519.
576. *New York Times,* 10/5/63.
577. Davis, *The Kennedys,* p. 844.
578. Rowe, *Bobby Baker Story,* pp. 46, 54.
579. Newman, *Assass. of JFK,* pp. 437–438.
580. Summers, *Conspiracy,* p. 586 nt. 93.
581. *New York Times,* 10/10/63.
582. Ibid.
583. *HSCA,* vol. 5, p. 452.
584. Haley, *A Texan Looks at Lyndon,* p. 115.
585. Newman, *Assass. of JFK,* p. 441.
586. Scheim, *Contract on America,* pp. 223–225.
587. Newman, *Assass. of JFK,* p. 441.
588. Garrow, *FBI and Martin Luther King, Jr.,* p. 252.
589. Newman, *Assass. of JFK,* p. 441.

590. Schlesinger, *RFK and His Times,* p. 623.
591. *New York Times,* 10/13/63.
592. Newman, *Assass. of JFK,* p. 442.
593. Ibid., pp. 442–443.
594. Ibid.
595. Ibid., pp. 443–444.
596. Ibid., pp. 455–456.
597. Ibid., pp. 443–444.
598. *HSCA,* vol. 5, p. 447.
599. *New York Times,* 10/15/63.
600. Newman, *Assass. of JFK,* pp. 447, 449.
601. Ibid., p. 447.
602. Ibid., p. 449.
603. Ibid., pp. 449–450.
604. Ibid., p. 526.
605. *New York Times,* 10/17/63.
606. Newman, *Assass. of JFK,* p. 451.
607. Ibid., pp. 450–451.
608. Ibid., pp. 493–494.
609. Ibid., pp. 26, 487.
610. Ibid., p. 453.
611. Ibid., pp. 455–456.
612. Ibid., p. 464.
613. *New York Times,* 10/20/63.
614. Newman, *Assass. of JFK,* p. 458.
615. Ibid.
616. *New York Times,* 10/21/63.
617. *Warren Commission Hearings,* vol. 3, p. 214.
618. Newman, *Assass. of JFK,* p. 459.
619. Ford, *Portrait of the Assassin,* p. 327.
620. Newman, *Assass. of JFK,* p. 459.
621. Theoharis, *The Boss,* pp. 388–389.
622. Newman, *Assass. of JFK,* p. 461.
623. *New York Times,* 10/24/63.
624. Ibid.
625. Ibid., 10/25/63.
626. Ibid., 10/26/62.
627. Ibid.
628. Newman, *Assass. of JFK,* p. 464.
629. Ibid.
630. Ibid., p. 519.
631. Scheim, *Contract on America,* p. 225.
632. Newman, *Assass. of JFK,* p. 470.
633. *New York Times,* 10/28/63.
634. Ibid., 10/29/63.

635. Newman, *Assass. of JFK,* p. 454.
636. *New York Times,* 10/30/63.
637. Ibid.
638. Summers, *Conspiracy,* p. 424.
639. Newman, *Assass. of JFK,* p. 471.
640. Kantor, *Who Was Jack Ruby?,* p. 133.
641. *New York Times,* 10/30/63.
642. Scheim, *Contract on America,* pp. 94, 226.
643. *New York Times,* 10/31/63.
644. Ibid.
645. Ibid. The same article reveals both the fact that the gubernatorial primary was to be held December 12 of that year, and that "Mr. Morrison . . . is running for the third time as the 'good government' candidate." Further, one of Morrison's opponents, Kennon, ". . . is a bitter foe of the President. . . ." The other, Rep. Gillis Long, ". . . has the full support of Senator Russell B. Long, Huey's son. . . ." Recall that it was Senator Long who attempted to intervene on Marcello's behalf in early 1961. When Gillis Long entered the Governor's race on 6/24/63 he ". . . accused President Kennedy of encouraging 'mob demonstrations and violence in the streets." See *New York Times,* 6/25/63.
646. Ovid Demaris, *The Director: An Oral Biography of J. Edgar Hoover* (New York: Harper's Magazine Press, 1975), pp. 175–177.
647. Ibid., p. 192.
648. *New York Times,* 11/1/63.
649. Ibid.
650. Ibid.
651. Ibid.
652. Summers, *Conspiracy,* p. 403.
653. Newman, *Assass. of JFK,* p. 474.
654. *Warren Commission Hearings,* vol. 22, p. 110.
655. *U.S. Master Tax Guide,* 1963–64, p. 20, see Semi—monthly Withholding Table.
656. Ibid.
657. Summers, *Conspiracy,* p. 394.
658. *U.S. Master Tax Guide,* 1963–64, p. 20.
659. Ibid., p. 430.
660. *CCH-Standard Federal Tax Reports,* 1963, see "Adjustment of Errors in Withholding," p. 56, 177.
661. *U.S. Master Tax Guide,* 1963, see "Short—Period Return," p. 85.
662. Newman, *Assass. of JFK,* pp. 475–477.
663. Ibid., pp. 475–477, 488–489; Ford, *Portrait of the Assassin,* pp. 292–295.
664. *New York Times,* 11/2/63.
665. Rowe, *Bobby Baker Story,* p. 82.

666. Newman, *Assass. of JFK,* p. 480.
667. Summers, *Conspiracy,* pp. 403–404.
668. Newman, *Assass. of JFK,* p. 480.
669. Ibid.
670. Ibid., p. 481.
671. Ibid., pp. 480–481.
672. Blakey, *Plot to Kill the President,* p. 246.
673. Summers, *Conspiracy,* p. 404.
674. Ibid., p. 394.
675. Newman, *Assass. of JFK,* p. 480.
676. *HSCA,* vol. 10, p. 112.
677. Newman, *Assass. of JFK,* pp. 482–483.
678. *New York Times,* 11/6/63.
679. Scheim, *Contract on America,* pp. 243–244.
680. *FBI Law Enforcement Bulletin,* January 1964, p. 10.
681. *New York Times,* 11/7/63.
682. Newman, *Assass. of JFK,* p. 486.
683. Ibid.
684. *New York Times,* 11/7/63.
685. Scheim, *Contract on America,* p. 196.
686. *New York Times,* 11/7/63.
687. Summers, *Conspiracy,* pp. 395–396.
688. Newman, *Assass. of JFK,* p. 488.
689. *New York Times,* 11/8/63.
690. Scheim, *Contract on America,* p. 226.
691. *New York Times,* 11/9/63.
692. Summers, *Conspiracy,* p. 406.
693. Meagher, *Accessories after the Fact,* p. 365.
694. Summers, *Conspiracy,* pp. 427–428.
695. Newman, *Assass. of JFK,* pp. 489–490.
696. Ibid., p. 489.
697. Ibid., pp. 490–491.
698. Scheim, *Contract on America,* p. 226.
699. *New York Times,* 11/10/63.
700. Summers, *Conspiracy,* p. 429.
701. Ibid., p. 430.
702. Scheim, *Contract on America,* p. 51.
703. Newman, *Assass. of JFK,* pp. 491–493.
704. Summers, *Conspiracy,* p. 403.
705. Meaghers, *Accessories After the Fact,* pp. 351–352.
706. Summers, *Conspiracy,* pp. 404–405.
707. *New York Times,* 11/10/63.
708. Ibid.
709. Blakey, *Plot to Kill the President,* p. 307.
710. Newman, *Assass. of JFK,* pp. 493–494.

711. Ibid., p. 496.
712. *New York Times,* 11/12/63.
713. Newman, *Assass. of JFK,* p. 496–497.
714. Ibid.
715. Kantor, *Who Was Jack Ruby?,* p. 23.
716. *New York Times,* 11/13/63.
717. Newman, *Assass. of JFK,* p. 497.
718. Ibid.
719. Kantor, *Who Was Jack Ruby?,* pp. 22–23.
720. Scheim, *Contract on America,* p. 227.
721. Davis, *Mafia Kingfish,* p. 171.
722. *New York Times,* 11/13/63.
723. Ibid., 11/14/63.
724. Newman, *Assass. of JFK,* p. 498.
725. Ibid., p. 497.
726. *New York Times,* 11/15/63.
727. Ibid.
728. Ibid., 11/14/63.
729. Ibid., 11/15/63.
730. *Warren Report,* pp. 31–32.
731. Newman, *Assass. of JFK,* pp. 499–500.
732. *New York Times,* 11/16/63.
733. Ibid., 11/14/63.
734. Newman, *Assass. of JFK,* pp. 500–501.
735. Summers, *Conspiracy,* p. 474.
736. Kantor, *Who Was Jack Ruby?,* p. 24.
737. Scheim, *Contract on America,* pp. 240–241.
738. Newman, *Assass. of JFK,* pp. 499, 505–506.
739. *New York Times,* 11/16/63.
740. Summers, *Conspiracy,* p. 406.
741. Ibid., pp. 404–405.
742. *New York Times,* 12/10/63; Meagher, *Accessories after the Fact,* p. 370; Mark Lane, *Rush to Judgment* (New York: Holt, Rinehart & Winston, 1966), p. 334.
743. Lane, *Rush to Judgment,* pp. 334–335; Meaghers, *Accessories after the Fact,* p. 371.
744. Rev. Nicholas A. Schneider, ed., *Religious Views of John F. Kennedy* (St. Louis: B. Herder Book Co., 1965), pp. 58–60.
745. Newman, *Assass. of JFK,* pp. 501–502.
746. Ibid., p. 502.
747. *Congressional Record,* Appendix, 11/20/63, p. A7179.
748. *New York Times,* 11/18/63.
749. Summers, *Conspiracy,* p. 398.
750. Ibid., p. 599.
751. *Warren Report,* pp. 39, 41; Newman, *Assass. of JFK,* p. 504.

752. Newman, *Assass. of JFK,* p. 505.
753. *New York Times,* 11/19/63. The stay is inferred in part from the fact that the paper stated he returned from Florida that day, and from the fact he traveled to Miami on 11/18 to deliver his speech.
754. Summers, *Conspiracy,* p. 406.
755. Newman, *Assass. of JFK,* p. 507.
756. *LBJ Library,* JFK assassination file, Hoover report to LBJ 11/23/63.
757. Davis, *Mafia Kingfish,* p. 172.
758. Summers, *Conspiracy,* p. 430.
759. *New York Times,* 11/19/63.
760. Newman, *Assass. of JFK,* pp. 507–508.
761. *New York Times,* 11/20/63.
762. Ibid.
763. Kantor, *Who Was Jack Ruby?,* p. 24; Summers, *Conspiracy,* p. 474.
764. Summers, *Conspiracy,* p. 431.
765. *New York Times,* 11/20/63.
766. Schlesinger, *A Thousand Days,* p. 30; Schlesinger, *RFK and His Times,* p. 655.
767. Lane, *Rush to Judgment,* p. 334.
768. Harold Weisberg, *Whitewash,* vol. I (New York: Dell, 1966), p. 161.
769. Scheim, *Contract on America,* p. 31.
770. Summers, *Conspiracy,* p. 545.
771. Scheim, *Contract on America,* pp. 253–254.
772. *New York Times,* 11/21/63.
773. Ibid.
774. Ibid., 11/20/63; 11/21/63.
775. Ibid.
776. Reid, *Grim Reapers,* p. 36.
777. Ibid., p. 248.
778. Davis, *Mafia Kingfish,* p. 273.
779. Newman, *Assass. of JFK,* pp. 513–514.
780. Ibid., p. 514.
781. Ford, *Portrait of the Assassin,* p. 315.
782. Scheim, *Contract on America,* p. 256.
783. *New York Times,* 11/22/63.
784. Ibid.
785. Blakey, *Plot to Kill the President,* p. 306. *HSCA,* vol. 9., pp. 422–423 elaborates on the significance of Dolan. "In March 1963, it was learned that Dolan had been on a trip to New Orleans. . . . It was said that Dolan, while in New Orleans, had spoken to Carlos (last name unknown, possibly Marcello), a 'big-time New Orleans hoodlum,' who told him that the FBI was checking on

him and showing his picture around. . . . On May 21, 1963, it was reported that Dolan had a 'large score' set up in the New Orleans area . . . to take place during the week beginning on May 26, 1963. . . . The FBI contacted several informants who stated . . . that Nofio Pecora possibly might assist Dolan. . . . Dolan was also associated with R. D. Mathews, another Dallas hoodlum associate of Jack Ruby. . . . Mathews also assisted Dolan in collecting a 'bonus' from a nightclub owner in Hot Springs, Arkansas. On May 29, 1963, Dallas police intelligence advised that Dolan had recently been in contact with R. D. Mathews. . . . Dolan was interviewed by the FBI [after the assassination] regarding his association with Jack Ruby, but was not questioned regarding his organized-crime associates or criminal activities. He also was not questioned regarding any knowledge of Ruby's connections with organized crime. . . ."

786. Summers, *Conspiracy*, p. 476.
787. *New York Times*, 11/22/63.
788. Ibid.
789. Ibid.
790. Newman, *Assass. of JFK*, pp. 516–517.
791. Ibid.
792. Newman, *Assass. of JFK*, p. 520.
793. Scheim, *Contract on America*, pp. 258–259.
794. Blakey, *Plot to Kill the President*, p. 313.
795. Ibid.
796. Scheim, *Contract on America*, p. 246.
797. Summers, *Conspiracy*, p. 476.
798. *Warren Commission Hearings*, vol. 1, pp. 72–73; Weisberg, *Whitewash*, vol. I, p. 29.
799. Newman, *Assass. of JFK*, p. 525.
800. Ford, *Portrait of the Assassin*, p. 332.
801. Newman, *Assass. of JFK*, p. 526.
802. Lane, *Rush to Judgment*, p. 146.
803. Ibid., p. 144.
804. *Warren Report*, p. 132. As revealed by Lane's *Rush to Judgment*, p. 143, "The original bag was also shown to witnesses, but the Commission conceded that it had been practically destroyed by the FBI insofar as identification was concerned. . . . The bag into which the rifle had been placed by the Commission . . . had been manufactured by the FBI."
805. Lane, *Rush to Judgment*, pp. 145–146; *Warren Commission Hearings*, vol. 6, p. 376–377.
806. Newman, *Assass. of JFK*, p. 527.
807. Jim Marrs, *Crossfire: The Plot That Killed Kennedy* (New York: Carroll & Graf Publishers, Inc., 1989), p. 265.

808. *New York Times,* 11/22/63. Aside from his association with Levinson, Dalitz had long been a friend of attorney and Hoover intimate Roy Cohn. As detailed by Messick, in *John Edgar Hoover,* p. 177, "Cohn had invested in such syndicate projects as the Sunrise Hospital in Las Vegas. In 1960 he was Dalitz's guest of honor at a New Year's Eve party in Las Vegas." Further, in the fall of 1963, ". . . Cohn was indicted [by RFK] on perjury charges. It developed that Cohn . . . was deeply involved with Dalitz and his friends. The government accused him of . . . blocking indictments of the gamblers, and then lying about [it] under oath." Through Dalitz, yet another direct avenue of communication between Hoover and the Levinson/Lansky/Marcello Mafia element is revealed. Obviously, Hoover and Cohn had a mutual goal in stopping JFK, the political destruction of RFK. Cohn was also very close to a politically powerful New Orleans newspaper owner by the name of Si Newhouse. Interestingly, when Cohn was indicted, Walker media manipulator Robert Morris stepped into the fray, stating ". . . this evidence reflected serious badgering and abuse of witnesses. . . ." See *New York Times,* 9/9/63.
809. Schlesinger, *RFK and His Times,* p. 294.
810. Walter Sheridan, *The Fall and Rise of Jimmy Hoffa* (New York: Saturday Review Press, 1972), p. 459.
811. Jim Bishop, *The Day Kennedy Was Shot* (New York: Funk & Wagnalls, 1968), p. 20.
812. Ford, *Portrait of the Assassin,* p. 442.
813. Garrow, *FBI and Martin Luther King, Jr.,* p. 259. It is presumed Hoover dictated the memos prior to the assassination, for obvious reasons.
814. *Congressional Record,* Appendix, 12/10/63, p. A7522.
815. Newman, *Assass. of JFK,* pp. 528–529.
816. Ibid., p. 529.
817. Summers, *Conspiracy,* pp. 106–107.
818. Ibid., p. 107.
819. Ibid.
820. Ibid., p. 106.
821. Ibid., p. 107.
822. Ibid., p. 108.
823. Ibid., p. 111.
824. Ibid., p. 58.
825. Josiah Thompson, *Six Seconds in Dallas* (New York: Bernard Geis Associates, 1967) See frames from Hughes Film.
826. Ibid., pp. 32, 37, 38, 39, 41, 44.
827. Ibid., pp. 61, 62, 63, 66, 68.
828. Ibid., pp. 84, 85, 86, 89, 90.
829. Ibid., pp. 93, 94.

830. Ibid., pp. 96, 98.
831. Ibid., pp. 99, 100, 101, 102.
832. Summers, *Conspiracy,* p. 56.
833. Thompson, *Six Seconds in Dallas,* p. 123.
834. Summers, *Conspiracy,* pp. 80–82.
835. Thompson, *Six Seconds in Dallas,* p. 244.
836. Meaghers, *Accessories after the Fact,* pp. 71–72.
837. Ibid., p. 72.
838. Summers, *Conspiracy,* pp. 112–113.
839. Ibid., p. 476.
840. Moldea, *The Hoffa Wars,* p. 160.
841. Blakey, *Plot to Kill the President,* p. 397; Summers, *Conspiracy,* p. 476.
842. Summers, *Conspiracy,* p. 478.

Scienter (11/22/63—5/8/64)

1. Arthur M. Schlesinger, Jr., *Robert Kennedy and His Times* (Boston: Houghton Mifflin Company, 1978), p. 635.
2. *Dallas Morning News,* 11/23/63, p. 4.
3. *The Official Warren Commission Report on the Assassination of President John F. Kennedy* (hereafter *Warren Report* or *Hearings)* (Garden City, New York: Doubleday, 1964), *Hearings,* vol. 2, pp. 80–81, 124, 141.
4. *Daily Express,* 11/23/63, p. 2.
5. Josiah Thompson, *Six Seconds in Dallas* (New York: Bernard Geis Associates, 1967), p. 105.
6. *Washington Post,* 11/23/63, p. 1.
7. *Seattle Post Intelligencer,* 11/22/63, p. 1.
8. Thompson, *Six Seconds In Dallas,* p. 107.
9. Robert J. Nash, *Citizen Hoover* (Chicago: Nelson-Hall, 1972), p. 150.
10. Schlesinger, *RFK and His Times,* p. 636.
11. Nash, *Citizen Hoover,* p. 150.
12. *Washington Evening Star,* 11/23/63, p. 18.
13. *Warren Report,* pp. 156–157; Mark Lane, *Rush to Judgment* (New York: Holt, Rinehart, and Winston, 1966), pp. 190–208.
14. Henry Hurt, *Reasonable Doubt* (New York: Henry Holt and Company, 1985), pp. 165–169.
15. *New Orleans States Item,* 11/23/63, p. 30.
16. *Dallas Morning News,* 11/23/63, Sect. 1, p. 15.
17. G. Robert Blakey and Richard N. Billings, *The Plot to Kill the President* (New York: Times Books, 1981), p. 397.

18. David E. Scheim, *Contract on America* (Silver Spring, Md: Argyle Press, 1983), p. 253.
19. Anthony Summers, *Conspiracy* (New York: McGraw-Hill Book Company, 1980), p. 497.
20. Albert H. Newman, *The Assassination of John F. Kennedy* (New York: Clarkson N. Potter, Inc., 1970), p. 542.
21. Harold Weisberg, *Whitewash: Vol. I* (New York: Dell, 1966), p. 143.
22. Ibid.
23. Newman, *Assass. of JFK,* p. 543.
24. Weisberg, *Whitewash I,* p. 144.
25. Ibid., p. 223.
26. Ibid., pp. 145, 146.
27. Sylvia Meaghers, *Accessories after the Fact* (New York: Vintage Books, 1976), p. 171.
28. *Warren Commission Hearings,* vol. 3, pp. 214–216.
29. Summers, *Conspiracy,* p. 135.
30. *New Orleans States Item,* 11/23/63, p. 30.
31. *Washington Post,* 5/16/76.
32. *Washington Post,* 11/23/63, p. B9.
33. Newman, *Assass. of JFK,* p. 544.
34. Weisberg, *Whitewash I,* p. 146.
35. *New York Times,* 11/30/63.
36. Thompson, *Six Seconds in Dallas,* p. 166.
37. *New York Times,* 11/23/63.
38. John H. Davis, *Mafia Kingfish: Carlos Marcello and the Assassination of John F. Kennedy* (New York: McGraw-Hill Book Company, 1989), p. 297.
39. Henry Hurt, *Reasonable Doubt* (New York: Henry Holt and Company, 1985), p. 412; Summers, *Conspiracy,* pp. 576–577.
40. Summers, *Conspiracy,* pp. 578–579.
41. Ibid., p. 497.
42. Hurt, *Reasonable Doubt,* p. 19; *Dallas Morning News,* 11/23/63, p. 4; FBI memo, Hoover to Tolson, Belmont, et al., 11/22/63.
43. *New York Times,* 11/23/63, p. 11.
44. *Washington Evening Star,* 11/23/63, p. 1.
45. Author's files, letter from AP, 1/4/91. While nothing in the newspaper coverage suggests Hoover was there, it is possible he, like RFK, entered the immediate area of the plane without being seen by reporters. Protocol would seem to require his presence. No doubt, however, he was preoccupied by the consequences of his act of treason and may well have been at SOG. In the final analysis, his absence would be more disturbing than his presence.
46. *Honolulu Star Bulletin,* 11/22/63, p. 6.
47. *Washington Evening Star,* 11/23/63, p. 5.

48. Scheim, *Contract on America,* p. 114.
49. Blakey, *Plot to Kill the President,* p. 317.
50. *Washington Evening Star,* 11/23/63, p. 1.
51. Scheim, *Contract on America,* p. 50.
52. Summers, *Conspiracy,* p. 496.
53. Ibid., p. 88.
54. Ibid., p. 483.
55. *Washington Evening Star,* 11/23/63, p. 5; *Lyndon B. Johnson Presidential Library,* Austin, Texas, *Daily Diary,* 11/22/63. Examination of White House phone logs reveals heavy phone usage by Johnson. Calls between him, Hoover, and Warren Commission members have been included in this portion of the Chronicle to demonstrate the fact that Johnson maintained very close contact with all concerned. Undoubtedly, some of his calls to these people dealt with unrelated subjects. However, such interaction and ready access, by the man who had appointed them, does make apparent the opportunity for Johnson's control, perhaps even intimidation. At some points his manipulation of events is obvious.
56. John H. Davis, *The Kennedys: Dynasty and Disaster 1848–1984* (New York: McGraw-Hill Book Company, 1984), p. 846.
57. Ibid.
58. *Washington Evening Star,* 11/23/63, p. 1; *Four Days in November.* CBS, New York. 11/22/88 TV mini-series.
59. *Washington Evening Star,* 11/23/63, p. 1.
60. *The Fabulous Sixties: 1963 End of a Thousand Days,* Maljack Productions, Inc. 1970 video.
61. Weisberg, *Whitewash I,* p. 137.
62. Scheim, *Contract on America,* p. 120.
63. *Washington Evening Star,* 11/24/63.
64. *New York Times,* 11/23/63.
65. Ibid.
66. Ibid.
67. Ibid.
68. Ibid.
69. Ibid.
70. *Washington Evening Star,* 11/23/63, p. 6.
71. *Dallas Morning News,* 11/23/63, p. 15.
72. *Washington Post,* 11/23/63.
73. *Denver Post,* 11/23/63, p. 2.
74. *Los Angeles Times,* 11/23/63, p. 10.
75. *New Orleans States Item,* 11/23/63, p. 1.
76. Hank Messick, *John Edgar Hoover* (New York: David McKay Company, Inc., 1972), p. 221.
77. Blakey, *Plot to Kill the President,* p. 77.
78. Ibid., p. 21; *Daily Diary,* 11/23/63; *New York Times,* 11/23/63.

79. Blakey, *Plot to Kill the President,* p. 21; *New York Times,* 11/23/ 63; Davis, *The Kennedys,* p. 847; Schlesinger, *RFK and His Times,* p. 657; Robert Rowe, *The Bobby Baker Story* (New York: Parallax Publishing Company, 1967), p. 87.

80. William C. Sullivan with Bill Brown, *The Bureau: My Thirty Years in Hoover's FBI* (New York: W.W. Norton & Company, 1979), p. 55.

81. Blakey, *Plot to Kill the President,* p. 21; LBJ Library, JFK assassination file, Hoover report to Johnson, 11/23/63. See Hurt's *Reasonable Doubt,* photo inset between pages 138 and 139, for analysis of FBI Lab's report on the bag. It determined that the materials used to make the package did *not* come from the Depository, but the report that Hoover apparently made available to the Commission concluded the opposite. The falsified report was but one more instance in his efforts to implicate Oswald and hide his own crime.

82. *LBJ Library,* JFK assassination file, Hoover report to Johnson, 11/23/63.

83. Rowe, *Bobby Baker Story,* p. 87.

84. Newman, *Assass. of JFK,* p. 549.

85. Gerald R. Ford with John R. Stiles, *Portrait of the Assassin* (New York: Simon & Schuster, 1965), pp. 202, 297, 302.

86. *Four Days in November,* CBS.

87. Ibid.

88. Ibid.

89. Ibid.

90. Newman, *Assass. of JFK,* p. 550.

91. Ibid., p. 551.

92. *Dallas Morning News,* 11/24/63, p. 6.

93. *Ft. Worth Star Telegram,* 10/1/78.

94. Ford, *Portrait of the Assassin,* p. 371.

95. Scheim, *Contract on America,* p. 115.

96. *Denver Post,* 11/24/63, p. 33.

97. *Washington Evening Star,* 11/24/63, p. 1.

98. Newman, *Assass. of JFK,* p. 552.

99. *Seattle Post Intelligencer,* 11/24/63, p. 1. The public demeanor of Oswald hardly suggested the profile of a lone nut. Considered against genuine contemporaneous cases prior to the assassination, the absurdity of Hoover's and the Commission's position becomes all the more apparent. To quote just four newspaper excerpts, "A North Carolina man created alarm . . . at the White House today by crashing his truck through a street gate and nearly reaching the North Portico entrance. . . . 'I want to see the President. The Communists are taking over in North Carolina,' the driver screamed as he was taken into custody. . . ."; ". . . Bradburn

. . . was sentenced today to . . . five years in Federal prison. [He] was arrested July 31 for having written a letter demanding that Mr. Kennedy give $3 million to an Everett, Wash., cemetery, or be killed."; "A state legislator was fined $500 and given a 30-day suspended jail sentence today for making a false bomb report last Friday night on the eve of President Kennedy's visit to the University of Maine."; and "A visitor shattered a mirror in the Red Room of the White House today. . . . At District of Columbia General Hospital, where he was sent for mental observation, attendants said [he] was still uncommunicative tonight. The incident occurred . . . as the visitor stepped suddenly from a sightseeing group, grabbed one of three urns from a desk . . . and threw it." (See *New York Times*, 9/27, 10/15, 10/22, 11/6 respectively).

100. Newman, *Assass. of JFK*, p. 553.
101. Weisberg, *Whitewash, I*, p. 145; *Warren Report*, pp. 624–625.
102. Weisberg, *Whitewash, I*, p. 141.
103. *Denver Post*, 11/24/63, p. 3.
104. *Los Angeles Times*, 11/24/63, p. 1.
105. *The Fabulous Sixties*, Maljack Productions, Inc.
106. Newman, *Assass. of JFK*, p. 554.
107. Summers, *Conspiracy*, p. 483.
108. *House Select Committee on Assassinations, John F. Kennedy*, vol. 10., p. 113. Hereafter, *HSCA*.
109. Summers, *Conspiracy*, p. 474.
110. Davis, *Mafia Kingfish*, p. 302.
111. Scheim, *Contract on America*, p. 52.
112. Hurt, *Reasonable Doubt*, pp. 407–408.
113. *FBI*, Hoover memo re Oswald and Ruby, 11/24/63.
114. Ibid.
115. *New York Times*, 11/24/63, p. 5.
116. *Los Angeles Times*, 11/24/63.
117. *New York Times*, 11/24/63, p. 2.
118. *Dallas Morning News*, 11/24/63, p. 13.
119. Ibid.
120. *Washington Evening Star*, 11/24/63, p. 5.
121. Ibid., p. 15.
122. *Los Angeles Times*, 11/24/63, p. 1.
123. *Dallas Morning News*, 11/24/63, p. 6.
124. *Chicago Tribune*, 11/24/63, p. 1.
125. *Los Angeles Times*, 11/25/63.
126. Davis, *Mafia Kingfish*, p. 196.
127. Newman, *Assass. of JFK*, p. 560.
128. Weisberg, *Whitewash, I*, pp. 148–150.
129. Blakey, *Plot to Kill the President*, p. 320.

130. *The Killing of President Kennedy: New Revelations Twenty Years Later.* Syndacast Services, Inc., 1983 video.
131. Seth Kantor, *Who Was Jack Ruby?* (New York: Everest House, 1978), p. 228.
132. Ibid., p. 174.
133. Ibid., p. 76.
134. Meaghers, *Accessories after the Fact,* p. 137.
135. Summers, *Conspiracy,* p. 137.
136. Ibid., pp. 100–102.
137. Ibid., pp. 396, 397.
138. Hurt, *Reasonable Doubt,* p. 251.
139. *New York Times,* 11/25/63.
140. Ibid.
141. *Daily Diary,* 11/24/63.
142. *HSCA,* vol. 3, pp. 471–473.
143. Scheim, *Contract on America,* p. 183; Blakey, *Plot to Kill the President,* p. 258.
144. *New York Times,* 11/25/63. Inferred in part from the fact that at afternoon, 11/24, press conference a reporter had stated to Wade: "You talked with the FBI this morning."
145. Meaghers, *Accessories after the Fact,* p. 367; Weisberg, *Whitewash I,* p. 258.
146. *Los Angeles Times,* 11/25/63, p. 2.
147. *New York Times,* 11/25/63.
148. Ibid.
149. Summers, *Conspiracy,* p. 497.
150. *Daily Diary,* 11/24/63.
151. *Los Angeles Times,* 11/26/63, p. 14.
152. *New York Times,* 11/26/63.
153. *Denver Post,* 11/25/63, p. 16.
154. *Los Angeles Times,* 11/25/63, p. 11.
155. *Dallas Morning News,* 11/25/63.
156. *New York Times,* 11/26/63.
157. Blakey, *Plot to Kill the President,* p. 23.
158. *Daily Diary,* 11/25/63.
159. *New York Times,* 11/25/63.
160. Blakey, *Plot to Kill the President,* p. 23.
161. *Washington Daily News,* 11/26/63, p. 4.
162. Summers, *Conspiracy,* p. 506.
163. Ibid.
164. Davis, *Mafia Kingfish,* p. 196.
165. Ibid., p. 251.
166. *New York Times,* 11/30/63.
167. Ibid., 12/1/63.
168. Ibid., 11/30/63.
169. Summers, *Conspiracy,* pp. 406–407.

170. *New York Times,* 11/27/63.
171. Summers, *Conspiracy,* p. 545.
172. Ibid., p. 601 n. 479; *Daily Diary,* 11/25/63.
173. Summers, *Conspiracy,* p. 321.
174. *New York Times,* 11/26/63, p. 2.
175. *Washington Daily News,* 11/26/63.
176. Ibid., p. 4.
177. Ibid.
178. *Boston Record American,* 11/26/63, p. 2.
179. *Chicago Tribune,* 11/26/63, p. 9.
180. *New York Times,* 11/27/63.
181. Ibid.
182. Ibid.
183. Ibid.
184. Ibid.
185. Ibid. The foreign press, and average citizens of such countries perceived the obvious nature of the Mafia's involvement early on. An additional sampling illustrates both this point as well as Hoover's efforts to conceal the truth. " 'You can't tell me,' said the Belgian, 'that there wasn't a conspiracy. . . . We know better. Someone arranged for Ruby to murder Oswald to cover the tracks. Isn't that the way your underworld operates?' That assertion is typical. . . . Despite stories about the FBI report finding no evidence of a plot, few here will believe it. The plot . . . is said to involve . . . Cosa Nostra. . . . [it] . . . has 'deep-rooted political branches' in every American city and state. 'Who says that Dallas is not under its control?' One of the major actions of President Kennedy and Attorney General Robert Kennedy . . . was to move against Cosa Nostra. Hence the organization had to counterattack." (see *Washington Post,* 12/17/63). Articles such as this reveal American naïveté in the early 1960s. That a country as young as ours would suggest to citizens of civilizations thousands of years older that assassination by conspiracy could not happen in the U.S. was to them no doubt, laughable. It is small wonder Johnson was never able to develop significant credibility in foreign policy.
186. Ibid.
187. Ibid.
188. *Daily Diary,* 11/26/63.
189. Ibid., generally 11/26/63 to 5/64.
190. Scheim, *Contract on America,* p. 197.
191. Ibid.
192. Kantor, *Who Was Jack Ruby?,* p. 79.
193. *New York Times,* 11/30/63.
194. Davis, *Mafia Kingfish,* pp. 250–251.

195. *HSCA,* vol. 3, pp. 474–475.
196. Harold Weisberg, *Photographic Whitewash, vol. III* (Hyattstown, Md.: Harold Weisberg, 1967), p. 210.
197. Ibid., p. 211.
198. Summers, *Conspiracy,* pp. 597–598.
199. Blakey, *Plot to Kill the President,* p. 314.
200. *New York Times,* 11/28/63.
201. *Washington Daily News,* 11/27/63, p. 2.
202. *Boston Record American,* 11/27/63, p. 23.
203. *New York Times,* 11/28/63.
204. Davis, *Mafia Kingfish,* p. 202.
205. *New York Times,* 11/28/63.
206. Ibid.
207. Davis, *Mafia Kingfish,* p. 252.
208. Summers, *Conspiracy,* p. 493.
209. *New York Times,* 11/28/63.
210. Ibid.
211. *Washington Evening Star,* 11/27/63.
212. *New York Times,* 11/28/63.
213. Ibid., 11/29/63.
214. Ibid.
215. *New York Times,* 11/28/63, p. 29. Castro also observed, rather astutely, ". . . 'ultra reactionaries' of the far right were responsible." His foreign ministry stated, ". . . powerful forces of reaction in the United States are using all resources and influences to cover up the intellectual authors and the true motives behind the assassination of Kennedy." (See *New York Times,* 11/27/63, p. 17.)
216. Scheim, *Contract on America,* p. 216.
217. *Washington Daily News,* 11/28/63, p. 2.
218. Blakey, *Plot to Kill the President,* p. 23; FBI Hoover memo to LBJ; *Washington Daily News,* 11/26/63 three investigations developing; *New York Times,* 11/27/63 Senate investigation.
219. Kantor, *Who Was Jack Ruby?,* p. 132.
220. *New York Times,* 11/29/63.
221. Davis, *Mafia Kingfish,* p. 195.
222. Ibid., pp. 252–253.
223. Ibid., p. 253.
224. *New York Times,* 11/29/63. Johnson's activities and ego had driven him to fear the press long before this. A consistent pattern exists. On 5/11/63, during an address before ". . . a dinner of the nation's political cartoonists, the Vice President stressed the responsibilities of those who lead American opinion." (See *New York Times,* 5/12/63). Another example is revealed by Schlesinger in *RFK and His Times,* p. 379. "Hoover . . . dispatched DeLoach

to offer newspapermen [the FBI's] dossier on King's private life. When Ben Bradlee of *Newsweek* reported this to Katzenbach, now acting Attorney General, 'I was shocked,' Katzenbach testified, '. . . and felt that [Johnson] should be advised immediately. . . .' [He was on 11/28/63]. . . . Johnson['s reaction] . . . was to instruct Bill Moyers to warn the Bureau that Bradlee was an enemy."

225. Ibid.
226. Ibid.
227. Ibid., 11/30/63.
228. *Daily Diary,* 11/29/63.
229. *HSCA,* vol. 3, p. 476.
230. Athan G. Theoharis and John Stuart Cox, *The Boss* (Philadelphia: Temple University Press, 1988) pp. 390–391.
231. *Daily Diary,* 11/29/63.
232. Ibid., Blakey, *Plot to Kill the President,* p. 24.
233. Blakey, *Plot to Kill the President,* p. 24; Edward Jay Epstein, *Inquest: The Warren Commission and the Establishment of Truth* (New York: The Viking Press, 1966), p. 46.
234. *Daily Diary,* 11/29/63.
235. *New York Times,* 11/30/63.
236. *Daily Diary,* 11/29/63.
237. Davis, *Mafia Kingfish,* p. 256.
238. Dan E. Moldea, *The Hoffa Wars* (New York: Paddington Press, Ltd., 1978), p. 132.
239. Sullivan, *The Bureau,* p. 53.
240. *New York Times,* 11/30/63.
241. Davis, *Mafia Kingfish,* p. 234.
242. *New York Times,* 11/30/63.
243. *Life,* 11/29/63, generally. The caption describing Kennedy's wounds read as follows: "The President's wave turns into a clutching movement toward his throat. . . . Mrs. Kennedy suddenly becomes aware of what has happened and reaches over to help. . . . The President collapses on his wife's shoulder and in the last two small pictures the First Lady cradles him in her arms." No mention is made of the double head shot. *Life* paid $150,000 for the film rights, a figure equivalent to several times that amount in today's dollars. To pay such a sum for a product and then not be allowed to capitalize on it implies overpowering governmental intervention. It remains unknown whether *Life* received compensation from the government at some point for its cooperation. Note it was *Life* that asserted that Kennedy had turned at the last minute to face the Depository, "explaining" the "entrance" wound in the throat. Just as it was also *Life* that asserted that frames Z208-212, capturing that time interval, had

inadvertently been destroyed while in its possession, necessitating the obvious splice at that juncture.

244. Ibid., p. 39.
245. Ford, *Portrait of the Assassin,* p. 29.
246. *New York Times,* 11/30/63.
247. Ibid.
248. Ibid.
249. Ibid.
250. Ibid.
251. Ibid.
252. *Daily Diary,* 11/30/63.
253. *Dallas Times Herald,* 11/30/63. See Harold Feldman, "Oswald and the FBI," *The Nation,* January 27, 1964, p. 86. Feldman states "The Western Union office in Dallas handled frequent messages for Lee Oswald, but inquiries there brought the reply that 'any details or comment would have to come from Washington headquarters of the Federal Bureau of Investigation'. . . . if . . . money [was coming] . . . from a government source, then the agency's reticence is understandable."
254. Schlesinger, *RFK and His Times,* p. 657.
255. Scheim, *Contract on America,* p. 86.
256. Weisberg, *Whitewash III,* p. 278.
257. *New York Times,* 12/1/63.
258. Ibid.
259. Ibid.
260. Ibid.
261. *FBI Law Enforcement Bulletin,* December 1963.
262. *New York Times,* 12/2/63.
263. *Dallas Morning News,* 12/2/63.
264. Summers, *Conspiracy,* p. 407.
265. *New York Times,* 12/2/63, p. 1.
266. Ibid.
267. Davis, *Mafia Kingfish,* p. 279.
268. *New York Times,* 12/2/63.
269. Ibid.
270. Ibid.
271. Ibid.
272. Kantor, *Who Was Jack Ruby?,* p. 181.
273. *Warren Report,* p. 183.
274. Ford, *Portrait of the Assassin,* p. 459.
275. *Warren Report,* p. 413.
276. Davis, *Mafia Kingfish,* p. 222.
277. *New York Times,* 12/3/63.
278. Ibid.
279. Ibid.

280. Ibid.
281. Ibid.
282. Ibid.
283. Davis, *Mafia Kingfish,* p. 297.
284. Kantor, *Who Was Jack Ruby?,* p. 222.
285. *HSCA,* vol. 3, p. 476.
286. Harold Weisberg, *Whitewash II: The FBI—Secret Service Cover-Up* (New York: Dell Publishing Company, Inc., 1967), p. 200.
287. Ibid.
288. Mark Lane, *Rush to Judgment* (New York: Holt Rinehart and Winston, 1966), pp. 195–196.
289. Ibid., p. 199.
290. Ibid., pp. 198–199.
291. *New York Times,* 12/4/63.
292. Ibid.
293. Ibid.
294. Ibid.
295. Ibid.
296. Ibid.
297. Ibid.
298. Ibid., 12/5/63.
299. Ibid.
300. Ibid.
301. Schlesinger, *RFK and His Times,* p. 637.
302. Davis, *The Kennedys,* p. 851.
303. Summers, *Conspiracy,* p. 102.
304. Kantor, *Who Was Jack Ruby?,* pp. 224–225.
305. *New York Times,* 12/8/63 article stating Marina turned down offer from *Stern* prior to 12/7. Inferred also from fact that she was under FBI control during this time period.
306. *New York Times,* 12/5/63.
307. *259 F. Supp. 567.*
308. *Daily Diary,* 12/4/63.
309. *New York Times,* 12/5/63.
310. Ed Reid and Ovid Demaris, *The Green Felt Jungle* (New York: Pocket Books, Inc., 1964), p. 219.
311. *New York Times,* 12/5/63.
312. Weisberg, *Whitewash,* II., p. 294.
313. *Congressional Record—Senate,* 12/5/63, p. 23544. The intense nature of Hoover's focus on morality just before and after the assassination becomes all the more apparent when one considers the range of topics discussed in his monthly *FBI Law Enforcement Bulletin* "messages" during the Kennedy administration. Of the thirty-four that preceded the revealing 12/1/63 essay, none focused on morality as a theme. Twelve dealt with aspects of crime,

eight with law-enforcement responsibilities, five with citizenry responsibilities, four with communism, three with patriotism, and two with civil rights.

314. Richard Gid Powers, *Secrecy and Power: The Life of J. Edgar Hoover* (New York: The Free Press, 1987), p. 385. Hoover's fascination with simplistic explanations for the public continued as late as into 1965. That year he endorsed and wrote the forward for a book entitled *How the FBI Gets Its Man,* (David Sentner, Avon Books) which opens with the following lines "ELEVEN CLEAN-CUT, neatly dressed young men—their topcoats blowing in the brisk wind and their teeth clenched against the bitter cold. . . ."
315. Schlesinger, *RFK and His Times,* p. 657.
316. Blakey, *Plot to Kill the President,* p. 25. Warren's fear was apparent from the start. " 'I am sure that there is not one of us but that would rather be doing almost anything else. . . . Our job . . . is essentially one for the evaluation of evidence as distinguished from . . . gathering evidence. . . . We can start with the premise that we can rely on the reports of . . . the FBI. . . .' . . . Some Commission members expressed concern about some actions by the FBI. There had been numerous stories leaked to the press attributed to FBI sources. . . ." (See *HSCA,* vol. 11, p. 32).
317. Ibid., p. 73.
318. Scheim, *Contract on America,* p. 183.
319. Epstein, *Inquest,* pp. 46–47.
320. *New York Times,* 12/6/63.
321. Davis, *Mafia Kingfish,* p. 258.
322. Kantor, *Who Was Jack Ruby?,* p. 131.
323. *New York Times,* 12/6/63.
324. Ibid.
325. Ibid.
326. Epstein, *Inquest,* pp. 74–75.
327. Ibid.
328. *New York Times,* 12/6/63.
329. Ibid., 12/7/63.
330. Ibid.
331. Kantor, *Who Was Jack Ruby?,* pp. 224–225.
332. *New York Times,* 12/7/63.
333. *Life,* 12/6/63; Hurt, *Reasonable Doubt,* p. 139 (see photo inset opposing page). Between this date and 5/22/64, the editors of *Life* apparently realized their situation and came to oppose Hoover. Just two weeks after he obtained his retirement waiver, the magazine featured an editorial viciously attacking him. Entitled "Must J. Edgar Go On and On?" it states in part, "Under extraordinary circumstances the Roman senate conferred god status on a few emperors while they were still in office, and more or less the same

thing has just happened to J. Edgar Hoover. Not that he hasn't been at least a demigod for a long time. . . . the most serious defect in this business of Mr. Hoover's continuing one—man rule centers around the Bureau's preoccupation with *him*. . . . The trouble with this deification . . . is that the FBI gets lost in all the flack about its Director. . . . crime is flourishing. . . ." (see 5/22/64 issue, p. 25).

334. *HSCA.,* vol. 11, p. 32. Also, ". . . the Commission members kept wondering what the FBI was doing. . . ."

335. *New York Times,* 12/7/63.

336. Ibid.

337. *Daily Diary,* 12/7/63.

338. Scheim, *Contract on America,* pp. 80, 107.

339. Davis, *Mafia Kingfish,* p. 144.

340. *Daily Diary,* 12/6/63.

341. *New York Times,* 12/8/63.

342. Ibid.

343. Ibid.

344. Ibid.

345. *Daily Diary,* 12/7/63.

346. Ibid.

347. Ford, *Portrait of the Assassin,* pp. 15–16.

348. *New York Times,* 12/9/63.

349. Kantor, *Who Was Jack Ruby?,* p. 82; Epstein, *Inquest,* p. 22.

350. Blakey, *Plot to Kill the President,* p. 77.

351. *New York Times,* 12/10/63.

352. Kantor, *Who Was Jack Ruby?,* p. 86. The opinions of other staff members, as stated in HSCA, vol. 11, pp. 43–53, reveal the fear among the group concerning Hoover. "Redlich had a skeptical attitude toward the FBI when he joined the Warren Commission staff. . . . Griffin brought a very skeptical opinion of the . . . FBI to the Warren Commission staff. . . . Slawson . . . 'I understood immediately that *part of my assignment would be to suspect everyone. So included in that would be the . . . FBI. . . . We would sometimes speculate as to what would happen if we got firm evidence that pointed to some very high official. [deleted]* Of course that would present a kind of frightening prospect because *if the President or anyone else that high up was indeed involved they clearly were not going to allow* someone like *us to bring out the truth if they could stop us.'* . . . Griffin: '[deleted] there was . . . *concern that this investigation not be conducted* in such a way *as to destroy any of the investigative agencies* that then existed in the Government. *There was a genuine fear expressed that this could be done. . . . It would be bad for the country because it might be justified. . . .'* . . . . Slawson:'. . . *they all had a strong interest*

*in not being blamed for not having adequately protected the Presi-
dent.'* . . . . Redlich; '. . . the FBI report was a grossly inadequate document. . . . the Bureau . . . decided to produce
something very quickly. . . .' . . . . Griffin: 'I recall the Hosty
incident [deleted]. . . . It established in our minds that *we had to
be worried about them [deleted]* . . . we never forgot the incident.
We were always alert, we were concerned about the problem [de-
leted]' " (emphasis added).

353. Powers, *Secrecy and Power,* p. 384.
354. Epstein, *Inquest,* p. 165.
355. *Daily Diary,* 12/9/63.
356. Schlesinger, *RFK and His Times,* p. 643.
357. *New York Times,* 12/10/63.
358. Ibid.
359. Ibid.
360. J. Evetts Haley, *A Texan Looks at Lyndon* (Canyon, Texas: Palo
Duro Press, 1964), p. 78.
361. *New York Times,* 12/10/63.
362. Powers, *Secrecy and Power,* pp. 385, 574.
363. Edward J. Epstein, *Legend: The Secret World of Lee Harvey Oswald* (New York: McGraw-Hill Book Company, 1978), p. 16.
364. Powers, *Secrecy and Power,* p. 388.
365. Kantor, *Who Was Jack Ruby?,* p. 225.
366. Schlesinger, *RFK and His Times,* p. 642; Hurt, *Reasonable
Doubt,* pp. 193–194.
367. *New York Times,* 12/11/63.
368. Ibid.
369. Ibid.
370. Ibid.
371. Ibid.
372. Ibid.
373. Ibid.
374. Ibid., 12/12/63.
375. *Daily Diary,* 12/11/63.
376. Kantor, *Who Was Jack Ruby?,* pp. 9, 222.
377. Davis, *The Kennedys,* p. 852.
378. Kantor, *Who Was Jack Ruby?,* p. 86.
379. Blakey, *Plot to Kill the President,* p. 77.
380. Hurt, *Reasonable Doubt,* p. 32.
381. Kantor, *Who Was Jack Ruby?,* p. 221.
382. Powers, *Secrecy and Power,* p. 361.
383. Blakey, *Plot to Kill the President,* p. 77.
384. Weisberg, *Whitewash,* III, p. 34.
385. *New York Times,* 12/13/63.
386. Ibid., 12/14/63.

387. Ibid.
388. Epstein, *Inquest,* p. 23.
389. Davis, *Mafia Kingfish,* p. 258.
390. Summers, *Conspiracy,* pp. 80, 536.
391. *New York Times,* 12/15/63.
392. Ibid.
393. Ibid.
394. Davis, *Mafia Kingfish,* pp. 261, 280. HSCA, vol. 11, p. 33 states: "The members also considered that they may have been wrong in not hiring their own staff of investigators. . . . Rankin: '. . . The [FBI] report has so many loopholes in it. Anybody can look at it and see that it doesn't seem like they're looking for things that this Commission has to look for in order to get the answers that it wants and is entitled to.' . . . Rankin went on to say . . . the main reason they might need an independent staff of investigators was that there . . . were 'tender spots' for the FBI. . . . Warren suggested: '[deleted] perhaps we ought to have a thorough investigation [deleted] as to the relationship between the FBI and the Secret Service . . . so that we can do something worthwhile in the future.' Such a thorough investigation was never done."
395. *New York Times,* 12/17/63.
396. *Daily Diary,* 12/16/63.
397. Ibid.
398. *New York Times,* 12/17/63.
399. *Washington Post,* 12/16/63.
400. Sullivan, *The Bureau,* p. 52.
401. *New York Times,* 12/17/63.
402. *LBJ Library,* famous names box Hoover to Johnson.
403. Powers, *Secrecy and Power,* p. 393.
404. *New York Times,* 12/18/63.
405. Ibid. With regard to the autopsy "findings," there may have been other interests at work besides Hoover's. National security intervention seems apparent from Lifton's book, *Best Evidence.* That some form of preliminary autopsy (possibly as standard governmental emergency procedure) would have been performed on JFK, especially given the time interval between Dallas and Bethesda and obviously conspiratorial aspects of the killing, would seem logical. In my hours at the LBJ Library, quite by accident, I learned that there is indeed research currently being conducted in the area of national security reaction to the assassination. This involves extremely sensitive files, access to which is very carefully controlled.
406. Ibid.
407. Ibid.
408. Ibid.

409. *Daily Diary,* 12/17/63.
410. *New York Times,* 12/19/63.
411. Ibid.
412. *Washington Post,* 12/18/63. With regard to Kennedy's head wounds and Connally's, the *Post* stated "The second bullet to hit the President, . . . tore off the right rear portion of his head. . . . The one bullet that struck . . . Connally . . . could not be . . . traced to any rifle because it fragmented." Consider this description of the "fragmented" bullet that struck Connally in light of the Warren Commission's "magic bullet" which supposedly emerged from both Kennedy and Connally unscathed.
413. *New York Times,* 12/18/63.
414. Ibid., 12/19/63.
415. Ibid.
416. Ibid.
417. Davis, *Mafia Kingfish,* p. 234.
418. Kantor, *Who Was Jack Ruby?,* pp. 104, 226.
419. Ibid.
420. Ibid.
421. *New York Times,* 12/19/63.
422. Ibid.
423. Ibid., 12/20/63.
424. Ibid., 12/21/63.
425. *Daily Diary,* 12/20/63.
426. Ibid.
427. Ibid.
428. Kantor, *Who Was Jack Ruby?,* p. 80.
429. *New York Times,* 12/22/63.
430. Scheim, *Contract on America,* p. 139; Kantor, *Who Was Jack Ruby?,* p. 90.
431. Kantor, *Who Was Jack Ruby?,* pp. 9, 222.
432. *Daily Diary,* 12/21/63.
433. Kantor, *Who Was Jack Ruby?,* p. 131.
434. *New York Times,* 12/24/63.
435. Ibid.
436. Kantor, *Who Was Jack Ruby?,* p. 7.
437. *LBJ Library,* famous names box Johnson to Hoover.
438. David S. Lifton, *Best Evidence* (New York: Macmillan Publishing Co., Inc., 1980), p. 165.
439. Meaghers, *Accessories after the Fact,* p. 148.
440. *Daily Diary,* 12/23/63.
441. *New York Times,* 12/24/63.
442. Ibid., 12/27/63.
443. *Warren Commission Hearings,* vol. 23, p. 372.
444. *LBJ Library,* famous names box Hoover to Johnson.

445. Ford, *Portrait of the Assassin,* p. 425.
446. *New York Times,* 12/28/63.
447. Ibid.
448. Ibid.
449. Ford, *Portrait of the Assassin,* p. 427.
450. *New York Times,* 12/30/63.
451. Ibid., 12/31/63.
452. Ibid.
453. Ibid.
454. Ibid.
455. Ibid.
456. Lane, *Rush to Judgment,* p. 308.
457. Theoharis, *The Boss,* p. 391.
458. Powers, *Secrecy and Power,* pp. 398–399.
459. Theoharis, *The Boss,* p. 390.
460. Kantor, *Who Was Jack Ruby?,* p. 177.
461. *New York Times,* 1/2/64.
462. *FBI Law Enforcement Bulletin,* January 1964.
463. Ford, *Portrait of the Assassin,* p. 16.
464. *New York Times,* 1/2/64.
465. *Daily Diary,* 1/1/64.
466. *New York Times,* 1/3/64.
467. Kantor, *Who Was Jack Ruby?,* p. 187.
468. *New York Times,* 1/4/64.
469. Ibid.
470. Ibid., 1/6/64.
471. Ibid., 1/7/64.
472. Ibid.
473. Ibid., 1/19/64.
474. Ibid., 1/7/64.
475. Ibid., 1/8/64.
476. Ibid.
477. Ibid.
478. Ibid.
479. Ibid., 1/9/64.
480. Davis, *Mafia Kingfish,* p. 297.
481. *Daily Diary,* 1/8/64.
482. *New York Times,* 1/11/64.
483. Ford, *Portrait of the Assassin,* p. 29.
484. *Daily Diary,* 1/10/64.
485. *New York Times,* 1/11/64.
486. Ibid., 1/12/64.
487. *Daily Diary,* 1/11/64.
488. Kantor, *Who Was Jack Ruby?,* pp. 8, 167, 230.
489. *New York Times,* 1/12/64.

490. *Daily Diary,* 1/12/64.
491. *New York Times,* 1/14/64.
492. Epstein, *Inquest,* p. 59.
493. *New York Times,* 1/15/64.
494. Blakey, *Plot to Kill the President,* p. 314.
495. Ford, *Portrait of the Assassin,* p. 434.
496. *New York Times,* 1/15/64.
497. Ibid.
498. Ibid.
499. Ibid., 1/16/64.
500. *Daily Diary,* 1/15/64.
501. *New York Times,* 1/17/64.
502. *Daily Diary,* 1/16/64.
503. *New York Times,* 1/18/64.
504. Weisberg, *Whitewash* III, p. 280.
505. Rowe, *Bobby Baker Story,* pp. 88–89.
506. *New York Times,* 1/19/64.
507. *Daily Diary,* 1/18/64.
508. *New York Times,* 1/20/64.
509. *Daily Diary,* 1/19/64.
510. Weisberg, *Whitewash* III, p. 280.
511. *New York Times,* 1/21/64.
512. Ibid.
513. *Daily Diary,* 1/20/64.
514. *New York Times,* 1/22/64.
515. *Daily Diary,* 1/21/64.
516. Davis, *Mafia Kingfish,* p. 280.
517. *New York Times,* 1/22/64.
518. Ibid.
519. Ibid.
520. Ibid., 1/23/64.
521. Ford, *Portrait of the Assassin,* pp. 13–14. See also *HSCA,* vol. 11,
     pp. 34–36 for details of this meeting. Excerpts include, Rankin:
     "Why are they so eager to make . . . those conclusions [deleted].
     . . . Dulles: Lee, if this were true . . . I could see it would be in
     their interest to get rid of this man. . . . If he was not the killer,
     and they employed him, they are already it you see. So your argu-
     ment is correct if they are sure that this (i.e., conclusion Oswald
     acted alone and was not an FBI informant) is going to close the
     case, but if it don't *(sic)* close the case, they are worse off than ever
     by doing this (i.e., denying Oswald was an informant or part of a
     conspiracy)."
522. Davis, *Mafia Kingfish,* pp. 264–265.
523. Theoharis, *The Boss,* p. 480.
524. Rowe, *Bobby Baker Story,* p. 93.

525. Evetts, *Texan Looks at Lyndon,* p. 79.
526. *New York Times,* 1/24/64.
527. Ibid.
528. Weisberg, *Whitewash* III, p. 283.
529. *Daily Diary,* 1/23/64.
530. Epstein, *Inquest,* pp. 47–48.
531. Ford, *Portrait of the Assassin,* p. 20.
532. Ibid., p. 14.
533. Epstein, *Inquest,* p. 52.
534. *Daily Diary,* 1/25/64.
535. Ford, *Portrait of the Assassin,* p. 14.
536. *Daily Diary,* 1/26/64.
537. Ibid., 1/27/64.
538. Epstein, *Inquest,* pp. 48–49.
539. Ibid., pp. 49–50.
540. Ford, *Portrait of the Assassin,* p. 23.
541. Epstein, *Inquest,* pp. 49–50. Ford, *Portrait of the Assassin,* pp. 22–24. Members also stated: "Boggs: 'You have got to do everything on Earth to establish the facts one way or the other. And without doing that, why everything concerned, including everyone of us is doing a very grave disservice [deleted]'. . . . McCloy: '. . . Does the embarrassment supersede the importance of getting the best evidence in a situation [such] as this?'. . . . Rankin: '. . . there will be more friction, more difficulty with his carrying out his responsibilities, and I think we have a very real problem in this Commission in that if we have meetings all the time and they know what it is about [deleted]'. . . . McCloy: '. . . I don't think that we could recognize that any door is closed to us, unless the President closes it to us, and in the search for truth [deleted].'. . . . Dulles: '. . . Hoover would say certainly he didn't have anything to do with this fellow.'. . . . Dulles said that he could not imagine Hoover hiring anyone as stupid as Oswald. . . . McCloy: '. . . I have run into some awfully stupid agents.' Dulles: 'Not this irresponsible.' . . . Chairman: 'If we are investigating [Hoover], we are investigating the rumor against him, we are investigating him. . . .' " (See *HSCA,* vol. 11, pp. 36–40).
542. Hurt, *Reasonable Doubt,* p. 43.
543. Blakey, *Plot to Kill the President,* p. 28.
544. Ibid., p. 27. Before Rankin even met with Hoover, the Director sent a memo to the Commission denying Oswald was an informant. He stated in part, "In the event you have any further questions concerning the activities of the Federal Bureau of Investigation in this case, we would appreciate being contacted directly." (See *HSCA,* vol. 11, p. 41).
545. *Hearings Before the Subcommittee of the Committee on Appropri-*

ations, House of Representatives, Eighty-Eighth Congress, Second Session, 1/29/64, see first page (hereafter *FBI Appropriations Testimony);* Ovid Demaris, *The Director: An Oral Biography of J. Edgar Hoover* (New York: Harper's Magazine Press, 1975), p. 84.

546. Kantor, *Who Was Jack Ruby?,* p. 37.

547. *Daily Diary,* 1/31/64.

548. Myrna Blyth and Jane Farrell, "Marina Oswald: Twenty-Five Years Later," *Ladies' Home Journal,* November 1988, p. 236.

549. Scheim, *Contract on America,* p. 196.

550. Weisberg, *Whitewash* III, p. 277.

551. Robert J. Groden and Harrison Edward Livingstone, *High Treason* (New York: Berkley Books, 1990), p. 225.

552. Epstein, *Inquest,* p. 50.

553. *Daily Diary,* 2/4/64.

554. *Congressional Record,* Appendix 2/6/64, p. A566. Interestingly, as late as 1/17/64 no public suggestions had been made by Johnson that he intended to waive Hoover's retirement. To the contrary, conservative elements were still calling for such an endorsement. "We continue to seek the inspiring leadership of this dedicated American." (See *Congressional Record,* Appendix, 2/18/64, p. A723.) This enhances the probability that the timing of Johnson's ultimate decision was triggered by the rising tide of hostility directed toward Hoover from within the Warren Commission between 1/22/64 and 3/10/64.

555. Blakey, *Plot to Kill the President,* p. 27.

556. *Daily Diary,* 2/7/64.

557. Blakey, *Plot to Kill the President,* p. 27.

558. Rowe, *Bobby Baker Story,* pp. 95–96.

559. *Daily Diary,* 2/19/64.

560. Rowe, *Bobby Baker Story,* pp. 96–99.

561. *Daily Diary,* 2/25/64.

562. Rowe, *Bobby Baker Story,* p. 145.

563. Ibid., p. 69.

564. *Daily Diary,* 2/26/64.

565. Ibid., 2/27/64.

566. Kantor, *Who Was Jack Ruby?,* p. 87.

567. *New York Times,* 9/27/78, p. 2.

568. Kantor, *Who Was Jack Ruby?,* p. 87.

569. Epstein, *Inquest,* p. 51.

570. *Daily Diary,* 2/28/64.

571. Moldea, *The Hoffa Wars,* p. 166.

572. John Edgar Hoover, "The War on Organized Crime", *De Paul Law Review,* spring—summer 1964, vol. 13, no. 2.

573. *Washington Post,* 3/1/64, p. 23.

574. *HSCA,* vol. 5, p. 453.

575. *Hearings Before Committee on Rules and Administration U.S. Senate, Eighty Eighth Congress, First and Second Session,* part 15, p. 1466 (hereafter *Bobby Baker Hearings*).

576. *Washington Post,* 3/3/64, p. 1.

577. *LBJ Library,* famous names box Hoover to Johnson.

578. *Washington Post,* 3/4/64.

579. *HSCA,* vol. 5, p. 304.

580. Ibid., p. 453.

581. *Washington Post,* 3/6/64, p. 8.

582. *Daily Diary,* 3/9/64.

583. *Congressional Record,* Appendix, 3/25/64, pp. A1541–42. Newspaper editorials were already commenting on LBJ's decision to waive Hoover's retirement by this date. A letter to Johnson from a private citizen, which I came across at the *LBJ Library* (WHCF, Name File "H," 3/10/64), illustrates. "I have just read M. Lyle Wilson's column on the editorial page of the Macon [Georgia] Telegraph, telling the world that you will sign an executive order waiving with respect to Mr. J. Edgar Hoover, . . . the requirement [that he] retire at age seventy." In this same letter, the following statement was also made: *"I know all about the big movement on, here, to oust Mr. Hoover"* (emphasis added). Thus, this letter supports the conclusion that in early 1964 there was indeed some plan developing to remove Hoover. More importantly, and perhaps profoundly, consider the source of the letter, Macon, *Georgia.* Warren Commission member Senator Russell (Dem.), the Commission member who initially refused to sign the *Warren Report* (he had to be ordered to do so by Johnson), and never would accept Hoover's lone-nut thesis, represented *Georgia.* Recall that on 1/27/64, it was Russell who openly attacked Hoover in executive session, saying "[Hoover] ha[s] tried the case and reached a verdict on every aspect." Boggs had replied, "You have put your finger on it."

584. *Washington Post,* 3/10/64.

585. *Bobby Baker Hearings,* part 17, p. 1588.

586. *Daily Diary,* 3/12/64.

587. Ibid., 3/13/64.

588. Ibid., 3/19/64.

589. Davis, *The Kennedys,* p. 853. Perhaps coincidentally, this same day FBI generated a report which ". . . indicates [Las Vegas Ruby associate] McWillie solidified his syndicate connections through his association with Santos Traficante." Lansky was also mentioned in the same context. (See *The Killing of President Kennedy,* Syndacast Services, Inc., video.)

590. Rowe, *Bobby Baker Story,* p. 66. Also in April 1964, RFK gave an interview in which he ". . . told an interviewer Hoover was

'dangerous' and was 'rather a psycho.' . . . the FBI was 'a very dangerous organization . . . and I think [Hoover]'s . . . senile and rather frightening.' " (See Powers' *Secrecy and Power,* p. 397).

591. *Daily Diary,* 4/1/64.

592. Kantor, *Who Was Jack Ruby?,* p. 87.

593. *Daily Diary,* 4/7/64.

594. Ibid., 4/9/64.

595. Ibid., 4/14/64.

596. Ibid., 4/18/64.

597. *Warren Commission Hearings,* vol. 17, p. 857.

598. Kantor, *Who Was Jack Ruby?,* p. 155.

599. *Daily Diary,* 4/29/64.

600. *Warren Commission Hearings,* vol. 17, p. 858. This same day, the Commission, apparently on a split vote, voted to go ahead with the decision to call Hoover before the group and question him under oath. ". . . Some Commission members were . . . reluctant to get involved in a confrontation with Hoover." (See HSCA, vol. 11, p. 41.)

601. Kantor, *Who Was Jack Ruby?,* pp. 156–157.

602. *Warren Commission Hearings,* vol. 17, p. 855.

603. *Daily Diary,* 5/8/64.

604. Epstein, *Inquest,* p. 51.

605. *Daily Diary,* 5/6/64.

606. *Warren Commission Hearings,* vol. 17, p. 855.

607. Ibid., vol. 5, pp. 97–120. Rankin, a man very careful with his words on this subject, hinted at his position when he testified before the HSCA. " 'I went to see Mr. Hoover before we finally put out our report . . . He was pretty feisty when I saw him, any friendship we had had in the past was not very apparent then.' . . . Rankin told the committee, 'Who could protest against what Mr. Hoover did back in those days?' " See *HSCA,* vol. 11, p. 49.

608. *Daily Diary,* 5/8/64.

609. *New York Times,* 5/9/64.

610. LBJ Library, famous names box, Hoover to Johnson, 5/8/64. In what was apparently a final insult to RFK, Johnson, on 5/11/64, had a *clerk* formally notify him of Hoover's waiver. "[Johnson] on May eighth signed an Executive Order entitled 'Exemption of J. Edgar Hoover from Compulsory Retirement for Age,' a copy of which is enclosed." See *LBJ Library,* WHCF, Hopkins letter.

X

Bibliography

Articles

Blyth, Myrna, and Jane Ferrell. "Marina Oswald: Twenty-Five Years Later." *Ladies' Home Journal.* November 1988.

Demaris, Ovid. "The Private Life of J. Edgar Hoover." *Esquire.* September 1974.

Demaris, Ovid. "The Office Politics of J. Edgar Hoover." *Esquire.* November 1974.

Feldman, Harold. "Oswald and the FBI." *The Nation.* January 27, 1964.

Goettel, Gerard L. "Why the Crime Syndicate Can't Be Touched." *Harper's Magazine.* November 1960.

Hay, Jacob, and Robert F. Sisson. "The FBI, Public Friend Number One." *National Geographic.* June 1961.

Hoover, John. E. "Communist Youth Campaign." *Follow Up Reporter.* August 1, 1962.

————. "The Indispensable Supports." *Sunday Visitor.* February 17, 1963.

————. "Protecting the Innocent-Law Enforcement's Sacred Task." *Notre Dame Law Review.* March 1961.

————. "Shall It Be Law or Tyranny?" *American Bar Association Journal.* February 1962.

————. "The War on Organized Crime." *De Paul Law Review.* Spring—Summer 1964.

————. "What I Would Tell a Son." *Christian Science Monitor.* September 21, 1963.

————. "Why Reds Make Friends with Businessmen." *Nation's Business.* May 1, 1962.

"J. Edgar Hoover and the FBI." *Newsweek.* December 7, 1964.

Kennedy, Robert F. "What's Wrong With the $2 Dollar Bet?" *Parade.* October 29, 1961.

Levine, Jack. "Hoover and the Red Scare." *The Nation.* October 20, 1962.

——————. "The Next Mr. Hoover." *The Nation.* February 16, 1963. *Life.* November 29 and December 6, 1963, generally.

Moley, Raymond. "The Faith of the FBI." *Newsweek.* March 4, 1963.

Phelan, James. "Hoover of the FBI." *The Saturday Evening Post.* September 25, 1965.

Solow, Herbert. "How Not to Award a Navy Contract." *Fortune.* December 1960.

The Texas Argus. April 1962.

"The Truth About Hoover." *Time.* December 22, 1975.

Wainwright, Loudon. "Must J. Edgar Go On and On?" *Life.* May 22, 1964.

Books

Altman, Dennis. *The Homosexualization of America.* Boston: Beacon Press, 1982.

Bishop, Jim. *The Day Kennedy Was Shot.* New York: Funk & Wagnalls, 1968.

Blakey, G. Robert, and Richard N. Billings. *The Plot to Kill the President.* New York: New York Times Book Company, 1981.

Bullough, Vern L. *Homosexuality:* A History. New York: Garland STPM Press, 1979.

Cook, Fred J. *The FBI Nobody Knows.* New York: The Macmillan Company, 1964.

Davis, John H. *The Kennedys: Dynasty and Disaster 1848–1984.* New York: McGraw-Hill Book Company, 1984.

——————. Mafia Kingfish: *Carlos Marcello and the Assassination of John F. Kennedy.* New York: McGraw-Hill Book Company, 1989.

Demaris, Ovid. *The Director: An Oral Biography of J. Edgar Hoover.* New York: Harper's Magazine Press, 1975.

de Toladano, Ralph. *J. Edgar Hoover: The Man in His Time.* New Rochelle, New York: Arlington House, 1973.

Epstein, Edward Jay. *Inquest: The Warren Commission and the Establishment of Truth.* New York: The Viking Press, 1966.

Legend: The Secret World of Lee Harvey Oswald. New York: McGraw-Hill Book Company, 1978.

Facts on File—World News Digest. September 26, 1963—October 2, 1963.

Ford, Gerald R., with John R. Stiles. *Portrait of the Assassin.* New York: Simon & Schuster, 1965.

Garrow, David, J. *The FBI and Martin Luther King, Jr.* New York: W.W. Norton and Co., 1981.

Groden, Robert J., and Harrison Edward Livingstone. *High Treason.* New York: Berkley Books, 1990.

Haley, J. Evetts. *A Texan Looks at Lyndon.* Canyon, Texas: Palo Duro Press, 1964.

Holy Bible, Revised Standard Version, Micah 6:8.

Hoover, J. Edgar. *Masters of Deceit.* New York: Holt, Rinehart and Winston, 1958.

————. *A Study of Communism.* New York: Holt, Rinehart and Winston, 1962.

Hurt, Henry. *Reasonable Doubt.* New York: Henry Holt and Company, 1985.

Ianni, Francis A. J., and Elizabeth Reuss-Ianni, eds. *The Crime Society.* New York: Meridian, 1976.

Kantor, Seth. *Who Was Jack Ruby?* New York: Everest House, 1978.

Lane, Mark. *Rush to Judgment.* New York: Holt, Rinehart and Winston, 1966.

Lewis, Eugene. *Public Entrepreneurship: Toward a Theory of Bureaucratic Political Power.* Bloomington, Indiana: Indiana University Press, 1980.

Lifton, David S. *Best Evidence.* New York: Macmillan Publishing Co. Inc., 1980.

Look, eds. *The Story of the FBI.* New York: E.P. Dutton & Co., 1947.

Lovegrove, Richard and Tom Orwig. *The FBI.* New York: Exeter Books, 1989.

Maas, Peter. *The Valachi Papers.* New York: G.P. Putnam Sons, 1968.

Marrs, Jim. *Crossfire: The Plot That Killed Kennedy.* New York: Carroll and Graf Publishers, Inc., 1989.

Meaghers, Sylvia. *Accessories after the Fact.* New York: Vintage Books, 1976.

Messick, Hank. *John Edgar Hoover.* New York: David McKay Company, Inc., 1972.

————. *Lansky.* New York: Berkley Publishing Corporation, 1973.

Moldea, Dan E. *The Hoffa Wars.* New York: Paddington Press, Ltd., 1978.

Nash, Robert J. *Citizen Hoover.* Chicago: Nelson-Hall, 1972.

Navasky, Victor S. *Kennedy Justice.* New York: Atheneum, 1971.

Newman, Albert H. *The Assassination of John F. Kennedy: The Reasons Why.* New York: Clarkson N. Potter, Inc., 1970.

O'Reilly, Kenneth. *Hoover and the UnAmericans.* Philadelphia: Temple University Press, 1983.

Overstreet, Harry and Bonaro. *The FBI in Our Open Society.* New York: W.W. Norton & Company, 1969.

Powers, Richard Gid. *Secrecy and Power: The Life of J. Edgar Hoover.* New York: The Free Press, 1987.

Reid, Ed. *The Grim Reapers: The Anatomy of Organized Crime in America.* Chicago: Henry Regnery, 1969.

Reid, Ed, and Ovid Demaris. *The Green Felt Jungle.* New York: Pocket Books, Inc., 1964.

Rowe, Robert. *The Bobby Baker Story.* New York: Parallax Publishing Co., 1967.

Rutledge, Leigh W. *The Gay Book of Lists.* Boston: Alyson Publications, 1987.

Scheim, David E. *Contract on America.* Silver Spring, Maryland: Argyle Press, 1983.

Schlesinger, Arthur M., Jr. *Robert Kennedy and His Times.* Boston: Houghton-Mifflin Company, 1978.

——————. *A Thousand Days.* Boston: Houghton-Mifflin Company, 1965.

Schneider, Rev. Nicholaus A., ed. *Religious Views of John F. Kennedy.* St. Louis: B. Herder Book Co., 1965.

Schott, Joseph L. *No Left Turns.* New York: Praeger Publishers, 1975.

Sentner, David. *How the FBI Gets Its Man.* New York: Avon Books, 1965.

Sheridan, Walter. *The Fall and Rise of Jimmy Hoffa.* New York: Saturday Review Press, 1972.

Sherrill, Robert. *The Accidental President.* New York: Pyramid Books, 1967.

Slatzer, Robert K. *The Curious Death of Marilyn Monroe.* New York: Pinnacle Books, 1974.

Sullivan, William C., and Bill Brown. *The Bureau: My Thirty Years in Hoover's FBI.* New York: W.W. Norton & Company, 1979.

Summers, Anthony. *Conspiracy.* New York: McGraw-Hill Book Company, 1980.

——————. *Goddess.* New York: New American Library (Onyx ed.), 1986.

Theoharis, Athan G., and John Stuart Cox. *The Boss.* Philadelphia: Temple University Press, 1988.

Thompson, Josiah. *Six Seconds in Dallas.* New York: Bernard Geis Associates, 1967.

Turner, William W. *Hoover's FBI: The Men and the Myth.* New York: Dell, 1971.

Unger, Sanford J. *FBI.* Boston: Little, Brown & Co., 1975.

Watters, Pat, and Stephen Gillers, eds. *Investigating the FBI.* Garden City, New York: Doubleday & Company, Inc., 1973.

Weisberg, Harold. *Whitewash, vols.* I, II, III. Hyattstown, Md: H. Weisberg, 1965, 1966, 1967.

Welch, Neil J., and David W. Marston. *Inside Hoover's FBI.* Garden City, New York: Doubleday and Company, Inc., 1984.

Zion, Sidney. *The Autobiography of Roy Cohn.* Secaucus, New York: Lyle Stuart, Inc., 1988.

Government publications and reports

Annual FBI Uniform Crime Report. July 24, 1961.
Attorney General's Conference on Organized Crime. Report of February 15, 1950.
Congressional Directory. 1961–64.
Congressional Record. 1960–64.
FBI Crime Condition Report—Dallas. March 1, 1962.
FBI Handbook. Years 1961–63.
FBI Law Enforcement Bulletin. January 1961—January 1964.
Federal Records Act of 1950.
Hearings Before the Committee on Rules and Administration, United States Senate, Eighty-Eighth Congress, First and Second Sessions. Parts 15, 17. (Bobby Baker hearings).
Hearings: Subcommittee of the Committee on Appropriations—House of Representatives, Eighty-Sixth Congress, Second Session, Department of Justice. February 8, 1960.
Hearings: Subcommittee of the Committee on Appropriations—House of Representatives, Eighty-Seventh Congress, Second Session, Department of Justice. January 24, 1962.
Hearings: Subcommittee of the Committee on Appropriations—House of Representatives, Eighty-Eighth Congress, First Session, Department of Justice. February 1, 1963.
Hearings: Subcommittee of the Committee on Appropriations—House of Representatives, Eighty-Eighth Congress, Second Session. January 29, 1964.
Hearings: Subcommittee on Civil and Constitutional Rights of the Committee on the Judiciary—House of Representatives, Ninety-Fourth Congress, First Session, FBI Oversight. February 27, 1975.
Hearings: Subcommittee of the Committee on Government Operations—House of Representatives, Ninety-Fourth Congress, First Session. "Inquiry into the Destruction of Former FBI Director J. Edgar Hoover's Files and FBI Recordkeeping." December 1, 1975.
House Select Committee on Assassinations. Investigation of the Assassination of President John F. Kennedy: Hearings, Appendix, Report. Ninety-Fifth and Ninety-Sixth Congress. vols. 1–12. March 29, 1979. (HSCA).
Internal Revenue Bulletin (IRB), 1959-1, p. 583.
Internal Revenue Code. 1954, 1986.
John Fitzgerald Kennedy Library, Boston, Massachusetts.
Lyndon B. Johnson Presidential Library, Austin, Texas.
18 *United States Code* 1. (1948 ed.).
42 *United States Code* 1985, 1986. (1958 ed.)
U.S. v. Gilbert Lee Beckley. 5th Cir., Eastern District of Louisiana, June 27, 1961, Crim. No. 28247.

U.S. President's Commission on the Assassination of President John F. Kennedy. Hearings, Exhibits, and Report. 1964 (Warren Commission).
U.S. Senate Intelligence Reports, Foreign Assassinations.
U.S. Senate, Permanent Subcommittee on Investigations of the Committee on Government Operations. Gambling and Organized Crime. Eighty-Seventh Congress. August—September 1961, Parts 2 and 3.
U.S. Senate, Select Committee on Improper Activities in the Labor and Management Field. Eighty-Sixth Congress, Second Session. March 1959, Part 48. (McClellan Committee).
U.S. Senate, Select Committee to Investigate Organized Crime in Interstate Commerce, Eighty-Second Congress. January—February 1951, Part 8. (Kefauver Committee Hearings and Report).
U.S. Senate, Select Committee to Study Government Operations with respect to Intelligence Activities—Hearings. vol. 6, FBI, Ninety-Fourth Congress, Second Session, 1976.

Legal publications

Black, Henry Campbell. *Black's Law Dictionary.* St. Paul, Minn: West Publishing Co., 1983.
CCH-Standard Federal Tax Reports. New York: Commerce Clearing House, Inc., 1961–63.
Corpus Juris Secundum, Vol. 87. St. Paul, Minn: West Publishing Co., 1956.
259 *Federal Supplement* 567. (U.S. v. Beckley, collateral action).
Federal Tax Coordinator 2nd. Research Institute of America, 1990.
U.S. Master Tax Guide. New York: Commerce Clearing House, Inc., 1962–64.

Newspapers

American National Bookstore News, June—July, 1961.
Associated Press, December 22, 1960; May 20, 1963.
Austin American Statesman, September 24, 1989.
Boston Record American, November 26–27, 1963.
Charlestown Gazette, April 17, 1963.
Chicago American, June 26, 1961.
Chicago Tribune, May 25, 1962; November 24, 26, 1963.
Christian Beacon, May 21, 1961.
Daily Express, November 23, 1963.
Dallas Morning News, January 29, 1963; September 26, 1963; November 23–25, 1963; December 2, 1963; May 1, 1977.
Dallas Times Herald, April 24, 1963; September 13, 1963; November 21, 30, 1963.
Denver Post, November 23–25, 1963.
Fort Worth Star Telegram, June 9, 1962; October 1, 1978.

Gannett News Service, July 23, 1962.
Honolulu Star Bulletin, November 22, 1963.
Houston Post, January 1, 1964.
Los Angeles Times, see August 1961, 1962, 1963; November 23–26, 1963.
Las Vegas Review Courier, September 6, 1963.
London Sunday Times, December 3, 1961.
Memphis Commercial Appeal, February 25, 1961.
New Orleans States-Item, December 28, 1960; November 23, 1963.
New Orleans Times-Picayune, August 13, 1963; September 13, 1963.
New York Herald Tribune, October 5, 1961.
New York Journal American, August 24, 1963.
New York Mirror, April 3, 1961.
New York Post, July 15, 1963.
New York Times, November 1960—May 1964. See individual footnotes.
The Pecos Independent and Enterprise, February 12, 1962.
Philadelphia Inquirer, December 8, 1963.
St. Louis Globe Democrat, July 16, 1962.
San Francisco Chronicle, May 3, 1961.
Seattle Post Intelligencer, November 22, 24, 1963.
Texas Observer, January 29, 1963; December 13, 1963.
Tulsa Daily World, December 1961; December 1962—March 1963. See individual footnotes.
Washington Daily News, May 10, 1961; November 26–28, 1963.
Washington Evening Star, February 5, 1963; November 23–24, 27, 1963.
Washington Post, November 1960—March 1964, see individual footnotes; May 16, 1976.

Radio, television, videocassette

The Fabulous Sixties: 1963 End of a Thousand Days. Videocassette. Maljack Productions, Inc., 1970.
Four Days in November. CBS, New York. November 22, 1988.
Hoover vs. the Kennedys: The Second Civil War. Videocassette. Sunrise Films, Ltd., 1987.
The Killing of President Kennedy: New Revelations Twenty Years Later. Videocassette. Syndacast Services, Inc., 1983.
The Manchurian Candidate. Videocassette. MGM/UA Home Video, 1988.
Monitor. Radio. NBC, New York. July 15, September 2, 1962.
Secret Intelligence: The Only Rule Is Win. Community Television of Southern California—PBS, California. 1988.
Who Shot President Kennedy? NOVA-WGBH, Boston. 1988.

XI

Index